# LIGHT
# &
# TRUTH

## Volume Three
# The Nauvoo Years

A Historical Novel
Based on a True Story

Visit us at www.harrispublishing.com.

Library of Congress Control Number: 2005926512
ISBN: 0-9747376-2-3.

First printing July 2005

Printed at Falls Printing, Idaho Falls, Idaho, U.S.A.

Dedicated to my children—
Chuck, Mike, Jason, Stephanie, and Ryan—
that they may appreciate their heritage.

# Foreword

*The Nauvoo Years*—Volume Three of *Light and Truth*—is historical fiction based on a true story using mostly real characters. It begins shortly after our characters arrive in Nauvoo after their emigration from England, and ends with the exodus from Nauvoo. The viewpoint, therefore, is British.

Two volumes have been written as a prologue to this one, *The Field Is White*—the story of our characters' conversion—and *The Gathering*, the story of their trip across the Atlantic Ocean and up the Mississippi River to Nauvoo. Volume four, *The Mormon Battalion*, will deal with the Mexican-American War and with Winter Quarters.

The theme of this volume is sacrifice. Saints who came to Nauvoo in the early 1840s sacrificed their time, talents, and money to build the Nauvoo Temple and build the Kingdom of God on earth. It goes without saying that research for this book was extensive and required trips to Nauvoo. Robert and Hannah Harris, my grandparents—and two of the main characters of this book—owned a lot near the temple, and so did Daniel and Elizabeth Browett. Attempting to reconstruct their lives through traditional family history efforts and through this historical novel has been fun, educational, and inspirational.

Every good novel requires the element of conflict. Those who have studied the Nauvoo period in Church history know that conflict existed in plural marriage, apostasy, conspiracy, persecution of the Saints, attempted kidnapping of the Prophet Joseph Smith, attempted murder, murder of Joseph and Hyrum Smith, and the trial of those murderers. The characters of this book find their lives entwined with all those conflicts.

# Principal Characters

All characters are real except those indicated with an asterisk. Bold face indicates main characters. Ages are as Volume Three opens in December 1842.

### THE ROBERT HARRIS FAMILY
**Robert**, 33, the father.
**Hannah**, 28, the mother.
Joseph, 8.
Lizzy, 6.
William, 5.

### THE BROWETT FAMILY
**Daniel**, 31.
**Elizabeth**, 29, sister to Robert Harris.
Martha Pulham Browett, 58,
    Daniel's mother.
Rebecca, 24, Daniel's sister.

### THE EAGLES FAMILY
*Henry, 36.
*Katherine, 31.
*Annie, 2.

### THE BLOXHAM FAMILY
Thomas, 31, the father.
Dianah, 29, the mother.
Charles, 8.
Lucy, 7.
Tommy, 6.
Johnny, 4.
Isaac, 2.

### OTHERS
**John Benbow**, 43; wife, Jane.
Jacob Kemp Butterfield, 31.
John Cox, 33.
John Hyrum Green, 39; wife, Susannah.
Joseph Hill, 37.
Orson Hyde, 39, Apostle.
**Thomas Kington**, 50.
William Pitt, 30.
Edward Phillips, 30.
Levi Roberts, 33.
Joseph Smith, 38, President of the Church
    of Jesus Christ of Latter-day Saints.
**Wilford Woodruff**, 36, Apostle.

# The
# Nauvoo Years

# 1

*December 1842*

MORNING BEGAN WITH AN ANGRY shiver for Elizabeth Browett. With tired bloodshot eyes she sat up in bed and peered out of the small frosty window that overlooked the Illinois prairie to the east. There were no pink clouds, no yellow-colored glory to lift her spirits. The coming day promised no more than a dim silver disk in a gloomy gray muslin sky. A cold wind howled through cracks in the clay-and-grass chinking of her small log home.

Normally a good sleeper, she had tossed and turned all night. For the first time in her married life, she and Daniel had slept in separate rooms. For the first time since her conversion to Mormonism, she had not said her evening prayers. She had gone to bed without eating one bite of the birthday dinner she had prepared for her husband. Worst of all, she had not been able to get out of her mind the fact that Daniel had been asked by Joseph Smith, Wilford Woodruff, and Orson Hyde to take a second wife. Call it what you want, plural marriage or polygamy. Despite the fact that the doctrine had given her mind no trouble when she first heard about it, that had changed the moment it threatened to come into her life.

Early last evening, Elizabeth had locked herself in the bedroom of their two-room cabin on Warsaw Street in the Kimball Addition, six blocks east of the temple site. Daniel, the "brethren," and the Church had stepped over an unseen line as far as she was concerned.

Her skin tingled with a clamminess that told her that a morning confrontation with Daniel would not be pleasant. She frowned, bringing to remembrance the conversation of the previous evening.

"They asked that both of us present it to the Lord in prayer," Daniel had stammered, his eyes watering. At first, the statement struck Elizabeth as typical of Daniel's faith. He had always supported the "brethren" in every cause, in every commandment, without hesitation.

Normally swift in her comebacks, the remark caused Elizabeth to be at a loss for words. She felt an emptiness and couldn't speak for several seconds. She could only think of this biting question: "I'm to pray and ask if it's okay to give half my husband to another woman?"

There was no answer from Daniel. Tears streaming down his cheeks failed to soften her. She pushed locks of blond hair out of her green eyes, and turned her back. "I'm going to bed. Enjoy your stew. Sleep in front of the hearth. I want to be alone."

The small cabin shook on its foundation when she slammed the door. She threw herself on the wood-and-rope bed and beat on the pillow. Then she remembered. Daniel had not even mentioned the name of the proposed second wife. She buried her head in humiliation.

Still fuming, Elizabeth now slowly crawled out of her straw tick mattress. She touched her stocking feet on the freezing rough-sawed planked floor, and listened for any evidence that Daniel was awake. For a moment her mind flared back to her honeymoon in Bath, England, seven years ago. She could picture Daniel's mouth curling in his old beguiling grin, feel his tousled blond hair in her fingers, and feel the touch of his hands. What a dry death-in-life this was—the thoughts of him taking another wife!

She hoped that Daniel had already awakened, dressed, and left the house. But where would he go this early in the morning, with the sun not even up? With the temperature hovering below zero, there was nothing productive to do except milk the orange and white cow. She peeked out her small window. Through the cheap bull's eye glass she could barely make out his neatly stacked woodpile, covered with a new dusting of snow. Construction on the temple was lagging because of the unusually cold weather, so it was unlikely he would be there, especially this early.

*If he's still here, I'm leaving.*

A burst of warm air greeted Elizabeth as the planked door that separated the two rooms groaned open. A red and orange fire glowed in the hearth. The ghostly image of Daniel was a blur at first. He was seated backwards on a wooden chair, facing bright embers that revealed a worried unshaven face. For a moment, grief strafed Elizabeth's heart. She wondered if he had been sitting there all night.

As her husband's sad blue eyes rose to hers, Elizabeth had a feeling that he longed to jump to his feet and embrace her. There would be her typical delightful way of complaining that his whiskers scratched and tickled her face. But her current emotions wouldn't allow it; there would be no cuddling this morning. As she detected a muscle movement, and before he could form words, Elizabeth's sharpness curdled the air. "*Don't* speak to me," she roared.

Daniel lurched to his feet, fumbling for a lantern.

"*Don't* light that just for me," she hissed. "I can *see* just fine." She felt the urge to leave the house, to get away from her pathetic husband. She found her black wool coat, draped it around her nightgown, and pulled on her boots.

Light filled the room as Daniel managed to ignite the lantern. For a split second Elizabeth glanced up. She could see lips curled in a lonely grimace and eyes that seemed to plead with her to stay and talk. She felt her resolve stiffen.

"*Don't* ask me *where* I'm going, or *when* I'm coming back," she steamed.

Daniel sat the lantern on the table and quickly poured a cup of composition tea. "Want some?" he asked.

Without comment she snatched the cup and sipped so quickly the tea burned her mouth and throat. She knew that Daniel expected the tea to calm her. Instead, the mixture of bayberry, ginger, cayenne, and cloves seemed to liven her anger. Still sipping, she stepped toward the door. *"Don't* follow me," she lashed out. "Stay here and draw your dream cabin plans for your new wife." She took her last sips of tea and then slammed the teacup on the table. She tied a crimson wool bonnet to her head and threw a dark gray scarf around her neck.

"It's freezing out there ..." Daniel pleaded.

"I said *don't* speak to me."

"Did you ...?"

"Not a word!"

The door opened, and then shut with a slam. Icicles fell from the shake shingles to the ground in a haunted and wasted musical shattering. As Elizabeth stomped away, she missed Daniel's final question:

"Did you ... pray?"

Smoke billowed from the chimney of her next-door neighbor's cabin. Inside, Elizabeth could see her brother, Robert, who had celebrated his thirty-first birthday three days ago. He was opening a yellow curtain, revealing the warmth of a happy home. A bright lantern beamed from inside. Hannah was bent over the hearth, fixing food. Four children, wiping sleepy seeds from their eyes, stood watching. Elizabeth caught the odor of bacon cooking. This scene grated on Elizabeth. Where were *her* children? Why did God choose to punish *her* with a barren womb? And why this sudden intrusion into her life? Must she share Daniel with another woman? Why wasn't this happening to Hannah, instead of her?

Cabins occupied by the Roberts, Cox, and Pitt families were dark except for a faint hint of coals that needed to be stoked in the hearths. Elizabeth let her eyes drift to the Phillips cabin. Surprisingly, newlyweds Edward and Susannah were up already, laughing and cooking something for breakfast in a black pot hanging over the fireplace on a swing crane.

Elizabeth scoffed. *Wait until Susannah has to face what I'm facing.*

The cabin shared by Daniel's mother and sister was also dark. A preposterous thought came to Elizabeth's pensive mind. *Has Daniel promised his sister, Rebecca, as a plural wife for one of his friends? Or for one of the brethren?*

The sky was a dark slate color with a faint inky hue of purple to the east where the sun would be coming up in an hour or so. Pampering the gloom that had swept over her during the past twelve sleepless hours, Elizabeth could barely make out Ripley Street as she turned west. Two inches of snow blanketed Nauvoo. A crunching sound came with each step, causing flushes of more irritation to crawl up her spine. The frosty air began stinging her nose and cheeks. Her nostrils stuck together when she drew deep breaths.

Mulholland Street ran straight for a considerable distance before it hit the top of the bluff and Elizabeth had her eyes fixed on it. Soon she was walking downhill toward the river. Within a few blocks, Elizabeth could make out the faint image of the small wood-frame home occupied by Wilford Woodruff. She crept closer. Her green eyes blazed with a defiant hatred that shocked her. The thirty-five-year-old Apostle, until yesterday a man she literally idolized, was sitting at a table studying by the light of a lantern. She looked for a rock about the size of her fist. Along the barrow pit she scuffed at the snow. All the rocks were buried by snow and frozen to the turf. She gave up her plans to throw one through the window.

In her madness, Elizabeth thought about hiding near the Ebenezer Robinson home where Orson and Marinda Hyde were staying temporarily. The dimness of the morning sky revealed a dead tree with brittle branches. She pondered tearing one off and fashioning a club with it. She could put an embarrassing knot on Orson's head as he left the house for wherever this miserable day would take him.

Elizabeth came to Water Street and the Red Brick Store, site of the meeting between her husband, the Prophet, Elder Woodruff, and Elder Hyde. In addition to being a general store, it had become a center for social and civic activity, even a public school. She had attended a meeting there nine months ago when Joseph Smith had organized the Relief Society. Now, she silently wished for a whirlwind to dash it into pieces, and all of the holy city of Nauvoo for all she cared. She cast a spiteful glance at Joseph's log cabin near the river. She paused in the street as Emma Smith opened a curtain and poured a pitcher of water to fill her basin. As Elizabeth raked Emma from head to toe with a hot gaze, she wondered how Emma was handling her own challenges about women who had also been sealed to Joseph. Despite Elizabeth's previous tolerance—even acceptance—of what she had heard about the doctrine of plural marriage, she now wished she had never heard of Joseph Smith or Mormonism. She stomped onward.

A plum sky from the east revealed the dim images of the Nauvoo Landing and a frozen-over Mississippi River. Ice coated the water in a ragged, treacherous layer. Trees lining the bank were also covered with ice, the branches cracking against each other in the wind. Piers that held the wooden landing looked as though they might shatter in the sub-zero temperature.

Elizabeth recalled her feelings twenty months ago when she stepped onto the landing from a steamboat called the *Goddess of Liberty*, with Daniel and one hundred eight English immigrants. Most had been former United Brethren congregation members, converted to the Church by Wilford Woodruff. Her arrival in Nauvoo had been followed by the happiest days of her life—selecting a lot in a beautiful, rapidly growing city; building a cabin; sharing a forty-acre farm with Robert and Hannah; and getting lost in happy service as a midwife and herbalist.

And now this. Her dreams were literally shattered. Zion was supposed to be a place where one was expected to live a life of purity, unity, friendship, and Christian love. Right now she felt a loss of dignity, ripped apart, and full of hate.

Elizabeth let her eyes trace the banks along the frozen river. She wished for a curse to melt the ice and for a steamboat to come by and pick her up. She longed to reverse the steps that brought her to Zion: back to St. Louis, back to New Orleans, catch a ship to Liverpool, and return to Apperley, Gloucestershire, England.

The thought of returning to England further depressed her and she began to despise the idea. Only one member of her family remained in Apperley, her older brother, John. He managed the Ferret's Folly, a pub. Her parents were interred in the Churchyard of the St. Mary's Priory Anglican Church. So was her brother, William. Her two other siblings, Robert, and her sister, Dianah Bloxham, were both in Nauvoo. She wondered if the brethren had plans for Robert. Luckily for Dianah, her husband wasn't Mormon. Dianah was safe.

Depression was practically a new emotion for Elizabeth. It usually came over her only when she thought about her barrenness. Until today at least, she had desperately wanted to give her husband a houseful of children. And until last evening she had been Nauvoo's epitome of optimism: spunky, spontaneous, adventurous, daring, full of energy, a risk taker, communicator, entertaining, and the ability to turn a crisis into a comedy.

Her old strengths were failing her now. The prospects of losing Daniel's full devotion was real, no comedy. She began to weep. Without realizing it, she collapsed to her knees, sinking into the snow. Alone on the Nauvoo Landing, she cried her heart out.

# 2

DANIEL BROWETT CRINGED AT THE slam of the door. Through a frosted pane he watched the faint image of Elizabeth march away like an angry bull. Puffs of powdery snow flew with every raging step.

Daniel wiped tears from his eyes, thinking. He had been on his knees most of the night. The Spirit had witnessed to him that the principle of plural marriage as taught to him by the Prophet Joseph Smith was true. But the Spirit had also told him that his wife must consent to the practice. If not, he should not enter into it.

He felt an inner devastation as he thought about the awkwardness of telling Joseph Smith, Wilford Woodruff, and Orson Hyde that Elizabeth had rejected the whole idea. Daniel recalled the events of yesterday afternoon. Chopping wood when Orson made his surprise visit. Orson asking him to come to the Red Brick Store to meet with the Prophet. The interview about his worthiness. The utter shock he felt when they asked him to marry Harriett Barnes Clifford, the widow, and take care of her. The hour they spent discussing the principle of plural marriage. The instructions to present the question to the Lord in prayer. The numbness he felt walking home. And how he bumbled the whole thing with Elizabeth.

He couldn't help but think of Sister Clifford. He felt genuinely sorry for the lady. An English convert, Harriet Barnes Clifford had lost her husband, Elijah, to cholera last May. The courtship that began in the fall between Sister Clifford and James Pulham, his own cousin and employee in the cooper shop back in England, seemed so perfect. James had lost his wife, Nancy—Hannah Eagles Harris' sister—on the ship *Echo*. He contemplated how lonely James had been, and how James had looked forward to marrying Harriet. Then came the accident at the well, the tragic death of James, buried by forty feet of dirt. The result was emotional devastation for Harriet, who had lost both a husband and the prospect of a new one.

Daniel felt a chill. He turned to the warmth of the hearth and clasped his hands together in a gesture of sorrow. Minutes later, in deep distressed thought, he used a poker to stir the fire, sending sparks spiraling upward. He placed two new logs onto the coals. New flames erupted, but they failed to fortify him.

*If only Elizabeth would pray.*

He stared through the doorway into the bedroom and at the empty bed, the quilts in a heap. He longed to be cuddled together with his wife, sharing his body warmth, talking about their commitment to their baptismal covenants, their marriage covenants, life in Nauvoo, the hope of a pregnancy, a family, the building of the temple. He missed Elizabeth's company over an early morning breakfast. The creative flare she brought to each new day, her normal willingness to bend her will to anyone else's just to please him or her, and her pleasing conversation topics ranging from serious to superficial.

Daniel was tempted to follow the footsteps in the snow.

There were many reasons why he didn't. He recognized Elizabeth's need to be alone for a while, to cool down. Sometimes she had a tendency to speak without thinking; at least she had partially held her tongue so far. If pushed, she might vocally threaten to end their relationship, although it would be pretended and not real. In the past she had sometimes displayed a tendency to be quick-tempered in unpleasant circumstances requiring patience. She was the kind of forthright woman who called men by their first names, even in the Church, and when riled she was known to salt her speech rather freely with criticism.

This was definitely an unpleasant circumstance for her. One that would require lots of patience.

Right now, Daniel knew, it required prayer.

# 3

"WHERE DO YOU SUPPOSE ELIZABETH is going this time of morning?" Robert asked. He had seen his sister rush out of the Browett cabin, slamming the door behind her. "She must be in a hurry."

Hannah did a quick calculation. Harriet Ann Roberts was not due for another month. Eliza Cox was not due until February. "Maybe someone other than our English friends have called her to midwife a delivery, or someone's sick we don't know about," she said. "Get back, Lizzy. Don't lean over. When the bacon gets hot it'll spit on you."

"Can I stir it, Mama?" Lizzy asked. "Remember, I'm your best helper."

"If you're careful," Hannah replied.

"I think it's time we told the children," Robert said, letting his gaze settle over his wife's figure.

"Told them what?" Hannah asked, handing Lizzy a spatula.

Robert winked. "Number five. In May."

Seven-year-old Joseph, the oldest, caught on quickly. "Mother, are you in a family way again?"

"That's true, son," Hannah said as she blushed slightly. She drew Joseph to her and gave him a warm embrace. "One more helper around here." She suspected it would be another boy, one that would grow up to be like his father—tall and sturdy, with rippling muscles and ribs close-knit.

Lizzy perked up. "Can I feel your tummy, Mama?"

Hannah laughed and gave her only daughter a sweet smile. "I hope it's a sister for you. We girls are outnumbered, aren't we?" She shook her finger at the children. "But don't tell anyone about Mama for a while. This will be our secret."

"I understand, Mama," Lizzy said as she went back to the bacon.

"Tell Papa he'd better add onto the house," Hannah said with a big smile.

Robert let his gaze trickle up to the loft. "Plenty of room up there for more kids," he said. With the help of Daniel and other English converts, Robert had built their log home in early 1841, right after their arrival.

"Just so you don't get any ideas—I never want to live out on the farm," Hannah said.

Robert scoffed inwardly at Hannah's insecurity. As he watched Joseph, Lizzy, William, and even little Thomas poke at their mother's tummy in awe, Robert marveled at how attractive his wife was, despite four children and nearly seven years of marriage. He still admired her cute pug nose, her dark eyebrows over deep-set brown eyes, and her creamy full lips circled by an oval chin.

"I suspect Elizabeth won't want to live out on the farm either," Hannah stated. "Too many people right around here rely on her too much." Hannah's only aim in life was to raise her children in a peaceful atmosphere. Nauvoo was her heaven on earth.

"It would be nice to live on the farm someday," Robert said. "That's where my work is."

"But we're so close to the temple site here," Hannah complained. "And out there, you'd be too close to Henry again."

Robert ran his hands through his coarse brown hair. "I think Ole Henry's gonna end up moving to Carthage one of these days. That's what he keeps claiming. Besides, we could get into a daily tussle. I need the exercise."

Hannah shuddered at the thought of her brother Henry and his wife Katherine moving to Carthage. She wished Henry would let his guard down and join the Church. However, it was comforting to her to know that Robert and Henry hadn't actually had a serious come-to-blows fight for several months. For that, she was grateful. All the years she had known Robert, it seemed there was always someone for him to hate. Back in their courtship years, and in the first years of their marriage, it was all the opponents Robert had as he contended for the British heavyweight championship. Here in Nauvoo, other than former mayor John C. Bennett, whom Robert often said he would like to give a good whipping, Robert seemed to have no one other than Henry to particularly hate. An exception might be enemies of the Church in Missouri that he had never met. But she didn't have to worry about Robert lining up an official fight with them. He just grumbled whenever he heard the Missourians threatening the Prophet, and privately told Hannah that he wished the Prophet would commission him to fight the Missourians one at a time. After a while, he would have them all so black and blue they would leave poor Joseph Smith alone.

Leftover cornbread was served with the bacon for breakfast. Robert stood, wiping his mouth when he was done. "I'll never get used to cornbread, but I do like honey." He had to use a forefinger to capture the absolute last drop of the sweetener, which was just as sweet licked off a finger as it was when eaten on American cornbread.

"You're just too English," Hannah said, taking the hint that she needed to bake some regular bread. She took Robert's dish and carried it to the wash-tub.

Robert turned to his oldest son. "Let's do our chores, Joseph." He loved his three sons, but the apple of his eye was his daughter, Lizzy. He fancied her marrying an Apostle one day.

"You bundle that boy up good, Robert," Hannah warned. "Two pairs of trousers, two shirts, and his overcoat. I don't want him frostbitten. I think it set a record for cold during the night. Bring in some more wood, too."

# 4

DANIEL MOMENTARILY SNAPPED OUT OF his bleakness when he saw Robert and his son step outside their cozy cabin to begin their morning chores. Daniel desperately needed someone to talk to who knew him well, and nobody fit that bill better than his best friend, his brother-in-law. He dressed himself, threw on his coat, and stepped outside where a gripping cold wind was still blowing from the north. The wind had drifted the snow into ripples, scattered across the road and the landscape. He thought of Elizabeth and where she might be, and how she was faring in the cold. The sun was rising as a faint disk in the eastern sky, casting the gentle hills and leafless trees into a shadowless twilight.

With legs that felt like a boneless chicken, Daniel crossed his lot and found Robert under his lean-to on a one-legged milk stool, his head in the flank of a black-and-white cow. Steam rose from a pail of white foamy milk. A brown dog approached, offering a friendly lick at Daniel's hand. Two horses neighed from a corral, signaling their need for a pitchfork full of hay.

"Morning, Daniel," Robert said, without looking up.

Daniel exhaled slowly. "Morning," he said, his voice soft.

"You sound sick," Robert said. "Does he sound sick to you, Joseph?"

Joseph brought his shoulders high around his ears, not answering.

"I'm not sick," Daniel said, allowing a little more volume from his five-foot-ten-inch frame.

"Old Victoria's about dry," Robert said in his English accent. "We'll have to quit on 'er in a couple more weeks. Good thing your cow's giving lots of milk." He squeezed the final strippings in the wooden pail, which was less than half full.

"I haven't milked yet this morning, but I'll give you all you want when I do," Daniel said. At the mention of Victoria's name, Daniel thought of Robert's curious habit of naming animals after English royalty. Victoria the cow. Duke the dog. In England, Robert had named the two family horses Old Earl and Queenie. It had always given Robert great pleasure to give orders to aristocrats, or to anyone in authority. In Nauvoo, Robert had slightly departed from the practice. He had named the two farm horses Tapper and Bendigo, nicknames of famous British fighters. But then Robert ordered them around, too, and even punched them in the gut when they didn't behave.

The horses neighed again and pawed at the frozen turf, begging for a pitchfork full of hay.

"My hands nearly froze off this morning. If it weren't for Old Victoria's warm flank ..." The former pugilist and butcher thrust his right hand between the cow's leg and udder. Victoria didn't flinch.

Daniel thought of Elizabeth again, and wondered how she was coping with the cold morning. He drew a deep breath of courage. "I need to talk to you about your sister."

Robert withdrew the pail and stood. Daniel was grateful that Robert seemed to sense the urgency in his voice.

Duke whined for his share of the milk, trotting to a snow-covered pan. Robert kicked the snow off the pan and poured a little milk. "Now, or shall we go inside?"

"My place," Daniel replied, motioning with his head. "Just you and me."

"I'll give this to Hannah," Robert said, referring to the pail. "Turn Victoria out of the stanchion for me. And feed the horses."

When Robert opened the door, Hannah called out. "I've got some bacon and cornbread left over, Daniel. Want some?"

"No thanks," Daniel said, waving her off. He reached out to touch Tapper and Bendigo's muzzles. Right now, he thought how relieved he would be to trade one of them places. He would rather be a horse, a cow, or any barnyard animal right now. The horses were blowing steamy air out their nostrils.

"Where'd Elizabeth go so early?" she asked.

"The usual," Daniel lied, meaning her midwife duties. He retreated toward his own cabin, beckoning Robert.

"Someone froze to death out on the prairie yesterday," Robert said, walking toward Daniel's place. "I can't remember the name. Brother Roberts told me."

Daniel closed his eyes, thinking of Elizabeth again. He was still fighting the urge to follow her tracks.

"Joseph, go inside and help your Mama before you go off to school," Robert said, pointing.

Daniel watched the boy obey. Daniel found himself wishing he had a young son who could be his chore boy—run errands, carry water, fill the wood box, and clean ashes from the fireplace. Joseph would wear blisters on his hands come spring, using a hoe handle to plant and weed rows of beans, onions, corn, and potatoes.

When they got inside and closed the door, Daniel said, "What I'm about to tell you is just between you and me." He took off his cap, revealing tussled blond hair.

The words put Robert into a slight fidget. "What do you mean?"

Emotion spilled into Daniel's throat. "It's not even for Hannah."

Raised eyebrows and a shrug of the shoulder signaled Robert's acceptance of the terms. "Fine."

Daniel rehearsed everything—from the time Orson Hyde made his visit yesterday afternoon to the huffy manner in which Elizabeth stormed out of the house early this morning. There was a broad sweep of emotions that ran through Daniel as he related his story. One moment he was practically sobbing, and the next he was taking a firm resolve. One moment he expressed strong support of the Prophet, the next he weakened.

Robert made a wide range of facial expressions, stood for part of the time, sat on the chair, moved to a wooden bench, and stood again. He acknowledged to Daniel that he had heard about plural marriage. Daniel could tell that the conversation clearly shocked Robert, especially the fact that Daniel had been asked to participate. Robert said he thought it was something only a few handpicked Church leaders had been asked to do. He asked questions about details of the three Church authorities' explanation of the principle, and about Daniel's willingness to enter into the practice.

Daniel related the only conversation he had with Elizabeth about plural marriage prior to last night. It had happened two months earlier, shortly after Hannah's brother, Henry, had accosted Rebecca and tried to take her as his own secret "spiritual" wife. And it was a conversation Elizabeth had initiated.

"I have to ask you this question," Elizabeth had said that night, probing.

"About polygamy? Would I take another wife if the brethren asked?"

Daniel watched Elizabeth's jaw drop. The subject had been off limits by mutual agreement. Elizabeth blinked hard and then smoothed her hair, searching for her next words.

"It would break my heart," she said, through misted green eyes. She dabbed at them with her apron.

"And mine," Daniel answered without hesitation.

"But if the brethren asked?"

Daniel took several seconds to answer, thinking. "I don't know," he said honestly. "It would have to be a matter of prayer and fasting."

Elizabeth bowed her head, and stared at the floor. She wiped her eyes again. "I feel so *terrible* that I have not given you a child yet."

"Elizabeth. Please. It's not your fault."

"I think about my blessing from Brigham Young every day. At least *one* child. That's what Willard Richards said Brigham's blessing meant. A mother in Zion."

Daniel reached for his wife's hand. He squeezed it.

Elizabeth looked mournful. "Perhaps another wife could give you a child."

"Elizabeth, that's enough for now. I love you."

More tears. "I love you, too."

Robert took a deep breath, contemplating all he'd heard. Nearly an hour had passed and he felt genuine sorrow for Daniel, thankful this terrible situation was not happening to him. In a low, mild voice he asked a question. "Are you certain you're committed to take Sister Clifford to wife if Elizabeth changes her mind and accepts this whole business?"

Daniel looked thoughtful, as he always did. His eyes seemed to be traveling over scenes from the past, giving the impression that he was a man of sorrows. "You need to know I did not seek this in any manner. I never once mentioned to Elder Woodruff, or anyone else, that I would be willing to take another wife. I never suggested to anyone that I could take Sister Clifford into my home."

Robert slowly pulled his shoulders up. "I believe you."

Daniel stood to throw three more logs onto the fire. In seconds, huge flames licked at the hearth's interior. "I was shocked when they asked me," he said, gnawing on his bottom lip.

Robert nodded. He was not a patient man and he was anxious to hear the rest of the details. "It would be a shock to anyone's system."

"I love your sister more than life itself. I can't wait to be sealed to her. But she's not in the right spiritual frame of mind right now."

Robert accepted Daniel's response. "I know."

"If she says no, I have no hesitation in telling the brethren. I just won't do it."

"What about Sister Clifford?" Robert sensed that the Spirit had already whispered to Daniel that the widow should be under his care.

"She's not the only widow in Nauvoo. We can all help her. Chop her wood. Milk her cow. Things like that. I wish poor James were still alive. They would have made a perfect couple."

"So Elizabeth blew her cork?" Robert asked.

"That's an understatement," Daniel said.

"Well, she's always been the kind of girl who's emotional. You have to keep the reins laid on her loose."

"You can say that again. I cringe at the thought of having her this mad at me."

Out of the corner of his eye, Robert caught the image of a person approaching the cabin. It was Elizabeth. Almost unconsciously, he retreated toward the hearth.

# 5

DANIEL RECOILED AS ELIZABETH BURST through the door. She brought powdery flakes of snow with her, pushed by the wind. For a second, she seemed distracted at the sight of her brother. But it didn't stop her from marching toward Daniel, her face red and her green eyes flaring with anger. She thrust a bony finger into his chest.

"You're not the *only* one who's read the Book of Mormon," she squealed. "The Prophet Jacob condemned this whole *scurrilous* business." Again and again, she jabbed her finger into his chest.

Daniel felt helpless and cast a quick glance at Robert, who closed the door. *Don't leave!* Daniel screamed with pleading eyes.

Daniel was retreating now, until his back touched the log wall. He was unable to express his thoughts in defense of the doctrine. Jacob had condemned the *unauthorized* practice of plural marriage among his own people. Plural marriage had been the norm among just about all the civilizations of the past: the Far East, Middle East, Near East, and the Book of Mormon lands. He suspected it had been practiced throughout the entire history of the earth, in every gospel dispensation.

Elizabeth continued her angry ranting. "Jacob said that men should have only *one* wife. Do you hear me? *One wife.* And *don't* lecture me about those *frail* old men of the Bible—Abraham, Jacob, David, Solomon, and Moses. I *don't care* if they had one wife, two wives, or a thousand. That was *another* time. Women in these *modern* times aren't going to put up with that nonsense. Having more than one wife is an *abomination!* So says the Prophet Jacob!"

Daniel hoped Robert wasn't fighting back the urge to laugh, but in a way the scene was a comic one. Here was his wife, the woman both he and Robert oft times described as the lioness of England—the woman who always did as she pleased and everyone else could get out of her way—devouring her husband with an anger Daniel had never seen. Just as always, she was over accentuating certain words for effect, a habit she acquired from her mother. And here he was, in full sight of his brother-in-law, backed against the wall, biting his tongue, elbows pushed out in defense, bracing for possible slaps to the face.

Suddenly, Elizabeth whirled. Somehow she detected the silent communication between Robert and Daniel. "And *you!*" Elizabeth withdrew her accusatory finger and pointed it at Robert.

Robert cowered to a corner of the house.

"I suppose you have been here all morning having a good *laugh* over this, haven't you? Have the *brethren* talked to you, too? Where are *you* going to build *your* new wife's cabin? Right next door to Hannah? Now wouldn't *that* be cozy? I suppose Levi, John, and Edward are in on this, too. My, my. Aren't we going to have a *cozy* little community right here by the new temple?"

Daniel watched the smirk disappear from Robert's face. The lioness had attacked the both of them. She had even reverted to her old southwestern English accent, the brogue sounding like that of her parents. He felt a thickening shroud of absurdity settle into the room. He had seen and heard enough. "Elizabeth, it's time you calmed down."

She whirled again. "I told you earlier this morning *not* to speak to me. *I'm* doing the talking here. And I'm *far* from finished."

"Fine," Daniel said, sitting in the chair. "Just let me know when you're done. Then I've got a few things to say, and I *will* say them."

"You must think I'm *blind,*" she ranted, flaring her index finger again. "I happen to have seen a copy of the *Messenger and Advocate* published in Kirtland way back in 1835. Joseph declared that one man should have one wife. Want me to get you a copy?"

Daniel bit his lip, taking mental notes.

Elizabeth threw off her coat. *"Don't* answer that. He said the same thing in the *Times and Seasons* just two months ago. One wife! Hear me?"

"Harriet Clifford."

Daniel felt a flush of relief and paused to let his words sink in.

Elizabeth took a deep breath. For a second, she rolled her eyes. She failed to catch the implication. "I told you to be quiet. What does *she* have to do with all this?"

"Think," Daniel said, hoping she would reach the obvious conclusion.

Elizabeth's voice cracked. *"Don't* play games."

"That's who the brethren asked me to take in."

There was dead silence in the room for a few seconds. The fire crackled and popped. Daniel glanced at Robert, who fought the urge to smile. Daniel let his eyes return to his wife. The look on her face turned incredulous. Daniel hoped she was thinking of the evening when Harriet Barnes Clifford lost James Pulham in the well accident.

Elizabeth seemed to be wallowing in astonishment while silence pervaded the room.

"But you have to approve," Daniel said quickly. "Or it's off. They'll find someone else to take care of her. That's why you need to pray about this."

For a moment it appeared that the light of possibility was going to shine through Elizabeth's soul. There seemed to be a glimmer of contentment and peace. She tilted her head to one side, as though in deep thought. She had always been one to accept others into her circle of friends, even energized by people who were once strangers. This was especially true as long as the new friend didn't overshadow her: Elizabeth liked being the center of attention.

She saw in herself the ability to be the social glue of society, a genuine people connector.

A heavy iron teapot hung over the fire. Robert approached it slowly. "I'll bet you're freezing, dear sister. Let me pour you a cup of tea."

Daniel grimaced. The distraction seemed to somehow rekindle Elizabeth's anger and resentment. The peaceful look on her face vanished. He felt her reverting to an old weakness: an unwillingness to commit to long-term needs of distressed friends. His wife was totally capable of focusing on herself and ignoring the feelings of others.

"Harriet Clifford? *Fine*. Go *live* with her. You two *lovebirds* can stay in *her* cabin. Or for all I care, you can *finish* the cabin James started for her."

Daniel shrank in disbelief, almost giving up.

Elizabeth snatched the teapot from her brother. She poured her own tea. "See this teapot? It's *mine*. See this cup? It's *mine*. See this cabin? It's *mine.*"

Robert retreated to his corner.

"Elizabeth," Daniel stammered, "you're being ridiculous."

She pushed the cup into Daniel's chest, spilling composition tea onto his shirt. "You already know what's *really* ridiculous. Plural marriage. You can't unspill a glass of spilled milk. Gather up your things and *get out.*"

Daniel cast another helpless glance at Robert. He wondered if he could ever forgive Elizabeth for this emotional outburst of hers.

Elizabeth threw Daniel's coat at him and pointed to her brother and to the door. "Take your things and *leave.* I'm going to catch up on my sleep."

"But where …?"

"Stay in the lean-to with the *cow* for all I care. Maybe Robert will take you in. He has a *small* family—only *four* children. Better yet, stay with your new *sweetheart*, Harriet."

Robert opened the door to Elizabeth's acrimonious scowl. "Come on, Daniel. Let's get your cow milked."

The two men walked out.

Elizabeth stared morbidly at the door for a few seconds, and then went into the bedroom and collapsed onto her bed, sobbing again.

# 6

*January 1843*

GOVERNOR THOMAS FORD sipped his coffee in a grumpy mood. Carpenters and painters coming in and out of his office irritated him. Ford loved the new statehouse in Springfield because of its Greek revival architecture and handsome cupola, but he hated the fact that continuing political and financial problems meant that the structure wouldn't be completed for several more years. The Senate Chamber and the Representatives Hall were being used, but like all the offices, workers were still scurrying around like ants.

Whigs were another source of irritation to the governor. He hated them. One Whig—a young, brash lawyer by the name of Abraham Lincoln—had published satirical letters attacking Ford's auditor, James Shields, a fellow Democrat.

"You should have killed Lincoln when you had a chance," Ford told Shields, over a cup of coffee laced with brandy on this cold December morning. As a strong personality who moved forcefully through life, he found himself again cursing at his political enemies. "All the Whigs ought to be six feet under."

Last year Shields and Lincoln almost faced off in a duel with cavalry broadswords on a sandbar in the Mississippi River. Friends parted them just in time. And just a few days ago, Lincoln had been the first person to borrow a book from the state library that had just opened. That also rankled Ford. As far as he was concerned, the library ought to be off limits to Whigs.

Shields nodded his agreement through spectacles that hung over the end of his nose. He was a thirty-four-year-old Irishman with a hot temper.

"Back to the Mormon problem," said Ford, pulling on his thin upper lip. He had no compunction about parading his values and opinions in the faces of all others, including his political friends. The Mormons were another irritant to Ford. "What's your latest count?" He glared at the five-foot-nine-inch Irishman, who stood a few inches shorter that himself. Ford wished he were as witty and energetic as Shields. Shields was single and a successful womanizer. But both men had at least one thing in common. They had a passionate hatred for Mormonism.

"We estimate there are sixteen thousand of them in Hancock County alone," Shields answered, the Irish accent evident. "Several thousand more scattered in the other counties." Previous to his election as auditor, Shields had been a lawyer and a member of the state legislature.

"Good Lord, what if they vote Whig in the next election?"

"It'll throw Democrats out of office."

Ford shook his head in anger, brown hair spilling over his eyes. The thought gave him a bleak outlook. Unlike Shields, he was not a good conversationalist; he liked to lecture rather than listen. This limitation caused him to experience long periods of loneliness, although he would never admit it. He conveniently blamed his loneliness on others. "Doesn't look good for us right now. The Democrats in Missouri and Illinois procured the arrest of Joe Smith. But right under our nose he was released by a Whig judge."

Shields poured two jiggers of whiskey as he shook his head. "And his case was handled by Whig lawyers."

Ford sneezed, wiped at his long nose, and then poured his whiskey into his coffee and drank it. "Funny thing about it, Joe Smith is probably too stupid and ignorant of the law to know whether he owes his discharge to the law, or to the favor of the court and the Whigs."

When Ford had come into office, the previous governor—Thomas Carlin—had issued a warrant for the arrest of Joe Smith as a fugitive from justice from Missouri. The warrant had never been executed and was still outstanding when Ford came into office. The Mormons were desirous of having the cause of arrest legally tested in court. Upon the Mormons' application, a duplicate warrant had been issued and placed in the hands of the sheriff of Sangamon County. Thus, Joe Smith had come to Springfield and surrendered. A writ of habeas corpus—a writ requiring an imprisoned person to be brought to a stated place at a stated time for the legality of his imprisonment to be examined—was granted.

The governor pulled at his dimpled chin and cursed. *That imbecile Judge Pope—the Whig—discharged Joe Smith!*

Ford went off on the Mormons again, pacing the floor, letting his tenacious nature take over. "Seems to me that every time the government bores down hard on the Mormons, however legal, they look upon it as wantonly oppressive. But whenever the law is administered in their favor, they attribute it to partiality and kindness. What kind of people are they?"

"Peculiar," Shields said. "Quite peculiar and quite clever."

Ford ground his teeth together. His normal tendency was to remedy problems quickly, exhausting every possible avenue to do it. "How many spiritual wives does Joe Smith think he needs?"

Shields grinned. "Smith should have just stayed single, like me. No one thinks I'm peculiar." He was thinking of a long line of mistresses.

"I just hope them rotten peculiar people don't vote Whig in the next election," Ford said. His inner competitive nature was eating at him. "If we think hard enough, Mr. Shields, we'll find a way to get rid of the Mormons."

When Shields left, Ford was left alone to fret about the Mormons. He took another drink and admitted to himself that his opinion of Joe Smith and his Church had eroded quickly these past few months. At first, back in 1839, just before his appointment to the state Supreme Court, he had held a neutral view of Joe Smith and the Mormons, almost tolerant. At first the Mormons were nothing more to him than religious refugees fleeing from their former settlements in Missouri. That first winter they huddled in and around Quincy, but with the coming of spring they moved seventy miles up the river into Hancock County. There, they commenced building a new settlement called Nauvoo, if anything now the most worthless community in all Illinois. The Mormons had never become Missourians; and they had never become Illinoisans, either.

Ford laughed to himself. These "spiritual wifery" Mormons were peculiar all right. He viewed them as a collection of former Baptists, Methodists, Presbyterians, Campbellites, Millerites, and whatever. They came not only from western New York—where Smith started the religion—but seemed to pour into Illinois from the Northeast, the Ohio Valley, the South, and even Great Britain. They were a strong-willed people, and that was part of the problem.

To Ford, Mormonism was an unorthodox sect whose ways shocked not only him, but the world—and probably its own members as well. Yes, they had abundant self-confidence, a sense of mission, pragmatism under-girded by faith, and a high degree of social idealism. But Ford believed that their doctrines were too radical, too different. Smith claimed to have both seen and talked with God. He claimed an angel had given him gold plates, and the writings on them had become the Book of Mormon. Although the Mormons professed belief in Jesus Christ, they seemed to almost worship Smith. Now Smith claimed that God had told him to practice the ancient custom of multiple wives!

Ford recalled how varied his early opinions of Joe Smith were. Smith seemed to be an enigma, unfathomed by both his followers and his enemies. Sometimes Smith came across as simple, even superficial, sometimes complex and profound, sometimes arrogant, sometimes contrite. Smith was definitely a passionate man, loving his friends and hating his enemies with equal fervor. He seemed to excite rather than soothe rising passions. But he was a poor judge of character, placing key people around him who later became his most bitter enemies—John C. Bennett as an early example. And Joe Smith was a man naïve in temporal affairs, an easy mark for sharpies and flatterers.

Despite Smith's character flaws, Ford had long ago become aware of the Mormon Prophet's extraordinary influence over his followers. The appeal of Smith's vision could not lightly be dismissed, despite his inexperience and naivety. There seemed to be no end to the sacrifices Smith's Mormon people would undertake and the zeal they would manifest. Nauvoo had quickly become the largest city in the state.

Ford had never understood why Joe Smith chose to locate his Zion in western Illinois. Didn't Smith know that mean, rascally characters would quickly surround him? Thieves, counterfeiters, and rogues of all kinds? There was little or no chance of religious tolerance here. There had always been a strong tendency against religion in Illinois, especially along its western frontier. Folks out here didn't want interference of any kind with their liberty to drink, hunt, race horses, and gamble every day of the week, including Sundays. They didn't want to address such questions as immorality, intemperance, vice, or tobacco-chewing. Frontier people tended to be agnostic, rejecting notions of salvation and damnation.

Ex-Mormon and non-Mormon charges against Joe Smith and his Saints these past few weeks and months had been both sensational and alarming, in Ford's view. Did the Mormons really want to conquer the states of Ohio, Indiana, Illinois, Iowa, and Missouri? Did Joe Smith really want to set up a despotic and religious empire, ruled by Smith and his ministers and viceroys? Did the Mormons really want to wage a holy war of revenge against Missouri? Or were they more apt to pull up stakes and establish an independent empire in Oregon Territory? Or in Texas? And what of the internal strife, disunion, and schism within Smith's church? The Mormons condemned secret societies, but encouraged a Masonic lodge in Nauvoo. The Mormons denounced "priestcraft," but employed a priestly hierarchy of control that grew stronger and more absolute day by day. Church leaders had insisted on strict morality among its members, but now Ford was hearing rumors that polygamy was widespread among the Mormons. He chuckled over the fact that the spiritual wife doctrine was unsettling to many Saints and the cause of some apostasy.

Lately it seemed that nearly everyone hated Joe Smith and the Mormons: apostates within the strange religion, non-Mormons from Carthage and Warsaw, all the Missourians, and even some of the Whigs.

And most Democrats.

Hannah knew that Elizabeth and Daniel were having problems, but she didn't know the cause. A warm day in January found her sauntering between their two cabins, on her way to visit Elizabeth. Daniel was sitting outside, making Elizabeth a new butter churn. Lately, it seemed, he was always doing something to curry Elizabeth's favor. His blond hair glistened in the morning light. Near him, long icicles hung from the eaves, dripping in the sun.

"Oh, Elizabeth's going to just love you," Hannah said with a tinge of jealousy. "I wish Robert had your skills."

Daniel, the former cooper and carpenter, had cut cedar strips in the fall, when the sap was down, and left the wood drying under his lean-to. He had already split the cedar into staves with his stave froe, cut sixteen of them to a twenty-one-inch length, and shaved their sides so they were narrow at the top and thicker at the bottom. Now he was using his long jointer to plane the edges, getting ready to fit them into his temporary hoops.

"Elizabeth's complained about the old churn Sister Roberts gave her ever since we arrived in Nauvoo," Hannah said, her big brown eyes following the jointer. "Maybe it'll cheer her up. I don't know why she's been such a grouch lately."

Hannah wondered why Daniel took such a deep breath. "I hope so," he said. His eyes almost seem to water. His formerly good-natured wife had dissolved into a puddle of unhappiness.

With song sparrows flying out of the way, Hannah pushed open the door to the Browett home. "Elizabeth? Got a minute? I need to talk to you."

Elizabeth was at her table and had an unusual look—the look of a woman who was somewhere else. She had a fine head of blond hair but today it looked unkempt, wiry and gnarly. Her cheeks were hollowed a little, which normally gave her a distracting beauty. This time she looked pale and angry. Experience had taught Hannah that Elizabeth's demeanor could be dangerous when she had that certain angry look. The hearth fire was nearly out, a victim of neglect. Elizabeth's tone was stiff and cool. "I suppose. You're halfway in, so you might as well come all the way in."

Bristling at Elizabeth's iciness, Hannah scanned the small cabin. Dirty dishes littered the table. The black kettle was swung away from the fire, nothing cooking. There was no evidence of knitting, or an open book. Elizabeth's spinning wheel was collecting cobwebs, half covered by a dirty apron. Her bag of herbs and remedies lay in a corner, catching soot dust from the hearth. All of this appalled Hannah.

"Haven't you been feeling well?" Hannah asked. In past times, Hannah had always thought how youthful and attractive her sister-in-law looked— sharp features, long Roman nose, dark eyebrows under blond hair, and fair skin. Today Elizabeth looked like a forlorn crab.

Elizabeth yawned behind her hand. "I'm just fine," she fibbed.

Hannah furrowed her brow and closed the door. "But you haven't been out and about. You haven't even delivered any babies lately, have you?"

Elizabeth's dedication as a midwife and herbalist had always amazed Hannah. Elizabeth had entered into the practice at the behest of Elder Willard Richards, who suggested she enter the practice following a personal blessing given to her by Elder Woodruff back in England, in 1840. She restricted her practice mainly to Woodruff's converts, former members of the United Brethren congregation. There were many other midwives in Nauvoo, ranging from the busiest—Patty Sessions—to others like Ann Green Duston, another English convert from Herefordshire, and Sarah Marinda Thompson from Scotland.

Elizabeth scowled. "Nothing wrong with me." Methodically and placidly, without inviting Hannah, she began to devour a loaf of bread, chunk by chunk, with a cold stew, sopping up brown juice from her plate. Each time she broke the bread, her gestures and dull countenance showed disgust at the feel and smell of the loaf.

There were a few moments of awkward silence as Hannah assessed the look on Elizabeth's face.

Elizabeth finally looked up. This time her tone was laced with loathing. "And you?"

Hannah sighed, wondering why Elizabeth did not offer her any of the food. In her condition, however, she had no appetite. "That's why I came to see you. I'm going to have another baby."

The cool tone continued, the jealousy evident. There was a series of gasps and grunts as she devoured more bread and stew. "Tush. That's hardly news, considering it's the *fifth* time."

Hannah bristled but clung to her dogged determination to make a conversation. "I get scared, actually, thinking about the baby's future." She glanced through the small window in the Browett cabin. Outside, her three oldest children were playing in the snow.

"What do you mean?" Elizabeth queried.

"I'm worried about the coming years here," Hannah said, wagging a finger at her sister-in-law. "The Prophet's trial in Springfield. How the Missourians keep trying to arrest Joseph, like some kind of cat-and-mouse game. All the anti-Mormon articles in the Warsaw newspaper. What if our enemies get stirred up enough to start harming us bodily?"

Elizabeth's face remained sullen and withdrawn. She reached to her feet and pulled a red quilt over her, as though she felt a chill. Hannah wondered when Elizabeth was going to start to share the excitement of her pregnancies.

"Those Mormon-haters write essays like little kids making up a melody," Hannah continued on as she twisted one hand in the other. "They meander along, issuing snide remarks until they run out of energy, then conclude with the most vicious thing they can think of to kick down the doors of our religion."

Elizabeth didn't respond.

Hannah's patience snapped. "You could smile, you know. It costs nothing and would do you good. And you could comb your hair and put on a clean dress. Show a little enthusiasm, even if you don't feel like it. Make a cake and lick the spoon. Cheer up, woman."

Still, no response.

A feeling of helplessness came over Hannah, not knowing what to say next. Nothing worked, not even criticism. Patiently, she loosened her bonnet and waited for a reaction. Elizabeth's next words shocked her.

"Daniel wants to marry Harriet Clifford."

Hannah reeled, the words hanging like a pall. She was tempted to laugh. Elizabeth was given to some funny notions, but that was one of the funniest, to think that a man of Daniel's loyalty would marry another woman. "Marry Harriet? Elizabeth, I've never known you to make this kind of a joke."

Elizabeth made a despairing gesture with both hands. "Oh, I'm *not* joking. Surely you've heard of this spiritual wife stuff. Now it's *Daniel's* turn. I'd rather hear of someone who drowned or got stomped by a horse. It's more than I can handle."

*Spiritual wife.* Hannah hated the term used by John C. Bennett in his criticism of the Prophet and the Church. The doctrine of plural marriage suited her better. She detested the thought that it might someday enter into her life, but she had no problem with the rumor that some leaders of the Church had entered into the practice.

"You mean that the brethren have asked Daniel to take in Sister Clifford?" Hannah fought to keep her voice empty of the sentimental pity she felt.

Elizabeth went off on everything. "Life here in Nauvoo is just so *keen,* isn't it? Surely you heard about Judge Pope coming into the courtroom in Springfield, accompanied by all those *ladies.* He certainly made *his* point about spiritual wifery. Do you think Brother Joseph had a good *laugh* about it? The judge's little private joke about polygamy, and all the rumors it brought—it's just *great* for our Mormon community, isn't it?"

Hannah shook her head at Elizabeth's cynicism. Good news had actually come out of that courtroom. Judge Pope had ruled that Joseph Smith could not be extradited from Illinois to face old charges in Missouri. Pope threw out the extradition order because of its vagueness and legal inadequacy. Joseph's attorney had said afterward, "It is a momentous occasion in my life to appear before the Pope, in defense of a Prophet of God, in the presence of all these angels."

"I don't know *why* you and Robert participated in the day of thanksgiving that was held just because Joseph was freed," Elizabeth hissed.

Hannah looked away. Everyone in her ward, except Elizabeth, had responded enthusiastically when an assembly had been held where the Saints could hear details about the proceedings in Springfield.

Elizabeth's prattling went on. "And I suppose you heard the statement that Joseph made about the Negro. He's *asking* for more trouble."

*Yes, and it was a good statement,* Hannah thought, wondering where Elizabeth was going with all this. The Prophet had said, "Change their situation with the whites and they would be like them. They have souls, and are subjects of salvation. The slaves in Washington are more refined than many in high places, and the black boys will take the shine off of those they brush and wait on."

"Trouble?" Hannah scoffed. "I suppose so. If Brother Joseph continues his advocacy for the black people, the southern people and everyone who owns slaves will grow to hate him." *But what does all this have to do with Daniel and Harriet Clifford?*

Elizabeth was not done with her ranting, flitting from subject to subject. "Orson Pratt was *rebaptized* and reinstated as an Apostle. Do you *agree* with that? I'll tell you another thing I think is bunk. Joseph's article in the *Wasp.* Despite what he says about wanting to be left alone to attend to the spiritual affairs of the Church, I think he'll get *involved* in politics. I heard he was caught playing ball with some of the brethren. Can you imagine? A Prophet playing *ball?* Elder Kimball needs to lecture the *Prophet* on loose style of morals, instead of the young people that were at his home the other day. What do you think of the name, 'Young Gentlemen and Ladies Relief Society' for the youngsters here in Nauvoo? Is that where they're going to *teach* them about spiritual wifery? Are you going to *vote* for Joseph as mayor next week? Maybe I'll write in Daniel's name. Get him out of the house."

Hannah grimaced. As far as she was concerned, Nauvoo was still the closest thing to a paradise on earth. True, she lived in a modest log cabin. But it was *hers*. It didn't belong to some American aristocrat. She had despised Squire Hastings and the hold he had on her husband back in England. Here, the economy was strong. In England, people were still starving. Here, people could actually vote. There were Whigs and Democrats, statewide and nationwide. Here in Nauvoo, people could vote for mayors and councilmen. State politicians fell over themselves currying favor from the Mormon-voting bloc. A solid Mormon vote had put Thomas Ford into the governor's chair. Here, a charter granted the city by the state gave power to the municipal court. Mormons didn't have to be hauled off to Carthage or the state capital, Springfield, on most charges. The local Nauvoo Legion was becoming the largest military body in the nation, except for the U.S. Army.

Personally, Hannah took little interest in the rumors that non-Mormons in surrounding communities were nervous. She felt it was *their* problem if they were jealous of the labor and materials lavished upon the construction of the temple. Or that its completion someday might somehow symbolize Mormon dominance in the area. As far as she was concerned, persistent whispers of the practice of polygamy within the Church, even by the Prophet Joseph, was none of their business. If the Lord decreed that the doctrine of polygamy be restored in the latter days, so be it. Thomas Sharp and his Anti-Mormon Party, and his newspaper, could be flushed down the Mississippi for all she cared. Let them rant and rave about the claim that Joseph Smith ordered Porter Rockwell to shoot ex-Governor Boggs of Missouri. She believed the Prophet's statement: "It wasn't Port. Port wouldn't have missed." And it didn't bother Hannah that ex-Mayor John C. Bennett was striking back at the Church with vindictive fury. He was merely a tool of Satan. Let him try to take the lid off Nauvoo with lies about Joseph, lurid stories about women and plural marriage, a Nauvoo underworld, a city with a depot for stolen goods, and plans for world domination. Hannah's testimony of the gospel was rock solid, and she was not affected by Bennett, Thomas Sharp, Boggs, or Elizabeth Browett. Or the fact that Joseph was in hiding, trying to avoid arrest by the devil and his Missouri followers.

But Hannah was sorely saddened by her sister-in-law's deteriorating attitude. She tried steering the conversation in another direction. "Have you seen Sister Kington in the last week or two? Is she still battling the flu?"

Thomas Kington, founder of the United Brethren in England, had lost both his wife and mother in death shortly after his arrival in Nauvoo. A year ago, he had married again, this time taking a widow to wife, the former Margaret Peizel Myers. But she had been ill since the birth of their first child in October.

"Haven't seen her."

The stark briefness of Elizabeth's answer chilled Hannah. Her lack of interest seemed rude compared to Elizabeth's old way of caring for all her "patients." Last month, Elizabeth relished the praise heaped on her for being a midwife and an herbalist. Now, she didn't care. Last month, Elizabeth was at center stage with all her involvement. Now, she was pouting on the back row. Last month, Elizabeth was one of the most popular wives among the English immigrants. Now, everyone avoided her.

Hannah fixed her dark brown eyes on her sister-in-law, now probing her to the very core. An uneasy feeling came over Hannah. It spoke of darkness. *What has happened to your spirituality, Elizabeth?* She wanted to scream the words. Instead, she decided to politely excuse herself.

"Got to get back to the children. Robert's going duck hunting this afternoon with Levi and John." Hannah wanted to invite Elizabeth over for a roast duck dinner, but she tucked the words back in.

Elizabeth's parting shot did not make Hannah feel any different. "Be glad Robert's not going hunting with Wilford Woodruff or Orson Hyde. In their sly little way, they'd shoot you in the back."

Hannah tied her bonnet around her dark auburn hair and left the Browett cabin, grateful for the fresh air outside.

CHAPTER NOTES

Ford's viewpoint on Mormons is taken from his book, *A History of Illinois* (Chicago: S. C. Greggs & Co., 1854), pp. 313-315.

On September 22, 1842, Auditor James Shields challenged Abraham Lincoln to a duel after Lincoln published satirical letters attacking Shield's official practices. Their friends, however, settled the dispute just before the duel began. Sandburg, Carl, *Abraham Lincoln,* Volume One (New York: Harcourt, Brace and Company, 1954), pp. 76-77.

# 7

MARY ANN PRICE GREETED ORSON HYDE at her doorstep with an accepting smile. She didn't know, however, that the invitation to accompany him to his house for dinner would also include an invitation to become his third wife.

Mary Ann had left England in September 1841, nearly a year after her baptism in Gloucestershire. Her husband had opposed her baptism and had grown intensely adverse to the Mormons. They separated. Petite and attractive, she was yet another single woman in Nauvoo, having arrived in November 1842 as the influx from the British missions continued. She considered herself another victim of the industrial revolution in England, but Church officials had been successful in constantly reducing the fare to get to America to less than five British pounds.

The appointment to dine with Orson and Marinda Hyde had been made a week earlier. It had driven her crazy all week: she could not figure out why she would be invited to dine with an Apostle and his wife. Mary Ann knew only basic information about Elder Hyde—that he had been called as a member of the Quorum of the Twelve Apostles in 1834, and that he had dedicated the Holy Land in 1841. The thing that most impressed Mary Ann about Elder Hyde was the fact that he had memorized the Bible not only in English, but in German and Hebrew as well.

Orson was bowing deeply as a curious Mary Ann opened the door. He held his tall beaver hat in his hand, letting his brilliant red hair glisten in the afternoon sun. A heavy application of bear grease was apparent. "The carriage is waiting," he said, pointing to the street. Two matched bay horses were harnessed to the carriage where Marinda Hyde sat waiting.

"Thank you," Mary Ann said, stepping out of her home in graceful swoops of her arms and legs.

"We have a surprise waiting at dinner," Orson said, smiling tightly. He was dressed in a black suit with a long topcoat.

"A surprise?"

"The Prophet will dine with us."

Mary swallowed hard and tried to steady her senses. "The Prophet?"

"Yes," Orson replied, escorting her toward the carriage. "Isn't that wonderful?"

Mary Ann was still swallowing her astonishment when Marinda Hyde greeted her, shaking her hand. Tall and slender, dressed in red satin, Marinda's expression was friendly. "Good to see you again. I'm not as formal as Orson. Do you prefer to be called Mary or Mary Ann?"

Mary Ann let her gaze meet Marinda's energetic hazel eyes, admiring her dark lustrous hair and olive complexion. "It was always Mary Ann back in England. Most everyone calls me Mary now. I thought you would be at your home preparing the meal."

"Everything's prepared," Marinda said, an open smile emanating from her long oval face. "It wouldn't look good for Orson to pick you up alone, would it?"

Mary thought for a few seconds, contemplated the meaning, and then nodded her agreement. She had heard that Marinda was from Kirtland, Ohio, and was the sister of Luke Johnson, one of the first members of the Council of Twelve Apostles. He had apostatized in 1838, long before Mary had joined the Church.

For an instant Mary recalled the occasion five days earlier when Orson had knocked on the door of her small log cabin, standing there alone in well-pressed clothes, handing her letters of introduction. Other than being aware that he was a Church leader and that he had returned from Jerusalem in December, she knew little about him. After watching him place his hat over his bright red hair and disappear into the Nauvoo landscape, she began reading the letters. They told about his mission to the Holy Land and to England, his return trip, and the frustration he felt when the frozen Mississippi delayed his return. Her wondering began right there. *What does all this mean?*

"Have you ever met the Prophet in person?" Marinda asked as Orson clucked the horses into a trot. Nauvoo was alive with construction. Both log and frame homes, and even some new brick homes, dotted the streets. Now that spring was here, new arrivals were literally pouring into the city. The population had exploded to near fourteen thousand. Neighbors were busy in their gardens, turning over the soil, obedient to their dreams.

"Yes and no," came the answer. Mary gripped the carriage tightly, displaying her nervousness. "I was able to shake his hand at the grove after his talk once. There were so many people, I'm certain he wouldn't remember me."

Orson flashed a warm smile. "You'd be surprised."

"You understand we're still living in the Ebenezer Robinson home," Marinda said. Her voice was apologetic.

Mary nodded yes. "But I've heard…"

Marinda was right on queue. "Brother Joseph has been very helpful. With Orson away for so long, he authorized Orson to publish a plea for assistance last month in the *Times and Seasons*. The Saints in Nauvoo have been very generous. We've purchased a lot for a new home. And now that Orson is on the city council, he has a little income."

Mary nodded her approval.

"I'm sure you're aware that our Church authorities don't get paid for their service in the Church. Even the Apostles. Elder Hyde has to leave tomorrow on a two-week speaking tour to the Quincy area. He's very busy. But it won't be long until we have a home of our own."

To Mary Ann's curiosity, Elder Hyde seemed content to let Marinda do most of the talking. Orson tended to his driving duties.

"Let me tell you about the last time Orson was on a speaking jaunt. He went with the Prophet a month ago to Shokoquon. The second day, the sleigh he was riding in with Orson Pratt was turned over by a runaway horse. Orson's hand was hurt that time, wasn't it dear?"

Elder Hyde nodded.

Mary Ann grimaced. "Did your hand heal?"

Orson placed the lines in his lap and held up both hands, working his fingers. "The Lord did wonders when he created us. We get hurt, but in time we heal. Good as new."

The response disarmed Mary Ann a bit, and she began to relax.

Marinda continued making conversation. Her deep-set brown eyes were glistening. "That was right after Brother Joseph talked to three hundred men at the temple, exhorting them to continue the work after the cold weather of December and January. There's always something to worry the poor man. Did you hear the Illinois legislature has repealed part of the Nauvoo city charter?"

"Yes," came the answer.

"First the legislature gives our city the freedom and flexibility to do the things every other city has power to do, then they take it away," Marinda said, shaking her head in obvious frustration. "This anti-Mormon business sure distresses me."

Mary Ann nodded her agreement.

"Drives people like Orson and Joseph plum crazy trying to keep up with everything. Now Joseph is really worried about Porter Rockwell. Poor Brother Rockwell. I feel sorry for him, held illegally in that Missouri prison." Rockwell had been captured in St. Louis, trying to return to Nauvoo from Philadelphia.

Mary smiled, impressed with Marinda's awareness of nearly every detail of political and Church events in the city.

"Seems we're surrounded by horse thieves, counterfeiters, and all sorts of riff-raff here along the American frontier," Orson said. "For some reason, the Lord has plopped us right in the middle." He pointed to the temple site. "And there's the reason. We've got to get that temple built."

Orson, Marinda, and Mary Ann were inside the Robinson home only minutes when the Prophet arrived. As others before her, Mary Ann was impressed with Joseph Smith's noble bearing, his gentle manners, his thoughtful deep-set blue eyes, his strong rounded shoulders, and his spirituality. Over a dinner of roast goose, boiled duck eggs wild and tame, potatoes, turnips swimming in hog's lard, and boiled squash, the conversation covered a variety of subjects—the battle with the legislature, Porter Rockwell, John C. Bennett, Sidney Rigdon, and the news that another immigrant ship had left England, the *Yorkshire*. She chuckled openly at Joseph's story about his wrestling match with the toughest man in Ramus—William Wall. Joseph had won, as he always did. Joseph's physical strength was exceeded only by his spiritual strength.

When the Prophet and Orson guided the conversation to marriage, Mary Ann still did not have an inkling why she had been invited to the Hyde home for dinner. She listened to the two men as they traded ideas about the marriage covenant, almost in oratory fashion. They spoke of the fact that the trial of separation from loved ones belonged to earth life only. That in the glorious realms of Heaven, worthy husbands and wives could have the privilege of being together in an eternal covenant.

Suddenly, Mary Ann gasped inwardly. *Am I being considered as a plural wife for someone? If so, to whom?* Mary Ann became convinced of that perception as the conversation turned decidedly toward plural marriage.

"Let me give you a brief history of the marriage covenant in the modern Church," Joseph said.

Unsettled, Mary sat back in her chair. She turned down an offer of brown betty, a pudding of apples and breadcrumbs. She took in a deep breath and slowly let it out.

Joseph's cultured voice projected outward. "As you know, we published the Book of Mormon in 1830. During the translation process, I was overwhelmed with the plain and precious teachings of the gospel. I began to contrast the teachings with that of the Bible, which had gone through so many translations over many centuries."

Mary Ann blinked, wondering where the Prophet was going with his conversation. The mention of the scriptures brought a warm feeling to her, however.

"Under the direction of the Spirit," Joseph continued, "and by command of God, I began the almost insurmountable task of revising the Bible text. Of course, I began with the Old Testament, dealing with the Age of the Patriarchs."

Mary Ann thought of the term, *insurmountable task.* Her Bible had more than a thousand pages. Even with the personal revelation accorded to a Prophet of God, it would take a long time to find and correct errors that had crept into Biblical translations over the years. *Age of the Patriarchs.* She immediately thought of Abraham, Isaac, and Jacob.

"I was struck with the favor in which the Lord held our Biblical patriarchs of that period; notwithstanding they had a plurality of wives," Joseph said. "I kept praying to the Lord, asking: *Why, O Lord, didst thou justify thy servants, Abraham, Isaac, and Jacob; as also Moses, David, and Solomon, in the matter of their having many wives and children?* In answer to my inquiries, a revelation came."

Mary stiffened and cleared her throat. "This was when?"

Joseph's tone continued somber. "Back in 1831. The revelation was burned into my mind, with exact wording. But I never wrote it down."

"Why?"

The Prophet paused for a few seconds. "I knew there would come a time that I would be expected to practice it, and I shrank at the thought. Although I was passionately curious as to why the patriarchs engaged in the practice, never for one moment did I wish to enter into the practice myself. After all, this was the 1830s, not Biblical times. I knew the world would not accept it, nor the governments of the world, and without a testimony of the practice, neither would my wife or other members of the Church."

Mary bit her lower lip, contemplating the words. "So what did you do?"

"I had enthusiastically embraced all the principles of the restored gospel—priesthood authority, baptisms for the dead, temple work, and on and on. But with this doctrine, I just plain dragged my feet. To make a long story short, I taught the principle, in strict secrecy, to a few close friends in the Church. For example, I told Oliver Cowdery and Lyman Johnson about it."

Lyman Johnson was Marinda's brother. He was the first Apostle called to serve in this dispensation, ordained in February of 1835. His apostasy from the Church began two years later over a merchandising venture in Kirtland. He claimed his loss of six thousand dollars was the fault of Joseph Smith. The charges were dismissed in court, however, and a year later Lyman was excommunicated on a bevy of charges, including assaulting another member, not attending Church, not keeping the Word of Wisdom, and other unrighteous conduct. Marinda prayed every day that he might someday return to the Church.

Mary did not know whether to shrink or bask in her newfound knowledge. Dumfounded, she continued asking questions. "When did you take your first plural wife?"

"Not until an angel of the Lord commanded me, in 1840. Then I began preaching that the restoration of all things had to include the patriarchal or plural order of marriage. I taught the principle to Joseph B. Noble, and on April fifth of that year, he sealed Sister Louisa Beaman to me. After the members of the Twelve returned from their missions to England, I taught the principle to them. They dragged their feet as well."

Mary shot a glance at Orson. *I don't blame you.*

"Sister Price," Joseph said, his voice chiseled with conviction, "I testify to you that the commandment of eternal marriage is now in effect for the Dispensation of the Fullness of Times. That means now. Today. The principle *must* be believed among the Saints. I was startled when the Lord made the pronouncement to me, but I have *no choice* but to be obedient."

As Joseph took over the conversation, Mary cast a quick glance at Orson and Marinda. They sat on a sofa holding hands, smiling at each other from time to time, gauging Mary's reaction.

The Prophet's tone continued decidedly serious. "Sister Price, the reason for the restoration of plural marriage is best explained by a scripture from the Book of Abraham—*to prove you all, as I did Abraham, and that I might require an offering at your hand, by covenant and sacrifice.* If we live in accord to divine edict, the Lord promises us that plural marriage can bring rewards during mortality as well as during immortality. Men and women sealed by true priesthood authority remain together in eternal bonds."

Mary sat on her hands, swayed back and forth on her chair, and tried to disguise her agonizing inner throbs. Slowly, she regained her composure. As she did, she began a polite dissent. But Joseph had heard objections before. Bible times. Modern times. Old tradition. New tradition. Repulsive to traditional beliefs. Reconciling the practice to the Gospel of Jesus Christ.

Mary sat in stunned silence as her Prophet, in a calm voice, handled each objection with the charm of a master. The Lord wanted his children to spurn plural marriage except when He required compliance. The greatest external principles not only earn the greatest rewards, he said, but also the greatest punishments. People could not, without severe divine censure, choose for men to have more than one wife at a time. The Lord had decreed to him, Joseph, that in righteousness the Saints should live this law to hasten the purposes of the Kingdom of God. And finally, from a human reasoning standpoint, more women than men seemed to be attracted to the gospel. Future exaltation in eternal worlds would require a means for the entrance of every worthy person to be sealed in the marriage covenant. Plural marriage provided this, he said.

With the suddenness of a man with more to do than time permitted, Joseph pushed himself away from the table and stood up. "Please excuse me, Sister Price. I must get back to my family."

Mary extended her hand for a farewell handshake. Joseph wrapped his right hand around hers, and placed his left hand on Mary's shoulder. "God bless you, Sister Price. May the Lord bless you with understanding. The answer is very simple. Please take the doctrine of plural marriage to the Lord in prayer. The Spirit of the Holy Ghost will confirm it to you, I promise."

He turned to Orson and Marinda, uttered several sentences filled with thanks, shook their hands, and disappeared into the dusk, walking toward his log cabin by the river.

Mary let her puzzlement about the purpose of the evening cross her face. "Elder Hyde, what does all this mean? Surely the Prophet is not considering me..."

Orson smiled again at Marinda. "No, no. Not Brother Joseph."

Mary furrowed her brows. "Then what...?"

Orson approached slowly. "Joseph gave you a lot of personal teaching. What did you think of his explanation about plural wives?"

Mary's mouth went dry.

Orson suddenly locked eyes with Mary. He threw his shoulders back and let his lower jaw protrude toward her. She felt an awkward awareness. "Sister Price," Orson said, "would you consent to enter my family?"

Mary's heart screamed a very loud *no,* but for several seconds words would not form in her mouth. She hung her head and refused to return the Apostle's gaze. She felt tears sting her eyes. Finally she said, "I cannot think of it, even for a moment."

Marinda cleared her throat. "Mary..."

Mary turned away. "I'm sorry, Sister Hyde. I cannot look you in the face right now. Please."

"Sister Price," Orson said, pressing the issue now, "I know this is difficult. Joseph himself lacked the courage to teach the revelation until an angel of the Lord threatened to slay him if he did not reveal and establish this celestial principle. Joseph commanded Heber C. Kimball three times before he agreed to enter the practice. Then Heber became distraught over his compliance, until his wife received her own witness from the Lord of its correctness. Please follow the Prophet's admonition and pray about it."

Mary put her hands to her ears. "That's enough for one night. I want to go home."

Orson drew a deep resigning breath. "I agree." He stood up. "We'll take you home."

"No thank you," Mary said, her eyes now swimming in tears. "I would like to be alone, if you don't mind."

Reluctantly, Orson handed Mary her coat. "It's chilly out. And it's a long walk."

"I can manage."


CHAPTER NOTES

The meeting between Orson and Marinda Hyde, Joseph Smith, and Mary Ann Price is documented in the book *Orson Hyde, The Olive Branch of Israel,* by Myrtle Stevens Hyde (Salt Lake City, Utah: Agreka Books, 2000), pp. 153-161.

# 8

ELIZABETH'S REACTION WAS SKEPTICAL and cynical, as expected. Daniel had just told her that Joseph Smith, Wilford Woodruff, and Orson Hyde wanted to meet with the Browett family.

"I *won't* have them in my house," she said in a steely voice. Outside, a strong breeze was blowing—typical for a spring day in mid-April.

One thing Daniel prided himself on was his skill at cooking a basic meal, proving he could get along without his wife's food preparation. Daniel toyed with pepperpot stew of his own fixing, his trousers barely clinging to his narrowing mid-section. The spring farm work had caused him to lose a few pounds of winter fat. The aroma of the stew had him famished. Rarely did Elizabeth cook him meals anymore. Rarely did she do anything productive. In his estimation, she held her own pity party daily, criticizing the Church, its doctrine, its people, and its leaders. In the old days, she obtained her spiritual fix every morning with her prayers and scripture study. Lately, she had blatantly tossed her spiritually aside.

"They're not coming here," Daniel said, containing his emotions. He added more tripe and dough balls to his stew. "This cooking for myself kind of suits my tooth. From now on, I'll be the cook. You milk the cow and do the plowing. The meeting will be at Mother's home."

The statement seemed to deflate his defiant wife. Under normal circumstances, he was certain, she would have turned on her charm and done cartwheels for the opportunity to entertain the Prophet in her home. It was an opportunity few enjoyed. Unless she changed her mind, which was unlikely, she was going to miss it.

"I'm *not* going," she said. "Not unless you want me to give a *tongue* lashing to all three of them."

Daniel scoffed at his wife's pride; lately she generously salted her speech with bits of criticism. "I didn't say you were invited."

Elizabeth's cynicism faded. "Don't *lie*. You just said they were coming to meet the Browett family."

"The *Martha* Browett family."

There was a flush of humiliation in Elizabeth's cheeks. "You men have to have *more* help? *Ganging* up on me? Need your mother and sister to convince me that it's *fine* for you to marry that Clifford woman?"

Daniel waved at Elizabeth dismissively. "How many times do I have to tell you? The brethren know of your opposition to plural marriage. The matter is dead. I'm not even thinking about it. Get over it, Elizabeth. Please. You're making life miserable for both of us."

The hardened look remained. Elizabeth rose from the table. "I'm going for a walk. *Don't* expect me at the meeting tonight. I'm *too* busy."

Daniel rolled his eyes, shook his head, and blew on a spoonful of stew.

Daniel laughed to himself. It was a comical sight to see Elizabeth sneaking looks through a narrow slit in her curtains next door. Inside his mother's cabin, Daniel settled in front of a plate filled with fried potatoes and onions, dandelion salad, headcheese, boiled turnips, cornbread, and buffalo tongue imported from St. Louis. His mother, Martha, was having the time of her life entertaining the three Church authorities. She wore her favorite blue gabardine dress, the one she wore in England the night she told Elder Woodruff that she would be baptized.

Daniel placed both hands on his face. When he was certain none of the others were looking, he waved his pinky finger at Elizabeth. Scowling, she withdrew from sight.

The early conversation drifted back and forth. Wilford asked about Robert's family. They were doing just fine, Daniel reported. The baby, Thomas, turned two years old the end of March. Lizzy turned five April first. Hannah was due to have her fifth baby soon.

General conference, held on the unfinished temple floor six blocks away, was discussed. For the first time in two years, Sidney Rigdon, Joseph's counselor, had given a talk. He claimed poor health had kept him away. In part, Joseph told the Browetts, that was true. Since Sidney's Missouri imprisonment, Sidney had been moody and uncooperative. Also, some one hundred fifteen elders were called on special missions. Since the conference, members of the Twelve had been training the elders.

A few days ago, Joseph had preached to around two hundred fifty new British immigrants who had just arrived in Nauvoo. Most of the former United Brethren converts had gathered at the Nauvoo Landing to welcome them. Some arrived on the steamboat *Aramath*. Others, after being forced to live in St. Louis during the winter until the ice melted on the Mississippi, had come on the *Maid of Iowa* the next day.

The temple itself became the dominant topic.

Wilford Woodruff was talking. He seemed to direct his words to Rebecca. Temple building, he said, was not new to Church members of the latter day. After Kirtland, they had dedicated two temple sites in Missouri— at Independence and Far West—all with the intent that *the Son of Man might have a place to manifest himself to his people.* However, they had been forced from those locations before construction could begin. Nauvoo, unlike any other city, had been a child of necessity. The Saints had gathered not to eke out a living in the wilderness, but to build a temple. The effort had become more than a demonstration of the spiritual strivings of its people; it was an expression of their willingness to sacrifice all they had: strength, time, goods, and funds. Even though everyone was poor, and had little to give, the sacrifice was expected.

As Wilford spoke, Daniel thought of the dozens of masons and stonecutters. He conjured up images of mallets, chisels, sanding devices, and ropes to haul one-ton stones into place. He thought of the carpenters—himself included—and he thought of the donated labor of most of the men in Nauvoo. One day in ten each worked on the building.

Following the same pattern the night the Hydes invited Mary Ann Price to their home, the Prophet took over the conversation. He preached the same message, plural marriage, first committing the Browetts to confidentiality. He talked of its practice by ancient prophets; how the revelation came from the Lord to him, that the Saints must practice it as part of the restoration of the gospel. He appeared to Daniel a picture of confidence, outlining five kinds of priesthood sealings between husbands and wives.

Joseph's voice was commanding and he appeared to be enjoying his teaching moment. "First of all, you need to understand that a living woman can be sealed to a living man for time and for eternity. This can be done at the time of their original marriage or later in a separate ceremony."

Daniel had heard this explanation before, but it was new to Rebecca and her mother.

The Prophet's self confidence was solid and deep as he continued. "Second, a living person can be sealed to a deceased person for eternity, with someone standing as the proxy for the deceased person. Ordinarily, this involves living widows or widowers being sealed to their deceased spouses."

Martha accepted those words with a nodding smile. Daniel suspected she was thinking of Thomas Browett, his father and her deceased husband, lying in a grave in Tewkesbury, England, near a small Quaker Church. Someday, Daniel knew, he would be able to be sealed to his father and mother in the temple—as soon as it was complete.

"Third," the Prophet continued, "a deceased man and a deceased woman can be sealed to each other for eternity, with two living people acting as proxies. We will eventually do this in the temple for persons married to each other on earth, who die before receiving their priesthood sealing."

Daniel thought of Robert and Elizabeth's parents, interred in the yard of the Deerhurst Anglican Church, thousands of miles away.

"Fourth, a living man and a living woman can be married for *time* only, or mortality, only. Generally, this involves widows previously sealed for time and eternity to their first husbands. These women could be married to later husbands for *time* only."

There were many people in Nauvoo who fit into this category, thought Daniel.

"And fifth, the power of the priesthood can seal a living man and a living woman for *eternity* only. They would not be husband and wife during their sojourn on earth, but would be *after* death."

Daniel stole a quick glance at Orson Hyde, who appeared to grimace. Marinda Hyde, although married to Orson in this life, was sealed to the Prophet Joseph Smith for eternity. Daniel wondered if it were merely a test of Orson's faith, something that would be corrected later. He couldn't imagine it otherwise.

Daniel could see his sister's attention drifting. Rebecca at times had appeared fascinated by the Prophet's oratory, but at other times she fidgeted in her hard wooden chair. At the end, to Daniel's eyes, she seemed aloof, almost in a trance, wishing the evening to be over. Rebecca's mind, he guessed, was on her seamstress work. Stored near a log wall were two skeins of silk, three yards of linen, and an assortment of scarlet cloth, red flannel, coating, buttons, and other sundries.

Suddenly, the Prophet was talking to her. "Sister Rebecca, Brother Orson Hyde has something to ask you."

Rebecca sat up straight in her burgundy dress, momentarily startled. A lone mosquito buzzed at her ears. She swatted it away. A spring breeze fluttered through a partially open window. Her hand reached for a pendant hanging from her necklace. "A question for me?"

Orson smiled at her. She wondered if he remembered the first time they met, that cold day in December when he had come looking for Daniel to tell him that the Prophet wanted to meet with him.

"Sister Rebecca—you have met my wife, Marinda, haven't you?" Orson asked.

Rebecca hesitated only briefly. "Just once. At the conference last week." A thought came to her. *Was the meeting happenstance, or arranged?*

Orson was smiling at her. "I want you to know that Marinda totally supports what I am about to ask you."

Rebecca's blue eyes widened. A premonition was building inside her. She brushed aside locks of blond hair and waited for Elder Hyde to speak again.

Orson took a curious deep breath. "Marinda and I would like you to join our family."

Rebecca blanched openly and blinked hard. She felt a wave of apprehension.

Wilford folded his arms and waited for a reaction.

Rebecca glanced at her mother and at her brother. Martha's mouth was wide open in astonishment. Daniel was pulling on his sideburns, deep in thought.

Rebecca brought a hand to her mouth as she weighed Orson's words. *Marriage? To an Apostle? Become a plural wife?* "I don't know," she stammered. "I'd have to think…"

"Of course," Orson said, nodding. "We would expect you to take your time, to think, to pray, to fast."

Vivid images of past encounters with men came flashing to Rebecca's mind. Even though Daniel kept reminding her that he considered her the "Belle of Apperley," no one had come calling. She was twenty-three, prime marrying age. She never had the chance to court in England, before the family emigrated. There were far more single women than men her age in Nauvoo, so it sometimes seemed as though she were pining her life away. There was the time on the ship that Henry Eagles told her that he had married the wrong girl, that he should have married Rebecca. That frightened her.

Then came the night she was physically attacked by John Poole, the sailor. That scared her, perhaps permanently. And there was the night that Henry asked her to become *his* spiritual wife. That upset her.

"What do you think, Mama?" Rebecca queried, her face flushed with red now.

Rebecca's stare took in her mother, Martha Browett, fifty-seven, her head graced with long gray hair tied in a bun. Her mother's mouth was still open, trying to digest the implications. If Rebecca accepted, it meant her mother would live alone in the little log cabin Daniel had built for her. Rebecca was concerned for her mother and wished she could get married, too. But it seemed as though every man her mother's age that came to Nauvoo to settle was already married.

Martha picked up a shriveled apple from a bowl and fondled it. "Honey, it's an Apostle asking."

Rebecca bit her lip, thinking. Next, she turned to her brother. "Daniel?"

Daniel's face was blank, his mouth compressed to a straight line. "You better fast and pray about this, Rebecca. Next to your baptism, it's the most important decision you've ever made."

A smile crossed Rebecca's face and her eyes widened. She thought of sitting next to Orson Hyde at Church gatherings, riding in his carriage with him to visit the nearby Mormon communities of Zarahemla, Ramus, Knowlton, Lima, and Payson. Living in a new wood-frame home, maybe later in a brick home. Dancing with Orson at a Christmas ball. The social status. Bearing children to an Apostle.

"When will the wedding be?" Rebecca asked with imploring eyes, turning her gaze back to Orson.

It was Orson's turn to blink. "Is this a *yes?*"

Rebecca was studying Orson intently now. His red hair, his ruddy complexion, large blue eyes framed by an intelligent face, prominent eyebrows, straight nose, dimple in the middle of his chin, squarish face accented by very square jaw. To her, he suddenly looked strikingly handsome.

Rebecca sat still for a moment, taking stock of her mother and brother.

She heard no objections. Surprisingly, her mother suddenly gave a faint nod.

Rebecca turned to Orson again. "I have lots of experience as a seamstress. Could I make my own wedding dress?"

Orson's eyes sparkled. "Of course, my dear."

A thought came to Rebecca's mind and it caused her to change her tone and facial expression. "But we've never courted."

Orson tilted his head and cast a quick glance at Joseph and Wilford. "In these cases, meaning plural marriage, courtship is somewhat out of the question. What would people think if we were seen in public together? I'm a married man."

Rebecca winced. "So we just get married?"

Orson nodded up and down.

"When?" Rebecca asked.

"Whenever you would like," he answered. "Assuming your mind is made up, of course."

Rebecca bit her lip, thinking. *Finally, marriage. An Apostle's wife. A home of my own. Children.*

"What do you think, Daniel?" she asked again, unsure of herself.

Daniel seemed to force a smile. "Perhaps you need to let Elder Hyde know in a few days."

Rebecca blinked at her brother, and then turned to face her new suitor again. A new feeling came over her. "That's not necessary. My answer is yes."

Orson obviously was entering new territory. "I don't know whether to shake your hand or give you a little hug."

Rebecca blushed, her transformation complete. "A hug would be nice."

As Orson and Rebecca stood, leaning over to touch their shoulders and cheeks in a light embrace, Daniel peered through the window at his next-door cabin. Elizabeth was there again, taking in the scene through the slit in the curtain.

Daniel wondered what his wife was thinking as Orson and Rebecca embraced.

# 9

DANIEL LAUGHED OFF ELIZABETH'S scandalous look when he walked through the door. She was pacing before an open fire of the hearth.

After three months of enduring his wife's insolence, Daniel had learned to survive by matching cynicism with cynicism, with the hope of giving her enough rope that one day she would realize she was hanging herself with her stubbornness.

"What did those three rum dog *mucky-mucks* want?"

"A good dinner," Daniel answered, highly aware of his wife's raging curiosity. "Mother is a splendid cook, you know." *Much better than you, lately.*

Elizabeth turned up the lantern on the table. The light spilled out onto a floor littered with soiled clothing. She sank into a chair, glowering. "I think it's *impolite* for everyone to sit around talking about me like that."

"Next to the buffalo tongue, it was the highlight of the evening." Daniel tossed his coat on the floor.

"Wilford *hates* me."

"I could have your brother train you in the art of pugilism. You could duke it out with Elder Woodruff somewhere."

*"Funny."*

"You shouldn't peek through the window. Everyone saw you."

Elizabeth's tone came tinged with impatience. *"Quit* playing games. What's going on?"

"They gave me a new list."

"A *list?"* Elizabeth's face turned ashen.

"More than a hundred names."

"Bah! What names?"

Daniel's voice was a little hollow. He didn't enjoy fibbing. "Widows. Unmarried women."

"Let me see it."

"I committed it to memory. There is no piece of paper."

"Does this mean you're a member of some *clandestine* committee to find husbands for all those women?"

"Not at all. Just new choices for me. You turned down Sister Clifford. Maybe you'll like one of these new ones. Shall I spit out some names?"

Elizabeth scanned the room for something to throw. Her green eyes clouded with confusion. "I warn you, don't tease me. It's not that *Clifford* woman. It's the whole *idea* of plural marriage."

"Oh. I would have never known. You've been so quiet these past three months."

A woman's leather shoe came flying across the room. It glanced harmlessly off the log wall, two feet from Daniel's head. Elizabeth was screaming now. "Just tell me what's going on, or I'll…"

"Throw the other shoe? Your aim is terrible. Not cook breakfast? I've grown to enjoy my own cooking. Not wash clothes? I don't mind looking for my cleanest dirty shirt."

The other shoe thumped against the wall.

Laughing now, Daniel blurted it out, emphasizing each word. "Rebecca is going to be sealed to Elder Orson Hyde." He waited for his wife's stomach to tie in knots.

"Your sister? Marry an *Apostle?* That's *absurd.*"

Daniel laughed some more, pleased at his wife's baffled look. "You're right. It is. Guess I'll go to bed. Do you want to change rooms tonight? I'll take the soft tick mattress. You take the hard floor in front of the hearth."

"When is this *glorious* wedding supposed to take place?" she scowled.

"April twenty-seventh."

"Quit lying. That's only *two* weeks from now."

"Don't worry about it. You're not invited, anyway. Mother and I will represent the family."

Elizabeth stood, looking rigid. "I'm going to bed."

"No kiss goodnight?"

"You'd catch my cold."

"You have the grumpies, not a cold. Grumpies aren't catchable."

"The hard floor is still *yours.* Don't speak to me anymore."

The little log cabin shook on its foundation as she slammed the door.

Daniel cringed, and fought the temptation to pick up his coat and Elizabeth's shoes. In his loneliness, he reached for the candlesnuffer. End of another day.

The Prophet Joseph Smith officiated at the wedding between Orson Hyde and Martha Rebecca Browett, held on the second floor of the Red Brick Store. Two men holding the Melchizedek Priesthood, Wilford Woodruff and Daniel Browett, functioned as the official witnesses. Also witnessing the wedding, and hearing the words of the ceremony, *for time and all eternity,* were Rebecca's mother Martha, Robert and Hannah Harris, and Marinda Hyde, Orson's first wife.

Elizabeth Harris Browett told Daniel she was staying home.

No one knew it, but she hid behind a tree across the street from the Red Brick Store during the entire ceremony.

CHAPTER NOTES

The marriage between Orson Hyde and Martha Rebecca Browett is documented in the book *Orson Hyde, The Olive Branch of Israel,* by Myrtle Stevens Hyde (Salt Lake City, Utah: Agreka Books, 2000). They were married April 27, 1843.

# 10

*June 1843*

GOVERNOR FORD SCRUTINIZED THE STRANGER who wanted to see him. The man looked worn out and smelled like a sweaty horse. Ford trusted few men and felt no need to trust this man, who seemed to have a loose manner. Besides, the swigs of whiskey he had nursed during the day had slowed the governor's thinking down to a crawl.

"I'm sorry," Ford said from the circular staircase of the capitol building in Springfield, "but I have a long list of people waiting to see me. If you don't have an appointment you'll have to wait. I might have time tomorrow."

"My name is Sheriff Reynolds and I'm from Missouri," the stranger replied. "And I have an indictment against Joe Smith." He pulled a letter of introduction from his vest pocket.

Ford's countenance brightened suddenly. His imagination took flight. "My office is right over there, adjacent to the reception room. Let's talk."

From across his desk, Ford continued his scrutiny of the man from Missouri. He was tall and stout looking, swarthy, a narrow nose showing through a full beard, thick wavy black hair that needed cutting, and fierce, bulging, muddy brown eyes. "When was this indictment issued?" Ford asked.

"Two days ago, on the fifth of June." Reynolds' voice was low and gruff. His hair looked as though it had a can of secondhand lard poured over it.

"Didn't take you long to get here."

"Nope. Our governor is anxious."

Ford exhaled, feeling good. He looked over the warrant. "For the attempted murder of your ex-governor Boggs?"

Reynolds nodded patiently. "We already have Rockwell."

"I know. Weren't you the one who investigated the attempted murder of Mr. Boggs?"

Reynolds smiled, pleased that Ford remembered. "I'm the one who found the revolver, still loaded with buckshot. Rockwell lost it while trying to escape. I found it in the mud. It had been raining that night."

Ford smiled back. He knew, as well as everyone else in Illinois and Missouri, that the true owner of the pistol had never been found and that the pistol likely was not Rockwell's. "That was careless of Porter Rockwell, wasn't it?"

"I need you to sign a new warrant, authorizing me to arrest Smith here in Illinois."

Ford motioned to an aide. The aide darted out of the room, seeking the attorney general, James A. McDougall. Ford smiled wickedly. "Dr. John C. Bennett must be behind this."

"Yes, sir."

"Mormonism is a cockroach religion, and the Smiths are toying with their own extinction," Ford said. "You have my cooperation." While they waited, Ford launched into a tirade of anger against the Mormons, relishing the chance to express in a manner that no one would dare refute. He gave Sheriff Reynolds his version of why Mormons were now unwelcome in Illinois. He came to the conclusion that the Missourian had better have some help from someone from Illinois, finding the sheriff a little lacking in mental sharpness and common sense. Ford fought back an urge to saddle up and take charge of the effort to find the Mormon Prophet and drag him into Missouri

In less than a half hour, Ford had signed the warrant and was issuing his own orders. "In pursuance with the constitution of the United States, this warrant will have to be served by a law authority from Illinois. I recommend the constable of Hancock County, who lives in Carthage. He'll be more than happy to arrest Joe Smith. His name's Wilson and here's a letter of introduction you can give to him."

Sheriff Reynolds stuffed the warrant and the letter into his vest pocket In seconds he had disappeared.

Governor Ford drew a deep breath and crossed his fingers. If the Missourians could convict and hang Joe Smith, the Mormons would probably disappear from off the face of the earth. That was his fondest hope.

The letter was marked urgent. Hyrum Smith wondered why Judge James Adams in Springfield would be sending him an express letter. With a jerk of his opener, Hyrum tore the envelope apart. His blue eyes read it in disbelief His jaw dropped. He darted for the door in front of his wife.

"Where are you going?" Mary Fielding Smith asked.

"To find Stephen Markham," he answered, trying to recover from his shock. "There's an emergency. I've been informed that Governor Ford has issued a writ for Joseph on the requisition of the Governor of Missouri."

Mary blinked rapidly. "What does that mean?"

Hyrum's answer was swift. "It means that both governors are following master plan devised by Satan."

Mary blinked again. She understood perfectly. Satan had been trying to destroy Joseph Smith and the work of the restoration for years. "Oh."

Hyrum tried to explain it in more modern terms. "Mormon-haters like Governor Ford and Governor Boggs have some kind of psychological block their minds are fine, but the alliance with the devil wells up in them."

Despite the fact that Porter Rockwell was still in jail in Missouri, the pas two or three months had been a happy time in Nauvoo for Hyrum and Mary. The community was growing rapidly, business was expanding, and shops and commercial buildings were going up at a brisk pace. The City Council had passed an ordinance to establish a ferry across the Mississippi at Nauvoo. Converts were still pouring into the city. The missionary program had expanded ambitiously, with elders called to serve in Russia and the Society Islands. The temple, rising tier upon tier, was assuming an imposing appearance on the bluff.

June had proved another matter, and Hyrum felt the heavy burden in connection with the internal problems of the rapidly growing force of Mormonism. Joseph and Hyrum's longtime and faithful friend, Judge Elias Higbee, had suddenly died of a fever. His two sons were horses of a different color, causing problems. Emma Smith had become ill the same day Judge Higbee died. And John C. Bennett had renewed his agitations to have the Prophet arrested.

"Constable Wilson of Carthage and Sheriff Reynolds of Jackson County are on their way to Dixon to arrest Joseph at this very minute." Hyrum exclaimed. "I'm going to send Brother Markham there. I hope he can warn Joseph before Reynolds gets there." Hyrum reasoned that Wilson and Reynolds had looked for Joseph in Nauvoo first, but somehow found out that five days earlier Joseph had left by carriage, taking Emma north to visit her sister, who lived on a farm near Dixon, Illinois, some two hundred twenty miles north. He didn't know who would divulge such information, but the thought infuriated him.

"I'll have prayers with the children and put them to bed," Mary said. The baby, Martha, was already asleep. Hyrum's sixteen-year-old daughter, Lovina, was tending the other three children, John, Jerusha, and Sarah.

"Kiss them goodnight for me," he replied. With those words Hyrum jumped his six-foot-two-inch frame down the steps from his house on the northeast corner of Water and Bain Streets, near the office of the *Times and Seasons*. It was June eighteenth, one of the longest days of the year. However, the sun had set two hours ago. In near darkness, he ran past his office, located on the other side of the street. Stephen Markham, Joseph's chief body-guard, lived just a few blocks away, on the northeast corner of Young and Partridge Streets.

In Hyrum's eyes, Markham had proven his loyalty time and time again. In Missouri, when Joseph and his fellow prisoners were taken from Liberty jail for trial, Stephen Markham had testified in their behalf at risk of his own life. In fact, after testifying, Markham had been called outside by one of the guards, a man named Blakley. Blakley attacked Markham with a club. Markham caught the club, wrenched it from the Missourian, and threw it over the fence. At this, ten other Missourians charged him, but as Markham began knocking them aside one at a time, they retreated.

And during the exodus from Missouri, it had been Markham who brought Emma and her children safely to Illinois. Emma and her children had walked across the ice-encrusted Mississippi River in the dead of winter.

Nearly out of breath, Hyrum knocked on Markham's door. No answer. He knocked again, louder.

A voice from upstairs came. "Who is it?"

"It's me, Brother Markham. Hyrum."

Soon Hyrum was standing face-to-face with Joseph's chief bodyguard, a large barrel-chested man, who had been asleep. Hyrum thrust the letter at Markham. "The governor of Missouri is up to his old tricks. He's convinced Governor Ford to issue a warrant for Joseph's arrest. John C. Bennett is behind the whole thing. Him and Sam Owens." Sam C. Owens had headed the mob that ran the Mormons out of Jackson County.

Hyrum could see the concern on Markham's face as a lantern was lit. "Did the Missourians send a posse?"

Fear lined Hyrum's face and he felt the need for immediate action. "Judge Adams thinks there's just two men after Joseph. Constable Harmon T. Wilson of Carthage is one of them. The other is a sheriff from Jackson County, Missouri. Joseph Reynolds."

*Thank God for a few good friends in Springfield,* Hyrum thought to himself.

"When did they leave?" Markham asked.

"Yesterday. Apparently, they know where Joseph is."

Markham narrowed his eyes. "How do they know that?"

"I really don't know. Someone has betrayed us."

Markham pulled a face.

"You need to warn Joseph," Hyrum said. "If they get Joseph back into Missouri, they'll kill him."

"I'll ride out tonight."

"Not alone."

"I'll take William Clayton."

"How soon can you leave?"

"I'll have to find a horse. Mine's gone lame on me."

"Take Joseph's horse, Joe Duncan."

Markham nodded his approval. In the 1842 election for Illinois governor, one of the candidates—Joe Duncan—pledged that if elected he would ride Joe Smith and the Mormons out of town. Joseph promptly renamed his sorrel horse "Joe Duncan." It gave Joseph great pleasure riding Joe Duncan out of town whenever he wanted.

"I'll get to Joseph before Wilson and Reynolds do, I promise," Markham said.

Hyrum nodded back. He believed him. Nobody could ride as fast and hard as Stephen Markham.

At midnight, Markham rode Joe Duncan out of town with William Clayton. Destination: Dixon, Illinois.

# 11

A STARTLED JOSEPH SMITH PULLED BACK on the lines. The two horses pulling his carriage arched their necks and stopped in the middle of the road leading from Dixon back to the Wasson farm. It was Wednesday, June twenty-first.

"Brother Markham, Brother Clayton—what are you doing here?" The Prophet shot his two friends an incredulous look. His sorrel horse, Joe Duncan, was totally lathered under his bodyguard friend, his head hanging and his chest heaving. Likewise, Clayton's gray horse. Swarms of mosquitoes and flies soon converged on the animals and the men.

"The Missourians are at it again," Markham said from his saddle. Pain was written on his face. He had more saddle sores than warts on a toad, some festering and bleeding. "It's for your security we have come." Markham was amazed at Joseph's confident smile. The dangers of his calling seemed to sit lightly on him.

"Something has excited you," Joseph said as he examined the horses. "You've rode Joe Duncan right down to the bone. But I'm not worried. I shall find friends; the Missourians cannot hurt me."

Markham furrowed his brow, feeling a slight irritation. "But you don't understand. Two lawmen are on their way here to arrest you. Sheriff Joseph Reynolds of Jackson County. And Constable Wilson of Carthage." He winced in pain as he dismounted.

Markham was still puzzled at Joseph's lack of worry. Markham and his companion had made it all the way to La Harpe by sunup Monday morning. While they had breakfast, a local blacksmith shod their horses and fed them. Then they headed north to Monmouth, where they stayed overnight to rest. In all, they traveled two hundred and twelve miles in sixty-six hours. Today was Wednesday the nineteenth. Sheriff Reynolds and Constable Wilson had been beaten, just as Markham had promised Hyrum. But then he knew where the Wasson farm was located; the two lawmen did not. When he and William Clayton arrived at the farm, Emma had told them there had been no word of the deputies. Joseph, she said, had gone into Dixon to arrange for preaching there tomorrow night. Markham and Clayton had climbed back onto their horses and spurred toward Dixon, twelve miles away.

Half-way to Dixon, they had seen the Prophet driving his carriage.

Joseph seemed to read Markham's thoughts. He laughed. "I've already been to Dixon. There's no sign of any Missouri sheriff. I made an appointment to preach there, tomorrow. Members of the Church told me there's nothing new going on. There are a couple of Mormon elders in town, but I didn't get to meet them."

Joseph smiled again. His Mormon elders were everywhere, preaching the gospel.

"So what do we do now?" William Clayton asked, still wincing in pain.

"Let's go back to the Wasson farm and get you two rested up."

Friday, two days later, Markham was a bundle of nerves. For him, time was standing still at the Wasson farm. He had no choice but to endure his Prophet's chaffing at the constant inactivity. Joseph wanted to preach somewhere and felt he had disappointed the people in Dixon; their hearts were set on hearing him give a talk. The Prophet had sent William Clayton into Dixon to see if anything was happening there. Clayton had instructions to find the two Mormon elders that were seen there, and to invite them to the Wasson farm for dinner. After Clayton was gone, Joseph had suggested a wrestling match, a footrace, pulling stakes—anything to keep him busy. But Markham was still too tired and too saddle sore to do anything. Besides, Joseph always beat him anyway.

Yesterday, a lawyer by the name of Edward Southwick had ridden from Dixon out to the Wasson farm. He had heard that a writ had been sworn out for Joseph by the Missouri authorities in cooperation with Illinois. Joseph had thanked him for his kindness, introduced him to Markham and Clayton, and paid him twenty-five dollars.

"How about horseshoes or quoits?" Joseph suggested, headed for the barn. Quoits was a contest to see who could throw heavy rocks the farthest.

"Think I'll just stay here in the shade," Markham said, sitting on a chair under the Wasson back porch. He began admiring the butterflies flitting around nearby, some tortoise shell colored, some red-spotted purple, some blue, and some yellow. Violets had taken over the yard, bearing dark purple-blue flowers on long stems among the grass.

As he sat, Markham heard a buggy pull up to the Wasson farmhouse. He peeked around the corner. There were three men aboard. Markham smiled. Brother Clayton must have found the Mormon elders. A third man, not dressed like a missionary, stayed in the buggy as the other two knocked on the front door. Markham, too sore to care, sat back in his chair again as he heard Emma Smith direct the elders outside, pointing in the direction of her husband.

"Is that the Prophet walking toward the barn?" one of the men asked Markham as they walked past the porch.

Markham groaned and took a deep breath. "Yep." Out of the corner of his eye, he could see Joseph walking toward the house. Joseph obviously had seen the buggy arrive.

The man speaking was tall, lean, and dark. "A nice man named Clayton directed us here. We're elders of Israel."

"We want to shake the Prophet's hand," said the second elder, chunky and sandy haired.

Joseph Smith extended a right hand as he approached. "Where are you brethren from? Who called you on your mission?"

The tall, dark man quickly drew a pistol from under his coat. "Lilburn W. Boggs called us on this mission."

Markham's jaw dropped as he watched this. With surges of protective instinct, he ran toward the Prophet.

"You must be from Missouri," Joseph was saying.

The imposter's voice was well oiled with hatred. "Sheriff Reynolds from Jackson County, taking you back to justice. And this here is Constable Wilson from Carthage. We have a writ for your arrest."

The other imposter, a chunky man, pulled his pistol as Markham arrived. He wheeled, pointing it at the approaching bodyguard. "Back off," he warned.

The chunky man, Constable Wilson, reached inside his coat as well. He brandished his pistol and aimed it at Joseph's chest.

Markham balled his fists, thinking how he had failed Joseph.

Joseph appeared still stunned. "Let me see the writ." He took a step toward the two men.

Reynolds cursed, taking the Lord's name in vain. Then he said, "If you stir, I'll shoot!" He reached out with his free hand and grabbed the Mormon Prophet by the collar. "If you stir one inch, I'll shoot you."

Markham's eyes quickly raked over the two lawmen. Reynolds' missionary disguise did little to mitigate the evil he projected. He was tall and stout looking, swarthy, a narrow nose showing through a full beard, thick wavy black hair that needed cutting, and fierce, deep-set brown eyes. His leathery skin had turned purple with rage. Wilson had a rounded, deeply scored red face, showing stained tobacco teeth, a wide nose, and a sandy beard.

"What's the meaning of this unwarranted intrusion?" Joseph asked, his eyes narrowing.

"I'll show you the meaning," Reynolds said, pulling Joseph closer, blaspheming again. "I'll shoot you. You're going back to Missouri!"

Markham ground his teeth in frustration. The Missourians already had Porter Rockwell. If he didn't do something, they would have Joseph, too. He suspected Reynolds would be paid a handsome reward if he succeeded in getting Joseph into Jackson County.

Markham kicked himself for not being more vigilant. Joseph's options were deteriorating. A chill raked Markham's flesh.

Suddenly, Joseph seemed overcome by a higher power. He stretched out his six-foot frame, holding his chin high, and jerked himself free of Reynolds's grip. Then he arched his face toward his captor. "I am not afraid of your shooting. I am not afraid to die. I have endured so much oppression, I am weary of life."

Sheriff Reynolds paused, radiating confusion and some fear. "I swear, I'll shoot you."

Markham watched in horror as his Prophet unbuttoned his shirt, baring his chest. "Shoot away. Try to kill me, if you please. But you should know that with my own natural weapons I could soon level both of you. If you have any legal process to serve, I am at all times subject to law, and shall not offer resistance."

Once Markham had heard Joseph say, "Angels shall bear me up until my time." Markham prayed for angels to help right now.

Reynolds' eyes were still locked onto Joseph. His language was not angelic. Foul deprecations sprang out. "If you say another word, I'll shoot you."

"Shoot away," Joseph repeated. "I am not afraid of your pistols."

Markham took a menacing step forward.

Reynolds wheeled. He aimed his pistol at Markham's head. "I'll kill you if you come another step closer," Reynolds screamed, taking the Lord's name in vain repeatedly.

Markham thought about the angels. He took another step toward Joseph's assailants.

Perplexed, Reynolds turned away and aimed his pistol at Joseph's chest.

again. "Stop, or I shall shoot this man this instant."

Markham forced himself to stop. In frustration, he took a deep breath and let his fists drop to his side.

A cryptic smile broke over the face of Joseph Smith. "Brother Markham, you are not going to resist the officers, are you?"

Markham's shoulders dropped like weights. "No, not if they are officers. I know the law too well for that." A thought came over Markham. Since the two men had not shot Joseph, perhaps they were under orders to take him back alive.

Reynolds took a step backward. "There's a buggy over there. Get in it." He motioned his pistol toward the house, where the driver from Dixon stood holding two horses.

A woman's scream pierced the air. Markham whirled to see Emma Smith running toward Joseph. "Keep the children inside," she yelled at her sister, who stood on the porch weeping.

Reynolds waved his pistol at Emma. "That's far enough, woman," Reynolds stated. He cursed again.

Using the distraction of Emma, Markham ran to the buggy and seized both horses by their bridle bits. His gaze at Reynolds and Wilson was blistering. "There is no law on earth that requires a sheriff to take a prisoner without his clothes." He turned to Emma, whom he was certain was having vivid negative images of her husband rotting away again in some Missouri jail. "Sister Smith, fetch your husband's coat and hat."

"Who are these men?" Emma asked, tears coursing down her cheeks.

"Do as Brother Markham says, Emma," Joseph said, his voice calm. "Get my coat and hat. One man is from Missouri, the other from Carthage. Don't worry, they won't get me to Missouri."

Emma's expression remained clouded. Turning, she ran to the house.

Joseph stared into Reynolds' cold, leathery face. "Gentlemen, if you have any legal process, I wish to obtain a writ of habeas corpus." The writ would force his assailants to have the arrest charges examined by a justice of the peace somewhere in Illinois.

Reynolds thrust his pistol into Joseph's side and let forth another stream of filthy oaths. "You shan't have one. Now get into that wagon."

Markham screamed at Joseph, but the warning was too late. In horror, Markham watched Reynolds thrust his heavy pistol into Joseph's side, striking him over and over and over and over again, until the sheriff looked so fatigued he could scarcely raise his arm for another blow.

Joseph slumped to the ground, groaning and holding his side.

"Brave men you are," Markham yelled as he rushed to help Joseph, "beating an unarmed man."

Constable Wilson's oaths were blood curdling. "Get Joe Smith into that wagon."

"Go to Dixon," Joseph said to Markham as he staggered to his feet, breathing in short, labored spurts. "Get legal help." The driver helped Markham assist Joseph into the wagon.

At the urging of Joseph, Markham left the wagon and quickly saddled Joe Duncan. "I'm gonna have to kick the frost out of you, old boy. Forgive me." He wondered if the jaded horse could make it to Dixon. Suddenly, a thought came to him. If he left, there was a danger Reynolds would head southwest, toward Missouri, kidnapping not only Joseph but the driver, too.

The wagon, however, headed toward Dixon in a cloud of dust. Joe Duncan could barely keep up.

Markham taunted Reynolds and Wilson as the wagon lumbered along. "You two are the biggest cowards I've ever met."

Reynolds aimed his pistol at Markham. "I could shoot you, too." Markham backed off.

# 12

JOSEPH SMITH COLLAPSED INTO a chair as he held his side, as though it would somehow alleviate the pain. He scanned his temporary prison, a room above McKennie's Tavern in Dixon. Sheriff Reynolds towered over him, pointing the pistol at his chest. Constable Wilson had been sent across the street, ordered to bully the Dixon blacksmith for fresh horses for the run to Missouri. Markham was searching for William Clayton and a lawyer.

The room was Spartan—hardwood floors, a pine dresser, two oak chairs, and a single bed. The smell was rough frontier, with traces of pipe tobacco and an earthen aroma of pine. Joseph groaned as he rose to his feet. From a basin, he doused his face with water.

"Don't get too comfortable," Reynolds advised, his hand wrapped tightly around the pistol. "We'll be leaving as soon as the constable gets here with the horses."

Joseph wiped his face with a towel. "I have the right to legal counsel, you know."

Reynolds' eerie appearance exuded a fusion of evil from both the real and unseen worlds. "You shan't have counsel," he hissed, cursing again. "One more word and I'll shoot you."

Joseph narrowed his eyes. "I have repeatedly told you to shoot. And now I tell you again. Shoot away."

The Missouri lawman grunted and then threatened Joseph again, cursing loudly. "Wilson will be here soon."

Joseph cringed at the way Reynolds used the Lord's name in vain. He gave a grim sigh. He let his eyes trace the room, then fall to the street below. He thrust his head through an open window, yelling to a passing man. "I am falsely imprisoned up here, and I want a lawyer!"

The man looked up, puzzled.

"Get away from that window," Reynolds fumed. There were more foul oaths.

Joseph exhaled, savoring the fact that one more person knew of his captivity. He withdrew and collapsed into the chair again, praying. Several minutes passed.

Sheriff Reynolds wheeled at the sound of footsteps bounding up the stairs. Fists pounded at the door.

Joseph hoped it wasn't Constable Wilson.

"Open up! I'm Edward Southwick, an attorney."

Joseph heaved a sigh. It was the man who had ridden out to the Wasson farm to warn him of the writ.

Disappointment was written on Reynolds's face. He cursed again and slowly opened the door. He pushed his pistol into Southwick's face. "Leave, or I'll shoot. This man will not have you or any other lawyer."

"Have it your way," Southwick told Reynolds. "But I'll be back." He retreated down the stairs as Reynolds slammed the door.

With a dire sigh, Joseph sank into a chair, praying again. The dreamlike quality of late afternoon was settling around him. He tried to nap. A half hour passed.

Joseph's nap was interrupted by another knock on the door. Cursing again, Reynolds opened the door to find another attorney standing there. "I'm

Shepherd G. Patrick, attorney-at-law. I'm here to help that man," he said, pointing.

Joseph rose, hoping to talk. Reynolds used his gun to force the attorney back down the stairs and slammed the door shut again.

"Where's Wilson?" Reynolds said to himself, adding foul oaths to his question. Reynolds looked out the window and pulled a face. Below him, a crowd was gathering.

Joseph smiled. Word was spreading that the Mormon Prophet was in town.

More minutes passed. Another knock on the door.

"Go away!" Reynolds yelled.

A voice came back. "My name is Dixon."

Joseph grinned at the thought. *A Mr. Dixon from Dixon?*

Dixon's voice was sharp, directed at Reynolds. "I own this building. A citizens' committee has formed downstairs. I have two attorneys with me, a Mr. Southwick and a Mr. Patrick. Open up, Mr. Reynolds. Or you'll be in a lot of trouble. We are a law-abiding people, and Republicans. We aim to see that your prisoner has a fair trial, and that he is protected by the laws of this state. We have a very summary way of dealing with varmints like you."

Reynolds squinted his displeasure, his anger brimming. "Damned lawyers." He opened the door. Dixon, Southwick, and Patrick burst into the room.

Southwick pointed a bony finger at Reynolds, ignoring the pistol. "Judging by your rudeness, you must be from Missouri."

"Yes, and this man is my prisoner. You're interfering with my job."

Southwick was already earning his money. He held a hand in Reynolds' face. "You'll be quiet while we interview Mr. Smith."

Joseph could see a knot tightening in Reynolds' stomach. The lawman's plan to whisk him into Missouri without legal representation had faded considerably.

Another man bounded up the stairs. It was Constable Wilson. "I have the horses ready."

"What took you so long?" Reynolds growled.

"You two are not taking General Smith anywhere," Patrick growled back.

"Guard the door," Reynolds told Constable Wilson. "Don't let anyone else in."

Joseph did his best to ignore the continuing confusion. With Mr. Dixon at his side, he began explaining everything to the lawyers. He told of the insults and abuses heaped upon him by Reynolds and Wilson. He bared his shirt, telling how he had been punched with pistols. The skin on his side disclosed a mass of black and blue marks, eighteen inches in circumference. For several minutes, with Reynolds uttering angry but feeble protests, Joseph related the circumstances that brought him to Dixon as a fugitive.

There was another knock on the door. Sheriff Reynolds grimaced as Stephen Markham came into the room.

The lawyers continued giving advice to Joseph. A writ could be obtained from the master in chancery, a Mr. Chamberlain, who lived only six miles from Dixon. However, it would have to be made returnable before the Honorable John D. Caton, judge of the ninth judicial circuit, at Ottawa.

During the conversation, with Reynolds and Wilson looking away in disgust, Markham slipped a pistol into Joseph's shirt.

"Shall we proceed with the writ?" Southwick asked Joseph.

Joseph nodded his approval. "Yes. Get the writ."

Too late to see the pistol, Reynolds and Wilson turned. They snorted and frowned openly. Ottawa was sixty miles *southeast* of Dixon. Their destination was *southwest,* toward Missouri.

Joseph felt flushed with relief. His captors were losing control. He folded his arms across his chest. *I won't need this pistol,* he predicted to himself. But it felt good, anyway.

As the two lawyers began making arrangements for the trip to Ottawa, William Clayton came up the stairs. He bore good news. Cyrus Walker was in the vicinity.

"Who's Cyrus Walker?" Reynolds asked his companion.

Constable Wilson took off his hat and wiped the sweat from his brow.

"The Whig candidate for Congress in this district of our state. He must be campaigning here."

"A politician?" Reynolds asked with rising concern.

Old man Dixon thrust his wrinkled face in front of the Missouri sheriff. "Not just any old politician, you scoundrel. Cyrus Walker is the greatest criminal lawyer we have in these here parts."

Reynolds felt a chill. He put his gun away and shrank into a corner, fretting.

"Must be your lucky day, General Smith," Dixon said, winking.

*Or an answer to prayer,* Joseph thought.

Within an hour, Walker was interviewing Joseph. Reynolds cowered in a corner, clearly disgusted, listening to Joseph tell the story all over again. The conversation turned to the subject of a fee.

"My fee will be ten thousand dollars," Walker said without breaking a smile.

Reynolds chuckled.

Joseph pulled a face. "Too much."

"Take it or leave it," Walker replied.

Reynolds chuckled again.

"You drive a hard bargain," Joseph said, shaking his head in disappointment.

A mischievous smile came over Walker's face. "There's one other option."

"And what would that be?" Joseph asked, twisting his head in thought.

Walker's gaze was sharp. "As you know, I am seeking a seat in Congress. I'll represent you in exchange for your vote in the coming election."

Joseph understood the implication immediately. Nauvoo had grown to be the largest city in Illinois. Walker needed the Mormon vote to ensure his election. Joseph drew a deep breath, thinking. *What if I pledge my personal vote? After all, that's the way Walker had phrased it. Everyone else in Nauvoo can vote as they please.*

Joseph took a deep breath, and signaled his approval. "I agree."

Walked smiled. "Well, then, let's get started." He turned to Reynolds and

Wilson with an imposing glare. "You two will be interested to know that the first part of my defense plan will be to issue a warrant for your arrest."

Reynolds shot Walker an incredulous look, pondering his words. "For what?" he growled.

Walker's smile was bigger now. "I've compiled quite a list in my mind. For threatening the lives of Joe Smith and Stephen Markham. For private injuries, and false imprisonment. Ten thousand dollars damages sounds fair to me. And for a violation of Illinois law in relation to writs of habeas corpus."

Reynolds touched his pistol.

"I could add threats against my life, too," Walker said with an imposing look. "Take your hands off that pistol."

Joseph made no effort to wipe off the grin that swept over his face. *Walker is worth the vote,* he said to himself. Joseph took in the awkward glances Reynolds and Wilson exchanged with each other. Now they would need their own writs of habeas corpus.

Walker continued, enjoying the moment. "Since you and Wilson were unable to obtain bondsmen outside of Missouri, Sheriff Campbell of Lee County is waiting downstairs to take you into custody. I'm sure we'll keep merry company together on the way to Ottawa."

# 13

SHERIFF REYNOLDS HAD THE WORST headache of his life. He had just received news that Judge Caton of Ottawa was not available—out of town back east. Under his breath, he cursed again. Caton certainly would have rendered a favorable decision on Joe Smith's writ of habeas corpus, upholding the arrest. One of Smith's bodyguards, William Clayton, had fled to Nauvoo, sure to bring a Mormon rescue posse. Smith's wife and children were on their way back, too. *I should have arrested the whole lot of them!*

Worse, Markham's warrant against Wilson and him had been served. Now Reynolds had to put up with the ominous presence of a local sheriff, a man named Campbell. And Cyrus Walker, the attorney. Those thoughts caused him to think of more foul oaths.

In the restaurant of a Pawpaw Grove hotel, Sheriff Reynolds picked at his breakfast, thinking. Word had spread in town that Joe Smith, the Mormon Prophet, was in the hotel. That brought a crowd of curious onlookers, thronging to the lobby.

"What'll we do now?" Constable Wilson asked. Wilson seemed to be enjoying the breakfast of toast swimming in butter, ham, and eggs as much as Joe Smith, Markham, Walker, and Campbell at the next table. That irritated Reynolds.

"Don't rush me," Reynolds warned, his headache worse.

"We either have to go back to Dixon and get a new writ, or..."

Reynolds cut Wilson off and cursed again. "I know. You don't have to tell me." It appeared the only other option available was to head for Quincy, where Judge Stephen A. Douglas was holding court. That meant head south toward Nauvoo, directly into the path of a Mormon rescue party. More cursing.

The crowd in the lobby was getting larger by the minute. His pulse thundering, Reynolds rose from his chair.

"Where're you going?" Wilson asked.

"To handle that crowd."

Reynolds stomped into the lobby. He parted his topcoat, and then bared his holstered pistol.

For a moment, there was an eerie silence.

"I wish you to understand that Joe Smith is my prisoner," Reynolds yelled. "I want you to disperse, immediately."

There was a prolonged murmur.

From behind Reynolds, Sheriff Campbell emerged, pointing. "Reynolds, there's an elderly gentleman here in the crowd that wants to say something."

Reynolds reeled and swore. "What does he want?"

"His name is David Town," Campbell said. "He's an influential man in these parts. He's the head of the Regulators. That's an organization that prevents land speculators imposing their will on poor-folk settlers."

A gray-haired, bent-over man approach with a limp. The elderly gentleman raised his heavy hickory cane in the air, and brought it down with a thud. The noise echoed throughout the lobby. David Town stood glaring at Reynolds.

"See these people?" Town asked with a commanding sweep of his arm. "They've come to hear General Smith speak. You let him come forward. Bring him in here."

The Jackson County sheriff shook his head, cringing at the word, *general*. "Joe Smith will not be speaking today."

Reynolds cringed again as the cane slammed to the floor again. Town's eyes were on fire. "You damned infernal puke, we'll learn you to come here and interrupt gentlemen."

Reynolds put his hand on his gun. Tension, thick and hot, gripped the room.

Using the hickory cane, Town pointed to the lowest chair in the room. "Sit down there, and be still. Don't open your head until General Smith gets through talking."

The old man paused, waiting for Reynolds to comply.

The Missourian scanned the room. More men were filing in, some with guns. Several were laughing at the old man's panache. Reynolds exhaled deeply, swore, and shrugged his shoulders in resignation. He walked to the chair and sat on its edge. The only thing that made him comfortable was the frontier love affair with chewing tobacco and spitting. He reached for a plug and placed a pinch in his upper gum.

Town ground his teeth together and formed more angry words. "If you never learned manners in Missouri, we'll teach you that gentlemen are not to be imposed upon by a nigger-driver. You cannot kidnap men here as you do in Missouri. If you attempt it here, there's a committee in this town that will sit on your case. And, sir, it is the highest tribunal in the United States. From its decision, there is no appeal."

Reynolds sank deeper into the chair. Pawpaw Grove was a long way from Jackson County, Missouri. He spat sickening spittle, most of it settling on his own boots.

Pointing again with the cane, Town's eyes reached Joseph. "General Smith, you have the floor."

# 14

IN A SURREAL, DREAMLIKE IMAGERY, a late afternoon sun illuminated the magnificent contours of Tapper and Bendigo. The two horses shook their heads and stamped their feet as a gesture against their confinement. Kept in a wormwood corral between the Harris and Browett cabins, they were eager to work, eager to run. They were about to get more than they bargained for.

Inside his cabin, Robert was coddling his month-old son in his lap. His sister, Dianah Bloxham, and his wife, Hannah, were putting the finishing touches on a Sunday afternoon dinner. The garden already yielded fresh peas, onions, and radishes.

Duke barked. The figure of a short stocky man came sliding by the window. There was a knock on the door of the small cabin.

Robert handed baby Enoch to his brother-in-law, Thomas Bloxham. "I'd better get it. I think its Wilford Woodruff."

A solemn look greeted Robert as he opened the door. Wilford was ignoring Duke's friendly hand licks.

"Step outside a moment, please," the Apostle said, wincing. Gone was his normal cheery face. Nearby, the Bloxham and Harris children were playing marbles.

As he closed the door, Robert wondered what had come over Wilford. They had seen each other at the Church service earlier in the day on the unfinished floor of the temple, as Elder Lyman Wight addressed the congregation about charity. However, toward the end of the meeting a curious thing happened. A ragged-looking William Clayton had walked into the meeting and whispered something into Hyrum Smith's ear. The meeting was cut short. Several men, including Wilford, followed Hyrum and William Clayton to the Masonic Hall for some kind of emergency meeting. So many attended, the meeting was continued outside.

"How's your arm?" Robert asked, strolling toward the horses. Elder Woodruff had injured it twelve days ago, the day Joseph Smith and his family left to see Emma's sister, two hundred miles north, near Dixon, Lee County, Illinois. Wilford had gone to work on his farm fence outside Nauvoo, when the reach of his wagon broke. A wheel had fallen on Wilford's arm, bruising him severely. Then, to make matters worse, later in the day he had been severely bitten on the leg by a dog.

"Don't worry about me," Wilford began. "A crisis has developed with Brother Joseph."

Robert felt a rising trepidation. He had felt it since the meeting, when he saw William Clayton walk in.

Wilford was quick to come to the point. "We have a problem. Brother Clayton has informed us that two scoundrels disguised as Mormon elders have kidnapped Joseph in Dixon." It hadn't taken long for Clayton to return to Nauvoo. It was high water time on the river.

"Kidnapped?" Robert asked, blinking hard.

Wilford clasped his hands together behind his back and paced back and forth in front of Tapper and Bendigo. "They're trying to whisk Joseph into Missouri before Joseph can get legal help. I fear if they are successful, we may never see Joseph alive again. They could murder him before he reaches the border."

Robert's heart sank. Even if the two men did not kill Joseph, the Prophet likely would be held in another suffocating prison along with Porter Rockwell. They had captured Rockwell months earlier, in St. Louis. Although there was no evidence, Porter and Joseph were still being accused of conspiring to shoot and kill ex-Governor Boggs. Robert asked the man who converted him the obvious question, "What do you propose to do?"

"Send out the Legion. Rescue him. We've fanned out, knocking on doors for help."

Robert's fists rolled into balls. Disdain for these new enemies swept over him, and it pleased him greatly. He could see other members of the Twelve, and many others, pleading with the men of Nauvoo to join this hastily put together posse.

"You are to go with the Legion. Intercept the two men before they get the Prophet over the border."

Robert found his pitchfork, leaning against the corral. He stabbed it into the ground in useless anger. "We can't let the Missourians get away with this." His knuckles turned white as he gripped the handle. Previously, he had planned to begin his hay harvest tomorrow. He would change his plans.

Wilford reached out to touch Tapper's muzzle. The sorrel gelding snorted in appreciation. "Good thing you have your horses handy. You'll need to ride out immediately."

"Who's in command?" Robert asked, his voice tightening.

"You'll be under the direction of Generals Wilson Law and Charles C. Rich. I want you to get help. Get Levi Roberts and John Cox. You've all received training in the Legion as bodyguards for the Prophet. Take anyone else you can find. Brother Browett, and your brother-in-law too, if he'll come. I know Thomas Bloxham's not a member of the Church, but we can use all the men we can get."

Robert nodded his understanding. "How many men are going?"

"We need a hundred, more if we can get them in time. Once you get far enough north, you'll fan out and cover all the routes. In case there's a fight, we need five or six men in each group."

"Fight with our fists?" With a coy smile, Robert again balled his fists. He would like nothing more than to prove his loyalty to the Prophet.

"The Legion commanders will issue you firearms," Wilford said. "I've opened a barrel of powder. There'll be enough for every man to fill his horn or flask. Meet at the temple as soon as you can. I'm off to inform others."

Wilford walked a few steps away, and then turned again. "Remember, you represent the Church on this trip. Your every action must reflect that. This is a big responsibility. Don't let us down."

Robert couldn't believe his ears. Wilson Law, a man with the rank of brigadier general in the Nauvoo Legion, was arguing with Brigham Young, an Apostle.

"I'm not taking the Legion one step toward Dixon without money to fund our expedition," Law declared.

There was a stunned silence among the members of the Legion. More than a hundred men had gathered, many on horseback. More were seen coming up the hill toward the temple site.

Robert fondled his saddlebag, his mind racing. Inside, he had placed a two-day supply of corn fritters and dried meat. A wool blanket was strapped to the back of his saddle. Something in Wilson Law didn't quite stick. Something wasn't quite consistent. Law sounded like the most determined man in Nauvoo in one moment, and in the next, practically worthless. The man wasn't long on backbone. It seemed to Robert there was a better way, so he raised his hand.

"You have something to say, Brother Harris?" Brigham asked, his blue eyes searching and his golden brown hair blowing in the breeze.

"We can take our own food and sleep on the ground," Robert said.

Wilson Law paled and gave Private Robert Harris an acrimonious scowl. Robert didn't flinch at the bear-like man whose rough moon face was pockmarked by childhood acne.

Brigham spoke quickly. He let his eyes scan the assembled members of the Nauvoo Legion. Tension now hung like a pall over the gathered men. "How many of you brought your own food and bedding?"

About twenty hands went up, out of more than seventy.

"See?" Law said, his face drawing into a smirk. "We need money."

Robert felt somewhat at a loss, but did not want to give up. "The other men can go home and get equipped quite quickly," he said.

Law cut Robert off. "Just as quickly, you Church authorities can raise some money. We're not leaving without it."

Robert restrained an urge to leap at General Law and strangle him. Robert's chest began rising and falling in sharp, shallow little breaths. *Glory hounds always whine and plead.* Precious time was slipping away. Ghastly images of Joseph's kidnapping thrashed through his mind. He had heard William Clayton's vivid reports.

"How much?" Brigham asked, looking perplexed.

Charles C. Rich, the other general, threw his hands open. "We don't need much, if any at all."

"A thousand dollars," Law said as he pushed Rich aside. "We don't know how long we're going to be gone. We need money for food, for lodging. We might need to re-shoe some horses. Stephen Markham had two hundred fifty dollars for expenses when he left to warn the Prophet. William Clayton had two hundred dollars. What's wrong with our entire outfit having a thousand dollars?"

Daniel Browett raised his hand. "Missionaries go out without purse or scrip. We can do the same."

Law ignored the comments. His tone was icy, and to the point. "What if our horses become jaded? What if we have to make some quick horse trades?"

Robert could see Brigham wilting under the weight of Law's demands.

General Law was still on the offensive. Smiling smugly, he turned to Hyrum, Joseph's brother. "Are you willing to risk the life of the Prophet over a few hundred dollars?"

Robert shook his head, fighting his rise of adrenaline. To save the life of Joseph Smith, he was willing to beg, borrow, trade for, or steal fresh horses along the way. And give them back later. Law was a squeaky wheel, and sometimes squeaky wheels got kicked.

Hyrum and Brigham exchanged awkward glances. Both men were obviously embarrassed. "Wait here," Hyrum told Generals Law and Rich.

Robert watched as Hyrum and Brigham strolled a few paces away. Tapper whinnied in impatience. Bendigo, Daniel's roan horse, pawed at the ground.

"How long would it take to raise a thousand dollars?" Hyrum asked the Apostle, looking grim.

"I don't know," Brigham said, appearing unsettled. "We'll just have to start. Men like John Benbow will contribute."

"Organize a committee, and raise the money," Hyrum said. "General Law is a stubborn man. Time's a wasting."

Robert stood close enough to hear the conversation. So did William Law. A satisfied smirk came over Law's face. Robert grunted his disgust.

# 15

ROBERT COULDN'T GET WILSON LAW off his mind. Dusk was approaching, the mosquitoes thick. The Mormon posse, under full gallop, was only a few miles north of Nauvoo in mostly wild, raw country. There were stands of tall oaks, elms, maples, birches, dogwood, and thick underbrush. They had crossed swollen streams with no bridges and difficult sloughs where the grass was thickly matted together. General Law's stubbornness had cost the Legion more than two hours in delay, all for seven hundred dollars that Robert still didn't think was needed. Where was Joseph? Which road would he be on? Would the delay cost the Prophet his life?

Tapper was blowing like a whale, but experiencing a sense of wild, exhilarating freedom. As dirt kicked up from both sides, Robert patted his sorrel gelding on the neck in a gesture of appreciation. Tapper was accustomed to pulling a plow on Robert and Daniel's forty-acre farm east of Nauvoo, not galloping at full speed to the drumming of hundreds of hoofs toward Dixon. Tapper and Bendigo were the lifeblood of their farming success. Without the two horses, farming their forty acres would be near impossible.

In a cloud of dust, Robert finally slowed his mount to a trot, following the lead of Generals Law and Rich. Wilson's brother, William Law, Joseph's first counselor, also rode in the lead. Robert guessed there were around a hundred seventy-five riders surrounding him. Their goal was Peoria and then split up, riding north in all directions. They had passed knots of curious farmers, but no suspicious-looking Missourians. But then it was far too early to expect a sighting. Robert guessed there was less than one person per square mile living out in this part of Illinois.

To Robert, the Illinois prairie seemed peaceful beneath a glowering purple sky, fringed with pink, as if the clouds were a lid too small for the earth. The colors were rich. Boulders were shrouded in deep green grass. Nearby, a plum lake reflected the sky. Here and there, the riders flushed quail out of the tall, waving grass. White-tailed deer stared at them from bedding areas within groves of trees. Wrens, owls, sparrows, blackbirds, warblers, and robins sang the final lullabies of the day. Tall trees cast long peaceful shadows at the riders.

Robert's mind, however, was not peaceful. He thought of Joseph Smith's capture, and the distress of the Prophet being taken to Missouri.

Another seventy-five Mormon men had earlier boarded the *Maid of Iowa* under command of Captain Dan Jones. They were headed up the Mississippi River with the goal of turning up the Illinois River as far as Peoria to search every steamboat they could find. Hyrum had said that he suspected that his brother might be held prisoner on one of them.

As the horses slowed to a walk, Robert eased Tapper near Daniel Browett and Bendigo. With an emphatic shake of his head, Robert said, "I was tempted to reduce our force by one man back there in town."

His brother-in-law's jaunty bluntness confused Daniel. "What do you mean?"

Robert shot Daniel a disapproving look. Tan road dust covered both men. "Wilson Law," Robert said, steaming beneath his dark gray cap. "We could have been half-way to Monmouth by now." Dixon, where the Prophet was captured, was more than two hundred miles north of Nauvoo.

Levi Roberts, John Cox, Thomas Bloxham, and a man named Robert Pixton eased their horses near Tapper and Bendigo. Robert had gotten to know Pixton working alongside him at the temple. Pixton had been baptized after his immigration from England, and lived in Iowa Territory, at Augusta. He had been taught and converted by Elder Lyman Wight.

Blinking rapidly, not hiding his disgust, Levi agreed. "To a man, I think we all wanted to leave as soon as we could. We'd better watch General Law. Make him account for every cent."

"I've never liked him," John Cox said. "Nor his brother, even though he is the Prophet's counselor."

"I say, beware of the Law brothers," Robert added. "They'll pour honeyed potion into our ears."

"One day we'll wake up and find both of them are just another John C. Bennett," Levi added.

Thomas Bloxham found this Mormon talk intriguing. "Then why is Wilson Law leading us? He's a brigadier general."

Daniel shrugged, holding his musket tightly. "I don't know. I think the Prophet Joseph has been too kind and too patient with the Law brothers."

Robert set his jaw. "Well, if Brother Law does anything more that seems strange or out of place, I'll break his ribs and we'll have just one man to follow. Brother Rich." His voice rang with loathing.

The look on Thomas Bloxham's face was still perplexed.

Robert began to laugh, reading his brother-in-law's concern. With Daniel, Levi, John, and Pixton's help, he began telling Thomas what he knew about the Law brothers. They were born in Northern Ireland and immigrated as young boys to America in about 1820, settling first in western Pennsylvania, and then later in Ontario, upper Canada. William Law was converted to the Church in 1836 through the efforts of John Taylor and Almon W. Babbitt. The Laws met Joseph Smith a year later, when the Prophet visited that area of Canada. The two brothers were early settlers in Nauvoo arriving in 1839. Wilson resisted baptism into the Church until he was in Nauvoo. In Robert's mind, Wilson's baptism came out of convenience, no out of a testimony. The Laws were aggressive businessmen, wasting little time putting down roots. The two men purchased properties, opened a store on Water Street, and proceeded to build a much-needed steam mill along the river to make flour and saw logs. By 1841 the Prophet was so impressed with William Law's leadership abilities that he called him to serve in the First Presidency as a counselor. William served a mission to Philadelphia with Hyrum later in 1841. And William eagerly defended Joseph's character in 1842, issuing public statements condemning John C. Bennett's licentious conduct. Both Law brothers extended moral and financial support to Joseph during his trial in Springfield in January 1843.

Thomas' brow furrowed in apparent confusion. "Why would a man like General Law delay us for so long, to obtain money? He should be the first one to strike out without regard to where he's going to buy his first meal."

"I think it has something to do with the way he runs his businesses," Daniel said, his voice on edge.

"What do you mean?" Thomas asked, probing further.

"He and his brother are in the real estate business, too."

"So?"

Daniel continued his explanation. "They're the ones who have developed the business district near the temple."

"And they're selling building lots, too," Levi added.

"In direct competition with the Church, undercutting prices," Robert said bitterly. "I've heard that the Prophet has recently insisted that the English immigrants purchase building lots from only the Church."

"And everyone else," John Cox snorted.

"What's wrong with people having a choice?" Thomas asked. "In my mind, the immigrants ought to decide which lots they want. Especially if they are less money."

Daniel raised a free arm, emphasizing his next point. "Because. All those who can afford it pay a reasonable price to the Church. Profits from the sale of Church property can be used to defray the cost of lots to people who can't afford it. And to pay off the debts of the Church."

"What debts?" Thomas asked, his brow wrinkled.

"The money owed by the Church to the original landowners in Nauvoo extending way back to 1838 and 1839," Daniel said.

"The Law brothers put their profits into their pockets," Robert said. "In my mind, they're downright greedy. I think their attitudes show it." He thought of Wilson Law's lavish two-story brick home on Water Street, and his extensive commercial holdings in the business development near the temple. He was still bristling over his personal verbal encounter with Wilson Law.

Daniel spoke again, his tone still one of disgust. "I remember the time John C. Bennett poisoned himself. Obviously done to solicit sympathy from the Prophet. The Law brothers were in the George Robinson home with Bennett when Dr. J. F. Weld came to treat Bennett."

"As far as I'm concerned," Robert said, "Dr. Weld should have given an enema to both the Laws as well as to Bennett." He rolled a fist into a ball and raised it to the air, waving it at General Law's back.

The weight of reality bit at Daniel. "Better save your energy for the two men who've captured Brother Joseph."

The posse rode until well past midnight. They stopped at a grove of trees just as a gust of wind from the southwest brought showers that swept over the darkened Illinois prairie. Generals Law and Rich ordered the men to rest their horses, eat whatever food they brought in their saddlebags, and get a couple hours of sleep.

"In the morning we'll split up," General Rich explained as he unsaddled his horse. "We don't know which route Sheriff Reynolds is taking. Whatever it is, we need to find Joseph before they get across the border."

"We can't let that happen," General Law added, his voice desperate. "Do you know what real estate values will do if they assassinate Joseph Smith? People will start moving out of Nauvoo. You won't get anything for your houses or lots. Prices will drop like a lead ball."

Robert frowned in the dark and nudged Daniel with his elbow. "Is the general worried about real estate, or about the Prophet?" he whispered.

"Probably about his real estate holdings," Daniel answered.

Robert's voice stiffened. "And where's our comfortable beds, inside some warm inn?"

"I wonder if we'll ever stay in an inn on this trip," Daniel said, untying his wool blanket from his saddle.

"Then what's the thousand dollars for?"

"You have to remember, Brigham only gave General Law seven hundred dollars. We're three hundred dollars short."

"So we sleep on the ground," Robert concluded, laughing. "Just as we wanted, so who's to complain?"

As he rolled himself up into a single wool blanket, Daniel compared the prairie grass underneath an elm tree to the hard floor of his cabin, next to the hearth. Thankfully, Elizabeth had softened somewhat during the past month. He almost forced her to do that the day he invited an old friend from England, George Bundy, to stay with them. Bundy had arrived in Nauvoo on May thirty-first, one of the *Yorkshire* passengers. His mother, Martha, opened her cabin to accept John Gailey, Robert and Elizabeth's cousin. It was John Gailey, a fellow United Brethren lay preacher, who had accompanied Daniel and Elizabeth to the John Benbow farm to meet Wilford Woodruff for the first time. And all three were baptized that spring day, back in 1840.

Daniel assumed it was mostly for show, but Elizabeth had resumed her midwife and herbalist duties just before that. There was the birth of a daughter to Edward and Susannah Phillips on May ninth. And the birth of Enoch Harris, the fifth child of Robert and Hannah, on May twenty-ninth. She was also treating the first cases of ague of the season among her English immigrant friends, treating them with precious doses of quinine—now marketed on the frontier as Sapinton's Pills.

Otherwise, her attitude remained defiant and cynical regarding plural marriage and Church authorities. Not once had she visited Rebecca since his sister's wedding to Orson Hyde. She refused a birthday celebration for her and Hannah on June eleventh, also the day of their wedding anniversary. When

Daniel told her goodbye as he joined the rescue posse, she said, "Be sure to take Brother Joseph an extra wife or two."

In the dark, Robert asked his brother-in-law a question, whispering, "Things any better with Elizabeth?"

Daniel's answer was blunt. "No."

"When are you going to make them better?"

"I guess when she comes off her high horse."

Robert grunted his disapproval of the answer. "I said when are *you* going to make things better?"

"What do you mean?"

"You're letting her run right over you, with her attitude."

"So what would you do if she were your wife?"

"Take her over my knees and spank her."

Daniel spit out a scoff. "Funny."

"Take control."

"What?"

"Just take control. Tell her you've had enough of her insolence. Take your place back, as a husband. Sleep in your bedroom, with her."

"She'll explode."

"Nonsense. She's waiting for you to do just that. When you get home, try it."

"I'll think about it. Goodnight."

"Goodnight, chicken feathers."

Daniel rolled his eyes in the darkness. Robert had a different philosophy about life than he did. As he thought about it, Daniel finally decided that Robert's directness was just a by-product of his general vanity and overconfidence. Daniel himself spent plenty of time on self-appraisal. He knew what he would do under certain situations and what he might do if he was lucky, and what he couldn't do barring a miracle. The problem with Robert was that he always regarded himself as the miracle, in such situations as chasing after Missourians and rescuing the Prophet, or dealing with his wife. He treated danger with light contempt or open scorn, and scorn was about all he seemed to have for Missourians or for Elizabeth and her attitude. Robert's disregard for common sense in some situations bothered Daniel. But he was a cool customer, perhaps the coolest Daniel had ever known. Robert didn't scare easily. His disregard for danger was so complete that Daniel sometimes thought he didn't even fear death. That's the way Robert had been from the day they had met back in England, even before Robert had begun his pugilism career. The more fights he won, the more his confidence soared. He hoped Robert's overconfidence didn't get the Mormon posse in trouble during their hunt for Joseph. But he wondered if perhaps Robert was right about how he should deal with Elizabeth.

To the sound of crickets and the rushing water of a nearby creek, Daniel settled into a troubled sleep.

CHAPTER NOTES

Background information about William Law and his brother is taken from *William Law, Nauvoo Dissenter,* Lyndon W. Cook, Brigham Young University Library.

In the *History of the Church*, page 447, Joseph Smith writes: "Wilson Law declared he would not go one step unless he could have money to bear his expenses, upon which Elder Brigham Young said the money should be forthcoming, although he did not know at the time where he could raise a dollar. In about thirty minutes he got on the track, and in the course of two hours he had borrowed seven hundred dollars, and put it in the hands of Hyrum Smith and Wilson Law, to defray the expenses of the expedition."

# 16

JOSEPH COULDN'T HELP BUT SNORT AT Sheriff Reynolds' awkward dilemma. Reynolds was on horseback, escorting the private stage Joseph was riding in. Joseph was still Reynolds' prisoner, but Reynolds and Wilson were prisoners of Sheriff Campbell. Seated next to Joseph was the most clever attorney in northern Illinois, a fact that was clearly rankling the Missouri lawman.

In contrast to Reynolds' foul disposition, Joseph was jovial and relaxed. It showed in his teasing.

"Care to let me ride your horse for a while, Sheriff Reynolds?" Joseph asked. "Kind of hot and stuffy in this stage, you know. Besides, I want the best view of the road. There'll be a hundred Mormon riders coming this direction any time. There's no doubt in my mind that Brother Markham found my rescue posse somewhere south of here."

Joseph sensed Reynolds knew he was correct.

"Cat got your tongue?" Joseph asked. Long ago he had learned that no one, not even a prophet of God, could escape tragedy and suffering. But he had also learned that the Lord had promised not only him, but also everyone, that He would be with them. Joseph had always faced his problems with dignity and courage, along with the strength to be of good cheer instead of being resentful. To meet the most critical of situations with cheerful endurance and good spirits, he found it helpful to joke around a little, and that's what he was doing now.

Reynolds erupted, cursing again. "No, you're not riding my horse. A man should know when he's conquered."

Constable Wilson rode with his head hung low on a spent-out gray mare. Joseph suspected Wilson regretted the day he met Reynolds. It was not going well for either of them.

Joseph heard Cyrus Walker chuckle at Reynolds. Joseph had the sense that Walker's skills were going to earn him his legal freedom, whether in Quincy or in Nauvoo.

Sheriff Campbell, in contrast to Reynolds and Wilson, rode with his head held high on a fresh white gelding. This was probably the best day of Campbell's life, Joseph thought, having two other lawmen under arrest. However, Joseph wished Campbell had the courage to confiscate the other two men's weapons.

From the south, the faint whisper of a dust cloud appeared.

Joseph poked his head out of the stage, pointing. "See that, Sheriff Reynolds? What do you make of it? Is it the Mormons, or the Missourians?"

Reynolds' outward appearance remained hard as flint. Joseph knew there must be a ripple of fear going through him. After all, Reynolds was human even though he was an obvious tool of Satan. In a gesture of defiance, Reynolds touched his pistol and told the stage driver, Sanger, to slow his horses.

The dust cloud grew larger. Farther south, another dust cloud formed.

Joseph relaxed. God was smiling down on him.

Robert was riding in the advance party of Mormon riders, led by Peter W. Conover and William L. Cutler. Among the other riders were Daniel Browett, Levi Roberts, John Cox, Thomas Bloxham, and Robert Pixton.

"Stagecoach ahead," Cutler said, pointing his musket.

Robert shaded the noonday sun with a hand. They had come upon countless other riders, wagons, and stages during their long two-day journey. So far, their search had been fruitless. The huge Mormon posse had split up into several groups, fanning the Illinois countryside in search of their captured Prophet.

Robert patted Tapper on his neck. The sorrel gelding's hide was soaked in lather. *I hope this is it, old friend,* he thought. *Tapper can't take much more.*

There was a faint grin on Robert's lips, however. Tapper had withstood the trip. Wilson Law's bay mare had jiggered, worn out along with several other horses and their riders. Wilson had even thrust bottles of spirits down his mare's throat, to no avail. Wilson and his brother, William, were far behind, in a borrowed farm wagon, along with Albert P. Rockwood and three other men.

Cutler kicked his horse into a gallop. "That could be the Prophet and his captors."

Robert leaned forward in the saddle, hoping for a chance to use his musket or at least his fists.

*It has to be them,* Joseph said to himself as he watched nine horsemen draw nearer. He took off his hat and waved it. Sanger tugged on the lines and drew his six horses to a halt.

Reynolds gritted his teeth as the passengers stepped out of the coach onto the road.

A smile of recognition came over Joseph as he teetered on his tiptoes. He glanced at his captor, who sat perched atop the coach. Reynolds held one hand over his eyes, shielding the sun. He was trying to determine if the riders were friend or foe. In the warm June sun, he felt a chill.

Joseph looked up at the sheriff. "I'm not going to Missouri this time. These are my boys."

Reynolds seethed and his dark eyes were still defiant.

Sheriff Campbell inhaled deeply and let his air out. He spoke to both

Reynolds and Wilson. "I remind both of you. You are still in my custody."

Joseph chuckled.

Robert gripped his musket, sensing a fight. Cutler had confirmed that, indeed, the stage and riders comprised the party they had been searching for—Joseph Smith and the two lawless lawmen.

With muskets raised in the air, Cutler's search party approached the stage.

Sheriff Campbell rode his white horse forward, holding a hand up. "I'm the sheriff from Dixon. The Missourian and the Carthage Constable are under arrest. Joe Smith is quite well."

Robert scanned the group standing behind Campbell. *Then why do the other two lawmen still have their weapons?* He looked for signs of resistance. To his eyes, Reynolds looked like a human buzzard, his face craggy and permanently furious. Wilson reminded Robert of a coyote, pacing back and forth with a nervous twitch.

The Prophet rushed forward, drawing Cutler into an embrace. "God bless you Legion boys!"

Robert nudged Levi. "Keep your hands on your musket. I don't like the looks of those two men over there."

As the Prophet continued his happy reunion with Cutler and Conover, the second cloud of dust approached. It revealed another group of Legion soldiers, including Stephen Markham and Captain Thomas Grover.

Joseph's face lit up even more at the sight of Markham, who once again was riding Old Joe Duncan. Markham had taken the horse back to Nauvoo via the steamboat.

Joseph swung into the saddle and guided his horse toward Sheriff Reynolds. "I don't need to ride your old nag. I'm going to Nauvoo in style. On my own horse."

From his mount, Robert laughed out loud.

The laugh caught Joseph's attention. Pointing at all the Legion men, Joseph said, "You saved my life today."

"God smiled on us," Robert responded.

Reynolds and Wilson were not smiling. Reynolds' hot gaze was still raking the Mormons. Wilson was staring at the ground, kicking at it.

Grover fired an angry look at Joseph's captors, and then addressed the Prophet. "General Smith, we set out from Nauvoo with a hundred and seventy-five riders. More will be here soon."

A cloud passed over Reynolds' face. He began shaking as though he had a bad case of ague.

Robert laughed, beginning to feel just a mite sorry for the sheriff.

"Why are you trembling so?" Conover asked the shaking Missourian.

Sweat poured off Reynolds' brow. Turning pale, he tried to project his voice past a huge lump in his throat. "Is Jem Flack among your riders?"

"Yes," Conover answered. "You probably won't see him today, but surely tomorrow about this time you'll see him."

Reynolds held his head in his hands, as though his brain might erupt. "Then I am a dead man. I know Flack of old." He had issued a death threat to Jem Flack in Missouri, years earlier, during the Mormon War. Flack had returned the threat.

Markham thrust his face in front of Reynolds. "It appears Judgment Day is here."

Reynolds closed his eyes for a moment, trying to hide his fear.

"Don't look so shocked," Markham stated, giving the sheriff a hard look.

"Do I meet you as a friend?" Reynolds asked. "I expected to be a dead man when I met you again."

Markham chuckled. "We are friends, except in law. That must have its course."

From his horse, Joseph placed a hand on Markham's shoulder and addressed Reynolds. "We'll have to pass through Nauvoo on the way to Quincy."

Reynolds seemed to regain his composure. As his eyes hardened, he drew his pistol and began to swear, fouling the air with his oaths. "No, we won't. We will never go to Nauvoo alive!"

Following Reynolds' lead, Wilson drew his pistol, and waved it at the Mormons.

Robert raised his musket and cocked it. So did the other Mormon men. "Put that down or we'll make wolf meat out of you," he said.

Markham was quick to react. Using the cocked muskets as courage, he pointed at Sheriff Campbell. "When these men took Joseph as prisoner, then took everything from him, even his pocketknife. Reynolds and Wilson are prisoners of yours, and I demand that you take their arms from them."

Campbell drove his dark eyes into Reynolds and Wilson. "Drop your pistols," he thundered.

Both lawmen said no, and cursed violently.

"Shall I order our men to shoot?" Markham said.

"Surrender your arms," Campbell said, his voice rising.

A blank look.

Robert aimed his musket at Reynolds' chest. "The man says to surrender his arms. He means it."

Reynolds and Wilson returned Robert's icy stare, perplexed by the English accent. Robert had the urge to take off his shirt and show his rippling muscles. Slowly, however, Reynolds and Wilson wilted, their faces white with fear. They lowered their pistols. Campbell quickly confiscated them. "For the remainder of our trip, you'll be under armed guard," Campbell said.

Reynolds shook again, his eyes seeming to lose focus.

"Quit shaking," Joseph said in a soothing voice. "I'll invite you and Sheriff Wilson to my home for dinner. You're soon to find out that Mormons aren't the evil people you have been led to believe."

Robert let his eyes scan the ground, below the Missourian. Whispering, he leaned toward Thomas Bloxham. "The brave man wet himself," he chuckled.

Noting the pool below Reynolds trousers, Thomas laughed out loud.

# 17

JOSEPH'S TRIUMPHAL RETURN TO NAVUOO was dazzling
Thousands lined the road leading to the temple. It was a perfect Illinois day
hot sun, pellucid blue sky, scents of grass and wildflowers, a gentle breeze stirring waves of grain and corn. Near the Big Mound, not far from Daniel and
Robert's farm, English immigrants picked pungent wildflowers and placed
them in the bridles of the returning Legion mounts. A band was playing, led
by William Pitt, one of Wilford Woodruff's converts. With Hyrum Smith and
Joseph's wife, Emma, in the lead, hundreds of other Legion soldier
approached from the city, in full dress.

As the two groups converged, Daniel watched as Joseph swept a tearfu
Emma into his arms. Joseph, tired, frayed, and needing a warm bath, then
swung into the saddle of a fresh horse—Old Charley, his coal black stallion
With Emma riding at his side, the Prophet led the procession into Nauvoo
smiling, waving. William Pitt's band played *Hail Columbia*. Thousands o
happy Mormons, clogging Mulholland on both sides, waved and wept
Cannons boomed. Muskets spat fire in welcoming salutes.

Daniel wondered what Sheriff Reynolds and Constable Wilson were thinking as they peered out of Sanger's stage. Surely, Daniel thought, they must be impressed with the vast number of Mormons and their intelligent, gleaming looks. A bulging city of neat log, frame, and brick homes. And hundreds of armed Legionnaires.

With Robert, Levi, John, and Thomas, Daniel took his position ahead of the Legion, riding in front of the Legion with the heroic posse members. As the procession passed the Wells Addition close to his home, Daniel scanned the crowd, looking for Elizabeth.

"Daniel!"

The voice belonged to his mother, Martha.

"Welcome home! Good job!"

Daniel waved. Next to his mother stood his sister, Rebecca, waving with Orson and Marinda Hyde. The next group included Hannah and her children: Joseph, Lizzy, Willie, and baby Enoch. And Dianah Bloxham with Lucy, Tommy, Emma, Johnny, and Isaac. Next to them, Harriet Ann Roberts, and Henry, Caroline, and Phoebe Ann. Eliza Cox with Elizabeth, Ann, Johnny, and Mary Ann.

But no Elizabeth.

Other familiar families from England were there, too. John and Jane Benbow, and their two adopted children, Thomas and Ellen. Thomas and Margaret Kington. William and Caroline Pitt, and their son, Moroni. Edward and Hannah Phillips, and their newborn baby, Sarah. Mary Ann Weston Davis Maughan, and her new husband, Peter, and his six children. Henry and Katherine Eagles, and their child. The new arrivals from England: George Bundy and John and Ann Gailey.

Everyone waved except Henry. *What've you been up to?* Daniel thought.

Still, no Elizabeth.

The procession ended at the Nauvoo Mansion gate.

Daniel fought back tears as he watched Lucy Mack Smith embrace her son. The crowd, thousands in number, pressed forward.

Joseph's son, Fred, crawled up his father's leg. "Pa, the Missourians won't take you away again, will they?"

Daniel wiped at his eyes. Then he watched as Joseph placed little Fred in Emma's arms and mounted the fence surrounding the Nauvoo Mansion. In two months, Daniel guessed, the mansion would be ready for the Prophet's family to live in. Joseph spoke, thanking the posse, thanking the crowd, and telling them he would address them in the grove near the temple at four o'clock.

"Right now," Joseph said, "I'm so hungry I could eat a horse. I've invited the Missourians for dinner."

Daniel chuckled as the crowd roared its approval.

"But don't worry," Joseph continued, gesturing, smiling. "I've invited fifty of the brethren. We have Mr. Reynolds outnumbered."

The crowd laughed.

Daniel noted that Reynolds did not smile.


Exhausted, Daniel turned Bendigo toward home. He weaved his way through a dispersing, appreciative crowd, waving, smiling. Again, he looked for Elizabeth. Red patches of disappointment appeared on his cheek. His jaw hardened. *Robert's right. It's time I quit letting her get away with this silliness. When I get home, I'll....*

The sight of the Bundy family at his home shook Daniel back to reality. In all the excitement, he had forgotten that George and Mary Smith Bundy have moved into Martha's house on a temporary basis, along with their adopted son, Job Smith. That meant that Martha was living with Daniel and Elizabeth. Elizabeth, pretending that it was a genuine act of malevolent kindness, had invited Martha to share the bedroom with her.

*Drats.*

George was the first to greet Daniel. He stood at the corral as Daniel unsaddled Bendigo. "I must say, dear chap. Nauvoo is certainly an exciting place to live. You must tell me about your adventure, Brother Browett." At fifty-five, George was almost twenty years older than either Daniel or Robert. Wilford Woodruff had baptized him and his wife in March 1840, five days before Daniel and Elizabeth were baptized.

Daniel returned a fake smile. He ran a meaty hand across his tired brow. "Brother Joseph has called a meeting in the grove for four o'clock this afternoon. He can tell it better than I can. Where's my wife?" Daniel withheld his thoughts. But he was going to take Robert's advice. *I'm finding you another place to stay, and soon. Mother is going back to her own cabin. Elizabeth and I are going to start living like a man and wife ought to live: together.*

George pointed. "Inside with my wife and your mother."

Daniel sounded groggy and on edge. "I need to talk to Elizabeth, alone."

Bundy placed a hand on Daniel's shoulder. "I don't mean to sound inquisitive, old chap, but I remember Sister Browett as quite the outgoing lady back in England. What's happened to her? She's always been just a little sassy, but my word."

Drowning in humiliation, Daniel threw old man Bundy a challenging look. *If you only knew.* "Women. She's just having a bad month. She'll be back to normal soon." *Very soon.*

Bundy wrinkled his nose in confusion.

"Daniel!" Martha bolted from the door and embraced her son. "We're so proud of you. Welcome home."

"Thanks, Mother," Daniel said, kissing her cheek.

Still, no Elizabeth.

Sister Bundy emerged with her nephew and adopted son, Job. She gave Daniel a hug, congratulating him.

Daniel peered inside his cabin. He caught a glimpse of Elizabeth retreating into the bedroom.

"I'll take care of your horse, Brother Browett," Job Smith said, reading Daniel's anguish.

Daniel had already judged the long-faced sixteen-year-old boy extremely astute for his age. Daniel nodded his appreciation and strode toward the house. "Elizabeth?"

As he closed the door behind him, Elizabeth appeared in the doorway that separated the two rooms with a defiant scowl that was all too familiar and beguiling. She made a skeptical face. "The *great* defender of multiple wives has returned, it appears."

He ignored her cynicism. "I looked for you all along the route. There were thousands of people out there, welcoming us home. Where *were* you?"

Detecting a different tone, a demanding one that she had seldom heard, Elizabeth took a while to answer. "Right *here*. Where else?"

"You should have been out there."

Elizabeth smoothed her hair with both hands. "Why?"

Daniel's voice turned high, crisp, and very British. He placed his body directly in front of hers, and placed his hands on both her shoulders, almost digging his fingers into her flesh. "I'm totally out of patience with this nonsense. I'm not taking another wife. I've told the Prophet. I've told Elder Woodruff. I've told Elder Hyde. Get over it, right now. Put this behind you."

Her shoulders slumped and her face clouded. Momentarily, she stared into Daniel's glaring eyes, and then looked away.

Daniel remained adamant. "You're going with me to the afternoon meeting."

"I'm *not*."

"Oh, yes you are. The Prophet's going to speak to us about his kidnapping. You're going to stand right next to me, side by side, like a wife should. Furthermore, when we get home, I'm taking my place in my bed. Right beside you. And you're going to sleep in our bed, not on the floor, not outside, not next door at my mother's place. Got that?"

Daniel could tell his verbal thrusts found their mark. Tiny beads of perspiration were forming on Elizabeth's forehead and tears welled in her eyes.

"Not only that, but..." His voice cracked. He stopped to start again.

"Tonight?" Elizabeth seemed to fight to retain her composure.

"Yes, tonight."

Her chin trembled. She began to blink rapidly. Her damp eyes fell to the floor. She collapsed on the bed while tears flowed, and her heart-wrenching sobs filled the room.

Daniel let her cry, standing there motionless.

With her head buried into her pillow, Elizabeth's brusque voice was almost inaudible. "I'm not changing my mind. No Harriet. No second wife. Period."

A shudder ran through Daniel. "How many times do I have to tell you?"

Elizabeth's voice was full of anguish. "I've never believed you."

Daniel tried to firm himself against another disappointment. "Elizabeth. Believe me."

"Do you still love me?"

"Of course."

"Say it."

"I love you."

"What time is it?"

"Three thirty."

"If you'll have a bath, I'll let you kiss me. You smell terrible."

"I'm not waiting. Stand up."

Elizabeth's reaction was akin to that of a penitent who had finally been cleansed of the burden of sin. She gave Daniel a warm passionate kiss.

In Elizabeth's view, Joseph Smith's speech was interesting, but too long, too animated, and too full of details. He railed against illegal writs from Missouri, and against his enemies. He covered city laws, county laws, state laws, mob raising, and the U.S. Constitution. And the entire incident at Dixon, Pawpaw, Ottawa, Geneseo, and Monmouth. *When will he be done? I want to be at home, with Daniel.*

Each time Joseph mentioned the rescue posse, and the men's valor, Elizabeth squeezed Daniel's hand. And each time she whispered, "How *long* is he going to talk? Let's go home. We have a *lot* to make up for." She marveled at how many people were crowded into the grove to hear the Prophet speak. She guessed several thousand.

However, there were times when the Prophet's remarks sent a chill up her spine. Especially when he said, "Before I will be dragged again away among my enemies for trial, I will spill the last drop of blood in my veins; and I will see all my enemies in hell. To bear it any longer would be a sin, and I will *not* bear it any longer."

She chuckled at Joseph's remarks when the Prophet introduced Cyrus Walker, the attorney. "Mr. Walker," he said, gesturing at the crowd, "these are the greatest dupes, as a body of people, that ever lived, or I am not as big a rogue as I am reported to be."

Low laughter swept through the crowd.

"I told others that I would not discuss the subject of religion with you," Joseph said. "I understand the gospel, and you do not. You understand the quackery of law, and I do not."

Elizabeth gained the feeling that Joseph was in good hands, that Walker's knowledge of the law would ensure the Prophet's freedom tomorrow in the Nauvoo municipal court.

"I guess this means I have to vote for Mr. Walker in the election," Elizabeth quipped to her husband.

Daniel responded with a question. "Do you know who he's running against—the Democrat?"

"No, but whoever he is, he's sure to hate the Mormons if we all vote for Mr. Walker."

Daniel nodded. *Sure thing.*

On every street, the faint, sweet scent of flowers further lifted Elizabeth's spirits as the thousands of Mormons walked home. Golden shafts of sunlight pierced purple clouds overhead. People were jovial, waving, laughing, relieved that their leader was safe, and that good had triumphed over evil. As the Browetts, Harrises, Roberts, Coxes, Bundys, and Gaileys reached the top of the hill near the temple, the distant flashes of lightning and booming of thunder to the south, near Keokuk, provided a resplendent end to the day.

Elizabeth was her old self, laughing, dominating the conversation, over-emphasizing her words, asking about everyone's health, making appointments. She was both confident and self-assured.

"I'm glad you're feeling better," George Bundy told her.

"Oh," Elizabeth said. "We *forgot* to tell you. Daniel's mother will be staying at her *own* home tonight, with you, and your wife, and Job."

George blinked, frowning at the thought.

Elizabeth put her arm around Job. "A teenage boy can sleep outside tonight, *can't he?*"

Job's long, narrow face broke into a happy smile. "Makes no matter to me. I'm just happy you folks took us in."

"Then it's all set," Elizabeth said, her green eyes alive again. *"Hear that, Mother Browett?"* She sensed that her mother-in-law knew things had not been right between her and Daniel for more than six months.

"I know when I'm not wanted," Martha joked, laughing.

"I'm hanging a 'Do Not Disturb' sign on our door tonight," Elizabeth said, singing out the words.

CHAPTER NOTES

The account of Joseph's capture, and eventual freedom, was taken from several sources: Joseph Smith, Jr. *The Journal of Joseph* (Provo, Utah: Council Press, 1979); B. H. Roberts, *The Rise and Fall of Nauvoo* (Salt Lake City, Utah: Deseret News, 1900); Ivan J. Barrett, *Joseph Smith and the Restoration* (Provo, Utah: Brigham Young University Press, 1967); and William Clayton, *Nauvoo Diaries and Personal Writings, 1840 through 1846*, Robert C. Fillerup, compiler. Only a few names of the posse members are mentioned, so it is pure speculation on the part of the author that any of the characters of this book participated.

On July first, Joseph was tried by the Nauvoo Municipal Court on the writ of habeas corpus, and was discharged from his arrest warrant. Cyrus Walker made a brilliant defense, pointing out powers given by the state when Nauvoo had adopted its city charter. Despite the fact that his arrest was made illegally, the governor of the state had nevertheless issued the warrant. The City of Nauvoo, thus, had overruled an order of the state, which would bring future unfortunate implications.

At the conclusion of the trial, the citizens of Nauvoo held a mass meeting and passed resolutions thanking the people of Dixon and vicinity, and of Lee County, generally, for the stand they had taken in defense of Joseph Smith. A year later, a jury in Lee County awarded forty dollars damages, and costs, against Sheriff Reynolds and Constable Wilson, for false

# 18

*July 1843*

GOVERNOR FORD PACED HIS OFFICE with angry steps. He was think-ing of the disaster it would be for Illinois Democrats if the Mormons followed Joe Smith's promise to vote for Cyrus Walker, the Whig candidate for Congress.

"How did Walker get involved in all of this?" he asked Shields, the audi-tor.

Ford's office was filled with aides, advisors, lawyers, and Democrats hold-ing key state positions.

Shields rehearsed the story of Joe Smith's capture as he knew it.

Ford kicked his oak desk and cursed. Constable Wilson, Sheriff Reynolds, and an army of lawyers were pressuring him to issue a new warrant and to call up the Illinois militia to help them serve it—by marching into Nauvoo with a show of force and arrest Joe Smith. Ford knew that if he did

Walker would be a shoo-in and the Illinois Democrats would blame the governor for Hoge's defeat.

He kicked the desk again. Cyrus Walker and the Mormon, Stephen Markham, were in Springfield, waiting to see him. They wanted him to deny the warrant and to not use the militia to arrest Smith. But if he did, it would be a capitulation to the Mormons—a sign of weakness.

He flung foul oaths against Joe Smith and the Mormons.

For an hour, Ford huddled with the men in his office. He wrote a short, terse letter to Sheriff Joseph H. Reynolds denying the request to arrest Smith with help of the Illinois militia. When everyone had vacated his office, Ford kicked his desk again in frustration.

The "knight of the ribbons" on Daniel's stagecoach was a salty, red-faced man. This driver had a full beard and a slouch hat adorned his head. Despite the warm sultry weather, he wore a heavy long-sleeved beige shirt. A fine, powdery road dust covered the man, and sifted through the coach. He held the ribbons—the leather lines attached to the horses—with a loose hand and chattered nonstop at his six horses: two Cleveland bay mares, a black Kentucky-bred trotter gelding, a half-Percheron chestnut mare, and two matching sorrel German coach geldings. "Git up Bolly; gwan boys an' gals. Yer shirky today, Sam. You want touching up, Sally? If ya don't do better, Liz, I'll swap ya for a mule. Get goin', ya old hussy."

Daniel Browett, former carpenter and cooper, was seated next to his missionary companion, Jacob Kemp Butterfield, a teamster by trade. Both men had admired the Abbott & Downing Concord model from the moment they boarded it in Carthage. Before covered with dust, its deep red exterior had gleamed in the bright sunlight, trimmed with gold, vermilion, black, and yellow. Its top, floor, and ends were fashioned of solid oak. The graceful side panels were made of countless layers of paper-thin basswood, and curved to fit the stout ash frames. They had been painstakingly laminated, dried, and coated with a tough, glass-smooth varnish. The planks had been hewn of pine and birch, and the metal was all steel except for the brass trimmings. The wheel hubs were of seasoned elm, the rims made of the hardest hickory, and the spokes hand-hewn ash.

Daniel and Jacob were two of a hundred short-term missionaries called by the Church of Jesus Christ of Latter-day Saints to serve short-term missions throughout Illinois. Their assignment was to preach the gospel, and do everything in their power to counteract widespread negative feelings from Joseph Smith's success in the Nauvoo Municipal Court, evading Sheriff Reynolds' old Missouri charges. The governor of Missouri had protested to Governor Ford that Joseph had escaped custody illegally in the Dixon affair. The Missouri governor now wanted Ford to supply troops for Joseph's capture and extradition. Things were further complicated by the fact that Ford supported the Democratic candidate Hoge for Congress. Joseph Smith had pledged his vote to the Whig, Cyrus Walker. Ford thus was delaying action on the Missouri writ until after the elections—a political horse trade that put the Prophet Joseph Smith on the horns of a dilemma. He had promised to vote for Walker; yet unless Walker lost the election, Joseph faced extradition to Missouri and likely would never come back alive.

Daniel and Jacob had paid their own six-dollar fare. Along the way Daniel saw evidence of the western movement of American settlers. There was an occasional broken wagon wheel with grass growing up over the spokes and hubs—even whitened bones of horses and oxen. The stagecoach driver pointed and said, "Men have died here, too. The cowards never started and the weak ones died by the way."

At an overnight stop at Beardstown on the Illinois River, they preached to everyone who stayed at a two-story brick building that served both as an inn and as a store. That evening, they bent the ears of visiting Reverends Dyer, Dresser, and Richmond, who had convened at the local Episcopalian church. Daniel and Jacob stomped up and down Clay, Jackson, State, Main, and Washington Streets, talking to everyone they could see before the stage left the next morning. In return for their teachings about Mormonism and Joseph's side of the arrest, the two elders had to endure endless stories about the pork industry of Cass County, the best catfish holes, spectacular duck hunting, the

Black Hawk War of 1832, and the time during December 1836 when the temperature plunged from forty degrees Fahrenheit to four degrees below zero in less than eight hours.

As the stage lumbered along at nine miles an hour, Daniel and Jacob settled into another lengthy conversation. Springfield was a hundred and twenty miles from Nauvoo, and they were just over half-way. For the first half of the trip, their conversation was guarded. Now, both men opened up. They discussed the fact that Joseph Smith had just dictated the revelation on plural marriage, committing it to paper. Although it was still a somewhat secret practice, its acceptance as doctrine was required of the Church leadership and hierarchy. All of this seemed to have split Nauvoo wide open. William Law, Joseph's counselor, was now convinced that Joseph was a fallen prophet whose more recent revelations concerning baptism for the dead, the plurality of gods, and plural wives were of the devil. Law seemed to be gaining a following.

"I can't believe your wife remained so defiant for so long," Jacob said after hearing Daniel's story.

"I've learned a lot during the past six months," Daniel replied.

Jacob leaned forward. "Such as?"

"Perhaps the most important is that the Spirit gets up and leaves whenever two people are arguing." Daniel held no illusions about himself. He had been just as guilty as Elizabeth in participating in arguments, sometimes raising his own voice. But thankfully Elizabeth was reading her scriptures again, and saying her prayers. But she never prayed about plural marriage, fearing an answer that she would not agree with.

Jacob's voice cracked. "I've had my own problems. My father-in-law. He just won't accept me. It may end up ruining my marriage."

The coach disgorged its passengers near the capitol building in Springfield, at the intersection of Adams Street and Fifth. As he peered at the stately capitol, framed by arching oak trees, Daniel looked up at his companion. He had temporarily forgotten how tall he was. Jacob was six-foot-two, angular, stood ramrod straight, and had dark brown hair and glistening blue eyes.

"Where shall we go first?" Jacob asked.

There was an impressive collection of three-story brick buildings near the town square. Daniel could make out several businesses, The State Bank, the Spottswood Hotel, a provision store, a drug store, and a blacksmith shop.

Their mission calls had been issued during a huge Fourth of July celebration in Nauvoo, a day that had brought a thousand visitors to the city. Many came by steamboat. The Nauvoo Legion had marched. Cannons had been fired. More than fifteen thousand people had assembled at the grove later in the day to listen to sermons by Joseph, Orson Hyde, and Parley P. Pratt.

The hundred elders were assigned to visit every county in the state, preaching the gospel, and providing correct information about Joseph's illegal arrest. Orson Hyde was in Lee County. Wilford Woodruff was not one of the hundred. He was in St. Louis purchasing paper and ink for the Nauvoo newspaper.

Daniel contemplated Jacob's question for only a second. "Let's approach anyone and everyone." In training they had received at the hands of members of the Twelve, they were instructed to find men of influence, and women, too.

"You pick the first one," Jacob said.

Daniel's scanning eyes locked on a tall man moving cautiously toward the capitol, his long arms swinging at his side, his walk undulatory. The man was taller even than Jacob and looked to be about the same age as himself, in his early thirties. Daniel placed his own bulky frame in front of the man and extended his right hand.

"Daniel Browett from Nauvoo, Illinois," he said, his features set as warm as he could contort them. He found himself looking up at a clean-shaven man who was at least a head taller, but who had a poor, lean, lank face. Heavy eyebrows overhung deep eye-caverns where dreamy eyes were set. The man's cheekbones were high, mouth wide, and on his right cheek a solitary mole stood out. His hair was thick, black, and unruly, with stray locks falling across his forehead.

"Abe Lincoln from right here in Springfield," came the response. A large bony hand draped around Daniel's. "You must be an English Mormon. You accent gives you away. What are you doing here in Springfield? The judge ruled in favor of Joe Smith. He's not in more trouble, is he?"

Jacob thrust out his hand, introducing himself. "Yes and no to your question."

"I have important business both in the capitol and in the courthouse," Lincoln said, "so be quick with your message."

"You must be an attorney," Jacob said, staring at the odd-looking man.

Lincoln nodded and pulled out his pocket watch. He was dressed in a black suit with faint stripes. "Twenty minutes. Then I'll have to go."

Ignoring the tall man's time restriction, Daniel and Jacob traced Joseph's troubles back to the 1838 Missouri persecutions and expulsion. The Election Day battle at Gallatin, setting the stage for a frontier war between Missourians and the new Mormon settlers. The siege against Mormons at DeWitt, and its abandonment. Growing distress in Caldwell and Daviess Counties. The battle of Crooked River. The extermination order, and Haun's Mill massacre. The siege of Far West. The imprisonment of Joseph Smith in Liberty Jail. The turning of public opinion against Governor Boggs. Joseph's freedom. Refuge in Illinois, and the settling of Nauvoo. The seeking of redress for Missouri grievances. The influx of immigrants into Nauvoo, and growth of the city. The apostasy of John C. Bennett, leading to political complications and renewed threats from Missouri. How Bennett contacted Boggs and conspired with him. Charges that Porter Rockwell tried to shoot Boggs, under orders of Joseph Smith. Joseph and Porter's innocence. New charges of treason against Joseph from Missouri. The capture of Porter in St. Louis, and his continued illegal imprisonment. Joseph H. Reynolds' foray into Dixon, capturing Joseph. And, again, Joseph's release.

Lincoln pulled out his watch again. He put it back in his pocket. "How did Reynolds know that Joe Smith went to Dixon?"

Daniel pulled a face, the question gnawing on him. "No one knows."

"Wouldn't that suggest that you have more than one John C. Bennett in the woodpile?"

Bewilderment was etched across Daniel's face as he contemplated the possibility.

Lincoln continued. "I'm just a lawyer on the outside looking in. But I'll tell you what I know. A copy of the court proceedings in Nauvoo were sent to Governor Ford here in Springfield, as well as an account of the treatment imposed upon Joe Smith by Sheriff Reynolds and Constable Wilson. Governor Ford is not at all favorable toward you Mormons, but he did refuse to grant Reynolds' petition that he be allowed to take Joe Smith by force. Ford also refused a plea from the governor of Missouri to call out the Illinois militia to retake your Mormon leader."

Daniel knew all that, but was pleased that the stranger knew it as well.

In a drawl unique to Lincoln, he went on. "The rapid growth of Nauvoo has fueled antagonism in many parts of our state. People fear your political power. Some people hate religion altogether. Governor Ford is a Democrat, and most of you Mormons voted for him last year. But the governor hears the Mormons are supporting Cyrus Walker—a Whig—for Congress. He's had two cat fits and a duck fit over it."

"Mr. Walker defended our Prophet," Butterfield said.

"I know," answered Lincoln. "He's a very talented lawyer. Ford is not all that friendly toward you now, but if Walker wins the election...I don't know. The Democrats already are feasting on the rumor that the arrest of Joe Smith at Dixon was a Whig conspiracy, and that Walker had been planted near Dixon by the Whigs to agree to aid the capture of Joe Smith."

"What?" Daniel stammered in disbelief.

"It's true," Lincoln said, his voice firm. "Even Ford believes that it was all pre-arranged by the Whigs in exchange for the Mormon vote, that it was a trick to prejudice you Mormons against Governor Ford and the Democratic Party."

Daniel groaned. Politically, it appeared the Mormons were in a no-win situation in Illinois, now and in the future.

Jacob Butterfield interrupted. "Please pass this on, to whomever you can. Joseph Smith agreed to give his *personal* vote to Cyrus Walker. He did not pledge the *Mormon* vote. I feel free to vote for either candidate."

Lincoln blanched and then paused to look at his pocket watch. "I didn't know that. But I would advise all the Mormons to vote for the Whigs."

"You must be a Whig," Jacob said.

"Through and through," Lincoln said.

Jacob sighed.

"Something else you should know before I go," Lincoln said, drawing a big breath. "Governor Ford has sent an agent to Nauvoo, in the form of a Mr. Brayman, I believe. The governor wants more affidavits about Joe Smith's arrest, escape, and rescue by your Mormon military force. He is still trying to decide whether or not to use the militia to rearrest your Mormon leader. Probably not until after the election, but it could happen. You can't trust Ford and the Democrats."

Daniel shook his head in disbelief.

After taking a step or two away, Lincoln turned his tall and bony frame back to Daniel. "You can tell your prophet, Mr. Smith, that there's one thing in particular I agree with him on."

"What's that?" Daniel asked.

"His views on slavery," said Lincoln. "I went to New Orleans in 1831 and saw Negroes chained together, maltreated, whipped, and scourged. It would be nice someday to give the Negroes their freedom. If I ever get a chance to hit the system of slavery, I will hit it hard."

"I agree," Daniel said, remembering that he had seen the same things when he went through New Orleans in 1841, ten years after Lincoln.

CHAPTER NOTES

Daniel and Jacob's conversation with Abraham Lincoln is fictitious, of course. However, according to the Jacob Kemp Butterfield family history, Jacob was one of the elders chosen to serve a mission for the Church in the summer of 1843. Having Daniel serve with Butterfield is an invention of the author. The conversation accurately reflects the mood and feelings of political pundits of the time regarding the Mormons.

Jacob Kemp Butterfield is the great-great-great grandfather of the author, on his mother's side.

# 19

"REBECCA WANTS TO SEE YOU," Elizabeth said soon after Daniel returned to Nauvoo. "She's waiting at your mother's cabin. I don't think she's too happy."

Daniel drew a heavy breath as he walked next door. The last he knew Rebecca had been a picture of contentment. She shouldn't be otherwise Daniel thought. After all, she was married to an Apostle, she had been getting along with Marinda, and Orson was building them a new home. Perhaps the hot, sultry weather was disagreeing with her.

Rebecca was pacing the floor when Daniel walked in. Other than the sour look on her face, she looked beautiful. New yellow dress. Blonde hair curled. Just the right amount of makeup, with her lips painted red. Martha was sitting in her new rocking chair, one that Daniel had made before his mission to Springfield.

"Something wrong?" he asked.

His words brought a flood of tears from Rebecca. Martha stood. "She's upset. Orson Hyde is taking a third wife."

Bewilderment showed plainly in Daniel's face. *What did she expect?* He asked the obvious. "Who?"

"A lady by the name of Mary Ann Price," Martha said. "Her husband left her when she joined our Church in England. You've probably met her."

"Oh, yes." He was familiar with the woman Orson had proposed to, prior to taking Rebecca as a wife. Had she accepted, Mary Ann Price would have become Orson's second wife, not third. *She must have changed her mind while I was away.*

Daniel turned to face his sister. He restrained the urge to send her back to the Hyde home without comment. "I'm sorry if this upsets you, Sis. I don't know what I can do."

Rebecca's lower lip pushed to a pout. Stammering, wiping away tears, she began her railing. "I never thought Orson would do this to me. I found out that he asked this woman to marry him even before he asked me. How many more women is he going to ask? Most of the time he takes Marinda with him. He acts like he doesn't want to be seen in public with me."

Sitting in a chair, Daniel pulled on his chin. "Are you going to leave? Come back home? Live with Mother again?"

Rebecca whirled. "I *didn't* say that."

"When is the marriage?" Daniel asked.

"Tomorrow. I just found out yesterday."

"You mean you didn't know about Sister Price until yesterday?"

Rebecca sobbed again. "Oh, I knew. He told me about her several times. I just kept hoping that she would always tell him no. I didn't for a minute believe she would consent. I even went and talked to her. I don't know what came over her. Or what changed her mind. One day, she says 'no' to Orson. One day she says 'yes.' Then, presto, a marriage."

*Mary Ann Price finally prayed for a testimony of plural marriage,* Daniel thought, digesting the information. "How have you felt when you've prayed about Sister Price?"

Rebecca was silent.

"Rebecca?" Daniel repeated, with painful dignity.

"Bad feelings," she piped.

For a moment, Daniel regarded Rebecca with an impassive silence. *You haven't prayed at all.* "I think you ought to get on your knees. Soon. Mother and I will leave, and give you some privacy. And you need to quit wringing your hands and enjoy the life that you have."

Daniel contemplated his sister, knowing that her emotions were probably ranging between confusion, anger, and a feeling that he had no compassion for her. She evidently wanted sympathy but she had received a short sermon. In the past she had always had the freakish ability to turn things upside down and blame circumstances for her own unhappiness.

Rebecca whirled again, her eyes locking on her brother. "You're no help at all," she spat bitterly. "I'm going home."

After the slam of a door, Daniel turned to face his mother. "Well, at least she knows where her real home is now."

A rare smile graced the face of Governor Thomas Ford. He jumped in the air clicking his heels together.

"Pour me another drink, Mr. Shields," he said. "Pour one for everybody."

The August election results had just been finalized. Hoge had defeated Cyrus Walker, thanks to the Mormon vote. Joe Smith had voted for Walker as he had promised, but the members of his Church had overwhelmingly voted for Hoge.

"I'll never understand Mormons for as long as I live," Ford said to Shield jubilantly. The parlor in Ford's governor's mansion was full of celebrating Democrats. He drank half the whiskey in a single swallow. As the liquor hit his bloodstream he felt himself relax and his tongue loosen even more.

"It's because Hyrum Smith's revelation overruled that of his brother's," Shield laughed.

Ford wished he could have been there. Hy Smith apparently had announced to a great assembly of Mormons in Nauvoo that the Lord had personally appeared to him and told him that the Mormons must support Hoge, not Walker. And apparently Hy Smith and a man named William Law had

had a great argument over the subject. This threw the Mormons into a tizzy for a few days until Joe Smith spoke to a reassembled body of Mormons and told them that although he was voting for Walker, they were free to vote for Hoge. That decided the Mormon vote. The next day—Election Day—Hoge received some three thousand votes in Nauvoo and was elected to Congress by nearly an eight hundred-vote majority.

"The Whigs are furious," a fellow Democrat said to Ford, as he swirled a brandy.

"The Whig newspapers will renew their crusade against the Mormons," another predicted.

"And against us," another warned as he cut into a new hoop of orange cheese.

"At least we'll have spicy reading about the Mormons," said the first.

Thomas Ford smiled. He loved it when the Whig newspapers tore into the Mormons, exposing their wickedness, their corruptions, and the enormities of Nauvoo. But he was certain that because he had not supported Sheriff Reynolds in the demand to furnish a posse of state militia to arrest Joe Smith, the Mormons would be more arrogant, more overbearing, and emboldened by their every success.

# 20

REBECCA WAS STILL POUTING THREE days after Orson's wedding to Mary Ann Price. Her immaturity and insecurity were heavy on Daniel's mind as the Browetts treated some of their friends to a Sunday afternoon meal.

Earlier in the week, Robert had butchered a hog for the Bloxhams. Thomas Bloxham donated the head for the Sunday meal, so on Saturday Hannah, Dianah, and Elizabeth used the head to make scrapple. They removed the hair, eyeballs, and ears, then boiled the head in a large black pot over the hearth until the meat fell from the bones. After the pot cooled, they pulled the large bones out and strained everything else to remove the small bones. The liquid was put back into the pot along with the mashed up meat, sage, and pepper. The women stirred the mixture until it boiled, and then added plain corn meal until it was "plumb thick," ready to be poured into molds. On Sunday, all that was left to do was cut it into slices and fry it.

Fried pork, scrapple, garden vegetables, cornbread, and mulberry pie. Sunday dinner on tables set out behind the Browett cabin on the gentle grassy slopes of Nauvoo. Conversation was broad and tall. Joseph's Sunday sermon at the grove. The aftermath of his release from the arrest by Reynolds and Wilson. The article in the *Nauvoo Neighbor* about Joseph's kidnapping. Progress on the temple construction. The new Masonic Hall, and how Masonry fit into the Mormon community. Written copies of the revelation on eternal marriage. Missionary work. The continued growth of Nauvoo.

Despite the fact that anti-Mormon opposition was closing in from the outside, there was a surface of gaiety all around Nauvoo. Weeks earlier, Joseph had introduced dancing as a Church recreation despite the opposition of a few stiffnecks. And a theatre had been opened.

Daniel was filling his plate at the serving table, absorbing the conversation.

John Benbow was talking. "You know the most amazing thing about all the growing antagonism against us Mormons in Illinois?"

Thomas Bloxham, who still resisted offers to be taught and baptized, was quick to raise his eyebrows as he placed six slices of scrapple on his plate. "What would that be?"

Benbow sampled the cornbread before he sat down next to Daniel and Thomas Kington. Benbow replied, "The effect it has on missionary work."

Thomas grunted. "Your Church must be hurting for converts then."

"Quite the contrary," Benbow countered, pointing to Daniel. "Take Daniel here for example, and his companion, Brother Butterfield. After a few days they had to send word back to Nauvoo for more help to teach all the interested people."

Thomas shrugged his shoulders.

"How many persons did you baptize in Springfield, Brother Browett?" Benbow asked.

"Nine."

Thomas Kington cleared his throat, anxious to add what he knew. "Brother Levi Stewart and his companion were sent to Franklin, Williamson, and Johnson counties. The prejudice there was bad against our Church, they reported, but after hearing the real story, people began to discover the falsehoods for themselves. As a result, the people there developed an interest in the gospel real fast. Last I heard, Brother Stewart had baptized two dozen people.

As Thomas Bloxham rolled his eyes, Daniel thought how similar Thomas' attitude was to nearly all non-members, especially people like Robert's brother-in-law, Henry. Henry and others had reveled in the false stories that had circulated about Joseph Smith and the Church, and scoffed at reports of hundreds of new Mormon converts.

Daniel said, "I can't wait to see the impact of the missions of some of the Twelve this summer, back east." Heber C. Kimball and Orson Pratt had departed Nauvoo on July first. Wilford Woodruff, Brigham Young, and George A. Smith departed July eighth. Early letters revealed they were preaching to overflow crowds made up of members and investigators.

"Ready to sell part of your lot, Brother Harris?" Kington asked. "There'll be so many new converts roll through here that we'll have to divide up our farms *and* our lots."

Benbow added, "I hear good reports about missionaries serving in the southern states, too. That, despite opposition from sectarian preachers. The honest in heart are joining the Church."

Daniel regarded Robert's laugh.

"I don't think I want to sell any part of my lot," Robert said. "But I'd do it before I'd let someone buy property from William Law and his gang."

The subject among the women had turned to Rebecca and Orson Hyde. Elizabeth was her old self, spunky, chatty, and seeing to it that everyone was well fed.

"Has your daughter settled down?" Jane Benbow was asking Martha Browett.

"You mean about accepting Mary Ann Price?" Martha asked.

Elizabeth could see Martha's face turn a shade red in embarrassment.

Jane leaned forward, anticipating the answer.

"She's getting better, day by day," Elizabeth's mother-in-law replied.

"Who wouldn't?" added Margaret Kington. "That's a nice home Brother Hyde built for his three wives. When are they moving in?"

"Next week," Martha speculated. "Then Brother Hyde will have to leave on his mission to the East shortly after that. That's what Rebecca has told me."

Elizabeth thought about the new Hyde home, and how she would enjoy one like it some day. It was a clapboard frame dwelling, built in Greek revival style, measuring eighteen by twenty-four feet, with a second floor. There was a porch across the front with four squared posts, a door in the center flanked by two windows, four small upstairs bedrooms, and chimney sentinels at both ends of the rooftop.

"Rebecca is starting to get fond of Brother Hyde's six-year-old daughter, Laura," Martha added.

The lone figure of Hannah Simmons Phillips strolled across the street and onto the Browett property. She approached the tables and placed a hand on Elizabeth's shoulder. "There's a brother Ezra Allen waiting at our place. His whole family is sick. Especially their newborn baby. Can you come?"

Elizabeth found Ezra Allen talking with Edward Phillips at the Phillips cabin, just a block away. "You must be Sister Browett," Ezra said. There was deep sadness on his face.

"And you have the *ague*," Elizabeth replied, quickly recognizing the symptoms. The man was shaking in a cold sweat. *The sickness from the marsh miasma is striking again.*

Allen nodded. "So does my wife. But it's our baby that I'm concerned about."

"Brother Allen tells me he moved to Nauvoo in April, from Shocoquan," Edward explained. Shocoquan was a Mormon settlement on the Mississippi River, twenty-five miles north.

Elizabeth did not sit. "Where's your home?"

Ezra began walking. "About a half-mile, this direction."

During the walk, Elizabeth found that the Allens were from Madrid, New York, and that Ezra had been baptized a year ago. Shortly after the loss of a daughter, he and his wife had moved to Nauvoo late last year, selling their homestead in New York. They rented a dilapidated log cabin in Nauvoo until

spring, and then tried to make a successful life in Shocoquan. Constant sickness forced them to move back to Nauvoo. Their baby was born only day
ago, and was barely clinging to life.

Elizabeth began her questioning again. "When the ague came on, di
you yawn a lot, and want to *stretch* your sore muscles?"

"Yes."

"Let me see your fingernails."

Ezra extended his hand. The fingernails were a bluish color.

"Cold sensations all over your body?"

A nod, yes.

"Your sickness seemed to creep into your system in streaks? Faster an
faster, colder and colder, in successive undulations coursing down your back?

"Yes."

"Cold chills and body shakes? Then warm flashes that turned into
burning fever?"

"Yes."

"When we get to your home, I'll give you a little quinine."

Elizabeth cringed with horror as she stepped inside the Allen home
Ezra's wife, Sarah, had lapsed into unconsciousness. Two neighbor women sa
at her bedside, holding Sarah's hands. A daughter, five-year-old Cynthia, ha
eyes that were listless, and she had a constant cough that secreted a blood
mucus. A frail, newborn baby was barely breathing. A stench came from th
diaper.

"Has your wife taken any nourishment?" Elizabeth asked Ezra as th
women moved aside. Elizabeth searched for a pulse in Sarah.

"Very little," Ezra said with a sad face.

Elizabeth turned to the two women. "You live near here?"

They nodded yes.

"One of you go home and make me some broth. Beef or chicken, eithe
will do. Hurry."

One woman scurried out.

"What do you have for juice?" Elizabeth asked Ezra. "Any wine?"

The other woman spoke. "There's virtually nothing here. But I have some wine next door." She ran out, and within a few seconds returned.

Elizabeth mixed wine with water in a cup. She opened the unconscious woman's mouth and administered one teaspoon of the simple mixture. It ran out. Elizabeth filled the spoon again, forced Sarah's mouth open, and poured one spoonful behind her tongue. There was a weak swallow.

Elizabeth handed the spoon to the woman. "Keep doing that. Change to the broth as soon as you can. I'm relieved to know Sister Cox is not suffering from milk sick."

Drinking milk from cows that had been eating white snakeroot, which poisoned the milk, caused milk sick. The first symptoms were a whitish coat on the tongue and burning vitals. The next stage was marked by the tongue turning a brownish color, feet and hands growing colder and colder, and a slowing pulse. Death usually followed.

Ezra was on a chair, praying.

"Bring your daughter to me, Brother Allen," Elizabeth said. "I'll give you both some quinine." She didn't mention the cost. Made from the bark of the Cinchona tree in South America, an ounce of the medicine was as expensive as an ounce of gold, or the cost of a cow. Fourteen dollars an ounce. Elizabeth kept a supply of quinine in her satchel, made possible by generous donations of John Benbow and others.

"Will this stuff work?" Ezra asked.

"Sure will. With you, I'm going to mix ten or fifteen grains in a glass of water. For your daughter, just a couple of grains every hour or two. If your ears start to ring, then the dose is too high."

As Ezra and his daughter drank, Elizabeth stared at the infant. She had the morbid feeling there was not much she could do. Willard Richards, her mentor, was on a mission back east. She wondered if a new arrival to Nauvoo, a Dr. John Bernhisel, would be available.

# 21

ROBERT DID NOT LOOK FORWARD to Sunday dinner. Hannah had invited Henry and Katherine, who had just moved from the outskirts of Nauvoo to—of all places—Carthage. Despite a few outward gestures of friendliness for Hannah's sake, Robert still despised his brother-in-law. The recent Sunday dinner with a lot of Wilford Woodruff converts at the Browetts' had been a success. Hannah had doomed today's dinner to failure, in Robert's opinion. In any event, it would be a lively time.

Fortunately, the only other guests were Daniel and Elizabeth and the Bundys.

Henry Eagles was Hannah's older brother. It seemed to Robert that he and Henry had disliked one another forever. They had fought the first day they met, in the barnyard of the Nightingale Dairy that Hannah's father managed in Apperley, England. They fought again at the Gloucestershire Fair. To prevent Robert from marrying his sister, Henry and his thug friend ambushed Robert from the trees at night, breaking Robert's ribs. After he healed, Robert returned the favor, smashing not only Henry but his two pub mates as well. Then there was the incident on the ship, when Henry wanted the *Echo* to turn around and return to Liverpool because of the storms in the Atlantic. They fought again, with Robert breaking Henry's nose.

Henry rejected baptism into the Church but at the last minute married a Mormon girl—in Robert's opinion, to get a cheap ticket to America. He married Katherine Hill, sister to Robert's boyhood friend, Joseph.

Robert regarded Henry as he always had: arrogant, insecure, tenacious, taxing, insensitive, selfish—the self-appointed King of the Jungle. Henry had a preternatural gift for striking a position of altercation. You could be talking about doily making and he would instantly leap to the anti-Mormon position. Henry had the propensity to think by the inch and talk by the yard; he ought to be kicked by the foot.

Despite the fact that Wilson Law had almost replaced Henry as hated enemy number one, Robert still despised his brother-in-law.

Ever since Hannah's invitation, Henry had been brushing up on his criticisms of Mormonism. Fortunately for him, Joe Smith, the Mormon Prophet, and other leaders, had given him plenty of new ammunition. In Henry's opinion, the list was endless. The Nauvoo City Council's mistake in letting Smith out of the grasp of Sheriff Reynolds. Joe's lying promise to deliver the Mormon vote to Cyrus Walker. The aroused enmity of the defeated Whigs. Anti-Mormon meetings in Carthage. Failure of Mormon missionaries to sway public opinion. Failure of the Apostles to do any good back east. The refusal of Hancock County officials in Carthage to seat Mormons elected to county posts. Swindling money from common poor people in Nauvoo to build a lavish temple. And spiritual wifery.

Whenever Henry knew he was going to be around Mormons, he did four things. First, he read all the anti-Mormon newspaper articles and literature he could find. Second, he listened to the latest Mormon gossip from his friends in Carthage and Warsaw. Third, he studied how to refute Mormon doctrines. And fourth, he practiced his rhetoric on his six milk cows, night and morning.

Before he left home, he did what nearly every frontier man did to start the day. He had a couple of drams of whiskey. When Henry moved to Carthage, he was pleased that nearly all the men there had liquor on their breath more often than not. Ministers there imbibed before sermons. Doctors before surgery. Lawyers took a dram or two before trying cases. Farmers before plowing fields. The taverns in Carthage were for men what church was for women. Taverns were the center of social life there, a home away from home. Henry liked taverns, just as he had liked pubs back in England. Mormon bashing was the main sport in American taverns on the Illinois frontier.

Henry loved it.

He also loved cockfights, dogfights, craps, poker, faro, and monte.

And he loved riling up Robert and the Mormons.

Robert blanched as he watched Henry arrive with his wife and daughter in a buckboard pulled by a speckled gray horse and a brown mule. Henry was just an inch or so under six feet. The fit, dark-haired dairyman had morphed into a seedy individual. His shoulders were still broad, but he had developed a big belly since his arrival in Illinois. He was still a powerful man at thirty-two, with well-developed muscles in his arms and hands from milking cows all his life. He had a huge brown mustache, bulging dark eyes, a booming voice, and an enormous appetite. Henry arrived at the outdoor tables laughing, and laughed at whatever was said to him, and at almost everything he said himself. For all his gross jolly façade, he was a tough and ugly brute. He was a grotesque man, and his clothing did little to mitigate his grotesqueness. He wore a checkered green shirt, manure-stained brown trousers, and a once black felt hat that had faded to a combination of colors. Rivulets of sweat had broken out on his forehead, where wild black hair hung over his eyes.

At first, Robert avoided Henry. All his life Henry had been as willful a a child: show him what he ought to do and he would dig in his heels and do the opposite. But as Robert carried food from the house to the outdoor tables a collision was inevitable.

"Haven't seen you for months, Henry. So what's boiling in your evil cal dron of a brain?" Robert asked as he placed a roast turkey on a table. *And I haven't missed you one bit. Beat up your wife lately?*

Robert wondered how Thomas and Ann Eagles could have fathered children so wonderful as Hannah, and so obnoxious as Henry, all in one family. To Robert's mind, Henry was the Cain in the Adam and Eve family. Or Laman or Lemuel in the Lehi and Sariah family.

Henry approached laughing, complete in his self-absorption. "You look absolutely crumpled this afternoon, *Brother* Harris. And you smell like a butcher." Henry did not offer a handshake. He was murmuring something about wishing he had never heard of Mormonism or the town of Nauvoo.

Robert drew a deep breath. Hunting, killing, plucking, cleaning, and scalding a wild turkey had not left him in a good mood. Hannah had complained that he had not removed all the fuzz off the skin when he singed it in the fire, and he had sliced his finger cutting off the legs.

"Correction," Robert seethed. "Hunter. I'm a farmer, not a butcher. Enjoy the turkey."

"We've feasted on turkey all summer," Henry said. "No treat for me."

"You don't have the patience to hunt wild turkey, Henry."

"I've got a neighbor near Carthage that taught me. Made me a turkey call, in fact."

"Out of a bull's horn?"

Henry did not catch the inference.

Robert observed that Daniel caught it. In the old days, in England, Daniel had referred to Robert as the "wild bull killer" after Robert and Henry's fight at the Gloucestershire Fair.

Henry began to brag of his turkey-hunting prowess. "My good neighbor in Carthage taught me to split the end of a green dogwood branch and force half a laurel leaf into the split, then trim it off. Works every time."

Robert thought of the all-day effort it had taken him to find a bird and shoot it. It gave him peace to go into the woods and hunt alone with his dog.

Henry was talking non-stop. "When you call the turkey, you just do it once. By and by the turkey will come slippin' up. Might be an hour, maybe quicker. Maybe longer. If you call another time, he'll suspicion somethin'. After he quits gobblin', he'll make out like he's going the other way, and he'll slip back. That's the nature of a turkey. Most of you turkey hunters call too much. Then you just keep still. He'll walk up in shootin' distance. Then you just drop him."

Robert shook his head at Henry's futile attempt to use the slang of the American frontier. Mixed with an English accent, it sounded hokey.

"Next time you go a huntin' turkeys, give me an invite," Henry concluded.

"No, thanks," Robert answered. "I prefer hunting alone, or with friends."

As Robert contemplated Henry's narrowing eyes, Daniel interrupted with a disarming remark. "Your little girl sure is cute," he said, nodding in the direction of Katherine Eagles and her year-old daughter, Annie. Daniel, like Robert, had often wondered how sweet Hannah and rotten Henry could be from the same family, concluding that flowers and thorns grow out of the same dirt.

Robert wouldn't let go. He had practically forgotten how fond he was of goading Henry. "The little thing takes after her mother, fortunately. I hope you never have a boy, Henry. He'd probably look like you."

Henry's eyes narrowed more. Robert's biting words had hit home. Henry bent a finger into Robert's chest. "Rule number one this afternoon, mate. Keep our conversation confined to Mormon politics."

"You must not have heard about rule number two," Robert countered, smiling smugly.

Henry squinted one eye, looking perplexed. "Which is…?"

"Ignore rule number one. Did you bring your Book of Mormon? We're gonna teach and baptize you this afternoon."

Daniel Browett exploded with laughter. "Round one to Robert," he said. Henry scowled.

Hannah stepped in between Henry and her husband. "Robert, quit your horseplay. It's time to bless the food and start eating."

# 22

"HAD THE TIME OF MY LIFE the other day in Carthage," Henry said as he piled his plate high with turkey, boiled potatoes, gravy, string beans, fried okra, cooked cabbage, and brown bread. Beneath him a caterpillar fed on milkweed. Henry kicked it to the ground and squashed it beneath his leather boot.

"How long did they keep you in jail?" Robert asked, determined to keep ahead of the verbal sparring match.

Robert felt Hannah's sharp elbow. "You two are terrible," she said. Hannah turned to Katherine and the baby. "Come with me, Katherine. Let's get away from these horrible men."

Katherine Hill Eagles was a big-boned woman with a dish nose and rather large ears that she hid behind her long dark hair. She walked with a slouch, and when she talked her voice tinkled rather than tittered. She knew Henry married her for a chance to come to America as part of a Mormon travel group, but she tried not to let it bother her. She was bright but not formally educated. She was a voracious reader but never discussed serious things with

Henry because they went over his head. A relieved look came over her face, as though she appreciated Hannah's gesture of friendship. She dished up her plate and followed Hannah to a grassy area between the Harris and Browett cabins and sat with Hannah, Elizabeth, and Sister Bundy.

Robert remembered Hannah telling Katherine several times that she admired her for putting up with Henry. "Do your best," she said, "if you happen to love a fool like him. You have my sympathy. You made a bond with the man, and I admire you for it. It's just too bad he doesn't quite know how to keep his end of the bargain. If he doesn't, there comes a time to quit. I'll support you if you do."

Robert and Hannah's children were playing in the grass, waiting for their mother to serve them. Duke was chasing yellow butterflies. Chickens were clucking noisily, picking at bugs. Hogs in pens grunted their displeasure at the hot weather.

"Funny," Henry replied, trying to disregard of his brother-in-law's icy comeback. "Let's sit together. I'll tell you about all the anti-Mormon meetings that have been going on there."

Robert gasped. He had heard almost unbelievable rumors coming out of the Hancock County seat. Was Henry telling the truth? Had he been there?

"Round two to you, Henry," Daniel said, discomfitted. "I'm all ears."

Henry muttered through a mouthful of food. "A committee of nine men was appointed to draft resolutions against you Mormons. They wanted me to be one of them, but I'm too busy with my dairy. One of the resolutions pledged themselves ready to capture Joe Smith if Missouri makes another demand for him."

"Resolutions?" Daniel stammered.

Henry spat turkey gristle onto the ground. He cracked a bone with his teeth, sucked at the marrow a minute, and then threw the bone on the ground as well. "They even passed a resolution for the president of the meeting to actually write to the Missouri governor to formally make that request. I've been thinking about how that letter could be worded. Would you two like to help me?"

From a face scored with doubt, Daniel said, "Name *one* man who was in the meeting."

Henry erupted in laughter again, enjoying being in control. "Walter Bagby. He's the county collector. The man that gave Joe Smith a whipping."

Robert was speechless, absorbing the shocking reality of Henry's answer.

Daniel paused for a few seconds. Ashen-faced, he said, "You're wrong, Henry. Joseph would have thrashed Bagby soundly had not Daniel H. Wells interfered that day when Bagby called the Prophet a liar over a tax payment. And I suppose you could give old Bagby a whipping, too, if you had a good mind to do it."

A hearty guffaw came from Henry. "Easy as pie."

Daniel scratched his head. "Let's see. Let me get this straight. You say you could whip Bagby, but Bagby whipped Joseph Smith. The Prophet outwrestled Robert, and Robert has knocked you silly about a dozen times in your life. Doesn't make sense, does it?"

Henry growled at the inference, temporarily devastated. He tried to retaliate by calling the Prophet names, things he had heard in Carthage and Warsaw: Joe Smith was ignorant, vain, arrogant, coarse, stupid, and vulgar. Daniel countered by relating stories about how Joseph was, at times, so overcome by the Spirit of revelation that he had to be carried home. Henry scoffed, saying it wasn't the Spirit of God, but ardent spirits from a bottle.

Nevertheless, *round three to Daniel,* Robert thought.

Henry had one more foil. He sat back, pulled his mouth downward, and let his breath out slowly. "Bagby's on his way right now to Missouri. I suspect they'll treat him like a king there. Won't be long before we have an army of Missourians after Joe Smith."

*Round four to Henry.*

"More like Satan entertaining Satan," Robert scoffed, his tone set to remind Henry that he could turn on impressive anger at will. His brother-in-law was like a fish. Neither would get into trouble if they kept their mouths shut.

Henry let the words float off as he began eating again. He had a new subject. "Who did you vote for, Walker or Hoge?"

Robert refused to divulge his vote. "I suspect you voted for Bagby for Congress, Henry."

"It didn't do you Mormons any good, you know," Henry said. "The Whigs are whopping mad at you because they lost. Joe Smith lied. Went back on his word."

Daniel was incensed. "Wrong, Henry. Brother Joseph voted for Walker, just like he promised."

Disbelief colored Henry's words. "But you and the rest of the Mormons voted for Hoge, and Hoge only won by six hundred votes. The Whigs are going to stick Joe Smith with a fork. And you, too. At least when the people that hate Mormons come around and burn your houses and farms, they won't get me. I'm painting my doorway in lamb's blood. So's they'll leave me alone."

"You're a work of art, Henry," Robert said mournfully, losing his appetite. "How many wives did you take with you to Nauvoo?" It was an obvious inference to the time Henry accosted Rebecca on the back streets of Nauvoo, trying to force her to become his "spiritual" wife.

Henry shot his brother-in-law a despised look. "That's for you Mormons. Not me."

Robert scratched his chin. "Let's see now. Seems to me I threw you over the corral fence when you made a pass at Rebecca. I thought by now you'd have a dozen or two. How you going to hide all those women in the Carthage town square?"

A bitter laugh came from Henry, his arrogance showing. "That was just a test on Rebecca's part, to see if the Browett family was brainwashed by Joe Smith yet. I have one wife, old scab brain over there. The doddering Mormon. One of you want her? I'll get me a new one in Carthage. One that's not Mormon."

A muscle twitched in Robert's jaw and he bit his lip in disgust. He liked Katherine. "I'll pass the word around, Henry. I can think of a thousand men who would treat her better than you do. There're two things that are hard on a heart, Henry: running up stairs and running down people. She's your wife.

Be kind to her."

Henry ignored Robert's comeback. He turned to Daniel. "How many wives do you have?"

Daniel let his eyes flit in the direction of Elizabeth. She was seated at another rough-sawn outdoor wooden table, talking to Katherine. She returned an unfriendly stare.

"Elizabeth's been very good about it," Daniel stammered, his voice carrying across the yard, hoping Elizabeth could take the joke. "I've lost count. Even got them stashed in the other Mormon settlements."

Robert cringed, wondering if Henry knew about the few converts who had become disillusioned with Mormonism because of the plural wife issue, and had left to settle in places like St. Louis. A few had even returned to England. As far as he was concerned, however, those people had terribly weak testimonies and thin skin.

Henry was going off again. "I don't understand how you Mormons let Joe Smith manipulate and rob you. You're living in a log house, and right down the street Joe makes you build a million-dollar temple? Secret sealings are going on all over town. You don't need to be sacrificing your money and time building Solomon's temple."

Daniel paled at the words but quickly had an answer. "You're right, Henry. Sealing men and women together can be done without a temple. It's the authority of the priesthood, not the place, that validates and sanctifies the ordinance. But other ordinances, like sealing children to their parents, must be done in a temple. Robert and I work every tenth day there, so do all the other Mormon men."

Robert pulled a face. He wondered why Daniel was wasting an explanation about sealings and temples on someone who didn't care.

Henry took a deep breath as his eyes narrowed. "So if my friends in Carthage and Warsaw burn your temple, it won't be too great a loss?"

"You come around that temple and I'll sic Duke on you," Robert said flatly.

"I killed your dog once. I can do it again." Henry warmed.

Robert seethed as Daniel held up a hand, like a referee parting fighters. "Henry, its time we taught you the gospel. Robert warned you when you first arrived. Let's get started."

Henry rose to fill his plate again, his distrust showing. "Ha! And force your beliefs down my throat?"

Despite another surge of uneasiness, Daniel persisted. He followed Henry to the serving table, letting his voice project toward Elizabeth. "You might find out that the doctrine of celestial marriage is the most holy and important doctrine ever revealed to man on earth. Without obedience to that principle, no man can ever attain to the fullness of exaltation in the celestial glory. I'll get you a copy of the revelation. You ought to read it."

Robert rose to fill his plate again, regarding the smug smile that was coming over Henry's face.

"I've read it," Henry said.

Robert choked in disbelief. His Methodist brother-in-law had read Joseph's revelation on celestial marriage?

"Good," Daniel said. "Then you'll already know what I'm about to tell you."

Henry looked grim. "You're not telling me anything. I think I'll get old scab face and go home."

Daniel made a playful nod at Robert. "Let's teach him the gospel, Brother Harris."

Bristling at Henry's inconsiderate description of Katherine, Robert wrapped a large hand around Henry's arm. His voice was sharp and authoritative. "Hey, there, brother-in-law. We've listened to your ranting all afternoon. Think of yourself sittin' on your milk stool. We're gonna back the cow right up to you. Pay attention to Brother Daniel."

Henry's skin tingled with old fears. "No, thanks."

The grip tightened. "You'll listen, or milk your cows for the next six weeks with six broken ribs."

Henry frowned and then meekly sat again. "Then make your preaching quick," he said to Daniel.

Daniel inhaled deeply and looked Henry straight in the eye but talked again in Elizabeth's direction. "I testify in the name of Jesus Christ that every revelation that Joseph Smith has given us contains the mind and will of not only the Savior, but of Heavenly Father."

Daniel's testimony momentarily had a remarkable calming effect on Henry. Daniel pulled two sheets of crumpled paper from his pocket. On it, he had written with his own hand Joseph's revelation relating to the new and everlasting covenant of marriage. The Prophet had committed it to writing in July. Daniel scanned the notes he had made in the margins.

"I've studied this thoroughly," he said, giving Henry a hard look, and then softening it as he stole another glance at Elizabeth. "I've condensed this down and come up with six strong reasons why we have to accept this new covenant. These are the Savior's reasons, not mine, not Joseph Smith's."

A perplexed look came over Robert. In his mind, Daniel ought to start with faith, repentance, baptism, and the Holy Ghost. The new and everlasting covenant of marriage was a tall order to digest, even for a member.

Henry appeared disinterested, lost, and scared. The deep territory was new for him. He began to tremble a little; only Robert noticed it. He let himself chuckle. It reminded him of the time Robert broke Henry's nose on the ship.

Daniel continued. "Number one reason is this, Henry. The Savior said that all those who have this law revealed to them, *must* obey it. In other words, if I pray and get a testimony of the principle, then I *must* obey it."

Henry chaffed with cynicism. "Two, three, or four wives?"

A lump came to Daniel's throat. "Might be only one, if that's what I want. Eternal marriage with the first wife is the most important."

Suddenly, Robert's eyes brightened. *Daniel's not preaching to Henry. He's preaching to Elizabeth!*

Elizabeth had stopped visiting with Hannah and Katherine, and was bending her ear toward Daniel.

Robert broke out into a wide smile. Daniel had been well coached by someone—probably Orson Hyde or Wilford Woodruff. Robert elbowed

Henry for a response to Daniel's last statement.

Henry forced a self-righteous smile in return. "Oh, I see. How conven ient."

"Second reason," Daniel continued, speaking forcefully, "the Savior say we are damned if we reject the covenant."

Robert was now watching his sister. She dropped her chin and looked away. Robert guessed the words had strafed Elizabeth's heart.

"Damned?" Henry asked, his face twisted with confusion.

Robert could plainly see that Daniel was paying no attention at all to Henry's lack of understanding. Instead, Daniel was throwing his voice in the direction of Elizabeth. "*Damned* is the word used to describe a lack of progress in the eternities. If, for example, Robert wants to keep progressing, to keep becoming more and more like the Savior and like our Heavenly Father, Robert must be obedient to *all* principles and *all* covenants. The Savior tells us in this revelation that if we reject the covenants and commandments of God, we can not enter into the Father's glory, the Celestial Kingdom. That's the fourth rea son."

Robert blanched for a second, thinking of his hatred for Wilson Law and how it was probably hampering his own progress as a Saint.

Henry rolled his eyes, his patience waning. "Give me the fifth reason and then let me go."

"The last one relates to the fourth," Daniel said, "but expands it. The Celestial Kingdom has three parts in it. In order to reach to top, or have a full ness of glory, we have to abide by this law. We have to be sealed to an eternal partner."

Henry squirmed. "Are we done? Let go of my neck."

Robert looked at Daniel.

Daniel shook his head, and looked at his notes again. "No, Henry. You're getting the full load." He stole another glance in the direction of Elizabeth. "The Savior tells us there are three kinds of marriages. You've got the first kind. You tried to get the second kind. And unless you repent, get baptized and enter into this covenant, you'll *never* have the third."

Henry blew out his air in frustration, and gritted his teeth.

Daniel's voice rose in intensity. "One verse tells us that there are marriages for mortality only. That's how you got married, Henry. Robert and me, too. You remember our double marriage, don't you, Henry?" Daniel's voice cracked as he glanced at Elizabeth. For an instant, he was standing at the altar in the Apperley Methodist chapel eight years ago, with Elizabeth, and with Robert and Hannah. "I remember the Methodist minister saying the words, *until death do you part*. Neither we, nor our wives, are bound by any law when we leave this world."

A few moments of reverent silence was broken by Henry. "Good," he said. "I don't want scab face in the next life, if there is one."

Robert inflated with rage, and tightened his grip around Henry's neck. "I think it would be a good idea to apologize to Katherine when Daniel is done with you."

Daniel continued, thrusting his jaw toward Henry. "There is another type of marriage. You tried this with my sister."

Henry shrugged his shoulders and acted as though his head were aching. "What do you mean?"

"A counterfeit marriage," Daniel said, his voice hardening. "You call it spiritual wifery. I call it non-authorized celestial marriage, performed by a counterfeit authority. And not valid in the hereafter."

Ghastly images of the evening he had surprised Rebecca from the trees, and proposed to her, came vividly thrashing to Henry's mind. He gritted his teeth together in renewed frustration.

"Want to hear the third, Henry?" Robert asked, his grip still tight.

"No. But tell me, then let go of my neck."

Daniel didn't need any promptings. "The third is what this is all about. Celestial marriage. Eternal marriage. Making a covenant, before God and angels, by someone having the proper authority, to be sealed for time and all eternity." He paused, letting the words sink in.

Elizabeth sat with her face in her palms, spellbound, thinking.

"Good," Henry said. "We're done. Let go."

"Shall I let 'im go?" Robert asked.

"No," Daniel answered, shaking his head. "Let me tell him about the four promises that await those who enter into the new and everlasting covenant of eternal marriage."

Henry grunted and looked troubled. "How long is this going to take?"

Daniel let out a choked laugh. "An eternity."

Henry placed his elbows on the table. "Get on with it."

Daniel's voice was still projecting toward his wife. "This first promise is quite glorious, Henry. Listen to this." Daniel spoke the words slowly. "You will inherit thrones, kingdoms, principalities, and powers, dominions, all heights and depths. And your name will be written in the Lamb's Book of Life. Sound good?"

Henry's head shook side to side. "Hocus pocus."

Elizabeth's head was not shaking.

"The second promise is this, Henry. We will have the power and knowledge to pass by the angels which are set before the gate of the celestial kingdom." Daniel paused. "You probably don't know what I'm talking about, do you?"

Robert tightened his grip around Henry's neck again. "Shake your head in the negative, Henry, or I'll shake it for you."

Daniel's voice was remarkably calm now. "The third promise is even better. It means that everyone who makes this covenant, and keeps all of the commandments, and their baptismal covenants, will become gods, because they have no end. Because they have all power, and the angels are subject unto them."

Robert knew that inwardly Henry was laughing about the absurdity of all these statements. But it didn't matter if Henry rejected the notion that men and women could actually become like their Father in Heaven—become gods—it only mattered if Elizabeth understood this doctrine.

"Do you like making babies, Henry?" Daniel asked.

The question caught Henry off guard. He peered up at Daniel, and confusion seemed to sweep over him. "What do you mean?"

"I finally have your attention," Daniel said, laughing. "The fourth prom-ise is that the seeds of giving life will continue with us, forever. Henry, only resurrected and glorified beings can become parents of spirit offspring. To me, that's the crowning glory. It sounds wonderful." He fought back a tear, and looked at Elizabeth again.

Robert withdrew his hand from Henry's neck. Robert said, "That's where we draw the line, Daniel. We don't want a bunch of little Henrys running around up there, waiting for bodies to come down to earth. Heaven couldn't stand it, and neither could earth."

Henry immediately stood up and exhaled. His split personality was giv-ing him two disturbing conclusions. There were wisps of truth in what Daniel had said. But another voice seemed to somehow veto his astonishment.

Silence surrounded Elizabeth. Slowly, she began clearing the tables.

# 23

*October 1843*

THE LETTER FROM ANN EAGLES bore good news. Elias, Hannah's younger brother, had not only married but had plans to emigrate to Nauvoo. Elias and his wife, the former Mary Crooks, had booked passage on the *Fanny*, scheduled to leave England in late January. That meant Elias and his wife would arrive about April.

"Your mother's not coming?" Robert asked.

Hannah scanned the letter closely. It almost gave her a headache to look at it. To avoid writing on two sheets of paper, which would have doubled the postage cost, Ann had written vertically across the horizontal lines, and even diagonally.

"I guess not," Hannah said dejectedly.

"What other news?"

"Jane's still not married and my older brothers still haven't joined the

Church. George's wife had a baby. Another niece I'll never get to know. And your brother's wife had another child, a boy."

Hannah would never get to know her new stepfather, either. Ann Eagles had married Samuel Roberts shortly after the *Echo* sailed for America. For an instant Hannah was back in Liverpool, trying to convince her mother to board the ship and not return home. It was one of Hannah's greatest disappointments in life, having her mother change her mind about emigrating.

The fire hissed as the washtub boiled over. Hannah scurried to swing the huge tub away from the hearth. Every time she received a letter from her mother, she wondered if Robert felt bad that his brother never wrote. John still managed a pub in England.

Hannah returned to her letter and let her fingers trace her mother's words. "There are more than seven thousand members of the Church in England now, despite the thousands that have come to America," she reported. Elder Woodruff had already told them that the growth rate of the Church in the British Isles had slowed somewhat after the Apostles left, but evidently the number of new converts was still swelling.

A thought came to Hannah. She tried to dismiss it, but the thought surfaced again. "Elias and his wife will need a place to live when they get here."

A shoulder shrug came from her husband.

"What do you think about selling them our home and building a new one?"

Hannah crossed her fingers as she waited for Robert to answer. They had discussed it once before. But Robert had contended that although a family of seven in a two-room log cabin was getting to be a burden, a small addition onto their log house would be much cheaper than an entire new home.

"Look," he had said. "You've made a new rag rug that covers a portion of the floor. You've got curtains over the two windows. The well is only a few steps away from the house. You have your wooden tub hanging outside on a nail. I provide you with more than enough animal fat to make soap. You have a washboard, a rolling pin, buckets for sugar and flour, and a small tub for mixing bread dough. I provide two sheep to keep the grass eaten down around the house. What more could a woman want?"

"Give me your answer."

"No," Robert said flatly.

"I'm serious this time," Hannah said. "Let's build a frame house, with an upstairs. Room for a bedstead. Enoch is six months old now. Who knows when number six will come along."

"But the cost…and we'd have to dig a new well."

"We've saved more than thirty dollars since we've been in Nauvoo. You can't take it with you. Build me a house."

"Winter's coming. And it's going to be a bad one."

"How do you know?"

"Squirrels gathered their nuts early, and their tails are bushier this year. The rabbit we had for dinner the other day—the fur on its feet was thicker. Birds have eaten up all the berries. The hornets' nests are heavier. The onions grew in more layers this year. There's a heavy crop of berries and acorns."

Hannah rolled her eyes.

"Moss is growing heavy on the trees. Pine cones are opening up early."

"That's enough. You don't need to build the house this winter. Wait until spring."

"What if the cow dies?"

"What?"

"Don't you remember? Brother James Robins offered to buy Old Victoria a few weeks ago." Robins, seven years younger than Robert, was also an English convert from Apperley. He had been a passenger on the *Caroline* in 1841.

"What does his offering to buy our cow have to do with anything?"

"Lots of frontier folks say if somebody makes a reasonable offer for a cow and you don't take it, misfortune with overtake that cow. She may fall into a sinkhole, or get killed by wolves, or never be able to get in calf."

"That's nonsense. Build me a house."

"A new cow will cost half our savings."

"Sell her calf. He's worth twenty dollars. Twenty plus thirty equals fifty dollars."

"Twenty dollars might buy the planking for the floor and the loft."

"Be a butcher again. You could earn extra money."

"I'd rather die."

"I'd rather have a new house. Sell a piece of our lot to someone."

"Who would buy it?"

"Converts are streaming into Nauvoo all the time."

"What about Joseph's prophecy?"

"Which one?"

"The one about the Saints being driven to the Rocky Mountains."

Hannah stretched her memory. Joseph Smith had made the statement on August sixth, 1842, just a few months after the *Echo* passengers arrived in Nauvoo. The Prophet had witnessed the installation of officers of the Rising Sun Lodge Ancient York Masons at Montrose. While the Deputy Grand Master was engaged in giving instructions, Joseph had a conversation with a number of brethren in the shade of a bowery, erected in front of the schoolhouse there. He began talking about the Missouri persecutions.

Joseph held up a tumbler of ice water, drawn from a barrel. "This water tastes much like that of the crystal streams that are running from the snow-capped mountains."

Several brethren noted that the Prophet seem absorbed in gazing at something at a great distance.

Joseph continued: "I am gazing upon the valleys of those mountains. Oh, the beauty of those snow-capped mountains! The cool refreshing streams that are running down those gorges!"

The brethren noted that the Prophet seemed to switch directions in his gaze.

"Oh, the scenes that this people will pass through! The dead that will lay between here and there. Oh, the apostasy that will take place before my brethren reach that land! But the priesthood shall prevail over its enemies, triumph over the devil, and be established upon the earth, never more to be thrown down."

Joseph pointed to a group of men near him. "There are some men here who shall do a great work in that land…and shall perform as great a work as has been done by men…and many of the nations of the earth will be gathered in that land."

A vision seemed to envelop Joseph.

"The Saints will continue to suffer much affliction, and will be driven to the Rocky Mountains. Many will apostatize. Others will be put to death by our persecutors, or lose their lives in consequence of exposure or disease. Some of you will live to go and assist making settlements, and build cities to see the Saints become a mighty people in the midst of the Rocky Mountains."

Momentarily, Hannah was caught in a trance of her own, thinking of that occasion. She wondered what the Rocky Mountains were really like, and how her family might fare way out there. *Make settlements. Build cities. See the Saints become a mighty people.*

Robert's next statement shook Hannah back to reality. "Our little home here is fine. We don't know when we'll have to move west."

Hannah tossed her mother's letter on the table. "I don't doubt the prophecy. But he didn't say when. It could be another ten years. By then, at the rate we're going, we'll have ten children or more. Build me a house!"

Robert smiled and kissed her on the cheek. "I'll talk to Daniel about it. But don't hold your breath. He's still having a tough time with Elizabeth. Let's wait until things smooth out between them."

# 24

*November 1843*

ROBERT STARED AT THE SIGNATURE on the bill of sale. *Edward Martin.* He stared at the man facing him. Medium height, dark brown hair. Born in Preston, England, in 1818. Baptized in 1837 by Orson Hyde. Emigrated to Nauvoo in 1842. Worked full-time at the temple as a painter, with William Pitt, Alfred Brown, and John Hutchinson.

Edward Martin rose from the oak table in the Harris parlor and thrust out his right hand. "I want to thank you again for your willingness to sell me a portion of your lot, Brother Harris," he said. "I feel fortunate, being able to build me a home so close to the temple."

Robert heaved a big sigh and looked at Hannah. "I hope you'll be able to get along with your new neighbors when they arrive."

"What's your brother's name again?" Edward asked, turning to Hannah.

"Elias," she said quickly.

"It's a nice gesture, giving him your home," Edward said.

Robert pulled a face. *Who said anything about giving it to him? It's worth forty dollars!*

Hannah clutched eighty American dollars to her bosom. "I can see my new home now. Framed construction, not logs. Lots of rooms. A modern kitchen with a real stove."

"I suppose it's none of my business," Edward pressed, "but are you building your frame house next to your log home, or on your farm?"

"Out on the farm," Robert said, pointing to the east.

Hannah shook her head. "There's plenty of room right here. We've still got plenty of room on this lot."

Robert placed his hands on his hips. "Out on the farm."

"Robert…we've been over this before. I don't want to be stuck four miles out of town. Let's build it here. Brother Martin's right. We're only two blocks from the temple. It's a perfect location."

Robert planted his legs and folded his arms. "The farm."

"What about Elizabeth? How can she function as a midwife and an herbalist that far out of town?" Elizabeth at this moment was at the Jacob Kemp Butterfield home tending to Butterfield's oldest daughter, Persis Amanda, who had a fever.

"I've already talked to Daniel about it. The farm."

Edward Martin smiled and walked away, folding his deed. "I think you two need some time alone."

CHAPTER NOTES

According to records obtained from the Nauvoo Land and Records office, Robert and Hannah Maria Harris sold a portion of their lot to Edward Martin. The transaction occurred November 29, 1843. The lot sold for eighty dollars. Edward Martin, also an English convert years later returned to England on a mission. In 1856, he was bringing a handcart company of English converts to the Salt Lake Valley when a snowstorm trapped them. He was eventually rescued.

# 25

*December 1843*

ELIZABETH WAS AMAZED AND SHOCKED to find Joseph Smith standing at the door when she opened it. A lantern from inside the Browett cabin illuminated his cheery face. Two other men, indistinguishable, stood behind the Prophet, where a cold December wind blew from the southeast.

"Are you here to see Daniel?" she asked, her awed olive eyes colored with curiosity. Her voice was sweet but shaky and suspicious. *Why would the Prophet knock on my door this time of night?*

Daniel had been turning down the bed. He stepped into the main room. "Brother Joseph?"

Elizabeth stepped aside, planted her legs and let her jaw drop, still absorbing her disbelief. She let Daniel do the welcoming.

"Come in out of the cold," Daniel said as he approached, motioning. He caught sight of the two other men, bundled in layers of winter clothing.

"Elder Woodruff, Elder Hyde—is that you?"

"It's us," came the reply from Orson.

"I want to express to you again how badly I feel about the loss of your child," Daniel said, shaking the Apostle's hand. A son, Orson Washington Hyde, born to Marinda, had lived only two weeks. Daniel had attended the graveside service a few days ago.

"Thanks for your concern."

"How's Rebecca?"

"Doing better," Orson said. "I think she took the loss of the baby harder than anyone. Except for maybe Laura." Laura was Orson's six-year-old daughter. "Did I tell you Laura just finished reading the Book of Mormon? I had to help her once in a while with some of the big words, but we're sure proud of her."

A premonition was building inside Elizabeth, despite the friendly conversation. In silence, her head shot up. Her green eyes blazed with defiance and she retreated into the kitchen, still dazed. She had not attended the service for the Hyde baby.

"You'll have to pardon our late intrusion," Joseph said, a friendly smile gracing his face. Despite the time, and the obvious fact that he and his two Apostles had worked a long day, Joseph's blue eyes were alive and radiant. The three men shook hands with Daniel and, without invitation, took off their hats and coats.

"You're always welcome at our home," Daniel declared, feeling elated, and hanging the hats on hooks near the door. It was the first time the Prophet had ever been inside the Browett home.

"Thank you Brother Browett," Joseph said. "And thanks to you and many of your friends for your contribution to help Brother Porter Rockwell."

"You're welcome," Daniel stated. "Pleased to help." More than a hundred dollars had been raised from temple construction workers two months earlier. Both Daniel and Robert had contributed a dollar.

Elizabeth knew that her iciness made Wilford uncomfortable. She didn't care. But now he was stepping toward her, offering his hand. "We missed you at Ellen and William's wedding." Wilford had married Ellen Benbow, John Benbow's adopted niece, to William Carter, in a ceremony at the Benbow farmhouse two days earlier.

"I was busy," Elizabeth said flatly. *Why are you here with the Prophet? Going to strong arm me about plural marriage?*

"I hear you're thinking about building a new home," Wilford said.

The question softened Elizabeth a shade. "You know about Hannah and all her children. She's been bugging Robert about it for a long time. If they build a new house, I suppose we will too."

"Daniel the carpenter," Wilford laughed, remembering Daniel's skills back in England.

"We're thinking about building on the farm," Daniel said.

"Quite the little community out that way nowadays," Wilford said, referring to an area now referred to as The Great Mound, near Daniel and Robert's farm. John Benbow owned plots of farm ground in and around the area.

Elizabeth kept her tone icy. "But Hannah and I want to stay in town," she said.

"I'll make the Browett version of composition tea," Daniel said. He poured water into a pot and pushed the pot into the fire. "It'll warm you up." He pulled a bench and wooden chairs together.

Elizabeth bristled at Daniel's change of subject. She pulled one chair a couple of feet back, sat down, crossed her legs, smoothed her blue dress, and brought a scowl to her face.

Small talk ensued, led by Wilford. There was more about the Ellen Benbow wedding. Following that, they talked about the tragic death of Thomas Kington's baby in October, a son that lived less than three weeks. The death of an eight-month-old son of William and Mary Jenkins, in November, was mentioned.

Elizabeth gritted her teeth at the remembrance of the two deaths. She had not been as devoted to her herbal practice for the past two months, and inwardly felt guilty. Outwardly, however, she assumed no responsibility.

Without much help from Elizabeth, Daniel told of the welfare of other

Wilford Woodruff converts. Robert Harris had just sold part of his property, a lot, to a new English immigrant, Edward Martin. The Harris children were healthy, as were the Bloxham children. But Thomas Bloxham was still withdrawn and unbaptized, blaming God for both the death of a new baby in England and the drowning of Charles during the steamboat trip to Nauvoo. On down the list they went for a few minutes. John and Ann Gailey, who had lived with the Harris family for a while, were now in their own log home. George and Mary Smith Bundy, and their adopted son, Job Smith, had stayed with the Browetts for a period of time, but were now staying with another family. Other families were discussed: the Roberts, Coxes, and Hills.

The mention of Henry Eagles brought a report from Joseph, Wilford and Orson about recent kidnappings of Mormons in the Warsaw area, more charges of sedition again Joseph, more problems with Sidney Rigdon, the Church's petition of Congress for redress of the Missouri sufferings, and a current effort to gather signatures on a petition to ask the federal government for a memorial containing a summary of the conflicts in Missouri.

Orson produced the petition. Daniel signed it willingly. Elizabeth grimaced, but signed it anyway.

Orson then told of his mission back east, leaving Nauvoo in mid-August, laboring in Boston, returning in early November, and going through the sorrow when he and Marinda's baby died after living only two weeks. He talked openly about Rebecca, but said little of his third wife, Mary, and the jealousy Rebecca had vocalized.

Following the same pattern, Wilford gave a brief account of his mission in the East. He had left in July, buying paper and ink supplies in St. Louis. He then traveled to Cincinnati, Pittsburgh, Philadelphia, and afterward continued a three-month proselyting campaign into New York, Connecticut, Massachusetts, and Maine. He had returned to Nauvoo a month ago, on November fourth.

Wilford expressed elation over the continued success of Daniel and Jacob Kemp Butterfield's mission to Springfield and elsewhere in Illinois during the past summer. As he wound down, he began chewing on his lip. He briefly alked about the construction of his new brick home, and then lapsed into silence.

As if on queue, the Prophet took over the conversation. He spoke briefly about the importance of Orson's petition, the new Missouri charges against him, his concern about the imprisoned Porter Rockwell, and all the continuing anti-Mormon sentiment in Warsaw, Carthage, and Springfield. He didn't mention how pleased he was to be living in the newly completed Nauvoo Mansion—finally out of the small log cabin he had lived in for three years.

Elizabeth's features hardened and she sat back in her chair. She felt uncomfortable as the Prophet turned his full attention to her. "I'm sure you know, Sister Browett, that we didn't come here for chit chat, even though all these things are important."

She maintained a tight grip on her stony outward appearance. "I suppose not."

"We're here to seal you to your husband," Joseph said suddenly.

Elizabeth flushed and looked away, not catching the implication. *And how does Harriet Barnes Clifford fit into all this?*

Daniel leaned forward in his chair. "Tonight? Here in our home?"

Joseph nodded, his smile wide. "For the past several months, as time permits, we have been taking the brethren into as many homes as possible and sealing husbands and wives together."

Wilford spoke again. "Brother Hyrum Smith sealed Phoebe and me together in November, on the eleventh."

"But what about the temple," Daniel stammered, "Isn't…?"

"Yes," Joseph began, anticipating Daniel's question, "many ordinances of the gospel must be performed in a temple. We're building the temple expressly for that purpose. Ordinances such as sealing children to deceased parents. Sealing deceased ancestors together, such as your grandfathers and grandmothers. In due time, all faithful members will receive their endowment in the temple."

Daniel and Elizabeth had already heard about the "endowment," a ceremony that teaches the eternal purpose of life on earth. The Prophet had first administered the ordinance to a few Church leaders a year ago May. He also instructed them in the principles and in the communication of keys pertaining to the Aaronic Priesthood, and the highest order of the Melchizedek Priesthood.

At the mention of the word *endowment,* Wilford recalled the Prophet's words following the instruction. Joseph had rejoiced, exclaiming; "Now if they kill me you have got all the keys, and all the ordinances, and you can confer them upon others. The hosts of Satan will not be able to tear down the kingdom as fast as you will be able to build it up."

Elizabeth blinked in deep thought at the Prophet's words and touched hand to her chin.

Joseph continued, speaking more rapidly now. "But we can seal living men to living women without a temple. And that's what we've been doing. That's why we're here. To seal you and Elizabeth together, for time and for all eternity. If the temple were complete, of course we would do it there."

Wilford Woodruff cleared his throat. "Sister Browett, how do you feel about that? May we seal you to Brother Browett tonight?"

Elizabeth hesitated. Her face took on a sullen, puzzled look.

"Just to make it clear, Sister Browett," Wilford emphasized, "we are not here to discuss plural marriage. The three of us know of your opposition to that principle. We thought both you and Brother Browett would like the opportunity to be among the first couples in Nauvoo to be sealed together. As we have time, we'll approach Brother and Sister Harris, the Roberts, the Coxes, the Pitts. All the faithful couples here in Nauvoo."

She remained silent, thinking.

It embarrassed Elizabeth to know that Joseph had detected her apprehension. He began to talk again, stating emphatically that he was not going to ask for her permission for Daniel to marry Harriet Clifford. Instead, he preached the doctrine and blessings of eternal marriage and sealing husband and wives together.

Elizabeth's mind was racing. Was this a trick? Would they soften her up with a sealing, and then twist her arm to get her to consent to plural marriage

Would another name be brought up, in addition to Harriet Clifford?

She bit her lip and closed her eyes. Tender thoughts of her marriage and relationship with Daniel began to sift through her mind. In that regard, her testimony of marriage was bedrock solid. Yet, she still harbored doubts as to the three men's real purpose.

"Sister Browett?" the Prophet repeated.

Elizabeth bowed her head. Tears sprang to her eyes.

"Brother Browett, I think your wife is saying yes," Wilford said.

Daniel paused for a few seconds. He leaned over and took his wife in his arms. "I think you're right, Elder Woodruff."

Elizabeth sobbed, burying her face in Daniel's chest.

Within minutes, Joseph, Wilford, and Orson had completed the sacred task. Elizabeth Harris Browett was sealed to her husband, Daniel Browett, for time and all eternity.

# 26

DANIEL AWOKE FROM A DEEP SLUMBER to find himself alone in bed. At first, pitch black greeted his eyes. He turned his head. A crack between the door and the frame revealed a faint light.

*Where was Elizabeth?*

In dead silence, Daniel slipped out of bed and peeked into the main room. What he saw shred him to tears.

Elizabeth was on her knees, in front of the hearth. Her head was bowed and her arms folded. Her lips were moving slowly. Red embers from the hearth revealed a tear trickling down her cheek.

Daniel swallowed hard. Despite the fact that he could not hear what his wife was uttering, the Spirit told him that Elizabeth had voluntarily returned to a relationship between her and Heavenly Father. In stunned silence, Daniel watched for a few moments and then returned to bed, his mind racing. What did this mean? A confirmation of their sealing? A full return to her old, charismatic personality?

Another thought came to Daniel. What if she were praying about

Harriet? What if the Spirit confirmed to her that Harriet should be part of their family? For the past several months Daniel had tried to get Harriet off his mind. At first, he had wondered if he could ever learn to love Harriet, and if so, what kind of relationship it could be. He loved Elizabeth so deeply he harbored doubts as to whether or not another woman could enter his heart.

Elizabeth had refused to talk about the sealing after Joseph, Wilford, and Orson left. Daniel's sixth sense concluded that she was overwhelmed by the whole thing and needed time to process the implications in her mind. She had been kind, cordial, and her personality even bordered on the verge of chattering about things again.

Sleep had almost overcome Daniel again when he heard Elizabeth slip through the door and crawl back in bed. He guessed that nearly an hour had passed. He decided to feign sleeping and not to try and force a conversation, despite his curiosity. If she wanted to talk now, let her wake him. Or they could talk in the morning or anytime.

For a few moments he lay stiff as a board. Elizabeth's breathing was slightly labored and there were sniffles. Daniel rolled over, as if his sleep were restless. Still, there was no conversation. *Let's talk, Elizabeth!*

A half hour passed. Daniel guessed Elizabeth had finally dozed off.

"I'm ready to talk about Harriet."

Daniel whirled, almost spilling his mixture of flour, eggs, and milk.

"Here, let me do that," Elizabeth said as she buttoned her red-checkered dress. Her eyes had an eager aroused sparkle. "You make *terrible* griddlecakes. What else shall we have for breakfast? Get some potatoes out of the root cellar. Bring up some blackberry preserves and a bottle of peaches. I'm *famished.* Throw another log or two on the fire; it's *cold* in here."

Daniel found himself groping for words. "What did you say?"

"*I said* stoke up the hearth, and light another lantern. What *time* is it?" She peeked out the window, heavily laden with frost. "It must be close to eight. The sun's about to come up."

Daniel fumbled at a lantern. "You said something about Harriet."

"Look at this house. I can't *believe* the mess. Will you heat me some water? Where did you put the tub? Gather up all those *soiled* clothes from of the floor. How many bars of soap do we have?"

Daniel felt dizzy with excitement. It was true. Elizabeth was emerging from a fog. "I'll get the potatoes," he said.

"Bring up a *pumpkin*. I feel like baking a *pie* today. A bottle of *cherries* too. While I'm baking, we'd just as well have two kinds of pie. Fetch us a *Hubbard*. Baked squash for dinner sounds good, doesn't it? How much preserved meat is down there? Or shall we reduce our poultry flock by one today? Got a *plump* rooster out there?"

Daniel donned his heavy black wool coat and danced toward the door. *She's back!*

"Bring up a *cabbage*, too. And some beans."

"Yes, dear!" *Are we expecting company?*

Moments later Daniel returned and his heart was thumping. He began to peel potatoes.

"Let *me* do that," Elizabeth said. "You haven't fed the fire yet. We've got a *lot* to talk about."

"Where do you want to start?" he asked as he opened the door again. He eyed his pile of chopped wood.

"Get *lots* of wood and stack it by the hearth."

Daniel returned, blowing flakes of snow off the blocks of firewood. Elizabeth was greasing her pan with suet, ready to add the sliced potatoes.

"I feel *good*, Daniel," Elizabeth began.

"About our sealing?"

"Yes. The sealing. The words. The Spirit that was with the Prophet as he sealed us."

"I belong to you forever, Elizabeth. Death cannot separate us."

Daniel suspected Elizabeth was recalling the Prophet's words, as he was. *A lasting bond of legitimacy. Eternal family unit. The nucleus of heaven. Heirs for God's highest blessings. Become like God. All celestial beings linked in an unbroken family chain. Divine parenthood.*

Elizabeth felt so full of feeling that she could hardly speak. "I want a *child,* Daniel. I want a son or daughter to be part of that sealing."

"Me, too. More than anything."

"We've been married eight years. I don't understand."

"I don't either."

Elizabeth bit her lip in frustration. "I think it's me. Something's *wrong.* I just can't conceive."

"It's possible the Lord is just testing our patience."

"Maybe *Harriet* could give you a child."

Daniel choked at the inference. "Elizabeth, I don't want Harriet. I just want you."

"But the brethren asked *you* to take care of her."

"I know, but I've thought it over. I don't want to have a second wife."

Elizabeth shook her finger at Daniel. "Obedience is the first law of heaven."

"Elizabeth, please. I've never wanted Harriet, even after they asked me. I've hated the thoughts of it."

"Selective obedience is *not* good, Daniel. You taught me that."

Daniel recalled the story of Saul in the Old Testament who was commanded to smite and destroy the Amalekites and all their possessions. Saul held back some animals, claiming he wanted to use them for sacrifices. *To obey is better than sacrifice, and to hearken than the fat of lambs.*

"Saul lost his kingdom. You don't want to lose yours."

"You're not implying…"

Elizabeth's eyes were blazing, taking in Daniel's astonishment. "From now on, *whatever* the Prophet asks, that's what we'll do. My stubbornness has brought me *nothing* but pain and sorrow. I missed being close to the Spirit. The Holy Ghost withdrew from me when I quit praying and when I quit studying the scriptures."

"But…"

"Let's go see Elder Woodruff today and tell him we've decided to accept Harriet."

Daniel drew a deep breath, unsure of himself. "But Elizabeth, we've never even talked about it. Wouldn't you feel awkward and even angry if there was another woman living under the same roof?"

"Build me a house out on the farm, next to Hannah and Robert."

"And leave Harriet here, in this cabin?"

Elizabeth was silent for a moment, thinking. "If you wish. Or build a large house on the farm, with extra bedrooms. One for me, one for Harriet, one for your mother, and one for future children. Mine or hers, makes *no* difference."

"I don't love Harriet. I don't know if I ever could. I just love you."

"The Spirit will change you. It changed me."

"Let's give this some time."

"Your birthday is next week. Why don't we have Elder Woodruff do the ceremony on your birthday?"

"That's too soon."

"I'm certain Sister Harriet Barnes Clifford is a *very* lonely woman. Someone needs to care for her. Thanks to *selfish* me, I've extended her loneliness for an entire year."

Daniel took Elizabeth by the hand. "Sweetheart, don't beat yourself up."

"Ta, ta, ta. Remorse is a part of *repentance,* remember? I'm *sure* it is not a *coincidence* that Brother Joseph has not asked any other man to take Harriet as a wife. I think he *knows* that the Lord has intended for her to be part of your eternal family. *Our* eternal family. Quit dragging your feet."

"Elizabeth…we're rushing this too much."

"We'll go see Elder Woodruff right after breakfast. Perhaps we *will* have guests for dinner. Harriet. And Elder Woodruff."

"Today?"

"Daniel, I know I have to do this. Let's pray together. We haven't said our prayers together for a long time."

Daniel knelt. "I think the Lord will allow us more time."

"Let's find out."

# 27

ELIZABETH WAS NOT SURPRISED AT HOW eagerly Harriet Barnes Clifford accepted the invitation to dine with the Browetts that evening. Putting herself in Harriet's place, Elizabeth understood perfectly.

Nor was she surprised that Elder Woodruff changed his schedule so quickly to make himself available.

Elizabeth had worked herself to a frazzle preparing for the meal. Her old adroitness—acquired from her mother—was returning: the adroitness for providing a home where the food was appetizing, the rooms well furnished and clean, and the atmosphere happy. For twelve months, those qualities had escaped her and now she was making up for lost time. Feelings of guilt haunted her.

As she accompanied Elder Woodruff and Daniel to Harriet's cabin, they hastened diagonally through their snow-covered lot, passing the filled-in well site where James Pulham had been trapped and suffocated. Elizabeth shuddered morbidly as she recalled that tragic day a year and a half ago. At first, she had thought that Daniel, too, had lost his life in that well opening. There were other tragic events to consider—things that led up to the triangle that was bringing her, Harriet, and Daniel together. First, how James had lost his wife, Nancy—Hannah's sister—at sea, a victim of seasickness and dehydration. And second, how Harriet had lost her first husband, a victim of cholera. Months ago, it had seemed so perfect that Harriet and James were to be married. They would have been so good for each other.

Harriet was quiet and subdued as she greeted Elizabeth and Daniel at the door. She donned her overcoat and they began the trek through the snow to the Browett cabin. Along the way they talked mostly about Orson Hyde's departure from Nauvoo. He had been sent to Washington, D. C., to again petition the federal government for assistance. He carried a memorial containing a summary of the conflicts in Missouri, and the threats that prevented Church members from returning to Missouri to recover their holdings or sign deeds to sell them. The petition also asked for redress for grievances and "to shield us from harm in our efforts to regain our lost property."

It was Elizabeth's personality to normally dominate the conversation. This time, however, she was glad to let Wilford do most of the talking.

"Orson's assignment," he was saying, "is to visit as many places as he can back East and get signatures on copies of the memorial. He's also going to buy paper so we can print a new edition of the Doctrine and Covenants. And he's after some new type and metal for stereotyping the edition."

Elizabeth more or less let Wilford's words go in one ear and out the other. Although she was genuinely concerned about the Missouri problems, she hadn't even been a member of the Church when most of those things happened back in 1838. But she had learned about the siege of DeWitt, hostilities in Daviess County, the battle of Crooked River, the Haun's Mill massacre, the siege of Far West and the imprisonment of Joseph Smith.

A scant five or six years ago, Elizabeth had been watching her brother climb the success ladder toward the British heavyweight championship. Both he and Daniel had been given the rights to lease a hundred acres of land near the hamlet of Apperley, thus reaching yeoman status. And she, along with Daniel, had been serving as a lay preacher in the United Brethren congregation. She had never heard of Missouri. Or Mormons. Or polygamy. Now here she was marching toward her little log cabin in Nauvoo, stride by stride along-side Harriet Barnes Clifford, the woman who was going to become her hus-band's second wife.

Funny thing—Elizabeth sighed to herself—she was actually happy about it. A few days ago, she had gagged at the very sound of the name Harriet Barnes Clifford.

There was no conversation between Elizabeth and Harriet. Elizabeth was content to listen to Wilford talk about Orson and the trip he was on. Bundled up against the biting wind of the cold December day and listening to the snow crunch beneath their feet, Elizabeth walked alongside Harriet. She wanted to reach out and hold her hand. Harriet Barnes Clifford—twenty-seven years old, sad brown eyes, long dark hair, olive skin, medium build, an inch or two shorter than Elizabeth.

*I'd give a hundred American dollars to read her mind right now,* Elizabeth thought.

Harriet was mum as they walked. Elizabeth contemplated her all the way. Surely, she thought, Harriet's mind had to be racing. Certainly Harriet wasn't naïve. Even though plural marriage wasn't openly discussed with outsiders, it was a constant topic of conversation among Nauvoo residents. *If that were me,* Elizabeth mused, *I'd know what's up.*

Elizabeth was full of regret, almost drowning in humiliating anger. She kicked herself that she had not reached out to Harriet and had not cared. Surely, for the past year Harriet had been the loneliest woman in the world. Lost a husband to cholera. Lost James in the accident. Who had been there to talk to her? To be her friend? Elizabeth bit her lip hard, thinking how she had been so self-centered. So irresponsible. So focused on herself, instead of on someone who had more trials and tribulations than one could imagine.

She and Harriet could have had so much fun together. Making confects out of fruit boiled in syrup and dried in the oven. Canning peaches and pears. Pickling cucumbers. Making apple cider. Sewing a new Sunday shirt for Daniel. Making lunches for Daniel and Robert and taking them out to the forty-acre farm with Hannah. Listening to Daniel and Robert's friend William Pitt, as he directed the Nauvoo Brass Band. Training her to help as a midwife and in the use of medicinal herbs. How many of Elizabeth's English convert friends had been neglected during the past year? All because of her selfishness. All because of her inward thinking.

The thing that haunted Elizabeth most was the prospect that by now there was a possibility that Daniel could have had his first child by Harriet. That would have meant the beginning of a Browett posterity, a descendant, a namesake, a baby—boy or girl, it made no difference to Elizabeth. Baby blankets to make. Layettes. Diapers. Clothing.

Elizabeth began thinking of names. If it were a boy—would Daniel want it named after him? Daniel Browett, Jr.? Sounded wonderful. What about Thomas—after Daniel's deceased father? Or after Thomas Kington, founder of the United Brethren? Or John, or William, after Daniel's brothers, still residing in England? Or Wilford—in respect for the man who brought them the message of the restored gospel? Or Joseph—after the Prophet? What about a Book of Mormon name? Like Nephi, Lehi, or Moroni?

What if the child were a girl? Would Daniel and Harriet want to name her Harriet, after the mother? Or Martha, after Daniel's mother? What was Harriet's mother's name? Elizabeth kicked herself. That's how little she knew about the woman who was going to become Daniel's wife—and her best friend. She was determined to make that happen. *My best friend.*

Elizabeth hung her head. *What little spirit is still up there, in heaven, in the pre-existence, waiting to come to Daniel's family, that I have delayed?*

Tears of regret came to Elizabeth's green eyes. She made no attempt to dash them away. They spilled down her cheeks and froze there.

The shock of Elizabeth's complete acceptance of plural marriage was still settling over Daniel as the four figures trudged along Mulholland toward the Browett cabin.

One day Elizabeth had been adamantly opposed to Harriet and the whole idea of plural marriage. The next day she was more than ready to embrace it. As for himself, the invitation by the Prophet a year ago to take Harriet as a wife—to provide for her, to protect her—had been the biggest challenge of his life. He had not sought a second wife within the practice of plural marriage. He harbored no intimate emotions for Harriet Barnes Clifford, none whatsoever. Pity, yes. Sadness, yes. A certain responsibility, yes. After all, James Pulham had been a faithful employee in the cooper shop back in Apperley. James had been a cousin, on his mother's side. James had married Hannah's sister, Nancy. Nancy had died on the *Echo*. James had needed a new wife and Harriet had been the perfect match. Daniel had helped James build a new cabin for James and Harriet. He had helped dig the well. *The well.* The end of James. Luckily, it had not caved in on the both of them. Now, James was buried near the well site. Harriet had two scars seared into her persona— the loss of a husband and the lost of a potential husband. How could he, Daniel, replace either of them? He felt so inadequate.

Daniel, too, wondered if Harriet had any idea of what was about to transpire. For him, life was an emotional double-edged sword. He had given the Prophet, Elder Woodruff, and Elder Hyde a positive answer about taking Harriet to wife without even thinking or praying about it. The Spirit had witnessed that it was the right thing to do during the meeting with the three brethren.

At first Daniel had been patient with Elizabeth, but for the past few months he had been inwardly unforgiving and too sensitive about the whole issue. Then he had given up on the whole idea and had gone into a form of depression about it. When Elizabeth suddenly had a change of heart, he experienced a desire to hang onto his "moody blues." Although he refused to admit it, he had begun to resent Elizabeth's stubbornness, and the whole idea of plural marriage. It was only then that he realized Satan was taking a grip on him, and only then did he shake himself back to reality.

As for Wilford, the master of resourcefulness, he continued to mask his emotions by talking about Orson's mission back East. However, he knew exactly what to do when he, Harriet, Daniel, and Elizabeth stepped inside the cozy

Browett cabin.

As they entered, Wilford smiled at the cleanliness of the home and contrasted it to the littered cabin he had seen during his visit just a day earlier. Elizabeth's transformation was complete. She was back to being immaculate, optimistic, spontaneous, endearing, lively, and entertaining. A slow-cooking pot radiated with the scent of roast chicken. Squash and homemade bread were baking in the oven. Cabbage, beans and bacon were simmering on the stovetop.

Wilford chuckled to himself. *A handsome meal, but hardly necessary.* He was prepared to soften Harriet up about the doctrine of plural marriage and then let Daniel ask the big question. Then he would go home. Back to Phoebe, back to his children, back to his warm brick home.

To speed things up, Wilford spoke as he ate. All the while he wondered what Harriet might be thinking. Would she accept Daniel's proposal? Would she accept the doctrine? Was she ready to be married again? Would she get along with Elizabeth? Was she through her mourning period for James?

Wilford thought it curious how Daniel worded the proposal when the time came. It wasn't, *Harriet, will you marry me?* It was, *Harriet, will you become part of my family?* Wilford suspected that Orson Hyde must have used the same wording when he proposed to Rebecca.

Harriet's eyes filled with tears as she spoke. "I've known for a year that I would be Daniel's second wife."

Wilford absorbed Harriet's response with surprise at first, which lessened the more he thought of it. *Of course she had known. That's how the Spirit works.*

Nothing could dim Wilford's elation as he waited for Harriet's revealing statement to be absorbed by Daniel and Elizabeth. Wilford peeked in their direction. Both sat in silence. Embers from the hearth crackled and popped. Daniel's cow bellowed outside, wanting to be grained and milked.

Elizabeth's jaw was slowly dropping.

Daniel closed his eyes in deep thought, grimacing.

Harriet began to speak again, trying to explain. "Daniel and I have not spoken to each other at all, other than a few words of greeting as we've seen each other at the grove on Sundays, and once when I brought food to the workers at the temple."

"Then how…?" Elizabeth stammered. She gave Harriet an unwavering stare.

"It was on a cold wintry day," Harriet explained, her voice soft, "almost exactly a year ago. A feeling came over me as I said my evening prayers. I don't know quite how to explain it, but I *knew.*"

Wilford accepted Daniel's knowing glance. One year ago Daniel had been summoned to the Red Brick Store. In a room above the store, a calling and responsibility had been extended to Daniel by the Prophet Joseph Smith to marry, care for, and cleave unto the widow, Harriet Barnes Clifford. It was now a fact that the Holy Ghost witnessed that fact to Harriet that very night.

Elizabeth's mind went numb as she bore the weight of Harriet's claim. While she had been defiant, exploding with temper tantrums, insensitive to the Spirit, obnoxious in her relationship with Daniel, unable to confront the truthfulness of the doctrine Joseph had brought forth, unwilling to follow the Prophet—Harriet Barnes Clifford had quietly, patiently, tolerantly, and empathetically waited for her new husband-to-be in the lonely solitude of her one-room cabin. Elizabeth shook her head in shame. She wanted to rush to Harriet's side, apologize, cry on her shoulder, and ask for forgiveness.

Elizabeth sensed Elder Woodruff knew it was time to leave.

Wilford stood. "There's an old saying. Two's company, three's a crowd. Tonight, it's more like three's company, four's a crowd. I think you three have a lot to talk about." He stood.

Elizabeth fought tears, drawing a series of rapid breaths. "I'll get your overcoat."

Daniel opened the door for Wilford. Light spilled out of the Browett home into the darkness. "Thank you, Elder Woodruff," Daniel said.

"Let me know what I can do to help," Wilford responded and he stepped outside.

Elizabeth came to the door wiping her eyes. "Elder Woodruff, I think *you* should perform the ceremony."

Wilford was buttoning his coat. He accepted her suggestion with a wide smile. "I'd be happy to. Just let me know when."

Elizabeth reached deep down, emphasizing her words. "One week from today. On Daniel's birthday."

"Are you sure?" the Apostle asked. "It's not too soon?"

Daniel remained silent.

Elizabeth brought Harriet into focus. "It's not too soon for Sister Clifford. She's been *waiting* for a year. And perhaps Daniel's child has been waiting too."

Daniel took on a puzzled look. "My child?"

Harriet blushed as she caught the meaning.

Wilford, too, understood perfectly. He began nodding. "Goodnight," he said, disappearing into the darkness.

Elizabeth closed the door. Turning slowly, she looked at Harriet, sitting quietly on an oak bench, her head bowed, and her hands folded together. Elizabeth strode toward the woman and then collapsed to her knees. Tears flowed. "Sister Clifford. Please forgive me."

Harriet shook her head slowly. "Sister Browett, there's nothing to forgive."

"Oh, yes, there is. I've been so wrong."

"No. No," Harriet cried. "You were perfectly within your rights."

Elizabeth sobbed again as she shook her head.

"Elder Woodruff just said what I've heard time and time again, Sister Browett," Harriet said, finding new strength. "These things cannot happen without the consent of the first wife."

"But I've been so *stubborn* for so long. You don't *understand*. I didn't pray. I even quit reading the scriptures."

"Sister Browett, had I been you, perhaps I would have done the same thing. You must love Brother Browett with all of your heart."

Tears streamed from Elizabeth's eyes again. "Yes, yes," she stammered. "With *all* of my heart."

Harriet blew her nose. She seemed to regain her composure. "Both of you need to understand something."

Elizabeth wiped her eyes with her forearm. She sensed Harriet was about to say something important.

"Brother and Sister Browett," Harriet said, her voice soft and meek. "Expressing myself has always been difficult. These words are hard for me to say. But although I have somehow known I would be included in your family some day, I want you both to know exactly how I feel."

Elizabeth let her eyes reach Daniel's. She bit her lip, fighting emotions.

Harriet continued. " Sister Browett, I have not coveted your husband. In some unexplained way, I do love him. But it is not the kind of love you would think. It is not a flirtatious love, nor filled with any kind of lust. It is deeply spiritual. I hope you know what I mean. I hope you can accept me, both of you. I would rather go back to England than not be accepted. I would rather die. I would rather join my first husband in his grave."

Elizabeth let her head fall into Harriet's lap, sobbing again. "Dear, dear, Sister Clifford. I accept you. I *love* you. I hope with all my heart that you can *forgive* me, and accept me as your friend. Your *eternal* friend."

Daniel witnessed this spectacle with a measure of insecurity. His love for Elizabeth had just grown by another magnitude of unmeasured greatness. He felt a place in his heart growing for Harriet and knew that it would expand tremendously. In Biblical cultures, when parents arranged marriages, it had been the responsibility of both the young man and the young woman to accept the arrangement and learn to love their spouse. That seemed to be his lot now. But he wondered how he could actually demonstrate that love equally to both women, without one or the other feeling jealous. How could he care for both? How could he raise two families, if children came? How could he get over the awkwardness of living with two women? Should he have two houses or one? Should he move Harriet in with Elizabeth and him, or leave her in her own cabin? Should a new frame home be built on the farm, as Hannah was coaxing Robert to do? Could he afford it? And what would

Elizabeth's true emotions be once he consummated the marriage with Harriet

Daniel's thoughts were interrupted as Elizabeth suddenly rose to her feet tugging at Harriet's hands. "I think it's time we both stood up. I don't know about you, Sister Clifford, but I want to feel my husband's arms around the *both* of us."

Harriet stood, anxious to please Elizabeth. Daniel waited for Harriet to look at him, but she did not. It was an awkward moment for her, he surmised

Daniel could not fight his emotions any longer. The sight of Elizabeth pulling Harriet toward him was too much. He began to cry. He extended his arms, pulling the two women to his chest. Sobbing, he managed some words "There are going to be three of us now."

For nearly an hour, the three of them talked. They tried to reach some decisions. Until a larger frame home could be constructed on the farm Harriet would continue to live in her own log cabin that her first husband built for her. Daniel would spend one night a week there, but watch over Harriet's needs on a daily basis. A goal was set to move into the frame house by sometime in the fall. They would build near Robert and Hannah and ask other English immigrants to help in the construction, men like Levi Roberts John Cox, Edward Phillips, William Jenkins, Joseph Hill, Thomas Bloxham John Hyrum Green, John Gailey, George Bundy, and Job Smith. Even Daniel's former missionary companion, Jacob Kemp Butterfield.

Elizabeth word's remained conciliatory as she and Daniel walked Harriet home in the dark. "We can work this out, Sister Clifford. Things will be fine.

"I have one small request," Harriet said, her mind dazed with the happenings of the evening.

"*Anything* at all," Elizabeth responded.

"Beginning now, could we call each other by our first names?"

Elizabeth smiled. "Of course."

# 28

TWO DAYS BEFORE THE SEALING AND MARRIAGE, Daniel's mind was in a troublesome turmoil. In desperation, he sought out Wilford Woodruff. "I need to speak to you in private," he said as he stood on Wilford's doorstep.

"Let's go for a walk," Wilford suggested as he reached for his coat. "I've got some time before I have to meet with the quorum."

Daniel's voice was apologetic as they began to stroll down the street. "Sorry to trouble you when you have so many worries of your own," he said. His words smoked in the frigid air. Snow was falling out of gray curtains in Nauvoo, hissing against each house, sometimes drifting hurriedly by. On the rooftops snow was thickening in pristine softness, and on the sheds, the pumps, the woodpiles, and all the trees. In the empty lots, rabbits had written their graffiti in forked paths, dancing, crisscrossing lines that obliterated each other.

Days earlier, a Church member had arrived from St. Louis with news that the governor of Missouri had issued another writ for Joseph Smith and was now appealing to Governor Ford of Illinois to arrest Joseph. The city council had quickly passed an ordinance that called for the immediate arrest and imprisonment of any Missourian who tried to arrest Joseph without consent of both the governor of Illinois and the mayor of Nauvoo. The quorum and the city council were also dealing with the news that Missourians had kidnapped two Church members—Daniel Avery and his son, Philander. Both were being held in a Missouri prison.

The two men walked along Durphey Street and then turned right on Monson Street, passing the Heber C. Kimball home—a log house with three lower rooms and a small second floor. Daniel wondered how long it would be until Heber replaced it with a brick home, similar to that of Wilford's.

"What can I do for you, Brother Browett?" Wilford asked, his shoulder hunched over. He turned his head sideways, avoiding the cold wind.

"I'm having second thoughts about my sealing to Sister Clifford," Daniel said quickly, getting the matter off his chest.

Wilford acted surprised. "What makes you say that?"

"From out of nowhere, negative feelings have come to my mind. It's hard to explain."

"What kind of feelings?"

Daniel gave a shoulder shrug. "That I won't be able to share my love with another woman. That the whole thing is wrong. That I'll begin comparing the two women with each other, and that wouldn't be fair."

"And how's Elizabeth been reacting?"

"Fine, until last night."

"And?"

"I find her regressing to some of her old attitudes. Now's she's testy again and has clammed up."

Wilford snorted and returned a sly smile that suggested this was not the first time he was hearing something like this.

"Do you think we should go through with this?" Daniel asked. "We felt so good about it that night you were there, and afterward. I'm confused. So Elizabeth."

"I'm going to ask you a question," Wilford said. "Think about the convert baptisms you had on your mission with Brother Butterfield." He paused.

Daniel nodded his head. "I'm thinking. What about them?"

"Did you ever have any of them change their mind after you taught them and after the Spirit had witnessed to them that the gospel is true?"

"Of course."

"Did their testimonies get challenged? Did they, all of a sudden, have additional trials and tribulations in their lives?"

"Yes."

"Is the same thing happening to you and Elizabeth? Is Satan challenging your testimony about the doctrine of plural marriage?"

"I believe so."

"I suspect you've had more than your share of trials and tribulations during the past few days, since my visit."

Daniel scratched his head, deep in thought. Wilford was right, as usual. The rope to his well bucket had broken. The cow had suddenly dried up. Fungus was discovered growing in precious bottles of canned fruits and vegetables. Weevil had infested their wheat storage. A wolf had carried off one of their sheep. Weasels had broken into the chicken coop, killing three hens. Elizabeth couldn't find one of her mittens. Some of her herbs were missing. A woman blamed her for an ailment. Elizabeth had come down with a bad cold, with severe headaches. He had fallen through the ice while fishing on the river. Now he had a cold. They had argued over plans to build a frame house. The rock chimney almost seemed plugged, fanning smoke into their home. A block of wood had slammed into his shin while chopping, almost breaking his leg. He still walked with a noticeable limp.

Wilford motioned to the sky with one arm. "Brother Browett, a third part of the hosts of heaven were cast out because of their rebellion. I suppose we may say that there may be a hundred thousand million followers of Satan on this earth, eager to do the devil's bidding. Where are they?"

Daniel grimaced wryly. "I suppose some are here in Nauvoo."

"Correct. Certainly there are plenty in Missouri and elsewhere here in

Illinois. Some are in places like Amsterdam, Constantinople, Jerusalem, and London. I wrestled with Satan in London, when I opened my work there back in 1841."

Daniel did a double take. "You did?"

"He injured me severely and I in turn injured him. Three men dressed in white tended to my wounds afterward."

Daniel wondered if the battle with Satan had been physical, with a man possessed of a demon, or with Satan himself, which would have been spiritual. Either way, Daniel reasoned, Wilford was telling the truth. He wondered if the three men who administered to Wilford afterward were the Three Nephites.

Wilford continued talking. "What happened to the Prophet Joseph when he went into the grove to pray as a young man, back in 1820?"

"Satan tried to destroy him," Daniel responded quickly.

"I testify to you in the name of Jesus Christ that Satan wants to destroy this work, Brother Browett," Wilford said, his voice rolling with thunder. "Satan wants to destroy every element of it. He does not want families sealed together. He does not want husbands sealed to wives, or any element of the restoration to succeed, including the doctrine of plural marriage."

Daniel gulped.

"As soon as the Spirit testifies to a Church member that something is true, Satan's followers move in. They are clever, cunning, and smart. They've been at this for thousands of years. Satan is a personage of great power; he has great influence and knowledge. The devil did not make this earth. It never belonged to him, and never will. But Lucifer was cast down to earth, he and his angels, and they remain her yet. They have their effect upon the hearts and minds and lives of the children of God. Lucifer has sought to overthrow the gospel from the beginning. He does not like you very well, Brother Browett. He does not like the idea of revelation. He has inspired the hearts of many men since the gospel was restored to the earth, to make war against you and me."

Daniel shook his head. He was beginning to understand that the adversary was behind his negative thinking. And behind the negative thoughts of Elizabeth.

"Brother Browett, you have to do as the Savior did. The devil followed Jesus everywhere, continually trying to draw him from his purposes and to prevent him from carrying out the work of the Father. You see this manifested when he took Jesus to the loftiest pinnacle of the temple and showed him the glory of the world. He told Jesus that he would give him all this if he would fall down and worship him. But the poor devil did not own a foot of land nor anything else! The earth was made by and belonged to the Lord, and was his footstool. Yet the devil offered that to Jesus, which was not his own."

Daniel hung his head.

"Brother Daniel, do as Jesus did. Say to Satan, *'Get thee behind me, Satan'.*"

A tear came to Daniel's eye.

"Two principles do exist, Brother Browett. Good and evil. God and the devil. Whatever leads to good and to do good is of God. Whatever leads to evil and to do evil is of the devil. God has labored from the creation of man to lead him to keep the celestial law, that he may inherit a celestial glory, and partake of eternal life. The devil, with all his fallen angels, has labored from the creation to lead man astray. To lead him down to the perdition of ungodly men, that he may have dominion over him."

"I should have brought Elizabeth with me."

Wilford stopped in front of the Brigham Young home, on Kimball Street. He pointed east, toward the temple. "Satan opposes the work of the temple. It's been a chore, getting that building constructed. But it will one day be ready so that you can receive your endowment there. You will be endowed there with your wife, Elizabeth. And with your second wife, Harriet."

Daniel recalled his work as a carpenter there. Receiving rafts of prime lumber from tracts of forestland in Wisconsin. Helping saw the lumber into boards. Using the lumber in the temple. In every other community along the frontier, one or more church meetinghouse had been constructed, whether Presbyterian, Catholic, or Baptist. Not in Nauvoo. Church meetings were held outdoors, or in homes. Not a single Mormon chapel. Not even a building like the little Gadfield-Elm chapel he had helped construct in England Every effort focused on the construction of the temple.

"I guess this means I should go through with it."

A smile crossed Wilford's face. "Brother Browett, plural marriage is part of the restoration. It is part of the gospel and we are asked to practice it in the Church right now. The time may come when we will not, but for right now, it is an essential part of building up the kingdom. I promise you in the name of the Lord that if you will return to your home right now, take Elizabeth by the hand, and get on your knees, the Spirit of the Holy Ghost will again confirm to your minds that you should bring Sister Clifford into your family. She is a lonely widow. She needs help."

The two men walked in silence for a few minutes, up Granger Street, turning right again on Hotchkiss Street, toward Wilford's home.

"I know what you're thinking, Brother Browett."

Daniel blanched.

"You're wondering why I haven't taken another wife."

"The thought has crossed my mind."

"The time is not right. I have to be away too much, in my duties in the Church. But I know the time will come, in the not too distant future. The Spirit has told me. Don't you worry about me. You just be obedient to the Spirit, and do what is right."


CHAPTER NOTES

Wilford Woodruff's thoughts concerning the adversary are taken from *The Discourse of Wilford Woodruff*, compiled by G. Homer Durham (Salt Lake City, Utah: Bookcraft Inc. 1969), pages 237-239.

Daniel's conclusion is correct about Nauvoo. There was never an effort to construct a single LDS chapel there.

# 29

FIVE TO ZERO. THAT WAS THE SCORE. Elizabeth and Hannah had been married in the same double ceremony more than eight years ago, in England. Today, as Elizabeth and Daniel met with Hannah and Robert to discuss plans for their new homes out on the farm, Elizabeth's barrenness still haunted her.

It seemed to Elizabeth that Hannah and Robert did not know how *not* to have children. They came like clockwork, every eighteen to twenty-four months.

"The more the merrier," Hannah kept saying, with a shoulder shrug.

"More help on the farm," Robert would say, his eyes sparkling. Joseph would turn eight in three months, almost old enough to drive a team of horses or oxen by himself.

Elizabeth marveled at the health of the Harris children, given the mortality rate in Nauvoo and the American frontier. Among most settlements along the Mississippi, childhood illness and death was a horror to contemplate. People used leeches at the back of the neck for headaches. Lancing of the gums or leeches behind the ears for teething. Chalk and powdered rhubarb for hiccups. A sticky paste of rhubarb and magnesia for stomachache. As for herself, Elizabeth still relied on the Thomsonian method of herbology as taught to her by Elder Willard Richards. That, along with generous doses of castor oil and an emphasis on fruits and vegetables in the diet, had kept Robert and Hannah's children amazingly healthy. Same with the majority of their close English converts, the former United Brethren people.

Elizabeth's namesake—Lizzy—was nagging her aunt to play jackstraws. "Well," Elizabeth said, "its obvious that our homes will have to be *totally* different this time," Lizzy's homemade rag doll lay crumpled behind a chair behind Hannah, Robert, and Daniel.

Hannah was nodding in agreement.

"You and Robert just as well have ten extra bedrooms for children, plus a ten-acre loft," Elizabeth said. "At the rate you're going, you'll have more than a dozen, maybe two. That eighty dollars you received from Brother Martin won't go very far."

"Your patriarchal blessing got it right," Daniel said, turning to Robert. "References to all that posterity you're going to have."

"I can repeat the exact words," Hannah said. Patriarch John Smith had given the blessing a few months earlier. "Thou shalt have a *numerous posterity* to keep thy name in remembrance," she said. She patted her tummy, laughing now. "Enoch is nearly seven months old now. Who knows when number six will start growing in there again."

"Am I going to have another little brother?" six-year-old Lizzy asked, her eyes searching her mother.

"Maybe when the next one comes it will be a little sister," Hannah said.

Elizabeth blanched. She quickly recalled the wording on her and Daniel's patriarchal blessings. She wondered why the patriarch couldn't have been just as specific about their posterity.

Robert got down to business. "If we build new homes this spring, are you going to actually build two houses, or have a large house with two wings, or just a regular house?" Robert asked Daniel.

"Your future *you-know-who* complicates things doesn't it?" Hannah asked, avoiding saying the name of Harriet Barnes Clifford in front of the children just yet.

"It's however Daniel wants it," Elizabeth said with a shrug. Her morning prayers made her feel good all over again about the decision to bring Harriet into the Browett family. But the day had brought more trials and tribulations to test her. She had cut her finger peeling potatoes for the meal they had just eaten. She had slipped on the ice walking between the two cabins, bruising a knee when she fell. And earlier in the day, a woman had accused her of prescribing fried mouse-pie for bedwetting.

Daniel got a gleam in his eye. "I don't think we need to make a decision about that this early. Right now, we need to be thinking about what kind of wood to buy. Oak plank is almost two dollars per hundred feet now, and walnut and curly maple is about three dollars. And we've got to find someone to plaster for us."

"First job will be to dig two wells," Robert said. "I hope we don't have to go down too far. Both Brother Benbow and Brother Kington had to dig forty-five feet out where they are."

The remarks brought a sad remembrance of the well that collapsed on James Pulham. Otherwise, Harriet would be happily married to him and not about to become Daniel's second wife.

Over a generous helping of apple pie, the evening concluded when Daniel stood up to leave. "See you in the morning. Elder Woodruff will be here at ten o'clock sharp."

"We'll be wearing our Sunday best," Hannah promised. "Sister Roberts is taking the children. I don't suppose the sealing will take long, will it?"

"I can't imagine that it would," Daniel said.

"We should save some of your apple pie for Elder Woodruff," Elizabeth said as she scanned Hannah's kitchen for another pie.

"I'll bake two more in the morning. I'll have time," Hannah said.

Elizabeth wondered where the woman got so much energy. Five children. And time to make pies.

As Hannah watched Elizabeth and Daniel walk through the snow to their own cabin, Hannah wondered about Harriet. She was probably sitting in her cabin, alone again. But tomorrow she would be sealed to Daniel Browett. The Browett family was about to become three. On December eigh teenth, Daniel's birthday.

CHAPTER NOTES

It is a historical fact that Daniel Browett took Harriet Barnes Clifford as a second wif while living in Nauvoo. The exact date of the marriage between Daniel and Harriet is no known. However, Daniel, Elizabeth, and Harriet are all listed together in the Nauvoo Templ Endowment Register. Harriet Barnes was born 10 October 1810 in Hempstead Gloucestershire, England, according to the Family Group Record. Her first husband wa Elijah Clifford, and they were married 25 December 1835. He apparently died shortly afte the couple's arrival in Nauvoo.

# 30

*April 1844*

HANNAH WAS AS NERVOUS AS A CAT. She had not seen her brother, Elias, for more than three years. She recalled that day in Liverpool when her mother, Ann, changed her mind about emigrating to America. Ann had returned to Apperley, taking Elias and Jane with her. Now, Elias and his new bride, Mary Crook Eagles, were about to step onto the Nauvoo Landing. They were among two hundred ten Mormon passengers who had been carried across the treacherous Atlantic on a 529-ton bark called the *Fanny*, and brought up the Mississippi on the Church-owned steamboat, the *Maid of Iowa*.

Curiosity tugged at Hannah's mind. How had Elias changed now that he was twenty-two? How strong was his testimony? What was his young wife like? And would there be a surprise on board? Was her mother, Ann Eagles, among the passengers? Hannah crossed her fingers.

The afternoon crowd waiting at the Nauvoo Landing was large. Hannah guessed more than two thousand. There had not been an immigrant company arrival at the Nauvoo Landing from Great Britain since November, when the *Metoka* passengers arrived.

It was a beautiful spring day in Nauvoo. Brief morning showers had passed, giving way to intermittent sunshine and temperatures in the fifties during the day. Now, near five in the afternoon, it was beginning to cool again. Northbound Canadian geese flew overhead. Ducks swam in the water of the Mississippi. Squirrels chattered from the treetops. Willows were beginning to show the fringe of yellow and green. Impatient youngsters fished off the banks of the river. But the main body of the Saints had broken out singing hymns, raising their voices as the *Maid of Iowa* drew nearer.

Wilford Woodruff pulled out a rumpled sheet of paper from the vest of his suit coat. He began sharing the contents with Daniel Browett, John Benbow, and Thomas Kington. The *Fanny* passengers comprised the twenty-fifth Mormon immigrant company to arrive in Nauvoo since the summer of 1840 when the first company of Saints arrived. By Wilford's calculations, the *Fanny* passengers would increase the number of Great Britain converts that had immigrated to Nauvoo to nearly four thousand. Wilford tried hard not to swell with pride. After all, he had been in a large part responsible for around eighteen hundred converts himself, during his mission to England in 1840-41. Most of them from the Malvern Hills and Cotswold Hills area of England in three counties: Gloustershire, Herefordshire, and Worcestershire.

"Whoever thought our mission to England would lead to this?" Wilford asked, appearing delighted.

Daniel, arm-in-arm with his two wives, smiled. "Brother Joseph certainly knew what he was doing when he sent members of the Twelve to England."

Wilford shook his head up and down. "Those were tough days for the Church, back in 1839. We had been driven out of Missouri. We were just getting settled here on the river. Nauvoo was just a swamp that nobody wanted. Now look at it."

With a majestic arm sweep he turned to the east, and pointed to a collection of new brick and frame homes, and the temple construction site. A
crane for lifting and moving large wooden beams and heavy stones seemed to
dominate the site, where the stone walls stood at around twelve feet tall, well
short of their intended overall height.

"Thanks again, Elder Woodruff, for bringing the light and truth of
gospel to us," John Benbow said.

Wilford put his arms around Benbow and Kington. "And thank you for
organizing the United Brethren, and being prepared for the light and truth of
the gospel." Wilford had baptized six hundred members of that congregation
within just a few months back in 1840.

Benbow, who celebrated his forty-fourth birthday on April first, was now
an established farmer east of Nauvoo. He had purchased his first eighty acres
from his brother, William, in 1841, for one hundred twenty-five dollars. A
year later he purchased another eighty acres from Francis McSperitt for two
hundred seventy-five dollars. His farms were the envy of the community, neat,
criss-crossed with fences, modeled after the Hill Farm in Castle Frome,
England. Joseph Smith and his wife had visited his farm right after April conference, just a few days ago, and had commented on how beautiful everything
looked, especially the peach tree blossoms.

"How's Ellen doing? And William?" Wilford asked. They were Benbow's
adopted children, fathered by Benbow's brother, in England.

"Both married, both doing well," Jane Benbow answered, showing an
appreciative smile for Wilford's concern.

Wilford pulled Thomas Kington to his side and peered into the eyes of
Thomas's wife, Margaret. "And how are the Kingtons doing these days?"

"We're fine," Thomas replied, implying that the couple had mostly
recovered from the death of their baby, Ephraim. The baby had been born in
October, but died two weeks later. Thomas' first wife, Hannah Pitt, had died
shortly after his arrival in Nauvoo. She had been a sister to William Pitt.
Thomas' mother had died, too. Thomas had married Margaret Pisel shortly
afterward. After living a short time in a rented house in the Nauvoo Third

Ward, the Kingtons had purchased a farm from Owen Bosworth, farther out on the Illinois prairie, east of the Benbow farms. Elder Woodruff had been there in February, to conduct a meeting in the Kington home for the rural members of the Church.

Margaret whispered into Wilford's ear. "I'm in a family way again."

Wilford broke out into a grin. "That's wonderful news. When?"

"September," she answered. "I've already told Sister Browett."

"I guess you know how responsible your husband was back in England for preparing a large body of people to receive the gospel," Wilford said. He was referring to the fact that Thomas Kington had organized the United Brethren congregation in the early 1830s. Benbow had provided the financing.

"Oh, yes," Margaret smiled. "I'm very proud of him." Many times she had heard Church authorities credit the Mormon immigration from Great Britain for strengthening the Church when it needed it the most. There were those who were of the opinion that the immigrants, with their strong testimonies, even saved the Church. "I suppose you are very busy these days."

Wilford nodded. Earlier in the day he had attended a meeting with the Twelve. Elder John Taylor had delivered a discourse on the political problems the Church was having with the authorities in Missouri, and in Illinois. April conference had just concluded. Joseph's counselor, Sidney Rigdon, had delivered a major address. Wilford hadn't told anyone yet, but he had not been impressed. Sidney, who had some personal problems and had been away for a long time—five years—did not sound just right to him.

Just before conference, Wilford had planted his spring wheat on his farm, out on the prairie. He had attended the dedication of the Nauvoo Masonic Lodge on April fifth. He was still working in the *Times and Seasons* office with Elder Taylor. At the end of March, they had printed and bound the fourth volume.

On Sunday March twenty-fourth, Wilford had listened to the Prophet make a troubling speech. Joseph reported that two men had informed him that there was a conspiracy taking place for the purpose of taking his life. That was old news of sorts, except for the fact that the men behind the conspiracy were members of the Church—William and Wilson Law, Chauncey and Frances Higbee, and Dr. Robert Foster and his brother, Charles. *If it's true,* Wilford thought, *they ought to be ex-members.* Two of them had been disciplined before—one of the Higbees, and one of the Fosters—for immorality.

In late February, Wilford had been sick. John Benbow and Job Smith had come to administer to him. On March first, Wilford had reached his thirty-seventh birthday.

Daniel Browett listened to parts of the conversation between Wilford and the Benbows and Kingtons, but his mind was elsewhere as he stood waiting for the passengers to disembark. He had two wives now and he was going through an uncomfortable stage.

His immediate reaction after his sealing to Harriet was to compare her to Elizabeth. He knew it was wrong, but he was fighting the "natural man." Elizabeth, for example, was more affectionate. Harriet seemed more passive about their relationship. Elizabeth liked to cuddle, to be touched, and to accept big hugs. Harriet did not. Elizabeth was highly intimate. Harriet had problems that way. Harriet was content to have Daniel spend one or two nights a week at her little log home. Elizabeth wanted him every night. Elizabeth was more optimistic about life, excited about building a new home. Harriet seemed bored and detached. Elizabeth was spontaneous, flashy, and spunky. Harriet was bashful and unsure of herself. Elizabeth was easy to talk to. Harriet seemed fearful of confrontations, and unable to verbally respond quickly in some conversations.

Harriet had her strengths, however. She seemed satisfied with her new life, and never complained. Elizabeth was flighty and uncommitted about a lot of things; that had been apparent during her testy twelve months of opposing plural marriage. Harriet was quiet, but she seemed at peace with herself. Sometimes Elizabeth was self-centered and egotistical. Harriet enjoyed the simple life. Elizabeth wanted to be involved in everything and sometimes that aggravated Daniel. Harriet was always receptive to suggestions. Elizabeth *gave* the suggestions. Daniel judged Harriet to be the best potential mother; she liked to spend quality time with children. Elizabeth loved children, but quickly became bored with them.

One thing troubled Daniel more than anything else, however. He had been married to Harriet for four months now. Harriet was not pregnant. Neither was Elizabeth.

Joseph Smith, as usual, stood in a prominent place on the Nauvoo landing, waiting for the steamer to arrive. He had learned on March twenty-fifth that another company of immigrants from England was expected soon. His blue eyes bright and alert, he stood ready to greet the Saints. Everything was organized to his satisfaction. The newcomers would temporarily stay in the home of other Saints until new homes could be constructed. Plots of land would be offered at a reasonable price to those who could afford it and given free of cost to those who could not.

Despite Joseph's outward appearance, there was a lot on his mind. He had just come from an ugly Municipal Court hearing against Dr. Robert. D. Foster. Days earlier, he had concluded the April conference of the Church. His counselor, Sidney Rigdon, had spoken for the first time in five years. Joseph was not happy with his talk. Sidney seemed incoherent, talking about the early history of the Church. Joseph liked the other addresses. John Taylor also spoke about the history of the Church. Joseph's brother, Hyrum, appealed for more donations to finish the work on the temple—twenty thousand shingles were needed, for example. As for himself, Joseph—because of ill health—delayed giving a talk until Sunday. Twenty thousand members of the Church had listened to him preach what would later be known as the King Follett sermon. The next day, Monday, he had given another short talk, followed by addresses by Heber C. Kimball, Hyrum Smith, and Brigham Young.

Thus far, 1844 had proved to be a challenging year for the Prophet Joseph Smith. Following the unsuccessful attempt to kidnap him into Missouri, the hatred of his enemies had become even more intense. Anti-Mormon newspapers had turned up the heat, publishing outright lies. Those led to more threats of mob attacks. The Nauvoo Legion was kept in constant readiness. The growth of Nauvoo—now reaching fourteen thousand—augmented the jealousy and hatred of neighboring towns, where thrift and unity were lacking. Citizens there feared the voting power of the Mormons. So strong were the Latter-day Saints now that they held the balance of power in elections.

In January, a political convention had been held in Nauvoo. Because candidates for the presidency of the United States had either ignored Mormon requests for a course of action in relation to the cruel oppression the Saints had suffered, or had given unsatisfactory responses (as in the case of Henry Clay and John C. Calhoun), the citizens of Nauvoo had nominated Joseph as a candidate for president. There was little thought that Joseph would actually be elected, but it gave them an opportunity to express their feelings.

In February, Joseph had published to the world his "views on the powers and policy of the government of the United States." He advocated sweeping changes. Reduce the number of congressmen by two thirds. Pardon prisoners in state prisons. Use the prisoners to build roads and improve public works. Turn the prisons into seminaries of learning. Abolish slavery in all the states. Have Congress pay slave owners a reasonable price for their slaves. Make honor the standard of all men. More economy, less taxes. Greater equality, less distinction among classes of people. Establish a national bank. Spread the boundaries of the union. Include Oregon, Texas, Canada, and Mexico.

Joseph chuckled to himself. Already, his platform for the presidency had created unprecedented commotions and favorable comment. But Joseph was a realist. In February, he had instructed the Quorum of the Twelve to begin sending out delegations of men to seek out a new location for the Church, somewhere in the West. "Where we can move to after our temple is completed, and where we can build a city in a day, and have a government of our own, set up into the mountains, where the devil cannot dig us out, and live in a healthful climate, where we can live as old as we have a mind to."

Joseph shook his head. It was not Washington, D. C., that was giving him the most trouble. It was corruption from within. When he had increased the police force in Nauvoo in January, he had instructed them in their duties and said, "I am exposed to far greater danger from traitors among ourselve than from enemies without, although my life has been sought for many year by the civil and military authorities, priests, and people of Missouri."

Those remarks, and others, seemed to bring his enemies out of th woodwork. Soon, men that had been loyal to Joseph were secretly plotting hi death. Joseph's enemies were soon exposed. Among them William Law, hi second counselor. William Marks, president of the Nauvoo Stake. Now Law Marks, and others—including Wilson Law, Leonard Soby, and Dr. Foster— had joined forces with John C. Bennett, the former mayor of Nauvoo. Josep suspected that they were in league with the Missourians. Secret meetings wer being held. Thanks to two young boys, Denison Harris and Robert Scott, th secret plots of Law and Marks had been exposed. Joseph knew that Law an Marks were leading a group of apostates to form a church of their own.

Joseph shook his head again. Those men faced excommunication by th Church.

A dark feeling came over Robert as he watched William Law worm throug the crowd at the Nauvoo Landing. Law's hands were in his pockets as thoug he were concealing something. As one who had received training in th Nauvoo Legion as one of Joseph's bodyguards, he felt an urgency.

"I'll be right back, Hannah," Robert said, making his way towards Law He knew what to do in situations like this.

Law edged closer to Joseph Smith. Robert could overhear the questic he asked the Prophet. "Mind if I walk home with you? I have something I like to discuss, and alone would be best."

"Alone?" Joseph asked, his suspicion evident.

"Alone," Law repeated. "I want to talk about my repentance."

"It'll be a while," Joseph said as the Spirit whispered to him to leave. want to meet the passengers." The Prophet soon separated himself from Law

Robert approached Law. "What do you have in your pockets, Brother William gave Robert an apprehensive stare. "Who are you?"

Robert ignored the question and returned the stare. He seldom lost eye-to-eye confrontations and was not about to lose this one. "It's all over town, the story that you've had illicit relations with a young lady. Does your wife know? Or do I need to spill the beans?"

"How did you find out?"

"That's not important. If you're not out of sight by the time I count to ten, I'll break every bone in your body."

"I remember you—from the posse last year," Law said with a newfound seething hatred. "You're an Englishman. I've never liked Englishmen."

"And this Englishman is the new czar of Nauvoo. One—two—three…"

Law, the Irishman, disappeared.

"Can you imagine living in this country with Joe Smith as president?"

Governor Thomas Ford cringed at the question posed by James A. McDougall in a barroom on Adams Street near the state capitol building. It was a horrific thing to contemplate. "What's the world coming to?"

The tables were full of Democrats, narrowly bounded by their own perceptions of political life. Both houses of the legislature had adjourned for the day. Raucous laughter filled the room, as did smoke from cigars and pipes.

There were no Whigs—they frequented a different bar.

McDougall, the attorney general, was scanning a pamphlet distributed by the Mormon Prophet. He appeared slightly stimulated by what he had read. "On the surface, he pretends to have some good ideas. His platform will attract a lot of people who don't know better."

"That's on the surface. In reality he'd be a disaster," Ford replied. He knew all about Smith's platform. Ford had been speaking out publicly against Joe Smith's candidacy, calling it an effort to "crown the whole folly of the Mormons."

"You're not going to vote for him?" McDougall joked as he ran his fingers through his thick beard. He drank straight gin.

"The man won't be satisfied until he rules the whole world," Ford said, shaking his head. "In Nauvoo, he's made himself the temporal prince—he's a self-anointed king and priest. His priesthood order is his nobility. He force his followers to take an oath of allegiance to him. He deduces his descent by an unbroken chain from Joseph, the son of Jacob."

"You learn all this from the Law brothers?" The attorney general had seen William and Wilson Law go into the governor's office on occasion.

Ford took a gulp of bourbon whiskey. "Interesting men."

McDougall ordered more gin. "I suppose."

"At one time William Law was Ole Joe's first counselor," Ford explained. "He and his brother come to see me on a regular basis now. It's too hot fo them to live in the holy city now; they live in Carthage. Wilson was majo general of the Nauvoo Legion. Of course William and Wilson's been denud ed, but now they appear to be quite conscientious and candid. Ole Joe tried to take William's woman as a spiritual wife."

McDougall almost choked on his drink.

"Now they say Joe's established a recorder's office in Nauvoo, and that the only way titles of property can be recorded. Gives a total advantage to Joe in the sale of real estate. Same with issuing marriage licenses, liquor licenses—everything."

"Then why do so many Mormons keep coming to Nauvoo?"

"A lot of them are leaving. Not only the Laws, but also two men named Higbee and two men named Foster. And lots more. They hate Smith's des potism. Nauvoo, they say, is totally corrupt and unprincipled."

McDougall gasped and took the Lord's name in vain.

"And now Joe Smith wants to be president."

CHAPTER NOTES

According to an affidavit recorded in the *History of the Church*, Volume 7, page 227 William Law tried to shoot Joseph Smith sometime in the middle of April 1844.

# 31

HANNAH'S HEART JUMPED TO her throat. She squeezed eight-year-old Joseph's hand. "There's your uncle Elias. See him?"

Joseph, who had been baptized by his father in the Mississippi River just weeks earlier, stood on the tips of his toes. "I think so," he said.

Hannah was too excited to consider that the boy really couldn't see his uncle. There were more than two thousands Saints converging on the Nauvoo Landing. And more than two hundred passengers were being disgorged from the *Maid of Iowa*. Even to her, it was a mass of confusion. She clung to Robert and her three other children, Lizzy, Willie, and Enoch. Hannah scanned the passengers looking for her mother.

Elias looked alarmingly like Henry—dark, unruly hair and a big barrel chest. Nevertheless, she plunged herself into his arms, tears welling in her eyes. "Mama's not here, is she?"

"No," Elias said slowly. "Sorry."

"Welcome to Nauvoo anyway."

"Thanks," came a deep voice. Elias had matured a lot in four years. His five-foot-eleven-inch frame carried a muscular, sinewy body. "Meet my wife, Mary."

Hannah pulled back to find herself looking at a petite five-foot-three-inch brunette, draped in a blue dress and bonnet. Mary Crook Eagles looked fatigued but happy, and was holding out a hand expecting a formal greeting.

"And welcome to you, too," Hannah said, pulling Mary to her bosom. "I'm so happy you came here."

Mary's nervousness was apparent. Hannah had another icebreaker. "You'll be staying with us for a few weeks. Then you can have our house. We're building a new one, out on our farm ground."

Mary looked pleased. "Really? We brought a tent...."

"A tent gets boring after a few weeks," Hannah said. She was still trying to cover her disappointment over the fact her mother was not in the Mormon company. "Mama's well, I assume?"

"And happy," Elias said. "Brother Roberts is good to her." Ann Eagles had married Samuel Roberts, father of Levi Roberts, shortly after returning home from Liverpool.

Elias was shaking hands with Robert and asking the obvious. "Where's Henry?"

"He avoids Mormon crowds," Robert said. "He lives near Carthage, several miles from here. You'll see him in a few days."

Hannah read Elias' disappointment. She changed the subject. "Robert had just been asked to serve on the Nauvoo police force. I'm really proud of him."

The welcoming crowd broke out into another hymn. A tear came to Mary's eye. "This is all so wonderful. I've dreamed of this for months."

Mary Crooks Eagles' dream city stood on two levels, one called the flat and one called the hill. She was standing only a half dozen feet above the Mississippi River high water mark where the city leveled off for seven blocks and then began a gradual ascent of sixty to seventy feet where it leveled off again into the Illinois prairie. Joseph Smith's home was nearby on the flat. The temple was on the hill, located on a bluff in the center of the city. Beyond the temple was the vast Illinois prairie. Most of the state's population of more than six hundred thousand people lived south of Springfield, in scattered settlements. Much of the state was hilly, some heavily timbered. Mammoth oaks, poplars, hickories, pecans, and other trees were abundant. Hillsides abounded in springs of clear water.

As Hannah contemplated Mary, she wondered what Mary's brother was like. Thomas Crook had married Hannah's younger sister, Jane. Hannah couldn't wait to ask the obvious question. "Do you think Jane will come to Nauvoo some day?"

Mary shrugged her shoulders. "They're thinking about it. But my parents are not well. My brother feels he needs to stay there, at least for a while."

"How's the Church doing in England these days?" Robert asked Elias.

Elias returned a shoulder shrug. "Fine, I suppose."

Robert guessed Elias was showing his disappointment over Henry not being here.

Nonetheless, Mary showed her knowledge. "The Cheltenham Conference is still one of the largest conferences in the Church there," she answered, referring to the general three-county area that included Apperley hamlet and Deerhurst parish. "A lot of people are joining the Church. Most of them want to come to America. I think there will be a lot of ships crossing the Atlantic Ocean carrying members of the Church. But poverty is still a huge problem at home. England is going through bad times, still."

Hannah was chagrined that Elias seemed a little tightlipped. Perhaps he would be more talkative later. Right now there was a large litany of tasks set before both the arriving and greeting Mormons. Dealing with the luggage and baggage. Listening to the Prophet's welcoming remarks. Reviewing assignments for temporary lodging. Finding lots and farm acreage. Utilizing tents for temporary housing. Constructing mud wattle huts, also for temporary housing. Organizing work forces to help build log cabins. Assessing the men's work talents, and assigning them to work on the temple.

And there were dozens and dozens of new immigrants to meet, such as William Kay, the company leader; the Thomas Steed family; the Richard

Slater family; and the Henry Wooley family.

In the White House, Orson Hyde sat staring at the President of the United States, John Tyler. Tyler, age fifty-four, had quickly impressed Orson with his plain, homespun, farmer-like personality and his religious convictions—an Episcopalian, the name given in America for followers of the Church of England. Tyler was tall and thin but looked a little unhealthy. He had a long hooknose under a receding gray hairline.

"It's hard to predict what will happen to your bill in Congress," Tyler was saying to Orson and his traveling companion, Orson Pratt. "But I don't think you ought to get your hopes up." Tyler had not been elected to office. As vice president, he became president upon the death of William Henry Harrison in 1841, the year Orson's second wife, Rebecca, had arrived in Nauvoo from England.

Orson already had a feeling that the President was correct. He and Elder Pratt had made several alternations in the Mormon Memorial Bill since they began lobbying members of Congress earlier in the week. As presently constituted, the bill still asked for a hundred thousand men from the United States to extend protection to people wishing to settle in Oregon territory and other portions of the United States, and extend protection to the people in Texas. That portion of the Mormon position especially appealed to President Tyler because he openly advocated the annexation of Texas into the Union. Orson had dropped Joseph Smith's request that Joseph be made a member of the U.S. Army, learning that Congress had no constitutional authority to appoint Joseph a member of the army with the power to raise troops as the original petition requested.

"But sir, our people have never been reimbursed for our losses in Missouri," Orson pleaded. The Mormon bill requested two million dollars to be deposited with the Nauvoo City Council, which would then allocated the money to members of the Church who had suffered property losses in that state.

As a father of eight children, Tyler had expressed sympathy over the murders of Mormon women and children in Missouri.

"I'm inclined to say that I would probably sign that bill if it came to my desk," the President said. "But your enemies have a very powerful lobby here. Members of Congress are in no enviable position, as you might guess. They get tugged at from both sides and they make decisions based on their ability to get re-elected."

Orson reluctantly nodded his understanding. The President had already expressed deep regret over what had happened in Missouri and had congratulated the Church for making a swampland in Illinois productive and building an impressive city there. The President spoke from a position of experience. As a Whig from Virginia, he had served in the U.S. House of Representatives and as a U.S. senator.

Orson didn't mention Joseph's candidacy for president, or his platform. But he had done just that to dozens of other influential men.

After spending a full hour with the President, Orson and Elder Pratt left the White House determined to spend more time with the committee on the judiciary for the Senate, which still held the original Mormon Memorial Bill.

"Joseph is serious about moving us out West some day, isn't he?" Elder Pratt asked.

"And equally serious about making certain it will safe out there," Orson stated.

The White House had impressed Orson, as did all the mammoth government buildings—as well as the wide expanses of green lawns, attractive pools, and many kinds of trees. But while the area immediately around the Capitol was impressive, the city was not. Structures ran from cheaply constructed buildings to outright shacks. The street lighting, except in the immediate area around the White House and the Capitol, was so bad that travel after nightfall involved the risk of stumbling into a chuckhole, crossing a vacant lot that might be filled with all sorts of refuse, or becoming the victim of a crossman with a pistol or knife in his hand. Creeks that flowed into the Potomac River carried raw sewage and gave off a sickening odor from rows of overused privies. These same creeks often became accidental swimming pools for stumbling drunks. During rainstorms, open sewers overflowed the banks and flooded Pennsylvania Avenue. When the weather turned warm, the same streets became a breeding ground for dust storms whipped by hot summer winds.

Washington, D. C., in Orson's view, was a city of magnificent intentions, but in reality a place of misguided plans, accidents of vision, and an obvious display of bad taste. All these things were carried to an ultimate height in this collection of incomplete villages that ran into each other in a helter-skelter manner, failing to produce anything other that chaotic ugliness.

Someday, Orson thought, it would be nice for President Tyler to visit Nauvoo—the beautiful city, a city planned and managed by a Prophet of the Lord.

It would be even more beautiful if the nation would reimburse Church members for their two million dollar loss in Missouri.

CHAPTER NOTES

The influx of new converts from the British Isles is amazing to contemplate. Source is *Saints on the Seas*, Conway B. Stone, University of Utah Press, 1983.

**Mormon Immigrant Companies**

| Vessel | # LDS | Port | Departure | Arrival | Port | Leader |
|---|---|---|---|---|---|---|
| Britannia | 41 | Liverpool | 6/6/1840 | 7/20/1840 | New York | J. Moon |
| North America | 201 | Liverpool | 9/8/1840 | 10/12/1840 | New York | T. Turley |
| Isaac Newton | 50 | Liverpool | 10/15/1840 | 12/2/1840 | New Orleans | S. Mulliner |
| Sheffield | 235 | Liverpool | 2/7/1841 | 3/30/1841 | New Orleans | H. Clark |
| Caroline | ? | ? | ? 1841 | ? 1841 | ? | T. Clark |
| Echo | 109 | Liverpool | 2/16/1841 | 4/16/1841 | New Orleans | D. Browett |
| Alesto | 54 | Liverpool | 3/17/1841 | 5/16/1841 | New Orleans | T. Smith |
| Rochester | 130 | Liverpool | 4/21/1841 | 5/20/1841 | New York | B. Young |
| Harmony | 50 | Bristol | 5/10/1841 | 7/12/1841 | Quebec | T. Kington |
| Caroline | 100 | Bristol | 8/8/1841 | 10/22/1841 | Quebec | T. Richardso |

| Tyrian | 207 | Liverpool | 9/21/1841 | 11/9/1841 | New Orleans | J. Fielding |
|--------|-----|-----------|-----------|-----------|-------------|-------------|
| Chaos | 170 | Liverpool | 11/8/1841 | 1/14/1842 | New Orleans | P. Melling |
| Tremont | 143 | Liverpool | 1/12/1842 | 3/10/1842 | New Orleans | Unknown |
| Hope | 270 | Liverpool | 2/5/1842 | 4/1/1842 | New Orleans | J. Burnham |
| John Cumming | 200 | Liverpool | 2/20/1842 | 4/26/1842 | New Orleans | Unknown |
| Hanover | 200 | Liverpool | 3/12/1842 | 5/2/1842 | New Orleans | A. Fielding |
| Sidney | 180 | Liverpool | 9/17/1842 | 11/11/1842 | New Orleans | L. Richards |
| Medford | 214 | Liverpool | 9/25/1842 | 11/13/1842 | New Orleans | O. Hyde |
| Henry | 157 | Liverpool | 9/29/1842 | 11/10/1842 | New Orleans | J. Snyder |
| Emerald | 250 | Liverpool | 10/29/1842 | 1/5/1843 | New Orleans | P. Pratt |
| Swanton | 212 | Liverpool | 1/16/1843 | 3/16/1843 | New Orleans | L. Snow |
| Yorkshire | 83 | Liverpool | 3/8/1843 | 5/10/1843 | New Orleans | T. Bullock |
| Claiborne | 106 | Liverpool | 3/21/1843 | 5/13/1843 | New Orleans | Unknown |
| Metoka | 280 | Liverpool | 9/5/1843 | 10/27/1843 | New Orleans | Unknown |
| Fanny | 210 | Liverpool | 1/23/1844 | 3/7/1844 | New Orleans | W. Kay |

# 32

*May 1844*

DANIEL FOUND HIMSELF STARING INTO the faces of Brigham Young and Willard Richards. Willard was seated and Brigham's five-foot-ten-inch frame was pacing back and forth in an elaborate room in the Masonic Temple, the new three-story building located on the corner of White Street and Main. Light flowing into the room through open windows made Brigham's sandy-brown hair seem a shade lighter. The fresh air brought smells of flowers blooming outside.

"Brethren, we've called you here for some advice," Brigham began. "Brother Richards and I have been assigned by the Prophet to write a letter to Brother Reuben Hedlock. He's our mission president in England. We wish to give him Church counsel regarding mission policy and future immigration."

Daniel slid his notebook onto a table. With all the commotion and controversy going on in Nauvoo right now, this was a welcome break. He felt a tinge of pride, rubbing shoulders with such good men.

Brigham pointed to William Kay, leader of a company of 210 Mormons who had recently arrived in Nauvoo. "Brother Kay carried a letter from Brother Hedlock. There are many questions to be answered. Policies to make."

Willard Richards spoke from a chair. "Each of you brethren led a company of Church members from Great Britain to Nauvoo. Your experience is valuable to us."

Daniel felt good, hoping he could contribute. His mind fell back to 1841 when he had been company leader on the *Echo*. He recalled the deadly weather, the immense ocean, and the crew of the ship.

Taking a deep breath, Daniel scanned the room. Not all the former company leaders had been able to respond. His gaze took in Theodore Turley—one of the first converts in England back in 1838. Theodore had built the very first new log home in Nauvoo. He went on a mission to England early in 1840, accompanying Wilford Woodruff and John Taylor. In late 1840, Theodore brought a group of converts to Nauvoo on the *North America*.

Seated next to Theodore was Daniel's old friend Thomas Kington, now fifty years old. Thomas was founder of the United Brethren congregation in England and had been company leader of the *Harmony* in 1841.

Around the room Daniel's eyes went: Joseph Fielding, former mission president in England, *Tyrian*, 1841. Lorenzo Snow, *Swanton*, 1843. Thomas Bullock, *Yorkshire*, 1843. And the most recent, William Kay, *Fanny*, 1844.

Brigham's blue-gray eyes seemed to read Daniel's mind. "I know what some of you brethren are thinking," Brigham said with a chuckle. "Where's Elder Wilford Woodruff?"

Daniel nodded, chuckling with Brigham. He had always appreciated the Apostle's humor and positive attitude. Brigham would turn forty-three in two weeks, but in some ways, Daniel thought, he looked and acted younger, despite the weight of his responsibilities.

"Elder Woodruff is probably more qualified than anyone to write this letter," added Brigham. But he's so busy right now trying to finish his new brick home, and getting ready for his summer mission back east, that the Prophet didn't include him in this assignment. But we'll certainly get his input."

Brigham had been company leader aboard the *Rochester,* in mid-1841 "The Spirit has whispered to us that Brother Hedlock should remain in England a little longer. He has done a good job."

William Kay raised his hand with the first suggestion. "The Saints in England are anxious to know about the temple. Give them some news about when you expect it to be completed."

Daniel agreed. After all, the Saints had gathered to Nauvoo for the express purpose of building a temple so that saving ordinances could be received.

"Our guess is about a year from now, maybe longer," Elder Richards said taking notes.

Daniel had the image of the temple and its dimensions emblazoned firmly in his mind: one hundred twenty feet long, eighty-eight feet wide, and sixty-five feet to the roof—reaching a staggering hundred feet above that when the spire was completed. To Daniel's satisfaction, the dazzling white temple built on the bluff overlooking the river and the surrounding farms, had been the subject of adoration among visitors to Nauvoo for several months. Its dramatic walls could be seen from more than a mile away.

Daniel felt himself in a near-trance, thinking about future temple ordinances, when William Kay spoke again.

"I think the brethren in England could use some more help," Kay added

Brigham nodded. "We met with the Prophet Joseph earlier today. More missionaries will be called and sent to Great Britain."

To Daniel's left, Willard was the one chuckling now, his chunky frame quaking. "Brethren, I can remember when Wilford Woodruff wrote me in England, in 1840. He had a similar problem. I call still recall his words: 'I can not do the work alone,' he said. 'I am called to baptize four or five times a day I want no better man than yourself to connect and labor with me here, and help me reap this mighty harvest.'"

Daniel let his gaze take in Thomas Kington, the man who had celebrated his fiftieth birthday just days earlier. No one in the world better knew what Elder Richards was saying, except perhaps John Benbow. Kington was smiling in remembrance. Back in those days, Elder Woodruff was in the process of baptizing all six hundred members of the organization Kington had started—the United Brethren. Daniel suspected that if a count were made, a third of them had immigrated to Nauvoo already.

William Kay was still making suggestions. "They could use more printed materials, more tracts, more everything." Taking a deep breath, Kay reported on the growth of the Church there. He also made a brief report of his trip from Liverpool to New Orleans, saying that Captain Patterson of the *Fanny* had been exceptional in his kindness to the Mormon passengers; the captain frequently let the Mormons use supplies from the ship's store whenever it was required.

That had been Daniel's experience, too, on the *Echo*. But not on the *Lady of New Orleans,* on the first leg of the trip up the Mississippi.

Daniel noted that Brigham and Willard were exchanging a quick glance. "I think we are at liberty to authorize Elder Hedlock to print as many pamphlets, hymn books, tracts, and cards as the missionaries and members can sell," Brigham said. "Including issues of the *Star.*"

It was Daniel's turn to say something. He cleared his throat. "I suppose it is assumed that they will emphasize sales of the Book of Mormon."

Daniel still cherished his personal copy, taken from one of the first boxes of the first printing in England. It had been given to him by Brigham Young, in Liverpool. John Benbow, with some assistance from Thomas Kington, had covered the cost of the printing.

Still writing, Willard nodded his approval. "You're correct, Brother Browett. It's the greatest missionary tool we have. We'll tell them to print all they need. They just don't need to print anything we can print in Nauvoo, and we're sending them a supply of materials."

"What about immigration policy?" Brigham asked. "We feel that all the British converts who can manage ought to come to Zion. There are those who

feel that we keep depleting the strength of the Church in England, Wales
Ireland, and Scotland. How do you brethren feel?"

Thomas Kington spoke. "Brethren, I have a question. Is the doctrine o
the gathering still in effect?"

Willard Richards stopped writing and locked eyes with Thomas. "It certainly is. The Prophet has strong feelings about it."

"Then that's what we should do—follow the Prophet," Kington said.

Thomas Bullock was next. "The economy is still in sad shape in Great
Britain. Folks are a lot better off here. Better to be anywhere in the United
States than stay in England."

Kington again: "We need more men like John Benbow. There's apt to be
many Saints who have the desire to come, but can't afford it. We started the
policy of the rich helping the poor. Let's continue it. If not, we won't be able
to continue bringing in skilled workers for the temple construction."

Daniel nodded his agreement. He thought of people like William W
Player, a master stonemason from Staffordshire. Player's arrival in 184
brought much-needed expertise to the pool of inexperienced laborers. At thi
very moment, nearly a hundred stonecutters were at work at the temple. He
also thought of Miles Romney, from Preston, who specialized in circular stair
cases. Daniel enjoyed the days when he helped Brother Romney.

"We've talked about the importance of maintaining a strong genera
shipping office in Liverpool," Brigham said.

To Daniel's right, Lorenzo Snow made a comment. "Our shipping agen
there has got to be loyal to the mission president. He needs to have a good
office, sleep on a good bed, shine his boots, wear good clothes, and put on a
good appearance."

Willard was writing again.

"I have a motion," Daniel said, raising his arm.

"Go ahead with it," Brigham said.

"Keep the letter positive."

Brigham responded with a smile. "Absolutely. We have no intention o
belaboring the Saints back in the British Isles about threats on the life of th

Prophet. Or that a bunch of apostates have organized a church right here in Nauvoo."

Daniel cringed, thinking of William and Wilson Law, Robert D. and Charles Foster, Chauncey L. and Francis Higbee, and others. There was a rumor circulating in Nauvoo that the apostates had ordered their own printing press. It was scheduled to arrive within a week.

"But if the apostates go through with their plans of establishing a mission in England, just to give us a bad time, we'll certainly send a warning," Brigham added. "But we can do that later. Right now, I agree, keep it positive."

The suggestions were coming fast now.

"Tell them about plans to build a dam opposite Montrose, to facilitate travel up the river to Nauvoo," Joseph Fielding said.

"Tell them that Latter-day Saints can be found almost everywhere in America," Thomas Bullock added. "If they can afford to only make it to the east coast, that's just fine. It's widespread knowledge that the gathering will continue here in Nauvoo until the temple is finished, so that the Saints can get their endowments. Remember that Hyrum Smith talked about this in April conference. After that, he said, the gathering will be from the nations to North and South America, which is the land of Zion."

Brigham interjected. "I suspect that before we fill North and South America, we will be removed to the Rocky Mountains."

Daniel thought seriously about that comment for several minutes as the western movement of the Saints was discussed. He thought about the construction of his frame home on the Illinois prairie, four miles east of Nauvoo. The thought entered his mind that perhaps he and Robert and their wives had acted in haste, that they should have saved their money for the move West—if it came.

Daniel recalled the day last month—April ninth to be exact—when the Prophet, along with his wife and a Dr. Goforth, had visited the English immigrant settlements, including the farm he and Robert owned. The Prophet had complimented everyone out there for the way the farms looked. Joseph had especially liked the peach trees.

"Or to the Republic of Texas," Lorenzo added. "Or New England, where Elder Woodruff has lots of relatives. Or Kirtland, where the Church is stil strong."

CHAPTER NOTES

Brigham Young and Willard Richards wrote a letter dated May 3, 1844, containing instructions on immigration matters to Reuben Hedlock, the mission president in England *(History of the Church*, Volume Six, pages 351-354). The author assumes that the two Apostle counseled people like Thomas Kington, Daniel Browett, and Thomas Bullock, for advice in what to say in the letter. The meeting purported in this chapter is fictional, however.

# 33

ROBERT SHOOK HIS HEAD NO. "Over my dead body will I be in the same room as the Law brothers. But I'd sure like to catch either of them in a back alley."

Seconds earlier, as they hoed weeds in their potato crop, Daniel had proposed that he and Robert listen to William and Wilson Law explain why they had formed their own church after their excommunication. The non-Mormon press in surrounding communities regarded it as a secessionist movement in the Kingdom of Joe Smith.

The Illinois prairie was bathed in balmy sunshine. Birds sang in the bushes. Beyond the rows of potatoes, Robert and Daniel's spring wheat had sprouted. Corn was three inches high. There was still a lot of work to tame their forty-acre farm—clearing timberland, cutting brush and burning it, splitting rails, pulling crosscut saws and whipsaws, plowing, harrowing, spading, planting, hoeing, fighting crop pests, cradling grain, killing hogs, raising houses...

"Why would I listen to a couple of apostates?" Robert asked. It made his mind gloomy just thinking about it. It was one thing for Daniel to be committed to his religion and his two wives, but showing even a spark of commitment to the apostates was beyond the possibility of imagination. His skin tingled with hatred as he thought about the Laws and their hooligan friends. The Laws, along with two other sets of brothers—Chauncey and Elias Higbee, and Robert and Charles Foster—were wicked opportunists in Robert's opinion. The six men had taken advantage of the element of mystery in the Prophet Joseph Smith's private teachings regarding plural marriage. They had spread the falsehood that Joseph approved of promiscuous intercourse between the sexes—that there was no harm in it if it were kept secret. But when their own wickedness was discovered, and when the Prophet boldly denounced it, it had brought the wrath of those apostates upon Joseph Smith.

Robert stopped hoeing for a minute, thinking about the excommunicated apostates. William Law had fallen about as far as a member of the Church could fall. William had served as Joseph's second counselor in the First Presidency for two years. Wilson Law had been suspended as major general of the Nauvoo Legion. Dr. Robert D. Foster had been relieved of his office as surgeon general of the Legion. Francis Higbee had contracted venereal disease from prostitutes. Chauncey Higbee had seduced three women with the promise of making them his spiritual wives. In Robert's opinion, the men epitomized the bad children of the world—willful, egotistical, and poised to break up faltering patterns of order.

"I asked you a question," Robert repeated, leaning on his hoe. "Why would I be in the same room with those apostates? Why would I court the devil?"

Daniel drew a deep breath, thinking. "Simple. We need to protect our wives and all our friends in the English community."

There was a peevish toss of Robert's head. "What do you mean?"

"I'd be the last one to join this crazy church the Laws have started," Daniel said, wiping sweat from the side of his bulbous nose. "But I want to hear all their arguments firsthand. That way, I can learn how to counter their logic, point by point. Then if anyone asks, I'll be prepared."

Robert rolled his eyes. This was a poor way for Daniel to show his insecurity. He had created an unappetizing dilemma. "Then you can tell *me* later, too."

"Come, go with me," Daniel pleaded. "A lot of our friends will be there."

"No." The peculiar knot in Robert's stomach was still there.

"It'll be interesting. We'll not invite our wives. It'll just be us, and the Law brothers."

"I thought the Higbees and the Fosters were part of this. And William Marks."

"They are. But all the apostates had a meeting a couple of weeks ago at Wilson Law's place. They organized themselves into committees to visit different families in the city, to proselyte converts. The Law brothers were assigned to the English immigrants."

"I'm warning you," Robert said, balling his fists. "If I'm in the same room with Wilson Law, I'll break his jaw. Hey…that rhymes."

Against his better judgment, Robert went to the meeting. It was held in the spacious William Law home, on the northeast corner of Water and Granger Streets. It smelled of spice cake just out of the oven and the hint of an unemptied chamber pot from the bedroom. William's wife, Jane, smelled of expensive French perfume. She touched Robert's hand with her cool jeweled fingers, crinkled her blue eyes at him and the others, and then set pieces of cake in front of each man. She then excused herself. "I'm going for a walk."

Robert felt sorry for Jane, who obviously made a mistake when she married William. And he felt sorry for the recently deceased Elizabeth Sikes Law, former wife of Wilson Law. A former schoolteacher, she had died of an unknown ailment in March. In Robert's mind, she probably died of disappointment in her apostate husband's actions. The Laws had lost their spiritual compass and their wives and children were going to suffer.

Two sights struck Robert as he and Daniel took a chair with a handful of other English converts in the William Law home. First were the two Law brothers, looking nearly alike with their sandy hair, full mutton-chop side-burns, beards growing under their chins but not on it, and dressed in fine gray suits with gold watch chains apparent. Second was the absence of wall deco-rations. Most homes in Nauvoo displayed some kind of a painting of the Savior on the wall. As to the gaudy wealth of the ostentatious Law brothers so boldly displayed, Robert refrained from envy. He had long ago learned that envy was the source of much unhappiness.

"I feel awkward being here," Robert whispered, pensively fingering his sideburns. "What if the Prophet finds out? Or his brother, Hyrum? Or Elder Woodruff?" Robert had refused to shake hands with the Law brothers as he entered the house. Right now, the Laws were greeting George Bundy and John Gailey.

"Don't worry," Daniel shot back, the opposite of nervousness. "All we have to do is come out of here as more fervent defenders of the faith. This new religion isn't going to amount to anything. Trust me." He relaxed and sat back in his chair.

Suddenly, Robert found himself exchanging appraising glances with Wilson Law, but no words. Stone-faced, Robert had no doubt that Wilson remembered him from last year when the posse rescued Joseph Smith. The majority of people with weak or no testimonies were harmless, nothing worse than a low capacity to irritate—worse than chiggers but not as bad as bedbugs. But the apostates in this room gave Robert a dark feeling. He wasn't about to lay aside his caution.

Robert remained skeptical as William Law, a blue-eyed Irishman, began speaking. His voice was high, authoritative, smug, and impatient. Hatred of the Prophet quickly became apparent, citing Joseph's political and financial influence. His words expressed a world of contempt for the way things were in the Mormon kingdom.

Robert balled his fists and visualized pounding the apostate's face. At only five feet nine and a hundred seventy-five pounds, William wouldn't be much of a match for him.

Robert nibbled on the spice cake as he scanned the small crowd assembled on the expensive imported furniture. His fellow Englishmen—John Benbow, Thomas Kington, John Cox, Levi Roberts, Joseph Hill, William Pitt, George Bundy, John Gailey, and newcomer Richard Slater—were glued to their seats. Their expressions were giving way to cold, mutinous glares, aimed at the Law brothers.

"I know you folks are wondering why I turned against Joseph Smith and started this new church," William was saying, appearing dark and potent. William stood in the center of the parlor, purposefully towering over his seated audience. His lips had curled into a proud smirk.

Robert felt tense. He suspected Daniel would be taking both mental and real notes. As for himself, he was learning how to hate all over again. He suspected that after tonight he would hate these apostates far more than he had ever hated Henry Eagles.

William Law spoke in oratory fashion, bringing up old charges against Joseph Smith—that the Prophet had been disobeying the laws of the land for his own convenience, and that it was wrong for the Prophet to unite both church and state in Nauvoo, even though the city charter allowed it. "Joseph has been manipulating politicians for his private purposes for too long."

As he talked, William seemed to lock eyes with Robert all too often. This disconcerted Robert. He seldom lost eye-to-eye confrontations, but this time Robert shifted his glance to Daniel, and then to the others, who were watching with lively interest. Robert fumbled at his cake, not eating.

Scarlet-faced Wilson Law, three inches taller and thirty pounds heavier than William, rose to join his brother. He had a large defiant mouth, half-closed analytic eyes, full sandy hair, and a somewhat sloping face suggesting an obstinate will. Convulsing as he talked, his blue eyes flaring with anger, he sounded off about economic matters. He took offense that Joseph Smith openly promoted Church building lots on the flats in preference to the Law brothers' privately offered lots on the bluff. He accused the Prophet of using Nauvoo House donations to buy land and sell it to converts at a profit. Wilson advocated that work on the Nauvoo House, and even on the temple, be postponed until everyone in Nauvoo had a decent lot and house.

The thought of halting work on the temple shook Robert and a renewed seething hatred for Wilson Law came over him. Greed of the Law brothers was apparent. Things in Nauvoo would be fine, in their eyes, if everyone bought *their* lots, and bought *their* lumber from *their* sawmill.

It was a well-known fact that the Laws and the Fosters were buying lumber from Wisconsin, running it through their mill, and reselling it for home and commercial construction. That despite the fact that the Wisconsin lumber was really intended for the temple. The apostates had further complicated matters by hiring away temple workers, paying them cash to join their construction crews. Those things had angered Joseph Smith and other Church authorities. In turn, Joseph was now trying to persuade the brethren not to work for the Fosters and the Laws, and to return to their duties at the temple despite the fact the Church paid them in kind—with goods instead of with cash.

"Joe Smith has too much control," Wilson said, his tone acid. "He must be stopped."

Wilson Law's prejudiced, half-mad, somewhat pathetic air made Robert laugh. And Robert bristled at the words, *Joe Smith.* That's what the enemies of the Church and the outside world called the Prophet.

Robert balled his fists. He had disliked Wilson Law ever since the day Wilson had delayed the Mormon rescue posse eleven months ago, whining about money. Robert still didn't know if Wilson Law accounted for all seven hundred dollars Brigham Young had given him.

As suddenly as he had begun speaking, Wilson stopped and sat down. William took over again. His eyes became tiny slits as he leveled more charges at Joseph Smith. "And more important than all these, I believe your Prophet has corrupted the Church by introducing some very damnable doctrines," William added.

The words took a long moment to register in Robert's mind. He scratched his head, and then his arm shot up. "And what would those be?"

William whirled like an angry ox to face the man who had interrupted him. "The plurality of gods, for one."

Robert dried up for a moment, thinking. Then it came to him. "You did-n't like the King Follet sermon, I take it."

"Calm down, Robert," Daniel said, trying to restore order. "Let him have the floor."

A groan escaped Robert's lips. He felt a fury rising from deep within. "Next he's going to attack you, Daniel. I can feel it coming."

William Law stood for a moment in utter bewilderment. Until now, he thought that plural marriage had been practiced only by Church leaders. Like Joseph Smith and Orson Hyde. "This must mean that Mr. Browett has an extra wife or two."

Robert rose to his feet. He was in a black fidget, the veins on his neck showing. "What of it? Do you and your brother have a suicide pact? Keep spouting off and you're apt to get your wish. I've feelings all bottled up inside and I'm dying to let them out."

Wilson Law rose to his feet also, and stepped between Robert and William. "We didn't invite you here to start a fight," he said. "But if you want one, step outside."

"Nothing would suit me better," said Robert, glaring at Wilson now. The two men were about the same height and width. "Besides, I think it was you who wrote that article in the *Warsaw Message* last February."

Wilson played dumb. His down-curved mouth was rigid and tense. "What article?"

Robert's laugh was an eerie chortle. "That piece of doggerel you called 'Buckeye's Lamentations for the Want of More Wives.'"

"I did not," the apostate sputtered.

Robert felt his skin crawl. "Yes, you did. You're Buckeye."

Wilson Law was defiant. "Not me."

"You probably have it memorized, since you wrote it." Robert drew a crumpled piece of paper out of his pocket, unfolded it, and thrust it into Wilson Law's face.

Law hesitated, like a child caught in the act of lying to his parents.

Robert glared at the apostate, his focus total. "Clever words, Irishman. I ought to shove them down your throat."

An uneasiness crossed Wilson's face. "You've always had a quick mouth I never did like Englishmen. You talk funny."

Robert felt Daniel's arms wrap around him. "We promised these men we would listen politely. Sit down, Robert."

"I didn't make any such promise," Robert said, grunting in disgust.

"Then leave," Wilson said. "Or you'll get blown down, just like the Seventies Hall did a few weeks ago." The younger Law brother referred to the fact that a strong wind from the west blew down a portion of the west wall of the new building, located on Bain Street.

Robert glared at his new enemy. "I suppose you were behind that, too. Wouldn't surprise me if you weakened the supports."

"Get out, or I'll throw you out," Wilson said, his anger brimming.

"You and who else?"

Daniel's arm wrap tightened as the two men stood scarlet-faced, regarding each other, glowering. "Robert?" Daniel said, pulling now.

"I didn't want to be here in the first place," Robert growled. He found the door and stormed outside. The door slammed behind him.

Daniel threw his arms apart. "I think the rest of us will stay and hear you out," he said, trying to sound regretful. He found his chair and sat down.

CHAPTER NOTES

Wilson Law's poem appeared in the Feb. 7, 1844, issue of the *Warsaw Messenger:*

### Buckeye's Lamentations for the Want of More Wives

1.

I once thought I had knowledge great,

But now I find 'tis small;

I once thought I'd Religion too,

But now I find I've none at all —

For I have but *One lone wife,*

And can obtain no more;
And the doctrine is, I can't be saved,
Unless I've *half a score!*.

2.

The NARROW GATE that Peter kept,
In ages long ago,
Is locked and barred since he gave up
The keys to BEARDLESS Jo.
And Jo proclaims it is too small,
And causes great delay,
And that he has permission got
To open the BROAD WAY.

3.

The Narrow gate did well enough
When Peter, James and John,
Did lead the Saints on Zion-ward
In SINGLE FILE along;
When bachelors, like good old Paul,
Could win the glorious prize
And MAIDS without a MARRIAGE-RITE,
Reach "mansions in the skies."

4.

But we have other teaching now,
Of great glories far;
How a SINGLE GLORY'S nothing more
Than some lone twinkling star.
The TWO-FOLD glory's like the moon,
That shines so bright at night,
Reflecting from her gracious Lord

Whatever he thinks right.

5.

A TENFOLD glory — that's the prize!
Without it you're undone!
But with it you will shine as bright
As the bright shining sun.
There you may shine like mighty Gods,
Creating worlds so fair —
At least a WORLD for every WIFE
That you take with you there.

6.

The man that has got ten fair wives,
TEN worlds may create;
And he that has got less than this,
Will find a bitter fate.
The one or two that he might have,
He'll be deprived of then;
And they'll be given as TALENTS were
To him who has got TEN.

7.

And 'tis so here, in this sad life —
Such ills you must endure —
Some *priest* or *king,* may claim your wife
Because that you are poor.
A REVELATION he may get —
Refuse it if you dare!
And you'll be damned perpetually,
By our good *Lord* the *Mayor.*

8.

But if that you yield willingly,
Your daughters and your wives,
In *spiritual marriage* to our POPE,
He'll bless you all your lives;
He'll *seal you up,* be damned you can't,
No matter what you do —
If that you only stick to him,
He swears HE'LL take you through."

9.

He'll lead you on through the broad gate,
Which he has opened wide —
In SOLID COLUMNS you shall march,
And enter side by side.
And no delay you'll meet with there,
But "forward march" you shall; —
For he's not only our LORD Mayor
But Lord Lieutenant Gene-RAL.

10.

This is the secret doctrine taught
By Joe and the red rams —
Although in public they deny —
But then 'tis all a sham.
They fear the indignation just,
Of those who have come here,
With hands that's clean and honest hearts
To serve the Lord in fear.

11.

Thus, all the TWELVE do slyly teach,

And slyly practice too;

And even SAGE PATRIARCH,

Won't have untied his shoe;

For sure, 'twould be quite impolite,

If not a great disgrace,

To have a WIDOW sister fair

Spit in a Prophet's face!

12.

But Jo at snaring beats them all

And at the rest does laugh;

For *widows* poor, and *orphan girls,*

He can ensnare with *chaff.*

He sets his snares around for all, —

And very seldom fails

To catch some thoughtless PARTRIDGES,

SNOW-birds or KNIGHT-ingales!

13.

But there are a hundred other birds

He never can make sing;

Who won't be dragged to hell.

By *prophet, priest nor king.*

Whose sires have bled in days gone by,

For their dear country's cause;

And who will still maintain its rights,

Its *liberty* and *laws!*

# 34

*May 1844*

THE MORE WILLIAM AND WILSON LAW whined the more Daniel wished he had left the house with Robert.

William was talking again, pacing the floor in his imported suit. A pure gold watch chain glittered in the light. William complained that the Nauvoo charter ought to be wholesale repealed, that it gave the municipal court too much power. He contended that the court should not have freed Joseph last July after the kidnapping incident. Incredibly, he said that Joseph should have been extradited to Missouri. William also whined about the election—in which the Whig candidate, Cyrus Vance, lost, even though Joseph Smith had promised him the Mormon vote. William said that he overheard Joseph promising Vance that "nine out of ten Mormon votes," would go his way. Yet nearly all the votes were given to the Democrat, Hoge, who was ultimately elected. William whined about Hyrum Smith's passionate plea to a Mormon assembly, asking Church members to vote for Hoge.

Daniel came unglued when William alleged that Joseph Smith had ignored the established order of the Church when the Prophet excommuni cated William from the Church. *What do you expect if you don't support th Prophet, your priesthood leader?*

William's eyes were puffy, and he was wilting in disappointment. "I con fess I was annoyed very much by such unprecedented treatment. It was all ver much illegal. I was appointed by so-called revelation and sustained by a unan imous vote at general conferences. Joseph and Hyrum weren't even there at m trial of excommunication. I didn't even learn of my excommunication until day after the trial."

*That's right. That's the way it should be,* Daniel recalled. The trial had bee presided over by Brigham Young, president of the Twelve Apostles. Becaus the Prophet had dropped William Law from the First Presidency in Januar of this year, the court handled the case as if William were an ordinary mem ber of the Church.

Daniel neared the end of his patience when William launched a tirad against plural marriage. William complained that he knew nothing c polygamy until the spring of 1843. "I was just turned upside down when th Prophet told me about plural marriage last summer," William said. "I talke to my wife about it."

Daniel turned his head, trying to hide his laugh.

"Brother Browett," William said. "This is no laughing matter. Do yo know that Joseph tried to make my wife, Jane, one of his spiritual wives? Ho do you suppose that made me feel?"

Daniel swallowed hard, holding his tongue. He knew the true stor Shortly after the revelation about celestial marriage had been made publi William approached Joseph Smith. William requested that he and Jane k married for eternity. Joseph presented the matter to the Lord. Receiving a answer, Joseph said it could not be done because William had been disobed ent to several gospel principles, including the law of chastity. When Jane aske why the ceremony could not be performed, Joseph refused to tell her, hopir to spare her feelings. As Joseph was passing her neighborhood several days later, Jane beckoned to him. She said, "If you won't seal me to my husband, seal me to you." Joseph gently rejected her proposal, and left. Spurned, her feelings hurt, Jane twisted the truth. She told William that Joseph proposed that she become one of his "spiritual wives."

Tirade after tirade followed, with William spinning his side of the argument. He told how he had demanded that Joseph either confess his desire to marry Jane, repent before the High Council, or have his sins "exposed to the world."

Daniel colored at William's version of the story.

"Joe Smith told me that such a confession would mean the downfall of the Church," William said. "I told him that was inevitable. He then replied to me, 'Then we can all go to Hell together and convert it into a heaven by casting the Devil out.' He also said, 'Contrary to the opinion of this world of fools, hell was quite an agreeable place.' Can you imagine such logic?"

Daniel scanned the room. His English friends had doubt and disgust scored on their faces.

Next, William talked of how Joseph's "Destroying Angels" were after him. How he and his brother began exchanging views with other disaffected Mormons, including William Marks, Austin Cowles, Leonard Soby, the Higbees, and the Fosters. He told about secret meetings, defending himself in the Nauvoo Municipal Court, and reacting against articles in the *Nauvoo Neighbor*. In one of the articles, Francis Higbee was openly accused by Church editors of seduction, adultery, perjury, and contracting a venereal disease from prostitutes. The other Higbee—Chauncey—was confronted with old charges of the Bennett days, having seduced three women with the promise of making them his spiritual wives.

Daniel held up a rigid palm, cutting William Law off in mid-sentence. "William, we came here to learn about your new church. All you've done is complain about ours—the Church of Jesus Christ of Latter-day Saints."

William Law put a hand to his chin. "Oh, I see."

"*Well?*" Daniel put forth.

"It's really very simple," William said. "Joseph Smith is a fallen Prophet We still accept the Book of Mormon, and most of the revelations in the Doctrine and Covenants."

"Most?"

"All except the one about sealings, and plural marriage. And we reject the doctrine of the gathering. It is contrary to the will of God. Too much haste too much sacrifice. We are united in virtue and truth. We set hell at defiance and all her agents. That means God has rejected Joe Smith, and his followers."

John Benbow raised his hand. "And what do you propose to call your church?"

"The Reformed Mormon Church."

Daniel felt something cold and sharp dance along his spine, making him shudder, as he contemplated the name. He wished they had used something like the William Law Church.

"And the head of your Church?" Benbow asked.

"Me, of course."

"Your counselors?" Thomas Kington queried.

"Why, my brother, Wilson. And Austin A. Cowles."

Kington asked another question. "And I suppose you have a Quorum of Twelve Apostles?"

"In the process. So far, Robert D. Foster, James Blakesley, and Francis M Higbee."

*All adulterers,* Daniel said to himself.

George Bundy raised a question. "The bishop of your church?"

"Charles Ivins. With Dr. Green and John Scott, Sr., as counselors."

Levi Roberts: "All the men you have named are scouring the city for additional members?"

"Yes. We already have an impressive following. Last Sunday there was large crowd at my home. I preached a sermon. So did Brother Blakesley."

*A houseful of apostates,* Daniel thought. "What's your goal?"

"To discredit Joe Smith. Force his resignation."

Daniel's skin crawled in revulsion. He wished the Prophet had not toler ated these enemies for so long. "And I suppose you would take his place."

"That's what the Lord wants. Joe Smith is a fallen Prophet."

Quickly now, in his mind, Daniel recalled the first chapter of Alma in the Book of Mormon. Daniel compared the roomful of apostates to Nehor. Nehor had been guilty of *bearing down against the Church,* just as the apostates were doing. *Teaching doctrines that were popular with men, but not with God, for the sake of riches and honor. Establishing a church after the manner of their own teaching. Wearing costly apparel. Loving the vain things of the world.*

As Daniel was thinking of those things, John Benbow asked another question. "What do you propose to do next?"

"We're having a hard time getting our story out," William said. "Your Mormon newspapers are one-sided. So we've ordered a printing press."

Daniel acted aghast, as though he hadn't heard. "A printing press?"

"It'll arrive from St. Louis tomorrow. We'll have our own newspaper very soon."

# 35

HENRY EAGLES DELAYED THE VISIT TO NAUVOO to greet his younger brother until he had confidence he could win the verbal confrontation he would initiate with Robert and Daniel. Ignoring his wife and child, he sat on his buckboard behind a team of horses, plugging their way along a muddy road, constantly rehearsing his side of the arguments. He paid scant attention to the resplendent wildflowers mingled with rich prairie grasses that dotted the western Illinois landscape between his small farm near Carthage and the overflowing Mormon city of Nauvoo. Rain had pummeled the prairie the day before, but today, Wednesday, the eighth of May, a bright sun peeked through intermittent puffy clouds.

In Henry's mind, today would be a heyday. How could Robert and Daniel defend Mormonism with all that was going on in Nauvoo? Some of the biggest names in Mormondom had defaulted against Joe Smith and formed their own church. One of them, William Law, had been Joe's counselor in the First Presidency! Rumors about polygamy were running rampant throughout anti-Mormon communities such as Carthage and Warsaw. Even

Daniel had taken a second wife! For all Henry knew, perhaps Robert had a second wife, too. A Masonic Temple had been dedicated a month ago in Nauvoo. Now, Joe Smith had copied the rituals of the Masons for eventual use in the Mormon temple. Joe Smith was still the number one suspect in the attempted murder of Boggs in Missouri. In desperation, Joe had sent polygamist Orson Hyde to Washington, D. C., to beg the government for help. Ole Joe still wanted tax money to be used to pay Mormons for what they lost in Missouri. How absurd! Mormons shouldn't have riled up Missourians in the first place. Wilford Woodruff and other Mormon Apostles were expected to leave on begging missions within days.

A mischievous smile came to Henry's face. He had already fortified himself with several swigs of corn whiskey. By the time he got through with Robert and Daniel, little Brother Elias and his new wife would beg to become partners in the Henry Eagles Dairy, just outside Carthage.

The letter from Hannah had said to meet them at the Browett-Harris farm, east of the city. That's where two new frame homes were being constructed. Hannah had asked Henry to help with the construction, but Henry had ignored the requests. Today, he planned on winning his arguments, planting the seed with Elias about the dairy, and whisking himself back to Carthage and its friendly confines.

The sight of the two nearly identical frame homes going up shocked Henry. He experienced an inner devastation of sorts, that the houses could be framed so quickly. That's what infuriated him the most about the Mormons. They worked together too much. He didn't see that in his Carthage and Warsaw friends. It was every man for himself, in the true spirit of the American frontier. John Cox was shingling Robert's roof, along with Levi Roberts and Edward Phillips. Another crew, John Hyrum Green, Thomas Kington, and Joseph Hill were mixing plaster, obviously intended for Robert's interior walls. John Benbow and William Pitt were painting the exterior a bright white. Even Thomas Bloxham, a non-Mormon, was helping them.

"We have an extra paint brush," Hannah told her brother as he stepped out of the buckboard. "Work hard. You could store up manna from heaven."

Henry's dark eyes were the color of coffee and he outright spurned the invitation. He scanned the two new homes, and the work crews. He was massive and powerful looking. "Where's Elias?"

Robert helped Katherine Eagles and her small daughter, Annie, out of the buckboard. "He's inside, helping the plasterers."

Henry fumed, knowing that his brother-in-law was probably fighting to keep his voice empty of the sentimental pity he felt for her. The two men exchanged heated glances.

Outwardly, Henry pretended he was unaffected by his brother-in-law's fixed hostile expression. "Which bedroom is he working on—Elizabeth's or Harriet's? Or is it a room for wife number three?"

"Harriet's," he replied.

"And how many wives do you have now, Bobby?"

"Robert," Hannah corrected her brother.

Henry could tell by Hannah's tone that he was getting on her nerves. That pleased Henry. Hannah hated for him to use Robert's old nickname. "That's his pre-baptism worldly pugilistic name," she had told him time and time again.

Henry did not flinch. He waited for an answer, glaring at his despised brother-in-law. *Let the games begin.*

Robert began to laugh. "Just one wife for me, Henry. For now. But I'm having a dozen new ones imported from Philadelphia. Brother Orson Hyde has my order."

Henry scoffed for a second and then smiled when he saw his sister give Robert an elbow. As always, her self-control was giving away.

"Don't say things like that to Henry," Hannah said. "He might take you seriously."

Daniel Browett approached, holding out a friendly hand. "Good to see you, Henry."

Henry accepted the handshake, suspecting that Daniel was feigning the jovial tone. "How's Rebecca?" he asked. "Has she left the red-headed Apostle yet? My offer still stands. I'd love to have her as my spiritual wife." He took off his hat, wet his fingers with his mouth, and smoothed his coal black hair. "She's fine," Daniel bristled, his tone sharp. "Just leave her alone."

Henry contemplated Daniel's warning as Elizabeth sauntered up, over-dressed in a yellow cabriolet bonnet with flaring blue trim that matched her blue crinoline skirt. She ignored Henry, preferring to talk to Katherine. "You're just in time for lunch. Can you give us a hand?"

"I should have brought something," Katherine said, looking at the ground, but clutching her two-year-old daughter tightly.

A sheep barbecued whole over coals of wood burned in a pit, covered with green boughs to keep the juices in.

"*Nonsense,*" Elizabeth said, pointing to a collection of sawbuck tables, their X-shaped trestle legs holding a collection of food. "Sister Roberts brought plenty of bacon and collard greens. Sister Benbow made succotash. Sourdough bread from Sister Cox. Pan-dowdy from Sister Kington. There's Dutch oven prairie chicken fixins. Bullock heart. Calf's head. Corn pones. We've got *everything* except fresh garden vegetables. But we've *already* planted a new garden patch, see over there?"

"You've been busy," Katherine replied, mystified. She had no personal friends at all in Carthage. She clutched at her daughter, holding on tight.

"This is my new *best* friend," Elizabeth said as she reached toward Harriet. Daniel's first wife had her same old naïve mushy charm.

Harriet was bareheaded, her dark hair wound in a topknot. She was dressed in green, with a paisley shawl draped over her shoulders. She returned a warm smile, and then gave Katherine a little hug. "Nice to meet you, Sister Eagles."

Henry overhead the greeting. "None of that 'Sister Eagles' business," he said in a sharp voice. "I don't let Katherine attend Mormon meetings, so I reckon she's not a Mormon anymore."

Katherine ignored Henry. "Do we have time to peek inside before lunch? I'd like to see the interior of both homes."

Elizabeth whisked Katherine and her young daughter away, with Harriet and Hannah following. "Sure—we'd be delighted to show you."

"Come along, Henry," Hannah said tentatively. "Inside is where you'll find your brother. Elias is anxious to see you." She walked toward the two-story framed Browett house, set on a stone foundation. Its symmetry was pleasing, borrowed from the Orson Hyde home in Nauvoo, although a little larger to accommodate two wives and a mother. Its outside dimensions were twenty by thirty-two feet. There was a porch across the front with four squared posts. Two windows flanked a door in the center.

Henry and Katherine stepped onto finished planks that lined the floor. Henry glared at his wife indicating she was to say nothing at all about the planks or any feature of the house. Their cabin near Carthage had a dirt floor. Henry had refused Katherine's request to put down at least a puncheon floor—split logs, with their faces smoothed with a hatchet.

Elizabeth took over. "This is the parlor," she said, letting her arm sweep the room. The smell of plaster was strong.

Henry scoffed at Elizabeth. "I suppose you'll wreck Daniel's budget by wanting new furniture," he said.

Daniel's wife was up to the challenge. Her voice was high, crisp, and very British. "What you *don't* know won't hurt you, Henry, old chap. Daniel's ordered me a *new* spindle-backed Boston rocker, stenciled with gilt. It'll go *wonderful* with the Victorian furniture we also have on order. Our tables will have marble tops. Three beds: one for me, one for Harriet, one for Martha, all with turned bedposts. We chose mushroom-turned wooden knobs for handles for our chest of drawers."

Henry's jaw dropped. He had always considered Elizabeth a reckless self-dramatizer, but this was far worse than he had imagined. He failed to realize Elizabeth was pulling his leg.

Katherine, however, was chuckling.

Elizabeth was not done. She stepped into an equally large kitchen. "Of course Daniel *could* build me a nice dining table. But the black walnut Victorian table that's coming from New York will look *nice* in here, don't you *think,* Henry?"

Henry ignored Elizabeth this time. He was looking at the narrow staircase. "How many bedrooms up there? I assume you have one for Elizabeth, one for Harriet, and a couple of extra ones for any new wives that come along."

Ignoring her brother's jibes, Hannah yelled up the stairs. "Elias! Are you there?"

There was an echoing sound of footsteps above Hannah's head. Elias appeared at the upstairs doorway with dabs of plaster sticking to his shirt and britches.

"Hello, little brother," Henry said, his head tilting upward. An open mouth revealed a few missing teeth, a by-product of his pub-brawling days in England.

Elias bounded down the stairs. "It's about time you came to see me."

As the brothers embraced, Henry said, "We live in Carthage. That's why we weren't there to greet you at the landing."

"But you could have come earlier," Elias said with a puzzled look. His brother's hand felt warm and damp as he shook it. "It has been three weeks."

Henry waved Elias off and abruptly changed the subject. "How much money did you bring? We could buy more cows and expand the dairy. You can be my partner."

Mary Crooks Eagles followed Elias down the stairs. Lines of determination graced her face. "Elias, I don't want to live anywhere but Nauvoo. I like the thoughts of living in Hannah's cabin as soon as she moves out here."

"This must be your wife, Elias." Henry held out a hand. She refused to take it, which pleased him all the more. To his eyes, she looked worn out and pale, unworthy of his brother. He looked forward to the days that he could draw her into arguments over religion and any other subject of his choosing.

The two Eagles brothers talked for a few minutes about their mother's marriage to Samuel Roberts, the dairy in Apperley, and the trip across the Atlantic. During the conversation, Henry looked into the upstairs bedrooms. There were four. Obviously one for Elizabeth, one for Harriet, one for Daniel's mother, and another for future children.

"How long do you expect to live here?" Henry asked, glancing around, aware of prying eyes.

Daniel flashed a contemptuous smile. "We haven't even moved in yet."

"But I've heard Ole Joe Smith is already talking about you Mormons moving West. If you have to give this place away, I'll take it."

"Give it away?" A smoldering rage was building in Daniel's chest. He had not poured blood, sweat, and tears into his new house and farm just to give it away.

"If all you Mormons move away at once, your property won't be worth much. Maybe I'd buy it, if the price is low enough."

Elizabeth drew her mouth to a pout. "We plan on being here for a long time."

"Don't stay too long," Henry warned, a wild look crossing his face. " know some folks around Carthage and Warsaw who would just as soon burn you out as look at you."

Elizabeth gasped. "Are you one of them, Henry?"

"What difference does that make?" Henry replied. "There're so many people out there who hate Mormons it doesn't matter."

"Every drop of rain adds to the ocean, Henry. It matters to me. If you're one of them, I'm going to take a frying pan and mash your head in." Elizabeth sounded serious.

Henry suspected that Elizabeth's mind was seeing the new home going up in flames. He smiled wickedly. Since his move to Carthage, and rubbing shoulders with the people there, Henry had a vision of his own. He could see the homes of all the English immigrants east of Nauvoo going up in flames.

Hannah tugged at Henry's gray shirt. "Want to see our house before lunch?"

"I suppose it looks the same," Henry said, sounding disinterested.

"Well, I want to see it, Hannah," Katherine responded.

The new Harris frame home was, in fact, a carbon copy of the Browet house. Chimneys stood as sentinels at both ends of the top roof, protecting four bedrooms. In the Harris home, the bedrooms would be used for children not an extra wife, nor a mother, or even a mother-in-law.

# 36

MINUTES LATER, ELIZABETH SIGNALED Susannah Green, who picked up a small bell and rang it. Rich smells hung in the air: roast meat, wood smoke, and the fragrance of blooming flowers. Soon the workers were piling their pewter plates high with food. The women sat at the tables. The men sat on the prairie grass in a circle. Elias sat on one side of his brother. Robert sat on the other side of Henry. *Family togetherness,* Robert thought.

Henry wolfed down his food without chewing, to Robert's disgust. First to finish, he rubbed his nose, a mannerism that signaled an itch to argue. His square face remained placid. "I hear Joe Smith's best friend has started another church. I believe his name is William Law. Ole Joe's trusted counselor?"

Robert rolled his eyes as Henry's words floated through the group. "You oughta publish a newspaper, Henry. You're plumb full of information."

John Benbow did not see the humor in Henry's remarks and he was clearly ruffled. "William Law is *not* the Prophet's best friend. Joseph Smith has long suspected that there was a right hand Brutus near him."

"Proves that Joe Smith is not a Prophet after all," Henry exclaimed. "No

Prophet of God would have a traitor as a counselor."

Benbow appeared to be fighting an urge to throw his plate at Henry. He responded with a searching question. "What about Judas? You mean to say that the Savior was not a Prophet?"

"Didn't William Law serve a mission with Ole Joe's brother, Hyrum?" Henry asked, his voice steely. "Hyrum, your Church patriarch, didn't detect any evil spirit in William Law either."

"All it proves is that Satan is doing his best to destroy the true Church of God," Kington added. "William Law is not the only Judas we've discovered."

The Mormon men nodded their heads. Wilson Law. The Fosters. The Higbees.

Henry was frowning, which tensed his large face up and made his deep pockmarks look like holes that went clear through his cheeks. The prospect of getting the better of Henry was increasing and Robert broke out in a smile. But his smile turned into a frown as bad as Henry's as he thought about the bunch of apostates. Last evening Robert had a dream about the apostates. He had hidden in the trees at night, waiting for the apostates to come by, one at a time. And one at a time, he had jumped them, beaten them, and left them in a pool of blood. Just like Henry had done to him, in England. And just like he had done to Henry, in retaliation. Right now Robert could visualize his fists crashing into their jaws, for real.

"Henry," Robert began, his eyes turning into flecks of cold steel, "do me a favor. You seem to have a special attraction for men like the Law brothers. Round them up for me. Bring 'em here, and let me have a crack at 'em. Remember how I broke your ribs that time? I'd like to see the Law brothers doubling over in pain, like you did. What do you say?"

To a round of laughter, Henry's face went red in embarrassment. In desperation, he changed the subject. "Been endowed yet, brother-in-law?"

A creeping numbness came over Robert. *How do you know about such sacred terms, Henry?* He bit his lip in deep shock. "No. I think that's a special blessing that awaits Hannah and me when the temple is finished."

Henry's dark eyes bore into Robert's. "I hear Ole Joe is transferring the ceremonies of his clandestine Masonic Lodge to Mormonism, adding a few new frills and furbelows he says he learned from the Mormon God."

Robert scanned his semicircle of friends. It appeared Henry had struck another painful chord.

At the prodding of John Benbow, Thomas Kington spoke in defense of Mormonism. His close relationship with Wilford Woodruff had given him a good background about Henry's chosen topic—Mormons and Masonry. Kington's face had reddened. "Henry, you're way off base. I'll tell you why."

Robert knew that Kington had always been a student of religion and history. Kington fully understood why Joseph brought the Masonic fraternity to Nauvoo. There were few organizations in the world in which the spirit of brotherhood abounded as it did in Freemasonry. They preached fraternity and brotherly love as much in their lodges as was preached in most churches. Masons carried the teachings into daily life. Joseph had reasoned that because many of the prominent officials of the state were Masons, they likely would extend that special spirit of fraternity to Nauvoo Mormons. That special relationship was hoped to provide an impetus that members of the Church could use to thereby escape the prison dungeons and ugly persecutions heaped upon them in Missouri. Furthermore, many Mormon men had been admitted to Masonry before they joined the Church. Those men—including Newel K. Whitney, Heber C. Kimball, and John C. Bennett—realized the advantages of membership and encouraged the Prophet to seek a special dispensation for all the Nauvoo brethren. There was a simple logic. If the Mormons could attend Masonic conventions and freely mingle with prominent jurists and lawmakers of the state, they could make key friends who might save them from the misfortunes of Missouri. Somewhat like Mormonism, Masonry stood as an island of sanity in a world of confusion.

"Don't quibble with me, Mr. Kington," Henry said smugly. "I'm a member of the Lodge in Carthage now. I know all about our emblems, and how Ole Joe pilfered them."

Kington boiled over. "I don't think we ought to be discussing sacred things that will be practiced in our temple."

Henry scoffed. "You mean things like the square and the compass?"

John Benbow held up a palm and shook his head. "Careful, Mr. Eagles.'

"Nothing sacred about the square," Henry added, grinning smugly "Masons believe in squaring our actions, to keep them within bonds."

"Too bad you weren't a Mason earlier in your life, Henry," Robert said "We might have ended up close friends. Does all this mean you're changing?'

Henry ignored his brother-in-law. His tone hardened and was very British. "Ole Joe has stolen the beehive, the all-seeing eye, the hand, the apron, and the sun, moon, and stars for use in Mormonism. I saw your temple the other day, mate. You can't deny the fact you Mormons are using al these ideas."

Thomas Kington set his plate aside and drew his arms around his knees "I'm a Mason, too, Mr. Eagles. So is John Benbow, and several of us in this circle. There are some things about Masonry and Mormonism that you need to understand."

"I understand Masonry," Henry said. "I want nothing to do with Mormonism."

Robert suspected Henry had joined the Carthage Lodge out of necessity and greed. And survival. He was married to a Mormon and looked upon with a great deal of suspicion. Joining the Masons gave Henry what it gave Joseph Smith. Friends. Trust. A chance to sell his dairy products to a wider base of customers.

Henry had been a member for nearly two years and knew of the Mason claim that their rites dated back to the time of Solomon's temple. He had been schooled to understand that the Master Mason's degree revolved around a ritual drama in which Hiram Abiff, grand architect of Solomon's temple, was murdered because he refused to reveal certain secrets until the temple was completed. Because of Abiff's death, a keyword, called the "Master's word," was lost. Master Masons receive a substitute word in its place. The lost word is restored during the Royal Arch degree, which reenacts events said to have occurred during the rebuilding of the Jerusalem temple, following the

Babylonian captivity. The candidate plays the part of a Master Mason who, while helping to rebuild the temple, discovers an altar hidden behind a veil. On that altar is a golden plate containing the sacred name of God, which is also the lost Master's word.

Robert had long suspected that Henry regarded the whole thing as hocus pocus, the same way he regarded Mormon doctrine. Henry just did not admit that fact to anyone.

Robert reached to his right and took Henry by the wrist. There was an intended force in the grip. "You started this Henry. I suggest you listen to Brother Kington and to anyone else who might want to say something."

Henry pushed his lower lip out and curled his mouth. "I've always been a good listener."

Robert returned a droll grimace. "I'm serious, Henry." He turned his head toward Thomas. "You can begin now. Henry will pay attention."

Thomas Kington stared at Henry Eagles through thick eyebrows, his head erect. "As Masons, it is our proud boast that our order descended from the Temple of Solomon, which was located on Mount Moriah. If you know anything about Masonry, you know that's true."

Henry nodded his head up and down, pretending he knew everything about it. "You're absolutely right," he said.

"We believe that ancients such as Noah, Enoch, and Moses practiced Masonry. Right?"

Henry was a picture of authority now. Kington was his mouth. With a sarcastic, one-sided grin Henry said, "You and me are on the same page, brother."

Kington let his eyes trace the circle of Mormon men. "None of us have been endowed, brethren, but Henry has opened up the subject. When we complete our temple, and when we receive our endowment, we are going to find some similarities in the rituals of the Masons."

Everyone in the circle, including nonmembers Thomas Bloxham and Henry, understood that the purpose of the endowment was to teach the eternal purpose of life on earth. Joseph Smith had given the endowment to several Church leaders, including the Apostles, two years ago May. Joseph had also taught them about other principles and the order of the Priesthood, including washings, anointings, and keys of the Priesthood.

Henry's cryptic smile widened. "Similarities, yes. Because Joe Smith stole them."

Kington sipped his drink, ignoring that last remark. "Here's where we part, Mr. Eagles. Just because there may be a few likenesses in a vast realm of rituals in both Masonry and our Church's temple endowment, it does *not* mean that the Prophet Joseph simply borrowed them from Masonry."

"You're wrong, Mr. Kington," Henry said, screwing his heavy feature into a mask of disagreement. "That's exactly the point. Joe Smith knew *nothing* about all this stuff until he became a Mason."

All the Mormons in the circle laughed. They knew better.

Kington's eyes brightened. Gaining confidence, he locked his eyes on Henry, who was seated directly across from him. "I suppose we must conclude that no institution has a monopoly on truth, Henry. Divine truths that were revealed to early Hebrew Prophets have filtered into all nations of the world. Unfortunately, those truths have been altered and corrupted as they descended from one generation to the next."

Daniel Browett was listening to all this with keen interest. To him, Kington was almost entering territory Kington had covered in a similar setting years ago, when Daniel and Elizabeth began exploring the United Brethren. That day they sat under the shade of an oak tree in Benbow's pasture, on the Hill Farm, near Castle Frome. And that day, Kington taught Daniel the origins of Methodism, Quakerism, Anglicanism, Catholicism, the corruption of the original Christian Church, and the reformation. Again, Daniel marveled at Kington's ingenuity and knowledge.

Daniel could see that Henry's expression was pained. "You can't connect Mormonism and Masonry," Henry warned.

"You just don't understand Mormonism and the restoration of the gospel," Kington explained. "Not a single feature of the Church of Jesus

Christ of Latter-day Saints is taken from Masonry, certainly not the temple endowment. Henry, you might just as well argue that the features of our endowment were taken from the American Indians, the early Druids, or the ancient Essenes. All those people preserved fragments of truth about the endowment, the very endowment that was anciently administered within the sacred institutions of ancient Israel."

Daniel knew Henry was lost. Henry had no idea what Kington was talking about. But Kington sounded so authoritative. Henry let his mouth drop, and his arms became weak. He could not offer a wave of protest.

Kington continued. "When all of us in this circle finally enter the temple in another year or two, quite frankly we are going to find a few similarities in the rites performed there and what we do in Masonry. But the evidence demands that we look higher than Masonry for the inspiration that the Prophet Joseph received to restore the temple ceremony again to the earth."

With his mouth still open, Henry watched and listened as the conversation sped out of his control. He sank heavily into the green grass.

"Do you understand what I am saying, Henry?" Kington asked.

Henry gave a grim sigh.

Kington remained solemn. "I testify to all of you that Jesus Christ, the Savior of the world, revealed the temple ceremony rites and wording to the Prophet Joseph Smith as part of the restoration of the gospel. The Prophet didn't need to borrow anything from Masonry."

The heady situation made Daniel feel philosophical. "What you are saying is true, Brother Kington," Daniel said, alternating his glances from Kington to Henry. "I know the Prophet began promising the Saints that the endowment was coming as early as 1841. He certainly was under no influence of Masonry way back then."

John Benbow cleared his throat, wanting to add a statement. "In fact," he stated, "There were washings and anointings performed in the Kirtland Temple, even years earlier."

The verbal free-for-all continued. John Cox had something to add: "Given the Prophet's patent interest in lost scripture and ancient teachings, I can totally understand why he was attracted to Masonry. Masonry offered him a whole new world of knowledge. There are teachings connected to Biblical figures, as well as to ancient Greek and Egyptian knowledge."

Henry sank deeper, caught in a crossfire.

Levi Roberts spoke next. "And he liked the Masonic idea of advancing our lives degree by degree, kind of like 'grace to grace,' or receiving 'knowledge upon knowledge.' Masons have three degrees of advancements."

Thomas Kington threw out a challenge. "Name those three degrees of advancement, Henry."

The challenge seemed to break Henry's stance. He regarded his Mormon enemies for a few seconds while he bit his lip in deep thought. "Entered Apprentice, Fellow Craft, and Master Mason."

"Very good, Henry," Robert said.

Kington invited Henry to relate everything he knew about Masonic rites and how they use symbolism drawn from stonemasonry. In Daniel's view Henry seemed quite knowledgeable. He spoke of stoneworker aprons and an assortment of tools—compass, square, gauge, plumb, and the level. Next came the five points of fellowship and penalties invoked in non-disclosure oaths. The Masons had two grips, or tokens, and a set script; they also imparted signs and passwords to initiates. There was more: the making of oaths at an altar using a Bible, acting out parts, played by the Worshipful Master, Senior Warden, Junior Warden, and the three ruffians who assault Hiram Abiff—Jubela, Jubelo, and Jebulum. The Masons knocked three times at an entrance and recited syllables in the Hebrew language. Henry said the Masons gave initiates a new name of virtue, donned their masonry aprons, and passed from one room to another. At the conclusion, the Masons gave a lecture to review the ceremony and expound its meaning, and passed through a veil wearing priestly robes of an Old Testament pattern.

Robert could see through his brother-in-law. "And I suppose you buy into all of these Masonic rites, Henry?"

"Some," Henry admitted. "But most of it is all hocus pocus rubbish same as Mormonism. But I go along with it."

Daniel had a thought to throw Henry further off balance. "Henry, in Masonry, is the ritual a drama, or is it Biblical?"

Henry rolled his eyes, confused. "Well, they read selections from Ruth, Judges, Psalms, and Ecclesiastes."

"But is Hiram Abiff a character of the Bible?"

"I suppose," Henry guessed.

The men in the circle snickered.

"Are women included in the rites of Masonry?" Daniel asked.

"No, of course not."

"Will women be endowed in our Church?"

Henry was clearly irritated. "Probably not."

"You're wrong, Henry. Does Masonry have any concept to save the dead? People who have not been endowed in Masonry, or baptized by someone holding the true priesthood?"

"Of course not." With that admission, Henry rose to his feet, clearly defeated.

"I have more questions, Henry. About Masonry."

Henry glared at Daniel. A gentle breeze blew east, toward Carthage. "I have cows to milk. I'd like to stay and answer your questions, but I need to get home."

"But I thought you came to help," Robert said. "There's more painting to do. Afterwards we're having an outdoor dance. I brought my fiddle. There'll be the two-step, the waltz, the double shuffle, and cotillions. Foot races for the kids."

Henry waved Robert off and let his eyes fall on his younger brother.

A confused Elias Eagles rose to his feet. "Good to see you again, Henry."

Henry motioned to his brother to follow as he walked away from the Mormon men. "My offer still stands, little brother. Come to Carthage and go into the dairy business with me."

"I don't know what to do," Elias said in a condescending voice. On one hand, he had to laugh at Henry's weak attempt to discredit Mormonism. But on the other hand, Henry was the only big brother he had in America. There was a natural affection, but it troubled him.

"Come with me now and stay for a few days."

"I need to stay and help Hannah. And Mary wants to dance."

"We have dances in Carthage. At parties, weddings, apple-pairings. More fun than here, though. Out our way we keep the double doors swinging. We have hard cider and corn liquor. If you want real entertainment, come to the basement of our tavern. You've never seen ratting."

"Ratting?"

"We put live rats in a ring and then put a dog or a weasel in there, too. We bet on how long it'll take for the rats to be killed."

Elias winced.

"I'm raising cocks, too. I bought me some steel gaffs. Put 'em on their feet. They really tear up the other rooster at our cockfights."

There was a side of Elias that somehow found all this appealing. "What else?"

"Gander-pulling."

"Which is…?"

"Outdoors sport. We hang a duck or goose upside down by its feet. We ride on horseback under it and see who can twist its head off."

Elias pulled a face. "That sounds gruesome."

"Everybody does it, all my friends."

"That doesn't make it right, Henry," Elias countered, registering a little of his good side. "Remember what Mother used to teach us about sin?"

Henry wrinkled his chin. "What do you mean?"

"Sin is still a sin, even if millions are doing it."

Henry ignored the clever little saying. "But the best sport is talking about the Mormons. They've given us so much to talk about. Spiritual wifery. What's gonna happen inside their temple. Their politics. Did you know Joe Smith is running for President?"

"What's wrong with that?"

"Look at it from the viewpoint of the Missourians. If Ole Joe is President, he'll raise the devil with Missouri. Even if he's not, he'll raise the devil anyway. And what'll happen to Illinois? The Mormons will take it over. There's so many people coming to Nauvoo, the Mormons control the vote."

Now Elias was gnawing on his bottom lip.

"There's been a lot of indignation meetings going on in Carthage during the past winter and spring."

"Indignation meetings?"

"To decide what actions we need to take to eliminate the Mormons." Henry had quickly discovered that the anti-Mormons in Carthage had a gift for striking a position on the side of hatred.

Henry told about similar meetings held in Warsaw. There, a sectarian minister by the name of Levi Williams had promoted a resolution compelling the Mormons to give up their guns or leave the state immediately. If not, Williams and his companions were prepared to drive them out.

"Mormons are a disgrace to the human species," Henry said. "Most people around my parts want Joe Smith cut down; make him a public example. We've talked about wolf hunts. To do violence to Mormons."

"But Henry, I'm Mormon, too."

"Foolery. You won't be for long."

Elias pulled another face. "What about Hannah? She is too, you know."

"Hannah's so narrow-minded that if she fell on a pin it would blind her in both eyes."

"I didn't know you felt that way about your own sister."

"There's a nasty border war coming, Elias," Henry said. "It's inevitable. Governor Ford still doesn't believe it, but I do."

"But Joseph Smith just told us all not to buy guns from salesmen that come calling. He says to use our money to buy plowshares and raise our crops."

"If I were you, little brother, I'd get out of Nauvoo. Somebody's gonna kill Joe Smith."

With those words of finality, Henry marched away. He whistled. Katherine came running. In minutes, the Henry Eagles family disappeared over the Illinois horizon.

# 37

## June 1844

JOSEPH SMITH'S SKIN CRAWLED when he saw Dr. Robert D. Foster. Just outside his office at the Masonic Lodge, Foster approached like an angry ox, his right hand hidden inside his cloak. With a nod of his head, Joseph motioned Porter Rockwell, Hyrum Smith, and others to his side.

To Joseph's relief, Foster withdrew his right hand and let it fall to his side. The two men exchanged uneasy looks. Foster spoke first, a bead of sweat dripping off his nose. "Would you meet me in private?" he asked, locking his gaze on Joseph. "I'm willing to make some concessions in return for my membership in the Church."

Joseph's eyes were riveted on a bulge under Foster's cloak and vest.

Quickly, Joseph's mind flashed back to the first time he met the doctor. It had been in Springfield, five years ago, in October. Joseph had been on his way to Washington, D. C., to present legal affidavits regarding the Missouri persecutions. Porter Rockwell, Sidney Rigdon, and Elias Higbee were with him. The four of them were staying overnight with a Mormon family in Springfield, with plans to leave as quickly as possible. Rigdon, however, was sick. Dr. Robert D. Foster was recommended. Foster treated Rigdon with medicine, bled him, placed a blistering poultice on the soles of his feet, and sweated him. Rigdon was no better the next day, so Foster agreed to travel with the group to Washington, D. C.

Although highly qualified and a charming personality, Foster had his problems. Foster was not only a doctor but a land speculator as well. His partner in land transactions was Isaac Galland. But it seemed to Joseph that at every stop Foster struck up a conversation with the prettiest girl around. It was surprising to Joseph and his traveling companions that so many young ladies, who otherwise seemed to be in perfect health, required his medical attention. It soon got him into trouble—immorality.

Joseph's wrath was upon Foster and continued in the months following the trip to Washington, D. C. Foster continually tried to justify his action on medical grounds instead of cleansing his soul with repentance. This made Joseph more indignant. But Foster finally repented. Joseph forgave him. Soon, a pattern in Foster's life in the Church developed. In December 1840 the High Council tried him for lying, slandering, and profane swearing. He repented. He was forgiven. Charges were brought against him again in May 1840 for abusive language toward Samuel H. Smith. Again, he was forgiven. Gradually he earned the trust of the Prophet. He rose to the position of surgeon general in the Nauvoo Legion. He also served as a county school commissioner. Again, moral problems arose. Confronted, this time he began to attack Joseph and the Church. Publicly, he began to criticize Joseph for having "spiritual wives." Joseph became a tiger after this, however, disappointed that Foster had swallowed the rumors to be true. Foster realized he was on the brink of excommunication, which would mean heavy financial losses. To be cut off would ruin him. Again, he faked repentance. For the sake of Foster's wife and children, Joseph forgave him one more time. Foster, however, returned to his old ways. He fell in with the Laws and the Higbees, who by now were conspiring against Joseph. His brother, Charles Foster, became so caught up with the apostates and overcome by evil that Charles tried to shoot Joseph on the steps of the Smith home in late April. Charles, along with his brother and Chauncey Higbee, were all arrested over the incident. Each man was fined a hundred dollars.

Joseph shook his head in sorrow. After all the repenting and forgiving, Dr. Robert D. Foster stood before him as one of the worst examples of spiritual hypocrisy Joseph had ever seen or known. His former surgeon general of the Nauvoo Legion had not only been drummed out of the Legion the day the prospectus was issued, but also excommunicated from the Church.

Dr. Robert D. Foster's reason for wanting to meet privately with the Mormon Prophet was diabolically simple. He wanted to kill Joseph Smith.

Foster was visibly shaken when Joseph said "no" to his proposal that they meet in private.

"What I have to say is for your ears only," Foster said, his visage ice cold and his heart pounding. He could feel the hidden pistol against his ribs. "I plead with you. I repeat. I'm willing to make concessions for my membership in the Church." Foster pictured Joseph on the floor, bleeding from a gaping hole in his heart

"What else do you want?" Joseph asked.

Joe Smith's skepticism riled Foster. "My position in the Legion. I wish to be reinstated."

Incredibly, another question came from the fallen Prophet. "And what else?"

The presence of Porter, Hyrum, and other Mormons irked Foster. He was reaching the end of his patience. "I want all the affidavits of the anti-Mormons under my control. Withdraw all your lawsuits against my friends."

Control of the affidavits meant the Higbee brothers, both lawyers, could litigate all the cases, charging fees. Their profits would be enormous.

"No," came the answer. "That won't happen." Joe Smith acted as though he were the sole guardian of all that went on in Nauvoo and the Mormon

Kingdom.

Foster winced in disappointment. "Just give me some time with you, alone."

Joseph appeared unmoved. He threw his hands apart. "I'd be happy to meet with you, but only in the presence of some of my friends. I'll choose three or four. You do the same."

Foster felt his hopes sinking. "But I want to meet you alone." *A new Ramage printing press is being set up as we speak. I'll blow the lid off Mormonism.*

"No. Only with my friends. We'll settle everything on righteous principles."

"Alone. Please?" *And you'll be a dead man.*

"No."

CHAPTER NOTES

The account of Dr. Robert D. Foster's early encounter with Joseph Smith on the trip to Washington, D. C., is taken from several sources, but mainly from *Nightfall at Nauvoo*, Samuel W. Taylor (New York, N.Y.: Avon Books, 1971), pages 52-54.

A summary of Foster's later relationship with Joseph and the Church is taken from *History of the Church*, Joseph Smith, Volumes 4, 5, and 6.

# 38

TONIGHT'S MEETING UNDER RAINY SKIES was clandestine. A committee composed of eight men gathered in the basement of a brick building in Nauvoo had several things in common. First, and foremost, the committee wanted Joe Smith dead. Second, the committee wanted to see the demise of Joe Smith-style Mormonism. Third, the committee wanted to take control of the real estate transactions in Nauvoo. And fifth, the committee was about to launch a new newspaper in Nauvoo.

The eight men—the Law brothers, the Foster brothers, the Higbee brothers, Charles Ivins, and Sylvester Emmons—had been denied space in Joe Smith's newspapers. Now the committee had a press of its own, purchased in Adams County from Abraham Jonas.

"Too bad I failed this morning," Dr. Robert D. Foster said, his voice apologetic. Possibly as a result of years of conniving, Foster's eyes were permanently marked with what looked like laugh lines. Strangers mistook him for a genial man. He was not. Today, he had been anything but genial. He had just tried to murder Joe Smith, the fallen Prophet.

"If he would have agreed to meet with you," Wilson Law said, studying Foster with sallow eyes, "it would all be over by now"

"Joe deserves to be dead," Foster scoffed, feeling a chill. Outside, the rain was pouring. Lightning flashed, followed by a tremendous thunderclap. "Someday soon he will be."

"Amen to that," Francis Higbee added, revulsion plain on his face.

Foster cast his eyes at the printing press. It had arrived by steamer in Nauvoo on May seventh, a month ago. Its arrival had caused great excitement in the city, but no one had interfered with its setup first in his home, then later in its current location. It was now housed in the basement of a two-story brick building in the upper business district, one block east of the temple, on Mulholland Street. The building was leased as a store to Charles Foster and Francis Higbee. Foster and his associates began work at once. Within three days they had issued a prospectus in which they espoused "unmitigated disobedience to political revelations," and proposed to "censure and decry gross moral imperfections wherever found."

Everyone in Nauvoo knew what the eight men meant. They were after Joseph Smith's hide.

In a corner of the basement, Sylvester Emmons, the editor, was working as a compositor now. Smirking calmly, he stood in front of two type cases and began picking up foundry type letters. Capitol letters came from the upper case. Proportionate quantities of each letter of the alphabet used in ordinary composition came from a lower case. Placed together, they began to form menacing words written by the Foster brothers, the Law brothers, the Higbee brothers, and Charles Ivins. The words slowly became sentences on a composing stick. Sentences became paragraphs on a long shallow tray called a galley. Paragraphs became columns and articles.

The columns and articles accused Joseph Smith of spiritual wifery, whoredoms, abusing political power, teaching the plurality of gods, and claiming power to seal up men to eternal life. Joseph was branded as a base seducer, a liar, and a murderer. Church leaders were accused of controlling politics.

With guards posted at the door, the first issue of the *Nauvoo Expositor* was about to go to press.

In the back of his mind, Foster wondered who would emerge as the lead-ing personality of the *Expositor.* It could be him, or William Law, but thei main goal was to take control of the Mormon kingdom. A side benefit woulc be they would get rich off real estate sales in Nauvoo. Mormon converts wer still flooding into Nauvoo. The Higbees were lawyers, like their father. Bu then their good friend Thomas Sharp, editor of the *Warsaw Signal,* had beer a lawyer, too.

Foster took a press-reading galley proof from Emmons and handed it t William Law. "President Law, we believe this to be correct. But as president o our new church, you need to approve it."

Membership in the Reformed Mormon Church had stalled at abou three hundred members. Foster was confident the newspaper would give hi organization new strength. If the committee could upend Joseph Smith Nauvoo would be a prize spoil for him and his friends. The men could tak over the entire Church. Law would be Prophet and trustee-in-chief. All re estate would come under his control.

William Law fondled the galley proof as though it were a new soft baby He had fathered the idea for the newspaper. Its gestation time had taken les than nine months. Labor: eighteen hours to set the type for each page. In jus a few hours more, the great anticipated birth would occur. Printed copie would hit the streets, enough to flood the city. Joe Smith was about to be trie by headline, to be attacked in his most vulnerable spot—the soft underbell of public opinion. This baby carried muckraking words of rebellion. A chal lenge to the power of a fallen Prophet.

Law's smile was wicked. *The power of the press will soon be turned agains Joe Smith, the Goliath of Nauvoo.*

Dr. Robert D. Foster pulled out a quill and paper. He sat at a table an began to write.

"What are you doing?" Chauncey Higbee asked.

"Writing a letter to Joe Smith," Foster said, smiling. "A saucy one. When he reads our newspaper, he'll realize he should have paid attention to us, and to the new church we've organized. Joe seems to hate lawyers and doctors. We hate him right back, don't we boys?"

"We do," Chauncey answered. "Joe better have a fast horse waiting. We're about to run him out of town."

# 39

IN HIS LOG HOME ON AN OVERCAST, raw, windy Friday, Robert sa
reading his copy of the *Nauvoo Expositor*. The newspaper had hit the street
early. Anticipating its printing, Robert had dashed the three blocks from hi
house to the red brick building on Mulholland Street where the press wa
located. It was a sore trial to Robert to read the paper, and his mood darkene
as he turned the pages. He brushed Lizzy off his lap. He scolded Joseph fo
not helping his mother with the dishes. And he snapped back at Hanna
when she told him Victoria hadn't been milked yet, and that he ought to b
leaving for the farm to work on her new house.

"Robert, you sound like you've got a sour stomach," Hannah sai
"What you need is a dozen cows to milk, enough to keep you out of our hair.

"It's just this cursed newspaper," he shot back. "Here—read it. It'll pu
you in a bad mood, too."

For the first time in his life, Robert wished he weren't a member of th
Church. In his seething madness he reasoned he could hunt down the me
responsible for this outrageous newspaper, leave them in a pool of their ow

blood, and then get baptized. His sin of revenge could be simply washed away in the waters of the Mississippi.

The *Expositor* condemned the Prophet's "moral imperfections," an obvious swipe at polygamy. No woman was specifically named, but a story told of a hypothetical convert, a young girl from England, arriving alone in Nauvoo, taught the "fullness of the gospel" in person by Joseph Smith, with the obvious intent of making her one of his wives. Austin Cowles, William Law, and Jane Law published statements that they had seen, or heard, Joe Smith's revelation allowing men to marry up to "ten virgins." In short, they charged that Joseph had perverted the restored gospel and fallen from grace by introducing heretical doctrines.

Just as Robert suspected they would, the apostates also complained of the Prophet's control of land in and around Nauvoo. They also bellyached about land prices being regulated and limiting competition by encouraging immigrants to buy building lots from only the trustee-in-trust, Joseph Smith. They accused Joseph of abusing the rights of the Nauvoo charter. They wanted the charter repealed outright. They opposed all "political revelations and unconstitutional ordinances." Joseph's candidacy for President of the United States was challenged, and the paper said God never raised a Prophet to Christianize the world by political intrigue. "We will not acknowledge any man as king or lawgiver to the Church," they said, "for Christ is our only king and lawgiver."

Robert threw the newspaper at Hannah. "The group that published this has the makings of a first-rate funeral party. They all ought to be dead."

Hannah reacted to the apostate newspaper in typical womanly fashion, and it further griped Robert. "If the Fosters and the Higbees and the Laws don't like the way things are here in Nauvoo, why don't they leave? No one's forcing them to stay."

The remark put Robert in such perplexity of spirit that he could hardly focus. When it came to tolerance, Hannah had no close rivals. "I might be the one who forces them to leave," he said in a huff, pacing back and forth in his cabin. He glanced out the window at Elias and Mary's tent. He wondered what they would think of the controversial newspaper. As yet, Elias had not decided whether to buy Robert's log home or move to Carthage and go into the dairy business with Henry.

"Calm down," Hannah replied, her eyes scanning the *Expositor*. She raised her shoulders and let them settle again. "Personally, I like the fact that the Prophet is not only the President of the Church, but the mayor and Lieutenant General of the Nauvoo Legion. How else can we guarantee that Nauvoo can be the place of refuge we need, unless we have trusted people in key positions?"

The publication of the apostates' newspaper only added to Robert's fading utopian view of Nauvoo. Plural marriage seemed to be splitting the Church. There had been unrest among workers at the temple over wages and living conditions. A scandal had broken out a few months ago in public about embezzlement of temple contributions by agents collecting for its construction. Robert and Daniel's crops had been poor last year. Corn, grain, and other commodities had brought the Harris and Browett families scant income on the open market. It had taken more money than they could afford to build their new homes. Construction had taken longer than expected. Yet thousands of converts from Great Britain were still pouring into Nauvoo and—like Elias and Mary Eagles—were totally unprepared to cope with the challenges.

Robert stared into Hannah's brown eyes, pounding his fists. "I'd like to get my hands on Wilson Law, or any of the others. They've printed all the lies that Satan could think of and some that even he couldn't think of."

"I agree," she answered. "They have their nerve, calling our Prophet and his brother apostates. But honey, you need to let the Lord take care of them in his own way."

"The Lord needs helpers. I could run them out of town by nightfall."

Whatever subject Robert had on his mind when he went to bed was generally still there when he woke up, even minor items. Publication of the *Expositor* was no minor event in Nauvoo, and it was the expected topic of conversation Sunday morning when Robert and Hannah walked to the grove with Daniel, Elizabeth, Elias, and Mary. Robert hoped Hyrum Smith would rail against the apostates and their newspaper in his address. Dr. John Bernhisel had confined Joseph to bed. Joseph's lungs were worn out by too much public speaking.

Robert led a chorus of hot criticism against the *Expositor* publishers. "I don't see how they can call the *Expositor* a newspaper. There's not a spec of news in it. It's just full of slander against our Prophet and our Church. It's worse than the Bennett letters."

Daniel nodded his agreement. "If those men get away with actually repealing our city charter it will ruin Nauvoo, and make it unsafe for all the members of the Church around here."

Robert pounded a fist into his hand. "We ought to hang the whole lot of them without benefit of clergy."

"Now, now, sweetheart, don't boil over," Hannah said. "That would make you just as bad as them." She was seeing in Robert a return to his old pre-baptism temperament.

"Well at least the truth of those men's evil ways came out in the city council hearings yesterday," Elizabeth said. "It makes me feel a *little* better."

It was a widely circulated fact around Nauvoo that because the publishers had lost their Church membership they were beyond further reprimand from priesthood councils. The only recourse had been for city officials to bring charges against the apostates for current and past crimes.

"What else have they done?" Elias asked, talking as though he regretted missing all the excitement of Nauvoo over the past three or four years.

Robert was quick to reply. William and Wilson Law had been charged with counterfeiting, ending months of speculation in Nauvoo about who had been circulating bogus money. The most damaging testimony had come from Theodore Turley, a gunsmith, the man who had accompanied Wilford Woodruff and John Taylor to England in 1840. Turley testified that the Law brothers had brought bogus dies to him for fixing. William Law had also been charged with adultery, oppressing the poor, and offering five hundred dollars to someone to kill the Prophet. It was learned that Francis Higbee had caught a dose of pox from a French harlot on the hill. And it came out that Emmons, the editor, had a scurrilous past. He had been blackguarded out of

Philadelphia. Emmons had claimed that he had been a judge there, but it was proved that he had been lying.

"Sounds like the paper was put out by a group of model citizens," Mary said, shaking her head in disbelief.

"Indeed," Daniel responded. "I wonder what Elder Woodruff and Elder Hyde would think of the *Expositor,* and all the controversy?" All of the Twelve except for Willard Richards and John Taylor, were out of town on a two-fold mission for the Church: to preach the gospel and electioneer for Joseph Smith's candidacy for President. Willard stayed in Nauvoo to be Joseph's scribe, and John Taylor remained to edit the two newspapers and direct the Prophet's political campaign. Joseph now had a disdain for both Whigs and Democrats.

The face Mary Eagles wore was clouded with confusion. "Where did all these evil men come from?"

Other than the controversies that seemed to be stewing on a daily basis, Mary had grown to enjoy her new home. People in her home country of England were out of work and starving. Here, gardens around Nauvoo home furnished vegetables, herbs, fruits, and berries. Meat came from herds outside the city. Corn, ground into meal for boiling, baking, and frying, was a staple as were potatoes and wheat. Around the homes grew larkspur, sunflowers, phlox, cannas, and heartsease. Streets and lanes were lined with hollyhocks. Each morning from the temple site a bell tolled at seven, signaling the start of another workday. The bell rang again at noon, one, and six o'clock. During the day the air was rent with the whistles of riverboats going up and down the Mississippi. Evenings passed pleasantly, usually reading the Book of Mormon and the Bible. Women could be found at neighbors' homes, quilting. There were corn-husking parties, pie suppers, cotillion parties, entertainment at the Masonic Hall, listening to the debating and dramatic societies perform dances, and amateur theatre nights. Mary's favorite pastime was dancing on the deck of the *Maid of Iowa* when she docked at one of the landings. Mary loved the twinkling of lights on the water, the swish of full skirts, and the cool breeze off the water.

Daniel contemplated Mary's question. He began by telling Mary and Elias that mobocracy was common on the American frontier, especially in states like Illinois and Missouri. For the past several years horse thieves and counterfeiters had overrun Hancock County. Even past sheriffs, judges, and constables had been convicted of such crimes. A gang in Pope County had become so strong that they constructed their own fort. Throughout the state "regulator" groups had been formed, banding together law-abiding citizens to fight against lawless men. Lawlessness had become even more rampant during the term of Governor Ford. It was literally impossible, Daniel concluded, to keep wicked, lying men out of the Church. Satan worked harder on members than non-members, in his opinion. But men like the Law, Higbee, and Foster brothers were indeed evil. Dark, evil men.

Daniel began with former mayor John C. Bennett. He related how Bennett took unauthorized "spiritual wives" to himself, and told of the time when he poisoned himself. When a doctor was summoned to the house where Bennett had been taken, the Law brothers were there. So were Chauncey and Francis Higbee. The Higbee brothers were sons of Judge Elias Higbee, a trusted lawyer friend of the Prophet.

"The doctor should have let Bennett die right then and there," Robert fumed. "And he should have taken the same poison, and given it to the Laws and the Higbees. It would save me the trouble of hunting them down and finishing them off myself."

An elbow crunched into Robert's ribs. "Be civil, and be Christian," Hannah warned.

"Is Bennett the one who left the Church, and went to Missouri?" Mary asked.

"That's right," answered Daniel. "He was not only the mayor of Nauvoo, but our Prophet's counselor. Brother Joseph exhibited a lot of patience and forgiveness with him, but when the Church finally had to excommunicate Bennett, he turned out to be our worst enemy. Because the Law brothers were good friends to Bennett, they kept pushing Joseph for reconciliation, but it didn't happen. I'm certain back then both William and Wilson Law were caught between a rock and a hard spot, trying to remain both loyal to the Prophet, and sympathetic to Bennett. Bennett had been using the Prophet's name to continue his hellish practices too long. As a doctor, Bennett was taking advantage of both unmarried and married women."

"I think I'll hunt him down, too," Robert said. "Even if I have to go to Missouri."

Another elbow came from Hannah.

Daniel quickly related the kidnapping incident and the involvement of William and Wilson Law. He also explained how the Laws, Higbees, Fosters, and others became increasingly critical of the Prophet, particularly regarding rumors that Joseph Smith had taken plural wives.

"So," Daniel added, "when Joseph Smith committed to writing his revelation about plural marriage, and circulating it, William Law, along with Joseph's other counselor, Sidney Rigdon, openly denounced it."

"Sadly," Elizabeth added, "so did William Marks, the Nauvoo stake president. And high council members Austin Cowles and Leonard Sobey."

Elias shook his head, evidently confused by too many new names.

"The rift between the Prophet and William Law seemed to reach a crescendo during the election last year, not too long after Joseph's kidnapping," Daniel explained. "Joseph had promised his vote to Cyrus Walker, the Whig candidate for Congress. Remember what we told you before. Walker was in the area of Dixon when the Prophet was kidnapped. Walker agreed to represent Joseph in return for a large fee and Joseph's vote."

Elias shrugged, again with a lost look on his face.

"Anyway," Daniel continued, "there was a political rally at the grove. Joseph's health was bad at the time, still weak from being poisoned."

"Undoubtedly poisoned by the Laws, the Higbees, and the Fosters," Robert said, still seething.

Daniel nodded. "Probably. But anyway, he stayed home from the rally. He was also weak from preaching and talking so much. At the rally, Hyrum Smith gave a speech. He asked the Saints to vote for the other candidate. The Democrat, Joseph P. Hoge. William Law was furious. He jumped up right in the meeting and denounced Hyrum as a false Prophet."

Elias blinked hard.

"You wouldn't believe the *sensation* that caused, right in our meeting," Elizabeth said, wincing in remembrance. "William Law took the stand and said he didn't think the Lord ought to meddle in Illinois politics. *Imagine that.*"

"Law went on to say that Hyrum's pretended revelation was a shabby ruse by a man with his own political ambitions," Daniel went on. "Apparently Hyrum wanted to be in the state legislature. Which was a good idea, in my mind. We need to have Church members in key positions, to protect us."

Robert thumped Elias on the shoulder. "Want my opinion? I think the Law brothers had something going on with the Whigs."

"So who did you all vote for?" Mary asked.

Hannah answered. "We took it to mean that Joseph had promised his *personal* vote to Walker. But we were free to vote for whomever we pleased. Hyrum was urging us to vote for Hoge, so that's what I did. And most everyone else did, too."

"Obviously: Hoge won," Elias said.

"Yes, and the Whigs were whopping mad," Daniel said. "But the Democrats didn't seem too happy, either. Both sides knew how unpredictable Mormon voting power was, and how strong. We could sway an election either way."

Elizabeth spoke again. "All the outside newspapers began to lambaste us Mormons. Governor Ford, the Democrat, said there was only one final solution to the Mormon problem. We would have to leave Illinois."

"*Leave?* But we just got here," Mary said, almost crying.

"We're not going anywhere," Robert said, a note of defiance in his voice. "We outnumber 'em."

"But I heard bad things have started to happen," Elias said.

"That's right," Robert acknowledged. "Anti-Mormon mobs burned out a farmer at Ramus last December." Ramus was twenty miles east of Nauvoo, near Carthage.

"What if they try that at your new homes?" Mary asked, tears welling up. "And I've heard that the Missourians are going to send twenty thousand armed men across the river to capture our Prophet and raze Nauvoo."

She spoke of a report that Walter Bagby, the tax collector who had scuffled with Joseph near Moeser's grocery, was active in stirring up anti-Mormon sentiment, visiting Boggs in Missouri. Bagby returned to Illinois to align himself with the Warsaw editor, Thomas Sharp, and other notorious anti-Mormons such as Levi Williams. Soon mobs were organized at Carthage, fueled by articles in Sharp's newspapers.

Robert clenched his fists. "Just let them try." He was overjoyed that the city council had recently passed an ordinance that stipulated that anyone attempting to arrest Joseph on old Missouri charges would be slapped into the city jail for life, and not even the governor could pardon him without the consent of the mayor—who happened to be Joseph Smith. There were reports that John C. Bennett was drilling a Missouri mob, whipping it into a crack military force for the invasion of Nauvoo.

Hannah shook her head sadly. This entire conversation spoke of the evidence that a state of war now existed between members of her Church and the surrounding world. Innocent people were being persecuted because of religion. In her eyes, it almost appeared that—with the exception of the traitors—the vast majority of the Saints were good. The Gentiles were almost all bad. Friend and foe. Communication and compromise no longer existed. Law and order was breaking down. The Prophet had increased the police force which affected her own circle of friends. John Cox and Levi Roberts were on the police force. If not for the fact that they would soon be moving to the country, her husband, Robert, would be on the police force.

"Mary," Daniel explained, "I guess you know that by now Brother Joseph is convinced there are traitors within Nauvoo." During the last conference, Joseph had lashed out at his old companion and first counselor in the first presidency, accusing him of tampering with Joseph's mail. Someone had revealed Joseph's whereabouts in Dixon, resulting in Sheriff Reynolds hunting him down.

"Yes," Robert said, rolling his fists tighter, "and now we know who they are. And one of the is old Buckeye himself."

"Buckeye?" Elias asked.

Daniel spoke again. "Thomas Sharp published a poem obviously written by a high-up member of the Church, called 'Buckeye's Lamentation for Want of More Wives.' The poem viciously targeted Joseph Smith and the women allegedly sealed to him. When those closest to the Prophet—Dr. John Bernhisel and Porter Rockwell—asked Joseph who Buckeye was, the answer came immediately. William Law. Joseph's other counselor."

"No kidding," Elias said.

"You should have been here," Robert said. "It was sickening. "The Prophet alerted the Nauvoo police that there was a traitor within the gates, using the word 'dough-head.' William Law immediately came forward and denied that it was him."

Daniel again: "By April conference things had deteriorated so badly that both William and Wilson Law were tried for their membership, and Dr. Foster, too. So now the rebels realized it was impossible to work their reforms within the Church. So they organized their own church, with the intention to use it to combat Brother Joseph, who they felt was a fallen Prophet."

"Over the revelation on plural marriage?" Mary asked.

"That was the big issue," Daniel explained. "But there were other differences between the Laws and Joseph Smith. The Prophet didn't want William and Wilson to develop the business tract on the hill by the temple. Joseph felt like it would detract from the temple."

"And be a detriment of his own real estate projects in the lower town," Elias suggested, repeating what Henry had told him. "Not even the Prophet should have a monopoly on real estate."

"I guess you're right," Daniel admitted. "But when someone from England arrives with no money to buy a lot, guess where the money comes from?"

Elias gulped.

"Not from Buckeye and his gang."

# 40

JOHN COX AND LEVI ROBERTS arrived at the new Robert Harris home east of Nauvoo on horseback in a panic. Robert was painting an inside wall with Hannah holding her baby, thirteen-month-old Enoch, on her hip, wondering how to place her furniture in the parlor.

"We've got a job to do," Levi said, bursting into the house, tracking mud onto the new floor.

Robert had a premonition building within him. "Do we get to do something about Wilson Law and the gang of apostates?"

"Under pressure of everyone in Nauvoo, the Prophet called a special session of the city council this morning," John said, a wild look in his eye. "They passed an ordinance prohibiting libel on penalty of a five hundred-dollar fine and six months in jail. To make a long story short, the *Expositor* has been declared a public nuisance."

Robert smiled. "So I finally get to crack Wilson Law's jaw?"

"Maybe," Levi said. "The Prophet, acting as mayor, has asked the city marshal to destroy the press and pi the type."

"Pi the type?"

"Scatter it. Stomp it into the street. So it can never be used again."

"But I'm not on the police force anymore." Robert had resigned last week, in anticipation of his move to his new home.

"Marshall Greene has asked for you anyway. Besides, the entire Legion is being asked to be there, as a show of force. Either way, you're going to be part of the action."

Levi went on to explain that under common law in the United States, public officials could remove or destroy a nuisance if lesser means failed.

Robert appeared delighted. "I'll saddle Tapper," he said. He rushed outside into the rainy weather.

Near sunset, Robert found himself near the front row of hundreds of Legion members, marching up Mulholland Street toward the two-story brick building that housed the Foster and Higbee store. Only a few Legion soldiers and city policemen separated Robert from Porter Rockwell, Marshal John P. Greene, and acting Major General of the Nauvoo Legion Jonathan Dunham. Robert marched to the sharp cadence of the Legion's drill sergeant. The *clump, lump, clump* of leather boots was music to the former pugilist's ears. As Robert approached Moeser's grocery store, across the street from the building used by the apostates, he flashed a broad grin at the gathering crowd. They didn't smile back. Their eyes were glued on Porter Rockwell, the marshal, the major general, and three men set to guard the brick building.

Inside the building, Robert could see several men peering out. Their faces were lined with a mixture of fear and anger.

"Don't let anyone in!" a voice yelled to the three guards.

Marshall Greene approached the three guards. His voice was oratorical. "I have an order from the city council." He flashed a piece of paper.

"So?" said John Eagle, one of the guards, setting his jaw. He was a big man. His arms were folded in defiance across a barrel chest.

"I am ordered to destroy the printing press and pi the type," the marshal said, his features set in an icy mask. He had no fear. Hundreds of men backed him up.

The door to the brick building opened. A man stepped out. Robert recognized him. He was Charles Foster, brother to Dr. Robert D. Foster. "I'll
handle this, John," Foster said.

Robert wondered where Wilson Law was hiding. The first floor? Second
floor? Cowering in the basement? Or already on the run? Robert stared at his
fists, amused at the thoughts that he might be able to use them on Law.

The marshal narrowed his eyes at Foster, a bantam of a man. "I'll need
the key to the building. Hand it over."

"You can't have it," Foster said, spreading his legs in a defiant stance. His
dark eyes radiated a fiery clarity that forecast his reputation for being an evil
tough man. His message was clear: nobody goes through the front door.

Marshall Greene motioned to two men, Jesse B. Harmon and John Lytle.
They stepped forward, each brandishing a large sledgehammer.

The door to the building opened again. This time Robert recognized the
man emerging as Francis Higbee. He locked the door behind him.

"Just a moment," Higbee said, thrusting his palms forward and up. "If
you lay hands on that press, you will date your downfall from this very hour."

Marshal Greene cast a quick glance at Major General Dunham, who gave
a quick nod. Green, in turn, motioned at Harmon and Lytle. "Break down the
door."

Reacting to all this, Higbee waved at his three guards. They were quick
to respond.

"No, you don't!" Eagle yelled, lunging at Levi and John.

Robert watched in horror as Harmon and Lytle were knocked off their
feet. Robert sprang into action, needing no encouragement. Quick as a cat, he
lunged at big John Eagle, spinning him around. Robert crashed a wicked right
cross to Eagle's jaw. The big man sank to the ground, half unconscious.

"Somehow you remind me of another man I know, with just about the
same name," Robert said, shaking his fist.

Stunned momentarily, the other two guards reacted. But so did Porter.
He lunged, catching one guard and knocking him to the ground. Robert side-

stepped the other guard, and then pounced on him, pinning him to the ground. Three blows to the man's head rendered him helpless.

Robert rose, looking for the third guard. The guard dropped to his knees. "Don't hit me," he pleaded. To Robert's right, John Eagle crawled away, moaning.

At a signal from the marshal, Porter took a sledgehammer from Lytle. One blow weakened the door, the lock, and the hinges. Other men inside scurried away, quickly disappearing. With a powerful leg kick, the door exploded open. Rockwell turned, smiling back at the marshal.

Marshal Greene motioned to his city policemen. "Do your job, men."

Robert ran inside the building, looking for Wilson Law. He felt as though the floor were tilting beneath his feet, so complete was his exhilaration. The inside of the building was dim, but revealed shelves stocked with leather, textiles, crockery, glass, and paint. Barrels, kegs, and boxes filled every available floor space. Wall hooks held animal pelts, buggy whips, and hand farm implements. A desk was littered with papers, a daybook, and ledgers.

There was not a human being in sight. A back door was open. Robert ran outside. The form of a man skulked in the alley. Robert approached, his fists clenched.

"That's far enough," a voice said.

Robert whirled to face three men, one brandishing a pistol.

"Freeze, or I'll shoot," said Wilson Law, the flare of annoyance on his face apparent.

More men poured out of the shadows, all with angry, mean looks. Robert locked his eyes on Wilson with an unwavering stare, visualizing a confrontation. Wilson had a solid build, about the same size as him. Someday, Robert promised himself, when he and Wilson were alone, there would be a fair fight.

"Turn around," Wilson ordered. "You were the smart-off during the meeting, weren't you?"

"My memory's a little cloudy these days," Robert replied.

Robert slowly turned his back on Wilson Law, facing the other men.

One by one, he recognized them. William Law, Robert D. Foster, Charle: Foster, Chauncey Higbee, Elias Higbee, and Francis Higbee.

Robert could hear Wilson's footsteps. "Maybe you'll remember this."

*Crack!*

A searing pain scorched the back of Robert's head as Wilson's pistoi crashed into his skull. Robert collapsed to his hands and knees, barely hang ing onto consciousness.

"Let's get out of here before the others find us," a voice said.

Robert was barely aware of the sound of footsteps running away. Hi rolled over on his back for a few minutes, waiting for the fog to clear. Finally he staggered to his feet. Wilson Law and the others were long gone.

Robert returned to the building with a splitting headache to find throng of city policemen and Legion soldiers carrying cases of type up the stairs ani out into the streets. Others followed, carrying and spilling leads and slugs Spaces and quads. Brayers. Quoins. Ink. Oils. Composing sticks. Type forms Galleys still full of type that made up the one and only edition of the *Expositoi* Contents from desks: papers, articles, and quill pens. Soon, the desks them selves.

Despite the pain, Robert managed to smile. He wobbled downstairs Legion soldiers were dismantling the press, piece by piece: the platen, th screw, and the frisket. Piece by piece the press was hauled up the stairs, alon. with printed copies of the *Expositor,* and extra sheets of paper.

Robert picked up a piece of the press and lugged it up the stairs, follow ing other men. He wondered if the extra paper would be taken to the *Timi and Seasons* office, or the *Neighbor* office.

In the middle of the street, Jesse B. Harmon was emptying a can of clean ing fluid onto the heap that had once been the *Expositor.* John Lytle added can of coal oil. Robert threw his load onto the heap. Porter Rockwell struck sulfur match. Huge flames erupted to the cheers of policemen, Legion so. diers, and the gathering crowd.

"Throw all the paper into the fire," Marshal Greene ordered. "Bur everything. Everything except the building. Leave it intact."

Soon, young boys were tripping over Robert's boots, scrambling for type souvenirs. Type had been scattered all over the street.

Robert reached down. There was every letter of the alphabet, some in capital letters, and others in lower case. There was type of every size and he picked some up. In his hand, Robert began forming words. Upside down and backward, like a mirror the words spelled out: *Wilson Law. You'd better run.*

"Come on, boys," Major General Dunham said, finally. "Follow me to the Nauvoo Mansion. The Prophet wants to commend you for a job well done."

# 41

*Thursday, June 13, 1844*

AGAINST MARY'S BETTER JUDGMENT, Elias Eagles went to vis
Henry in Carthage. "How can you think of going there when mobs are form
ing?" she had warned as he saddled Tapper, Robert's sorrel gelding.

"You worry too much," Elias countered as he mounted the horse an
looked down on his wife. "I'm not Joseph Smith. No one will harm me." H
dug his heels in the horse and galloped away.

The Illinois prairie between Nauvoo and Carthage looked the same t
Elias as the area around Robert's farm: a wide expanse of gentle sloping hill
sparsely filled with farms. Here and there were stands of mammoth oak
poplars, hickories, and pecans. Following Henry's explicit directions, he ha
no trouble finding the Eagles Dairy after the fifteen-mile trip over a well-tra
eled wagon road. Henry's farm was not as Henry portrayed it. It was nothin
like the Nightingale Dairy in Apperley England, where Elias had grown u

There was no tidy red brick building—sheltered by rows of apple trees—that housed copper milk vats, butter churns, and cheese molds. Henry's milk barn was a crude log lean-to instead of a whitewashed clapboard building.

"You're just in time," Henry said as Elias rode up. Henry's dog, a big black one, acted as though he wanted to tear into Elias' leg. Henry pointed to a tin milk can, filled with the morning's milking. "I have two clients in town waiting."

To Elias, Henry's rough log home was not much better than the barn. He caught a glimpse of Katherine, her sad eyes peering out the window. A garden next to the house was well kept. Elias guessed it was probably the product of Katherine's hard work. Six cows grazed in a small pasture. A red hog snorted in a pen, rummaging through household scraps, skim milk, and discarded shells of last year's squash storage.

Elias caught himself sounding like Mary. "Is it safe to go into town?"

Henry grunted. "Not for Mormons. But with me, you'll be fine."

Henry's horse-drawn wagon reached Carthage in less than fifteen minutes. Elias was struck by the sharp contrasts between Carthage, Nauvoo, and Apperley—his hometown in England. Carthage was small, similar in size to Apperley, with just four hundred residents. It seemed infested with burrowing animals—rats, rabbits, and prairie dogs. There were few stone cottages. As in Nauvoo, people here lived in a collection of log homes and frame homes, wrapped around a town square. The three most important buildings in the village were the Hamilton House—a traveler's inn with nearby stables— the Carthage Jail, and the Hancock County Courthouse. The town square in Nauvoo was really the temple grounds. Here, the courthouse was a pleasing new granite structure, but Elias was not impressed with the homes; they were not nearly as neat as those in Nauvoo.

Henry told Elias that Hancock County got its name from a man who was the first governor of the Commonwealth of Massachusetts and first signer of America's Declaration of Independence. Henry also said that eighteen small communities surrounded Carthage, with names like Ramus, Fountain Green, St. Mary's, Green Plains, Plymouth, LaHarpe, and Macedonia.

The number of people in town, mostly men, also struck Elias. "Is thi normal?" he asked.

A devious smile crossed Henry's face. "Normally, only during cour week."

"Court week?"

"The circuit court comes to Carthage only twice a year, in May anc October. You practically can't get into town then. Everyone comes. It's almos impossible for visitors to find sleeping space, even on a floor."

Elias arched his eyebrows. "This is June thirteenth."

Henry pointed to the town square. "These folks are gearing up for a mas meeting," he said. "We're going, too. You'll meet some of my friends."

Elias gulped, his face a mirror of nervous apprehension. Henry was th same as he had remembered him, reckless and impulsive. Elias said, "Abou the Mormon question, no doubt."

"No doubt," Henry replied.

"Is everyone in Carthage against the Mormons?"

"Just about."

"Including you?"

"It seems common sense to ride the horse in the direction it's going."

Elias furrowed his brow. "Not if the horse is going over a cliff."

Henry let the words float off. "First things first. Let's get this milk deliv ered. It's early. We've got time to go to Warsaw. We'll be back in time for th meeting."

To Elias' eyes, Warsaw was similar to Carthage—a small village with a tow square and a narrow but straight main street lined with shops and businesse on both sides. Henry pointed out the offices of the *Warsaw Signal,* where h once met the editor, Thomas Sharp, face-to-face. Henry told Elias tha Warsaw, located on the Mississippi, was a major competitor with Nauvoo fo river trade and political dominance in Hancock County. That caused a fierc rivalry between the two communities and was part of the reason for the hatre of Mormons. Nauvoo had grown quickly, from a few hundred in 1839 t nearly fourteen thousand residents currently. There seemed to be no end to the projected growth of the thriving, bustling city. Warsaw, however, was less than a thousand. Like Carthage, Warsaw had a mayor and a five-member board of trustees. The trustees appointed a justice of the peace, policemen, assessors, and tax collectors.

"There's Mr. Sharp," Henry said, his voice excited.

"He's the man who invented the myth of Mormon threats?" Elias asked, repeating what Robert and Hannah had told him. Where there is hatred, there is repression, torture, and mass murder, they had said.

"The Mormon myth is real, little brother. They want to control the world, beginning with Hancock County politics. Want to meet Mr. Sharp?"

"Sure," said Elias, letting his gaze fall onto a stocky man in his mid-twenties. Sharp was walking across the street at an energetic pace, a few sheets of paper in one hand, accompanied by another man, older, probably in his early forties.

Henry bent his head and walked as though he were bucking a high wind. "Remember me, Mr. Sharp?" Henry asked, his dark eyes alive with anticipation.

Sharp studied the square-faced, dark-haired man with an English accent. "I think so. One afternoon in the tavern here? Two or three years ago?"

"That's me," Henry said, beaming.

"The one with the Mormon wife?" Sharp asked, his mouth turning downward.

"I moved out of Nauvoo, to Carthage. I don't let that dish-nosed wife of mine go to church."

The words immediately disarmed Sharp. "This your brother? He looks just like you."

"His name is Elias."

Sharp did not offer a handshake. "Mormon or not?"

"He just arrived from England. After today, he'll be a former Mormon. We're going to the mass meeting in Carthage together."

Sharp laughed slightly, locking eyes with Elias. "I have some advice, young man. Drop Mormonism, and do it now. Your Prophet is a vulgar imposter of religion, snowing just the gullible. He's a rumpled imposter, without pedigree. There are titters about the Mormon scare that are sweeping not only the state but also the entire nation. From now on, it's going to be dangerous around these parts for Mormons. Watch yourself."

The *Warsaw Signal* editor turned to the man with him. "This is Mark Aldrich. He doesn't like Mormons, either."

Henry stuck out a hand. Aldrich, the older man, accepted it. Henry said, "We've got something in common. You work for Mr. Sharp?"

"No. I'm a land agent. Mormons broke me."

"That so? How?"

Aldrich narrowed his eyes, finding old anger. "Joe Smith promised to send Mormons to a new settlement near here. Called Warren. Quicker than they arrived, they moved out. On Joe's orders. It bankrupted me."

"Mr. Aldrich helped me form the anti-Mormon political party," Sharp said in a tone that discouraged further conversation. He walked away studying the papers in his hand. Then Sharp and Aldrich entered the office.

The men attending the mass meeting in Carthage were assorted in their looks, temperament, and expression. To Elias, they were passionate to the point of madness about the destruction of the *Nauvoo Expositor* press. Elias wondered why citizens in towns other than Nauvoo were so up in arms, and what business it was of theirs. He quickly concluded that it wasn't freedom of the press that had lit their fire. It was pure anti-Mormon sentiment, and it intrigued him. He recalled his study of the Book of Mormon. If ever there were secret combinations controlled by Satan, this was it. Initially, the meeting was unruly, with men raising their fists and voices in threat against not only the Mormon hierarchy, but also all Mormons in general. Eventually, a president of the mass meeting was appointed, two vice presidents, and a secretary. Restoring order, they called for resolutions. Suggestions came quickly, almost to the point of disorder again.

Several men from Nauvoo were asked to testify. Their names were

Francis M. Higbee, Wilson Law, and Robert D. Foster. Within seconds, Elias realized they were the men described by Daniel Browett and Robert Harris on the way to the grove last Sunday. They were avowed enemies of Joseph Smith, and partners in the *Expositor*. Elias quickly concluded that if one were to believe Higbee, Law, and Foster, all Mormons—including himself, Hannah, and Robert—were the worst form of humanity on the face of the earth. They used foul and colorful language to describe members of the Church and the history of Mormonism. They were allowed to talk as long as they wanted, and painted a dark and diabolical picture, spinning their version of what had happened to them and their friends and the printing press, and churning the crowd into a frenzy.

When Higbee testified, he said that "one of our valued citizens," Thomas C. Sharp, editor of the paper, had been publicly threatened by Hyrum Smith.

Elias quickly thought of Sharp, his curt greeting, and the sight of him disappearing into his office on the main street in Warsaw. He could visualize him with pen and ink, writing another scathing article against the Mormons.

A man named Henry Stephens was introduced. He passionately urged the Carthage assembly to adopt the same resolutions passed by a similar meeting held in Warsaw. Stephens said it would demonstrate a show of unity and strength against the hated Mormons.

The first resolution castigated the recently passed Nauvoo city ordinance that allowed Joe Smith to destroy the opposition press. The second stated that legal remedies no longer were of any force against Joe, that a mob would be necessary to fight against the Mormon mobs. The third called for an "immediate stop to the career of the mad prophet and his demoniac coadjutors," and that Carthage County citizens must "resolutely carry war into the enemy's camp." It also stipulated that citizens should unite to protect Thomas C. Sharp and his newspaper at all costs, and to "utterly exterminate the wicked and abominable Mormon leaders."

Elias sat silent, not daring to make a remark of any kind. In his opinion, these men were making a feverish pact with the devil. Henry, however, participated in the discussions as the participants sprang naturally to their

Mormon hatred positions.

The fourth resolution said that "a committee of five men would be appointed to notify all Mormons—persons in our township suspected of being the tools of the Prophet—to leave immediately on pain of instant vengeance." A fifth resolution stated that "the adherents of Smith, as a body, should be driven from the surrounding settlements into Nauvoo." The final resolution stipulated that "every citizen arm himself to be prepared to sustain" all the other resolutions.

As each resolution passed unanimously, a shudder went through Elias.

There was no pro and con debate, only fervent pleas from angry men that the resolutions be adopted, which they were. The men's attacks on Mormonism were enlivened with personal venom without pause and with no restraint for decency. Before they adjourned, they voted three thousand dollars for ammunition, and resolved to beat Joe Smith's expected appeal to Springfield with a delegation of their own.

The return trip to the dairy was marked by a bevy of questions from a confused Elias Eagles. He asked about the history of Nauvoo, the liberal powers granted the Nauvoo City government, provisions for a militia that had grown into a powerful independent army known as the Nauvoo Legion, and all the other issues Warsaw and Carthage citizens seemed to oppose. He also asked questions about all the other controversies swirling around Mormonism: plural marriage, plurality of gods, and Joseph Smith's presidential candidacy.

The idea that Joseph Smith could actually be a candidate for President intrigued Elias. In England, only a member of the royal family could hope to be king or queen. In America, any common man could rise from the ranks of the unknown to become president.

Henry's response to Elias' questions mostly took the typical anti-Mormon approach. The answers shook Elias' testimony and bulged his eyes into a state of shock. Then came the clincher: "Elias, it's time to move here with me. We'll be partners."

Elias sighed. Perhaps it *was* time.

# 42

*Monday, June 17*

THE DOOR TO GOVERNOR THOMAS FORD'S office hissed open. His aides parted as Wilson and William Law and their *Expositor* partners entered the room like a swarm of angry wasps. A secretary pointed to a semi-circle of velvet-padded chairs. The governor's office had once again become a refuge for Mormon-haters. Governor Ford stood behind his desk, shuffling a handful of letters. A thought came to him. He wished the *Expositor* had been destroyed by an unruly Mormon mob rather than by legal means. That fact was surely to complicate matters.

Livid in his mannerisms, Wilson Law asked the governor to read the letters out loud. They were from Joseph Smith, Sidney Rigdon, and John M. Bernhisel. The governor had already read them to himself, many times over, his reactions ranging from shock to horror. They explained the destruction of the *Expositor* from the Mormon point of view.

In an odd way, Governor Ford saw a trace of humor in General Smith's written description of the ex-Mormons in his office. Ford looked up at Wilson Law. "Says right here, in black and white, that you men are nothing more than unprincipled, lawless debauchers, counterfeiters, bogus-makers, gamblers, and peace-disturbers."

Law let an almost tortured gasp escape from his gaping mouth "Governor, how can you believe that?"

The governor chuckled, sensing that Wilson Law would love to arrest Joe Smith on any charge and throw a celebration party with the devil. The ex-Mormons in his room were once General Smith's most trusted supporters One a counselor in his First Presidency. One a major general in the Nauvoo Legion. Another a surgeon general in the Legion. Two of them Mormon attor-neys. Still another a successful businessman.

Ford also marveled at how quickly Mormonism had deteriorated and how it seemed on the brink of absolute destruction. For a moment, he com-pared Mormonism to religions like the Quakers, the Shakers, and the Methodists—all of which had be persecuted greatly until the world got used to them. It seemed to Ford that Mormonism was so different, so weird, that the world would never accept it. Smith had allowed his followers to steal manufacturer counterfeit money, and take multiple wives. He had heard that some Mormons were so bound to Smith that were committed to obey all orders from him, even to commit murder if so commanded. To him Mormonism was becoming the most intolerable collection of rogues ever assembled.

Ford read a few lines. The letters claimed the destruction of the *Expositor* was done legally and without harming anyone seriously.

Wilson cursed and jumped to his feet with a sinister look. "Lies! All lies The policemen and Legion were armed. They threatened to kill me."

Wilson's brother William erupted. "Joe Smith's been trying to pin crime on us for months. He's the criminal, not us."

Ford took a deep breath, glad that Joe Smith, Rigdon, and Bernhisel had sent letters and not come in person. It was much more fun to meet with the opposition.

"General Smith readily admits to destroying your newspaper," Ford said, thrusting the letter at Wilson. "He claims it was done without riot, noise, tumult, or confusion."

"Ha!" countered Wilson. "You should have been there, governor. The thundering of the Legion troopers as they stomped up the street. Thousands of them. The threats against us, the foul language. Smith himself ordered the press destroyed. Now he's trying to destroy us."

Ford sighed heavily. "But according to Bernhisel's letter, General Smith is a bright, shining example of integrity."

The floodgate was now open. The six ex-Mormons pounded Ford's ears into submission with tales of the many spiritual wives of Joe Smith, false doctrines of plural marriage and the plurality of gods, and everything else. They related how they had been forced out of Nauvoo, and that their wives and children were in hiding across the river in Iowa. They charged that Nauvoo was an armed fortress with soldiers ready to kill any non-Mormon who dared venture within two miles of the city.

Ford reeled as though knocked backward by the words. An armed fortress? The possibility of a war between the Mormons and their enemies? The press in places like Warsaw and Carthage were calling for the death of Smith and the extermination of Mormons.

"You've got to arrest Smith," Wilson charged without a shred of remorse.

Ford nodded, allowing himself to become more combative now, as if he sensed the reality of the situation. "I'll do it, even it we have to search the city for a month."

A lopsided grin crossed Wilson's face. "We could raise enough men in Carthage to attack Nauvoo."

"How many?" Ford asked with a devilish smile, speculating.

The six ex-Mormons glanced at each other. For a few seconds they discussed numbers. "There's nearly five thousand men in the Nauvoo Legion," Wilson answered. "We need to outnumber them two to one."

"You can raise ten thousand men?"

"If we have to," Wilson said.

The other ex-Mormons were silent for a moment. Robert D. Foster posed a question. "But what if we can only raise a thousand or two?"

"Then we need to incite things more," was the quick reply.

"How?" asked Chauncey Higbee, his eyes wide open with skepticism.

"I'll sneak back into Nauvoo at night and set our building on fire," Wilson said, showing the depth of his fertile imagination.

"Which building?" Ford asked. He tilted his head to one side, his skepticism evident.

"Where the *Expositor* was housed. We'll blame it on Joe Smith."

Governor Ford smiled. He was in good company. He liked the way these ex-Mormons thought. He just didn't want it to go too far, this inevitable clash of cultures. Mormons had to be driven out, but Ford did not want to experience an all-out war in Illinois.

After all, he had to face re-election sometime.

# 43

*Friday, June 21*

ROBERT HARRIS WAS ON EDGE. Two hours ago he had arrived at the eastern boundary of the farm he shared with Daniel Browett. And for two hours he had been digging with other troopers, Levi Roberts, John Cox, Thomas Bloxham, John Hyrum Green, and Edward Phillips. They were digging bulwarks for the protection of their wives, children, homes, and farms.

Out of breath, Robert stopped to rest and leaned on his shovel. He rubbed a small lump on the back of his head where Wilson Law had struck him with the pistol. Had it really come to this? War between the Mormons and the non-Mormons? Would the mob strike from the east, from the Carthage area? Would Henry be in the mob? And what about Elias? Sadly, Elias had moved in with Henry to be his partner in the dairy.

There were reports of mass meetings in Warsaw and Carthage. Resolutions called for all-out war against the Mormons and the death of

Joseph and Hyrum. There were other resolutions that would temporarily push all the Mormons into Nauvoo, and then ultimately exterminate all member of the Mormon Church from the state. Additionally, Colonel Levi William of the Carthage Greys had threatened to cut off the arms of all the Mormon around his area. There had been attempts to tar and feather Mormons. Ther were rumors of mobs with bloodhounds collecting at Carthage and on th Missouri border. Further rumors held that Wilson Law was going to burn th *Expositor* office and blame it on the Mormons. And there were reports of cannon arriving in Warsaw from Quincy.

In Nauvoo, Joseph and other Church leaders had been arrested fo destroying the *Expositor* press. But a non-Mormon justice of the peace, Danie B. Wells, had closely examined the charges and dismissed them. Delegates ha been sent from Nauvoo to all the surrounding towns, explaining the Church side of the *Expositor* issue. Affidavits had been sent to Governor Forc Notwithstanding all this, the Prophet had called up the Legion to be availabl twenty-four hours a day. In full uniform, Joseph had marched them as a sho of strength. He had declared martial law and made plans for the defense of th city, and plans to feed a city under siege. Already he had inspected the bu warks and was expected to do it again. Pickets had been established, guardin all roads that led to Nauvoo, and along the river.

There were also reports that Robert D. Foster, president of the Reforme Church, had just informed the Prophet that he would allow Mormons n willing to join with Foster to leave freely, but only after they sold their prop erty. Apparently a handful had already sold out even though Foster was offe ing less than ten cents on the dollar.

And worst of all, there was a report that Governor Ford had arrived i Carthage and that he had ordered a mob to be assembled under his comman Ford apparently had not believed the article written in the *Nauvoo Neighbo* by John Taylor. It said that Wilson Law and the other renegades had le Nauvoo of their own accord, that they were not threatened or menaced, th their mills and properties were not burned as claimed, nor was the *Exposit* building burned or destroyed.

Robert stared to the east and shook his head in anger. Out there, more troopers were digging bulwarks on Joseph Smith's farm, and on John Benbow's, and Thomas Kington's. And on the farms of new English immigrants, such as William Kay and John Gailey.

Robert wiped his brow and spoke in a direct tone laced with hate. "If they burn our new houses, Wilson Law is a dead man. I'll lay the wrath of the world on his doorstep." Robert threw down his shovel and picked up his rifle, a Legion issue owned by the state of Illinois. He drew it to his shoulder and aimed to the east. In his mind he could see Wilson Law's begging eyes.

"It won't be Wilson Law who'll set the fire," Daniel said as he dug. "It'll be some crazy anti-Mormon from Carthage or Warsaw."

Squinting, Robert set the hammer and pulled the trigger. Without a load in the muzzle, there was only a deadening click. "Maybe. I don't care. It'll still be Wilson Law's fault."

Despite the sound of shovels moving dirt, the area around the farm seemed perfectly calm. Birds sang in the bushes. A gentle breeze fanned stalks of wheat. Daniel wondered if an invasion would actually come. After all, the Nauvoo Legion was five thousand strong.

Daniel felt an upsurge of dread as he considered Robert's hardened view of Wilson Law. Robert had been going off on the Mormon apostate for days. It was probably because Wilson was the only one of the *Expositor* gang who was built like Robert—six foot tall, two hundred pounds, rippling muscles, bawdy personality—and the only one who likely could give Robert any kind of fight in an actual personal battle. Wilson's brother, William, was just as responsible for the predicament Church members were in than just about anyone else. So were Dr. Robert D. Foster and his brother, and the Higbee brothers. But they were smaller, weaker men.

There were a host of other villains as well, such as Thomas Sharp, the editor. Words of Sharp's recent article were seared in Daniel's memory: "It is sufficient! War and extermination is inevitable. Citizens arise ONE and ALL!!!...We have no time for comment: every man will make his own. LET

IT BE MADE WITH POWDER AND BALL!!!!"

Daniel had never met Sharp, but had formed a biased opinion of him. Sharp was a loose cannon with that press of his, a man who demanded tha the world treat sinners like friends and true Christians like enemies. A mar who wanted to attack Mormons without anyone making an issue of it, yet nc one was allowed to cast the slightest aspersion on Sharp and his tactics. In fact Sharp went into a diarrhea panic if anyone criticized him or his friends. He was a man who maligned Mormonism and held parties and secret meeting with other Mormon-haters.

There were others that Robert could turn his wrath on, in Daniel's opin ion. Mark Aldrich, the Warsaw land agent. Levi Williams, colonel of the Carthage Greys. And Governor Thomas Ford, who wouldn't meet personally with the Prophet or his representatives to hear the Mormon side of the *Expositor* issue. Yet he would meet with the *Expositor* apostates.

Daniel's dread would not fade away. "Maybe we ought to sell our farm and our new houses and get out of Nauvoo."

For the past couple of weeks, no work had been done on the new homes With the danger of invasion, there was no point in moving in. It was safer in the city. Daniel closed his eyes and thought of a future day when he could build steps, finish painting, and move into his new frame house with Elizabeth and Harriet. His garden was planted, but because of neglect it was full of weeds.

"And give in to that white-livered thief Wilson Law and the gang of crooks?" Robert answered. "No way."

Daniel shuddered. Robert's attitude had deteriorated to his pre-baptism days in England. Robert seemed to look forward to a fight; to him, life was daring adventure, or nothing at all.

At Daniel's side, Levi Roberts tossed his shovel aside. "Let's go forward and see how the others are doing," Levi said.

John Cox wiped his brow. "Maybe they need help at the Benbow farm.

Robert aimed his rifle again. "Let's go to Carthage and find Wilson Law and his friends. That's probably where they're hiding."

# 44

*Thursday, June 20*

THEODORE TURLEY SEEMED A MITE CONFUSED, in Daniel's view. On the one hand, Turley was telling the assembled men that he needed their immediate help to begin manufacturing artillery in his arms factory and repairing small arms. But on the other hand, he related Joseph Smith's promise that "a gun would not be fired in Nauvoo on our part during this fuss."

Joseph had summoned Turley earlier in the day, giving him orders as commander-in-chief of the Nauvoo Legion to commence the manufacture of arms. All of the rifles used by the Legion were state-issue and subject to confiscation. "The governor could order them back into the state's control just as easily as they gave them to us," he had said.

Many of the men assembled in Turley's building were British converts, willing to help their fellow Englishmen. Daniel knew Turley as the man who had accompanied Wilford Woodruff to England in 1840. The two men, along

with John Taylor, had traveled to England together as missionaries. After serving nine months, Turley—like Daniel—had been named a company leader
over a group of emigrating saints. Turley departed Liverpool on September
eighth with two hundred one Mormon passengers. After his arrival in Nauvoo
he became the second polygamist in Nauvoo—a sign that he was one of
Joseph Smith's most trusted associates.

Turley began organizing his emergency workers. Edward Phillips. John
Hyrum Green. Levi Roberts. John Cox. George Bundy. John Gailey. Joseph
Hill. James Robins. Thomas Bloxham. And many others.

Daniel thought about the temple. This was a major distraction that
would slow the final stages of construction. Minutes earlier he had passed the
limestone walls, still not finished, gleaming in the morning sunshine.
Sunstones were in place, however. So were the moonstones and the starstones,
emblematic of the celestial, terrestrial, and telestial kingdoms. And the arched
windows, even the round ones that Joseph had insisted on, despite the objections of the architect.

Theodore handed Daniel his first gun to repair.

Daniel stared at it. He hoped it would never have to be used. He thought
of Book of Mormon times—people who at one time followed the teaching
of Christ, but later fought against the Prophets. The men out there who
threatened to kill Mormons professed to be Christians. Yet they seemed to
have no aversion to murder.

"You've got three days to make up your mind."

Hannah glared at Henry. Her brother sat in the wagon he had driven
from his dairy farm near Carthage. "How can you come riding into Nauvoo
and give that kind of ultimatum to your own sister?"

"Don't shoot the messenger," Henry shot back, returning the glare to
both Hannah and Robert. He had just told them that mobs were forming in
Carthage. "Think of the kindness of the people who sent me. They could have
taken up arms and invaded Nauvoo without warning."

Hannah was appalled and began to wish she had never heard of Nauvoo

Henry had told her that all Mormons would be destroyed unless they did three things: deny that Joseph Smith was a Prophet of God, take up arms and help the mob arrest Joseph and his brother, and afterward give up their personal weapons and remain quiet.

"You tell whoever sent you that we reject the ultimatum," Robert fumed. "If they want to invade Nauvoo, let them start with me. My musket is in the house. Want to try to take it from me right now, Henry?"

Henry fumed as he stroked his gun. "Don't disappoint me. I'm mean as a tom turkey when I'm disappointed."

Hannah pulled on Robert's arm. "You two have had enough fights in your lifetime."

Henry's dark eyes glared at Robert. "You've got three days to make up your mind. That's the message. Tell your neighbors. It's my duty to warn you."

"We don't need three days," Robert answered in a gruff tone. "Go back to Carthage."

# 45

**Friday, June 21**

THE RUMBLE OF GUNSHOTS FROM THE west shook Hannah. *Pleas* *God! No! Not an invasion!* She exploded from the house screaming the nam of her children. "Joseph! Elizabeth! William! Thomas!"

*Boom! Boom!*

The skies were cloudy and it had been raining. But clearly, the soun echoing throughout Nauvoo were not thunderclaps.

Robert was at the corral saddling Tapper and Bendigo. He swooped tw year-old Thomas in his arms and ran toward Hannah, pointing wildly towa the Nauvoo Landing. "Gunshots!"

"Where're the other children?" Hannah screamed.

"At the Greens'," Robert said, motioning three blocks east. "Ta Tommy."

Daniel trotted up, leading the horses. Obviously, the two men wou have to change their plans. Work on the farm would have to wait. "If that was our troops at the river, they may need our help," he said, a sense of urgency rising within him. "But why would they invade from the river?"

Elizabeth and Harriet had burst from the Browett cabin. "We'll find the children," Elizabeth said.

Robert and Daniel swung into the saddle. In seconds they had disappeared over the hill, descending on a muddy road that led to the river.

Elizabeth and Harriet ran toward the John Hyrum Green cabin. Hannah streaked to the safety of her own cabin, slamming the door behind her.

Hannah peered out the window. Harriet Ann Roberts was scurrying her three children indoors. So was Eliza Cox, clutching her two-month-old infant. It was just past four in the afternoon, a warm and humid first day of summer. Hannah thought of Joseph Smith, in an emergency session with the city council. He would probably be rushing toward the Nauvoo Landing as well. He had just reviewed Robert and Daniel and all the other Nauvoo Legion troops, talking to them from ten in the morning until two thirty. Hannah sensed that the Prophet was terribly depressed. Brigham Young, Wilford Woodruff, Orson Hyde and all of the Twelve were away. Sidney Rigdon was in Pittsburgh. William Law had apostatized. George Miller, the presiding bishop of the Church, was at the pineries.

Hannah pulled Thomas tightly to her bosom, and then she wiped a tear from her cheek.

When Daniel and Robert returned they found their wives huddled together in the Browett cabin, fearing the worst. The children were locked in the bedroom.

"Is there an invasion?" Hannah asked, her eyes darting from the two men to the west, where they had been.

Robert held up a palm and waved it. "False alarm."

Hannah's mood brightened.

"It was the crew of the *Maid of Iowa*," Daniel explained. "They fired five of their guns."

"Contrary to their orders, too," Robert added. "Some of the men are probably in trouble." He went on to explain that guards at the Stone House were reporting the incident to on-duty officers of the Legion.

From the look in Hannah's eyes, Robert wondered what her reaction would be if an invasion actually did come. There was plenty to be concerned about, the signs not good. Joseph Smith, as Commander-in-Chief of the Nauvoo Legion, two days earlier had ordered picket guards to be posted on all roads leading to and from the city. Plans had been formulated for defense of the area. An order had been issued to secure all powder, lead, and arms. Joseph was reviewing the Legion twice a day. All outgoing mail had been cut off by mobs. Express letters had been sent to members of the Twelve on missions in the E'ast, telling them to come home. And worst of all, the Prophet had urged his brother, Hyrum, to flee Nauvoo by steamboat to Cincinnati. Rumor was circulating throughout the city that Joseph wanted Hyrum to succeed him as President of the Church and had actually ordained him to take his place.

"Are you going to take us out of here?" Hannah asked, tears welling up.

Robert shook his head, no. "Where would we go?"

Hannah shrugged her shoulders. All she knew was that it appeared Nauvoo was surrounded, or in the process of becoming so. She glanced at the Browett bedroom, where the children were playing as though nothing was wrong. "I'm afraid," she said.

# 46

JOHN TAYLOR FELT HIS SKIN TINGLE with fear as he entered the Carthage town square in pitch darkness. Even with Dr. Bernhisel at his side, Taylor had not been this terrified since his mission to England in 1840 when anti-Mormons stormed a baptism ceremony he was conducting in an outdoor pond. Actually, this time was worse, he thought to himself. He could feel the presence of Satan's tentacles wrapped around a collection of frontier rabble and rowdies hovering around the Hamilton House. Liquor was flowing freely. Taylor was glad to have a pistol hidden beneath his vest.

"They're under the influence of Bacchus," Taylor said to Bernhisel with a wave of disgust. Taylor was certain the Mormon doctor understood. Bacchus was the mythical Greek god of wine and fertility. Festivals honoring Bacchus were typically drunken orgies.

John felt the wavy brown hair on his head stand straight out. He sensed Bernhisel's was too. The drunken men surrounding them were whooping and hollering, vociferating as if bedlam had broken loose. Even though John stood just under six feet tall and weighed a hundred eighty pounds, he felt he was no match for this swarm of tipsy drunkards.

Matching Taylor's cleverness, Bernhisel whispered back, "They seem to be holding a grand saturnalia." His remarks were in reference to a Roman festival held in honor of the god of agriculture, Saturn, the mythical father of Jupiter. Held in December, the festival was also characterized by unrestrained orgiastic revelry.

Joseph Smith had dispatched Apostle John Taylor, editor of the *Nauvoo Neighbor,* and Dr. Bernhisel to Carthage. Joseph did it because Governor Ford had invited one or more "well-informed and discreet persons" who would be able to accurately give the governor Joseph's version of the *Expositor* matter. Ford had arrived in Carthage that morning and had immediately sent a letter to Joseph. Joseph received it at two thirty in the afternoon. Because heavy spring rains had left the roads a quagmire, Taylor and Bernhisel had ridden horseback instead of by carriage.

"Where did the governor get such a collection of crackpot base characters?" Bernhisel asked as they entered the hotel and walked to the registration desk.

"The American frontier, unfortunately, is full of them," Taylor said shaking his thirty-six-year-old head. After tonight, there would be more gray flecks in the sideburns that graced his temples. "I hope the governor is still up. I'd like to meet with him tonight and get it over with."

Even with a pistol hidden under his vest, John did not feel safe. Every man in the square—literally hundreds of them—had displayed a collection of rifles, pistols, and swords. All were members of various militia units surrounding Carthage, and some from units as far away as Springfield.

Both Nauvoo visitors were disappointed to find that Ford had already retired. "If he's really asleep," Taylor commented warily, "then he's the only one. All are at least half awake, owing to the fact they are at least half drunk."

An aide said they would have to wait until morning for their interview.

Taylor was shocked to find they had to pass through another bedroom to get to their room. To his dismay, Joseph H. Jackson, one of the apostate desperados, lay in the bed. Jackson lay on his back, head sunk in a pillow, staring at the two new arrivals. Jackson gave John an evil grin. "Welcome to Carthage," he said. "Have a good night's rest."

*The clerk gave us this room on purpose,* Taylor quickly surmised. He closed the door. The partition between the two rooms was a flimsy affair, a layer of single boards. Taylor held a finger to his lips. "Shhh. He'll be able to hear everything we say."

Taylor and Bernhisel quickly undressed and blew out the lantern. Minutes after they had snuggled into their beds a knock came to the door.

"Who is it?" Bernhisel asked, leaning his head toward the door and cupping his hand over his ear.

There was a voice with an English accent, speaking as though he had a couple of missing teeth. "Henry Eagles."

"What do you want?" Bernhisel asked as he held onto the doorknob, not about to twist it open.

"I'm a messenger, on duty with the Carthage militia. A member of your church was arrested tonight. He's in jail now and needs your help. He wants you to bail him out."

John Taylor shook his head and grimaced. He pulled out his pistol just in case. "What's his name?"

"They didn't give it to me."

Taylor shook his head again, his anger brimming. "It's a ruse," he whispered to Bernhisel. "They want us outside. Those men out there would kill us."

"It'll have to wait until morning," Bernhisel told the voice. "We're not coming out."

There were a few seconds of silence. "This won't make your man happy," the voice said. "They'll probably send me back."

Taylor and Bernhisel placed their pistols under their pillows and closed their eyes. Not more than a half hour passed and a knock came to the door again.

"Go away," Bernhisel pleaded, half asleep.

"We're not kidding about someone needing bail," a new voice said.

John Taylor sat up straight in bed. The voice was hauntingly familiar "Brother Higbee?"

"Chauncey, to you," the voice said. "I'm not your brother anymore. The name of the man in jail is Daniel Garn, a policeman from Nauvoo. Really, he's in jail. It's a dismal hole. He pleads for your help."

Bernhisel lit a lantern and began to dress.

Taylor leaned toward Bernhisel. His voice was a low whisper. "Brother Garn is not the sort of person who would be in trouble. Besides, it would be quite remarkable that a court would convene in the middle of the night. It's still a scheme to get us outside."

A pained quietness came over Bernhisel. "I agree," he whispered back.

"We're not coming out," the Mormon Apostle said, his voice firm "Goodnight. Tell all your friends hello."

"Friends?"

John Taylor couldn't help himself, feeling a wave of disgust. "Brother William Law. Brother Wilson Law. Brother Robert D. Foster. Brother Charles A. Foster. And your brother, Brother Elias Higbee. Your poor old father is rolling over in his grave. He was a faithful member of the Church. Not a hapless apostate like you."

Just as before, there was a prolonged period of silence. "We won't leave you alone tonight," Chauncey's voice said.

"Goodnight, former brother," Taylor said. "Be sure to say your prayers."

# 47

*Saturday, June 22*

GOVERNOR FORD WAS IN HIS USUAL bad mood as he waited in his room at Carthage's Hamilton House to meet with two Mormons sent from Nauvoo. He had been awakened in the middle of the night with a frightful report that the Mormons had already commenced the work of burning, destroying, and murdering. Terrified militia officers had banged on his door, awaiting orders. Ford had told them to go back to bed, that he had been hearing those false stories even before he had left Springfield.

Ford leveled his gaze at the assembly of men in the room who had seceded from the Mormon Party. "Who did Smith send?" Ford asked them.

"John Taylor and Dr. Bernhisel," William Law replied. "But be wary of them. They will utter any lie to protect their leader."

Ford shuddered. He suspected the rumor to be true that Nauvoo by now was one great military camp, strictly guarded and watched. "Do they have the affidavits?"

"I'm sure they do," William answered. "Mormon affidavits are lies, too, you know."

"They committed a crime when they destroyed our press," whined his brother, Wilson. "If it takes the whole force of the state, you must bring Joe Smith to justice."

Ford thought for a long moment. "What if I march into Nauvoo with the militia I have with me?"

"You'd be destroyed. The Nauvoo Legion has five thousand men," Wilson said, exaggerating a little. "You need to call up the whole state. Go into Nauvoo and wipe them out."

The governor drew a deep breath. Wilson Law probably knew what he was talking about. After all, he was the former major general of the Nauvoo Legion. Law had given him valuable information about the Legion, although Ford suspected that Law had widely exaggerated the number of arms and cannon in its possession.

However, as governor, Ford had another problem. June was the time of high waters on the Mississippi and on all the rivers and creeks in the western country; astonishing floods were ravishing the countryside. The Mississippi was several feet higher that it had ever been in the memory of even old-timers. Not only that, but the unusually wet spring had not given farmers a chance to plow and plant. Farmers who served in the militia were grumbling; no one wanted to be called to active duty right now.

Ford sank his head into his hands. Being governor was tough business.

The morning meeting with Governor Ford was turning out to be one of the greatest disappointments in John Taylor's life. He had expected Ford to give him and Bernhisel a *private* interview. Instead, after waiting outside Ford's room for a full hour, Taylor found himself inside a room filled with what he thought were the vilest men in all creation. Not only the Laws, the Higbees and the Fosters, but the two apostates who had signed the complaints against Joseph and Hyrum—Augustine Spencer and Henry O. Norton. And there was a handful of men from Warsaw, including longtime enemies Thomas C. Sharp and Mark Aldrich.

With a smug look, Ford began. "I take it you two are General Smith's duly authorized representatives from Nauvoo."

Taylor fought to focus his thoughts. The situation in Carthage and Nauvoo was almost too bizarre to grasp rationally. "We are. But I think you owe us the courtesy of an interview without anyone else in the room."

Ford's comeback was icy. "I will hear both sides."

Taylor let his eyes rake across the evil men who surrounded Ford. They seemed to suck light from the room. He felt like telling the governor that he was certain he had heard the other side a dozen or more times. And he felt like leaving, except that Joseph expected him to deliver the affidavits.

"I haven't much time," Ford said matter-of-factly.

Taylor shot a spiteful glance at Wilson Law. Law looked ready to burst, eager for a chance to rebut anything he or Dr. Bernhisel had to say. John asked Bernhisel to speak first. Bernhisel related the difficulties facing members of the Church in Nauvoo and the surrounding communities, and the course pursued by the Saints and their leaders.

Ford gave disinterested nods. "Get to the heart of the matter," he said angrily.

Taylor stared at Ford with a horrified look. He had the sinking feeling the governor was going to pay little attention to his affidavits. He reached for his satchel.

The first affidavit in Taylor's hands had been signed by John P. Greene, the Nauvoo marshal. Taylor began reading it, revealing that Greene swore that on May twenty-seventh Robert D. Foster called Greene into a private room in Carthage's Hamilton Hotel. Foster told Greene, "If Joseph Smith steps outside this door, his blood will be spilt."

Foster's jaw fell and his face glowed hot and he cursed vehemently. "What? That's a lie!"

Taylor fought the urge to laugh. "Why, Brother Foster—what language."

There was a rumble of murmuring among the Mormon apostates.

"When you regain control, Mr. Ford, I shall continue," Taylor chimed The governor, in his eyes, was becoming more diminutive and insecure by the minute.

Ford rolled his eyes. "Continue anyway."

Taylor took a deep breath. The affidavit went on to charge Joseph H Jackson with saying that Joseph Smith was the "damnedest rascal in the world and he would be damned if he did not take vengeance on him," even if he had to follow Joseph to the Rocky Mountains.

Jackson jumped to his feet, waving his fists and fouling the air with more cursing. "That's also a lie!"

Teetering on two shaky legs, Taylor turned to the governor. "Mr. Ford are you going to allow these interruptions? Common courtesy demands that you allow me to present these affidavits."

Ford shrugged his shoulders. His scowl deepened. "Get on with the nex one."

John Taylor sighed in disbelief. It was going to be a long morning.

The next affidavit was signed by William W. Phelps. It alleged that right after the destruction of the *Expositor* press Phelps overheard Francis M Higbee say that the owners of the newspaper not only meant to destroy Nauvoo, but to kill Joseph and Hyrum Smith as well.

Now it was Francis M. Higbee's turn to explode. Using language fit only for a barroom, he denied making the statement.

Taylor tried to block Higbee out of his mind and then took a deep breath in resignation. There seemed to be no intent on Ford's part to cut Higbee short.

A final affidavit, this one also signed by Phelps, stated that a mob led by Joseph Jackson fired at him, that there were more than a hundred guns, and that the noisy, cursing mob swore they would kill "every damned Mormon."

Again, more denials. More cursing. More smiles from an entertained governor.

Taylor threw his hands in the air.

Ford's devious smile seemed permanent. "You say that General Smith i willing to submit to the law. If that's true, it would be best for him, and all concerned, to come to Carthage for cross-examination."

"But, sir," Taylor rebutted, "everyone has already been examined before two competent courts on those charges—the municipal court in Nauvoo and also before Daniel H. Wells, the justice of the peace. I remind you that Mr. Wells is not a member of our Church. Both courts have acquitted Joseph Smith and everyone else charged in the destruction of the press."

Taylor felt his spear hit home.

Immediately, there was a whisper conference with the Higbees leaning toward the governor. Taylor watched the governor nod his head.

Ford looked angered as he cleared his throat and spoke. "It is my decision that the Nauvoo courts have exceeded their authority in the granting of writs of habeas corpus. Mayor Smith and the city council members must submit to arrest by the same constable who previously arrested them in Nauvoo, by virtue of the same warrant, and come to Carthage for trial before the same magistrate who issued the warrant."

John Taylor understood this legal double-talk mumbo-jumbo perfectly. It meant Joseph must appear before Constable Bettisworth in Carthage. No other. The apostates wanted Joseph in Carthage so that they could kill him.

Ford was sounding authoritative, like the former state Supreme Court justice he was. Now he was saying, "Nothing short of this can vindicate the dignity of violated law, and allay the just excitement of the people. Tell General Smith he *must* come to Carthage to answer the charges."

Wilson Law flashed a winning smile at Taylor. His little committee had done the job. Wilson concluded by saying to the governor, "Better tell General Smith, too, that he must leave his arms at home, and the Legion."

Taylor took a long moment to respond. "In consequence of the excitement prevailing in this place, it would be extremely unsafe for him to come to Carthage. In Nauvoo, we have men and arms enough to defend ourselves. But if those forces and those of our enemies are brought into close proximity, the most probable result would be a collision."

Ford's eyes narrowed. "As chief executive of the state, I forbid General

Smith to bring the Nauvoo Legion and their arms into Carthage."

John Taylor felt himself bristle. He knew Governor Ford did not want a collision. If the Prophet Joseph Smith became a martyr, Ford stood a fair chance of being dragged down to posterity like Herod, who approved the crucifixion of Christ.

"Then how … ?" Taylor's words trailed off. In his opinion, it would take at least a thousand members of the Legion to protect the Prophet in this hostile town.

Ford looked confused. There was another whispering conference and then Ford spoke. "I'll prepare a written communication guaranteeing his safety."

Bernhisel quickly responded. "How can you guarantee safety in this environment?"

Ford stole quick glances at the men surrounding him, first to the right and then to the left. He crossed his arms. "I pledge my faith as governor and the faith of the state. I guarantee General Smith's perfect safety."

Apostle Taylor stared at Ford's crossed arms. He didn't believe one word the governor had just uttered. He stalled, saying nothing.

Ford's impatience showed again. "Mr. Taylor, Mr. Bernhisel, this meeting is over. Please wait outside. I will prepare a letter to General Smith and you will take it to him."

"How long must be wait?" Taylor asked.

"Not long," said the governor.

Nearly six hours later, the door opened and Taylor had his letter. All the while, the apostate Mormons had influenced Ford.

John Taylor sat in an upper room of the Nauvoo Mansion, his head down. Tired and saddle sore, he felt he had let the Prophet down.

Joseph Smith was reading the letter from Governor Ford out loud to a room full of faithful Mormons, including Hyrum, Bernhisel, Willard Richards, and William W. Phelps.

In the letter, Ford called the destruction of the *Nauvoo Expositor* a "gross outrage upon the laws and the liberties of the people." Ford also contended that the Mormons had violated at least four principles of the Constitution, including freedom of the press.

Taylor visualized Ford writing the letter with advice freely flowing from the Laws, Higbees, Fosters, and others while he and Bernhisel waited for hours outside the room at the Hamilton. Taylor squirmed in his chair, his saddle sores festering.

Joseph was shaking his head back and forth in disbelief, reading that if he and the city council members refused to submit to Ford's demands to surrender to the court in Carthage, Ford feared the anti-Mormons would destroy Nauvoo and exterminate the members of the Church.

John Taylor saw in Joseph's blue eyes a profound exhaustion. The Prophet shook his head again in disbelief. "I thought the American system of government supposed everyone innocent until proven guilty."

Taylor sat back in his chair as the men in the room began to deliberate on what to do. Many options were discussed over a period of several hours. Joseph considered traveling to Washington, D. C., to lay the case before President Tyler, but quickly decided against it. Line by line, carefully worded, Taylor helped craft a written response to Governor Ford. Taylor liked the crux of the letter. Willard Richards, acting as scribe, read it out loud: "We would not hesitate to stand another trial to your Excellency's wish, were it not that we are confident our lives would be in danger. We dare not come. Writs, we are assured, are issued against us in various parts of the country. For what? To drag us from place to place, from court to court, across the creeks and prairies, till some bloodthirsty villain could find his opportunity to shoot us."

As the letter was being finalized by Willard Richards, Taylor noted that Joseph's countenance suddenly brightened. The Prophet raised a hand and began to speak. "The way is open. It is clear in my mind what to do. All they want is Hyrum and myself."

Taylor blinked hard as he slowly digested the implications.

Joseph continued, ignoring initial objections. "They will not harm you in person or property," he said, sweeping his arm across the room, speaking of

all the defendants. "Not even a hair of your head. We will cross the rive:
tonight, and go away to the West."

Taylor began thinking of how the Church would survive in Nauvoc
without Joseph and Hyrum. There was a temple to be completed, endow
ments to be done. Would their enemies truly leave them alone if Joseph anc
Hyrum left? Would they perceive the Mormon threat over? How long woulc
it be until the body of the Church followed them West?

As these thoughts raveled through John Taylor's mind, Joseph was giving
instructions for his and Hyrum's families—and their personal belongings—t(
be put on board the *Maid of Iowa* and carried down the Mississippi and u
the Ohio River to safety. Plans were made for Porter Rockwell to accompan
Joseph and Hyrum across the river.

"Tonight?" Taylor asked the Prophet.

"Tonight," came the firm answer.

CHAPTER NOTES

John Taylor and Dr. Bernhisel's detailed hearing with Governor Ford and events fo
lowing are taken from several sources, including: Roberts, B.H., *The Life of John Taylo*
Bookcraft, Salt Lake City, Utah, 1963; Smith, Henry A., *The Day They Martyred the Prophe*
Bookcraft, Inc., 1963; Smith, Joseph, *History of the Church,* Volume 6, pages 520-546; Taylo
Samuel W., *Nightfall at Nauvoo,* the Macmillan Company, New York, N.Y., 1971.

# 48

### Sunday, June 23

WHEN HENRY AND ELIAS EAGLES RODE into Nauvoo with a posse from Carthage, Hannah felt as though she had been stabbed in the heart. Her own brothers! Out to capture Joseph Smith!

Earlier in the day, more rain spread a hazy pall over all Hancock County.

Hannah and Robert had been standing outside, staring at the grassy slope that cascaded downward to the river and the Nauvoo Mansion, where the Carthage posse had gone thundering by only a short time earlier. Clusters of riders were riding throughout the city, searching for Joseph. Hannah recognized her brothers instantly. Riding a heavily lathered dark gray mare, Henry's bloodshot eyes bore into her as he rode up the hill with Elias and four other riders.

As if to accentuate the drama, Henry jumped off his horse and pulled a pistol from his belt. "We're here to take Joe Smith back to Carthage. Where is he?"

Both Henry's looks and words were hideous, in Hannah's estimation. She would be the last one in Nauvoo to know where Joseph Smith had gone. She had no idea that Porter Rockwell and Willard Richards had escorted Joseph and Hyrum across the Mississippi during the night. Henry's eyes were red, sign that Hannah knew well. He had been drinking again, probably for hours or even days.

Hannah was both angry and bewildered. She cast a wary eye at her brothers. "Why are you and Elias riding with these men?" Her heart pounded, not knowing the intentions of the four men she did not know. Could this be the beginning of war between Mormons and their enemies? She had no idea how the posse had slipped inside the city.

"It's a state law that all men serve in the militia," Henry snapped, his voice slurred slightly.

Hannah wheeled to face Robert. "Is he telling me the truth?"

"Yes," Robert answered. "But the problem is that your brother seems to take great delight in what he's doing."

Hannah noted the glare from Henry's dark eyes. "If you hurt my Prophet, I'll personally thrash you. It'll be a worse whipping than Papa ever gave you."

Henry caressed his pistol "If you know anything about Joe Smith, you better tell me." His words whistled through his two missing front teeth.

Hannah wondered if Henry ever thought about their deceased father lying in his grave in Apperley, England, near the Methodist chapel. *Probably not,* she concluded. She had never known Henry to even so much as write one letter to their mother.

"Elias, you'd better not relish this," Hannah said, pointing a bony finger at her younger brother. "After all, Joseph is *your* Prophet, too." She cast a wary eye to her right and to her left, hoping that Henry and Elias would disappear before Elizabeth, Harriet, or any of the neighbors knew that she had two brothers in the Carthage posse.

Robert pushed Henry's pistol aside. "Elias, we're going to have a sacra ment service in our house soon. Want to join us?"

"Not the grove?" Elias asked.

Robert pulled a face. "Joseph and Hyrum are gone, remember?"

Henry flashed the pistol again. "Stay with us, Elias. You'd be in big trouble."

An intense chill was now raking through Hannah. She pointed toward Carthage. "Leave. All of you."

Henry riveted his eyes on Hannah and Robert again. "Pass the word. The governor wants everyone to know that he's going to send more troops to find Joe Smith. We'll find him, even if it takes three years to do it."

Hannah watched as an old hatred swelled within her husband. She repeated her words. "Leave. Do it before Robert gets mad. He hasn't been in a good mood the past few days."

Darkness was settling over Carthage. The eeriness of the town left Theodore Turley feeling prickly, just as John Taylor said it would. With his riding partner, Jedediah M. Grant, he asked a member of the Carthage Greys where to find Governor Ford. To Theodore, the guard looked like a serpent from the forgotten depths of hell.

Turley's head was swimming as he dismounted, tied his horse, and walked to the Hamilton Hotel. It had been a busy, confusing day in Nauvoo. Joseph and Hyrum had crossed the river during the night, with plans to flee to the West. A Carthage posse had stormed Nauvoo by surprise. After scaring men, women, and children half to death, they left empty-handed, without the Smiths. Nauvoo Legion soldiers were digging more entrenchments. Emma Smith had convinced Joseph and Hyrum to return. Some had accused them of cowardice.

A powerful right hand reached from the darkness and grabbed Theodore by the shoulder with almost maniacal vigor. Theodore whirled to face Wilson Law.

"The end is near for Joe Smith," Wilson said. "You understand that, don't you?"

Theodore's muscles constricted, especially in his throat. "Leave me alone. I have a message for the governor."

"Follow me," Wilson said. "We've been expecting a messenger."

A door opened on the second floor to reveal the presence of the governor, Joseph H. Jackson, and two of the governor's aides. Introductions were quick. Ford snatched the letter from Theodore's hands. Joseph and Hyrum had signed it, offering to meet a Carthage escort at a location east of Nauvoo called The Mound, inhabited mostly by English immigrants.

Ford's smile seemed to indicate to Theodore he was ready to agree.

Theodore was surprised when Wilson Law began cursing as though he had never been a Mormon. Then Law said, "I tell you, you can't trust the Smiths, governor. They might have thousands of militia waiting in ambush."

Governor Ford motioned to the door. "You two men wait outside. I'll have my response in a few minutes."

Theodore's head began to ache. He sensed an answer that Joseph would not like.

An hour dragged by with men passing in and out of the governor's room. Finally, Joseph's two representatives were allowed back in.

Ford looked barely in control. He was still surrounded by the apostates. "You tell General Smith that the escort he desires will not be accorded. Such as escort is an honor not given any other citizen. So it will not be accorded to him."

Theodore's shoulders dropped. "But your Excellency, General Smith is offering to surrender. Earlier, you promised an escort for his safety."

Ford's certitude was hypnotic. "We sent an escort this morning. They couldn't find either one of the Smiths."

Theodore scoffed. *That was no escort. It was more like a lynch mob.*

The governor stood and pointed. "Get on your horses right now. Tell the Smiths two things. First, they must surrender the state arms."

Theodore gulped. Except for privately owned arms and those he was repairing in his shop, the order would leave Nauvoo almost defenseless.

"Second, tell the Smith brothers to be in Carthage by ten in the morning. If General Smith doesn't show up I'll send the militia into Nauvoo. We'll destroy everything in the city."

Wilson Law shot a mean glance at Theodore. "I'm sure you saw the men hanging around Carthage on your way in."

Theodore nodded, yes.

"They have the capacity to kill not only the men, but women and children, too."

Fear, Theodore realized, was an intense motivator. He believed Wilson Law and he believed the governor. Quickly, Theodore thought of the two jaded horses that had brought them to Carthage. "I don't know if our horses can make it back tonight. They're worn out. Besides, it's almost eleven o'clock."

"Leave now," Law said, pointing to the door.

Theodore felt as if he were being roasted alive.


CHAPTER NOTES

The account of Theodore Turley's encounter with Governor Ford and Wilson Law is contained in *History of the Church,* Volume 6, page 552.

# 49

*Monday, June 24*

ROBERT WAS SICKENED WHEN HE heard the order to surrender his rifle. It had been the first gun he had ever used, a Model 1816 smoothbore Musket with a flintlock ignition system. The first time he fired it, three years ago, it had left his shoulder black and blue because he had not held it tightly as he should have. It was nearly fifty-seven inches in length, a standard issue among all the Illinois state militia. As he thought about the ridiculous turn of events that had caused Church leaders to issue this order, he pounded his fist against his thigh as he contemplated the order. The popping sound largely went unnoticed. There were more than four thousand Nauvoo Legion members assembled in front of the Masonic Lodge.

The more Robert thought about it, the more he trembled with anger. "This is madness," he said to Daniel, not caring who might be listening.

"I agree," Daniel replied. "But the order came from the Prophet. We've got to comply."

A vision of sorts came to Robert's mind. "I'll bet somehow Wilson Law and the gang of apostates are behind this."

Daniel shrugged his shoulders at Robert. "No doubt."

His face still contorted in anger, Robert recalled the events of the day as he understood them. Theodore Turley and Jedediah M. Grant arrived in Nauvoo at four in the morning, their horses nearly dead from exhaustion. By six-thirty, Joseph was on his way to Carthage with everyone who had been named in the Carthage indictment, plus legal counsel and bodyguards. Just past The Mound, Joseph took what he thought would be a last look at his farm. Located not far from Robert and Daniel's farm, it looked beautiful in the morning light. Corn and wheat were waist high. Joseph bid a farewell to his farm manager, Cornelius Lott. By ten o'clock, the Mormon group had reached the Albert G. Fellows farm, almost half-way to Carthage, where they stopped to water their horses. Meeting him there was a friendly militia from McDonough County, the Union Dragoons, under command of Captain Dunn. An aide of Governor Ford, a Mr. Coolie, presented Joseph with the order to surrender the state-issued arms that were in control of the Nauvoo Legion. He pointed to a baggage wagon, sent with Dunn to collect the arms. Joseph complied, thinking it might help ensure the peace. Joseph immediately sent a messenger into town, ordering compliance.

The messenger, Henry G. Sherwood, was now addressing the Legion. He said that the Prophet saw in Governor Ford's order to surrender the arms a move designed to madden the citizens of Nauvoo to do something rash. If they did so, Ford would have an excuse for his mob militia to begin the systematic destruction of all Mormons in Illinois.

Robert immediately sensed the Prophet was right. "I repent," he whispered to Daniel. For a few seconds he had visualized going home to a nightmare worse that he could imagine: Hannah and his children shot to death by a ruthless mob.

As Robert relaxed his grip on his rifle, a faint cloud of dust rose from the area of his house.

"It's the Prophet!" a voice yelled.

The Legion soldiers snapped to attention.

Robert watched as Joseph rode up to the Masonic Hall and dismounted Joseph's voice was familiar, reaching deep within his lungs to project to the four thousand men who stood in the early afternoon sun. "God bless you men. Thank you for your obedience in surrendering your arms. I am going to meet inside and leave some instructions. As you know, I am on my way to Carthage."

Joseph broke for the building, with Willard Richards and the others trailing.

To Robert's eyes, Willard Richards looked terrible. Robert knew the Apostle had crossed the Mississippi during the night, rowing a skiff during a storm. The overweight man had been in the saddle half a day already, with a full eighteen miles to ride until the Mormon entourage reached Carthage.

Inside the hall, Joseph Smith was spreading out a map. Willard Richards watched as Joseph traced with his finger a route across Iowa.

The Prophet's countenance seemed to brighten. "Now I will show you the travels of this people. Here you will make a place for the winter."

Willard groaned. *I hope we don't leave today.*

Joseph's finger moved farther to his left. "And here you will travel west until you come to the Great Salt Lake Valley."

For an instant, Willard's eyes focused on the map, lingering on the Prophet's words. Joseph's meaning was barely registering. Willard could not comprehend leaving Nauvoo and the uncompleted temple.

Henry Eagles, his equilibrium fouled by drinking, nevertheless strode powerfully to the front of the mob with his brother, Elias. The mob was made up of local farmers, townsmen, and more than fourteen hundred members of various militia units. Henry wanted to get a good look at Joseph Smith and the Mormons as they approached the Carthage town square, bathed in the light of a full moon and torches held by mobbers. For five years, one year longer than Henry had been in Illinois, the Mormon leader had played cat-and-mouse, evading due process of law with his own lawmakers. With the other drunken militia waiting by lantern and torches in the darkness, Henry whooped, danced, and howled as the McDonough troops rode into town with Joe Smith and more than a dozen other Mormons.

Threats against the Mormon leader were music to Henry's ears.

"Where's the damned Prophet?" someone shouted, loud enough for even Governor Ford to hear.

"Stand back, you McDonough boys, and let us shoot the Mormons," another yelled and cursed.

"What do you think, old Joe? We've got ya now!"

"Clear out! Let us get a view of him!"

"He's seen the last of Nauvoo!"

"We'll use him up now, and kill all the Mormons!"

To Henry, the scene was more entertaining than anything he had seen at the Gloucestershire fair in England, or at any of the pub parties there. In the rear of the crowd, a platoon of Carthage Greys threw their guns over their heads, letting them curve down so that the bayonets stuck in the ground. They ran forward, picked them up, and yelled obscene curses, some imitating a band of savage Indians.

"Wave, Elias," Henry said as he elbowed his brother. "See if you can get old Joe to acknowledge us."

Henry slumped as the Mormon Prophet rode his black stallion with a rigid posture, his eyes trained straight ahead, paying no attention to the taunts. Near him, a fat man rode slumped in the saddle, looking half dead.

The Mormons dismounted at the Hamilton. Captain Dunn wore a worried look as he jockeyed horses and men.

Henry pressed forward, dragging Elias. "They're the men you call apostate Mormons." He pointed to a group of men with smug, vindictive expressions on their faces.

Henry also recognized John Taylor, the Apostle. He was a tall, sandy-haired man. Suddenly, Taylor was tapping one of the apostates on the shoulder.

William Law, Joseph Smith's former counselor, wheeled to face Taylor.

"Et tu, Brute?" Taylor said, pressing his face into Law's.

The Latin words took a few seconds to register. Law backed away, shrinking.

Henry tapped one of the Mormons on the shoulder. "What was that all about?"

The Mormon regarded Henry and his wild look. "You Mormon?"

"My wife is," Henry admitted.

The Mormon named Stephen Markham relaxed. "That was John Taylor. He was talking to William Law. John Taylor converted Law to the gospel, in Canada."


Minutes later, an incredulous and slightly drunk Henry Eagles backed away from the Hamilton to get a view of Governor Thomas Ford. A window on the second floor had opened and Ford's head was in plain sight.

All around Henry, militia troops and locals had been shouting, cursing, demanding to see Joe Smith, the captured Mormon Prophet.

Ford yelled, trying to project his voice. "I know of your great anxiety to see Mr. Smith, which is natural enough. I assure you, gentlemen, you shall have that privilege tomorrow morning. I will cause him to pass before the troops upon the square. Now I wish you to return to your quarters."

A trooper next to Henry and Elias threw his hat in the air. "Hurrah for Tom Ford."

To a chorus of cheers for the governor, Henry spun around, trying to remember where he had left his dark gray mare. It was time to go home.

# 50

*Tuesday, June 25*

DESPITE THE FACT THAT HENRY promised himself he would be back in the Carthage town square by sunup, he and Elias had already missed Governor Ford's speech. Henry had a splitting headache, so complete was his hangover. Henry had barked at Elias' wife, Mary, who seemed overly concerned for her husband's safety.

"Do you think Joseph is still in custody?" Elias asked on the way.

"We'll find out," Henry said. He hoped he wouldn't be subject to discipline. Both he and Elias were attached to the 57$^{th}$ Regiment, a local militia group. They had been ordered to be on duty again at eight in the morning. It was now nine o'clock.

Henry recognized a young member of the Carthage Greys, Tom Marsh. Henry pulled him aside. "Did they arrest Joe Smith yet?"

Marsh nodded the nod of a reluctant soldier. There was fear in his eyes.

"Happened at eight o'clock. Joe Smith submitted to the constable."

"Bail?"

"Five hundred for each man. Seven thousand five hundred dollars total."

Henry whistled. Constable David Bettisworth and Justice of the Peace Robert F. Smith were making certain Joe Smith stayed under custody. *Nobody* could afford that kind of money to spring the mayor of Nauvoo and his councilmen, Henry concluded.

"What did Governor Ford say?" Henry asked.

"He spoke from the top of an old table in the square. He said that Joe Smith and the Mormons were dangerous. And that they're guilty. But he said too, that since they were in the hands of the law, the law must take its course."

Henry understood. The law called for a trial. But Henry knew the mood of the mob. There likely would be a killing before a trial.

"Where's the governor now?" Elias asked, showing his concern.

"Inside the Hamilton," Marsh said, pointing. "He promised that he would parade the Mormons in front of the troops."

Henry took a deep breath and relaxed. He hadn't missed the big event after all.


"Brother Benbow! What are you doing here?"

Something about John Benbow's surprise appearance at Daniel's front door seemed profoundly strange, given all that was happening in Nauvoo. An unsettled feeling came over Daniel.

"I've been asked to go to Carthage immediately," Benbow replied.

"Why?" Daniel asked. Carthage was the most dangerous place on earth right now for members of the Church.

"To post bond for the Prophet and all the defendants in the *Expositor* writ."

Daniel's skin tingled. The move would keep Joseph and Hyrum and all the *Expositor* defendants out of jail. "Then why are you here, at my place?"

"The Legion has been disbanded, but we need some escorts."

Daniel responded to the word *we*. "Not just for you?"

Benbow pointed to half dozen or so men, waiting on their horses. "Between me and the men you see assembled here, we think we'll have enough sureties and property to post any kind of bond the Justice of the Peace in Carthage may throw at us. But we need protection from here to Carthage. I thought of you first."

Daniel tried to absorb the weight of the responsibility. "How many men do you need?"

"Ten or twelve. More if you can find them. We need to leave right away."

The morning sun spilled on Tapper and Bendigo, grazing in the small pasture between Daniel and Robert's cabin. "I'll start saddling the horses. You know where Brother Harris, Brother Roberts, and Brother Cox live. Get them. We'll find others, too."

Henry's heart danced a jig as Governor Ford emerged from the hotel with Joe Smith and the other Mormon prisoners. The jig stopped when the entourage headed north, instead of to the town square.

Henry pulled on Marsh's shirt. "Where's Ford taking them?"

"I think to General Deming's headquarters," came the answer.

Henry gulped, feeling torn between the two choices he had to make. General Miner R. Deming was *his* commander, the brigadier general in the state militia, with direct command of the 57th Regiment. Should he go to the square and fall in with his regiment? Or go with the mob and follow the governor and the Mormons? Pulling at Elias, he chose the latter.

The Carthage Greys were stationed on guard at the general's headquarters, muskets at charge, forming a three-sided protective square. Henry found himself pushed by the cursing, shouting mob until he was almost face-to-face with the Greys. Quickly taking charge, General Deming ordered the Greys to form around him, the governor, and the Mormons.

The general sounded authoritative, as usual. "Take us to the town square."

In Henry's view, General Deming was a Mormon sympathizer, but there were few who dared confront him about that.

Henry turned to Elias. "We'd better get up there with our unit." Using brute strength, Henry bullied his way through the mob. Elias followed. Without comment from other troopers, they melted into their unit.

The familiar voice of Henry's commanding general was making the introductions of the prized prisoners. "Gentlemen officers of the 57th Regiment, I introduce you to Joseph and Hyrum Smith, generals of the Nauvoo Legion."

There was a chorus of boos, hisses, and cursing from troops and the mob as they absorbed the words. "Joe Smith is no general," a trooper near Henry and Elias yelled. "He doesn't deserve the title! He's guilty of treason!"

*Treason?* Henry wondered. That's a new one. *I thought Joe Smith was charged with destroying a press.*

Henry smiled wickedly. The penalty for treason in Illinois was death by hanging.

The remark caused officers and soldiers of the Greys to throw their hats in the air, draw their swords, and curse. One screamed, "We'll introduce our selves to the Mormons in quite a different style." Simultaneously, the Greys waved their swords.

Elias Eagles shrank in clear astonishment. Although Henry was amused, Elias was not. Troopers and mobbers all around him were out of control. They wanted Joseph and Hyrum's blood and were not afraid to flaunt it openly.

From his back, another was yelling now. "This is too much like an honor guard. Joe Smith doesn't deserve an honor guard!"

To the utter amazement of Elias, the protection of the Greys was breaking down all around General Deming. Elias felt smothered. He wondered what Deming would do.

The general stopped in his tracks, spinning. "Men of the Carthage Greys. Form your lines! Or I'll place you under arrest!"

Robert F. Smith, captain of the Carthage Greys, leaped upon a wagon "Are we going to submit to arrest?"

The jaw of Elias Eagles dropped. Perhaps nowhere but in Carthage

United States of America, could a man serve as Justice of the Peace, a judge, and a captain of a militia unit. Smith's defiant attitude was amazing to Elias. He sensed that General Deming was not on the same side as R. F. Smith and most of the Carthage Greys.

"No! No! No!" came a unified chorus.

"Then load with ball cartridges!" the captain commanded.

Panic was now written on the faces of both General Deming and Governor Ford.

Elias held his breath. Would Joseph and Hyrum be slaughtered by powder and ball right in front of him, in the town square? Elias closed his eyes, wishing he were in back in Apperley, milking cows at the peaceful Nightingale Dairy.

Despite the madness around him, Ford managed to jump on another wagon, adjacent to Captain Smith. "Men! Listen to me! We have no intention of honoring the prisoners. We just wanted to exhibit them. Calm down!"

From the corner of his eye, Elias saw Henry withdraw a small flask from his pocket.

"You dare drink now?" Elias asked.

"Sure," his brother snapped. "This is grand entertainment."

Elias was reaching the conclusion that his brother had gone crazy. Behind them, troopers were yelling, cursing, making threats. Elias doubted there were a hundred troopers who did not want Joseph and Hyrum dead. Right now, they acted like they would kill the governor as well.

From behind Henry and Elias came more cursing and threats. The threats called for the deaths of Joseph and Hyrum Smith.

Elias forced himself to consider what was going on in the Prophet's mind. Fear? Doubt? Premonition of death? Since the restoration of the gospel, Joseph had been mobbed, beaten, tarred and feathered, chained, and imprisoned. Elias began to shudder, wondering what the conclusion to all of this would be. In his mind, the militia and mob's anger was far out of proportion to its provocation. The long-standing grudge against Joseph Smith and the Mormons was out of control. It was senseless, in Elias' opinion, that militia officers remained outraged just because Joseph had an exemption from regular military duty because of his license to preach, and that the governor had commissioned him a lieutenant general.

Elias was certain his disturbing conclusions would not be shared with Henry.

Governor Ford seemed to regain partial control over the Greys and the mob. With General Deming and members of the 57th Regiment, including Henry and Elias, Ford led his prisoners away, back to the Hamilton. Hellish threats, hissing, and cursing continued.

The past week had been the worst in Willard Richard's life. Saturday midnight, by the light of a smudged lantern, he had helped Joseph, Hyrum, and Porter Rockwell find Aaron Johnson's leaky boat. Willard had worked his guts out, rowing and bailing water with his shoes. Seeking refuge at John Killien's house at five in the morning, there was no one home. Exhausted, wet, and droopy from a lack of sleep, they were forced to walk another mile before they found a member of the Church at home, Bill Jordan. There was no time for sleep. Packing had to be done for the escape to the Rocky Mountains. Jordan donated flour and other supplies. Rockwell was sent back to Nauvoo for horses. A short time later Dr. Bernhisel arrived, bearing more bad news. Constable Bettisworth from Carthage had scoured Nauvoo with a posse, seeking Joseph and Hyrum.

With no sleep under his belt, Willard was devastated when Rockwell returned without the horses. Instead, he had a letter from Emma Smith, urging Joseph's return. Her cousin, Reynolds Cahoon, along with Hiram Kimball and others, had accused Joseph of cowardice, running away to the West. They feared that Nauvoo really would be destroyed if Joseph and Hyrum did not surrender. Back across the river they went, more rowing, more bailing.

Still without sleep, Willard mounted a horse with Joseph, Hyrum, and more than a dozen other members of the Church. Eight miles to the Fellow farm, eight miles back. Then a grueling eighteen miles to Carthage and a midnight arrival. Taunts, jeers, threats all night long. Very little sleep. Up at six

An appearance before the justice of the peace. Paraded in front of the 57th Regiment. Threats from the Carthage Greys.

His head splitting, his stomach nauseated, Willard Richards sought rest in his crowded room at the Hamilton. Not yet.

Willard cringed as a hand touched him. "Your fallen Prophet is about to meet his end," a voice said.

Willard whirled, facing three men. The first voice belonged to a familiar man, Wilson Law. His lips were turned down and his eyes burned with hatred.

Joseph Jackson's eyes were just as foreboding. "Holy Joe will rue the day he whipped me," snorted Jackson.

The third man, Thomas C. Sharp, thrust a bony finger into Willard's chest. "And so the stout doctor has come to Carthage with the fallen Prophet."

Willard took a step toward the hotel. He could not get away from Sharp.

"Can Joseph's wives save him?" Sharp taunted. "No. Not even God almighty will save him this time."

Lowering his head, Willard said nothing. He painfully climbed the stairs to the second floor and entered his room.

"Take the bed," John Taylor told him, pointing. "I'll open the window for some fresh air."

Willard Richards collapsed to the bed. He was nearly asleep when Joseph Smith was summoned out of the room under guard to meet with the United States Deputy Marshall for Illinois.

# 51

MARK ALDRICH STOOD SWEATING OUTSIDE a room at th
Hamilton cursing the Mormons. He had been cursing them since 1842 whe
Joe Smith told the Mormons in Warren to pull out and move to Nauvoc
Three months later, Aldrich took out bankruptcy.

Aldrich's purposes for wanting to meet with Joe Smith were simple. H
wanted the fallen Prophet to apologize, and he wanted to intimidate th
Prophet. He checked his pocket watch. It was two-thirty. He had less tha
thirty minutes to force an apology.

"Spread your arms please," said Stephen Markham, the Mormon body
guard. Aldrich, who commanded the Warsaw Independent Battalion, com
plied with the body search. Aldrich carried no weapons. With fourteen hur
dred militia outside, there was no possibility Joe Smith could escape. Smit
was a dead man—but that would come later.

Markham pushed the door open. Early afternoon light spilling throug
a single window revealed the man Aldrich despised more than any other ma
in the world. Joe Smith beckoned him in, pointing to a chair. The room w

stuffy. Seven men had slept in it last night.

"I presume this is a friendly call," the Mormon leader said. "It is on that premise I have agreed to meet with you."

Aldrich scanned the room. There were three other men. Hyrum, Joe's brother. And two men he recognized as "Apostles," one fat, one slender. Aldrich gave Joe Smith a tobacco-stained smile. "You know as well as I what this is about."

"You want me to send our people back to Warren?" the Mormon leader asked.

"It's too late for that."

In 1841, Aldrich's land development schemes had brought the two men into direct conflict. Aldrich had convinced the Mormons to make a settlement on a section of land he and his partners owned on the Mississippi River, one mile south of Warsaw. An English immigrant, Joseph Fielding, and two hundred settled there that summer. Abruptly, and without warning, the Mormon Prophet pulled them out in November.

Aldrich felt an old hatred swarming over him. "You don't regret what you did to my settlement?"

"You raised the price of flour by a dollar a barrel," Joe Smith said with a straight face. "You raised the rents. You forbade our people to collect wood in the area. Forced them to buy wood from you. What did you expect?"

"But we promised to change our policies about all that." Aldrich recalled how one of his partners had plead with Joe Smith, telling him that his temporal salvation depended upon the success of the Warren development.

Aldrich was shocked at the Mormon leader's icy comeback. "There was too much antipathy toward our people in the Warsaw area. We moved them to Nauvoo for their own safety."

The land developer was unimpressed. His heart pounded with hate. "You bankrupted me."

John Taylor sat on the edge of the bed scratching his head. Just before Aldrich had come in, Joseph had received word that the Laws, Higbees, and Fosters were organizing a mob to plunder Nauvoo. Would the evil ever end? Now another archenemy, Mark Aldrich, was trying to intimidate Joseph.

In his position as editor of the Mormon newspaper in Nauvoo, Taylor knew the ins and outs of the land business in the Nauvoo area as well as anyone.

Since the Church was the largest purchaser of land in Nauvoo, it also became the biggest land jobber. In the beginning there were a variety of *ad hoc* agencies dealing for the Church—bishops and other Church officials, and of course, Joseph Smith himself. The Church did not envision any real separation of powers between spiritual and temporal executives. The Nauvoo High Council made Joseph Smith treasurer of the Church, empowered to set prices and sell lots. To comply with state law, Joseph was also elected Trustee-in Trust. As new converts flowed in, John remembered how Joseph's expanding vision of the kingdom of righteousness on the Mississippi could not be dimmed. He foresaw that Nauvoo was not the only city that needed to be built up. He specified that communities such as Zarahemla and Nashville be organized across the river in Iowa. Same with Ramus, ten miles northeast of Carthage. And Warren, really an addition to the town of Warsaw, but separately platted by Aldrich and his partners.

John Taylor turned, his eyes blazing at Aldrich's remark. *You bankrupted me.* Truth was, Aldrich had concocted a clever scheme to take advantage of new national bankruptcy law. True, he had been badly hurt by the Mormon withdrawal, but it did not ruin him. Bankruptcy proceedings showed he had twenty-three parcels of land and numerous notes as assets. Liabilities consisted of judgments against him, and ten thousand dollars due to creditors on notes and open accounts. Then came the clever, crooked part. Aldrich's land was sold to his attorneys for one hundred sixty dollars. His bills and notes were sold to Dr. Robert D. Foster, the Nauvoo Legion surgeon general. As result of these and other proceedings, Aldrich's debts were totally discharged and he and his friends—acting as strawmen in his behalf—came back into possession of *all* their property.

John Taylor felt unsettled as the conversation continued.

Aldrich was making a hedonistic remark to Joseph. "Men like you deserve to die."

Joseph shrank from Aldrich's murderous gaze. In desperation, the Prophet threw his hands in the air. "You got your property back."

Aldrich drew a cold breath, pointing angrily at the Prophet. "You made some inflammatory remarks back then."

John Taylor knew where Aldrich was going. A discussion that Church leaders had back in 1841.

"I'd be happy to discuss it," Joseph said, showing no trepidation. "What remarks?"

"You said that the first thing toward building up Warsaw was to break it down, to break down them that are there. That was a declaration of war."

Joseph laughed. "You misquote me. I was telling our Church members that if they were to settle in Warren, and to make it a successful settlement, it would be better for them if they were to convert the people that were already there, or at least make friends of them."

"We don't want your religion. Not now. Not ever."

"And what is your religion? Certainly not your wife and three children, judging by your unfaithfulness to your wife."

John noted that Aldrich turned purple. Once again, the Prophet had clearly discerned the innermost thoughts of a man.

The Prophet was not done. "Or is your command your religion?"

Aldrich held a commission as a major in the Illinois militia. He commanded the Warsaw Independent Battalion, which consisted of two companies—the Warsaw Cadets and the Warsaw Rifle Company. His battalion was attached to the 59th Regiment, commanded by Levi Williams.

Aldrich seemed to recover. "My command will see to it that your life will end soon."

John Taylor had seen enough. Standing, he said, "Mr. Aldrich, shall I show you out or throw you out?"

There was a knock at the door. Taylor opened it to find Stephen Markham standing there. "There are more visitors. Mr. Aldrich, you'll have to leave now."

John Taylor's muscles tightened in dread fear as the room filled with officer of various militia units. Frank Worrell and Robert F. Smith of the Carthage Greys. Colonel Thomas Geddes of the militia. Colonel Levi Williams o Warsaw, and others. Taylor frowned, wondering about the outcome. He also fumed, thinking that the governor had overstepped his bounds. Joseph Smith was not a freak to be stared at. He was a Prophet of God.

Joseph looked remarkably calm. "Give me your honest opinion, gentle men. Is there anything in my appearance to indicate that I am the desperate character my enemies represent me to be?"

The remark caught the officers off guard. There were several seconds o silence. Finally, one said, "No, sir. Your appearance would indicate the very contrary, General Smith. But we cannot see what is in your heart. Neither can we tell what your intentions are."

Despite a lack of sleep, Joseph looked fresh and alert. He blue eyes were alive and full of depth. His hair was combed forward as always, and he had bathed and shaved early that morning. He was dressed in a blue suit.

As for himself, Taylor had a headache and felt that if had to answer a question like that he might skirt on the edges of rationality. The militia offi cers seemed to lean forward, like vultures seeking to devour an over-ripened carcass.

Taylor knew that Joseph Smith recognized evil, and evil was all around him. He noted that Joseph took a deep breath before he spoke.

"Very true, gentlemen," the Prophet replied. "You cannot see what is in my heart, and you are therefore unable to judge me or my intentions. But can see what is in your hearts, and I will tell you what I see."

The remark clearly unsettled the visitors; they were nowhere near to qualifying for manifestations of the Holy Ghost, let alone of the Gift of the Holy Ghost, thought Taylor. Manifestations are given to lead sincere seeker to gospel truths that will persuade them to repentance and baptism. The only manifestations these Mormon haters received came from the dark side.

"I can see that you thirst for blood," Joseph continued. "And nothing but my blood will satisfy you."

Levi Williams, commander of the Carthage militia, lowered his head.

"It is not for crime of any description that I and my brethren are thus continually persecuted and harassed by our enemies," Joseph said. "But there are other motives. And some of them I have expressed."

Joseph seemed to relish the heaven-sent words as they entered his mind. His mind was a conduit of light and truth and it had been that way ever since the day God and Jesus Christ appeared to him in the grove, at his father's farm near Palmyra, New York. From that day in 1820 until this gloomy day in 1844, Joseph had been the beneficiary of twenty-four years of remarkable schooling. He had been tutored by Moroni, the angel. He had translated an ancient record into the Book of Mormon. There had been that bestowal of divine authority, the priesthood, by heavenly messengers—John the Baptist, and Peter, James, and John. There were revelations, a number of them, in which Joseph heard the word of God again. The channel of communication had been opened between man and the Creator, and Joseph was the medium. The men sitting and standing in the room with Joseph comprehended none of this.

Joseph said, "Inasmuch as you and the people out there thirst for blood, I prophesy, in the name of the Lord, that you shall witness scenes of blood and sorrow to your entire satisfaction."

John Taylor began to regret Joseph's boldness. Did he mean that Joseph and all the Mormon prisoners would soon be lying in the streets dead? Or did Joseph refer to some future day, when the entire nation would be caught up in scenes of bloodshed?

There was no stopping Joseph now. "Your souls shall be perfectly satiated with blood. Many of you now present shall have an opportunity to face the cannon's mouth from sources you think not of. Those people that desire this great evil upon me and my brethren shall be filled with regret and sorrow because of the scenes of desolation and distress that await them. They shall seek for peace, and shall not be able to find it."

Joseph paused, letting the words bite.

Not one officer stirred.

"Gentlemen, you will find what I have told you to be true."

John Taylor opened the door.

In silence, one by one, the officers filed out.

CHAPTER NOTES

Page 565 of *History of the Church*, Volume 6, states, "After dinner, Mark Aldrich of Warsaw called to see Joseph. The dialogue between Aldrich and Joseph Smith is fiction, however. The author has not been able to find any record of the actual conversation between Aldrich and Joseph. Background information about Aldrich is taken from *Carthage Conspiracy*, Dallin H. Oaks and Marvin S. Hill, University of Illinois Press, 1979.

Joseph's conversation with the militia officers follows, on page 566 of the *History of the Church*, Volume 6. None of the officers knew it, but Joseph was speaking of the coming of the Civil War, seventeen years in the future.

# 52

WILSON LAW FELT A RUSH OF ADRENALINE. If all went according to plans, the Smith brothers would be dead by tomorrow afternoon, or the next day at the latest.

First, the Committee had to get Joseph and Hyrum officially behind bars. The Hamilton House was not suited for murder. With the cooperation of the governor and local authorities, within an hour the Committee would haul the Smiths to the courthouse. There, they would be charged with inciting a riot—to wit, destroying the *Expositor* press. And the Committee would surprise Smith's attorneys. Instead of the Smiths appearing before Justice of the Peace Bettisworth, a Committee member would be there—non other than Justice of the Peace Robert F. Smith, captain of the Carthage Greys.

Second, Robert F. Smith would keep the jail bond so high there would be little chance the Mormons could post it. That would likely ensure the Committee could next obtain a mittimus, or legal paperwork forcing the Smiths to jail.

Third, the Committee had a card up its sleeve that would cause the devil to applaud. If bail were somehow to be posted, Robert F. Smith was ready to serve an unexpected warrant against Joseph and Hyrum. To wit, treason against the state—for declaring martial law at Nauvoo without authorization by the governor.

Wilson smiled a devious smile. The Higbee Brothers and Robert F. Smith, key Committee members with legal backgrounds, had assured him that treason is a capital crime. Bail, they said, could only be fixed by a circuit judge. And even more delicious was the fact that the penalty of treason was death by hanging.

That move would guarantee that the fallen Prophet and his brother would end up in the Carthage Jail by nightfall. Then the Committee could get on with the rest of the plans.

The fourth part of the plan was diabolically simple. The Committee would get Governor Ford to agree to leave town. Constable Robert F. Smith would have the prisoners released to his custody. The Smith brothers would be turned over to the mob for execution.

Wilson took a deep breath and exhaled. Then he poured himself some whiskey from a bottle that sat on a table, surrounded by the Committee. Now that he was excommunicated, he didn't have to hide his drinking.

The Committee members poured themselves drinks, too.

Wilson liked the Committee's broad base. Aside from him and his brother, and the Higbees and the Fosters, there were others. Robert F. Smith, thirty-six, constable and sheriff in Carthage, and captain of the Carthage Greys; Colonel Levi Williams, thirty-four, a Carthage farmer, cooper, and sometimes Baptist minister; Mark Aldrich, forty-two, commander of the Warsaw Independent Battalion, a Warsaw land speculator; Thomas C. Sharp, owner and editor of the *Warsaw Signal,* and a former attorney; Jacob C. Davis, thirty-one, attorney of Warsaw, captain in the Warsaw Rifle Company; and an Illinois state senator, a Democrat; William Grover, twenty-six, also an attorney in Warsaw, captain of the Warsaw Cadets.

Swelling with a sense of accomplishment, Wilson Law toasted the other men. All he had to do now was sit back and watch. And smile. And laugh.

# 53

WILLARD RICHARDS SCOWLED, wondering what fate awaited Joseph and Hyrum in this morning's preliminary hearing concerning the *Expositor* charges. Ever since their arrival in Carthage, the cards seemed to be stacked against them and Willard reviewed events in his mind. Eight o'clock this morning, a voluntary surrender to Constable Bettisworth. Eight-thirty, paraded in front of the bloodthirsty militia and onlooking mobbers. Nine-fifteen, Governor Ford's refusal to see Joseph. Nine-thirty, Ford reverses, agrees to meet the Prophet for a few minutes, but refuses to look Joseph in the eye. Ten-thirty, revolt of the Carthage Greys, demanding Joseph's blood. Eleven-fifteen, rumors that Warsaw troops were approaching Carthage. One o'clock, news that the apostates were planning to plunder Nauvoo. Four o'clock, rumors that Wilson Law admits the riot charges probably won't stick, but "powder and ball will," and "Joseph will not get out of town alive."

Huddled in the lobby of the hotel awaiting the hearing were all the defendants, most of them members of the Nauvoo city council: Joseph Smith, Hyrum Smith, John Taylor, William W. Phelps, John P. Greene, Stephen C.

Perry, Dimick B. Huntington, Jonathan Dunham, Stephen C. Markham, Jonathan H. Holmes, Jesse P. Harmon, John Lytle, Joseph W. Coolidge, David Harvey Redfield, and Levi Richards.

From rowing the boat across the Mississippi and riding hard in the saddle, every muscle in Willard Richard's lumpy body was sore. Bent over in pain, Willard was trying to get some exercise limping along in the hallways of the Hamilton. He was clinging to the faint hope there might be a technicality that would temporarily spare Joseph and Hyrum. The brothers had been commanded to Carthage by Governor Ford to appear before Thomas Morrison, a justice of the peace. Morrison had issued the original writ, charging Joseph and Hyrum with inciting a "riot" when the printing press of the *Nauvoo Expositor* was destroyed.

Rumor was that Morrison was not in town. If so, Joseph's lawyers were confident Joseph and Hyrum and the others would be released.

With John Taylor and Stephen Markham, Willard walked up and down the hallway of the Hamilton with a glum feeling. He wished God would begin to smile down upon him. Then he saw two men who made him feel as though God were doing just that.

"John Benbow! Daniel Browett!" Willard gasped in disbelief. "What are you doing here?"

With a burst of confidence, Daniel put his arms around Willard. "Brother Benbow and some of his friends are going to post bail." Behind Benbow and Browett stood John Fullmer, Dan Jones, and Edward Hunter.

"You're just in time," John Taylor said. "For security reasons, the preliminary hearing is going to be held here in the hotel instead of at the court house."

"I'm surprised you got here safely," Willard said.

Benbow pointed out an open window. "We had an escort."

Willard looked out. He recognized several men in the Mormon posse still on horseback: Robert Harris, Levi Roberts, John Cox, John Hyrum Green, Robert Pixton, Jacob Kemp Butterfield, Richard Slater, and Ezra Allen.

Willard let his gaze take in the stocky John Benbow, his middle-aged chiseled features, his kind blue eyes, and the aura of dignity that always seemed to envelop him. Willard had known that an effort was being made to secure bond money, but he did not know how it would materialize, or who would come forth.

"Thank you for being here," Willard said. "Do Joseph's attorneys know?"

"No," Benbow replied, pointing to a handful of men who accompanied him, all of whom had agreed to help with bonds for the defendants. "We just barely arrived."

"Let's get down to the lobby," Willard said, limping again as he walked. "I'll tell the attorneys."

Willard felt an upsurge of confidence. He could imagine Joseph and Hyrum free again, galloping their horses toward Nauvoo.

*God bless you, John Benbow.* Willard smiled, thinking of his old friend. He had met Benbow in England, a few months after Wilford Woodruff arrived there on his mission in 1840. After Woodruff's initial success among the United Brethren, Willard had gone to the tri-county area of Gloucestershire, Herefordshire, and Worcestershire to assist. Willard had been overwhelmed with Benbow's goodness and generosity. Hundreds of converts had been baptized in a pond on the Benbow farm near Castle Frome. Benbow's donation of two hundred fifty pounds—coupled with Thomas Kington's donation of fifty pounds—made possible the printing of the Book of Mormon. Not only that, but Benbow had made generous donations to the Church to make it possible for poorer members of the Church to emigrate to America.

Robert sat on his horse, steaming. He wished he were inside the hotel, invited to the preliminary hearing sitting next to Wilson Law. Right in front of the hundred or so people crammed into the hotel lobby he would break Wilson's ribs, jaw, and arms.

Why not try?

Robert dismounted, handing the reins to Jacob Kemp Butterfield.

"Where are you going?" Butterfield asked.

"Inside," Robert answered. "They can squeeze one more in there."

"You can't get past the guards."

"Can't I?" Winding his way through dozens of militiamen, Robert strode toward the front door. Suddenly, Daniel stood in his way; he had just exited the hotel.

"You can't get in," Daniel said. "You need a pass. That's how I got in with Brother Benbow."

"Give me your pass," Robert said forcefully.

"I had to surrender it."

Robert took a few steps toward the hotel entrance. Six Carthage Greys blocked his way. They had weapons.

Sighing in disgust, Robert returned to his horse with Daniel.


To Willard's delight, Thomas Morrison was nowhere in sight in the crowded hotel lobby. "Is that a good sign?" he asked one of Joseph's attorneys, H. T. Reid.

"So far," Reid said. "We have a letter from Governor Ford. It's in my satchel. It states that in order to satisfy the law Joseph must submit to the same warrant, served by the same constable, and tried by the same judge. That means Morrison." The wording was explicit: *Nothing short of this can vindicate the dignity of violated law, and allay the just judgment of the people.*

There was a roar in the crowd as the door opened and a Justice of the Peace appeared, wearing court robes. Willard gasped. It was not Morrison. It was Robert F. Smith, the rabid Mormon-hater. Captain of the Carthage Greys.

R. F. Smith's first move was to summon the county prosecutor to the bench. Willard gasped again. One of the Higbee brothers, Chauncey approached. It was a bad development. Higbee had been sitting up front with the Laws and the Fosters.

"Your honor, the defendants destroyed the press of the *Expositor*," Chauncey Higbee began.

Joseph's attorney, H. T. Reid, quickly responded. "We've never contended that they didn't. I demand that the writ be dismissed."

"On what grounds?" R. F. Smith asked with devious eyes.

"This preliminary hearing is supposed to be held by Justice of the Peace Morrison, not you," Reid charged.

Willard was surprised by Smith and Higbee's next move. Higbee said, "I move an adjournment."

Willard's jaw dropped. Adjournment was bad news. Joseph's attorneys argued that the court was not authorized to take recognizance without the defendants acknowledging their guilt and having witnesses to prove it.

"Our chief witness is not available," Higbee countered.

"And who is your chief witness?" Reid asked.

"Francis M. Higbee," Chauncey replied.

Willard rolled his eyes. He smelled a continuing conspiracy.

"This hearing is adjourned," R. F. Smith said.

"Not so fast," Reid countered. "We can post bail for the defendants."

R. F. Smith was prepared for this move. He shuffled some papers. "I set bail at five hundred dollars per defendant."

Willard Richards reeled as the anti-Mormon crowd roared its approval. That meant a staggering total of seven thousand five hundred dollars! R. F. Smith clearly was attempting to overreach the wealth of the defendants and their friends.

The roar from the crowd melted when Reid summoned Benbow and Benbow's friends. "Your honor," Reid said, "you will find that these sureties and properties well exceed the amount you have requested."

R. F. Smith's jaw dropped a mile.

*Joseph and Hyrum are free!* Willard wanted to scream the words.

To Willard's discomfort, R. F. Smith huddled with Chauncey L. Higbee, the Law brothers, the Foster brothers, Thomas C. Sharp, and Mark Aldrich.

The huddle broke. Willard felt himself sink into the hard wooden bench. *What are they conniving now?*

"Each defendant will appear at the next term of the circuit court," R.F.

Smith declared.

Attorney Reid jumped to his feet. "Does that mean each defendant is free to go?"

"It will take a few hours to examine the sureties and properties that have been pledged for bail," R. F. Smith answered. "After that, yes."

Willard Richards' first reaction was to shake his fists in excitement. *Yes!* *Yes! Yes!*

Then he caught himself. *What does a few hours mean?*

CHAPTER NOTES

It is a historical fact that John Benbow and other wealthy Mormon members posted bail for Joseph and Hyrum in Carthage. However, historical records do not indicate whether or not a Mormon posse escorted them to Carthage. Having the characters of the novel participate in such a posse is an invention of the author.

# 54

JOHN TAYLOR RESPONDED TO A KNOCK on his door at the Hamilton. He pulled the door open, revealing the figures of Constable David Bettisworth and seven or eight deputies. It was almost eight o'clock. Three hours had passed since the preliminary hearing had been adjourned.

"I have a mittimus signed by Justice of the Peace Robert F. Smith authorizing me to arrest Joseph Smith and Hyrum Smith."

Bettisworth's icy statement shocked Taylor. He reeled backward. A mittimus was a fancy word from the court system. It was a warrant committing a person to jail or prison.

All the defendants in the *Expositor* case had been released except Joseph and Hyrum. Most of them had returned to Nauvoo under guard of the Mormon posse. Taylor, Willard Richards, along with Joseph and Hyrum, had feared the worst. Obviously, some type of delaying tactic was happening out here. Now, this. A new arrest.

Attorney Reid sprang to his feet from with the room at the Hamilton. "Arrest? On what charges?"

Joseph, Hyrum, and Willard Richards jumped forward, their jaws drop
ping.

Bettisworth drew his pistol, not answering. "I'm taking the two defen
dants to jail."

The deputies drew their pistols also, pointing them into the room.

Attorney Woods held up a rigid palm. "Hold on. Let's see the mittimus."

An evil smile crossed Bettisworth's face. He reached inside his vest and
drew out some legal looking papers. He thrust them at Woods.

Taylor gasped. *Does he really have a mittimus?* He gasped again as he
watched Woods' head drop to his chest.

"What is it?" Joseph asked his lawyer.

Woods shook his head. "Treason. They've charged you with treason."

Joseph's brow furrowed. "Treason? How can that be? This is nothing but
a barefaced illegal attempt to hold us in Carthage. It's tyrannical."

"They're claiming that when you declared martial law at Nauvoo it was
done without authorization from Governor Ford."

Hyrum was staring at the mittimus in disbelief. "According to the city
charter, we didn't need authorization."

"Why didn't this come up in the preliminary hearing this afternoon?"
Woods asked.

Bettisworth's answer was lame. "Because the key witnesses were not avail
able at that time."

John Taylor cringed. The apostates were causing more trouble than ever
imagined. For an instant he wished he had accepted the invitation to return
to Nauvoo with John Benbow and Daniel Browett.

Bettisworth motioned his pistol toward the Carthage Jail. "Follow me."

John Taylor placed his body between Bettisworth and his Mormon
friends. "I think we ought to talk to the governor first."

Bettisworth pulled out a pocket watch. "I'll give you five minutes."

"You'll give us all the time we need," Joseph said, his blue eyes glaring.

Bettisworth reconsidered. "Half an hour."

"Brother Taylor," Joseph said, "go with the attorneys. When Governor

Ford finds out about this patently illegal arrest, he'll have to countermand."

John Taylor's head ached and he felt low and heavy. As he trudged from Governor Ford's room in the Hamilton to the room where Joseph and Hyrum were being held, he knew for certain he had let the Prophet down. Governor Ford had acted like he did not care if Joseph was turned over to the mob. He had rejected every protest issued by Joseph's two attorneys, Reid and Woods.

Though at times Ford appeared sympathetic—which John Taylor regarded as a farce—the governor had said that he could see no way the chief executive of the state could interfere with the judicial process. "Let the legal process take its course," he had counseled.

*Hypocrisy,* Taylor thought. *Pure hypocrisy.*

The only bone Ford had tossed Joseph's attorneys was an offer to post a guard at the jail.

*Joseph will need a thousand faithful guards to keep him out of harm's way,* Taylor concluded.

Worse yet, the governor had submitted to a request from Robert D. Smith to let the Carthage Greys execute the arrest order. Because Justice Smith served as captain of the militia, he had ordered compliance to his own judicial ruling. *Incredible.*

John Taylor was still baffled as twenty Carthage Greys under the command of Captain James Dunn stomped their way into the Hamilton and posted themselves outside the room. After the report to Joseph and Hyrum, he had remained silent, staring at the floor. His mind was still grappling with the implications of today's developments. His brow sweating, he was trying to reject the obvious conclusions.

Meanwhile, Woods was telling Joseph, Hyrum, and Willard Richards about a message just received from R. F. Smith. He claimed he had issued the mittimus only to create a reason for placing Joseph and Hyrum under protective custody in the jail.

*Also incredible.*

# 55

ELIAS EAGLES FELT SMALL AND insignificant as he clamored to get into position along Main Street. It seemed that hundreds—even thousands—of militia and unruly mobbers lined the route that the captured Smith brothers would take from the Hamilton House to the Carthage Jail.

Elias and Henry's militia company were assigned to muster at the corner of Main and Marion, where the delegation, escorted by the Carthage Greys, would turn north and march the final block.

In fading daylight, Elias could hear a roar as Joseph and Hyrum emerged from the Hamilton. At first, Elias could see nothing but a mass of men, some uniformed, some not. Slowly, a wedge of Carthage Greys could be seen trudging toward him. Closer now, Elias could make out the images of the Prophet and his brother. Inside the wedge with them were two Apostles, John Taylor and Willard Richards. Following them were the attorneys, Wood and Reid. Trying to protect the Smiths were two bodyguards, Stephen Markham and Dan Jones.

After two days, Elias knew who all the prisoners were.

"What'll you bet I can get by the bodyguards and knock Joe Smith to his knees?" Henry suddenly said.

Elias considered the risk; Henry had been drinking again. "You're crazy," Elias responded.

The Carthage Grey wedge and its prisoners were within fifty yards. Another man, obviously drunk, belittled the Mormon prisoners, cursing, and approached swinging his rifle.

Using a large hickory cane that Markham called his "rascal-beater," Markham put a knot on the drunken man's head, sending him spinning backward.

"Sure you want to try that, Henry?" Elias asked.

Henry shrugged his shoulders. He found his flask and took a swig.

From the deep shadows of a building near the corner came a ghostly figure, slashing toward the wedge. Startled, Henry jumped back. Bracing himself, Elias crashed his shoulder into the approaching man's sternum. The man, heavily whiskered, looking to be in his early thirties, staggered backward.

"Dern you!" the man screamed. "Who's side you on?"

Elias didn't answer. He crashed a white-knuckled fist into the man's nose. There was a spurt of blood as the man crumpled to the ground.

Elias turned in time to see Stephen Markham wave his rascal-beater at the crowd.

"Any more brave men out there?" Markham asked. Markham nodded at Elias in a thanking gesture.

Henry continued to act as though Elias had betrayed him. "That was stupid."

"I thought our assignment was to protect the prisoners," Elias complained.

Henry shook his head. "You take things too seriously. You'd better hope that man with the broken nose doesn't find out who you are."

John Taylor knew Joseph and Hyrum's options had deteriorated to next to nothing. It was ten o'clock at night. Upstairs in the Carthage Jail, the door to an iron-barred cell reserved for rank criminals slammed shut. Taylor assessed the situation. The jail, constructed of native yellow limestone five years ago, certainly didn't look like as impenetrable as some of the old castles in England. That was to John Taylor's consternation. He feared a break-in of mobbers far more than he hoped for the possibility of a breakout by the prisoners.

Taylor sat in a corner while Joseph conferred with his attorneys. The possibility of a change of venue to Quincy was discussed. So was the possibility of asking a circuit court judge to hear a request for a writ of habeas corpus. If issued, it would require the Carthage court to examine the legality of Joseph and Hyrum's imprisonment. In the morning, another appeal would be made to Governor Ford. Perhaps finally, hopefully, he would consent to meet with Joseph.

Taylor put his ear to the thick wall of the jail. He sensed that the unruly crowd had finally dispersed.

Jailer George W. Stigall appeared again. Stigall moved Taylor and all the prisoners downstairs to a less secure but more comfortable room in the jail called the debtor's cell. It was furnished with a bench, some blankets, and a "night bucket."

As he rolled up into one of the blankets on the floor, John Taylor felt himself awaken fully to the unthinkable possibility that Joseph and Hyrum's lives were nearing an end. And perhaps his own.

# 56

### Wednesday, June 26

JOHN TAYLOR WAS SWELTERING ALREADY. It was going to be another hot, humid day in Carthage, especially for prisoners cooped up in the jail.

Taylor trained his eyes on Governor Ford who had just arrived to talk with the Prophet. Colonel Thomas Geddes of the Fountain Green Militia accompanied Ford. Taylor knew that Ford was the only man who could save Joseph and Hyrum, but as the conversation began, Taylor had the sinking feeling that Ford did not have the fortitude to do it.

"General Smith," Ford was saying, "you have given me an outline of the difficulties that have existed in Nauvoo, but there seems to be a discrepancy between your statements and those of your enemies."

Ford was referring to documents prepared by Taylor and Dr. John M. Bernhisel.

"What do you mean?" Taylor asked the governor.

Ford narrowed his eyes at Taylor, sending a message that he came to talk to General Smith, not to an underling.

"It is true, Mr. Taylor, that General Smith and his brother are substantiated by evidence and affidavit. But for such extraordinary excitement to be sweeping this part of the state, there has to be a cause."

Taylor took a deep breath. The governor was about to blame the Mormons again. He took out some paper and his pen. He hoped he could write as fast as Ford could talk.

Ford turned to face Joseph, who was sitting forward in a wooden chair. "General Smith, I attribute the last outbreak of violence to the destruction of the *Expositor's* press. And your refusal to comply with the writ issued by Justice of the Peace Morrison."

Joseph opened his mouth to protest, but Ford quickly cut him off.

"Let me finish before you reply, general," Ford said. "The press in the United States is looked upon as the great bulwark of American freedom. Its destruction in Nauvoo is looked upon as a high-handed measure. It manifests a disposition on your part to suppress freedom of speech and of the press. All this, combined with your refusal to comply with the writ, means that I must judge you as turbulent. And defiant to the laws and institutions of this country."

*Take a breath, governor,* Taylor screamed inwardly.

Joseph's rebuttal began. "Governor Ford, of all people, you should be aware of the persecutions I have endured."

Taylor noted that the governor gave a faint nod with his head. A *faint* nod.

"Our course in Illinois has been peaceable and law-abiding," Joseph continued. "Despite that, there has been every conceivable indignity and lawless outrage perpetrated upon me and the Mormon people since we settled here. I have attempted to keep you well posted of all these events. If you have not received some of my communications, it is not my fault."

Ford seemed resigned to hear the Prophet out.

Taylor was writing in a furious pace, sensing the historical importance of the moment. Joseph spoke of trying to protect members of the Church against armed bands of marauders, yet trying to keep the governor informed of events daily. Joseph spoke of how his motives were impugned, his acts misconstrued, and how his personal life was grossly and wickedly misrepresented.

"Was it the Mormons or our enemies who first commenced these difficulties?" Joseph asked.

Ford shrugged his shoulders.

"And who ordered out the Nauvoo Legion?" the Prophet asked.

Again, a shrug of the shoulders.

"I did," Joseph acknowledged, "but under your direction. And for what purpose? To suppress insurrectionary movements."

Ford was silent.

Joseph was on a roll. "It was at your insistence, sir, that I issued a proclamation calling on the Nauvoo Legion to be ready at a moment's notice to guard against the incursions of mobs. And now I am charged with treason? Why is it that I must be held accountable for other men's acts—including yours?"

Taylor looked up. Ford's discomfort showed.

Joseph began to justify his destruction of the *Expositor* press. He talked of the indignities he and the Church members had endured by "worthless vagabonds," that efforts by his enemies to "vilify and calumniate not only us but the character of our wives and daughters" should not have to be endured in any medium, including "that infamous and filthy sheet."

"It was a mistake to destroy the press," Ford said.

"There is not a city in the United States that would have suffered such an indignity for twenty-four hours," Joseph countered. "The publishers insulted the dignity of our community. Our people demanded that the city council redress the grievances. If not, they would have taken matters into their own hands."

Taylor agreed. He thought of Robert Harris, one of the few who wanted to do just that.

"But your city charter..." Ford began.

"Our city charter? It gave us power to remove such nuisances," Joseph said. "Our legal precedent goes back to an opinion cited by Sir William Blackstone."

Ford didn't have to be reminded that Blackstone was one of the most highly respected English barristers in the modern history of law.

"Blackstone has written that a libelous press may be considered a nuisance. Our own charter, given to us by the legislature of the state of Illinois, gives us that power to remove nuisances. By ordering that press abated, we were acting within strict accordance of the law. The city marshal carried it out."

Joseph paused, pointing to John P. Green, Nauvoo city marshal.

"It is possible there may have been some better way. But I confess that I could not see it."

Ford held up a hand to concede the point. "That's enough about the *Expositor* case."

"Then let's talk about our arrest," Joseph said.

"What about it?"

"All of us—I as mayor, and the city councilmen—were willing to abide the consequences of our acts. But we were unwilling to answer an illegal writ imposed upon us under the pretense of law."

Ford pulled a face. Joe Smith, unschooled, was lecturing a former justice of the state Supreme Court about law.

"Not withstanding the illegality of the writ, I told Constable Bettisworth—in the presence of twenty witnesses—that I was willing to go to any other magistrate, either in Nauvoo or any other place we would be safe. But not Carthage. We refused to put ourselves into the power of a mob."

Ford squirmed in his chair. The uneducated general was making a point.

"What right did Bettisworth have to refuse our request?"

Ford didn't answer

Joseph answered for him. "None, according to law. You know as well as I do, Governor Ford, that state law provides that the party on whom to writ is served shall, and I quote, 'go before him who issued it or some other justice of the peace.' Am I correct?"

Again, no answer.

"Of course I'm correct. Why, then, should we be dragged off to Carthage, where the law does not compel us to go? There are men serving as justices of the peace not only in Nauvoo, but in virtually every other community in the county."

Joseph had Ford on the ropes and he knew it. Joseph continued, talking about the breach of law, assumption of power, and how Bettisworth and the other conspirators were depriving him and other members of the Church of their legal and constitutional rights. Joseph related that even though Judge Jesse Thomas—a Mormon—had acquitted him and the city council of the *Expositor* charges, he and the council members even went before a non-Mormon judge—Daniel Wells—just to be certain. Even Wells acquitted Joseph and the council.

Joseph paused, waiting for a response. There was none.

"We submitted ourselves to the court in Carthage, sir," Joseph continued, "not because it was legal, but because you asked us to come. We desired to show you that we do not shrink from the most rigid investigation of our acts, as relating to the *Expositor.*"

Finally, Ford spoke. "I think you did the right thing. Thank you for coming to Carthage."

Joseph went for the juggler. "I now call upon you, Governor Ford, to deliver us from this place. Our arrest was illegal. We posted bond on the first charge. Now the second arrest, on the count of treason, is illegal. You know it is. I call upon you to rescue us from these infamous scoundrels."

Ford tried another approach. "But you, General Smith, have placed men under arrest, detained men as prisoners, and have given passes to others. I have both heard and seen of these instances."

John P. Green scooted his chair toward Ford. "Perhaps I can explain. Nauvoo has been placed under a very rigid police guard. We need to prevent against sudden surprises. Our guards have questioned suspected suspicious persons. We have given some passes out so that certain trusted people can get past the guards. No person, sir, has been imprisoned without a legal cause in our city."

Ford seemed to ignore Greene. He turned back to Joseph. "Why didn't you give a more speedy answer to the posse I sent out?"

Joseph had answers for everything. "Your letter showed anything but an amicable spirit. You know, sir, that we have suffered immensely in Missouri from mobs, in loss of property, imprisonment, and otherwise."

Joseph considered his eerie surroundings. It wasn't the same as the Liberty Jail, but it was close. On purpose, Joseph didn't disclose that he was on the other side of the Mississippi River when the posse arrived.

"Answer my question," Ford demanded.

"It took us some time to duly weigh everything. And your posse was too hasty in returning. I needed to consult with a lot of people. Vast interests were at stake. And another thing—you demanded that we come unarmed. We had to decide how much we could trust the posse, and how we might be protected from mob violence."

Colonel Geddes spoke, perhaps uninvited. "I agree with General Smith. It was not safe for him to come to Carthage unprotected." He was thinking of the mob violence that prevailed at the county seat.

Governor Ford seemed to concede the point. "Perhaps there wasn't sufficient time for you to get ready to submit to the posse. Perhaps they were too hasty. I suppose they found themselves bound by their orders."

It appeared that Joseph was about to exhale in a gesture of relief. Ford's next remarks prevented that.

"Let's go back to the matter of the *Expositor*. It was wrong for your city council to act in any kind of legislative capacity, or that of the judiciary. The council should have first passed a law in relation to the press. Then the municipal court, upon complaint, could have removed the *Expositor* press. Besides the owners of the press should have had a hearing before their property was destroyed. It was an infringement of their rights. It is contrary to the feelings of the American people to interfere with the press."

Now Joseph was squirming.

"And furthermore," Ford said, "you should have returned to Carthage with Bettisworth, even though the law did not require it."

Joseph shook his head. Ford was clearly on the side of the mobbers.

Ford continued. "As concerning your being here in jail, I am sorry for that. I wish it had been otherwise. I hope you will soon be released, but I cannot interfere."

Joseph held up a hand to protest. "There is one thing you have overlooked."

"What would that be?" Ford asked, looking surprised.

"Our arrest warrant was served by Bettisworth at the insistence of a brutal anti-Mormon mob. That mob had passed resolutions calling for the extermination of the Mormon leaders, including me. If they had taken us, it would have only fanned the excitement. That would mean all-out war. I thought it most judicious to avail ourselves of the full protection of the law."

Ford scratched at his chin. "I see."

Joseph went on countering. "In relation to the *Expositor*. You say you differ with me in opinion. Be it so. The thing, after all, is a legal difficulty. The courts can decide. Not a mob. If our act was illegal, we are willing to face it. If it is deemed we did a wrong in destroying the press, we will pay for it. We are desirous to fulfill the law in every particular. We are responsible for our acts."

Ford shook his head. "I understand your points, even though we disagree."

Joseph's eyes locked onto Ford's. "Governor, we look to you for protection. I hear you are going to Nauvoo. If you go, sir, we wish to go along. I refuse not to answer any law, but I do not consider myself safe here."

John Taylor stopped writing. With pleading eyes, he nodded his agreement.

The governor seemed unmoved. "I suppose if you are acquitted before I leave, you could go along. But I don't apprehend any danger for you."

"No danger?" Joseph asked.

Ford shrugged his shoulders again. "I think you are perfectly safe here in this Carthage Jail. I cannot remove you from jail. I cannot interfere with the law."

"But governor…"

Ford shook his head and looked down. "I am placed in peculiar circumstances and seem to be blamed by all parties."

John Taylor shook his head in disgust, still writing. *For the love of God do the right thing, governor!*

"I ask nothing but what is legal, governor," Joseph said. "I have a right to expect protection from you. Independent of law, you have pledged your faith, and that of the state, for my protection. I wish to go to Nauvoo where I will be safe."

The governor seemed to relent, in Taylor's view. "And you shall have my protection, General Smith. I did not make this promise without consulting my officers, who all pledged their honor to its fulfillment. I don't know if I'll go to Nauvoo tomorrow, but if I do, I will take you along."

Joseph stood. He extended his hand. "Thank you, governor. I expect you to keep your word."

John Taylor looked at his watch. The Prophet had talked with the governor for forty-five minutes.

The handshake was accepted by Ford. "Very well. I'm ready to leave."

Taylor opened the door. Ford and Geddes exited. Taylor closed the door and pressed his ear against it, listening. He overheard remarks that shook him to the core.

"This is all nonsense," Ford was saying to Colonel Geddes. "You'll have to drive these Mormons out yet."

Geddes answered, his voice trailing off. "If we undertake to do that, governor, when the proper times comes, will you interfere?"

Ford's voice was firm. "No. I will not."

There was a pause.

Ford's voice again. "Not until you are through."

# 57

ELIAS STOOD AT ATTENTION. The governor was passing by.

"I would give my right arm to know what Governor Ford and Joe Smith talked about in the jail just now," said a trooper in the same unit as Elias and Henry.

"When I left home I calculated to see old Joe dead before I returned," said another.

"So did I," said a third.

"I wonder if some damned Mormon is hearing all we have to say," said the first.

"If I knew there was, I'd run him through with my bayonet," answered the second.

Governor Ford walked by with a stern face. Colonel Geddes accompanied him. With the other men, Elias saluted.

In full view of Elias, an officer approached the governor. "The soldiers are determined to see Joe Smith dead before they leave here."

The governor frowned. "If you know of any such thing, keep it to yourself."

Elias felt Henry's elbow. "You didn't hear that," Henry whispered.

Elias checked his watch. Soldiers were leaving the jail. It was twelve-thirty. He felt himself sweating in his wool uniform. "They've changed the guards at the jail again."

"Let's make ourselves scarce," Henry said. "I don't want to pull guard duty."

"Why?" Elias asked. He felt a sudden, unexpected surge of protective instinct.

Henry scowled back at him. "Joe Smith and his brother preached to them—Mormonism stuff."

"What's wrong with that?"

"I'll show you." Henry motioned to one of the guards who had just left the jail.

"You want me?" the young guard asked. Elias judged him to be in his late twenties. He was a barrel-chested man with soft, putty-like features. He looked like he was on overload, in a hurry to get somewhere.

Henry pulled the guard aside. "What was it like in there, with old Joe preaching at you?"

The young guard suddenly looked electrified. "Those Mormons are innocent. I'm going home. No way will I fight against those men."

Henry pulled a face. "What's your name? I'll report you to your captain."

"Leave him alone, Henry," Elias said. Elias pushed the guard away. "Go home, where you belong."

The soldier was soon lost among hundreds of others.

Grinning, Elias stared at his brother. "Let's volunteer for guard duty. want to hear what the Smith boys had to say."

Henry looked furious. "Now you're the one who's crazy."

# 58

THE HANCOCK COUNTY COURTHOUSE stood in the center of the public square in Carthage. It was a two-story brick building, less than one block from the Hamilton House. But it was more than two blocks from the Carthage Jail. With attorneys for the two sides jockeying for control on the charge of treason against Joseph and Hyrum, the two defendants were about to make an appearance there.

Willard Richards peered out the window jail. What he saw frightened him. Constable Bettisworth was storming into the jail with a deputy.

"I'm here to take the prisoners into my custody," Bettisworth told the jailer Stigall.

"On whose order?" Stigall asked, his voice tinged with incredulity.

"Constable Robert F. Smith," came the answer from Bettisworth.

"And for what purpose?"

"Can't say."

Willard's aching body did a turn for the worse. The apostates were behind this, he reasoned. He prayed Stigall would not give in.

Joseph and Hyrum looked at each other.

"There's no law authorizing a justice of the peace to demand prisoner committed to my charge," Stigall replied.

"Quick," Joseph said to John Taylor. "Run to the hotel and get my attor neys."

Taylor bounded down the stairs as Bettisworth was leaving.

It seemed to Wilson Law that the Committee had to meet almost hourly to deal with one situation after another. The jailer's stubbornness irked him.

As he steamed, Bettisworth was asking Chauncey L. Higbee for advice.

"As a point of law, the jailer is correct," Higbee said.

"So now what?" Bettisworth asked, wiping his brow. Even inside the gov ernor's room at the Hamilton it was warm and sultry.

Robert F. Smith turned to Governor Ford. "What do you recommend?"

"We have plenty of troops," Ford answered. "The Carthage Greys are under your command. Bring them out."

The voice from the back of the room was loud and demanding. "I still say we settle this with powder and ball," Dr. Robert D. Foster said.

"Hear, hear!" chimed the other apostates—Foster's brother, the Law brothers, and the Higbees. They raised their whiskey glasses in a mock toast.

"I'll send Frank Worrell's command," R. F. Smith said.

Wilson Law smiled. Worrell had a reputation for meanness.

Willard could see the Carthage Greys coming. He checked his watch. It was twenty minutes to four. Just a little more than an hour had passed since Bettisworth tried to get Joseph and Hyrum. The Prophet and his brother were conferring with the attorneys in the debtor's cell. Word had been received from Nauvoo that Porter Rockwell had scuffled with Francis Higbee, during which a letter dropped out of Higbee's hat. The letter stated that seventy members of a mob in Iowa were ready to attack the Mormons. There were other rumors that a mob intended to attack the jail.

"R. F. Smith contends he wants a hearing on the charge of treason,"

Woods was saying.

The hair on the back of Willard's neck was standing out. "I don't like it. If they get you out in the open, anything could happen."

"What's the worst thing that could happen in court if we make it to the courthouse safely?" Joseph asked.

"R. F. Smith will rule for a continuation on the hearing. That means both of you will be legally incarcerated. At this point, I don't know how to avoid it."

Worrell banged on the jail door.

"They're not coming out unless the Greys form a hollow square for the protection of the prisoners," Reid demanded.

Worrell gave in. The Greys formed the square.

Willard shuddered. In his mind he could see Joseph and Hyrum falling in the streets to a barrage of muskets. In the midst of his gloom, he watched the Prophet put on his hat and drag Hyrum into the middle of the Greys. Reluctantly, Willard limped into the hollow square as well.

"Let's go boys," Joseph said boldly.

The march toward the courthouse began.

Incredibly, Joseph suddenly reached outside the protective custody of the square and pulled what Willard considered to be the wildest looking mobber and soldier into the square with him. Joseph locked arms with the man on one side, and Hyrum on the other. Willard held onto Joseph's other arm. John Taylor, Dan Jones, Stephen Markham, and John S. Fullmer trailed behind.

Joseph's move clearly shocked every Carthage Grey soldier, in Willard's opinion.

The man had locks of greasy black hair hanging from under his cap. His eyes were dark and bloodshot. "What's your name?"

Fear gripped the wild man. "Henry," he answered. There was an English accent.

"Well, Henry. Hang on tight. You're going to escort us to the courthouse."

The first floor of the courthouse consisted of four rooms that served as offices for the county sheriff, treasurer, clerks of the circuit court, and the county commissioner's court. Joseph and Hyrum had been taken to a large courtroom on the second floor.

Willard fumed at the assembly of attorneys representing the state Chauncey L. Higbee. Sylvester Emmons, the *Expositor* editor. Thomas Sharp the *Warsaw Signal* editor. Thomas Morrison, part-time justice of the peace for the county. They were huddled again with Wilson and William Law and the Fosters.

Woods and Reid immediately went to work in behalf of Joseph and Hyrum. They called for subpoenas for defense witnesses, and expressed their wish to go into examination as soon as witnesses could be brought from Nauvoo.

Higbee objected vehemently.

Woods demanded to see the original writ.

The court presented it, saying it was served June twenty-fifth.

Woods demonstrated it was false. The prisoners had been committed to jail without any examination whatever.

Once again, Reid demanded a continuance until the Nauvoo witnesses could arrive.

R. F. Smith, as justice of the peace, was stuck and he knew it. Reluctantly he postponed examination until noon the next day. Subpoenas were granted for the Nauvoo witnesses. R. F. Smith then issued a new mittimus remanding the Smith brothers to jail.

Joseph and Hyrum were thrust back into the Carthage jail.

By candlelight, Willard Richards sat writing the events of the day. The room in the upstairs of the Carthage Jail was crowded. Joseph and Hyrum occupied the only bed, trying to sleep. John Taylor, Dan Jones, Stephen Markham, and John S. Fullmer lay on the floor.

Earlier, Hyrum led a discussion about the Book of Mormon, the illegality of their imprisonment, and the deliverance of the servants of God for the sake of the gospel. Joseph bore testimony of the divine authenticity of the

Book of Mormon, the restoration of the gospel, the administration of angels, and that the kingdom of God was again established on the earth.

"It is for my testimony that we are incarcerated, not because I have violated any law of God or man," he concluded.

Willard felt a tear stain his cheek.

Outside, mobbers drank, sang, and shouted threats.

*Boom!*

Fear coursed down Willard's back. It was a gunshot. There were audible signs of a great commotion outside the jail, but the noise quickly died down.

Willard's candle flickered and went out.

Joseph removed himself from the bed and stretched out on the floor. "I would to God that I could preach to the Saints in Nauvoo once more," he said.

Willard laid his large, tired, still sore body on the floor.

Dim moonlight found its way through the window, revealing a worried Dan Jones. Willard closed his eyes, wondering the fate of them all. Jones had been called on a mission to Wales. Very likely he would never make it. Willard opened his eyes again when he heard Joseph's soft voice.

"Are you afraid to die, Brother Jones?"

Jones answered. "Has that time come, you think? Engaged in such a cause I don't think that death would have many terrors."

There were a few moments of silence before Willard heard Joseph reply.

"Brother Jones, you will yet see Wales and fulfill the mission appointed you before you die."

Willard believed the Prophet. Willard closed his eyes and wondered about his own fate.

# 59

*Thursday, June 27*

MARY CROOK EAGLES STOOD IN THE doorway crying. "Don't go back to Carthage," she pleaded with her husband, Elias. A light rain was falling and water was dripping off the roof of the Henry Eagles home, adding to Mary's discomfort.

"I have to," Elias said, exchanging looks with Henry.

"Not if we move back to Nauvoo," Mary said. "You could change your militia duty back to the Nauvoo Legion." She had been over this before, many times.

Katherine Eagles remained secluded deep within the floorless parlor of their cabin, feeding her young daughter breakfast. She had learned long ago that arguing with an Eagles was a waste of time.

"Come," Henry scoffed. "We'll be late. Today could be the day."

Mary knew what Henry meant. All morning he had talked about rumors that the mobs in Carthage were going to find a way to kill the Smith brothers. Night and day, she had been praying that their lives would be spared.

Mary's heart was pounding fiercely, as though a premonition was building. "With or without you," she said to Elias, "I'm going to Nauvoo."

Henry smiled faintly. He was holding the reins of both his horse and the horse that belonged to Elias. "How? Are you going to walk eighteen miles?"

"I will if I have to," Mary answered in a tone she hoped Elias and Henry would pick up on. She'd had all of Henry she could stand.

"I'll arrange it today if I can," Elias finally conceded. He mounted his horse. "Stay here. If possible, we'll return to Nauvoo tomorrow."

Mary watched as her husband galloped off with her despised brother-in-law.

Governor Thomas Ford wanted to scream. His breakfast eggs were overdone and the cook at the Hamilton had burned his toast. Wilson Law and his Committee were pressuring him to leave for Nauvoo. If he went, the Mormons were begging him to take Joe and Hyrum Smith with him. Colonel Geddes was throwing a fit, thinking he might give in. If he did release Joe and Hyrum Smith, Geddes was probably right—it would cause a bloody confrontation right in the streets of Carthage.

With his aides, Governor Ford was trying to sort out wild accusations right and left. The anti-Mormons claimed the Mormons near Lima had stolen sixteen horses, but at Lima the story was that the horses had actually been stolen in Hancock County. Plotters wanted to kill the Smiths. Mobbers warned of jailbreak attempts and told wild stories about the Nauvoo Legion coming in force to rescue their Prophet. Families caught in the middle were escaping Hancock County. The newest: Dan Jones had just come from the jail, pleading with him to replace the guards with men not so militant.

Ford barked at an aide to get him more eggs. He barked at another to get him some new cigars.

For a split second, Ford entertained the thought of letting Joe Smith escape. He recalled that when Governor Boggs of Missouri had the Smiths locked up at Liberty Jail, Boggs had gotten rid of a very sticky problem by allowing the prisoners to escape. That got the Smiths out of the state, and kept them out of the state by making fugitives of them.

Ford shook himself back to reality. If he let the Smiths escape, the mobbers in Carthage would try to follow, igniting an all-out war. In addition, they would turn their vengeance on him. There would be a dead governor. *Let them kill the Smiths,* he thought.

"To hell with the eggs," Ford said. He swiped at his breakfast plate, knocking it to the floor. He barked and cursed at another aide. "Pour me a drink."

*I should never have promised Joe Smith I would take him with me to Nauvoo!*

There was a knock on the door. The aide answered. It was Colonel Geddes.

"We're ready for the meeting," Geddes said, peering in.

Ford took a deep breath. "Tell them to come in."

Geddes motioned to the other officers.

"Is today the day?" Henry asked a Carthage Grey.

Henry knew the Grey understood. There was an undercurrent in Carthage that was apparent to everyone except the stupid blind. Tents of military units still covered the village square, and were spread out into the countryside. Carthage had swelled with men volunteering to fight against the Mormons.

"The governor's meeting right now with all the militia officers," Grey said, pointing up at the second floor of the Hamilton.

"Why do they need more meetings?" Henry asked. "Let's just get the job done."

"The governor is trying to decide whether or not to go to Nauvoo. Some of the officers want to take the militia to Nauvoo as a show of force. A few think it would rile up the Mormons, and that they would muster the Legion against us. Still others want all the troops disbanded as soon as the governor leaves."

"But wouldn't that turn the mob loose?" Elias asked. But if that happened, he and Mary could return to Nauvoo.

"But isn't that the idea?" Henry countered.

Willard Richards could see the anger in Cyrus Wheelock's eyes, and he felt it, too. Long one of Joseph's trusted bodyguards, Wheelock had entered the Carthage Jail with a pass issued by Governor Ford. A raincoat was draped over his hunched-over figure.

"Ford is as stiff-necked as a dead cat," Wheelock complained as he stormed up the stairs.

"You don't have to tell us that," John Taylor answered. "You must not have a good report."

Wheelock had been sent to enter a final plea with Governor Ford to take Joseph and Hyrum with him to Nauvoo. He turned to Joseph and Hyrum as he reported.

"I kept telling the governor that you are not safe here if he leaves. There're too many traitors and midnight assassins who thirst for your blood. He keeps saying that he does not believe the people to be that cruel. He underestimates the mob."

Willard's stomach had been cramping due to the food and worry over their situation. Now, he felt as though the world had crashed down upon him. "Then he's gone back on his word."

Joseph shook his head. "I was afraid he would."

Wheelock was still steaming. He stood unusually close to the Prophet. "The governor thinks that just because the militia has pledged to protect the jail, it will really happen."

Out of the corner of his eye, Willard saw Wheelock slip a revolver from his raincoat into Joseph's pocket.

Joseph pulled the pistol out, examined it, and put it back in his pocket without comment. Then he sent Wheelock out to help John S. Fullmer locate witnesses for the hearing set for later today. And Joseph sent Stephen

Markham out to get something to settle Willard's stomach.

Only four men remained in the jail. The two official prisoners, Joseph and Hyrum. And John Taylor and himself.

Willard wondered if they would all be dead before the hearing, and before the herbs could take affect.


Elias wilted when he saw Colonel Geddes approach. Elias expected to be crucified for asking to transfer out, especially since it was to Nauvoo.

"You Elias Eagles?" Geddes asked.

Elias could feel his throat tighten. He could hardly answer yes.

"I have an assignment for you," the colonel said.

Elias blinked his astonishment.

"I need a courier to relay a message to Colonel Levi Williams."

"Yes, sir." Elias saluted the colonel. *He obviously knows nothing of my request.*

"Colonel Williams is standing by at Golden Point with five hundred militia from the Warsaw area."

Elias scratched his chin. He was a newcomer to Illinois; he would have to ask Henry exactly where Golden Point was located.

Geddes handed Elias a sealed envelope. "Colonel Williams expects to rendezvous with Governor Ford's troops and accompany them to Nauvoo. This is an order from the governor. Colonel Williams is to disband his troops and tell them to go home."

"Go home?" Henry said the words in disbelief.

Geddes ignored Henry. He asked Elias if he had a horse. Elias said yes.

"Then get going," Geddes said. "And don't open that envelope."

Elias scratched his head at that last order. What was so secret about disbanding troops? "Can I take my brother?" Elias asked, pointing to Henry.

"Makes no difference to me. Your unit is going to be disbanded, too. After you deliver the message, you're free to go to your homes, too."


Golden Point was a landmark on the Mississippi roughly halfway between

Warsaw and Nauvoo. Colonel Williams and his five hundred soldiers were there, just as Geddes said. Their camp looked disheveled, with dirty clothes strewn on the ground and the camp cook passed out from a morning bout with his whiskey bottle. As Elias rode up with Henry in a light rain, the soldiers looked impatient, pacing in front of a collection of shanties that stood near the river.

Elias slid off his lathered horse in front of Colonel Williams. He felt a rush of dizziness. He, an English immigrant, had never had such an important assignment in his life. "I'm Elias Eagles, sir. And this is my brother, Henry. Colonel Geddes has sent us to deliver this message from the governor."

Colonel Williams fumbled at the envelope in disbelief. As he read the message, his bearded mouth opened vacantly. He planted his feet apart. To Elias, it seemed a gesture of defiance.

"Well I'll be damned," Williams uttered as he shook his head.

His officers immediately surrounded Williams. Shaking his head, the colonel mounted a wagon bed. He took a deep breath, to project his voice.

"This here paper says all militia units are to be disbanded, immediately."

A howl went up. The cursing reminded Elias of Henry's foul utterances. "Why?" one asked.

The order didn't say. Williams had his own opinions. He called Ford some choice names.

Despite their barroom language, most of the soldiers struck Elias as fairly important people, substantial citizens of Warsaw, and men of affairs. But their utterings soon gave another impression to Elias. They were united in their determination to rid Illinois of the "Mormon menace."

One soldier verbally recalled a recent resolution passed at a public meeting in Warsaw: "That we will forthwith proceed to Nauvoo and exterminate the city."

Elias cringed.

Although still shaking his head in disappointment, Williams issued the order. "You're free to go home, boys."

Several began gathering up equipment and taking down tents. One shook the camp cook, trying to sober him up.

"Let's get out of here," Elias told Henry. "Our job's done." He prepared to mount his horse.

Just then, one of the captains stepped onto the baggage wagon. "Men listen to me! I need volunteers."

Elias felt Henry's forefinger in his chest. "Hey, that's Mark Aldrich," Henry said. "Remember? We met him the other day in Warsaw."

Reluctantly, Elias nodded. They had met Thomas Sharp that day, too Suddenly, he recognized Sharp amid the gathering militiamen.

Aldrich was animated, red-faced and bug-eyed. "As members of the militia, we've been officially discharged. So I speak to you not as an officer, but a a fellow citizen. Geddes says in his letter that Joe and Hy Smith are left under guard of the Carthage Greys, and that they are all our friends. That implies that they wouldn't interfer with us if we were to take after the Smiths. Who will return to Carthage with me and use up Joe Smith?"

As several hands shot up, Elias motioned to Henry again. "It's time to go."

"Wait," Henry pleaded. "This is getting interesting." Henry jerked the reins out of Elias' hands. "I'm not gonna take part in shooting Joe Smith, but I'd like to watch."

Elias narrowed his eyes at his brother. "That's not the way we were brought up, Henry. Our parents always told us to refrain from applauding wickedness even though you don't participate in it. Sins of omission are our failures to do what's right. Let's get out of here."

His words fell on deaf ears.

Sharp was on the baggage wagon now, as energetic as a secular preacher "Are we going to be made tools and puppets of Tommy Ford?" he yelled.

The number of militant soldiers was increasing in front of Elias' eye "No!" they chanted in unison.

Sharp's next words seemed to Elias to be almost read verbatim from Sharp's own editorials. "There's only one way to quiet Hancock County," he said. "And that's to remove either the Mormons, or us! What'll it be?"

"The Mormons!"

"Is it possible for two sets of people to live together in peace, who regard each other with feelings of the most venomous hostilities?"

"No!"

"The remedy is apparent! Are you with us?"

Sharp had succeeded.

"Yes! Yes!" the men chanted.

Five minutes earlier, the men were unruly soldiers. Now they were a mob.

Elias was practically the only man in the camp to notice another rider approaching from Carthage. He came galloping in, his horse throwing mud from its hooves.

Elias didn't recognize the rider, but the rider wore sheer excitement on his face. The rider dismounted and asked a perimeter soldier to speak to the officer in command, just as Elias had done. As Sharp was working the mob into another frenzy, Elias could see Colonel Williams talking with the rider. With a tight expression of satisfaction, Williams worked his way to the baggage wagon. He jumped up, alongside Sharp.

"I've just received another communication," Williams said. "This one is from our good friend, Captain Robert F. Smith of the Carthage Greys."

Sharp's eyes opened wide in anticipation. "What is it?"

"With the governor on his way to Nauvoo, the Greys have been left to guard the jail."

The mob quieted. Men could be seen cupping their ears, anxious for the rest of the message.

"The way is open to settle the Mormon question, once and for all."

"Just what do you mean, colonel?" the Warsaw lawyer and newspaperman asked Williams. "In plain language?"

Williams smiled. "If a group of law-abiding citizens such as I see before me—driven in desperation—were to take the law into their own hands and storm the jail, there would be but token resistance. In fact, the guards would have their pieces loaded with blanks."

"Men, follow the colonel," Sharp said, his voice penetrating and loud "We're going to Carthage. You have a new name!"

"What's our new name?" a volunteer shouted.

"The Warsaw Regulators," Sharp cried back. "Joe Smith is a dead man!"

Williams held up a hand. "You men move toward Carthage. I'll ride into the town and talk to the Carthage Greys. I'll see what we can arrange. I'll be right back. I'll meet you just outside town."

Dumfounded, Elias found himself trailing after a body of eighty horse men. He had the distinct feeling that the whole thing was part of an overall plan. The worst elements of the militia were rushing back to Carthage with murder on their minds.

# 60

WILSON LAW paced the floor in the lobby of the Hamilton in front of the Committee members, waiting for the execution of the plan.

"Sit down, Wilson, you're driving me crazy."

Wilson flashed an angry look at his smaller, older brother, William. "It's plumb eerie out there. The governor is gone. Most all the militia is gone. What if the Nauvoo Legion comes riding in?"

"We'd be warned first," Chauncey L. Higbee surmised.

Wilson hee-hawed. "By the militia?" He bit into the pipe that he had started smoking only a week ago. There were plenty of other anti-Mormon sympathizers out there. Ford had posted a watch from McDonough County, half a mile out on the Carthage-Warsaw road. And Ford had ordered the Carthage Greys camped on the public square to continue a guard on the jail. Also, the Carthage Riflemen remained on alert.

*We are safe*, Wilson told himself.

Ford had left for Nauvoo mid-morning under protection of Captain Dunn's Union Dragoons. A short time ago, a messenger from Ford had come to the Hamilton, looking for R. F. Smith. The message: remind the guards of Ford's expectations to guard the prisoners.

Wilson shook his head. Ford was a nut case. One minute Ford sounded like he wanted the Smiths dead. The next minute he sounded like he wanted them protected. One minute he wanted to lead a powerful military escort to Nauvoo. The next minute he wanted only a small unit. One minute he wanted a continuance of the hearing. The next minute he wanted it postponed.

Wilson agreed with the governor on one point, however. A civil war *would* devastate property values in Nauvoo and cause the deaths of many including women and children. At this point, the Committee had no hope of gaining control of Nauvoo, the Church, and the politics there. All they wanted now was the death of the man they had previously revered as a Prophet. *Let the war between the Mormons and the mob come.*

"What's your guess?" Chauncey asked.

Wilson narrowed his eyes.

"When do you think Colonel Williams will get here?"

"A better question would be: with how many men?" Wilson stated. He thought of R. F. Smith's messenger to Colonel Levi Williams. The message had been penned in the Hamilton, with the Committee supervising.

"I hope enough to do the job," Robert L. Foster added.

Robert Harris thought of his musket hidden in cornrows at his garden spot. He didn't like what Governor Ford was saying to the collecting crowd at the Mansion House. For certain, he concluded, Wilson Law and his gang of apostates were responsible for the Prophet and his brother being unjustly stuck in the Carthage Jail. It was all he could do to restrain himself from running to the corn patch, retrieving the gun, and racing Tapper all the way to Carthage. If he had to, he would free Joseph and Hyrum single-handedly.

"You ought to be praying Saints, not military Saints," Ford was saying.

Robert cringed. *And you ought to be a praying governor, not a traitor to the Mormons.* In his view, Ford resembled the demonic-eyed, chin-jutting imperial bully he'd conjured up in his mind. As he had walked by the governor earlier, Robert could see how deep the creases of decision were folded into his face and how withdrawn from the Mormon position he was.

Ford earlier had railed against the Prophet and the city council, saying that the destruction of the *Expositor* had been an unwise action and that the heavily armed Nauvoo Legion posed a threat to the peace of the region. That's why it had been necessary to disarm the Legion. Yesterday, Ford had sent Captain Singleton with sixty members of the militia to Nauvoo to "protect" the city. While they were doing so, Singleton sent men to selected spots to search for three printing presses suspected of printing bogus money. They were reacting to a tip by Dr. Robert D. Foster. Nothing was found.

Robert smiled. He was certain he was not the only man in Nauvoo who was hiding a rifle somewhere.

"If any vengeance should be attempted openly or secretly against your enemies, literally thousands of people will assemble for the total destruction of your city and the extermination of your people," Ford was saying. He took a long portentous pause, and then spoke with a decisive nod. "No power in the state would be able to prevent it, not even me."

Several minutes later Ford asked for a vote. He wanted to know if the Mormons would strictly obey the laws—even in opposition to their leaders. He got his vote.

After the governor's unpopular speech, Robert started home with Daniel, Levi Roberts, John Cox, John Hyrum Green, Thomas Bloxham, Edward Phillips, and Joseph Hill. Robert witnessed an event that made his blood boil even more.

Governor Ford ordered Captain Dunn and his Union Dragoons to march full-width up Main Street with a show of military might. From the Mansion House all the way to Lyon's Drug the Dragoons demonstrated passes, guards, cuts, and thrusts just to intimidate the crowd.

Robert thought of his hidden rifle again. In his mind, he picked it up, loaded it, and aimed it at Ford's chest.

On horseback, Ford, Captain Dunn, and the soldiers trotted east past the temple on their way out of town, along Mulholland. A block away, Hannah stood watching the spectacle, clutching her children. She wished Robert were here, instead of in lower Nauvoo, where he had gone to listen to the governor's speech.

Hannah was in a nervous slump. "I'll be glad when all of this is over," she said to Elizabeth and Harriet, who were standing there with her.

"Me, too," Harriet responded with a gloomy face. "It's frightening. The apostates have sworn revenge. It looks like they're having it."

Hannah's thoughts turned to Joseph and Hyrum. Elizabeth's did too and she quickly said, "Daniel thinks the court will vindicate the Prophet."

Hannah listened as Elizabeth began to go off about everything—from the *Expositor* incident to the sudden appearance of Governor Ford in Nauvoo.

Elizabeth's prattling did little to comfort Hannah. Hannah's nerves were frazzled. She worried about Elias and Mary, wishing they would return to Nauvoo where they belonged. She worried, too, about Henry and Katherine and their daughter. Their home was too close to Carthage, where things might literally erupt.

Hannah especially worried about Robert. His hatred of Wilson Law and the apostates was consuming him.

Elizabeth was still chattering. She was pointing at the soldiers, who were nearly out of sight now. "Those men need to go home and let their wives take their place. What do you think would happen if the world were run by women, instead of men? The women guards at the Carthage Jail would open the doors and let Joseph and Hyrum out of there, don't you think?"

Harriet was nodding her agreement.

"And if the governor were a woman, she wouldn't have bothered to come to Nauvoo and show off like this, would she?"

Her sister-in-law was making a lot of sense, Hannah told herself. Women tended to be kinder, more sensible. Unless, of course, they were under the influence of Satan, as it seemed all the anti-Mormons were out here.

But the reality was, Ford was a man. And he was on his way back to Carthage.

And Joseph and Hyrum were still in jail.

# 61

WILLARD RICHARDS LAY COILED on a bed in the upper cell of the Carthage Jail, hands over his stomach. As a doctor of herbal medicines, he tried to diagnose the pain in his stomach. The lunch Stigall fed him? Nerves? Sheer exhaustion? Lack of sleep? All of the above?

The cell looked morbid from Willard's vertical position on the bed. Stephen Markham, using his pass, had left to find some herbs for him. Wheelock and Fullmer were still gone, looking for the witnesses the lawyers needed for Saturday's hearing. The attorneys were still in the Hamilton. Dan Jones had gone to talk to the governor, but had not returned.

There were four men left in the jail. Himself, Joseph, Hyrum, and John Taylor.

Taylor was singing verse after verse of the folk-hymn, "A Poor Wayfaring Man of Grief."

Hyrum sat with his hands in his face, listening. His pullover white shirt looked rumpled. He wore brown cotton serge trousers and a light brown sleeveless vest.

Joseph was pacing the floor, still dressed in a white lace-trimmed shirt and black trousers.

Elias Eagles was pacing back and forth in the woods, along the northwest edge of Carthage. He had tried to talk to the jailer, but the Carthage Greys had stopped him at the rail fence, threatening him. He had watched as the Greys forced one of Joseph Smith's bodyguards—a man named Stephen Markham—to leave town at gunpoint, with foul cursing and vivid threats against his life. Now Elias watched as, near him in the woods, members of the disbanded Warsaw militia assembled, their numbers growing by the hour. His dark eyes were wide open and darting here and there, rather like a deer being chased. Several men had just arrived toting an old wagon loaded with a barrel of whiskey. Now the whiskey was being passed around. It had an amazing effect on the men, in Elias' opinion. Their courage took a leap forward. The threats became more vocal.

"I want some of that whiskey," Henry said to Elias.

Elias stood dumbfounded as he watched his brother trudge through the trees. He could see the mobbers gesturing at Henry, not sharing the whiskey. Henry was walking back toward him now. Behind him, lightning flashed through lowering clouds and there was a thunderclap. The afternoon temperature was hot. The air was muggy.

"They told me to either go home or go out on the road and watch for the Nauvoo Legion," Henry said, appearing devastated. Elias surmised that it was the first time in Henry's life he had been turned down for a drink.

"Good advice," Elias admitted. The horses were tied to trees just a few feet away. Elias wondered who might be in the Hamilton. If there were any Mormon sympathizers there, he would like to talk to them about the men in the trees—Colonel Williams, Thomas Sharp, Mark Aldrich, and the other Warsaw militiamen who now formed an unruly mob. Incredibly, a group of men came from the direction of the Hamilton House. They joined the Warsaw group.

"Let's get out of here," Elias said, taking a step toward the horses. "It after five o'clock. I'm going home."

Henry pulled at Elias' shirt. "No need yet. Stick around. Look."

Henry pointed at the mob. Some of them were darkening their faces with a mixture of mud and gunpowder. Others were using colored mixtures, some red, and some yellow. To Elias, the men were beginning to resemble Indians. All were loading their rifles and muskets. Williams, Sharp, and Aldrich were still recognizable. They were doing a lot of arm waving and pointing.

Single file, the mobbers began moving through the woods toward the jail. Trees and a rail fence were helping to obscure them from the Carthage Greys and the Carthage Riflemen, who were posted at the jail. Elias gazed at the eerie scene. A separate four-rail fence and some trees surrounded the jail.

Henry pulled at his reluctant brother. "Come on." Keeping some fifty yards away, the two men followed.

For Henry and Elias, the jail was in full view now. The Greys seemed alarmed. They were marching double time from the square to the jail. Someone must have warned them, Elias guessed.

The Greys were too late. In front of Elias and Henry, the vigilantes from the woods had split into two groups, surrounding the jail. There were shouts and cursing. Mobbers jumped over the low fence in front of the jail.

Elias panicked. "They're storming the jail!"

Henry seemed pleased. "It's not just talk after all." Stumbling, running, pulling at Elias, Henry moved closer.

A guard was yelling at the mobbers. "Retire, or I'll fire on you!"

The one hundred fifty mobbers ignored the warning. Most were armed with muskets and spring breech rifles.

The guard aimed point blank at one of the painted men. There was a loud report and a puff of smoke from the musket.

To the amazement of Elias and Henry, the painted man did not fall. Elias could make out Thomas Sharp, the editor, and Jacob Davis, the lawyer, in the mob.

The guard was brushed aside. Two other guards fired point blank. Still, no one fell. Still other guards were firing wads straight into the air, covering their collusion.

*This looks too easy!* Elias concluded. *The flintlocks are loaded blank!*

Puzzling, too, was the fact that guards had sly smiles on their faces. Incredibly, now the guards were reversing their guns, breeches upward. Even more incredible, Elias could see Frank Worrell willingly open the door to the jail.

Mobbers were entering the jail; cursing, yelling, "Surrender! Surrender!" Just as the Keokuk stage was passing by, Levi Williams could be seen motioning and yelling for some of the men to surround the jail and to "shoot the scoundrels." Other mobbers could be seen wrestling innocent men to the ground, threatening them.

Elias wondered what the passengers in the stage thought of the scene surrounding the jail.

Elias could hear shots from inside, then a lull. Again, gunshots, some from pistols, most from muskets. From an open window on the second floor Elias could see flashes. Seconds later, gun smoke trickled out. There was a stench of burned powder.

Fear gripped Elias. His heart raced. Incredibly, more painted men standing on the ground fired at the building at random.

Even more incredible was the appearance of someone in a white shirt at the window. For a second, he poised on the ledge. There was a cry. "Oh, Lord. My God!"

More gunfire. Some mobbers were firing at the man; some were firing aimlessly at the jail building. Demonic oaths filled the air.

The white-shirted man tumbled eighteen feet to the ground, landing on his left side near the well curb. Briefly, the man lifted himself up, drew up one leg, and stretched out the other.

"He's leaped from the window!" a voice cried from the jail.

Elias' heart sank to his toes. "That's the Prophet!"

Joseph's drawn up leg went limp.

"Joe Smith is deader than a doornail," Henry said.

Elias turned away, tears filling his eyes. A painted man had propped up the Prophet's body. Others were firing into it on orders of Colonel Williams.

"Make certain the job's done," Williams was yelling.

There were more voices.

"Hyrum's the only one left up there!"

"Where'd the other two go?"

"Taylor's shot to pieces. He can't get far!"

"The fat one's lame—he's got to be around somewhere!"

"Find them!"

"Dig them out!"

Henry was pulling on Elias again. "Come on, let's help them search."

Elias looked for a gun. He might have to shoot his own brother. "Leave me alone!"

Suddenly, more voices.

"The Mormons are coming!"

Henry's eyes were as wide as saucers, scanning every direction. "Let's get out of here!" Henry let go of Elias and ran toward the horses, back in the woods.

Instinctively, Elias ran too.

Back in the woods, the paint-faced mobbers and "regulators" were in a panic. Elias could see men congregated around the whiskey wagon again, some wiping their faces clean, some jumping on frightened horses, some running deeper into the woods. Three men were wounded, one in the arm, one in the shoulder, and one in the cheek—as if a ball had taken the skin off.

Elias marveled how quickly the dastardly dead had been done. From the time the men had entered the jail until they fled from it, only three or four minutes had passed. Through his vantage point in the woods, Elias could see wagons flying out of town and men fleeing both on horseback and on foot. At the jail, a boy stood paralyzed over the body of Joseph Smith. Carthage Greys were slowly marching into the jail yard. None showed any inclination to pursue the fleeing mobbers. Lightning flashed again, filling the darkened skies with light. There was a tremendous thunderclap.

From the Warsaw Road a cannon was fired, no thunderclap. It shook the countryside. Elias suspected it was a signal from the mobbers to the people in Warsaw that the foul deed had been done.

Nearer to Elias, Williams, Aldrich, Davis, and Sharp were talking to the men who had come from the Hamilton. They were gloating over their accomplishment.

"We can't go back to the Hamilton looking like this," one said, referring to the blackened mixture on his face.

Another began wiping his face with a rag. "It's just mud and gunpowder. It comes right off."

"Where'll we go?"

"We'll head north."

Aldrich said, "And we'll go back to Warsaw."

Two abandoned muskets littered the ground between Elias and the whiskey wagon. He spied an ammunition box, with balls and powder.

Henry had reached the horses, his panic showing. "I'm leaving without you!"

"Then leave."

With no effort to hide his approach, Elias walked toward the whiskey wagon and picked up a musket. With amazing reflex speed, he had it loaded with powder and ball. He pulled the hammer back.

Henry's galloping horse could no longer be heard.

The last of Elias' control broke. He began to scream hysterically, his eyes bulging, and his hair seeming to puff away from his head. "You killed the Prophet!"

The mobbers whirled.

"You!" Williams exclaimed, suddenly recognizing the courier who had delivered the message from Colonel Geddes. He cursed. "What do you think you're doing?"

"You're all murderers!"

Elias read the fear on the faces of the four men, Williams, Sharp, Davis, and Aldrich. It pleased him. The musket was already cocked.

From behind Elias, a blast shuddered through the trees. The noise and the pain reached him simultaneously. His body felt paralyzed, barely enough control to pull the trigger. Falling, he could see only dreary gray skies and the tops of trees.

"This man is crazy."

"He fired straight in the air."

Footsteps approached. Elias found himself rolled over, looking into the faces of nearly a dozen men. One of them had a musket in his arms; smoke still curled from the barrel.

"Who is he?" one asked.

Elias was dying and he knew it. The ball had hit a rib and turned downward in his gut. There was no chance any of the men standing over him would get a doctor, or try to remove the bullet. He lay in a death sweat. He felt himself fading, his eyes heavy. He wanted to etch the memory of these killers into his mind. But if he died, what good would it do?

Elias still had strength to talk. "Don't let me die," he pleaded. One whole side of his body was wet with blood.

*Whoomp!*

Elias never saw the rifle butt hit him in the head.

"That'll finish him off."

"What'll we do with him?"

"Throw him into the wagon. When we get to Warsaw, we'll dump him in the river."

"No one will ever know."

"Let's get out of here."

# 62

"GOVERNOR FORD IS AT THE TEMPLE," Daniel said as he ran toward Robert's cabin. He found his brother-in-law at the horse corral. Robert had that look on his face—as though he wanted to ride off to Carthage and do something to help the Prophet.

A surprised look flashed on his face. "He is?"

Daniel and Robert had just returned from listening to the governor speak. They had also watched in anger as the soldiers escorting Ford put on their ostentatious display on Main Street, scaring the women.

Daniel motioned. "Let's get up there." He didn't know why, but he had a bad feeling.

Daniel and Robert ran the three blocks to the temple to find Ford circling the temple while his soldiers and their horses rested. While there were dozens of local members of the Church watching the spectacle, only one member appeared to be accompanying Ford and his officers on a sort of unofficial tour. Without thinking, Daniel led Robert to the side of that one member, Brother William Sterrett.

Sterrett looked surprised, but recognized the two approaching men.

"What's going on?" Daniel asked.

"Ford and his men stopped here unexpectedly," Sterrett said. "The temple committee sent me here to watch things. They thought it best to send just me in case it riled up the governor."

Daniel made a low whistle. "Want us to leave?"

Sterrett scanned the soldiers, glanced at Ford, and shrugged his shoulders. "They don't seem alarmed. You just as well stay. Makes me feel better, anyway."

Ford was circling the light gray limestone walls of the temple, a little awestruck by its size—one hundred twenty-eight feet long by eighty-eight feet wide. Suddenly he and his aides walked inside.

"Let's follow them," Sterrett told Daniel and Robert.

Nothing of note happened for a few minutes, but Sterrett seemed alarmed when Ford descended the stairs leading to the basement. Ford seemed perplexed at the wooden baptismal font, placed on the backs of twelve wooden oxen.

"It's a temporary font," Sterrett explained. "The new one will be made of chiseled limestone."

Daniel and Robert stood behind Sterrett. Ford paid no attention.

Ford stared at the oval font, constructed of pine lumber staves that were tongued and grooved, measuring sixteen by twelve feet at the top. The font stood seven feet high from the floor and was four feet deep, allowing full immersion. There were two sets of stairs leading up the font, lined with iron banisters, one for entering the font and the other for leaving.

Ford seemed intrigued with the twelve wooden oxen. One had a missing horn.

"We have a replacement being made," Sterrett explained.

Ford placed a hand where the horn was missing. He laughed. "This is the cow with the crumpled horn that we read of."

"That tossed the maiden all forlorn," piped one of his officers.

A wave of raucous laughter rose from the basement of the unfinished sacred temple. It rankled Daniel. He shot a quick glance at Robert and at Sterrett; they were clearly riled.

One of Ford's officers tested the strength of the other wooden horn. To Daniel's surprise, it broke off. The officer examined it for a few moments.

There was no reprimand from Ford. Instead, he approached another wooden oxen. "I'll be damned, but I should like to take one of these horns with me to show as a curiosity." Using the same motion as his officer, he broke off a horn. "It's a pity to break them off," he said to Sterrett, "but you Mormons can make new ones."

The men behind Ford laughed.

One said, "This temple is a curious piece of workmanship. It's a damn shame they didn't let Joe Smith finish it so we could see how it would turn out."

A dark feeling came over Daniel. But he sensed it would not be wise to tell Robert to smash the governor and his aides in the face.

Another said, "It's altogether a different style of architecture from any building I've ever seen or read about."

"Joe Smith may never see his temple again," said a third.

Daniel closed his eyes, praying. Ford's men began filing out of the temple basement. Daniel could hear Robert's labored breaths.

Sterrett spoke as Daniel said his silent prayer. "Our enemies may kill the Prophet, but they cannot kill his work."

There was a sickening sound of footsteps echoing through the chamber as the remainder of the officers and aides exited.

Outside, a nervous aide approached the governor. The aide pulled a watch from his pocket and rubbed the crystal. "Governor, it's time to leave. We've been here too long already."

"Tell the men to mount up," Ford said.

Daniel was relieved. He pulled his own watch from his pocket. It was twenty minutes to six. With Robert, he started his mournful walk home, three blocks away.

"I didn't like what I heard in there," Robert said.

"Me either," Daniel replied.

"Do you think Joseph and Hyrum are safe?"

Daniel pulled at his chin, assessing his feelings. "I don't know," he admitted.

"What can they do to them?"

"The charge of treason carries a death penalty," Daniel explained. "But first there would have to be a trial. Then there would be appeals. We all know that they're not guilty."

Daniel could tell Robert was getting more upset with each step.

"If a mob kills Joseph and Hyrum, I'll not only hold Wilson Law and his gang accountable, but Governor Ford, too."

Daniel knew Robert was telling the truth.

# 63

WILFORD WOODRUFF, ORSON HYDE, and Brigham Young sat on a bench in front of Boston's Faneuil Hall, literally arguing.

*Strange,* Wilford thought. *We've never argued before.* But an unexplainable dark mood had set over them.

Maps were spread on the three Apostles' laps. The disagreements centered on where they should labor next, and who should go where. They had been on their missions here in the east for several weeks. Orson and Brigham had left Nauvoo in early April, Wilford in early May. Orson had lobbied for the Church and Joseph's presidency in Washington, D. C., and preached and baptized in Philadelphia, Long Island, and Connecticut.

Above them, a grasshopper weathervane atop the hall's cupola pointed northeast, responding to lazy sea breezes. Boston shoppers and sightseers were lost in a wonderful panoply of colors, aromas, sights, and sounds. Market stalls on the first floor of the massive Faneuil Hall were packed full of people. They had choices of dried codfish, molasses, rum, crockery, tin ware, furniture, clothing, textiles, tea, sugar—nearly everything imaginable.

The three Apostles had choices, too. But nothing seemed to mesh for the future. The gloom deepened.

"We're not getting anywhere," Brigham finally said in frustration. "I've got an appointment in Salem. I'd better leave."

Wilford rose to his feet. "I'll walk you to the train depot."

Orson gathered up the maps. "I'll wait here for you, Elder Woodruff."

Wilford took a few steps toward the depot. Turning, his gaze took in the red-haired missionary. Orson's eyes were misted.

"Anything wrong?" Wilford asked.

"Yes, but I don't know what."

Wilford grimaced. He felt it, too.

"I'm going for a walk," Orson said. "Not too far. Just to the other end of the market and back. I want to be alone for a while."

Moments later, Wilford sat on a bench with Brigham at the train station.

Brigham took a deep breath. "I've never felt so sorrowful in my life."

Wilford nodded. "I feel it, too."

"And depressed in spirit," Brigham added.

"What time is it?" Wilford asked.

Brigham pulled out his watch. "Six-thirty. Five-thirty in Nauvoo."

# 64

HENRY'S GRAY HORSE WAS SPENT after its two-mile run from the Carthage Jail to the dairy. Henry had not looked back since he left the woods. He dismounted and fled to the house, leaving the horse standing untied. He looked as frail as the spindly yellow cat Katherine kept as a pet. It scampered out of the way, its matted tail reminding Mary Crook Eagles of a worn out bottle brush.

There was a chagrined look on Mary's face. "Where's Elias?"

Henry collapsed onto a chair. "Last time I saw him he was right behind me."

"What happened back there?" Mary asked, biting her lip.

A smile swept over Henry's face. "You should have seen it. The mob killed the Smith brothers."

"No! No!" Mary shrieked.

"Old Joe fell out of the jail window, right before my eyes."

Katherine came from the bedroom, her jaw dropping in disbelief. "You were there? I don't believe all this."

"Yep. Me and Elias. I'm telling the truth. The mobbers were in the same trees as us. They filled those Smiths with balls alright."

Mary sobbed, her face buried in her hands.

Katherine went to the door, tears streaming down her reddened cheeks. A family in a wagon went by, the horses trotting away from Carthage. "I don't see Elias. You sure he's coming? You shouldn't have left him behind."

Henry shrugged his shoulders, the insinuation seeming to offend him. "Don't worry. He can take care of himself."

"I'm going into Carthage," Mary said. She stood, waiting for Henry to respond.

"I wouldn't if I were you," Henry said, taking in Mary's rising concern. "Rumor is that the Mormons are coming from Nauvoo. Probably the Legion. Could get ugly in town, and dangerous."

"I don't care," Mary said. "Your horse is still saddled."

"You go with her, Henry," Katherine said. "Hook both horses to the wagon."

"Bug off, woman. If she wants to go bad enough, let her go. I don't suppose the Mormons would take their revenge out on an unarmed woman. Especially if she's one of their own."

Mary's dress fluttered in the evening breeze as she rode the gray horse toward Carthage. Instinct told her everything was wrong. A carriage filled with a man, woman, and children passed. They stared at her, as though she were going the wrong way. Mary was too worried to consider it.

Mary kicked the gray horse in the flanks. The mare resisted a gallop, trotting only for a few minutes. Mary slapped at the mare's neck. Foamy lather stuck to her hands.

Another carriage approached from Carthage, filled with men.

"Dig a grave for Joe and Hy Smith," they were yelling. "They're dead. Thank God!"

Mary flagged them down. "I'm looking for my husband, Elias Eagles."

"Who are you?" one of the men asked in a cold, precise voice.

"Mary Crooks Eagles, from here in Carthage. And you?"

"Wilson Law. Go back home, lady. The Mormons are coming. They'll kill you, woman or not."

The man lashed his whip at a team of black horses and sped away.

Carthage was nearly deserted, to Mary's disappointment. Elias had told her only this morning that fifteen hundred people, counting the militia, were in town. Both the Hamilton Hotel and the courthouse had been virtually emptied. A single room upstairs looked occupied.

Mary rode toward the jail. She saw a man. "Have you seen Elias Eagles?"

"Never heard of him."

"Is it true?" she asked. "Are Joseph and Hyrum dead?"

The man nodded.

Mary noted that the jail was the only hubbub of activity. Her breath was coming in ragged spurts. "Are the bodies in there?"

"They're bringing 'em out now. Taking 'em to the Hamilton. They've already taken the wounded Mormon, John Taylor, there. They had to talk the hotel owner into staying around. He wanted to get out of town like everyone else."

Mary approached the party coming out of the jail. "I'm looking for Elias Eagles."

The large man looked mournful. Mary guessed him to be Willard Richards.

"Sorry," the large man said.

Mary backed the horse away. In the rubble of her grief, she watched teary-eyed as men carrying the bodies of Joseph and Hyrum Smith trudged by.

A rider came storming toward them on horseback, the horse lathered. "Oh, my God! No! Dear Joseph! Dear Hyrum!" He fell onto the bodies, weeping.

"Who's that?" Mary asked.

"Must be Samuel Smith, a brother," the man said.

A flash of understanding swept across Mary's mind. Samuel Smith had been living in Plymouth, thirty-four miles south of Nauvoo on the road to Springfield. He was keeper of a public inn there. Mary surmised that word had finally reached Samuel that his two brothers were in trouble, that there were threats against their lives. Samuel looked terrible. His horse looked worse.

There were details that Mary didn't know. Samuel had started his journey for Nauvoo at daybreak. He had been stopped at Bear Creek by a mob stationed to report any movements or activities of the Mormons, especially the Nauvoo Legion. Turned back by force, he found a Mormon home where he learned that Joseph and Hyrum were not in Nauvoo but were being held prisoners in Carthage. He secured a fresh horse from the friend but found that every road or trail into Carthage was under heavy guard. Suspected to be a Mormon, Samuel was pelted with rocks. At one place the guards recognized him. They immediately gave pursuit, trying to kill him. The chase took him through bogs and brush. Thanks to the fresh horse, Samuel was able to elude them. A sentry posted on the outskirts of Carthage threatened him again. Tired to the point of recklessness, he had spurred his foam-lathered horse past the sentry.

Mary contemplated the sad scene and wept again. Suddenly, she pictured Emma's Smith's reaction, and Joseph's mother, too. It would be a horrible time when news reached them. Mary turned the gray horse away, looking for anyone else she could question. A grove of trees caught her eye. She headed there.

A young boy stood by the grove. He had never heard of Elias Eagles, either.

"That's where the mobbers came from," the boy said.

Out of curiosity, Mary dismounted and tied the horse. A walk in the woods revealed deep wagon tracks in the mud, along with tracks made by both horses and men.

More grief washed over her, but she missed the pool of blood. Discouraged, she mounted the gray horse again. She took in shallow breaths. "Elias? Elias?"

She was still calling his name when she returned to Henry's log cabin.

# 65

GOVERNOR FORD FELT FLUSHED WITH RELIEF. Joseph and Hyrum Smith were dead. He had suspected it when he heard cannon fire coming from the outskirts of Carthage: the agreed-upon sign. Confirmation had just come from Constable David Bettisworth and a Mormon, George D. Grant who lived near Carthage. Now Ford knew most of the grisly details.

"Everyone's on the run," Bettisworth was saying. "We heard the Mormons are on their way to Carthage."

Ford twisted in his saddle, scanning the horizon. "I don't see them on the move yet, but they will be."

The soldiers riding with Ford suddenly were overtaken with fear. Their eyes flared to the right and to the left. The officer in command, Singleton, said to Ford, "They'll kill everyone in Carthage, men, women, and children,"

Grant shook his head back and forth. "I don't believe for one minute my people would do that."

Ford ignored Grant's remark and began conferring with his officers "We've got to beat the Mormons to Carthage and protect the court records and all the public documents. They'll burn the courthouse and everything in town."

Again, Grant protested.

"You're going back to Carthage with us," Ford told Grant. "The Mormons may not be on the move yet, but we're not going to let you warn them."

"But governor, my people have a right to know," Grant said. "I have a letter from Willard Richards." Disappointment was written across his face. "I have every confidence they will not organize an attack on Carthage."

"Don't listen to him, governor," Singleton pleaded. "The Mormons will immediately countermand your order and be on the move. They'll have two or three thousand Nauvoo Legion soldiers called up within an hour after they find out what's happened."

Ford nodded his agreement. Now that the curse of Joe Smith had been eliminated from the state of Illinois, he didn't want to see the Nauvoo Legion make a systematic revengeful sweep of Carthage and Warsaw. The Whig newspapers would place the blame for that squarely on his shoulders. In Ford's mind, mob leaders and colluders needed time to split up and either return to their homes or go into hiding. He wondered where Wilson Law and the Mormon apostates would go.

"Put that letter from Willard Richards away," the governor told Grant.

"But governor … "

Ford snatched the letter away from Grant. It bore the signatures of both Willard Richards and John Taylor. He read it out loud to his officers and soldiers.

*Joseph and Hyrum are dead. Taylor wounded, not very badly. I am well. Our guard was forced, as we believe, by a band of Missourians from 100 to 200. The job was done in an instant, and the party fled towards Nauvoo instantly. This as I believe it. The citizens here are afraid of the Mormons attacking them. I promise them no!*

"It's a trick, governor," Singleton countered. "It might be a secret code. Don't believe a word of it."

Ford issued a command to his officer. "Turn Mr. Grant's horse around. We're all going back to Carthage. I'll take my aides and ride on ahead."

At midnight, Governor Ford galloped into Carthage an angry man. On his way he and his aides had intercepted a hundred troopers from Columbus who had been mustered on his forged signature. Making certain his disgust had been totally understood, he had sent the troopers home. In his mind, Ford could read all the negative articles in the Whig newspapers if any kind of war broke out between the anti-Mormons and the Mormons. Besides, when he had left Carthage he had issued the order that all militia units be disbanded. That was supposed to have served two purposes: it gave the men of Carthage and Warsaw a free hand to do what they had to do, and it prevented an organized effort on the part of the state militia to do anything that would further provoke the Nauvoo Legion.

As Ford dismounted and strode toward the Hamilton by the dim light of lanterns, he caught sight of more soldiers out of the corner of his eye. He began to curse and bark at his aides. "Who are those men?" he asked, trying to shake off the tentacles of fatigue.

The aide summoned one of the soldiers to the steps of the Hamilton. The soldier was in the dark green uniform of the Quincy Riflemen.

Ford flew into a rage and cursed again. "Get that unit on their way out of town, right now!" Ford wondered how many other units were on their way into Carthage under his forged signature.

The soldier turned pale and slipped away into the dark night.

"Wait!" Ford screamed as a new thought struck his mind. "Tell your men to round up every man in town and assemble them on the public square. I want to repeat my orders and have them understood. We've got to get this town cleared out."

Ford made no attempt to cover the frightened tone of his voice.

An hour later, Ford stood in the town square lit overhead by a half moon and on the ground by a few lanterns. It was a warm, humid night. Inside the Hamilton, General Minor Deming was assisting Willard Richards with the cleanup of the bodies of Joseph and Hyrum Smith. The sight of the bullet-riddled bodies had actually shocked Ford, and so had the sight of the terribly wounded John Taylor. Despite reports that Carthage had been emptied of her citizens, leaving windows and doors open in their haste, there were a few dozen people left in town, all with fear written on their faces. Ford had just given orders to hold George D. Grant captive for a few more hours and then release. Now Ford stood in front of Singleton's troops and the Quincy Riflemen.

"We don't know what the Mormons will do once they hear that the Smith brothers have been killed," Ford said, letting his voice project over the square. "I've done all I can to delay the message, but by morning word will penetrate Nauvoo from all over. For all I know, the Nauvoo Legion may be on its way. I'm allowing Mr. Richards to leave in the morning with the bodies. Mr. Richards is of the opinion that his people will not retaliate. I certainly hope he's right."

Ford paused while the crowd absorbed his words.

"Some of you soldiers have orders to remove the records from the courthouse. You'll take them eighteen miles south, to Augusta. Hopefully, they'll be safe there."

"Where are you headed, governor?" an officer asked.

"First, to the courthouse. And then south, away from the path of the Nauvoo Legion."

As he left the square, Ford let his gaze turn upward to the Hamilton rooms where all the meetings had been held to plan the deaths of Joe and Hyrum Smith. He was glad the whole grisly thing was over.

# 66

IN HIS FRUSTRATION, ROBERT PULLED the cinch so tight on Tapper'. saddle it caused the sorrel gelding to flinch. Robert didn't care. The devastating news that Joseph and Hyrum had died at the hands of murderers had settled over him to the point of numbness. He had a job to do, even if he had to do it alone. His Prophet was dead and nobody was doing anything about it. Willard Richards was a coward. His letter proved it.

"Where're you going, Father?" his eight-year-old son Joseph asked.

Robert ignored Joseph. He ran toward the corn patch and to the spot where he had hidden his musket. He drew it out and unwrapped the burlap that had kept it protected. He regretted that he had turned his legion musket in—at least he had his own. As he tossed the burlap on the ground and inspected the gun he was surprised at how fast life could suck you along; that morning he had awakened with no plans except to be a farmer, and now he was about to become a man-killer, which would put his whole future in doubt.

Hannah exploded from the house. She had been crying for an hour, eve.

since the first messengers had arrived bearing the tragic news.

"You can't go to Carthage alone," Hannah wailed. "Besides, what if the Missouri mobbers are on their way? What about us? They're asking the Legion to stay on guard all night. You're needed here."

Robert regarded his wife's sobbing as a female weakness. Weakness would not avenge the Prophet's death, he reasoned. The whole city was crying. His sister, Elizabeth, was sobbing in the Browett cabin with Harriet and Martha. Ditto the wives of Levi Roberts, John Cox, Edward Phillips, Richard Slater, and everyone else.

Dogs were wailing. Cows were bellowing. Horses were neighing. Pigs were snorting. It was as if the whole earth was in mourning.

Robert recoiled at Hannah's words. "Well, I'm going whether Daniel goes with me or not, or anyone else for that matter."

Daniel had already turned him down. So had Levi and John. The men were as bad as the women.

Robert checked the saddlebag for tightness. It held the powder and balls. He had counted out the balls. One for Wilson Law. One for William Law. And one each for Chauncey Higbee, Francis Higbee, Robert Foster, and Charles Foster. He even counted out one for Governor Ford. And he threw in a few extra for the Warsaw Regulators.

Tingling with anticipation, he swung himself onto Tapper's back. The desperate task before him required all his faculties and strength. He had never shot at a man before. He had never considered taking another life, no matter how disgustingly evil that person might be. He just savored the cleansing ritual of avenging Joseph and Hyrum's murders. It was a driving force that nothing could stop.

"Robert! No!"

Robert gripped the reins tightly and mashed his hat down on his head as he galloped away. He didn't look back. Tapper's hooves were throwing mud high into the air.

Daniel burst from the Browett cabin red eyed. He stared at the image of

Robert and Tapper disappearing in the distance. It seemed that Robert was being sucked into a low, black void. "I can't believe he's doing that."

"You've got to stop him," Hannah shrieked. She felt as though her world was being torn upside down. Her attempt to stop Robert had been futile and now tears coursed down her face.

Daniel ran to the horse pen calling Bendigo. Something told him he would never catch Robert, but he had to try. He had the uneasy sense that all Nauvoo had crossed over an imaginary threshold into another world, so bizarre was the news that Joseph and Hyrum had been killed. An enormous pain had wrapped around his heart with crushing force. He was in no mood to deal with Robert's maddening eruption. Daniel wanted to stay in the house and mourn.

"I wish he'd listen for once," Hannah sobbed.

Daniel shook his head as he saddled Bendigo. Robert was ignoring a letter received by Emma Smith and Major-General Dunham of the Legion. Sent from Carthage, delivered by George D. Grant, it was signed by Willard Richards, John Taylor, and Samuel Smith.

*Don't rush out of the city—don't rush to Carthage—stay at home, and be prepared for an attack from Missouri mobbers. The governor will render every assistance possible—has sent out orders for troops. Joseph and Hyrum are dead. We will prepare to move the bodies as soon as possible.*

Daniel also thought of General Deming's letter:

*Please deliberate on this matter—prudence may obviate material destruction. I was at my residence when this horrible crime was committed. It will be condemned by three-fourths of the citizens of the county. Be quiet, or you will be attacked from Missouri.*

Hannah was still sobbing. "I'm worried about Elias and Mary, too. If you see them, get them back to Nauvoo." She frowned, wiping at her tears. Suddenly she realized she was pleading with Daniel to stop her husband from even reaching Carthage, and on the other hand she was pleading with Daniel to reach the village and find her brother.

From behind Hannah, Daniel heard other voices.

"Was that Robert who just left?" Levi Roberts asked.

Hannah nodded while Daniel held his horse.

"He must be crazy," John Cox said. "What if those hundreds of militiamen are still there?"

"There are probably a dozen sentry posted at every intersection," Levi added. "He'll never get through."

Daniel expression clouded further as he thought of the musket Robert was carrying. At the sight of a gun, a sentry would shoot first and ask questions later.

"We'd better go, too," John said.

"Take your wagon," Hannah suggested with tear-stained cheeks. "Bring Elias and Mary home with you."

"If we get through," Levi said.

# 67

A DEEPENING SENSE OF URGENCY had struck Robert. It was mor
intense than the day he rode with a Mormon posse to rescue the Prophet
year ago in Dixon. That day he rode with more than a hundred other men
Today he rode alone. He shivered at the realization that it was too late for
rescue and inwardly he cursed at himself for not doing something earlier. Bu
it was not too late for revenge.

After galloping at full speed for nearly two miles, Tapper gave out by th
time Robert reached the farm. He had no choice but to let the horse strike eas
in a long trot. He had no idea how thick anti-Mormons would be as he neare
Carthage, but it occurred to him that he had to evade them in order to fin
the real culprits.

He had been sleeping when the first reports of Joseph and Hyrum's deat
reached Nauvoo. Two Mormon farmers who lived near Carthage had take
back routes into Nauvoo. Shortly after that, long before the sun came up, me
started congregating at the Mansion House, absorbing the news, and wor
dering how to tell Emma. Word spread from house to house like wildfire. Th

knock came to Robert's door at six.

Robert felt a rising trepidation that those responsible would never be brought to justice. It was up to him. There might be a hundred men he would have to hunt down, perhaps two hundred. He prided himself that he had the blistering determination to do it, even it he had to do it one man at a time. He knew who would be first. He clenched his teeth in rage and began to envision Wilson Law's pleadings before he shot him.

"Don't shoot me, please!" he would say as he sank to his knees.

"You murdered the Prophet!"

"Not just me! It was the mob!"

"But you planned it. You and your gangster friends."

*Boom!*

"Come on, Tapper," Robert yelled, digging his heels into the gelding. "Get me to Carthage before they get away!"

Tapper snorted and broke into a gallop.

Robert pulled at Tapper's reins. The gelding arched his neck and slid to a stop on all fours. For a few seconds Robert's brain was paralyzed with the realization that three men on horseback blocked the road ahead. Two worries seesawed in his mind: that he might get killed or that he might make a stupid blunder that would bring harm to the people of Nauvoo, including his family. Neither was pleasant to contemplate.

Tapper reared straight in the air, so tight had Robert jerked at the reins. The three men were pointing at him. They were only two hundred yards away. A dark feeling came over Robert as one of the horsemen charged at him, brandishing a rifle. Robert wheeled on the horse, dug his heels in, and sped away. There was not much left in Tapper. The horse groaned audibly as Robert kicked his sides.

"Go, Tapper, go! Don't be a jughead and fail me now," Robert screamed as he scanned the muddy road for a side trail. In a few seconds he found one and he reined Tapper to the left. Robert turned in the saddle. The rider behind him was closing fast on a horse much fresher than Tapper. The trail wound through wet, spongy ground rimmed with sphagnum moss, tamarack, and black spruce. Beaver ponds flashed by. A white-tailed deer scampered away. The trail left the boggy area and gained altitude into surrounding uplands grown to oak, hickory, and maple—where raccoons, cottontails, and red foxes scattered out of the way.

Robert turned again. The rider—obviously an anti-Mormon who had been guarding the road leading to Carthage—was gaining ground. In desperation Robert reined Tapper off the trail, to the right, and horse and rider plunged recklessly across the Illinois prairie. This time burrowing animals darted away.

There was a grunt from Tapper as the gelding fell to the earth, sending Robert tumbling and the gun flying. Robert scrambled to his feet. Tapper was rising, too, but the broken leg was evident. There had been too many holes for him to dodge.

The rider was closing fast.

*The musket!*

The gun was lying on the ground. Robert rushed to it and pulled the hammer back.

Less than a hundred yards away, Robert could see the approaching rider pull his horse to a stop. The man now appeared to take stock of the situation. Robert made certain the man could see his rifle. He took careful aim. Robert had no desire to shoot what might be an innocent sentry. He wanted the killers of Joseph and Hyrum. He didn't pull the trigger.

In a few seconds, the sentry yelled a few threatening words and then slowly rode away.

Robert put down his rifle and turned his attention to his horse. Tapper stood on the soft prairie grass, pawing aimlessly with his right front leg. The leg dangled helplessly from above the hock. The gelding had snapped it in two in an unseen hole left by a burrowing animal.

Robert grit his teeth in frustration as he unsaddled the horse that had become like a member of his family ever since his arrival in Nauvoo. Wilson Law had one more death to be accountable for. Standing back a few paces,

Robert took careful aim just behind Tapper's ear.

"Sorry, old chap."

*Boom!*

When Daniel, Levi, and John reached the spot in the road where the sentries had been posted, the sentries were no longer there. The three men also missed the horse tracks that led to a side trail. Their wagon continued along the Nauvoo-Carthage road unmolested. However, two miles out, other sentries were seen. There was a convenient side road. Daniel took it and continued on to Carthage.

Daniel could see that Carthage had been almost deserted. There were a few soldiers, aides to General Deming of the Carthage Militia. Daniel began talking to one of them, explaining that he had just come from Nauvoo.

An expression of fear clouded the soldier's face. "Is the Nauvoo Legion coming?" he asked.

"No," said Daniel. "Not that I know of."

Daniel let his eyes scan the streets. There was no sign of Robert. The soldier told Daniel he had not seen anyone riding into town matching Robert's description. And there had been no incidents of vigilante action—neither by one man nor a group of men. Daniel breathed a temporary sigh of relief. But then he asked himself, where was he?

"Are you certain you haven't seen a man on a sorrel horse?" Daniel asked again. He had to find Robert before he did something rash. There must be no excuse for the Missourians to get involved, or for men from Carthage or Warsaw to go on a rampage against Nauvoo. Daniel was certain Robert did not realize what a tinderbox Hancock County was right now.

"Nope, haven't seen anyone fitting that description," the man said. "The only Mormon left in town is Mr. John Taylor. He's being tended to." He pointed upstairs. "Mr. Willard Richards left with the bodies of Joe and Hyrum Smith not too long ago."

Daniel's heart jumped to his throat. If he hadn't taken the detour, he would have met Willard on the road. "How is John Taylor?"

"Surviving. The few local men who are still in town consider him a hostage of sorts. Taylor is their only trump card in case of a Mormon invasion."

Daniel scoffed and then thought of Robert and the Mormon apostates he was hunting. "What about the men from Nauvoo—Wilson Law and the others?"

"They were staying here but they got out of town, too. They left several hours ago."

A wave of relief came over Daniel. Robert was on a wild goose chase but not in much obvious danger. The militia had small presence in Carthage. The mob that had killed Joseph and Hyrum were long gone. Most everyone else had melted into the countryside. The town square was deserted. The courthouse appeared empty.

"Watch the wagon, Levi," Daniel said. "I'm going upstairs to see if there's anything I can do."

Daniel found John Taylor asleep, tended by men who introduced themselves as General Deming and Colonel Jones of the Hancock County militia. Taylor had been brought to the hotel in Hamilton's wagon early that morning, a pitiful sight, according to the men. He had bled a great deal. The worst wound had torn away a portion of his hip. He had a clean wound through his left thigh, and wounds below his left knee and on his left wrist. A local doctor, Thomas L. Barnes, had cut a bullet out of Taylor's left hand with a dull penknife.

"Mr. Taylor has nerves of steel," Deming said, describing the operation to Daniel. He told what he knew of the murders and how he had been jolted in amazement when he heard about them. Deming repeated what he had learned about the rush of the jail by the mobbers hidden in the woods, how they stormed up the stairs, forced the door open and killed Hyrum first and wounded John Taylor. A knot formed in Daniel's stomach as he heard all this and how Joseph fell from the window and was killed. Miraculously, Willard Richards escaped unharmed.

Like a peal of thunder, the reality of Joseph and Hyrum's deaths came crashing down on him. Daniel listened to the story in reverent silence, inwardly weeping. He had a warm feeling for Deming, sensing that by what Deming had said and what he was doing that Deming was a sensitive and deeply religious man. Deming told Daniel that he had settled on a farm in St. Mary's Township in 1838 and worked his way up to be brigadier general. He was rigorously opposed to mob activities.

After Dr. Barnes cut the bullet out of Taylor's hand, Deming said he and the others urged Taylor's consent to move him here to the Hamilton Hotel. "He was quite skeptical and angry, saying he was surrounded by assassins and murderers. We had to convince him that his enemies were gone, that he was among friends now, even though we weren't Mormons."

Daniel had another feeling come over him. Not all the people that had converged upon Carthage during the past several days could be considered enemies of the Church.

"Mr. Taylor expressed his anger over the coroner's inquest, too," said General Deming.

"Why?" Daniel asked.

Deming grunted, his embarrassment apparent. "It was conducted by Robert F. Smith."

Daniel threw his arms open. He had heard the name, but couldn't connect it.

"He's one of your enemies. R. F. Smith is not only the coroner; he's a justice of the peace, too. He's the one who issued the arrest warrant, charging Joe and Hyrum Smith with treason. Without a hearing, he jailed them. General Smith's attorneys pleaded that the whole thing was illegal, which it was, in my opinion. Then, a few hours later, R. F. Smith dragged them out of jail to appear before his own court."

"That is almost unbelievable," replied Daniel, the astonishment of it all suddenly taking a tight grip on him.

"That's not all," Deming said. "R. F. Smith is also captain of the Carthage Greys. He's got a lot of questions to answer to me. His men were guarding the jail. They didn't do a good job. Either he was in collusion, or he had some traitors in the guard unit. Early reports indicate that the guards had their guns loaded with blanks, and let the mobbers overrun them."

Daniel's initial reaction was one of stark disbelief. He was glad Robert was not hearing this. Robert might be tempted to put R. F. Smith higher on his hit list.

General Deming explained that Willard Richards had just left Carthage with the bodies of Joseph and Hyrum. Samuel Smith had accompanied him, along with Artois Hamilton, owner of the hotel, and a guard of eight soldiers provided by General Deming.

"If you hurry, you can catch them," Deming said, shaking Daniel's hand.

"I'm looking for my brother-in-law," Daniel responded. "Depends on how fast I find him." His next destination was the Henry Eagles dairy.

"Good luck," Deming added.

# 68

MARY CROOKS EAGLES BURST INTO Daniel's arms crying. "We can't find Elias."

Daniel was baffled. Now he had two men on his missing list. It was midmorning at the Eagles cabin. Dreary gray clouds floated overhead, serving as a gruesome reminder of the unbelievable events of the past several hours. When Daniel arrived at the Eagles cabin with Levi and John, Mary was pacing back and forth in the yard. A light rain had almost soaked her clothing.

Daniel let Mary sob on his shoulder a minute and then leaned back to look into her face. She appeared totally shattered; her eyes were red and teary, and she was shaking like a leaf, her terrible agony apparent.

"What do you mean?" he finally asked as Henry approached from the fields.

Mary was drawing short breaths and wiping away more tears. "He didn't come home with Henry last night. Both of them witnessed the murders."

"Is that true, Henry?" Daniel gasped.

Henry's shirt was black with sweat, an incredible sight to Daniel.

Apparently Henry was doing his regular farm work as though nothing had happened. He didn't answer Daniel's question.

"Do me a favor," Henry said. His mouth was turned downward in disgust as he pointed to Mary. "Take this worry wart back to Nauvoo."

Daniel fixed his blue eyes on Henry. "Where's Elias?"

Henry acted as though he were totally disinterested. "Beats me."

A voice behind Daniel broke the tension. It belonged to Katherine "Anything I can get you?" she asked as she tugged on her young daughter Annie. Annie was trying to touch Levi and John's horses. "I'll bet you three men are starved."

Daniel broke his prolonged stare at Henry. Katherine had reminded Daniel of a constant growl in his stomach. He had left Nauvoo without breakfast. "Anything will do, thanks. Just some milk and bread, if you don't mind."

"I'll have something fixed up in a few minutes," Katherine said.

Again, Daniel locked his eyes on Henry. "Tell me what you know."

Henry's tone hardened again but he tersely related his experience accompanying Elias to deliver the message to the Warsaw militia boys, riding back to Carthage, and witnessing the storming of the jail from the trees. "When someone yelled, 'the Mormons are coming,' I ran like everyone else," he explained. "I got on my horse and came home. Elias never showed up."

Grief stabbed Daniel's heart as he thought about Katherine and the crushing pain she was going through, not knowing what happened to Elias. Daniel turned to Mary and asked, "Would he have any reason to go to some place like Fountain Green, Pilot Grove, or Warsaw?"

"None at all," Mary said, still looking pale and sad. "I've thought of every possibility. I'm worried."

"Where have you looked, Henry?" Levi asked.

"Nowhere," came the quick reply. "He knows where we live. He's been here two weeks. He'll find his way back."

"Maybe Elias is on his way to Nauvoo," John suggested.

Mary heaved an ominous sigh and glanced at Daniel. "Without me?"

"As soon as we finish eating we'll load your things into the wagon,"

Daniel said, knowing that Henry was serious about wanting to get rid of Mary.

A feeling came over Mary. "What brought you out here, anyway? You didn't know about Elias and that all the members of the Church were asked to stay home."

"We're looking for Robert," Daniel answered.

Mary's jaw dropped. "He's missing, too?"

Daniel nodded. "He rode out here with his musket looking for anyone who had anything to do with the murders of Joseph and Hyrum."

Henry looked scornful. "Who does he think he is, God? Does he think he can hunt down a hundred men?"

Daniel felt his muscles tighten. "I suppose he does. That's the problem."

"I want to go to Nauvoo," Mary said, giving Henry a grimacing look.

John jumped out of the wagon. "We'll load your things, eat, and get on our way."

Mary rode in the wagon, slumped over. With Daniel, Levi, and John, she mournfully discussed every possibility as to the whereabouts of Elias. A dark gloom hung over the four passengers knowing that not only had Joseph and Hyrum been murdered, but that Elias was missing. Was he chasing the murderers? Had the trail led to Missouri? Or had the murderers kidnapped him? Was he being held hostage somewhere in Carthage or Warsaw?

The conversation left Daniel feeling turgid and distended. He had no answers and he didn't know what had happened to Robert either. A cold logic told Daniel that perhaps the sentries had blocked Robert's way into Carthage and had either caught him or were still chasing him. All of the questions pertinent to the disappearance of Elias suddenly applied to Robert's strange disappearance. Was Robert hot on the trail of someone like Wilson Law? Was he confronting Thomas Sharp at the newspaper office in Warsaw? Or had anti-Mormons killed him and buried his body in the woods?

Six miles out of Nauvoo, the wagon rounded a curve in the muddy road and began a gradual descent down a hill. Ahead, Daniel caught sight of a lone figure walking in the same direction they were. The man was carrying a saddle and a musket.

Daniel stood up suddenly, the revelation staggering. "Robert!"

Robert looked up at Daniel, tension ebbing from his body and a giddy wave of exhaustion shuddering through his core. The emotions knotting his chest were so many. Dozens of killers were running loose and here he was walking back to Nauvoo; he had shot his own horse in the head. He was dead tired, running on no food and no rest. He made no attempt to wipe the sweat away that dripped from his brow. He felt a total humiliation. "I guess I need a ride," he said in a sheepish voice.

Daniel was still standing, a stunned look of amazement on his face.

"What happened?" Levi asked.

"Where's your horse?" John asked.

"How long have you been walking?" Mary asked.

Robert threw his saddle and musket into the wagon. He ignored their questions and fired one of his own. "Are you moving back to Carthage, Mary?"

Daniel appeared too surprised to be angry at the obvious loss of the horse. "That's another story. Tell us what happened."

Robert gave a bleak sigh as he climbed aboard and considered running away and hiding in the trees. His shoulders dropped like weights. Reluctantly, he told his story—the chase by the sentry, Tapper breaking his leg, scaring off the sentry, and the painful decision to destroy Tapper.

Daniel winced in disbelief. "How are we going to do our farm work without Tapper?"

Robert felt his mouth go dry as he fumbled for an answer. "I dunno. Borrow one. Buy one." His mind was still on Joseph and Hyrum's killers. He considered asking Daniel to unhitch Bendigo so that he could resume his manhunt.

"We've put every penny we have into those new houses," Daniel said as he shook his head in disappointment. "How can we afford to buy another horse?"

Robert shook his head and fell silent, letting his personal devastation sink in.

Muddy ruts in the road shook the five passengers. Fresh wagon and horse tracks lay before them, going in the same direction.

"My guess is that Willard Richards is just ahead of us," Daniel said.

"I thought he was still in Carthage," Robert commented.

"He's taking Joseph and Hyrum's bodies back to Nauvoo," Daniel explained. He has an escort with him. I'm surprised you didn't see them."

"They must have come by while I was still walking toward the main road," Robert said. His voice was wrought with sadness as he thought about the Carthage tragedy again. Now he thought of Mary. When he asked, Mary, Daniel, Levi, and John explained what had happened to Henry and Elias' strange disappearance.

"How much is a good horse?" Mary asked Robert.

Robert experienced an eerie emptiness as he thought about Tapper lying in a pool of blood on the Illinois prairie. He brought his shoulders to his ears. "Eighteen, twenty dollars."

"Well," Mary said, "if you still haven't sold your cabin, we'll buy it. I refuse to stay with Henry another day. And I don't want to live in Carthage."

Robert nodded. "That'd be fine."

Once again, Robert's hostility was renewed. In his mind, the same men who had killed Joseph and Hyrum were somehow responsible for Elias' disappearance. He questioned Mary all over again, covering every possibility he could think of, including the possibility that Elias might be in Nauvoo waiting for them.

Mary began to cry again.

"I've been thinking," John Cox said. "Perhaps one of the militia officers commandeered Elias for some kind of special assignment."

Mary's eyes brightened. "I never thought of that."

Robert reached back for his musket and placed it in his arms. "If Elias is not in Nauvoo, I'll find him for you, Mary."

# 69

THE SIGHT OF THE WAGON CARRYING the bodies of Joseph and Hyrum devastated Daniel. Willard Richards sat in the wagon, his shoulders hunched over, his chin on his chest. Next to him sat Artois Hamilton, owner of the wagon and owner of the team of ghostly white horses that were picking their mournful way to Nauvoo. The bodies were contained in two rough oak coffins covered with branches and brush to protect the two bodies from the sun.

Samuel Smith, the Prophet's brother, rode ahead of the wagon and the soldiers. To Daniel's eyes, he looked worse for the wear than Willard. Daniel had heard of Samuel's desperate ride from Plymouth to Carthage. Daniel suspected Samuel's insides were all torn up from the ride.

Daniel edged his own wagon closer to the procession but caught the menacing stares of eight mounted soldiers, who turned in their saddles.

As Daniel backed off he began to think of the weight now on Willard Richards' shoulders. Willard would have to guide the Church for a few weeks until the other members of the Twelve returned from their missions, and until

John Taylor recovered. Daniel wondered how soon Wilford Woodruff would hear about the martyrdom and what his reaction would be. He guessed it would be a month or more before Wilford could make it back to Nauvoo.

In a few minutes Daniel could see Major-General Jonathan Dunham and his staff leading a solemn welcoming committee toward Hamilton's wagon and the white horses. There were a few exchanges of words and then a grand procession started to form. Led by the city marshal, the procession started for Nauvoo.

Trailing behind, almost unnoticeable, was Daniel's wagon with his passengers.

Daniel looked at his watch. It was three o'clock.

Hannah felt another thickening shroud of sorrow settle over her as the procession proceeded along Mulholland near the temple. People streamed out of their homes and lined up along the street. Hannah couldn't tear her eyes from the wagon carrying Joseph and Hyrum. She had been crying nonstop since early morning, staggering in horror at the thoughts they had actually been murdered. It took several seconds to process what she was seeing. The image of the oak coffins, she was certain, would remain etched in her memory forever. Choked up, she sobbed again, gasping for breath as she dropped to her knees. She seemed to cross an imaginary threshold into another world. Her beloved Prophet was dead. There was no doubt about it now.

And to top it all off, her husband had ridden off to Carthage trying to find the killers all by himself. Where was he? How long would he be gone? Had Daniel found him? Would he wind up in jail, arrested for murdering the murderers? Would she ever see him again?

Next to Hannah, Elizabeth and Harriet sobbed too, almost collapsing in one another's arms.

"Mother! Mother! Get up! Father is home!"

Hannah felt a tug on her green cotton dress. It was her son, Joseph.

"Your father is home?" she asked as she rose to her feet. Joseph's red cheeks were graced with an open smile.

"He just drove up on a side street," the nine-year-old boy explained. His chest was heaving after running three blocks.

Temporarily casting off her mournful shroud, Hannah broke for home followed by Elizabeth and Harriet.

Robert scoffed at Willard Richards' lame attempt to convince the men in a gathering throng near the Mansion House not to seek retribution against the murderers of Joseph and Hyrum. So what that Richards had promised Governor Ford there would be no retaliation and no war? Ford had broken promise after promise of his own!

"Brethren, think, think, and think again before you act," Elder Richards was saying. "God will avenge our wrongs in His way, in His time."

Robert shook his head in defiance. He thought of Bendigo waiting in the corral at home. Bendigo would help carry the sword of justice for him where Tapper had failed. Robert gazed upward at the Apostle he used to respect. Richards was speaking from atop the frame building called the Mansion House. He had told all the morbid details of the assassination, drawing dreadful outbursts of mournful cries from the audience. Nearby, Stephen Markham, William W. Phelps, and Joseph's attorneys stood poised to take their turns addressing the crowd of several thousand.

Robert remained skeptical as Richards continued to talk. To him Willard was coming across as a hungry man begging for food. If Willard's talk were a letter, Robert vowed he would crumple it up and lob it into the Mississippi. After four years of being a Mormon, he felt he could make his own decisions. He didn't need an overweight Apostle to tell him how to feel.

The women of Nauvoo were braver than Richards, Robert concluded as he thought of one event of the day. The wives of Hyrum Smith, John Taylor, W. W. Phelps, and a few others had found out that Robert D. Foster had returned to his home in Nauvoo. The wives had marched to his home and warned him that if he didn't leave town they would come back with a stronger force. The implication caused Foster to leave during the night. Robert wished he had arrived before the women. Foster wouldn't have been able to walk, ride or limp out of town. *I would have broken every bone in his body*, Robert thought.

Ironically, the event happened while Robert had been racing Tapper through the countryside. If he had stayed home, he realized, he might have been in town when Foster was here.

Willard Richards was concluding now, asking for a sign of support. From the crowd of thousands, hands went up high. Hannah dropped her grip and raised her right hand.

Robert balled his fist and let it hang at his side.

Stephen Markham's remarks were more to Robert's liking. He told the men to arm themselves and to prepare to defend the city. There was no guarantee that mobs from Missouri or elsewhere might strike, he said.

The implications chilled Robert. Why Willard Richards advocated staying at home cowering in fear he did not understand. Instead, the Mormons ought to be striking out in every direction. If Jacksonian democracy prevailed here and elsewhere along the American frontier, so be it. The majority of Mormons ought to wake up and take matters into their own hands. It wouldn't be hard to identify the men who killed Joseph and Hyrum. It was the same men who had been organizing anti-Mormon meetings in Carthage and Warsaw. And it was the Mormon apostates.

*Led by Wilson Law*, Robert thought to himself.

CHAPTER NOTES

In addition to the *History of the Church*, the author has used a wide variety of sources to extract information relating to the deaths of Joseph and Hyrum Smith. Among them are: Barrett, Ivan J., *Joseph Smith and The Restoration*, Provo, Utah: Brigham Young University, 1973; Hill, Donna, *Joseph Smith, The First Mormon*, Garden City, New York: Doubleday & Company, Inc., 1977; Leonard, Glen M., *Nauvoo, A Place of Peace, A People of Promise*, Salt Lake City: Deseret Book and Brigham Young University Press, 2002; Noal, Claire, *Intimate Disciple, A Portrait of Willard Richards*, Salt Lake City: University of Utah Press, 1957; Smith, Henry A., *The Day They Martyred The Prophet*, Salt Lake City: Bookcraft, 1963; Roberts, B. H., *The Life of John Taylor*, Salt Lake City: Bookcraft, 1963.

# 70

ROBERT WAS AT A LOSS WHEN IT CAME to finding a way to snap Hannah out of her depression. She took the deaths of Joseph and Hyrum worse than that of her own father. The wailing and crying was more intense almost constantly at first, then in spells every few hours. She wanted to stop the clock in the house at the exact hour of their deaths, just as they did in England for her father. Robert talked her out of buying a new black dress to wear to the viewing of the bodies. She searched in vain for black-edged paper so that she could write news of the Prophet's death to her mother in England and black wax to seal it with.

Robert had to admit that the scene at the public viewing was a bit morbid. He and Hannah and Mary Eagles, along with Daniel and Elizabeth arrived in line at mid-day Saturday. They stood in a line that consisted of thousands of Saints, not only from Nauvoo, but from surrounding communities as well. Robert's legs were tired when they finally were admitted to the main floor parlor in the Mansion House. The two bodies had been placed in coffins lined with white cambric. Hannah broke out in uncontrolled sobbing when she viewed Joseph and Hyrum's faces though a square of glass mounted in a lid attached to brass hinges to the coffin. Had she been closer, she would have spilled tears onto the black velvet—held taut with brass nails—which covered their bodies. Word passed through the line that English immigrant George Cannon made molds of the faces of the two deceased Church leaders, using plaster.

Robert had to tug hard at Hannah's arm to tear her away from the coffins. He had exhibited little tolerance for those ahead of them in the line who tarried too long, making everyone else behind them wait.

As for himself, Robert was still smoldering inside. When he looked at the two bodies in all-white clothing, he felt nothing but hatred for the men responsible for their deaths—the apostates from Nauvoo, and the low-life drivel from Carthage and Warsaw. There was a rumor that a letter had been received by Willard Richards from Sheriff J. B. Backenstos of Carthage. The letter identified every member of the Carthage Greys—all thirty of them— and every member of the Warsaw militia that had attacked the jail—all sixty of them. To top it off, Willard Richards had identified not only the Laws, Higbees, and Fosters as being members of the mob, but ten other apostates as well. This merely confirmed what Robert felt all along: that it would be simple to identify the murderers, organize a vigilante committee, and methodically hunt each guilty man down.

Robert wanted to scream. Was there no one else in Nauvoo who thought the same as he did?

Then there was the burning question: Where was Elias? Hour-by-hour, Robert was gaining the impression that if the truth were known, the same evil men who assassinated the Prophet knew something about Elias. But how could the truth be uncovered? Right now, roads between Nauvoo and Carthage and Warsaw were blocked. Hannah and Mary were beside themselves with worry. Elias had been missing from the very time Joseph and Hyrum were killed. Everyone hoped he would turn up in Nauvoo, but that had not been the case so far.

Elizabeth was filled with regret as she stared into the lifeless face of Joseph Smith. She thought of the year she had spent withdrawn from any contact with him and his teachings. She had refused to listen to his sermons at the grove and at the temple; sermons on the Kingdom of God, the mission of John the Baptist, the parables of Jesus, the resurrection, and the gathering of Israel, for example. She had missed counsel given to groups of immigrating Saints from England. And, worst of all, she thought again of her selfishness, depriving Harriet of not only Daniel's love, but also hers.

Even though she had placed a stumbling block over her testimony for nearly a year, it was back in full now. In the casket before her lay the Prophet, a man who bore an imprint in her mind of an infinite and divine intelligence. He was the man who ushered in the Dispensation of the Fullness of Times, a man whose visions and revelations brought the restoration of the gospel in the latter days. She remembered the night he came to her home to seal her to Daniel. The power of God rested upon Joseph to such a degree that he seemed transfigured before her. That was the beginning of rebuilding her testimony. After that, she began to pray again. And prayer had brought a witness through the Holy Ghost that it was time to overcome her pride and accept Harriet into the family.

Joseph Smith's life passed vividly through Daniel's mind not only when he stood in front of the two bodies, but all the time he waited in line. The Prophet was only five years old when Daniel was born, and Daniel had spent most of his life in England unaware that such a man existed on planet Earth. He was ten years old when Joseph had his first vision—when the heavens finally opened between God and man for the first time since the time of the ancient Apostles. While Moroni and other angelic visitors were tutoring Joseph, Daniel had been a young boy, an apprentice carpenter in Tewkesbury, Gloucestershire, England. Daniel's father died in 1824, a year after Moroni appeared to Joseph. In 1830, when the Book of Mormon was published and the Church formally organized, Daniel attended the Quaker Church with his family. In 1834, when Daniel met Elizabeth, LDS Church headquarters were in Kirtland and the first temple was under construction there. In 1835, when Daniel and Elizabeth were married in a double ceremony with Robert and Hannah, Joseph obtained the Egyptian mummies and papyrus from Michael Chandler—and a portion of the translation from the papyri eventually became the Book of Abraham.

Daniel smiled as he recalled the time in 1836 when he shared with Robert and Hannah the contents of a letter he had received from his relatives in France. It contained references to a statement from a Catholic priest living in Basel, Switzerland, made in 1739. *The old true Gospel and the gift thereof is lost*, it said. *False doctrines prevail in all the churches on the face of the earth. Prayer and purity may cause an angel to visit a deeply distressed soul, but I tell you, God will have spoken within a hundred years. He will restore the old church again ...*

That soul, Joseph Smith, lay before Daniel. Joseph had completely restored the gospel, and now had given his life for it.

In 1838, when members of the Church were being persecuted by Missourians, Daniel and Elizabeth were lay preachers in the United Brethren congregation. While Joseph was imprisoned in Liberty Jail, Daniel was enjoying being a yeoman farmer in England. When he joined the Church in March of 1840, Joseph Smith and the Saints had just settled in Nauvoo. As Daniel was preparing to leave England as company leader on the *Echo* in February 1841, Joseph Smith was working on city ordinances establishing the Nauvoo Legion and the University of Nauvoo.

Daniel recalled the first time he laid eyes on the Prophet. It was the first of May, 1841, when his *Echo* passengers stepped off the steamboat onto the Nauvoo Landing. Joseph was there to greet all one hundred eight passengers. Daniel remembered the indelible imprint Joseph made on him, and how he felt—overwhelmed by meeting a Prophet of God for the first time. Daniel recalled Joseph's commanding presence and his noble bearing. When he shook the Prophet's hand the first time, he remembered how it seemed to sap the strength from him, but immediately how serene and peaceful he felt. Later Daniel heard the Prophet and his brother preach Sunday sermons in the grove. And whenever he saw Joseph leading a parade of the Nauvoo Legion Daniel thought Joseph looked like a Prophet, and more: like a god.

"I knew the instant my eyes rested on him that he was a true Prophet of God," Elizabeth whispered to Daniel as they gazed on Joseph's body.

Daniel nodded his tearful agreement.

"I remember the day we arrived at Nauvoo," she was saying. "It wa almost as if I were having my own vision. I seemed to be lifted off my feet almost walking on the air as he came to greet me. I was electrified, just thrillec through and through, to the tips of my fingers, to every part of my body. I'v never really talked about it until now. It was such a sacred experience for me.

"Me, too," Daniel said, feeling spellbound by his wife's words.

Elizabeth continued on. "I just feel so terrible that I was so stubborn fo so long. I feel like I denied myself some very rich blessings during those eleve months."

Daniel took one last look at Joseph's face. He tried to picture Joseph aliv again: his light brown hair blowing in the wind, his large blue eyes full of ligh and peace, his cheeks full, his lips thin, and always a smile. He thought o death, how morbid it was, that if some persons died, and others did not die death truly would be a terrible affliction. But all men would have to die soon er or later, and all men would be resurrected.

Daniel smiled when he thought of the day that Joseph and Robert ha wrestled. He honestly thought that Robert would be the first to throw th Prophet to the ground, but not so. Joseph threw Robert, and then immedi ately launched into a gospel discussion as the men rested.

More tears came to Daniel's eye as he walked away from Joseph an Hyrum's bodies. Joseph had been such an incredible man. He had seen an talked to both God the Father and Jesus Christ, His Son. John the Baptist ha appeared to Joseph, restoring the Aaronic Priesthood. Likewise the ancien apostles—Peter, James, and John—who conferred upon Joseph th Melchizedek Priesthood.

Daniel wiped tears from his eye and then smiled for a moment. He wa thinking of something Joseph taught Church members about ministering angels. "Angels of God never have wings," he said one time. "Angels are not a special creation, an order of beings distinct from men. They are commissioned personages who either have come to this earth or will one day come and receive physical tabernacles."

That simple statement brought comfort to Daniel because it was so typical of Joseph's teachings.

William W. Phelps gave the funeral sermon to a crowd of ten thousand Saints at the grove, just below the temple.

When Phelps remarked that the deaths of Joseph and Hyrum signaled another failure in the justice system on the American frontier, Robert found his fists clenching in anger again. The Prophet and his brother, Phelps lamented, lost their lives and their freedom "to the popular will of mobocracy in this boasted realm of liberty."

Robert, however, differed with the assertion that Phelps made in regards to the evildoers being brought to justice. Phelps preached that he welcomed the future day of *heavenly* retribution. Robert scoffed. He was ready to use his God-given athletic prowess to hunt down the guilty apostates and mobbers one by one and given them *earthly* retribution.

As Phelps preached on, touching themes familiar to the Saints—appeals to the government for lost properties in Missouri and that the Church would continue onward without Joseph, but not without challenge from Satan and the world—Robert stiffened his resolve. Someday, sometime, when things calmed down, he vowed to do something about these deaths, even if he had to do it alone.

In another gesture of his strong will, he pulled two tearful women to his side with his powerful arms. He resolved also to find out what had happened to Elias Eagles: Hannah's brother, and Mary's husband.

Even if his search took him to the ends of the earth.

Carthage and Warsaw.

# 71

DANIEL THOUGHT ROBERT'S PLAN TO RIDE into Carthage and Warsaw was ludicrous. There were reliable reports that Governor Ford had ordered the commanders of militia in ten nearby counties to enlist volunteer and outfit themselves with arms and supplies for a campaign against the Mormons. Ford's people were everywhere, gathering information, assessing the mood of the Mormons.

"Just one little incident could touch off a war between us and our enemies," Daniel warned as he leaned over the corral fence, rubbing Bendigo's muzzle. The farm partnership between Daniel and Robert was down to one horse. Daniel didn't want to lose Bendigo over some other senseless action by Robert.

"How would they know we're Mormons?" Robert asked, pacing along the fence rails.

Daniel's skin tingled. "Your mouth would betray you," he said. "How're you going to track down Elias without asking questions? Besides that Carthage is deserted by now. There's something you don't understand, any way. Satan is the real enemy. He's the one who constantly stirs up wicked men to oppose the Lord's work. How are you going to shoot Satan? Or break his jaw with your fists? Satan doesn't have a body."

"The men Satan possesses have bodies. The only question here is whether or not you're coming with me," Robert shot back. "Mary's out of patience. So's Hannah. They've got to know."

Daniel felt another surge of uneasiness. "You'd shoot the first man you suspected of having anything to do with the Prophet's death. Besides, for all we know, Elias is at Henry's house at this very moment."

"How will we know unless we ride out there? Someone's got to do something. If Elias is not there, we'll take Henry with us."

"We need to follow the brethren," Daniel said. "The Lord will avenge Joseph's death in his own way."

Robert shook his head and grumbled to himself.

"This hatred for Wilson Law and the other apostates is no good for you, Robert," Daniel said. "It'll harm your testimony, not strengthen it."

"Remember Ecclesiastes," Robert hissed. "A time for war, and a time for peace. A time to kill, and a time to heal."

Daniel gave a dire sigh. "You're trying to masquerade your hatred for the killers under the guise of patriotism for Joseph and the gospel. That's dangerous, Robert. This will eat you up. Get over it."

"It's better than indifference," Robert said, standing his ground. "We don't stand a chance if we're indifferent to what has happened. I can't put up with the thoughts of doing nothing. Hate is good. There are men out there who sinned against God and his chosen Prophet. I have a duty to respond to my feelings, to find what happened to Elias, and who killed Joseph and Hyrum."

"Have you thought about Hannah and your children?"

"What do you mean?"

Daniel painted a gruesome picture. "One more widow in Nauvoo. Another home without a father."

Robert set his jaw. "You underestimate my tactics. I'll find them one at a time, when they don't know I'm coming."

"You don't even know where Wilson Law is. He could be in Iowa Missouri, or Ohio."

Robert's tone turned viperous. "He can't hide. He has blood on his hands. I'll smell him out."

"This won't make Elder Richards happy. And it won't make Elder Woodruff happy. He'll be back in Nauvoo in a few weeks."

"Elder Woodruff's not my mother."

Daniel shuddered at Robert's frankness.

"I want you to come with me," Robert said.

"It's wrong. Stay home."

"There're things that will change your mind."

"Such as?"

"When these murderers steal Joseph and Hyrum's bodies, take them away from here and desecrate them like they promise, then how will you feel?"

Daniel's mind flashed to the funeral of Joseph and Hyrum. As soon as William W. Phelps had finished his sermon, the entire congregation watched solemnly as a horse-drawn hearse stopped at the nearby graveyard. Daniel had wormed his way as close as possible to watch as the two coffins were lowered into the ground.

Robert was right, Daniel thought. He felt like guarding the burial spot day and night. *Had it been up to me*, Daniel thought, *I would have buried the bodies in a secret place.*

Wilford Woodruff stared at the July ninth issue of the *Boston Times* in utter shock.

"Do you think it's true?" his father-in-law, Ezra Carter, asked.

Tears were forming in Wilford's eyes. "This is awful, just awful," he moaned. From the front porch of Carter's home in Portland, Maine, Wilford shook his head back and forth in a gesture of disbelief. The newspaper carried the news of the deaths of Joseph and Hyrum Smith.

A minute or two passed in silence as the two men contemplated the news. The story also said that the Nauvoo Legion was expected to strike out in vengeance at the communities of Carthage and Warsaw, and that people there had fled to Quincy. Wilford pictured in his mind where he was on June twenty-seventh, the very hour when the martyrdom took place. He could remember how he and Orson Hyde and Brigham Young had argued about missionary work in front of Faneuil Hall in Boston, and the odd feelings they had.

Afterward, Wilford had attended the Boston conference of the Church with Brigham, Orson Hyde, Heber C. Kimball, Lyman Wight, Orson Pratt, and William Smith. Wilford departed Boston on July second, arriving in Portland the next day.

The seventy-four-year-old Carter asked the obvious. "Are you still going to Thomastown and the Fox Islands?"

Wilford dashed his tears with his arm, wetting his shirtsleeve. "No, it's time to go home."

"Phoebe and your children will be needing you," Carter said, his voice laced with sadness.

Wilford nodded his agreement. "Let's take a walk to the Post Office. I'll retrieve the letter I just posted to her, and rewrite it. And I'd better write to Brigham. I suspect he'll want to meet up in Boston. He's the senior Apostle. The Twelve will need to take up their duties in Nauvoo right away, I suspect."

At Daniel's urging, Robert waited for another week until he took the daring trip to Carthage. Robert flared up one day—the day that he heard Robert D. Foster was in town trying to dispose of his business interests. By the time Robert rode off searching for him Foster had already left town and no one knew where he had gone, so there was no ugly incident.

Daniel surprised himself by going with Robert to Carthage, riding Bendigo while Robert rode a new horse he bought with Mary Eagles' money—money that had been used to purchase Robert's log home. That transaction, however, worried Hannah, who was overcome with fear about living outside of Nauvoo. Anything outside the city limits exceeded her security blanket, she told Daniel and Robert.

Robert's new horse was a black gelding. He named the horse Lawless, an obvious reference to Wilson Law and the gang of apostates.

"I have a question about sealings," Robert said as they rode out of town. It had rained earlier, a good sign. The horses were not leaving a dust trail.

Daniel scratched his head, wondering why Robert would ask such a question on this occasion.

"When Elder Woodruff gets back in town, could he seal me to another wife?"

The question caused Daniel to blanch. "Have you talked to Hannah about this?"

"Not a live woman—a dead one."

"Who?"

"Elizabeth Sikes Law."

Daniel recoiled in disbelief. The woman had been Wilson Law's wife, a Nauvoo schoolteacher. She had died four months earlier. "Why her?"

"I met her once. Seemed like a nice lady. She'll never have Wilson Law in the hereafter. He's now a *son of perdition.*"

"Where'd you get that idea?"

"From Joseph Smith—don't you remember?"

Bendigo's gentle lope seemed to loosen Daniel's memory. The Prophet, indeed, had taught that some apostates entered into dangerous territory when they became enemies of the Church. Once they gained a testimony, then denied it, they took the first step. Second, if the apostate embraced the same spirit as those who crucified the Savior and sought to hunt down and kill leaders of the Church, the apostate had sinned against the Holy Ghost. Daniel could now hear Joseph's voice, in a sense. *You cannot save such persons; you cannot bring them to repentance; they make open war, like the devil, and awful is the consequence. When you find a spirit that wants bloodshed—murder, the same is not of God, but of the devil.*

Daniel shook his head. "You'd best leave those matters up to the Lord. Don't even bring up the subject to Elder Woodruff, or anyone else. It's weird thinking."

"It's not weird thinking," Robert countered. "Think of the woman in this case. She has the right to be sealed to someone worthy. Her first husband was bad news."

"What about Don Carlos?"

The name threw Robert off track. "Don Carlos? What are you talking about?"

"Joseph and Emma's little baby that died here in Nauvoo. Maybe someday the Lord could arrange a sealing between Don Carlos and Sister Law, after he grows to maturity in the next life."

"There you go," Robert said.

CHAPTER NOTES

The two coffins that were lowered into the ground at the Nauvoo graveyard contained bags of sand. At midnight, the bodies of Joseph and Hyrum were secretly taken from the Mansion House and across Water Street to a secret burial place in the basement of the unfinished Nauvoo House. Rain helped secure the hiding place. Unusually heavy thunder and lightning must have discouraged the mob because they did not show up. The bodies remained there until the fall of 1844, when Emma Smith had them reburied in a small outbuilding toward the river from the homestead. This resting place remained a closely held secret by the family. Later they were reburied to another location near the homestead, where the remains are today.

# 72

*July 1844*

THE TRIP TO HENRY'S DAIRY WENT WITHOUT incident, although the roads were extremely muddy. Two days earlier rain had descended the area in torrents, along with a tremendous wind. There was little traffic on the road between Nauvoo and Carthage, but a great many trees had fallen over, victim of the winds.

"God is angry with us for not doing his work, for not avenging the Prophet's death, " Robert said as he and Daniel passed the downed trees. "We've got to find the killers and bring them to justice."

Daniel grunted in disgust. "You're back to weird thinking again. Is there any way we can look for Elias without using Henry? I don't like being around him."

Robert laughed. "Toads aren't ugly—they're just toads. Henry's just Henry. He's the last to see Elias alive. We have no choice."

Robert and Daniel found Henry in his normally sour mood, separating cream from milk.

"What brings you two out here?" Henry asked in a clipped voice, glancing up only briefly from the shade of his porch. His black dog arched its back and growled.

"Elias," Robert answered as he dismounted. "He didn't show up in Nauvoo. Send that mean dog away. Mean dogs have mean owners."

"Well, he's not here," Henry said in a voice iced with loathing. "The dog's fine."

"Where have you looked?" Daniel asked.

Henry skimmed another cup of cream from his bucket. "I haven't. Folks are just now returning to town, from wherever they were hiding from the Mormons. Everyone's been on edge; it's dangerous out there. A man could get shot nosing around."

"Mary's worried to death," Robert said. "We've got to find him."

"What's going on in Nauvoo?" Henry inquired, his worry evident. "Are we facing war?"

"No war," Daniel replied. "Governor Ford addressed a public meeting in Nauvoo the other day and a large crowd was on hand. We all sustained his efforts to keep the peace. Our city council passed a lot of resolutions."

"What good will that do?" Henry asked.

"It's calmed everyone down," Daniel said. "The resolutions call for support of the governor's plea for a peaceful and lawful settlement of all the issues in question." Daniel stole a quick glance at Robert. "The city council has denounced those who might seek private revenge on the assassins."

Robert ignored the inference to his unremitting rebellion. "What's the mood around here?" he asked Henry.

"Some of the older folks still haven't come back to town, vowing never to live here again," Henry said as he poured more cream. "There are rumors that a reward has been offered in Nauvoo for the destruction of the *Warsaw Signal* and the death of Thomas Sharp."

"Now there's a good idea," Robert said, his hazel eyes alive with anticipation.

"Ignore Robert," Daniel counseled Henry. "What else?"

"We hear reports that mobs from the Iowa and Missouri side are gathering," Henry said. "I've heard that men from Carthage have gone house-to-house in some of your settlements and taken arms from the Mormons. They still think that you Mormons are gonna overrun the state. Vigilantes are still roaming around, looking for people just like you. The Warsaw militia is doing drills. They're demanding the expulsion of Mormons out of Lima. That's just for starters ... I could think of more."

Katherine stepped out of the house. "I've set the table. You two need some lunch. I've got cheese and bread and buttermilk."

"What's your thinking about Elias?" Robert asked Katherine as they sat at the table.

"It's puzzling," Katherine said. "Henry saw him ... "

Henry cut Katherine off in mid-sentence. "I saw him in town. In all the confusion, it's hard to say where he went. He could have gone crazy with fear and wandered off. He could be still chasing the murderers. Maybe the murderers feared he could identify them."

Daniel swallowed hard, digesting the implication. The thought had gone through his mind. Maybe Elias really was dead, killed by the same men who assassinated the Prophet and his brother.

"Henry," Daniel said, "exactly what did you see that day?"

Henry colored as he related how he had accompanied Elias to Golden Point on orders from Colonel Geddes. "We delivered the message to the militia waiting there, and then left. When we got back to Carthage, there were still a lot of people in town." Henry then said that he and Elias witnessed the shooting from across the street, saying nothing about what happened in the grove of trees. "Joe and Hy Smith lost the gunfight."

"What do you mean?" Daniel asked.

"Folks around here say Joe and Hy had weapons; it was a fair fight."

"Fair? How many mobbers were storming the jail?"

Henry didn't answer.

Daniel shot a glance at Katherine, who dropped her eyes.

"For Mary and Hannah's sake, we've got to make an effort to find Elias," Robert said.

"It's not a good idea for you and Daniel to just ride into Carthage on your horses," Katherine said. "No one knows you. You'll draw suspicious stares."

"Just go home," Henry scoffed.

"We could hitch up the farm wagon and all go into Carthage together," Katherine said, her courage showing. "Folks there know us. They wouldn't harm us, especially if there's a woman and a child with you. "

"They know you're a Mormon," Henry said, chaffing.

"But you've made certain folks know that you're not," Katherine added.

"I'll help you hitch up your horses, Henry," Robert said, leaving the table.

Henry threw his arms up in despair. "If you insist. Why is it that you Mormons have a way of making all others feel inferior?"

"No one can make you feel inferior without your consent, Henry," Daniel countered.

From Henry's farm wagon, Carthage appeared to Robert not yet quite back to normal. Very few rooms at the Hamilton were occupied. Court records had not been returned. Only an occasional citizen could be seen near the town square, crossing for some kind of business or personal activity. The Carthage jail stood a silent, deserted sentinel.

At Robert's insistence, they parked the wagon at the Hamilton and Robert soon had innkeeper Artois Hamilton engaged in a conversation. Hamilton shook his head in honest silence when asked if he had seen Elias Eagles.

"Wouldn't know him if I had seen him," Artois said in a bewildered frontier drawl. "There were hundreds of men in town."

"Tell me about Wilson Law," Robert quickly asked.

Daniel didn't interfere with the question.

Artois Hamilton shrugged his shoulders. "Mr. Law and his brother—and the others associated with him—all left town in a hurry after it was all over."

"Where'd they go?" Robert's gaze was riveted on the hotel owner.

Hamilton threw his hands apart. "Didn't say. Didn't ask."

"Let me see their registration," Robert demanded in a steely voice.

"Why?" Artois prodded.

"It might disclose their addresses," Robert said.

Artois reached for the guest book, seeing no harm in the request. He opened it and let his finger trace the records. "The Laws, Fosters, and Higbee all wrote down 'Nauvoo' as their residence."

Robert pulled a disappointed face, as though Hamilton had dealt a staggering blow to his private investigation.

Artois threw Robert a challenging look. "Why your interest in those men?"

"They killed Joseph and Hyrum Smith."

Artois snorted. "So did everyone from Warsaw. And everyone from here in Carthage. Conspiracy theories are running rampant."

"You don't think Wilson Law had anything to do with it?"

Artois Hamilton ran his fingers through his beard, deep in thought. "Beats me. There were a lot of meetings in their rooms."

Robert clenched his jaw as he went a purple-red shade. "Who with?"

Daniel could almost see Hamilton's guilt.

"It would make a long, long list."

"Give it a try."

"The governor. Robert F. Smith, our justice of the peace. Frank Worrell of the Carthage Greys. Levi Williams. Thomas Sharp. Mark Aldrich." Artois paused suddenly. "You're not here to start trouble are you? Our town doesn't need any more trouble."

Daniel let his eyes trace the interior of the hotel, and the stairs leading to the second floor. He sensed that Artois Hamilton didn't fully understand the seriousness of the clandestine meetings that had been held in some of the rooms in the days leading up to the assassination of Joseph and Hyrum. He also sensed that Hamilton was trying his best to continue his friendship toward the Mormons. Hamilton's wagon had carried Joseph's body to Nauvoo, accompanied by Willard Richards.

Robert pulled Henry to his side. "This is Henry Eagles, a resident of your town. He operates a dairy just outside of Carthage. Elias Eagles was his brother, and a partner in his business. Elias is missing. We're trying to find him. He's my brother-in-law."

Artois recognized Henry and seemed to relax again. "What's that got to do with the guests in my hotel, like Wilson Law?"

"It's all connected," Robert said. "You surely can't blame us for trying to find my missing brother-in-law, now can you?"

"No, I guess not," Artois concluded. "Just be careful. Don't dive deeper than you have breath for. Since you're a Mormon, be doubly careful."

The conversation at the courthouse between Robert and Robert F. Smith was short. Smith was rude and abrupt, not willing to talk. Most important, he claimed he had no knowledge of Elias Eagles. Same with the conversation with Frank Worrell, at his farm. Worrell's eyes seemed distrustful to Daniel, and Daniel pulled Robert away before feelings erupted on either side.

"What about Wilson Law?" Robert had asked Worrell.

Worrell's eyes narrowed with a dark, misty fate. "Don't know anything about 'im. Thought you were lookin' for a man named Eagles."

"We are," Daniel said, whisking Robert away.

The remainder of the day proved fruitless. There was not a single person who knew anything about Elias, although two or three men knew who he was. Robert and Daniel questioned the baker, the blacksmith, the postmaster, the druggist, the millinery shopkeeper, the cooper, the wheelwright, the newspaper editor, a midwife, courthouse clerks, bank clerks, and several farmers.

"Tomorrow we'll go to Warsaw, and talk to Thomas Sharp and Mark Aldrich," Robert said as Henry turned the wagon toward home and the Eagles Dairy. "And to Fountain Green, to see Colonel Geddes."

Daniel shook his head. There was farm work to do in Nauvoo.

# 73

THE MOOD IN WARSAW HAD BEEN SHAPED by Thomas Sharp and his newspaper. After obtaining copies of the *Warsaw Signal* that had been published since the martyrdom, Robert, Daniel, Henry, and Katherine sat in the wagon in the shade of a tree on the outskirts of town, assessing the articles. They had already seen a group of vigilantes going into a tavern for a meeting. Daniel had brushed by one man so closely that he had been able to read the inscription of his powder horn: "Warsaw Regulators. The end of Polygamist Joseph Smith, kilt at Carthage June 27, 1844."

Daniel read the articles with a tone of complete disgust. "How can an editor get away with these lies?" he asked. Sharp claimed the guards at the jail had killed Joseph and Hyrum because the Nauvoo Legion had rushed the jail in an attempt to free the prisoners. Daniel had always been amazed how an editor in a small town of only five hundred people could have so much influence on the western Illinois frontier. He suspected there never had been an objective article about the Mormons in the Warsaw newspaper, and that Sharp had done all he could to suppress facts that would reflect poorly on the anti

Mormon positions.

"You were there, Henry," Robert said. "Let's march over to the *Signal* office and you can tell Mr. Sharp what really happened."

Henry perked up. "Would I get my name in the paper?"

"You sure would," Robert said.

Daniel recoiled. "We'd be inviting trouble. Thomas Sharp is the worst anti-Mormon in Warsaw."

"I've met him twice," Henry admitted. "I brought Elias to Warsaw once. Mr. Sharp spoke with us for a few seconds. He remembered me from my first visit to Warsaw, right after we all arrived in Illinois."

"Finally," Robert said, "someone who has actually seen Elias and knows who he is. Let's go."

The wagon began rolling toward town. Henry appeared anxious, like a child leading children to the cookie jar.

"What's Mr. Sharp like?" Daniel asked.

"Younger than us. I'd say twenty-five or six. Real nice man. Looks honest as the day is long."

"Nice man, all right," Daniel snorted. "Remember, the bad guy doesn't always wear a black hat. He's been criticizing our Church ever since we came to Nauvoo. He's a tool of Satan, in my opinion, and he has lots of helpers around here. Sharp is absolutely morally blind when it comes to hate mongering. He's openly advocated the killing of Joseph and Hyrum."

Daniel reminded Henry about early editorials written by Sharp that criticized the Illinois legislature for granting the charter given to the city of Nauvoo. "He's always distorted the truth. He's waged a campaign of horrendous lies and disinformation to dull the discovery that Mormonism is a sound religion."

Henry shrugged his shoulders. "What lies?"

"Overstating the amount of arms we have in the Nauvoo Legion," Daniel said. "And saying that Church leaders issue counterfeit money and bogus coins. Criticizing the Prophet's land transactions, and his holding of too many positions—mayor, Legion general, presiding judge of the highest city court, and political boss. Lamenting the unified, powerful Mormon-voting bloc. Claiming that Governor Ford sides with the Mormons."

"That's all true."

"Not so, Henry" Robert charged, thumping his brother-in-law on the shoulder.

Daniel waved the newspapers still in his hands. "Now Mr. Sharp is calling for our extermination, saying that people around here have a right to take the law into their own hands. He says that the Warsaw militia has been drilling, preparing to fight us."

The door to the newspaper office was open. Warm air gushed from inside, carrying odors of ink and newsprint. Sharp was at his desk, a quill pen in his hand, writing. The newspaper editor did not appear alarmed as his visitors approached, which greatly relieved Daniel. Robert had made certain that Katherine and her young daughter were in plain sight.

"Hello, Mr. Sharp," Henry stammered. "Remember me?"

"The face, but not the name," Sharp responded from narrowing eyes.

"Henry Eagles. I have a dairy farm in Carthage."

"Oh, yes," Sharp acknowledged, the recognition disarming him somewhat.

"My brother is a partner. We're looking for him. Elias Eagles."

"An Englishman? Haven't seen him."

"He's been missing since June twenty-seventh."

Daniel noted that Sharp took a deep breath and that his muscles tightened.

"I saw the whole thing," Henry said.

"Saw what?" Sharp asked.

"The mob, when they killed Joe Smith. I was right by the courthouse."

Sharp seemed shaken. He placed his quill on the desk.

"Do you want to interview me?" Henry asked.

Sharp took a deep breath and let it out, his distress apparent. "No," he said in a matter-of-fact voice. "Lot's of people witnessed it. I don't need anything from you."

Henry's mouth turned down quickly, absorbing his disappointment. "But I thought…"

"I'm busy, Mr. Eagles," Sharp said. He pointed to the door.

Robert stepped in front of Henry, towering over Sharp. "Did any of your witnesses say who killed Joe Smith?"

Sharp rose from his chair. "Not a one."

Robert glared at the newspaper editor, tasting the bile of Sharp's servile words. "Do you know Wilson Law?"

Sharp froze for a second or two. "Yes, of course. I've made it a point to know a lot of men in my profession."

"Know where he is?"

The question was met with several seconds of silence.

"I thought you were looking for someone named Elias," Sharp said, looking suspicious.

"We had a lead back in Carthage—someone who thinks Wilson Law might know where Elias Eagles is."

Daniel gasped at Robert's aggressive lie, and at Robert's demeanor. Robert stood ramrod straight, his fists balled.

"Who was that?" Sharp asked.

Robert remained firm. "Can't remember the gentleman's name."

"Can't help you. I have no idea where Wilson Law went." Sharp pointed to the door again. "I've got work to do."

Robert retreated a few steps, following Henry, Katherine, the child, and Daniel. Robert paused, turning toward Sharp again. "By the way," he said, pointing to Henry, "this man claims not one member of the Nauvoo Legion could be seen the day Joe Smith was killed. Not one. That's a little different than what your newspaper article says."

"Who are you?" Sharp asked, his face beginning to twist in anger.

"Just another dairyman from Carthage."

Robert instructed Henry to drive the farm wagon away from the newspaper office to avoid Sharp's menacing stares through the window. Now Robert understood all of Daniel's fancy words. Sharp and his newspaper truly were the beachhead of Mormon hatred and believed in the politics of personal destruction. In Robert's opinion, Thomas Sharp was one of the men who enthusiastically backed Satan in the war in heaven. How Sharp ended up with a body here on earth, Robert could only speculate.

"I think that man was in the mob that killed the Prophet," Robert said "Am I right, Henry?"

Henry seemed to wilt as he changed his tune. "How would I know? I was too far away, and besides, the men had painted faces."

Robert grunted at Henry's answer, shaking his head. He let his eyes trace the main street of Warsaw. To him, Warsaw was, if anything, a more worth less community than Carthage, filled with people too weak-willed to follow basic principles of human decency. "While we're here, let's do what we did in Carthage. Let's talk to anyone we see, people on the street, people in the shops. It's the least we can do for Mary and Hannah."

"Stay together," Daniel advised. "Try to look like dairymen."

"Do I have to look like Henry?" Robert asked.

For the next two hours, they combed Warsaw, talking to whoever would speak to them. A man in a tailor shop, another in a comb factory. Three women in a general store. An elderly gentleman in front of the library. The blacksmith. A shingleshaver. A tinner.

On the way back to Carthage, Robert made a startling conclusion "There're a few men that we talked to that I have strong feelings about."

Henry looked perplexed. "What kind of feelings?"

"What did I say about Thomas Sharp?" Robert asked.

"You think he was part of the mob at the jail," Katherine recalled.

"Right," Robert said. "And I think we met some more mobbers today What do you think, Daniel?"

"You, first," Daniel said. "But I'll bet we're having the same thoughts."

"I'm thinking of Jacob Davis, the state senator we met in front of the tav ern. He said he was captain of the Warsaw Rifle Company. He was evi through and through."

"I agree," Daniel said. "He sure was nervous when we talked to him. If I'd met him before, I sure wouldn't have voted for him. But then again, what choice did we have? The man who ran against him was an anti-Mormon."

"Who else?" Katherine asked.

"The young lawyer, William Grover. Captain of the Warsaw Cadets. I didn't like him, either."

"I agree again," Daniel said, feeling gooseflesh over the conversation.

Robert went on, naming others they had met, men that had caused a dark feeling to come over him. Mark Aldrich, the real estate man. Levi Williams, a farmer from nearby Green Plains. And John Wills, a rough-looking Irishman dressed in a new suit of clothes, favoring an arm injury of some kind.

"See any of those men in the mob, Henry?" Robert asked again.

Henry's dark eyes flashed an old anger. "I told you, I was too far away."

Robert had the feeling that if he were to break Henry's jaw and ribs a different answer might fall from Henry's lips. "We haven't found anyone who knows a thing about Elias," Robert said.

Henry remained silent.

"That leaves one disturbing conclusion, Henry."

More silence from Henry.

"What conclusion?" Katherine asked.

"The only thing we know about Elias's disappearance comes from one man. Henry Eagles. If Henry truly doesn't know what happened to Elias, perhaps we'll never know."

Katherine poked at her husband. "Henry?"

"Everybody panicked after the shooting that day. Elias and me did too. I ran for my horse and came home, and didn't look back. I honestly don't know what happened to Elias."

Robert put his arm around Henry. "I think I believe you, Henry."

Governor Ford drew a deep breath as he sorted through a stack of newspapers that had accumulated on his desk. He was not mentally deficient; he had already considered the possibility that he was seeing.

State auditor Shields stood over Ford, pointing as he studied the pile of newsprint. "What'd I tell you? There's more newspapers critical of the death of Joe and Hyrum Smith than favorable."

Ford had spent the past month in Quincy. He had met daily with men from Warsaw who had been pressuring him to expel all Mormons from the state. He had made application to the U.S. Government for five hundred men of the regular army to help do the job, but had been refused. Ford's secret agents reported to him daily the movements of both the Mormons and the anti-Mormons.

"We're taking a beating from the Whig newspapers, especially," said Shields.

Ford's face was in his hands. He was turning green in frustration. "We're in a no-win situation."

"Precisely," Shields stated. "The Mormons blame you for the death of Joe Smith and so do the Whigs."

Ford knew the implication. The August elections were drawing near. Until the elections were over, he wished he could retract the things he had said about Joe Smith. He had been quoted as saying that Joe Smith was the most successful imposter in modern times, that he was a man with a dark and gloomy person with a long beard. He had also said that Smith was a man who dressed like a dandy, drank like a sailor, and swore like a pirate; that Smith was as rough and as boisterous as a highway robber; and that Smith had lusts and cravings of an animal nature.

Furthermore, he had labeled Smith's followers as men of broken down unprincipled talents; men who had nothing to lose by deserting their previous religions; men who were mostly infidels, who held all other religions in derision. Ford now suspected that his own lies would come back to haunt him during election time.

"The Mormons are meeting daily," Shields warned. "The incumbents in Carthage are worried."

"I know."

"They're going to vote, despite your appeal not to."

"I know." Ford had asked the Mormon people to stay out of the August election. "But the damn Whigs are telling them to ignore my advice and vote anyway."

"It's mostly Colonel Taylor."

"He ought to be shot."

"Congressman Hoge favors prosecuting those responsible for killing Joe Smith."

"I know."

"When he wins, you'll have to do it."

Ford slammed his fist to the desk. "I know." Shields had not used the term *if he wins*, but *when he wins*.

Ford put his hands to his face. He thought about the years ahead, as an ex-governor, out of office. That would be the time, in his opinion, to tell the truth about Mormonism. He would help see to it that schoolchildren of the future were taught to cringe with terror at the name of Joe Smith; that Smith's evil designs were frustrated only through the sacrifices of brave politicians like himself and brave journalists like Thomas Sharp.

# 74

**August 1844**

A PROPELLER-DRIVEN STEAMER CALLED the *Hercules*, with five members of the Quorum of Twelve Apostles on board, cut through the smooth waters of Lake Michigan on a course south by southwest. The ship had left Detroit five days earlier, sailing north on Lake Huron to Ft. Mackinac. By nightfall, August first, the *Hercules* was scheduled to reach Chicago. Elders Young, Woodruff, Pratt, Kimball, and Wight each paid a seven-dollar fare. From Chicago, the Apostles would take a stagecoach to Galena in the far northwest corner of Illinois. From there, they could catch passage on a steamboat down the Mississippi River to Nauvoo.

Orson Hyde had parted with the other five Apostles at Fairport in order to visit Marinda's family in Kirtland. Marinda had left Nauvoo shortly after the martyrdom, returning to her family until matters quieted. Rebecca and Mary Ann were still in Nauvoo.

Wilford Woodruff had met with Elder Young and the others in Boston on July eighteenth. That night they listened to Orson Hyde speak to a large crowd in Washington Hall about the murder of Joseph and Hyrum Smith. Donations from the people were enough to pay for Orson's passage home, and helped defray Wilford's costs, too. From Boston, the Apostles journeyed to Buffalo where they caught the *Hercules.*

The subject of the martyrdom clung to the Apostles like glue all during the trip. But the statement that shocked Wilford the most was one from Lyman Wight.

"Brother Joseph told me once that he would not live to see forty years of age," Lyman said.

Wilford reeled in disbelief, staring at Lyman and then letting his gaze reach across the peaceful waters of Lake Michigan. "He knew all along, didn't he?"

"Yes," Lyman said. "He made the statement to me when I visited him in Liberty Jail. He told me not to say a word to anyone until after his death. Joseph probably knew even before he died that he would be required to some-day give his life for the gospel."

A scripture came immediately to Wilford's mind: Hebrews 9:16-17.

*For where a testament is, there must also of necessity be the death of the testator. For a testament is of force after men are dead: otherwise it is of no strength at all while the testator liveth.*

Tears welled in Wilford's eyes. "The Church will go on," he said. "They have killed the First and Second Elders of the Church, but the work will go on."

Lyman nodded in agreement. "The Church is on the earth to stay this time."

"I worry about what is going on in Nauvoo," Wilford said. "I hate the thoughts of war breaking out between the Saints and Mormon-haters."

"I hope all our families are safe," Lyman said.

Wilford thought of Phoebe and his children, of little Wilford, who was staying with John Benbow and his wife. "Everyone in Nauvoo has got to keep a cool head. All it would take is one hothead bent on revenge to place every-one in danger."

Robert Harris pulled a wadded up piece of paper from his pocket and stared at it again. From the oak table near the hearth in his new frame home on the forty-acre farm, Robert held the rumpled paper under the light of his lantern. He dipped his quill in an inkwell, ready to write on the paper. It read:

*Men who must pay for the killing of Joseph and Hyrum: William and Wilson Law, whereabouts unknown. Robert and Charles Foster, whereabouts unknown. Francis and Chauncey Higbee, hiding out somewhere in Carthage or Warsaw. Thomas Sharp, editor of the Warsaw newspaper. Mark Aldrich, Warsaw land speculator. Jacob Davis, state senator from Warsaw. William Grover, Warsaw lawyer. Levi Williams, Green Plains farmer. Frank Worrell, Carthage, for failing to guard the jail properly.*

"Blow out the lantern and come to bed," Hannah groaned from the other room. "You're probably keeping the children awake." She had endured a long, laborious day, moving the family's belongings into the new house. Mary, Elias' wife, now lived in her old log cabin in Nauvoo.

Robert began pulling off his boots. "I'll be right there. Patience, woman, patience."

"It's probably past eleven," Hannah hissed. "What are you doing?"

"Reading the scriptures."

"Well, hurry up. I'm exhausted."

While loading the farm wagon with furniture during the day in Nauvoo, John Cox had made a startling statement to Robert. "There's a rumor floating around town about the Law brothers," Levi said.

Robert wheeled, his ears bristling. "Tell me."

John disclosed that Willard Richards had received a stinging letter from the Laws, meant for publication in the *Times and Seasons*. Taylor had ripped it up and thrown it away. But not without noticing the postmark.

Robert smoothed the paper and began to edit. *Men responsible for the deaths of Joseph and Hyrum—and their brother, Samuel.*

Samuel had died two days earlier, on July thirtieth, thirty-three days after Joseph and Hyrum were killed. To Robert, it was plain to see that Wilson Law and his gang of apostates were just as responsible for Samuel's death as the other two. Samuel, who had been living at Plymouth, some twenty miles or more southeast of Carthage, had ridden his horse at breakneck speed toward Carthage and Nauvoo the day he learned Joseph and Hyrum were in mortal danger. At Bear Creek he had met at mob. The mob refused to let him advance toward Nauvoo. He went to the home of a friend, changed horses— the new horse was one of the fastest in the country—and rode hard toward Carthage. Other mobbers chased him back and forth across the countryside until he finally made it into Nauvoo. The ride eventually took its toll, however. A victim of physical and nervous exhaustion, a severe fever broke out in him. He never recovered.

The thoughts of Samuel's passing grated on Robert. He crossed out the words *whereabouts unknown* next to William and Wilson Law's name.

With his pen dripping with ink, Robert wrote new words: *rumored to be in Galena*. His desire for revenge was about to triumph over his good sense.

Dawn found Robert riding Lawless into Nauvoo. He could see the outline of the temple as he approached, with a huge new crane towering over it. As he passed his old log cabin, he was surprised to see Mary Eagles hanging out her wash.

"You're up early," Robert said, pulling his horse to a stop. It was hot already; his clothes stuck to his skin.

"I couldn't sleep all night. I keep having nightmares about Elias."

Her words struck a nerve. "I'm sorry we haven't found him," Robert said, his head on his chest.

"And where are you off to so early in the morning?" Mary asked, her sad eyes fixed on the bedroll tied to Robert's saddle.

"Fort Madison," Robert answered, feeling sheepish about his fib. He took off his cap and wiped his brow. "Got some business there."

Mary gave him a concerned stare. "You don't look so good. Ague got you?"

Robert clouded over. "I'll be fine. It comes and goes."

They chatted for a few minutes more. Robert described how much Hannah liked her new home, despite being two miles out of town, and that he and Daniel were getting ready to harvest their wheat and barley. Mary put forth more theories about where Elias might be—held as a secret hostage somewhere in one of the outlying communities, kidnapped and taken to St Louis or Springfield, or suffering from amnesia and wandering around some far off American city like Chicago or Detroit.

"He could have just gone half crazy when he saw what happened at the Carthage Jail," Mary explained. "That's what would have happened to me if I had witnessed the martyrdom; I just couldn't handle it. We should never have come to Nauvoo."

Robert accepted the amnesia philosophy as the most reasonable, and was still thinking about it when he passed the Browning Gun Shop. He jangled the coins in his pocket, wishing he could afford a new pepperbox, or even a shotgun, to take with him. He continued onward to the Nauvoo Landing There, he boarded the *St. Croix*, a steamboat headed north. She was burning resinous pine knots and black smoke streamed out of her stacks. He purchased a ticket for both him and his horse from a man clad in a thick frieze jacket black trousers, and a tall hat. The steamboat was loaded with barrels of blasting powder for the lead mines up north.

Destination: Galena, Illinois.

"Have you seen Robert this morning?" Hannah asked Daniel.

Daniel was taking a break from his corn harvest. He jerked his head, startled by Hannah's question. He peered toward the new wooden horse pens "No. His horse is gone. Maybe he went to town, but I don't know why he would." He began to think that Robert's absence was nothing to be worried about.

Hannah pulled a face, thinking.

"Corn is high this year, thanks to the wet spring and summer," Daniel said. "Corn for supper tonight, silage for the cattle, husks to stuff mattresses, cobs to kindle fires and smoke meat. Good American crop, isn't it?"

"He was gone before I even woke up."

"Is it his day to work at the temple?"

"No," Hannah remarked. "You'd know that as well as I."

Daniel remained unconcerned. "We talked yesterday about seeing a rope manufacturer to buy our hemp. We need to find out who's taking over the Law's gristmill. There was a small bull running loose yesterday, maybe he's herding it home to its owner. Or perhaps he took a couple of buckets of gooseberries to town to sell."

"Or he's on another wild goose chase," Hannah sighed theatrically.

The remark caused Daniel to pull at his chin. "I hope you're wrong. We can't afford to lose another horse."

"I'm not worried about the horse. I'm worried about Robert. He's got the shakes."

Elizabeth jerked her head up. "Why didn't you tell me? I've got some quinine."

"It just started last night. I was going to get some from you this morning."

# 75

THE STEAMBOAT RIDE UP THE Mississippi reminded Robert of the trip from New Orleans to Nauvoo three years earlier, in the springtime. This time however, the river had a dank, musty smell as the summer weather was hot and humid. The heat rolled over and settled on the water like an oppressive blanket pulled from the great sprawling woodlands that surrounded the river. Overhead great thunderheads of clouds were riding oceans of wind in the endless blue sky, like some wondrous mountain ranges that had learned the secret of flight. Lawless was not the only horse on board; Robert could count five others. Swarms of mosquitoes and flies were tormenting them, causing them to be restless. There was also an assortment of pigs, cows, and chickens. In addition to the blasting powder, the *St. Croix* was loaded with freight from New Orleans and St. Louis. Commodities such as refined flour and sugar were dropped off at places like Fort Madison, Burlington, and Davenport, making progress slow. Robert learned that the *St. Croix* terminated at Galena. There the steamboat would be loaded with lead and furs, the most important export of the area. He thought of the time he rode with the Mormon rescue posse year earlier, when Sheriff Reynolds had kidnapped Joseph. Galena was eighty miles northwest of Dixon.

The traffic on the river consisted of every known vessel from dugout canoes to chugging steamboats dangerously overloaded with passengers, their funnel smoke fanned by a gentle northern breeze. Here and there the *St. Croix* passed wrecked steamboats, their hulls lying like corpses in upriver shallows, and their boilers and engines destined to make fossils for the future. A piano in the main cabin resonated with music for cabin passengers. When another steamboat passed close by, a wake reached the St. Croix and she bobbled in an undignified fashion. Loons, grebes, ducks, and herons by the thousands dotted the waters. A brown pelican dove into the water headfirst and came up with a fish.

For a while Robert settled his gaze to the west and wondered about Joseph Smith's prediction that the Saints would be relocated somewhere in Oregon territory, California, or even Mexico. Many Americans were already in the West; more were on their way, and still more would follow. Restless men, these Americans, Robert thought. They seemed to have a relentless desire to become a two ocean nation; distant promised lands seemed to be just waiting for the taking. Reports from western explorers had reached all parts of the East, including Nauvoo. Explorers and trappers had returned with wild tales of salt lakes, jagged mountain peaks that punctured the clouds, geysers that shot hot water skyward, deserts of alkali and endless sagebrush flats, rivers that vanished into the earth, and soil to make a farmer weep for joy.

Robert's mind soon returned to the purpose of his trip; he couldn't keep his feverish mind off Wilson Law. He couldn't picture the Law brothers fleeing so far north. What had attracted them to Galena? The rich lead deposits? Had they already sold their business interests in Nauvoo and invested their money into the mining industry? A bank, a dry goods store, a gristmill, or a hotel?

The farther north the steamboat traveled, the slightly smaller the Mississippi became. Overnight, the *St. Croix* passed points where the Wapsipinicon and Maquoketa Rivers emptied, filling Robert with anticipation. Soon the steamboat would veer off into the Galena River and travel six miles upstream to Galena. Arrival time was expected to be early Sunday morning. With red-rimmed tired eyes, he began to envision Wilson Law lying in a pool of blood, his jaw broken, and his ribs cracked.

"Mother, it's dinnertime now. I can give you Father's note."

Hannah wiped her hands on her apron and gave Joseph a blank stare "What note?" The farther the sun set in the west, the more worried she had become about Robert.

"Father made me promise not to give it to you until dinner." Joseph handed his mother a thrice-folded piece of paper.

"Sit still, Enoch. Mama will feed you in a minute," Hannah said as she opened the note.

*My dearest Hannah: There's someone up north that may know something about Elias. I'll be gone for a few days. Don't worry about me. Love, Robert.*

Hannah sank into a chair. How far north? Appanoose? Pontoosuc? Rock Island? Dixon? Or Wisconsin? How long were a few days?

"Joseph, watch the children for a few minutes. Lizzy—you'll eat your peas and carrots before your bread this time, or Mama will spank you."

Lizzy gave Hannah an obedient nod.

"Where you going, Mother?" Joseph asked, his face screwed into a picture of concern.

"I've got to talk to Daniel," she said as she scurried out the door.

Hannah found Daniel discussing the farm crop with Elizabeth and Harriett on the porch of their new home. To the west, a dazzling sunset painted the horizon. "Corn's worth twenty cents a bushel this year," he was saying "And wheat fifty cents. If our yield is fifty bushel an acre ... "

"What do you make of this?" Hannah asked. She thrust Robert's note at Daniel.

Daniel quickly scanned the short note. A perplexed look came over him

"Are you thinking the same thing I am?"

Hannah sighed heavily. "Exactly."

"Have you heard anything about the Fosters or the Laws or the Higbees hiding out up north somewhere?" Daniel asked.

"No, but obviously Robert has."

Robert was surprised that the region surrounding Galena was not flat. Instead, there were attractive hills, valleys, and bluffs. The froth of the bow-wave died away to a series of ripples as the *St. Croix* approached the dock. As he prepared to disembark with Lawless, a Galena businessman told him that although glaciers had flattened most of Middle America thousands of years ago, the glaciers must have missed Galena. He also said that Galena produced eighty-five percent of the nation's lead. Around fifty million pounds were expected to be shipped out this year.

"Do you know of a man named Wilson Law?" Robert asked as he stepped off the steamboat. *I've come to town to flatten him.*

The early morning light revealed eleven other steamboats docked along Water Street. A few blocks away Robert saw a busy railroad yard.

The man scratched his sweaty bald head. "Can't say that I do. He must be new. I've been away for two months on business. Sorry."

Robert sat on his horse in silence for a long time, studying the city. He soon found himself wandering aimlessly along the warehouses by the dock, and then along Prospect Street, wondering where to begin his search. A fever was still racking his body; his shirt was soaked with sweat. The sun had risen. Gaslights lining the street were being doused. He was surprised at the city's prosperous look. The "lead rush" had brought a wide assortment of interesting people, swelling the population to nearly ten thousand. The DeSoto House Hotel, the John Dowling House, banks, dry good stores, churches, and mansions were beautiful with their spectacular Italian, Gothic, Roman, and Queen Anne architecture. Robert picked up a copy of the *Galena Gazette,* but found no mention of Wilson or William Law. He felt confused; he had expected a small town of just a few hundred citizens.

"Come on, Lawless," Robert said to his horse. "I've got to lie down for a while and see if this fever will go away." With creeping edges of fatigue wrinkling the sides of his eyes, he looked at his watch. It was nearly eight o'clock and no doubt it would be another hot day. Soon the sky would lose its bluish hue and turn white hot.

For a second, Robert contemplated how luxurious it would be to put Lawless in the local livery stable and get a room at the DeSoto. Leading his horse, Robert strolled toward the hotel, stretching his aching legs. It had been a long, two-day ordeal on the steamboat.

Suddenly, a stagecoach pulled by six horses rounded the corner and headed for the same hotel. What Robert saw next shocked him beyond belief.

Five men stepped out of the stagecoach, all looking nearly as disheveled as himself—as though they had been on the stage for two or three days without sleep. Robert recognized them all; their names rolled off his tongue easily. Wilford Woodruff, Brigham Young, Lyman Wight, Heber C. Kimball, and Orson Pratt.

Robert stiffened in anguish and then began to shake. He hid behind his horse.

The Apostles talked of their fatigue as they disembarked, but their voices were cheery as always. Robert gathered that they had been on the stage twenty-four hours almost nonstop, traveling one hundred sixty miles.

In a low whisper Robert talked to his horse. "Come on, Lawless. Let's get out of here."

A small grove of trees on the outskirts of the city, on the banks of the Galena River, became Robert's camping spot. He unsaddled and hobbled his horse and let Lawless graze on the lush wild grass. Robert made breakfast out of dried meat and hard corn fritters, washed down with river water. He threw his wool blanket onto the ground. Although the fever had slowed his thinking down to a crawl, a debate began to rage in his mind.

Robert had never thought of anyone besides Joseph Smith as the leader of the Church. When Joseph and Hyrum died, Joseph was only thirty-eight and Hyrum forty-four. The shock of seeing five of the Apostles step off the stage in Galena made Robert wonder who would take over the role as Church leader and Prophet. Robert favored Wilford Woodruff. If it came to a vote, that's who he'd vote for. Robert wondered if the campaign for president of the Church would be similar to the campaign for governor of the state, or president of the United States. He slowly came to the conclusion that it probably would not be the same. But if not that, how would it happen? Would the presidency go to the most popular Apostle? The oldest? The one with most seniority? Robert thought of other possibilities. Would it go to Sidney Rigdon? Sidney had been Joseph's counselor for several years. The scorned apostate, William Law, had been Joseph's other counselor until April, when he was excommunicated. He had not been replaced.

Robert closed his eyes and thought again. Or would the presidency go to a member of the Smith family?

Robert sank into a gloom that matched the challenge of trying to find a needle in a haystack, or finding Wilson Law in a city of ten thousand. Days earlier, Samuel Smith had died. Dr. Willard Richards blamed the death on internal injuries Samuel suffered on his torturous ride to Carthage the day Joseph and Hyrum were killed. Of all of Joseph and Hyrum's brothers, Robert thought Samuel would be the most qualified to lead the Church. Another option would be William, Joseph's brother who served in the Quorum of the Twelve. Still, another possibility loomed. Joseph had a twelve-year-old son; perhaps the presidency should go to him. After all, there were several cases in Europe where kingdoms had been conferred upon young princes at the death of a King. The current Queen of England, Victoria, had been only seventeen when she took office.

Robert's thoughts were now torn between a desire to go back to Nauvoo as quickly as possible to see what events would transpire with the return of the Apostles, and the feeling he had to track down Wilson Law and make him pay for the deaths of Joseph and Hyrum.

Almost too wound up to sleep, he spread out his blanket under a shade tree. He pulled off his boots, removed his shirt, and sprawled out on the blanket. As he lay on the ground, the ague symptoms began to return. Cold sensations coursed down his back, followed by warm flashes that turned into a burning fever. His fever caused his sweat to become even harsher. He rolled over and let the cool morning air wash over his body. Next came a dull headache and dizziness. His right arm became numb and unconsciously he began to rub it. A prickling sensation from the area of his liver caused more distress. Drowsiness settled in, and he welcomed it. When the chills returned he rolled himself back into the blanket and began to slumber.

CHAPTER NOTES

Wilford Woodruff's journals contain details of his return to Nauvoo following the deaths of Joseph and Hyrum. According to Woodruff, he made the journey from Albany, New York, to Nauvoo with four other Apostles, Brigham Young, Heber C. Kimball, Lyman Wight, and Orson Pratt. Just as portrayed in this chapter, they went through Galena and caught a steamboat there, which took them to Nauvoo.

Here is an interesting side note. During the Apostles' trip on the stage, they encountered a company of Norwegians traveling by ox teams. One wagon was stuck in the road and several of the men were whipping the animals and cursing at them in their native language. Brigham Young took a whip out of the hands of one of the men and asked them to stand back. Brigham then talked to the oxen in a tongue neither English nor Norwegian. To the astonishment of the Norwegians the oxen then pulled the heavily loaded wagon out of the mud (see *History of the Church*, Volume 7, page 224).

Lyndon W. Cook's research paper, "William Law, Nauvoo Dissenter," reveals that William Law (and probably his brother) was a merchant in Galena and Hampton, located in northern Illinois, after he fled from Nauvoo.

# 76

THE WET NOSE OF HIS HORSE FINALLY woke Robert long after the dawn sun came over the horizon with the fiery thrust of a poker, spawning a slight breeze that felt like a blast from an open fireplace. Robert was lying on the damp grass. His rumpled blanket lay three feet away. His clothing was damp from his constant sweat and the high humidity. The pain from his liver area was excruciating. He urinated; blood was evident. Every muscle in his body ached. A long drink from the river did nothing to relieve his misery, nor did his nibbles on dried meat and stale corn pones. He became aware that he had slept off and on for a day and a night. The Sabbath had come and gone. It was Monday morning.

With dogged determination, he stiffly rose to a standing position. A blue jay scolded him lustily from the branches of a tree. Groaning all the while, he saddled Lawless and rode into town. He hoped his wide-brimmed felt hat would hide his disheveled look. He avoided the area immediately surrounding the DeSoto, but nearby he began his detective work. He picked on a man in a pinstriped gray suit walking into a real estate office.

"I'm looking for a man named Wilson Law. Just moved here." Robert inhaled and exhaled, feeling no relief from his body pain.

"Can't say that I know him," the man said, pulling on a long handlebar moustache. "If you find him, send him my way." He reminded Robert that today was Election Day in Illinois, and that a lot of people would be in town. Fighting had broken out in some of the barrooms the night before, caused by arguments over the election. Robert realized he wouldn't be able to cast his own vote in Nauvoo, where members of the Church were determined to win control of crucial county offices. Mormons had agreed to support Minor Deming as sheriff, Daniel H. Wells as coroner, and J. B. Backenstos and A. W. Babbitt as state representatives. Mormons were also trying to win control of the Hancock County commission. Robert gritted his teeth. He wished Governor Ford were up for re-election; he was certain the Mormons would vote him out of office. All over the country, people were casting their vote for president. Robert wondered how many votes Joseph Smith actually would have received had he not been killed. Now it was between the Democrat, James K. Polk, and the Whig, Henry Clay.

Robert posed the same question about the Law brothers to a barber, a trapper dressed in skins, three workers from the lead mines, an immigrant with a Swedish accent, and a stevedore. None had heard of men named Wilson or William Law. Perhaps they were using aliases, he reasoned.

*Nearly ten thousand people,* Robert groaned, his pain worse.

He came to Water Street. Columns of coal-black smoke rose from the steamboat that had carried him to Galena. Her flag was flying at jackstaff.

"What time do you leave down river?" Robert asked a Negro roustabout near the *St. Croix.*

"Ten o'clock," came the answer.

Robert jerked his pocket watch up to his face. He grunted in agony. Departure was less than a half-hour away. He scanned the main, hurricane and boiler decks. He reasoned that if the Apostles were on board they would be traveling in first-class cabins. He asked himself if it were possible to be on the same steamboat for two days and never run into them. He reasoned, yes.

Robert knew that Elder Woodruff would easily recognize him. After all, Elder Woodruff had stayed in his home in England a couple of nights during Wilford's mission there.

*Doesn't God want me to take vengeance on Wilson Law on His behalf?*

Robert dabbed at his sweaty forehead with a kerchief. With short labored breaths, he tugged at Lawless. "I'm going home," he whispered to the horse. He paid the fare, settled Lawless into a livestock stall, and to the shrill whistle of the steamboat Robert collapsed on top of boxes of freight, between hogsheads and barrels.

As the *St. Croix* paddled downstream and reached the confluence of the Galena and Mississippi rivers, Wilford Woodruff peered south thinking of Nauvoo. He felt anxious, wondering how Phoebe and his three children were faring, and all of the Saints there. He pulled a letter from Phoebe out of his satchel and read it again. It related a dream she had had about Joseph Smith and William and Wilson Law.

The Laws had cast Joseph into a pit, just as Joseph in the Old Testament had been cast in a pit by his brothers, and subsequently sold into Egypt. In her dream, Phoebe said that a bound Joseph Smith had struggled hard to climb partway out of the pit so that he could look out. Joseph saw William and Wilson Law a short distance away, and they had fear written on their faces. One brother was in the grasp of a snake, the other in the grasp of a tiger. Both William and Wilson were pleading for Joseph to free them from the beasts that were consuming them. Joseph replied that cords bound him, the very cords that William and Wilson had placed on him, and that he had no power to help them.

Brigham Young approached with a hand over his eyes, shielding himself from the bright sun. "What are you thinking about?" Brigham asked Wilford.

Wilford carefully folded Phoebe's letter and told Brigham about her dream. A thoughtful expression crossed his face. "I suppose the Lord will exact his own vengeance upon those who caused the deaths of Joseph and Hyrum," he said.

Brigham nodded his agreement. "In my opinion, men like that are truly sons of perdition. Perhaps that's what the dream signified."

"I've also been thinking about what Orson Hyde said in his talk in Boston just before we left," Wilford stated.

"Which part?"

Wilford ground his teeth together softly. "When he stated that just as the Jews were not satisfied with killing the Savior, and after He was dead a spear was thrust into his side, William and Wilson Law and the other enemies of the Church are not going to be satisfied with the deaths of Joseph and Hyrum."

"That's right," Brigham commented coldly. "Our enemies are going to thrust a spear into the side of the Church and her members."

"God help us," Wilford said in a sigh of exasperation. "Satan is still trying to destroy what the Savior and the Prophet have restored to the earth."

Robert's ears were ringing on two accounts. The double-dose of quinine given to him by Elizabeth was working, and Hannah had lit into him. Terribly weak, he lay on his bed with Daniel, Elizabeth, Harriet, and his children staring at him.

"Don't you ever do that to me again," Hannah was saying. "I don't care if you were looking for Elias or not. I don't want to worry about a missing brother *and* a missing husband."

"I don't suppose you saw Wilson Law up north?" Daniel asked.

The question shocked Robert. "You know?"

"It's all over Nauvoo," Daniel explained. "He and his brother are in Hampton."

"Hampton?" Robert kicked himself and his face reflected disappointment. He had passed right through it. Hampton was a small town of only a few hundred people, near Rock Island. "What are they doing there?"

"Finding a place to spend their money, I suppose. A group here in Nauvoo bought up all the Laws' businesses for fifty-cents on the dollar."

Hannah's face turned beet red with anger. "So that's what this is all about—finding Wilson and William Law?"

Robert was still suffering from fever and body pain, but his mind was quick. "I just have this feeling that Wilson Law and the others may know something about Elias."

Hannah shook her finger at Robert. "No more chasing after the bad guys."

Thomas Sharp took both written and mental notes as he met with other anti-Mormons lamenting the results of the election. In his view, both the state and county returns had resulted in a disaster.

"Hoge's win is going to mean that Governor Ford will be pressured to prosecute us for the murder of Joe Smith," Sharp said in a seething voice, the horrible consequences settling in. Just prior to the election, a prominent downstate democrat, Colonel E. D. Taylor, had persuaded the Mormons to vote for Hoge as U.S. representative in the Sixth Congressional District. Taylor did so on the premise that Hoge favored bringing the murderers of Joe and Hyrum Smith to trial. Ford had already written a letter to the Mormons that he was ready to enforce the law should the accused murderers offer resistance to legal process.

Mark Aldrich kicked at the table in Sharp's office and cursed audibly. Hoge had beaten the Whig candidate—a man by the name of Sweet who was on the anti-Mormon side—by less than fifteen hundred votes. Sweet received only fifty votes in Nauvoo.

Robert F. Smith was steaming. He had lost his position as coroner to Daniel H. Wells. He let go a stream of foul oaths against the Mormons.

"It's almost worse news that General Deming won the office of sheriff," Sharp lamented.

"I'll tell you what," Frank Worrell said, veins sticking out in his forehead and neck, "I hope Deming attempts to arrest some of us. If he does, we'll have some more sport, make no mistake about that. I'm mad as the devil about all this." He cursed.

"If Deming tries to use the militia to arrest us, he'll be lucky to find more than a handful to support him," Sharp advised thoughtfully. "By my count there were nearly three hundred men involved in getting rid of the Smiths, and the network of support in this county for those three hundred men runs far deeper than Deming could imagine."

With downturned lips, Aldrich said, "When we hold our 'Grand Military Encampment' here in Warsaw in a couple of weeks, it'll make Deming think twice about coming against us. I think all the militia leaders are on our side."

Levi Williams threw his hands apart in exasperation. "We've lost control of the whole county."

Sharp cringed and cursed again. Williams was right. County commissioners had the power to choose grand jurors. If the men in his office, including himself, were ultimately arrested by Deming and Ford, those grand jurors would determine whether they would be formally charged. The commissioners also had power to select the petit jurors, who would hear the evidence and determine their guilt or innocence at the trial.

"This is bad news," Williams said. "Very bad news."

CHAPTER NOTES

The dream Phoebe Woodruff had about William and Wilson Law is related in Wilford Woodruff's journal.

# 77

*August 1844*

WILFORD WOODRUFF ADMIRED John Taylor's tenacity. It had been just more than six weeks since he had suffered four wounds at the Carthage Jail, but John was looking forward to returning to his duties as a member of the Council of Twelve Apostles and as owner of the entire printing industry in Nauvoo. Taylor had purchased all printing assets from the Church eight months ago—the building and lot, press, bindery, and foundry. He was publisher of both Nauvoo newspapers—the *Times and Seasons,* the official Church organ, and the *Nauvoo Neighbor,* a secular publication.

In the comfort of the Taylor home, Wilford and Willard Richards sat for a short visit, telling John what had happened during a meeting at the Seventies Hall. Taylor's wife served apple cider and hot bread with peach preserves, and then took her children outside so the two men could visit about delicate matters of their apostleship. For the first few minutes, John talked about the distress he felt in getting back to his publishing business: getting timely world, national, and regional news; collecting from subscribers; and securing a reliable source for newsprint.

"I don't see how you get everything done," Wilford commented.

"One thing about it, we eat well," John chuckled. "Lot's of folks can't afford the two dollar per year subscription fee, so they pay in flour, meat, vegetables, or fruit. But my creditors won't accept a few bushel of apples for the paper I need."

John still did not have the strength to sit in a long afternoon meeting as Wilford had done, along with Brigham Young, Heber C. Kimball, Orson Pratt, Willard Richards, members of the Nauvoo Stake High Council, and all high priests in the city. They had listened to a passionate plea by Sidney Rigdon that Sidney be allowed to govern the Church.

"Sidney's been working on us pretty hard," Willard said as he spread peach preserves on his bread. Sidney had been in Pittsburgh when he heard the news of the martyrdom and left immediately for Nauvoo, arriving three days earlier than Wilford. "Ever since he got back he's been pressuring us, hasn't he Brother Taylor? He thinks he should be the modern Moses."

Wilford smiled and nodded. To him, the situation was almost amusing. Always the ambitious orator, Sidney had predicted impending judgments, including a destructive global warfare in which Sidney would personally lead a militant Church to a triumphant victory over the nations of Babylon. Sidney had even boasted that he expected to walk into the palace of Queen Victoria in England and "lead her out by the nose."

"Poor Sidney hasn't been right in the head ever since his ordeal in the Missouri jail years ago," Wilford said. Rigdon had served as first counselor to Joseph Smith since 1833, but had never been ordained as an Apostle. Members of the Twelve, along with the Prophet, found Sidney—with his independent mind—to be a valuable advisor in many matters, but a man subject to wild mood swings. Rigdon was self-centered, unreliable in doctrine, conspicuously absent from many important council meetings, uninterested in bearing his share of the burdens of leadership, and the subject of frequent rep rimands from the Prophet.

John appeared famished and he talked through a mouthful of bread and jam. "He's always been either in the bottom of the cellar or up in the garret window. In his early days, Sidney was more sanguine than he is now. I could see a few years back how valuable his experience was to Joseph as a counselor. But ever since the Church moved to Nauvoo, Sidney has been a different man. I feel sorry for him. But he's got to understand his place in the Church. He was a counselor. He holds no keys to leadership."

Wilford nodded his agreement. "I was disappointed in his talk. He said nothing about feeding the poor, building the temple, ministering to the Saints, or preaching the gospel. All he wanted to talk about was Queen Victoria, the Mount of Olives, and the sort. We need to build up the Church and the Kingdom of God. Never mind about Gog and Magog."

"Sad thing about it is that a few will be led away by Sidney," John lamented.

"And I suppose others will step forward, claiming they ought to lead the Church," Wilford said. "But as for me and my house, I'm following the keys of leadership. All the keys to leading the Church have been bestowed upon the Twelve."

"And Elder Young is the senior Apostle," John said as he wiped jam off his lips.

"I like the way Elder Young provides structure and direction, never coddling an indulgence," Wilford said.

John agreed; he did not need any further convincing.

"This will all come to a head in a few days," Wilford concluded. He felt that perhaps part of the problem was that Sidney, at age fifty-one, considered himself to be a father-figure of sorts to the younger Apostles, who were mostly in their thirties.

Brigham Young had called for a public meeting tomorrow so that the members could begin to consider whom they would support as their new leader. That would be followed by a special conference of the Church on August eighteenth. By that time the other members of the Council of the

Twelve Apostles would be in Nauvoo—Orson Hyde, William Smith, and John E. Page.

"More and more I'm impressed with Brigham Young," Willard said. "I liked what he said about the importance of seeking the mind and will of the Lord regarding who should lead the Church."

Wilford immediately thought of Brigham's remarks during the meeting. Elder Young had expressed one other key concern—ensuring the continuity of the keys of leadership in the event enemies of the Church were successful in hunting down and killing other Church leaders. Brigham had stated that Joseph and Hyrum Smith had been killed by the combined efforts of internal apostates such as William and Wilson Law, and outside opponents.

"I'm ready to give my life, too, if necessary," Brigham had said.

A stiff warm wind was blowing through the trees in the grove as Daniel Browett stood near the front of a massive crowd gathered to hear Church leaders speak on the subject as to whom should lead the Church. Elizabeth and Harriet were at his side, as was Hannah. Robert was still in bed, trying to recover from the devastating effects from the ague.

"It's good to see the Apostles home," Elizabeth said as Brigham Young rose to begin the meeting. "Despite the deaths of Joseph and Hyrum, we are in good hands."

"Brother Brigham looks healthy and confident," Daniel said.

"This mighty congregation makes me think of the days of King Benjamin in Book of Mormon times," Brigham began. His countenance seemed to reach infinity. "There was such a great congregation that the people couldn't hear. I hope all can hear me. We need your attention. We have important issues to deal with."

Brigham called on William W. Phelps to talk for a few minutes.

Afterward, Brigham spoke again: "For the first time in my life, and the first time in your lives, we are called on to walk by faith and not by sight. Our beloved Prophet is gone, and so is Brother Hyrum. They have sealed their testimonies with their blood. But I willingly, humbly, step forth to act in my capacity as senior member of the Quorum of Twelve Apostles."

Daniel bit down on his lip. This was an emotional time for him. With his right hand, he squeezed the hand of Elizabeth, and did the same to Harriet with his left hand.

Brigham was animate in his speech, drawing deep inside himself, projecting his voice to the crowd of many thousands. He immediately got to the heart of the matter. "I wish to speak of the organization of the Church. Sidney Rigdon was a counselor to Joseph. But where is Joseph? He is gone; he his now beyond the veil. If Sidney wants to continue as his counselor, then Sidney must go where Joseph is—beyond the veil."

Elizabeth turned to Daniel. Her voice was a low whisper. "I didn't think of it that way before, did you?"

Daniel returned a smile and a whisper. "Brother Brigham is right. The First Presidency has been dissolved."

"If you members of the Church want Sidney Rigdon to lead you, you may have him," Brigham was saying. "But I say unto you that the Quorum of the Twelve has the keys of the Kingdom of God on the earth. The Twelve now hold the keys to the presidency of the Church, and have power to ordain the man who will be chosen of God to be the next president. The members of the Church cannot choose that man; God must do it. You cannot appoint a man at your head. But if you want any other man to lead you, take him, and the rest of us will go our way and continue to build up the Kingdom of God."

Daniel gasped as Brigham's frankness. And Brigham was not done.

"Some think that Brother Sidney would not be honored if we do not choose him, as a former counselor to Joseph Smith, to be our leader. But if he does the right thing, he will not act against our decision. We must act together. The Prophet Joseph Smith has laid the foundation for this great work in the latter days, and we must build upon it."

"Amen to that," Daniel said in his low whisper.

Brigham went on to say that the same principle applied to Joseph's other counselor, Amasa Lyman. Lyman had been ordained an Apostle a year earlier, taking the place of Orson Pratt. When Orson Pratt was reinstated to his office,

Joseph Smith had solved the problem of having too many Apostles—thirteen—by placing Amasa in the First Presidency as a counselor, taking the place of William Law.

"Right now, who is the head of the Church?" Brigham asked, looking on the bright side. "It is no one man, it is a body of men. It is the Twelve. If one man or a thousand men break away and say they have the right to the shoes of Joseph Smith, I know they are imposters."

Daniel gulped, wondering what Brigham knew that he didn't.

Brigham yielded the stand to Amasa Lyman, who said that he supported what Brigham had just stated. William W. Phelps and Parley P. Pratt, who also voiced their support for the Twelve, followed him.

"It's our own fault that we have had wicked men arise in the city, because we have given them some support," Pratt said.

Daniel felt a cold chill of regret as he thought of William and Wilson Law, and the Higbees and the Fosters.

"Stop dealing with them, and they will go away with nothing," Pratt said. "I will not support them, and neither should you. Mobs and wicked men will cease when you cease to support them. I would rather die a natural death than to employ a wicked doctor to kill me."

Brigham Young rose again to sum up the meeting. "We of the Twelve are anxious to see how you, the congregation, feel about the situation. If you want Sidney Rigdon to lead you, vote for him. But if you don't intend to follow him, and support him as you did Joseph, then don't make a covenant to support him unless you intend to abide by his counsel. Same for the Twelve. Don't vote for us unless you intend to abide by our counsel."

*No doubt who I'm voting for when the time comes,* Daniel thought. He also thought of a handful of men who supported William Marks, the stake president, as the next Church leader. Another handful wanted the oldest son of Joseph; still others favored Stephen Markham, or Parley P. Pratt. *They just don't understand the keys of the priesthood,* Daniel concluded to himself.

"I want to know if this people will support the leadership of the priesthood," Brigham added. "If you build the House of the Lord, you will receive your endowments. If we do our best, but cannot finish the work on the temple, we will go into the wilderness and receive our endowments. But the work of the Lord will continue under the leadership of the Twelve."

Daniel thought of the wilderness and Joseph Smith's predictions that the Saints would someday have to remove to the Rocky Mountains.

Brigham called for the vote. "Do you want Sidney Rigdon to be the head of the Church, or do you want the Twelve to stand at the head? All in favor of the Quorum of the Twelve assuming the duties of the First Presidency, you may manifest it by holding up your right hand."

There was a swishing sound throughout the grove as Daniel joined thousands of other Saints in raising their right hands. Daniel glanced to his right and to his left, and behind him. He could not see one dissenting vote. He let his gaze take in Sidney Rigdon, seated behind Brigham. Sidney's eyes had narrowed and his face had reddened. But he sat in silence, still looking a bit arrogant.

Brigham was now in a mop-up mode. He pleaded with the Church membership to be faithful in the payment of tithing so that the construction on the temple could be properly funded. He recommended that Thomas B. Marsh be retained as president of the Nauvoo Stake and that the matter of choosing a patriarch to replace Hyrum Smith be left in the hands of the Twelve. "Had Samuel Smith lived, the position would have gone to him, in the patriarchal order of things."

There was another unanimous vote.

In a gesture of compromise, Brigham also recommended that Sidney Rigdon be allowed to sit in council with the Twelve, although he was not an Apostle, to guide the Church in all the work that must be done.

Daniel gave his vote.


CHAPTER NOTES

Details concerning the history of the Church during this time were taken from several sources, including *Wilford Woodruff's Journal,* Volume Two, pages 430-441.

# 78

FROM HIS WORKBENCH AT THE TEMPLE, Daniel saw his sister
Rebecca, approaching with her husband, Orson Hyde. The afternoon sun wa
a ball of brass that bore down relentlessly on the temple workers, turning thei
world into a sweltering, oppressive oven of heat. Wet, heavy air hung like .
pall over Nauvoo.

"I insisted that Orson come by and say hello to you," Rebecca said with
a wide smile.

Daniel tossed his hammer aside and shook hands with the Apostle tha
was his brother-in-law. "We've been expecting you. Welcome home. Whei
did you get here?"

"Last night, on the steamboat," Orson said, his red hair taking a tumbl
as he removed his hat. He wiped his brow. "I've been in meetings all day. Bus
times, I suppose."

"Tell him, Orson," Rebecca urged. She cast excited eyes at her husban
and then at Daniel.

"Elder Woodruff is going to return to England to preside over the mis sion there," Orson said. "The decision was reached the day before I arrived, actually. I just learned about it today." He also told Daniel of the Twelve's resolve to spread the gospel not only in Great Britain, but in all the world, and to fight wickedness in all forms.

Daniel's mouth fell open, basking in his newfound knowledge. It startled him to think that the Twelve would send one of their members on a foreign mission with all the turmoil going on in Nauvoo. "You're kidding!"

"Not in the least," Orson said. "He's scheduled to leave by the end of August."

Daniel gasped. That was only two weeks away. "Missionary work must be important." Rebecca looked as though she was glad it was not Orson going to England.

"And so is temple work," Orson added, letting his gaze rake the limestone walls of the temple. "You workers have made commendable progress in the four months I've been gone. I don't see how you can work in this heat. But I know the brethren hope that within a little more than a year it will be finished."

"That's what we think," Daniel said. He drank water from a canvas bag. "Unless more trouble comes."

"Do you expect it?" Orson asked, lifting an eyebrow.

"I'm not the one to ask, I suppose. The brethren know far more than I. But from my perspective things have quieted down a whole bunch. Maybe our enemies will back off now that Joseph and Hyrum are gone."

"I hope so," Rebecca said with weary resignation. "It was scary while you were gone, Orson."

"I know," Orson replied as he gave his second wife a little hug. Marinda was still in Kirtland and Mary Ann was at home.

"Where's Brother Harris?" Rebecca asked.

Daniel's face took on a sad look. "Sick with the ague. He hasn't been able to work at the temple and he's not much help at the farm, either."

Orson grimaced and shook his head. "Sorry to hear that. I hear you've moved out to your farm."

"Yep, and we like it there, too," Daniel said. "Elizabeth, Harriet, and Hannah will be excited to know that Elder Woodruff is returning to England. I'll bet they'll all have a letter or two to carry back with him."

"And maybe Brother Harris will, too," Rebecca added.

"I doubt it," Daniel predicted. "He'll let Elizabeth write to their brother. Robert's more intent on being a one-man vigilante committee."

Orson pulled a face, his curiosity aroused. "What do you mean?"

"If it weren't for the ague, he'd be on his horse, trying to find the murderers of Joseph and Hyrum."

Orson gave an audible snort. "I was going to volunteer to give him a blessing. Sounds like we'd better pray he stays so sick he has to stay in bed. We don't want a loose cannon out there riling things up again."

*No wonder my blessings and prayers haven't worked for Robert,* Daniel thought.


"What do you want me to say to John?" Elizabeth asked Robert. Her quill was filled with ink and writing paper lay on the table in Robert and Hannah's home. Robert sat with his face in his hands, elbows resting on the table, the ever-pale look still on his face.

"Tell him I could use him here to hunt a few people down," Robert replied, little beads of sweat evident on his brow. Truthfully, he thought little of his older brother these days.

"Get that off your mind," Hannah said as she swept the floor. She had just fed her children gingerbread and they had left a sprinkling of crumbs.

"It's the key to finding out what happened to Elias," Robert said, repeating his old claim. "Henry's never going to do anything about it."

Hannah went silent, sensing more trouble.

"I hate to tell John about all the awful news here in Nauvoo," Elizabeth lamented.

"I suppose by the time Elder Woodruff gets to England all the Church members will already know about Brother Joseph and Brother Hyrum," Hannah said, regretting the catastrophic events. "Mama will never come to

America now—she'll think it's too dangerous."

"And Sidney Rigdon is still challenging Brother Brigham's position as leader," Harriet said, thrusting her hands to her hips. "I think his lust for power is having the opposite effect. Everyone I know is more solidly behind the Twelve than ever before."

"I'll add his name to my list," Robert said, his hands still on his face.

Hannah slapped her husband on the shoulder. "He's not in the same category as Wilson Law."

"I'll just bloody his nose instead of break his arms and legs," Robert said, his voice growing more morbid.

"You're so sick you couldn't break a turkey drumstick," Hannah grumbled. "Go back to bed and grow up."

"Growing up is optional, growing old is mandatory," Robert countered. "When I grow too old to punch someone out I'd just as soon die."

"I would like you brethren not to sit on the stand today," Brigham Young told Orson Hyde and the other members of the Twelve. It was Sunday and Orson knew that Brigham's remarks today might likely be the clinching factor in gaining support from the few members who were wavering in their support. Nevertheless, Brigham had given Sidney every opportunity to remain in full fellowship, despite Sidney's stubbornness. Now there were rumors that George Miller and Lyman Wight were not going to support Brigham.

Orson gave Brigham a blank stare, waiting for further instructions. The sky was slightly overcast, a good sign. The crowd at the grove was expected to be in the thousands again and Orson didn't want them to suffer in the hot sun on another humid day.

"Disperse among the congregation and feel the pulse of the people," Brigham said. Earlier Brigham had told Orson and other members of the Twelve that he felt the spirit of Joseph had been with them ever since their arrival back in Nauvoo, but that it wasn't as good as having Joseph here in person.

Brigham was again bold in his address to the Saints, lamenting the rumors that certain Church leaders sought to lead away factions. "There is no man here that has any right to lead away one soul out of this city; there is no man who has any liberty to lead away people into the wilderness, unless it be by consent of the Twelve. I tell you in the name of Jesus Christ that if Lyman Wight or George Miller take a course contrary to our counsel, not acting in concert with us, they will go to their own destruction. And if men will not stop striving to be 'great and self-exalted,' and take a course against us, they will be damned; they will fall and not rise again."

Orson scanned the crowd. Every eye and every ear was glued to Brigham.

"I want you to distinctly understand that the Council of the Twelve is acting in the best interest of each family," Brigham continued. "We want you to stay here in Nauvoo, finish building the temple, and receive your endowments. Don't scatter. United we stand, divided we fall. It has been whispered that you might go into the wilderness with Brother Wight or Brother Miller and get your endowments there. But they cannot give an endowment. They do not have the authority. If we do not carry out the plan Joseph has laid, and the pattern he has given us, we cannot be endowed. Sink that fact deep in your heart that you may remember it!"

Orson blinked and blinked again. As Brigham said the word, "Joseph," Brigham began to look and sound like Joseph. Orson pinched himself, but Brigham still looked and sounded like the deceased Prophet.

Brigham was now talking about the importance of finishing the temple, paying a full tithe, the how to acquire personal revelation from the Holy Ghost. He then began talking about Joseph.

"The testator has always lived until now, but Joseph has sealed his testimony with his blood; his testament should now be put in force. While the testator lived the responsibility for the Kingdom was all in his hands, but now he is dead. There has been a great debt paid. There will be no need of more blood of the Saints being shed at present."

Orson took a deep breath, sighing in relief. The words were like music to him. He had worried about further bloodshed, but felt he could believe Brigham's words.

"But woe, woe, woe unto all who have shed the blood of the Saints, and the blood of Joseph and Hyrum," Brigham continued. "It must needs be that offenses come, but woe unto that man through whom they cometh."

Orson thought of men like William and Wilson Law.

"To those who want to leave Nauvoo, I say wait until the time comes," Brigham was saying now. "I will give you the key. North and South America is Zion. As soon as the temple is done, and as soon as you get your endowment, you can go and build up stakes throughout the land. But don't go in haste. Wait until the Lord tells you to go. The entire continent must be organized into districts, with elders called to preside over each district. The time has come when all things must be set in order."

Orson began to envision stakes and wards all over the United States, Canada, Mexico, and into Central and South America.

To Orson, Brigham's animate motions still reminded him of Joseph Smith. Brigham said, "The time has come for bickering to cease. There must be a strict order of things; we are no longer bound to harbor blacklegs, counterfeiters, and bogus makers. We know all about them. They have been in our midst long enough. I advise all the Saints to have no dealings with such men. Leave them alone. Let the ungodly dealers alone."

Brigham next struck out against doctors and lawyers. "They want you to believe that when you spell B-A-K-E-R it means cider or whiskey," he charged. "All ye lawyers, go away, and leave us alone. I ask all you Saints to cease to employ doctors, lawyers, and all other merchants who will empty your purse and then mob you. Store your grain in Nauvoo, for you will want it here to eat while you are building the temple. Be united as you build the temple. Do not turn a person away because he is an Englishman, Scotchman, Irishman, or from any other nation."

Brigham's next words shocked Orson even further.

"I'd rather pay out every cent I owned to build the temple and get an endowment. Then, if we are driven out, at least we have our endowments to take with us."

Orson pulled a face, wondering if those words were a harbinger of things to come. Was that a timetable that would prove to be a prophecy? Finish the temple, and then be driven from Nauvoo?

Next, Brigham related a dream he had. "I saw a fruit tree, and I went in search of the fruit. I soon discovered that some of the main branches of the tree were dead, those at the top. It seemed necessary to cut off those branches to save the tree. I told some others to help me cut them off, and they stepped onto a large green limb. They were afraid it would break, so I put my shoulder under it and held it up while they cut off those dead branches. The green limb cracked but it did not break. After the dead limbs were cut off, the tree healed and continued to grow just fine."

Orson knew what Brigham was saying.

"Brothers and sisters, the time has come to cut off the dead branches of the Church, that the good fruit may grow and the voice of the Lord can be heard again. Let us go and build Zion and the great temple of the Lord!"

Orson began to share what he saw and felt with Rebecca and Mary Ann as they walked home after the meeting.

"Did you notice the same thing that I did?" he asked the two women.

Mary Ann cast a knowing glance at her husband. However, Rebecca let a perplexed look cross her face.

"What do you mean?" Rebecca asked.

"Almost as soon as Brother Brigham opened his mouth, I heard the voice of Joseph Smith through him. His words went through me like electricity."

"Same thing with me," Mary Ann testified. Tears began to stream down her cheeks.

Orson said, "I kept pinching myself, asking if I were mistaken."

"Me, too," said Mary Ann.

"Brigham sounded just like Joseph," Orson said. "The voice was as familiar to me as the voice of you, Mary Ann, or you, Rebecca. Even Brigham's gestures were the same as Joseph's, and the very features of his countenance. Even the stature of Joseph."

Rebecca's look was still blank. "I don't know what you two are talking about."

Orson ignored Rebecca. "This tremendous feeling went through me, the thrill of conviction that Brigham Young is the man to lead the people."

"That's exactly how I feel," Mary Ann said. "I saw the same thing in Brother Brigham."

Rebecca twisted her head in confusion. "I certainly support Brother Brigham, but you two have been seeing things."

# 79

WILFORD WOODRUFF WAS AMAZED that everyone gathered at the John Benbow home east of Nauvoo had seen the same thing during Brigham's talk at the grove.

"That's what I saw and heard," Benbow said in a composed voice. His skin seemed to prickle in remembrance. "Brigham Young looked and sounded just like Joseph Smith. I'll remember it for as long as I live."

"It's a sign that we should unite behind Brother Brigham," Elder Woodruff said. It had been an inspiring event for him. He was at Benbow's home to say goodbye to Benbow and all the English converts who lived in the area. And goodbye to little eight-year-old Wilford, Jr., who was going to stay with the Benbows while Wilford and Phoebe served their mission in England.

One-by-one, the English immigrants shook hands with Elder and Sister Woodruff, testifying they saw the same thing at the grove, and wishing them Godspeed on their trip to England and success in the work there. Thomas Kington, Levi and Effie Ann Roberts, John and Sarah Cox, John Hyrum and Susannah Green, John and Mary Gailey, Dianah Bloxham, Hannah Harris.

Hannah handed to Wilford the letter she had penned to her mother. "I'm sorry to burden you with this," she said in a docile, placating tone.

Wilford accepted it with a smile and placed it in a leather satchel. "Comes with the territory. A hundred or so letters won't take up much space in a large trunk."

"Thanks," Hannah said. Then she gave Wilford a kiss on the cheek. "Deliver that to Mama, too."

"I will," he said in a vibrant voice. "How's Brother Harris? I hear he's got a bad case of the ague this summer, much like I did in the summer of 1840 when I left on my first mission to England."

"It's bad all right," Hannah said with a sad face. "The quinine reduces the fever, but the symptoms keep coming back. I've never seen him so discouraged."

"I'll have some time in the next two or three days," Wilford said. "I'll come by and give him a blessing."

Hannah was pleased. "Oh! Would you?"

"Which route are you taking?" Daniel asked Wilford.

"Probably the northern route," he responded, meaning Chicago, the Great Lakes, Detroit, and New York. "Going through New Orleans this time of year would be unbearable for heat and humidity."

"If you get to Cheltenham, say hello to my brothers," Daniel added. He handed Wilford a letter addressed to his brothers, Thomas, John, and William Browett.

Wilford smiled. "I remember the time we visited one of your brothers in Cheltenham when you took me there to catch the train to London."

"How long will you be in England this time?" Elizabeth asked.

"Probably two years," he answered. The brethren had not specifically said, but this was his guess.

"By that time we'll have the temple finished," Daniel said.

"I would hope so," Wilford said. "I would hope so."

Ten days later Hannah had all but given up on Elder Woodruff's promise to give Robert a blessing. But at five o'clock in the afternoon, as she was hanging out her wash with her young daughter, she saw three wagons loaded with baggage approaching.

In her shyness, Lizzy hid behind her mother's skirt. "Run inside and tell your father Wilford Woodruff is here," Hannah said. The eight-year-old girl scurried to the house.

"Sorry I've delayed this so long, but I've come to give Brother Harris a blessing," Wilford said as he stepped out of the wagon with Phoebe. Behind him, Dan Jones and his wife were stretching their legs near the second wagon. Jones had been set apart to serve in Wales, just as Joseph Smith had prophesied during their joint captivity in the Carthage Jail. Hannah also recognized Hyrum Clark and his wife. Several other brethren were with the five wagons, obviously there to help with the baggage and to drive the horses and wagons back to Nauvoo.

"We're grateful," Hannah said. "You must be on your way out of town."

"We hope to reach Chicago within a week," Phoebe said. "You'd think we'd get used to it as many times as we've been back and forth to New York, but I don't look forward to it."

Hannah was amazed at Phoebe's toughness. "When will you reach England?" she asked.

Phoebe turned her gaze to Wilford. "I suppose we'll spend Christmas on the ocean and be in Liverpool sometime around New Year's, the way Wilford thinks."

Hannah saw Robert stagger out the door. His dark hair was matted and his skin was pale. "I'll bring Elder Woodruff in, honey. He's here to give you the blessing."

Wilford motioned for Dan Jones and Hyrum Clark to accompany him.

"The roads leading out of Nauvoo might still be dangerous," Robert said to Wilford in an obviously weak voice. "I'll saddle up my horse and lead the way."

"You'll do nothing of the sort, silly man," Hannah said, pushing him out of the doorframe and into the parlor.

Hannah was surprised that Wilford was willing to sit and visit for a few minutes. He mentioned how pleased he was at the progress on the temple, that he and Phoebe had said a special prayer on top of the highest cornerstone just days ago. Robert promised to get back on one of the work crews as quickly as he felt better. Wilford talked about his mission assignment, mentioning that the Twelve had set him apart, with John Taylor as the spokesman. Brigham Young had given Phoebe a special blessing, and the three children accompanying them had also received blessings.

Phoebe told Hannah that she and Wilford had been given locks of hair from the heads of not only Joseph Smith, but from his brothers Hyrum, Samuel, and Don Carlos. They were gifts from Hyrum's wife, Mary Fielding Smith. That same day, Wilford had given a special blessing to Lucy Mack Smith, mother of the Prophet. Lucy was failing, Phoebe said, and the language of the blessing hinted that Phoebe and Wilford might never see her again in this life.

Tears welled up in Hannah's eyes again as she thought of the trials and tribulations the Smith family had endured. She couldn't imagine how Lucy Mack Smith was feeling, or Emma Smith.

"How many of the Apostles are going to England this time?" Elizabeth asked.

"Just me," Wilford answered.

"Good," Elizabeth said. "We need them at home."

Wilford chuckled. "You're not the only one who feels that way. There're a lot of good men who hold the office of seventy, so Brother Brigham is going to use them for extensive missionary work. Soon we'll have several quorums of the seventy."

Hannah wondered if someday her husband and Daniel would be called to that office in the priesthood. She had heard that the Seventies Hall was near completion in Nauvoo, and that it would be used as a missionary training center.

"We've learned a lot from the England experience," Wilford added. "The Twelve have the responsibility to bear off the kingdom in all the world. We'll be organizing more districts and conferences in the future. Brother Brigham along with Heber C. Kimball and Willard Richards, have divided North America into districts and will soon appoint a high priest over each district And we're going to call bishops to serve in the larger branches of the Church."

Robert sat in a chair slouched over, waiting for the blessing.

"Where's Brother Browett today?" Wilford asked.

Hannah was about to answer when Daniel burst through the door leaving a trail of wheat chaff. "I see my farm workers arrived," he joked. He had been cradling wheat all alone.

Wilford rose to give Daniel a warm embrace. "Sorry, but we're on our way to Chicago. We're here to give Robert a blessing."

"I'd appreciate a healing," Daniel said. "He hasn't been a bit of help around here since he went on his wild goose trip to Galena."

Robert turned his head in embarrassment. Daniel covered his mouth with a hand, suddenly aware of his error.

"Galena?" Wilford queried. "When?"

The room went silent.

Hannah watched as Wilford scanned the room. No one was willing to talk. Daniel was still holding a hand over his mouth looking at the floor. And Robert was fuming.

Elizabeth broke the ice. "My brother was on the *St. Croix* with you on the trip from Galena to Nauvoo."

"Well, I never saw you," Wilford said to Robert.

"I couldn't afford cabin class," Robert said sheepishly.

"And he was stretched out among the hogsheads and barrels, half sick and half hiding from you," Elizabeth said, glad the cat was out of the bag.

"Hiding?" Wilford asked. "Why?"

Robert hung his head.

"My brother went to Galena to find Wilson Law," Elizabeth said. "He's been on a one-man vendetta ever since the martyrdom, trying to find the murderers."

Robert drew on his reserve strength. "You all need to understand something. I think Wilson Law knows where Elias is. It's just something I feel. Besides that, didn't Elder Taylor and Elder Richards make a list of sixteen men they identified as the killers? And didn't the list include the Law brothers, the Fosters, and the Higbees? I'll bet all those men know something about Elias, too."

Wilford had a puzzled look on his face, so Robert and Hannah took turns telling about the disappearance of Elias.

When they finished, Wilford said, "Well I can't tell you not to look for Hannah's brother, but be careful. We think things have quieted down. Just don't give our enemies reason to start things up again. We're pressing the governor to find the killers and bring them to trial. Leave it in the hands of the law, Brother Harris. Do you understand?"

Robert gave Wilford a blank look.

"Answer Elder Woodruff, Robert," Hannah said. She clapped her hands together to get his attention.

"Yes, sir," Robert finally answered.

Wilford pulled a chair into the center of the room. "Sit here and I'll give you a blessing. Would you object if Brother Jones, Brother Clark, and Brother Browett stand in the circle with me?"

"Not at all," Robert answered.

Wilford handed Daniel a vial of consecrated olive oil. "You anoint and I'll seal the anointing."

Minutes later, when the blessing had been completed, the visitors went out the door to board the wagons.

"I just have one final question," Robert said to Wilford.

"What's that?" the Apostle asked.

"If Sidney Rigdon causes the Church any distress while you're gone, do I have your permission to run him out of town?"

Wilford laughed. "My prediction is that he'll soon leave on his own. But he'll probably cause a little trouble first. You behave."

Robert was astounded that he was already feeling much better. As he walked back to the house he began to reflect on the wording of the blessing he had been given. The wording was evidently on Hannah's mind, too, judging by her immediate comments.

"You'd better give up on your vendetta," she said.

"I suppose," Robert answered. Elder Woodruff had promised Robert that the men chiefly responsible for the murders of Joseph and Hyrum would be brought to trial. "But what about Elias?"

Hannah shrugged her shoulders. "I hate to give up, and I know that Mary never will. But more and more it seems to me that something dreadful happened to him and we'll never see him again."

# 80

*September 1844*

REBECCA WAS DISTRESSED and Daniel was at the end of his patience. Rebecca complained that Orson had to leave again, this time to get Marinda and bring her back to Nauvoo.

"You're a plural wife, Rebecca," Daniel had told her a hundred times. "You can't have Orson all to yourself."

Daniel was holding Rebecca's hand at the Nauvoo Landing while Orson said goodbye to Brigham Young, John Taylor, and Willard Richards. The Mississippi River was bathed in gorgeous fall sunshine. Daniel had another purpose to be in town. He had purchased a new seven-dollar plow from Hiram Kimball's foundry. Elizabeth was at the Kington farm; Sister Kington had just given birth to a daughter.

Rebecca's blue eyes were misty. "She left Nauvoo without Orson—why can't she leave Kirtland and come back alone?"

Daniel took a deep breath, exhausted at his sister's jealousy and immaturity. "He already delayed the trip once to support Brigham Young against Sidney Rigdon...you know that. And Brother Brigham has given him the assignment to warn the Saints in Kirtland and elsewhere to beware of Sidney."

Last Sunday, Orson had been one of the main speakers at the Sunday Church services at the grove. Again, thousands attended. A motion had been made at the meeting that Sidney Rigdon be cut off from the Church. Less than ten persons voted against the motion.

Sidney had gone off the deep end in Daniel's opinion. Rigdon's last sermon on the first of the month—ten days ago—had been a sad, complicated, animated, confused oration outlining millennial events through the final winding up scene. Strange, Daniel thought at the time, that he didn't give Church members much reason to throw their support behind him. Right after that, Sidney met privately with a few supporters and established his own leadership group. After he ordained a few men illegally, contrary to the order of the priesthood, and claimed a higher authority than the Twelve, Brigham Young and the Twelve had no choice but to take disciplinary action. Sidney had been excommunicated from the Church just yesterday.

Today, Sidney was leaving Nauvoo on the same steamboat as Orson.

"Sidney's just a silly old man," Rebecca wailed. "The danger is here in Nauvoo. Orson should stay here and take care of me."

"I'll take care of you," Daniel said. "Come and stay with Elizabeth, Harriet, and me for a while." Inwardly, Daniel admitted Rebecca had a lot to be concerned about, as did everyone in Nauvoo. Although victorious candidates that the Mormons had supported had taken office three days ago in Carthage, the outgoing county commissioners had pulled off an outrageous act. In anticipation of a trial for those who would ultimately be indicted for the murder of Joseph and Hyrum Smith, the commissioners had selected panel of twenty-three grand jurors—not one of them a Mormon! When that news reached Robert he had reacted in typical fashion, threatening to go to Carthage himself and straighten things out.

"No. Mary Ann will take over the entire house while I'm away. As soon as she has her baby, she'll get all the attention."

Daniel rolled his eyes. "Suit yourself."

The man had strutted into the Taylor home like a red rooster, but John Taylor took an immediate liking to him. John had never met an attorney from Jacksonville, Florida, but Murray McConnell fit the bill of a special prosecutor. He had a square jaw, deep-set green eyes, and a stocky build. John wondered how Governor Ford was able to attract a man like this to Illinois. Perhaps the Joseph Smith murder case was getting more national attention than John suspected.

"You feel up to this?" McConnell began.

John stretched his lanky frame up and out. His most painful injury was still his left hip where a ball had torn a large piece of his flesh away. There was also pain just below his left knee where another ball had struck a bone. His left wrist and forearm were healing, but still sore. His watch had stopped a fourth ball.

"I'd be most happy to tell you my story if it will help bring to justice those responsible for the death of Joseph Smith," John said. "Sit at my desk and make yourself comfortable."

"I'm curious about something," McConnell said as he sat down.

"Ask anything you'd like," John said

McConnell drew an affidavit out of a black leather satchel. "You've already sworn before Justice of the Peace Aaron Johnson that you have good reason to believe that Levi Williams and Thomas C. Sharp were involved."

"That's correct," John answered.

The newly appointed prosecutor dipped his quill in black ink. "Start from the beginning and tell me everything you know. Why are you Latter-day Saints treated with such hostility?"

For the first half hour, John tried to answer that question with his views on religious intolerance, block voting, Nauvoo Charter resentment, fear of the Nauvoo Legion, Masonic activities, Joseph's presidential candidacy, economic competition, the practice of plural marriage, apostate betrayal, the criminal element of anti-Mormon mobs, a national acceptance of mob violence and behavior, and the "Jacksonian democracy" that prevailed in the times.

"You may not have this as much in Jacksonville, where you're from, but there's a lot of lawlessness on the Illinois frontier," John said, his head shaking in sorrow. "People out here, unfortunately, are violence prone and Illinois i one of the most lawless states in the Union."

"Excuse me for asking, but why is it that some people say there are law-less men living right here in Nauvoo? If you profess to be people of God, why are there outlaws in your midst?"

John gave a lively little snort. "Unfortunately, we can't control who comes into the Church. We try, but if a person wants to deliberately lie and deceive us, unruly people get baptized and are received into our organization You have to remember, Mr. McConnell, we're the largest city in the state o Illinois. Lawless people are attracted to concentrations of population just because there is more opportunity. We try our best to weed out those outlaws but it takes time."

McConnell was making a lot of notes. "You mentioned something just a minute ago. What do you mean by a *Jacksonian* democracy?"

John suspected the prosecutor already knew, but he gave him his version "It's the belief that the majority opinion prevails over any law or even the con stitution. It's almost a 'mob-rule' belief. Around here—by that I mean Carthage and Warsaw—the lawless mob element held that it was popula public opinion that Joseph and Hyrum Smith be killed, and so they were."

"So Mr. Sharp and Mr. Williams—just to name two—feel justified ir murdering two Americans?"

"Yes, sir. You've got it right."

McConnell pulled a face for a few seconds and then smiled. "All right Mr. Taylor, let's get down to business. I have a pen and paper in my hand. need you to tell me the names of everyone you can positively identify who wa in that hallway shooting at you on the twenty-seventh of June, in the Carthag Jail."

John Taylor didn't flinch. "Some I cannot identify. There were a lot o men from Warsaw and Carthage. But I can identify seven. They are former residents of Nauvoo."

McConnell nodded. "Go ahead."

Taylor spoke slowly and enunciated clearly. "Wilson Law. William Law. Robert D. Foster. Charles A. Foster. Chauncey L. Higbee. Francis M. Higbee. Joseph H. Jackson."

"I have a warrant for your arrest."

The words startled Thomas Sharp. He had not expected Sheriff Deming to send a deputy so soon. Sharp reached to touch his chin, sorting out his thoughts, searching for words.

The deputy stood rigid. He held the warrant in his hand.

Sharp stood, surprised that he stood an inch higher than the young deputy. The deputy looked unsure of himself. "Who signed the warrant?" he asked.

"Justice of the Peace Aaron Johnson," came the answer.

"But he's from Nauvoo," Sharp snapped.

"That's where I'm to take you. Justice Johnson is acting on direction from Governor Ford and Sheriff Deming."

"They sent a boy to do a man's job," Sharp hissed, intending to break the young man's will. He could see beads of sweat collecting on the deputy.

"It's my duty," the deputy said. His voice remained light and crisp.

Sharp laughed. "Nauvoo? Are you kidding?"

The young deputy had a pistol in a holster. He placed his right hand on it.

"If my friends here in Warsaw say 'go,' I'll go. You understand?"

The deputy looked puzzled.

Sharp continued the staring match. He believed he had sufficient community support to resist with impunity any writ issued in Hancock County. "If we walk outside together, and I put up any kind of fuss at all, there'll be a hundred men running to assist me."

"You're exaggerating," the young deputy replied.

"Try me."

The deputy's balance seemed to falter a bit. "Sheriff Deming may have to arrest you in person."

Sharp cursed loudly. He told the deputy to take the warrant and stuff it up Deming's nose.

Robert and Daniel's farm bordered the road that led from Springfield and Carthage to Nauvoo. The two men were harvesting corn when Governor Ford passed by in a carriage, escorted by armed militia.

"He's got to be awfully embarrassed that his attempts to arrest Thomas Sharp and Levi Williams have failed," Robert said. He glared at the cloud of dust the horsemen had made. To him, Governor Ford was a paradox. In his opinion, the Governor had been part of the conspiracy that resulted in the arrest of Joseph and Hyrum. But Ford was now trying to save his political hide. If war broke out between Mormons and non-Mormons, he would go down as the worst governor in the history of the state. Ford was in a no-win situation, of sorts. He was disliked by the Mormons and hated by the men who actually killed the Prophet. The anti-Mormons all across the state were belittling the governor for using state funds to prosecute the killers of Joseph and Hyrum.

"I hope you're not thinking of trying to collect the reward he's posted," Daniel said, casting a suspicious glance at his brother-in-law. Notice of the reward had been posed in two neighboring newspapers. Ford wanted not only Sharp and Williams arrested, but also Joseph H. Jackson, a renegade Mormon.

"What can two hundred dollars buy nowadays?" Robert mused out loud. "A new wagon, a hundred dollars. A carriage, sixty. We could use a new hand cart, a grain cradle, wheelbarrow, another horse, and a pair of oxen. Think what six hundred dollars would buy if I captured all three of them."

"The curse of the ague will return if you start chasing after the men you think killed Joseph and Hyrum again," Daniel joked.

"I'll bet by now writs have been issued for the arrest of Wilson and William Law, and the Fosters and the Higbees," Robert speculated, letting his imagination run wild. He started walking toward the house.

"Where are you going?" Daniel asked.

"To lunch."

"It's not lunch time."

"It will be by the time I get to Nauvoo."

Against his better judgment, Daniel rode into Nauvoo with Robert. Governor Ford was in a private meeting with Brigham Young. While they waited the outcome, Robert suggested they visit Mary Eagles. They found her typically distraught and she asked what Robert planned to do to continue the search for Elias. Robert promised to do all he could, that he would question Henry again in a few days. Robert and Daniel timed their return to the Masonic Hall just right. Bishop George Miller was looking for volunteers to furnish and deliver boats to the governor.

"Governor Ford wants to use the boats to convey him and the militia to Warsaw under cover of night," Miller told Robert and Daniel.

"We volunteer to help," Robert said. "What's the plan?" Robert was also pleased to learn that Governor Ford had activated the Nauvoo Legion again, on an as-need basis to help with the arrest of those indicted.

Daniel gave a grim sigh. Robert slapped him on the back. "Perk up. It's the least we can do."

Robert, Daniel, and two dozen other men—most of them men who had worked for Miller in the Wisconsin forests—had no trouble locating five boats from people who lived along the river. They did it while Miller rode his horse to a point along the river where Ford and the militiamen were camped.

Miller returned just after dark, meeting Robert and the others at the Nauvoo Landing. "The governor's camp is three miles south, along the river. He's waiting for the boats."

Robert cast his eyes down the river. He had not been south on the Mississippi since his arrival three and a half years ago. Frogs croaked from the banks and crickets sang their songs. A lazy half moon peeked through scattered clouds. A warm breeze fluttered leaves in the trees. A year ago Robert and Hannah had danced on the deck of the *Maid of Iowa* while the steamboat was tied to the landing. This seemed like an easy job, delivering five boats three miles downstream. He wished he could accompany the militia and surprise Thomas Sharp and Levi Williams in their nightshirts.

The men in the first boat were jovial and singing an American folk song. Robert wished he had his violin. He could play the volunteers a few old English folk songs. He had a paddle in his hands instead. He dipped it into the water and helped keep the wooden boat close to the bank.

*Boom! Boom! Boom!*

Balls from muskets fired from the bank of the river splashed around the boats.

"What the…?" Robert said to himself.

*Boom! Boom!*

"Turn those boats around!" a voice from the bank commanded.

Robert squinted hard to make out a dark figure hiding in the trees. Then another, and another. He took a tight grip on his paddle, wishing it were a gun.

"Who are you?" a volunteer from the first boat yelled.

*Boom!*

"None of your business. Get those boats back to town and don't come back. The governor doesn't need them."

Daniel pulled on Robert's shirt. "Let's get out of here before they kill us. This is the last time I'm volunteering with you for anything."

Sheriff Minor Deming was furious. One minute he had Thomas Sharp and Levi Williams in his custody, and the next minute he did not. He rode into Nauvoo in the late afternoon, seeking Brigham Young. He found Brigham at the Mormon temple.

Deming was amazed at the beehive of activity at the temple. Dozens of stone masons were chipping away at limestone. Huge cranes were employed setting stones on top of what looked to be the very top. Carpenters were framing inside walls. All this despite his understanding that the Mormons were contemplating moving out west.

"I've got good news and bad news," Sheriff Deming said as he stood before Brigham, John Taylor, and Willard Richards.

"We're so used to bad news maybe you ought to give us the good news first," Brigham said, removing his hat.

Deming gave the three Mormon leaders a day-by-day, blow-by-blow account of the efforts to arrest Thomas Sharp and Levi Williams. Two days ago, on September twenty-ninth, Deming had joined Governor Ford and his three hundred troops at a camp in the vicinity of Warsaw. When he went to arrest Sharp and Williams with the governor and some troops, they found that the two men had slipped across the river to Alexandria, Missouri. Deming accompanied an angry governor across the river in a boat in the dead of night and led a raid on Sharp's camp near Churchville. For political purposes, Ford had three whigs accompany him on this expedition. The expedition came back empty-handed, but one of the Whigs—Colonel E. D. Baker—returned later in the night and made a secret deal with Sharp.

"What kind of secret deal?" Brigham asked.

"That Sharp and Williams would surrender themselves if they could be arraigned before Judge Thomas in Quincy rather than being taken to Nauvoo. And that the bail be reasonable."

Deming could see a thickening shroud of disappointment overwhelm Brigham, and also John Taylor and Willard Richards.

"I suppose you're going to tell us that Sharp and Williams are free again," John Taylor remarked.

"Sorry, yes. The judge set a nominal bail of two thousand dollars, which was met immediately. Sharp had nine of his friends pledge their goods, chattels, lands, and tenements."

Deming watched Brigham's eyes drop in disgust. The sheriff then did his best to explain all the legal maneuvering that went on. At first Judge Thomas held to the opinion that persons charged with a capital offense were not bailable. E. D. Baker, it turned out, had been retained as an attorney for Sharp, along with O. H. Browning. By having Sharp and Williams waive their right to a preliminary hearing, the judge let them execute a bond securing their later appearance before the circuit court, the next time it convened.

Brigham Young grimaced and shook his head sideways. "In three weeks?" The sheriff nodded, yes.

"Why didn't the governor do something about this?" Willard Richards asked, his uneasiness showing. "The whole county is on the brink of self-extinction again and our illustrious governor does nothing but strut his self-importance while bunched together with his political friends."

"Personally, I don't think he has the heart. Just about everyone that was in his company is against you Mormons."

"The whole thing is a farce," concluded John Taylor.

"What do we do now?" Brigham asked.

Deming's busy eyebrows arched. He knew the Mormon leaders understood that the struggle to obtain the arrest, indictment, and conviction of the murderers of Joe and Hyrum Smith had been inseparable from the struggle for control of Hancock County. Control of the county commission was key. This elected body chose the grand jurors who would determine whether the accused parties would be indicted, or formally charged. They would also select jurors who would actually hear the evidence and determine their guilt or innocence at the trial.

Deming said, "I'll be a busy man and so will the county commissioners. They'll have to select a grand jury. My officers and I will have to serve subpoenas to all the witnesses."

"How many witnesses do you think you'll have?" John asked.

"Two, maybe three dozen," Deming answered. "The most powerful witnesses will be you and Dr. Richards."

"And the trial will obviously be in Carthage," John said awkwardly.

"Yes, sir. That's the county seat."

"Brother Richards and I barely escaped with our lives. If we were to return, I fear we would be somehow murdered."

CHAPTER NOTES

The incident about the governor and the boats is taken from *The History of Illinois,* by Governor Thomas Ford (Chicago: S. C. Greggs & Co., 1854). It has been fictionalized, of course, to include Robert and Daniel. Bishop George Miller said that when he went to the governor's camp later that night the militia told him that the boats were no longer needed. Ford said in his book that the militia was infested with anti-Mormons.

# 81

## *October 1844*

ROBERT PICKED THE THIRD MONDAY of October to visit Henry again. That's because court week was beginning in Carthage. A grand jury had been convened to consider evidence of the murder of Joseph Smith—and to consider evidence against eleven members of the Church on the charge of inciting a riot in the destruction of the *Nauvoo Expositor*. Hannah had seen right through his timing. He had conveniently escaped volunteering to join a detachment of Nauvoo Legion troops formed to watch the eastern edge of the city during the proceedings at the courthouse.

"You can't fool me," she had said as he announced his plans days earlier. "You're pretending to look for Elias, but you just want to be where the action is."

"A lot of the people who were in Carthage when Elias disappeared will be in town again," he explained. "Sheriff Deming will have things under control. It's not as dangerous in Carthage as it was when Henry and I rousted around before."

Robert knew that Hannah couldn't argue much with his rationale, so he had left Sunday afternoon. As he rode the fifteen miles to Henry's cabin on Lawless, he reflected on the unusual October conference of the Church. A proclamation had been drafted to be sent to the Saints in the British Isles, naming Brigham Young president of the Church. The Council of the Twelve was sustained as having authority to act for the Church in place of the First Presidency. John Smith, Joseph Smith's uncle, replaced William Marks as Nauvoo stake president. And Brigham Young told Lyman Wight and George Miller that they were free to take members of the Church, known as the Wisconsin Pine Company, to Texas.

In two hours, Robert arrived at the Eagles Dairy. Henry, as usual, expressed his repugnance at seeing him again.

"You always seem to invite yourself," Henry said as Robert rode up. Henry had his head pressed against the flank of a brown cow, doing his milking.

Robert gave Henry a granite look. "I came to visit Elias. I thought maybe he just showed up today to help you do you're milking."

"You won't find anyplace to stay in town, so you'd just as well go home," Henry hissed. "It's court week."

"I brought my bedroll."

"All the trees around here hate Mormons."

Robert gazed at the groves of aspen that were turning orange and golden and shimmering with the lightest breeze. There were cottonwoods that looked like burnished silver. "That cottonwood right over there looks fine to me. It doesn't smell like you do."

By now, Katherine had made her way to the milking barn, her daughter trailing behind. "You'll sleep on the floor in the parlor, not out here," she said.

Robert marveled at her courage. When he first met her, Katherine didn't dare say "boo" around Henry, whose personality remained abrupt and prick-y.

Over dinner of baked squash, boiled string beans, fried potatoes, cheese and milk, Robert forced Henry to rehash the final hours with Elias. This time Henry mentioned that he and Elias had stood in the trees not too far from the painted men who killed Joseph and Hyrum. It was as though a new revelation struck Robert.

"If that's true, you ought to testify at the trial," he said.

"One Eagle inside that courtroom will be enough," Henry grumbled.

"What do you mean?"

"Old dish nose here got her a job at the courthouse. That new Mormon county commissioner—what's his name?"

"George Coulson," Katherine answered without hesitation.

"Coulson's hated by everyone else, but the Mormons sure like him."

A torrent of questions was running through Robert's mind. "Coulson helped get you a job? What kind of job?"

Henry looked put out. "Special deputy to the sheriff, Minor Deming, but in reality a clerk of sorts. She has to be at the grand jury hearings every day to keep a record for the sheriff."

"What's this I hear about not one Mormon getting seated on the grand jury?" Robert asked, feeling his blood warm.

A sly smile crossed Henry's face. "A good development, considering two out of the three commissioners are Mormon."

"Let's hear your version, Katherine," Robert said, trying to ignore Henry. Henry rose from the table and went outside, saying he had more chores to do.

Katherine surprised Robert with her astuteness. "There're two reasons why that happened. The clerk of the court, Mr. Thatcher, is now the ranking anti-Mormon in the county. He's been opposing the Mormons at every point. He didn't have any vote in the selection of the jurors, so he's been exerting his influence in other ways." She started clearing the table, so Robert helped.

"Such as?"

"He helped circulate printed invitations for the Grand Military Encampment, knowing that would serve to intimidate all the Mormons, including the commissioners. Lots of folks around here would welcome a civil war in Hancock County, thinking it's inevitable if they're going to settle the Mormon question once and for all."

"So that worked? The commissioners were intimidated?"

"I think so, but reason number two carries a lot of weight, too."

Robert was reeling was disgust. He threw dirty dishes into a metal tub.

"The Mormon commissioners are going out of their way, in my opinion, to cultivate support from the people you and I would consider middle-of-the-roaders, or uncommitted about the Mormon question."

"So by not placing Mormons on the grand jury, you think they are gaining brownie points from those people?"

"It makes a lot of sense."

Robert snorted. "Not to me. If I were one of the commissioners, I'd make sure every single one of the grand jury members were Mormon."

"Every single one?"

Robert rethought for a moment. "Well, at least I would stack it proportionately to the population. Out of twenty-three jury members—if they did it that way—how many would be Mormons, and how many would be non-Mormons?"

Katherine paused to do a quick calculation. "Let's use the election results as our guide. Commissioner Coulson received more than eighteen hundred votes, and the non-Mormon candidate got just over eight hundred. That's a majority of more than two to one."

"So there should be at least fifteen or sixteen Mormons on that grand jury," Robert concluded.

"That's right," Katherine said.

"Are the jury members rabid anti-Mormons?"

"Not in my opinion. The commissioners tried to select people who are in the middle."

"Such as?"

"Abram Lincoln, Abraham Lincoln's brother. He's a justice of the peace in Fountain Green. George Walker, another justice of the peace in Walker Township. Thomas Owen, a Baptist minister. Abram Golden, a non-Mormon officer in your Nauvoo Legion."

"Do you work for the non-Mormon clerk, Mr. Thatcher?"

"Nope. I was hired by Sheriff Deming as a special deputy to his office. My job is to write down the proceedings of the trial so they can be compared with those made by Mr. Thatcher's office."

Robert was tempted to ask her if the sheriff needed any more help.

Carthage looked more festive Monday morning to Robert than the time a traveling circus came to Nauvoo last year. Farmers and other citizens from Fountain Green, LaHarpe, St. Mary's, Plymouth, Augusta, Chili, Knowlton, Montebello, Appanoose, and Warsaw were streaming into town by wagon, carriage, on horseback, and on foot. Most of them were armed, fearing an outbreak of hostilities. Those who had already arrived were trading horses, swapping stories, learning of the news, and arguing about the impact of the August elections on Hancock County.

The county was the largest in Illinois at around twenty-two thousand inhabitants and it seemed to Robert that about half of them were crowded into Carthage, which still had a population of only a few hundred. Hamilton House was jam packed with American aristocrats, a lot of them politicians from Springfield and newspapermen from all over. That's where the circuit judge had slept and the lawyers representing the prosecution and the defense.

"See?" Henry said from his wagon box as they drove into town. "You're lucky Katherine let you in the house to sleep."

Henry was right. Robert could see makeshift beds in wagon boxes, on haystacks, and on porches. Dusty cavalcades of new visitors were yet trailing into town.

Wearing a new cabbage-green cotton dress trimmed with lace she had made for herself with her first paycheck, Katherine disappeared into the courthouse. Official-looking men dressed in tall black hats, tailcoats, and biled shirts with limp cotton collars rolling over their black neckerchiefs rambled toward the courthouse, too. Robert wished he could go in. The drama inside the two-story brick building today promised to be better than that of any the atre, concert hall, or opera. The judges and the lawyers were the stars—their wit and eloquence sure to bring a chorus of "oohs" and "ahs" from everyone inside. What happened in there in the next few days would be told time and time again in episodes in the cabins, schoolhouses, barrooms, and social gatherings of the county and state.

Robert knew it was fruitless to look for Wilson Law or any of the other Mormon apostates. If they were smart, they would be as far away as China. It was up to the grand jury to indict them. He wondered if Wilson and his brother were still in Hampton, defrauding the people there.

He and Henry had to wait to be seated inside the tavern at the Hamilton House. When they were, Robert found himself listening to men surrounding a nearby table talk about the very first court term in the new courthouse, when the only man ever hanged in Hancock County had been found guilty. He was a twenty-one-year-old Irishman who had been employed as a deckhand on a steamboat; he had killed a man in a drunken brawl in Schuyler County just east of Hancock County. A lawyer named Abraham Lincoln, who had been riding the circuit that spring, had defended the Irishman. After Lincoln failed to have the judgment set aside, the Irishman was hanged on a gallows in the center of a natural amphitheatre about a mile southeast of Carthage, where a large audience could be accommodated.

Carthage hadn't had a murder trial since the Irishman's hanging. Circuit judges mostly dealt with less serious crimes such as the stealing of livestock or household effects, riot, adultery, fornication, and assault.

While Henry consumed a few jiggers of whiskey, Robert closed his eyes. He visualized Thomas Sharp, Levi Williams, and all the Mormon apostates like Wilson Law hanging at another set of gallows southeast of Carthage.

He wondered what was going on inside the courthouse. It was almost too abhorrent to dwell on.

Katherine looked at the clock on the wall. It was nearly four o'clock and she was dead tired. The day had started at ten o'clock as she suspected it would. Judge Jesse B. Thomas of Quincy appeared to be unperturbed by anything, including the sight of armed spectators and the fact that one of the twenty three jurors had failed to show up. He quickly issued a court order fining Samuel Marshall, a Carthage politician and former clerk here in Hancock County, the sum of five dollars.

Slowly and methodically, every other juror was interviewed and cross examined by both the prosecution and the defense. Judge Thomas, a few minutes ago, had excused three jurors for cause, two of them because they had been summoned as witnesses in the Joseph Smith murder case. That being done, the remaining nineteen jurors were being sworn in. To function under state law, he only needed twelve.

"I keep hearing reports that the anti-Mormons are going to prevent this court from convening," Judge Thomas had announced as he began. "Everyone who is of that opinion is mistaken. Law and order prevails in Carthage."

Wedged between her employer, Sheriff Deming, and another deputy, Katherine felt a compelling reason to smile. She liked the sheriff and in her opinion he was doing an excellent job.

A rumbling swept through the crowd when a man who had rushed up the stairs told a guard there was cause for concern. Soon, everyone in the courtroom was buzzing. Katherine found out that a rumor was spreading throughout town that a portion of the Nauvoo Legion was camped out of town, accompanied by a large group of Indians.

"Do you think it's true?" Katherine asked the sheriff.

"I know the Legion part is, but the part about the Indians? Hogwash."

Deming told Katherine that a man named General Charles C. Rich had been authorized by Governor Ford to camp outside town, "just in case."

By now, the ringleaders in the courtroom were demonstrating in a violent, warlike manner. Katherine shuddered as they vowed to kill Mormons on site.

Abruptly, however, Judge Thomas adjourned the court. "It appears we cannot have order in this room until we know whether or not the Mormons and the Indians are in the vicinity."

Katherine was then struck by the strange sight of a group of armed spec tators surrounding the judge, demanding to talk with him. As she walked out of the courtroom she had the sinking feeling that the spectators were taking control.

Robert had spent the day nosing around about Elias but he found no one who knew anything, or would admit to it. Henry swore up and down that he could not identify any of the men in the grove that day because he was a little too far away and they had their faces disguised with mud and gunpowder. Despite the fact that he felt Henry still wasn't telling him the whole truth, Robert was amazed how the Elias tragedy had sort of bound him and Henry together for the first time in their lives. They had gone back to Henry's house for an hour to do some chores and were just returning to town when the court adjourned.

"What's all the fuss?" Robert asked Katherine when they saw her walking toward home.

"They think the Nauvoo Legion is on its way with two thousand Indians," she said laughing.

Robert stared at her in disbelief. "How many Indians?"

"The first reports we heard in the courtroom was about fifty, and then it grew to a hundred. Right now it's swelled to two thousand. I'd imagine by dark it'll be ten thousand."

Robert and Henry exchanged perplexed looks. Henry began to laugh with his two missing teeth showing. "The only Indians around here are that little band of Potawatamis on their way to Iowa to hunt muskrat." Henry laughed again.

Robert watched as swarms of anxious armed men cast their eyes up and down the streets and out to the countryside, looking for the thousands of Indians. By now, he concluded, these anti-Mormons probably suspected that every member of the Nauvoo Legion—all five or six thousand of them—were out there somewhere crawling on their stomachs, creeping through the tall grass, about to attack and kill every living soul in and around Carthage.

It gave him a good laugh, but only for a short time. He knew how volatile the situation was and how little it would take for these devil-followers to actually start shooting.

"Come on, Henry," he said. "Let's take Katherine home. Then we'll ride out and talk to the Legion. I think I know where they'll be."

Robert and Henry rode horseback four miles west of Carthage and easily found the Legion camped at Crooked Creek. The yellow-gold sun was creeping toward the horizon. A guard recognized Robert and let them pass. The detachment was composed of one hundred fifty men and thirty wagons under the leadership of Major General Charles C. Rich.

Rich welcomed Robert into the camp and immediately questioned him about the proceedings inside the courthouse and why the increase of activity of riders from Carthage. His guards had turned aside three or four unrecognized men. Four of Robert's old neighbors were in the detachment, Richard Slater, Robert Pixton, Levi Roberts and John Cox.  When Robert told Rich and the troops about the Indians, everyone roared with laughter.

"These are cheap accommodations," Robert joked as he scanned the bedrolls laid on the ground. "Carthage has a nice hotel. The steel welcome mat is out."

"We'd be murdered in our beds," Rich answered, not joking.

The next day the sheriff and Katherine were allowed in the jury room with the prosecutor, William Elliot. Most of the time was devoted to hearing witnesses against Mormons charged in destroying the press. Katherine, like the rest of the city, was largely disinterested. None of the Mormons charged, including Porter Rockwell, Jonathan Dunham, and W. W. Phelps, did little to protest the indictment. John Taylor, as expected, did not even show up to defend himself. At day's end, Judge Thomas allowed all the indicted Mormons to return to Nauvoo to "allay the excitement around here."

The charges for the murders of the Prophet Joseph Smith and his brother, Hyrum, proved more complicated. Katherine took notes Tuesday afternoon, Wednesday, Thursday, and Friday. Seventeen persons testified before the grand jury and several statements were read into the record, including statements from John Taylor and Willard Richards.

Robert stayed in Carthage the entire time, still asking about Elias, disturbed over the easy indictments against Porter Rockwell and the other Mormons, and fuming constantly that the apostate Mormons were not included as possible defendants. In Robert's mind, they were just as guilty. They may not have been the men who pulled the trigger, but it was widespread knowledge that Wilson Law and the others had been responsible for the illegal arrest of Joseph and Hyrum, and met regularly with men such as Sharp, Aldrich, Williams, Davis, and Grover.

It wasn't until Saturday that Katherine emerged with news that the judge had accepted signed indictments. Henry and Robert immediately drove her home, asking questions. She said that at first the grand jury voted on the entire sixty defendants.

"Good," Robert said, "they all ought to be hung."

"Sorry," Katherine explained. "The evidence was judged to be so inconclusive that very few jurors voted to indict them all."

Robert asked the big question. "So tell me, how many did they indict?"

"The jury struck ten names off, the ones with the least evidence. That made it fifty defendants, but time and time again the jurors failed to get the minimum votes for a lot of the defendants. So they just kept voting, and kept considering the evidence. It was tedious. I'm tired."

"Out with it—how many?" Robert snapped, out of patience.

Katherine was silent for a long moment, almost afraid to answer. "Nine," she said.

Robert scoffed derisively. "Nine? Only nine?"

Henry looked straight ahead, keeping out of the conversation. A lazy afternoon sun was setting in the direction of Nauvoo.

"Give me the names," Robert demanded.

Katherine knew them by memory. She spit them off alphabetically. "Mark Aldrich, Nathan Allen, Jacob C. Davis, William Gallaher, William N. Grover, Thomas C. Sharp, William Voras, Levi Williams, and John Wills."

After spending all week in Carthage, Robert knew quite a bit about these nine men.

Mark Aldrich was the oldest of the nine at age forty-two. He was a land speculator, one of the four original developers of Warsaw, its first postmaster, and served in the state legislature. But his land development schemes had brought him into direct conflict with the Church when he made an agreement with Mormon leaders to have English immigrants settle on a new section near Warsaw, called Warren. Some two hundred Mormons settled there, but moved out after Aldrich raised the prices of everything including flour and firewood. Aldrich took out fake bankruptcy soon afterward, using friends as strawmen.

Nathan Allen was a local rowdy who had been a member of Captain Grover's Warsaw Cadets at the time of the murders. He was tall, six feet two inches.

Jacob C. Davis was an Illinois state senator. He claimed to be a lawyer but no one had ever found any evidence of a law degree. But in 1842 Judge Stephen A. Douglas had appointed him circuit court clerk. Earlier in the year he had tried to get the democratic nomination for Congress, but the nomination went to the incumbent, Joseph P. Hoge. Davis blamed the Mormons for his loss of the nomination. Unmarried at age thirty-three, he held the rank of captain in the militia and captained the Warsaw Rifle Company, which consisted of four officers and sixty-five men.

Either Joseph or Hyrum Smith had shot William Gallaher in the face during the martyrdom. An ugly scar still marred his face terribly. He was also young, and came to Illinois from Mississippi. He was one of the first men at the door of the jail and probably fired the shot that killed Hyrum, and he shot Joseph as he ran to the window.

William N. Grover was the youngest at age twenty-six, married, but had no children. He was also a captain in the militia, in charge of the Warsaw Cadets that had four officers and forty-two men. Grover loved military service and was insanely jealous of the Nauvoo Legion.

Thomas C. Sharp by far was the best known of the nine men, in Robert's opinion. He was editor of the *Warsaw Signal*, a lawyer, and a previous justice of the peace. Only thirty-one years of age, he was born in New Jersey, the son of a noted Methodist preacher. He was the most hated and most feared anti-Mormon in the country. It seemed to Robert that Sharp must have devoted his entire life to slandering, lying against, and misrepresenting the Mormons. There was one consolation, however. As a businessman, Sharp was a failure. His newspaper enterprise had lost money to the point that the original owner took it back for a while in 1842 and Sharp had to resort to farming. Other anti-Mormons came to his rescue, however, because they needed the poisonous newspaper to continue its attacks against the Mormons.

William Voras was known as a half-grown hobbledehoy from Bear Creek and appeared in court still trying to recover from a shoulder wound suffered from a gunshot fired by Joseph Smith. He had the temerity to wear a new suit of clothes to court, given to him as a gift by the citizens of Green Plains for his part in killing Joseph and Hyrum.

Levi Williams, thirty-four, was a farmer, trapper, cooper, and part-time Baptist minister. He was married, had five children, and was a colonel in the Illinois militia. He had served two terms as a county road commissioner and lived in Green Plains. In 1843, Williams headed a mob that forcibly, at gunpoint, kidnapped a Mormon named Daniel Avery and his son. Williams threatened them with knives, bound them in chains, imprisoned them in Missouri on false horse-stealing charges, and finally released them for fear of retribution. Since then, Williams had been involved in many other mob actions. He hated the Mormons because they thought they ruled the county, and elected whom they pleased, and thought that killing Mormons was the only way to get rid of them.

John Wills, in Robert's estimation, was nothing more than a young Irish immigrant who had joined the anti-Mormon mob merely because he loved drinking and brawling. He had also been shot in the arm during the martyrdom.

After Robert raced these names through his mind, he asked Katherine more questions.

"The trial is not going to be until next May?"

"That's right," Katherine answered, "but attorneys for the nine defendants wanted an immediate trial."

"Why immediate?"

"Sheriff Deming calls it a 'pre-trial advantage;' their lawyers wanted to get on with it before the defense had a chance to prepare."

"But the judge didn't grant it..."

"Mr. Murray McConnell objected. Most of the witnesses had already left town. And no legal apparatus had been executed for them to appear at a later trial. On top of that, the state's attorney, Mr. William Elliot, had left, too."

Robert was stunned. He shook his head, seeing the hand of Satan in all this. "What a mess."

"That doesn't even begin to describe the mess. All you need to know is that the trial won't be until next May."

"Do you think these nine men will be found guilty?"

"Sheriff Deming says it's a lock."

Robert felt an angry chill. "But what about the other sixty men? They're guilty, too!"

Katherine shrugged her shoulders as she stepped out of the wagon. She looked weary as she trudged toward the Eagles cabin.

Robert followed her, throwing his hands in the air in an act of desperation. "And what about Wilson Law and the other apostates? They were on a list, I know they were. It's widespread knowledge. Both Willard Richards and John Taylor identified them. Governor Ford issued writs against them last month."

"I don't know, I just don't know," Katherine said as she collapsed on a chair.

"Why does it always seem that it's up to me?" Robert screamed. "Do I have to find them? Do I have to hunt them down one at a time?"

Henry stepped into the cabin, a pained look on his face. "Why all the yelling?"

"You wouldn't understand, Henry," Robert said as he ground his teeth. He felt difficulty breathing. "Let's go milk your cows. Then I'm going home."

# 82

*November 1844*

DANIEL FELT BAD FOR ORSON HYDE THAT Rebecca chose not to be at the Nauvoo Landing when Orson arrived from Kirtland with Marinda and his two daughters, Laura and Emily. Mary Ann was there, and so were Elizabeth and Harriet. The Nauvoo weather was chilly and the edges of the river showed traces of ice at mid-day.

"Won't be long until the steamboats quit coming up this far," Orson said as he shook hands with Daniel. "I don't see Rebecca—is she all right?"

"Just temperamental as usual," Daniel replied as he helped with the baggage. "How was life with Sidney Rigdon?"

Orson tossed his head. "I'll take temperamental any day of the week compared to volatile, difficult, excitable, and explosive."

"Tell me about it," Daniel said. "We've heard just bits and pieces."

"And you'll have to tell me about the indictments. I've heard the same, just bits and pieces. How about at dinner tomorrow night? That is, unless Brother Brigham has plans for me."

Daniel brought both Elizabeth and Harriet to the dinner. Marinda, Mary Ann, and Rebecca teamed up to cook a celebration of garden vegetables from the cellar—some fresh, some cooked—along with roast pork, pickles and canned pears. Rebecca looked happy in a new blue dress, but Daniel knew that underneath she was still miffed at her position as second wife in a polygamous family.

Orson expressed disappointment in the number of murderers arrested in Carthage, but relieved that at least a few men would stand trial for the murder of Joseph Smith. Like Robert, he couldn't understand why the Mormon apostates were not indicted. He had discussed this with other members of the Twelve in a meeting earlier in the day.

Daniel also told Orson that Robert Harris had sold another portion of his lot in Nauvoo to a man named Oren Jefferds for two hundred dollars.

"What's he going to do with the money?" Orson asked. "Buy some more farm ground out in your area?"

There was a low chuckle from Daniel. "That would be a good idea. I just hope he doesn't buy a new gun and go after those apostates."

"In a way, I don't blame him," Orson replied.

"Now tell me about Sidney," Daniel said as he dived into a serving of apple pie.

"I tried to befriend him all the way to St. Louis while we were on the steamboat together," Orson began. "We had been through a lot together, and we talked about old times a lot. He seemed to listen patiently, but with a lot of aloofness. In the end, he said that his course was marked out before him, and he was going to pursue it."

Rebecca filled his plate again, adding an extra helping of Orson's favorite serving—cooked red beets.

"I was surprised to find that the members of the Church in St. Louis already knew of his excommunication. Word travels fast, even out here on the frontier. I preached that night, and even invited Sidney. But he declined. I found all the members there very loyal to the Twelve and I reported that in a letter to Brigham Young.

"I preached again on Sunday, but on Monday I discovered that Sidney had begun his revolution, so to speak. He had an article published in the newspaper there, accusing the Church—and expressly me—of trying to blackmail him. I hurried and wrote an article to refute him, and the paper published it. The sparring match continued when we reached Ohio. I went to Kirtland, of course, and he went to Cincinnati. From there he wrote articles that appeared as far away as New York City. You wouldn't believe the whole length of his lies and slander. His tirade of abuse and slang is still going on. He'll probably never give up, but fortunately few people are attracted to him."

Daniel felt relieved at that final statement. "It's good to have you home again, isn't it Rebecca?"

From the other end of the table she nodded her agreement.

"It won't be for long."

"What do you mean?" Rebecca asked.

"Brother Brigham wants me to leave right away. I've been assigned to raise money and buy more supplies for the temple. We need iron, steel, nails, oil, paint, and turpentine."

A spasm crossed Rebecca's face. She excused herself and went upstairs.

Governor Ford followed Sheriff Deming up the main stairwell of the capitol building to the entrance of the Senate Chamber. "I'll wait here," Ford told the sheriff.

With his winter coat still bundled around him, Deming set his jaw. "This won't be fun, but it's got to be done."

Jacob C. Davis, state senator from Warsaw, never saw Deming coming. Davis was seated in the third row, tending to minor legislative business. It was December twenty-sixth, the day after Christmas. To Ford's eyes, Davis seemed bored almost to the point of distraction. Perhaps he was thinking of circuit court time in May, when he would have to face a jury trial for the murder of Joseph Smith.

Ford could hear Deming's voice clearly. It echoed throughout the chamber. Ford cringed. He knew Jacob's fellow senators wouldn't like what was about to happen.

"Mr. Davis," Deming said slowly. "I'm placing you under arrest for the murder of Joe Smith."

Jacob's jaw dropped a mile. "Deming, get out of here. We're in session."

Deming drew his pistol and pointed it at the politician's chest. "You're under arrest."

The state senator who occupied the speaker's stand cut short his remarks. The chamber went silent and every eye turned on Deming and Davis.

Ford hid himself by going around the corner. He had learned to despise Davis, who was acting more and more like a Whig every day. Ever since Davis had lost his bid for Congress—losing in the convention to Joseph P. Hoge, the incumbent—Davis had turned weird. In past weeks Davis had been spearheading a movement to investigate Ford's anti-wolf hunt campaign. "Wolf hunt" was a term used to describe the anti-Mormon terrorist activities. The anti-Mormons had even threatened to kill Deming and anyone else who stood in their way.

"I'm not going," Ford heard Davis say.

There was a sound of tremendous struggle. Ford peeked around the corner again and saw Deming dragging the smaller Davis up the aisle. The chamber was now in an uproar, but no one was assisting Davis.

One voice was heard above the rest. "There'll be an investigation—don't worry Jacob."

"Where're you taking him?" another senator asked.

"Back to Carthage," Deming said, fuming. "You'll find Mr. Davis in the Carthage Jail, where Joe Smith was murdered."

Ford slipped around the corner again. This murder trial business was getting serious. He had already been served a subpoena to appear at the May trial. So had a lot of other people, including the Mormon Apostle John Taylor.

"Happy birthday to both of you," Elizabeth chimed over two cakes dotted with candles—thirty-three for Robert and thirty-two for Daniel. As she lit the candles she led her little choir into a chorus of "Happy Birthday." The choir—Hannah and her four children, Martha, Harriet, and Rebecca—sang with happy faces.

Daniel accepted the birthday song with a reciprocating glad countenance.

Robert did not. His face was drawn up into a scowl. All he wanted to talk about was the fact that the legislature had repealed the Nauvoo Charter.

"What good is the Nauvoo Legion now?" Robert asked through a mouthful of ginger cake. The repeal placed the Legion directly under the control of Governor Ford and stripped the city of most of its independence, especially limiting the powers of the municipal court.

"Let's talk about a happier subject," Elizabeth countered.

"Well it won't be about Orson," Rebecca sneered. "He's never home."

Robert wouldn't let go. "I'd like to be in Springfield right now. I'd find every Democrat and every Whig who voted for that crazy repeal and start breaking arms until they reversed it. And I'd do more than break arms of the Anti-Mormon Party members."

Elizabeth sighed in frustration. It seemed that her brother would never change. He always threatened to use brute force to get his way. But she knew it was a fact that a leader of the Anti-Mormon Party, Jacob C. Davis of Hancock County, had led the charge for the appeal of the charter. Davis, a state senator, had already been arrested on the Joseph Smith murder.

The office of Governor Ford was unusually crowded for the signing of the bill that would strip the city of Nauvoo of its charter.

Jacob C. Davis spoke out of turn, as though he were in charge. "Governor, I congratulate your party on working with us to accomplish this bill. We should have stripped the Mormons of their power long ago."

Ford grimaced as he dipped his quill into his silver inkpot. He was tiring of Davis' tirades. For a half-dollar piece he would dip his quill into Davis' own blood.

He signed the document. Applause erupted from both Democrats and Whigs.

"Next, we must address the issue of all the illegal activities going on in Nauvoo," Davis said, obviously savoring the moment. "The Mormons are crooks. All we hear about Nauvoo centers around their thieving, bogus-making, gambling, spirituous liquors, bad houses, and swearing."

As he replaced the quill into its holder, Ford countered Davis. "You're grossly over-exaggerating. I've done my own investigations into those matters."

Davis cursed a blue streak as a toast of brandy was prepared. "Believe what you want. I have my opinion. You have yours."

"And we must face the fact that the Mormons will appeal this legislation," Ford said.

Davis cursed again. But the liquor made him feel good.

Five days after Christmas Elder Wilford Woodruff awoke from his dream in his cabin. He was a passenger on the new packet ship, the *John R. Skiddy*. The seas were rough, almost as rough as the day two weeks ago when some of the stern windows were broken and so much water taken in that some of the trunks and baggage were afloat, not only in the hold, but in his cabin as well. This time, however, the thousand-ton ship was making good headway toward England despite contrary winds.

In New York, before his departure, he had to conduct some uncomfortable business for the Church. He found William Smith, George Adams, and Samuel Brannan exploiting the Church members. They were sealing couples in polygamous unions without authority of the Quorum of the Twelve, and he suspected William Smith of pocketing tithing money. Wilford had written Brigham Young, suggesting that a member of the Twelve be sent to New York to take charge of the churches in the Atlantic States.

Wilford peeked out his window of the ship. Faintly, in the distance, he could make out the Irish coast. Phoebe was still asleep. So were his two daughters, two-year-old Phoebe Amelia and one-year-old Susan Cornelia. He thought how he missed his son, Wilford, Jr., who had been left with Brother and Sister Benbow, back in Nauvoo.

He rubbed his hands together as he thought about his dream. Several times since the death of Joseph, he had dreamed about the Prophet. This dream was a good one. He saw the Prophet Joseph at the door of the temple in heaven. Joseph told Wilford he could not stop to talk with him this time because he was in a hurry. The next man Wilford saw was Father Smith. He said the same thing, that because he was in a hurry he could not talk. Next, Wilford saw another half-dozen brethren who had held high positions on earth, and none of them could stop to talk.

Wilford rubbed his hands together, astonished at these recollections.

By and by, in his dream, he had seen Joseph Smith again. He asked Joseph why he was in such a hurry. Wilford told Joseph that he knew the business of God's kingdom on earth required men to be in a hurry, but that he expected that Joseph's hurry would be over when he got into the kingdom of heaven.

"I will tell you, Brother Woodruff," Joseph had said in the dream. "Every dispensation that has had the priesthood on the earth and has gone into the celestial kingdom has had a certain amount of work to do to prepare to go with the Savior when he goes to reign on the earth. Each dispensation has had ample time to do this work. We have not. We are the last dispensation, and so much work has to be done, and we need to hurry in order to accomplish it."

Wilford closed his eyes for a minute. What Joseph had said was new doctrine to him, but it rang true.

Strange, Wilford thought. Not once in any of his dreams had Joseph mentioned any concern about his death, the scoundrels responsible for killing him, or the trial for his murderers that would be held soon.

"Wake up, Phoebe. I can see Ireland."

CHAPTER NOTES

Wilford Woodruff's dream is related in his journal.

# 83

*March 1845*

FROM DANIEL'S VIEWPOINT, the meeting in the new Seventies Hal couldn't have gone better. He was on a new spiritual high as he walked into the house and faced Elizabeth. He was about to receive the shock of his life.

Elizabeth's smile was radiant, almost knocking Daniel over. Her greer eyes were twinkling. She was dressed in her best candy-stripe dress with a rose sash. "How was your meeting, sweetheart?"

"One of the best meetings I've ever attended," he answered, wondering why she was not in her nightgown. It was after nine-thirty. He and Robert had been ordained to the office of seventy in the Melchizedek Priesthood ir January. The Church had begun to expand the seventies Quorum at the las October conference when they filled eleven new quorums of nearly sevent men each. He and Robert were now members of the Seventeenth Quorum.

Joseph Young, president of the Quorum of Seventy, had spoken to packed house about the importance of receiving personal revelation.

Elizabeth's giddy, happy look puzzled him a bit, but Daniel began explaining Young's talk. Joseph Young was a brother to Brigham Young. "I thought I understood personal revelation somewhat," Daniel said, "but now I think I understand it a lot better. President Young challenged us to qualify for it on a daily basis."

"Give me a *quick* review, and then I've got something I want to share with you," she said.

The puzzled look remained with Daniel. "Well, President Young talked about faith, obedience, and application of gospel principles." He paused.

"You don't have to be *that* brief," she laughed.

Daniel laughed, too. "He talked first about the importance of studying the scriptures every day—not just reading the scriptures, but searching them, studying them."

Elizabeth pursed her lips. "We *try* to do that, don't we?"

"President Young talked about the difference between trying and doing. We've got to get into the habit of doing it every day, not nearly every day—and studying, not just reading."

"And if we do…?

"He taught us that the knowledge we receive by studying the scriptures would give us increased faith. He said that faith is a gift from God awarded to us for our personal righteousness."

Elizabeth retained her mushy smile and twinkling gaze. "That makes perfect sense."

Daniel continued. "As our faith increases so will our obedience to gospel laws and ordinances. Faith is the first principle of the gospel, and obedience is the first law of heaven."

"About done?" she asked.

"Do you have something to tell me?" Daniel asked.

"You're not done, I can tell," she said. "Go ahead, finish."

Daniel drew a deep breath. "President Young says that greater obedience leads to a desire to fulfill the law of Christ, which is to bear one another's burdens. That means to do anything the Church asks us to do, to help others, to give service. That's the gospel in action—application to gospel principles."

"You keep making a circle with your hands—what does that mean?"

"He taught us that the course of the Lord is one eternal round. Faith leads to obedience, obedience leads to greater application, application leads to more faith, more faith leads to more obedience. Get it?"

"Got it. But what does this have to do with personal revelation?"

"If we place ourselves in that circle—faith, obedience, application—savored by our daily study of the scriptures, President Young promises that we will be entitled to the Holy Ghost in our lives. We were given that gift at baptism, but we have to earn it. The Holy Ghost will tell us what to do and how to do it. Personal revelation."

Elizabeth's smile was infectious now, and she was beaming. "Well, dear Daniel, let's see if this works."

"What do you mean?"

"What is the Spirit telling you right now?"

Daniel let his imagination run wild. It didn't take long. After nine years of marriage, finally—a baby! He began to quiver as a lump formed in this throat. "Elizabeth, are you…?"

Tears began to course down the face of his wife. She tried to speak, but couldn't. She rushed to his arms trembling and there was a long embrace.

Between his own sobs, Daniel asked, "When?"

Elizabeth's grip was tight. "September."

A great happy shudder passed through Daniel. After a few more moments he said, "Do you want a boy or a girl?"

Elizabeth pulled away for a second and let her gaze meet his. Tears still filled her eyes and she made no attempt to dash them as they streamed down her cheeks. She was trying to keep control of her fragile emotions. "Oh Daniel, I'm so happy. It makes no difference. I'll take whatever the Lord sends."

"Does Harriet know?"

"Let's tell her tomorrow."

"What about Hannah and Robert?"

"I want to make certain I don't lose it. Let's wait until I start to show, then we'll tell them."

Daniel nodded his approval.

"For the first time in my life I'm not jealous of Hannah."

Daniel smiled. Hannah's next baby was due in June.

Hannah was getting more and more distressed about the upcoming trial in Carthage. At a Sunday dinner at the Browett home right after April conference, Hannah was sharing her concern with Daniel, Elizabeth, and Harriet. More than twenty thousand members of the Church had attended the conference. Brigham Young announced a change in the city's name; no longer would it be known as Nauvoo, but as the City of Joseph, in honor of the deceased Prophet.

"It's a no-win situation," she said as she finished a dessert of gingerbread. "If the jury finds those men guilty, about every non-Mormon in the county will be ready for an all-out war against us." She patted her tummy. "It's so dangerous out there—what about the future of our children?"

Robert was tired of hearing talk like this. He smashed a fist to the table. "If they don't find them guilty I'll …"

Hannah cut him short. "Don't say it. I'm tired of hearing about it. Isn't there something else we can talk about?"

This was Elizabeth's cue. She wiped her mouth with a blue napkin that matched the tablecloth. Happiness lit her face. "I have some good news."

There were a few moments of silence as Hannah searched Elizabeth's pretty face. "There's been so much bad news lately it wouldn't take much to qualify for good news." It was a given certainty that members of the Church were going to have to leave Illinois soon. Under the auspices of the Nauvoo Coach and Carriage Manufacturing Assn., covered wagons were starting to be made for the exodus. Orson Hyde was in St. Louis raising money. Lyman Wight was threatening to leave with a group for Texas—although Brigham Young was trying to get him to wait at least until the temple was completed so that they could obtain their endowments. It had taken a large armed Mormon posse to prevent the sheriff from illegally arresting a member of the Church by the name of Joseph Benjamin Brackenbury because the member was scheduled to testify at the trial; Church members feared he would merely be taken to Carthage and killed. There was no more Nauvoo Legion, but at least the Church had organized a priesthood quorum police force. And John Taylor and Willard Richards were trying to evade arrest by Governor Ford. Ford was trying to force Taylor and Richards to go to Carthage and testify at the trial. However, both Apostles claimed that they would be killed by anti Mormons there if they actually went, and claimed that Ford knew that as well as they did. Brigham Young was advising members of the Church in other Illinois settlements to move to the City of Joseph so that the temple could be finished more more quickly.

With all these thoughts racing through her mind, Hannah said, "So go ahead—what's the good news?"

Elizabeth began to chuckle. "Guess."

Hannah arched one eyebrow as Elizabeth sat there chuckling, patting her own tummy. Hannah's mouth dropped and she thrust her head forward as the realization came to her. She stood up. "Elizabeth! Are you …?"

Elizabeth jumped to her feet, grasped Hannah's hands and began to dance. "Yes! Yes! Finally!"

Robert threw Elizabeth a challenging look. "Is my sister in a family way?"

Tears came to Hannah as she let Elizabeth twirl her around the room. "I can't believe it's finally happened! I just can't believe it! It's so wonderful."

Out of the corner of her eye Hannah caught a glimpse of Daniel. Tears were rolling out of both eyes and down his cheeks. Harriet sat on a chair and watched the happy scene.

Hannah wiped her eyes. "When, Elizabeth? When's the baby due?"

"Middle of September," she said. "I'm *already* showing."

"You are? Why haven't I noticed?"

Elizabeth pinched each side of a loose yellow dress. The bulge in her stomach was clearly evident. "Well, notice me *now.*"

# 84

*May 1845*

KATHERINE EAGLES READ THE confident look on Sheriff Deming's face. Except for the unruly crowd openly displaying rifles and pistols, everything for the big trial was in order. It was Monday, May nineteenth. The fifty-by-forty-foot courtroom was packed. The Mormon-dominated county commissioners had appointed twenty-three grand jurors and another forty-eight to serve on the two panels of petit jurors. Witnesses had been subpoenaed. Defendants had been named.

Sandwiched between Deming and Josiah Lamborn, the prosecutor, Katherine glanced at the clock on the wall. It read two o'clock.

From one of the jury rooms, Judge Richard M. Young made his entrance. His posture erect, more than six feet tall, handsome in his appearance, he strode to the front of the courtroom and struck the gavel.

The trial for the murder of Joseph Smith was beginning. Katherine scanned the crowd. Of the two hundred people packed inside, less than fifty were Mormons. Far less than a proportionate share, Katherine thought. She hoped it wouldn't make a difference.

Sheriff Minor Deming had on his best confident smile. Forty-seven-year-old Judge Young was one of the most experienced justices of the Illinois Supreme Court and a former U.S. senator.

"The Mormon-haters won't pull anything over on Judge Young," Deming whispered to Katherine.

Katherine nodded her agreement. She wished the sheriff had been able to do something about the weapons in the courtroom. He had talked it over with the judge but both men felt that if they attempted to do something about it, bedlam would break out.

Robert though it was ludicrous that Hannah and Mary accompany him to Carthage, given the danger. After all, Hannah was eight months pregnant. But both women figured the trial event might be the last chance to figure out what had happened to Elias. As Robert scanned the armed men in town—more than a thousand of them—he wished he had at least left Hannah and Mary at Henry's house. Church leaders had instructed members of the Church to stay home unless they had specific business in court. Hannah and Mary rational ized that they did have official business—finding out what happened to Elias. But the men in town were armed to the hilt for the purpose of keeping Mormons and their friends away. Luckily, so far none suspected him and the two women; they recognized Henry as a non-Mormon and that apparently deflected their fears. Campfires had dotted the outskirts of town during the night; people had bedded down in wagon boxes and on porches in town. Despite the fact that Church leaders had instructed Mormons to stay home unless they had specific business in court, Robert came anyway. He viewed it as a final attempt to find any clues to Elias' disappearance.

"These men look like they want a war to start," commented Robert.

"If war starts, it'll be started by you Mormons," said Henry, his voice low.

"Don't say the word *war*, Henry," Hannah warned, digging her finger into Robert's arm.

"And it'll be started by some swagger named Bobby Harris."

Hannah ground her teeth together. She hated it when Henry called Robert by his old nickname, the name he went by before his baptism.

"All we want is to convict the men responsible for the death of Joseph and Hyrum," Robert said.

"I'll make you a bet," Henry said. "Not one man will be found guilty. No one will hang."

Robert bowed his neck, seething. Illinois law required death for all men convicted of murder. "They'll all hang, everyone of 'em. I'll take your bet. One milk cow."

Robert had every reason to be confident. The county commissioners— dominated by Mormons since the last election—had selected the jurors. Right now, in the courthouse that he was staring at, Judge Young was empanelling a twelve-man jury out of the twenty-four petit jurors selected by the commission. Sure, their names would be drawn out of a box by random. Sure, some would seek to be excused. Sure, some would be absent, forcing Sheriff Deming to send out a deputy to arrest them. If any vacancies occurred, Sheriff Deming had the power to choose the replacements.

There were witnesses galore. In Robert's view, it was an open and shut case, just as Sheriff Deming had predicted months ago. Thomas Sharp, Mark Aldrich and the others were cooked—they were sure to be hung by the neck until dead.

Then, Robert thought, he could get on to the business of hunting down the Mormon apostates. Not one of them—not even Wilson Law—could be seen in town.

When the court adjourned for lunch, Katherine found Henry, Robert, Hannah, and Mary in front of the Hamilton House where they had agreed to meet. Its lobby was packed with men, standing room only. Under a tree in the town square, they began a lunch of cold pork, cheese, bread, and lukewarm milk.

"You should have seen the look on Sharp's face when the jurors were announced," Katherine said.

Henry pulled his ugly features into a contortion. "You bring bad news."

"Bad news to you, Henry, but good news for the rest of us."

"Who got selected, Katherine—how many Mormons?" Hannah asked. She had her fingers crossed.

Katherine smiled, ignoring Henry's icy stare. "Ten Mormons for the first week; eleven for the second."

Robert slapped his thigh with a powerful hand. The sound echoed. "Ha! What milk cow you giving me, Henry?" Robert gloated. "Sharp is toast now."

"The trial ain't even started yet," Henry snorted. "Just wait."

For the rest of the lunch break Henry and Robert argued over the qualifications of the defense attorneys against the prosecutors.

"Them four lawyers got by Sharp and his boys are sharper than sharp," Henry jibed. He named O. H. Browning, Archibald Williams, Calvin A. Warren, and William A. Richardson.

Robert gasped at Browning's name. He had been the principal counsel for Joseph Smith when Joseph was arrested for extradition to Missouri on old charges in 1841, and did it effectively. Browning won the case and Joseph went free. Joseph, in fact, had dispatched a letter from Carthage Jail, asking Browning to come to his aid. He was killed shortly afterward, so nothing came of the request.

Browning, Katherine confirmed, was the leader of the four. To her, he already seemed bold and self-assured. He was thirty-nine, born in Kentucky where he served in the legislature before coming to Illinois, and as a powerful spokesman for the Whig party, he had served in both the state senate and the lower house in Illinois.

Katherine said that William A. Richardson, the other lead attorney, was in stark contrast to Browning. Browning was a Whig; Richardson a Jacksonian Democrat. Richardson, in fact, had faced Browning in elections to the state senate and U. S. Congress, winning every time. Browning was religious; Richardson rough, almost crude.

Robert gasped again. The Mormons were facing an experienced *nation-al* politician. Where did Sharp and the other defendants get all their money?

Calvin A. Warren, thirty-eight, before taking up residence in Quincy, had practiced law in Warsaw for several years, and was a Democrat. He, too, had served as a lawyer for Joseph Smith. That is, until 1843. In 1841, he and defendant Mark Aldrich had attempted to use Mormon immigrants to popu-late their real estate development near Warsaw—appropriately named "Warren." Katherine said she thought Warren viewed the trial as his way of getting back at the Mormons, because he blamed the Church for his business failures when the Mormons pulled out of the settlement.

Katherine said that the other lawyer, Archibald Williams, was the ugliest man in the courtroom.

"Uglier than Henry?" Robert said in jest.

Katherine didn't answer. She went on to say that the ardent Whig, forty-four, from Quincy, was not only homely but also careless in his dress. But he had a homespun manner, without pretensions to culture or superior knowl-edge. "The jurors will like him," she said.

"You just wait," Henry said. "These slick lawyers will find a way to get Sharp and the others off."

"But you're forgetting about Josiah Lamborn," Hannah said. "He's the best."

"He was damn near disbarred," Henry scoffed, spreading a rumor that he'd heard.

"That was due to an angry client," Katherine said. "His case went clear to the Illinois Supreme Court, and they took no disciplinary action."

Henry shrugged.

"You have to remember that he was elected attorney general of Illinois and held that office until a year and a half ago," she said.

"Yep, and he represented Illinois in its second attempt to arrest Joe Smith and return him to Missouri," Henry retorted.

"He did?" Mary asked. She had been in England during the time.

Robert dismissed Henry's statement. "Lamborn was just doing his job.

He's on our side now."

"Lamborn has political aims—he just wants the Mormon vote for something in the future," Henry charged.

"Well, he has an easy job," Robert said. "It's common knowledge that Joseph and Hyrum were killed by the men of the Warsaw militia. You saw them do it, Henry. Everyone knows they're guilty."

"They'll get off."

"How?"

Henry had become a self-taught expert on the law since Katherine's employment in the sheriff's office. "Don't look for Sharp and the boys to go on the witness stand themselves. The law don't allow for it. They'll make their defense out of the mouths of other witnesses. Nobody knows which men of the militia actually did it."

Robert pulled a copy of a twenty-four-page booklet from his back pocket. "What about this?" he asked. He had paid twenty-five cents for it.

Henry scoffed at the booklet. William M. Daniels, the prosecution's key witness, had written it. It contained the names of those who murdered Joseph and Hyrum, according to his personal eyewitness account.

"This man says how he overheard some Warsaw militiamen plotting to assist the Carthage Greys in the murder while the governor was in Nauvoo," Robert charged. "Daniels says they convinced him to join them. He describes the passionate speeches by Sharp and Aldrich in great length. He says that Levi Williams rode back and forth to Carthage, making arrangements with the Carthage Greys, and that finally a note was received from the Greys telling them that the time was ripe to murder the Smiths. The guns of the jail guards would be loaded with blank cartridges."

"I know, I know," Henry said. "I've read the dern thing too. Daniels said he tried to warn the prisoners, but that's a crock. He could've got through."

Robert thumbed through the pages. "This is irrefutable. I keep telling you, Henry. You're gonna lose your cow."

"We don't want Henry's cow, Robert," Hannah stormed. "Grow up."

"That book's been out for two weeks, dear brother-in-law," Henry said, smiling. "Sharp's attorneys appreciate it, believe you me. It's given them boys a long time to prepare a careful cross-examination. They'll know how to exploit it."

"I'll take your Holstein cow, Henry. And the calf, too."

Before court began, Robert had Katherine introduce Sheriff Deming to him. The conversation soon evolved around Governor Ford.

"Do you think the governor had anything to do with the murders?" Robert asked.

"That's a good question," the sheriff responded. "I've thought a lot about it myself."

Henry spit on the ground in derision. "You Mormons—you've got your conspiracy theories."

"John Taylor's given this matter a lot of thought," Robert explained. "He makes a good case against the governor."

"You've got my ear," the sheriff said.

Robert rolled his eyes skyward, searching his memory. "Let's see if I can remember what Elder Taylor said." Slowly at first, Robert recited what he had learned in Nauvoo. That Ford knew Joseph and the City Council had not broken one federal, state, or local law when it came to the matter of destroying the *Expositor*. That Ford knew that mobs in Carthage and Warsaw had passed inflammatory resolutions threatening to exterminate the Mormons, and that armed mobs were assembled and commencing actual hostilities.

Robert paused, letting the sheriff digest all this.

"I don't disagree with anything so far," the sheriff said, though deep in thought.

"Ford disbanded the Nauvoo Legion on purpose," Robert charged. "The Legion had never violated any law. But the governor took away our arms. Then Ford requested that Joseph Smith go to Carthage without any protection whatsoever, even though he said he promised protection."

Deming nodded his agreement.

Even Henry was silent.

"And when they took Joseph and the others to jail—illegally, the governor refused to interfere."

"You're absolutely right," Deming said.

"Time and time again, the governor refused to free Joseph and Hyrum's confinement in the jail, even though he promised to help. Then comes the worst part—Ford dismissed all the militia that might have been relied on to protect Joseph and Hyrum."

Deming was at a loss for words. He knew Robert and Elder Taylor were right. Governor Ford had dismissed all the men under his command—except the Carthage Greys.

"Elder Taylor claims that the governor knew full well that the Carthage Greys were bitter enemies of our Church. The Greys were made up of men who had been ringleader mob members in Carthage. They're the men who passed resolutions against us just weeks before."

"I didn't have a choice in the matter," stammered Deming. "Ford ordered me to do all those things."

"We're not blaming you by any stretch of the imagination," Robert said, taking a friendly grasp of Deming's shoulder. "It's all Ford's fault, not yours. You've been a great friend."

"Is that everything in this conspiracy theory of yours?" Henry asked.

"Not mine, Henry. Elder Taylor's," Robert retaliated.

"Be quiet and let Robert finish," Katherine said.

Robert spoke with authority, the words coming easily now. "Governor Ford was informed that the murders were about to happen, both before he left Carthage, and again on the road, by different parties. Yet he did nothing to stop it from happening."

Henry laughed as though the statement were absurd.

Deming was hanging his head.

"And that's not all," Robert said. "When the cannon was fired in Carthage signifying that the evil deed had been done, the governor immediately fled out of the area. He obviously knew what the signal meant."

Henry had a couple of friends who were in the Carthage Greys. "I don't think it was unusual to place a local unit in charge of the jail," he said. "I think it shows the governor really did expect some danger."

"It was like leaving a lamb in charge of a wolf," Katherine countered. "They put up no fight against the mob that charged the jail."

"But some of Ford's officers made a solemn promise to help protect the Mormons," Henry sneered. "You know that as well as I do."

"Promises, maybe, but some of those officers helped murder Joseph and Hyrum," Robert said, angry that Henry was arguing with him.

Deming held up a hand. "I'm sort of caught in the middle. Perhaps the strongest argument in the governor's favor would be that perhaps he didn't believe that the mobbers were capable of such an atrocity as killing the Smiths."

Robert was quick to respond. "But why the broken faith? Why the disregard of the warnings he was given? How did he understand the signal, the firing of the cannon? Why was he so oblivious to everything pertaining to our interests? And so alive and interested in everything our enemies were doing?"

"No good answer," Deming admitted.

"All theory," said Henry.

"I support Elder Taylor in his theories," Robert said in a stern voice. "Ford stands just as responsible as anyone else for the blood of Joseph and Hyrum Smith. It's dripping on his garments."

Henry shook his head. "You mean to say that Ford actually planned the murder of Joe Smith?"

"No, Henry," Robert explained. "He didn't plan it. The Mormon apostates along with the mob in Carthage and Warsaw planned it. But Governor Ford didn't have the firmness to withstand the mob; that's what Elder Taylor thinks. Ford lent himself to the plans and unwittingly became a partaker of their evil deeds."

On Wednesday noon, Katherine reached the shade tree where Henry, Robert, Hannah, and Mary were waiting. She was out of breath and had a wild, excited look in her eyes.

"You won't believe what just happened," she cried. Tears began to stream down her reddened cheeks.

Henry smiled, expecting good news. He was already eating his lunch—this time dried beef and radishes. "Spill it out," he said.

Robert felt a rising concern. "Something bad?"

"Could be, depending on what the judge does," Katherine wailed.

"Tell us," Mary pleaded.

"Judge Young is considering an outlandish motion filed by the one of the defense attorneys, William Richardson."

"I told you so," Henry said, appearing puffed up already.

"Shut up, Henry," Hannah snapped. "Let her talk."

"First of all, Richardson wants the judge to discharge all the jurors."

Robert's mouth fell open. "What? Why?"

"He produced an affidavit signed by the defendants. It swears that they believe that the three county commissioners were prejudiced against them and chose jurors that were prejudiced against them, too."

"What about the will of the majority of the people?" Robert asked throwing his dried beef on the ground. "We elected the commissioners. They have the right to select the jurors; it's that simple."

Everyone was silent for a few moments while Robert fumed.

"That's not all," Katherine said in a sad voice.

"What can be worse?" Robert asked.

"A second affidavit claims that Sheriff Deming and his deputies are very much prejudiced against the defendants. It used a lot of fancy words—like 'so influenced by partiality' and 'bias of opinion'."

"Told you them out-of-town lawyer sharpies were good," Henry gloated.

"What now?" Mary asked as she watched Robert continue to steam.

"The judge has to make tough decisions," Katherine said. "The defense proposal is simple. Disqualify the county commissioners, set aside the jurors they've chosen, disqualify the sheriff, bypass the coroner, and select a totally new jury."

Hannah bit her lip. "Does that mean you lose your job, Katherine?"

"No. The sheriff and I get to stay in the courtroom, but he'd be stripped of his power for this trial only."

"Select a new jury?" Robert exclaimed. "What bull crap!"

Henry was still smiling. "You have one cow or two, Bobby? I hate to take your only cow."

There was a long delay in the trial while Judge Young considered the unusual request in the privacy of his room in the Hamilton House, receiving guests who were giving him advice. Katherine went to the courthouse twice, but was turned back both times. Because she was not needed in the courtroom, the conversation between her and the others continued. It centered on the incredible fact that Judge Young could rule either way.

"Judge Young is no dummy," Henry said. "He knows all about the struggle for control of Hancock County. Folks around here don't like the thoughts that a Mormon-dominated county commission would control our criminal justice system."

"But if there are more of us than there are of them, so be it," Robert argued.

Henry asked a biting, astute question. "But aside from you, who's here representing the Mormons in Carthage?"

"Henry's making a good point, Robert," Katherine said. "Church members are conspicuous by their absence. There are less than fifty in the courtroom. Rumors going around inside the courtroom speak of Nauvoo's apparent indifference to the prosecution. No one expects John Taylor and Willard Richards to testify, and their testimonies would do the most damage to the defendants by far."

Robert knew her statement to be true. All winter and all spring Elder Taylor and Elder Richards had consistently said they would not go to Carthage for any reason, trial or not.

Henry shook his finger at Robert. "If Judge Young has any political ambitions, he'd better be careful. If he rules against the defense on these matters, his political future is ruined. People like me would never vote for him."

Robert narrowed his eyes. "I remind you, Henry, we Mormons outnumber you in Hancock County. And we make a big impact in the state, too."

"Rumors are you're moving out west sometime in the future."

That took the air out of Robert. Henry had a point.

"I hear Judge Young is even considering a run at the governorship," Henry quipped.

Hannah noticed Robert's blank stare. "What are you thinking, dear?"

Robert spoke derisively. "Funny how I can see a steady stream of anti Mormons knocking on the judge's door. Pledging their votes. Pledging money. Even offering bribes."

"But that's against the rules if it's really happening," Katherine said.

Henry's smile was wicked. "In war, there are no rules."

"Maybe I'll go back into training," Robert concluded.

Henry laughed. "Hey, if you want to beat up those defendants one at a time, or as a group, I'll help. Just for the fun of it."

"I won't need any help."


The three-hour break ended. Katherine was aghast that the judge seemed ready to make his decision so quickly. He began with a brief review of the law on the subject of quashing an array of jurors, followed by a statement of his determination to "do strict justice to both parties, so that there may not be any cause of complaint on either side."

*That's impossible,* Katherine thought. *The two sides are too far apart.*

"I will now announce my decision," the judge said.

Katherine said a silent prayer and closed her eyes.

"I believe it is my duty to quash the array, and to appoint persons as elisors, to select another jury."

Sheriff Deming was seated next to Katherine again. She could feel his body stiffen in anger. Likewise, so did the prosecutor's. Katherine gasped and covered her mouth.

All two hundred people in the courtroom broke out with a mixture of cheers and gasps.

Judge Young smashed his gavel to restore order and went on. H explained that he did not hold the jurors responsible, but he did hold the county commissioners and the sheriff responsible for trying to manipulate the justice system.

*Balderdash!* Katherine thought. The sheriff and county commissioners had acted in good faith, trying to follow the wishes of the majority of the citizens of the county.

"Since I am a stranger in the county," Young was saying, "I am appointing the prosecutor and the defense lawyers to agree upon two persons to act as elisors."

Katherine had a sinking feeling. There was one prosecutor and four defense lawyers. *In war, there are no rules.*

# 85

WHO WOULD BE THE NEW elisors? That question haunted Robert and dominated the evening conversation at the Eagles cabin two miles west of Carthage.

"Sheriff Deming has no influence as to whom they might be," Katherine was saying as the group sat on firewood blocks in front of the cabin at sunset. "It's all in the hands of five men."

Robert was clearly smoldering. "And four of 'em are Sharp's lawyers. This thing stinks."

"What about Lamborn?" Hannah asked.

Katherine's story about how William A. Richardson had made the motion that the jurors be discharged grated on Robert. Robert said, "Richardson and the other three lawyers probably have Lamborn hog-tied and whipped already. Just wait. In the morning the judge will announce the new elisors, and we won't like either one of them. What a farce."

Henry was his usual self. "Don't include me in that. I'll probably like both of them."

Katherine had a sinking feeling that Robert was right.

Sheriff Deming look concerned as he accompanied Katherine to the court-house the next morning—Thursday. "All the Mormons have gone home," he was saying. "The courthouse will be filled with the other side now."

"I don't blame them," Katherine responded.

"But there's something they failed to consider," he said.

A puzzled look came over Katherine. "What would that be?"

"When the new elisors are announced they'll be given the responsibility to select new jurors."

"So?"

"What if the judge is in a hurry and they have to select the new jurors right away?"

"We can send word to Nauvoo. We'll have plenty to choose from within a day."

"We may not have that much time."

Katherine studied the sheriff for a moment. A thought came to her mind. "My brother-in-law—what about him?"

"Fetch him, but hurry."

Katherine ran in the direction of the shade tree. Robert, Hannah, and Mary were in the farm wagon, headed back to the Eagles Dairy. Henry, they said, was in a tavern having a drink.

"Sheriff Deming thinks there's room for you in the courtroom," Katherine said, nearly out of breath. "All the other Mormons have gone home."

"Well, who can blame them?" Hannah asked, echoing Katherine's earlier thought.

Katherine could see Robert thinking. "Come on—it's an opportunity you don't want to miss, all of you. Hurry!"

"I'll have to tie up the horses," Robert said, shaking his head in the affirmative. "We'll meet you inside."

Katherine ran back to the courthouse.

When Robert, Hannah, and Mary arrived, a guard stopped them.

"Sorry, we're filled up now. No more passes."

Katherine kept staring at the door, but Robert, Hannah, and Mary did not come through. She turned her attention back to the judge. He announced the two new elisors—William D. Abernethy and Thomas H. Owen. Katherine scratched her head.

"Couldn't be much worse," Sheriff Deming whispered to her.

"Why?" Katherine asked, a blank look on her face.

In front of the courtroom, Abernathy and Owen were executing their oaths.

"Abernethy used to be sheriff," Deming said. "He lost his job in 1842 because the growing Mormon population refused to vote for him. Ever since then he's been active in all the anti-Mormon activities around here."

Katherine gasped. This news would be ridiculed by Robert and all of the Mormons in Nauvoo.

"And the other one?" Katherine asked.

"Not quite as bad," Deming confirmed. "Owen is a Baptist clergyman known around here as a Jack Mormon, meaning that he's been somewhat sympathetic to the Mormon cause. He's been on record as opposing violence against the Mormons."

Katherine nodded her understanding. She resigned herself to the fact that it was the best Lamborn could do against the defense attorneys. Owen was supposed to satisfy the Mormon end of the equation. *But he's not Mormon,* Katherine thought. In her mind, Owen may have opposed violence in the past but there was nothing to say he didn't oppose letting the killers off.

Young was now instructing Abernethy and Owen. Young told them to summon from the bystanders twenty-four "good and lawful" men to serve as the petit jurors in the Joseph Smith murder trial case.

Deming whispered into Katherine's ear again. "Are there any Mormons left as observers in the courtroom?"

Katherine cringed. *Where was Robert?* She quickly scanned the courtroom. She could see only three of four persons that she considered to be "militant Mormons," or members of the Church who were more sympathetic to their enemies than they were to their own Church.

Josiah Lamborn handed Sheriff Deming and Katherine a letter he had just received from Nauvoo, signed by George Albert Smith, one of the Mormon Apostles. Reading over the sheriff's shoulder, Katherine quickly scanned the letter. Smith expressed wonderment at laws that would permit the discharge of the jurors and the disqualification of the sheriff. He reaffirmed that the Church wanted to stay out of the "procuring witnesses" business—the Church had given Murray McConnell all the information in their possession when he visited them in Nauvoo. Smith further stated that Church leaders wanted nothing to do with the trial lest any effort on their part should be construed as "a persecution or desire to pick a quarrel on our part."

Katherine gasped out loud. She read on.

Smith added that in the opinion of Church leaders the trial in Carthage was not between Mormons and anti-Mormons, but between the state and the indicted prisoners. He said that while Mormons would like the state to prosecute the case to final judgment, they would submit peacefully even if the prosecution were abandoned.

"Your Church doesn't seem to care what happens here," the sheriff whispered.

Katherine whispered back. "That's not entirely true. The letter says the case should be prosecuted to final judgment." But in the back of her mind Katherine realized that the Church had ceased to place any reliance on Illinois justice and wanted only peace until they could plan and carry out their exodus.

What Judge Young did next shocked Katherine to the core.

Speaking to the two newly-appointed elisors, the judge ordered them to summon *from the bystanders* twenty-four men to serve as new petit jurors.

A roar of approval swept through the two hundred spectators.

But not Katherine; out loud she said, "But that's not fair! There are no Nauvoo Mormons in here!" She exchanged glances with the sheriff. "I'll be right back. I'm going to get Robert."

"Won't do any good," Deming stated. "Judge Young just said that the petit jurors must be selected from people *inside* the courtroom."

"Darn!"

That night, while Robert ridiculed the ruling and Henry laughed about it, the examination and selection of individual jurors began at a special session at the courthouse. Judge Young called the defendants—Thomas Sharp, Mark Aldrich, Jacob Davis, Levi Williams, and William Grover—before the bench for formal arraignment.

Katherine watched as Josiah gave them a copy of the indictment, a list of state witnesses, and a list of the persons the elisors and summoned for service on the jury. She cringed as the five men smiled at the list—of twenty-four names, there were only three or four Mormons.

The judge then asked the defendants how they would plead.

"Not guilty!"

Despite the increasing futility of it all, Katherine took impeccable notes as the process began in the jury selection. Deming told her it was one of the most important stages of the trial, but she was beginning to feel a little like George Albert Smith and the brethren of the Church.

The matter seemed rather complicated to Katherine. First, a clerk drew four names out of a hat, and those first four became subject to examination. Lawyers from both sides tried to determine if potential jurors were prejudiced in any way.

In Katherine's opinion, they were prejudiced, indeed. After all, the court-room had been packed with venomous anti-Mormons and the press. Newspapermen were not eligible, of course, to be on the jury. Nevertheless, out of the first twenty-four potential jurors on the first panel, the two teams of lawyers accepted only five. And only two from the next group of twenty-four. In all, the prosecution and defense examined forty-eight prospective jurors and selected only seven.

It wasn't until late the next morning that the final five jurors were selected. Judge Young told them that the trial would begin Saturday morning.

Daniel Browett rubbed his eyes and pulled his watch out of his pocket. The capstone to the temple was about to be laid. The sun was barely peeking over the eastern horizon, in the direction of Carthage, where the trial was taking place.

The watch said twenty-two minutes past six, Saturday morning, May twenty-fourth.

William Pitt's brass band was playing "The Capstone March" that Pitt had quickly composed. A crowd of several thousand people had gathered.

Brigham Young uttered a prayer with a teaching sermon attached. It talked about the importance of the temple endowment which members of the Church could not conduct until the temple was completed.

"The last stone is now laid upon the temple," Brigham said in his prayer, "and I pray the Almighty in the name of Jesus to defend us in this place and sustain us until the temple is finished and we have all got our endowments."

Brigham had purposely set the timing for the event at an early morning hour. He and the other members of the Twelve had been in hiding most of the time, fearful of repercussions from Carthage during the trial. There had been threats against the lives of John Taylor and Willard Richards because their testimonies of what happened on June twenty-seventh could be seriously damaging to the defendants at the trial.

As the temple crowd dispersed, Daniel checked his watch again. It was just before seven. He thought about the trial in Carthage and about Robert's absence from the farm. It perturbed Daniel that Robert had spent all week there. It was springtime. There was much to do. And in a few days Daniel would be in a group of carpenters raising the timbers for the attic of the temple.

In a strange way, Daniel felt that cultivating farm crops was more important than whether or not a rigged jury acquitted the indicted murderers of Joseph and Hyrum Smith. If not, certainly finishing the temple was.

# 86

IT SEEMED TO KATHERINE THAT NOW the trial was about to officially begin, Judge Young ought to do something about all the muskets, rifles, and pistols being hauled into the courtroom by the partisan anti-Mormon spectators.

Sheriff Deming threw his hands apart in exasperation. "Just goes to show you that this whole thing is out of control," he said. When the judge quashed the jury, he also quashed the sheriff's authority. His only duty was to send his deputies after reluctant witnesses. As of this moment there were three missing witnesses. Dangerous work, Deming had told Katherine, since they probably did not want to testify for the prosecution. Katherine remembered that last Tuesday a deputy had arrested a man named Henry Mathews. But Mathews pulled a gun on the deputy and escaped.

With preliminaries over, Josiah Lamborn was finally opening the case for the prosecution—reading the indictment, describing the legal theory of the case, and mentioning that the case was extraordinary because of the personalities and notoriety of the men who were killed—Joseph and Hyrum Smith.

Katherine shook her head at the contrast between Lamborn and Browning, the lead defense attorney. Drab clothing covered Lamborn's huge and crippled frame. Browning was dressed like a graceful cavalier—ruffled shirt, large cuffs, Prince Albert coat, and a yellow outside pocket-handkerchief.

Lamborn seemed to realize that he was a huge underdog. He was basing his prosecution on a conspiracy theory. Deming told Katherine that conspiracies were difficult to prove. Without conspiracy, only the man who pulled the trigger would be guilty of the actual murder.

*Wait until Robert hears this,* Katherine thought. *He'll blow his top.*

Pointing his finger at the five defendants, Lamborn reminded the jury that Joseph Smith had been a citizen of Hancock County, that he had been murdered by a mob while confined in jail, and that the crime was committed under protection of the law and with the "plighted faith" of the governor and the state. He identified the five defendants as the men who were the movers and instigators of the mob.

"It is not necessary to prove that these men entered the jail or shot the gun or any of these instruments by which Joseph's death was accomplished in order to convict them," he told the jurors, "but the mob got its spirit, impulse, movements, and blood-thirstiness from the minds and dispositions of these men ..."

Katherine scanned the faces of the jurors. Already they seemed unconvinced. *Why go on?* she wondered.

Twenty minutes later Richardson replied for the defense, saying he would be brief. And he was. He accused Lamborn of trying to work upon the feelings and prejudices of the jury. He reminded the jury that the defendants could only be convicted by specific evidence introduced by the prosecution. "At that task they will fail," he predicted.

Katherine could tell that a conviction of the five defendants would not come easily as she listened to Lamborn grill the first witness.

Lamborn was questioning a balding, mustached witness by the name of John Peyton, whose ownership of a two-thousand-five-hundred-acre farm three miles south of Warsaw made him one of the largest landowners in Hancock County. His wealth had helped elect him to the position of township supervisor. As evident from his testimony, Katherine judged Peyton to be over-confident and cocky.

Lamborn had already established that Peyton was at Golden Point the day of the Smith murders. Peyton said that he had been there with the Warsaw militia, and that Colonel Levi Williams' regiment had camped at what was called the "railroad shanties." Peyton could remember that Colonel Williams discharged the militia right after a courier from Carthage delivered a message.

Katherine nodded to herself. Elias and Henry had delivered the message.

Peyton seemed reluctant to admit that Mark Aldrich and Levi Williams pressured the militiamen for volunteers to return to Carthage. Finally he did, but Katherine felt that Peyton admitted it only because other witnesses were apt to say the same thing.

"Yes," Peyton said, "Mark Aldrich spoke of the grievances of the people, and that the Mormons had the power themselves and they must do something to stop it. Afterward, Thomas Sharp made a speech."

Katherine was smart enough to know that Lamborn needed Peyton to admit why volunteers were needed to go to Carthage. But Peyton remained stubborn.

"Did Sharp say anything about Joseph Smith?" Lamborn asked, letting his brown eyes bore into Peyton.

There was a very long pause. Peyton bit on his lower lip and blinked several times.

"Well?"

"I think he said that Joe Smith was now in custody, and the Mormons would elect the officers in the county, and by that means Joe would select his own jury and get free," Peyton replied in a slow, cautious voice.

Lamborn was relentless. "What else did Sharp say?"

Another long pause. "He told the men that the governor had said that whatever was done should be done quickly."

The courtroom erupted with gasps and murmurs.

Lamborn again: "Was anything said about killing Joseph Smith?"

"No."

"Did he say what should be done with him?"

"No."

"Was there anything said about coming in here, with the troops?"

Peyton paused again before he answered, blinking again. "Some of the officers, I think Aldrich, said something about it."

"Then it was Aldrich that was in favor of going to Carthage?"

"I don't know that it was Aldrich, or some other of them. There was something said in the crowd about going to Carthage, I think."

"What did the people there, upon the ground, in common with these men, say they were going to Carthage for?"

"I could not tell what their intention was. They did not say."

Peyton went on to testify that about half the disbanded troops—about a hundred men—started in the direction of Carthage, including all the defendants except Davis.

When the next witness—George Walker—testified, Katherine heard the first tangible evidence of conspiracy, which made both Lamborn and Sheriff Deming smile broadly. In a surprisingly forthright response, Walker said that he heard Davis say "he would be damned if he would go kill a man that was confined in prison."

*Bingo!* Katherine thought. *Lamborn—you're brilliant!*

There was quite a stir when Lamborn called the next witness. He was Frank Worrell, a young Carthage merchant who, as a lieutenant in the Carthage Greys, had been in command of the guard when Joseph was killed.

Katherine remembered Worrell as the man who had told Dan Jones—now on a ship with Wilford Woodruff headed to England and Wales—on the last night at the jail: "We have had too much trouble to bring Old Joe here to let him ever escape alive, and unless you want to die with him you had better leave before sundown."

However, Katherine was disappointed in Worrell's testimony and the way Lamborn handled it. Worrell said the mob came from the direction of

Nauvoo rather than from Warsaw, that the mobbers had disguised themselves, and that they stormed him by surprise. "There was a great crowd, as thick as in this courtroom. Their pieces were going off all the time and there was so much noise and smoke that I couldn't see or hear anything that was said."

Worrell admitted to seeing Aldrich and Williams in Carthage not long after the killing, but he said he did not see any of the defendants at the jail.

Katherine quickly tired of the parade of witnesses, gaining the sinking feeling that none of their testimonies would actually count with the rigged jury anyway. But Lamborn's strategy impressed her. His line of questioning for the next witnesses established the fact that the defendants arrived in Carthage at or before the time of the murders. Some witnesses identified them as members of the mob; others implicated them in a wicked collusion with the guards at the jail, or with members of the Carthage Greys. Others said they saw members of the mob everywhere, even atop the cupola of the courthouse.

Lamborn was embarrassed a few times, however, and Katherine felt bad for him. One witness said that he had been in Massachusetts at the time of the murders.

Laughter erupted from the courtroom.

Another witness, a tavern keeper from Warsaw, testified that he had seen the defendants in Warsaw at the time of the murders, and that none of the defendants had said anything about murdering Joseph and Hyrum Smith during the months following the event.

Katherine flinched at the obvious lie.

Low snickers erupted this time.

Clearly, in Katherine's mind, the courtroom was packed with Mormon-haters. She could feel the evil. She began to imagine what it would be like to be a member of the jury. She studied the weapons brandished openly by the crowd and the mean looks on their faces. She knew that if the jury issued a "guilty" verdict, there would be twelve more murders.

She was thankful that Robert was not on the jury.

All this became even more evident when Lamborn asked Judge Young for permission to recall Frank Worrell to the witness stand. Orville Browning jumped to the bench to protest, saying he had not yet cross-examined Worrell. Despite Browning's passionate plea, delivered with intensity and great fluency, Judge Young ruled that Worrell could be recalled so that Lamborn could examine him as to any material facts not already covered.

This time Judge Young almost lost control of the trial. The citizens of Carthage not only stomped their feet in an angry display, but beat their rifle and musket butts against the floor, yelled, cursed, and issued vocal threats. Katherine wondered how poor Judge Young felt. Deming had told her that Young was used to courtrooms that were models of decorum, and that these outbursts were obviously very distressing to the judge.

Lamborn dealt with only one subject in questioning Worrell. "Do you know if the Carthage guards loaded their guns with blank cartridges?"

Both Browning and Richardson jumped to their feet. Browning's eyes bore into Worrell. "You need not answer that question."

The crowd roared its agreement.

Worrell didn't miss the cue. "I will not answer that question," he said to Lamborn.

Undaunted, Lamborn pressed forward, repeating the question.

Most of the spectators were on their feet now, waving their weapons, cursing, and issuing threats.

"I will not answer," Worrell said.

Judge Young did the only thing he could, in Katherine's opinion. He ruled that Worrell was not bound to answer the question if he could not do so without incriminating himself.

The crowd roared its approval.

Worrell savored the cue, taking the Fifth Amendment.

Sheriff Deming leaned toward Katherine. "Worrell's answer is supposed to be neutral in the minds of the jurors. But to me—and to anyone else that is practical-minded—Worrell's refusal to testify seems to be an admission that Worrell and the guards at the jail were part of the plot. The guards obviously cooperated with the mob that killed Joseph and Hyrum."

Katherine scanned the unruly crowd again, and then the members of the jury. "But what about the jurors? How are they going to interpret this?"

Deming scoffed out loud. "You know the answer to that as well as I do. They're not practical-minded, and they're not neutral. Things are not going well for Lamborn."

Lamborn called a new witness, William M. Daniels—the man who had written the booklet.

Katherine crossed her fingers, hoping things would get better.

# 87

THE UNRULY CROWD HISSED, CURSED, and stomped their feet and weapons against the floor again as Daniels wiggled his way to the witness stand. The young cooper was the one witness who had been with the mob who was more than willing to testify. And Katherine felt his testimony might be so damaging it would turn the tide against the defendants.

Lamborn quickly got his preliminary questions out of the way. Then he said, "Mr. Daniels, stand up and tell the jury what you know about these five men."

Judge Young pounded his gavel as the crowd erupted again.

Daniels spoke at the jurors with unflinching boldness, leading them through what was now an all-familiar account: the militia's march to the railroad shanties near Golden Point, Levi Williams reading the order to disband, and the hot speech by Thomas Sharp. Daniels remembered that Sharp told of the necessity of "killing the Smiths to get rid of the Mormons" and that he wanted the troops to go on to Carthage. Daniels also testified that Sharp and Grover ridiculed Davis for Davis' initial reluctance to join the mob and go to

Carthage.

Responding to Lamborn's questions, Daniels said that nearly a hundred troops volunteered to join the mob and that most of them were on foot. Daniels did not see Sharp or Williams on the way to Carthage, but Aldrich was there—on horseback. But Aldrich disappeared about four miles from Carthage when the troops veered left into a timbered hollow. Daniels continued on the road to Carthage with several other men and two or three baggage wagons that accompanied them.

"Did you have any conversation with the guards at the jail when you got there?" Lamborn asked.

"No," Daniels answered.

"Why not?"

Daniels was firm in his answer. "Because they knew about it as well as anybody else," he explained. He added that he had understood from the other men that the guards were to have their guns loaded with blank cartridges.

Because of constant interruptions from the unruly crowd, Katherine had a hard time hearing every word of Daniels' testimony.

Next, Daniels described the scene at the jail. He was standing only twenty feet from the jail when the mob emerged from the timber, running single file along the fence. Some had their faces blackened with wet gunpowder. Most of the men had been drinking from the time they left Golden Point, he said.

"Did you see any of the defendants at this time?" Lamborn asked.

Daniels said yes, that Grover ran toward the jail carrying a double-barrel shotgun. Williams stood in the middle of the road telling his men to rush in, that there was no danger. Williams also motioned other men to the side window of the jail and told them "to shoot the damned scoundrel."

"Did you see Sharp, Aldrich, or Davis?"

Daniels said no, not in that specific group of men.

Lamborn held up a copy of the booklet. "Are you the author?"

"No. Lyman Omar Littlefield is the actual author. He's a typesetter for the *Nauvoo Neighbor.* I suppose he got it from what I told him; I told him the story a good many times."

Katherine glanced at Browning the lawyer. He was taking more notes than she was, especially about the part that talked about a miraculous light that was supposed to have appeared and baffled the mob immediately after Joseph's death. Katherine quickly surmised that Littlefield had embellished that part. There was a lot of lightning flashing in the skies that day, Katherine remembered.

Browning's attack on Daniels was devastating. In the eyes of the already-biased jury, he discredited Daniels on several accounts—Daniels sold the booklet for money, the typesetter had embellished Daniels' conversation with him, and although Daniels insisted he was opposed to the murder, he had been a member of the mob.

Katherine felt sorry for Daniels. To her, Daniels was an honest man who had had misgivings about being involved in the murder, and had told his story to the typesetter; it was not his fault the typesetter had embellished the story. Bottom line to Katherine was that Daniels was a key witness, that he had actually seen what happened at the jail and that the defendants were truly implicated, but a slick lawyer had managed to disparage his testimony so much that even an impartial jury would view it with suspicion. Browning even accused Daniels of accepting five hundred dollars to testify against the defendants in the case.

Daniel described in detail how three of the mobbers had been wounded in the attack. Katherine felt it was true. Those three defendants had fled the country rather than face a jury.

Robert finally wormed himself into the courtroom the next Monday. He had returned Hannah and Mary to Nauvoo Saturday evening, attended a worship service in the grove Sunday, and argued with Daniel over whether or not he even belonged in Carthage. But Robert's stubbornness prevailed and he returned to Carthage—leaving at five in the morning. Judge Young had given initial attention to some civil cases, so it was nine o'clock before the jury filed into the courtroom and the Joseph Smith murder case resumed.

Robert sat right next to Katherine.

"We didn't know if you'd be back," she said as Lamborn called his first witness.

"Wild horses couldn't keep me away," Robert answered. "I want to see the look on Sharp's face when he's convicted. Where's Henry?" Robert had bypassed the dairy, riding straight into town.

"I'm sure he'll be around somewhere," she said. "I hope he watches our daughter and doesn't take her into the barrooms."

Robert was not impressed with Lamborn or his first three witnesses—Thomas Barnes, thirty-three-year-old Carthage physician; John Wilson, a forty-nine-year-old tavern keeper; and an elderly farmer named Thomas Dixon. In Robert's opinion, the three witnesses knew far more than they told and Lamborn finally gave up in disgust. Lawyers for the defendants didn't even cross-examine the three.

Katherine and Robert met Henry at the usual spot for lunch and Henry was his normal cynical self, but was taking good care of little four-year-old Annie, their daughter.

The first witness in the afternoon session was a thirty-three-year-old member of the Church from Nauvoo, Eliza Jane Graham. Her appearance not only surprised Robert but all the Mormon-haters in the crowd. Lamborn himself had become aware of her knowledge only a few days earlier.

Miss Graham told the jury about her employment in the Warsaw House, a tavern. She said that Thomas Sharp arrived at the tavern the evening of the murder. Sharp said he was dry and needed a drink of water; he had come from Carthage in less than an hour. Graham's employer, a Mrs. Fleming, asked Sharp what he had been doing there. He answered, "We have finished off the leading men of the Mormon Church."

*Good,* Robert thought. *Her testimony will damage the defendants!*

A big smile came to Robert as she continued her testimony. Around midnight Graham and Mrs. Fleming began serving dinner to a small group of men, including Sharp, and the group gradually grew until it numbered sixty or more. Lamborn asked her to relate the conversation of the men to the jury.

"One man said that it was him who had killed Old Joe," Graham said sternly, refusing to be intimidated by the catcalling from the spectators. "Then another man claimed responsibility, that he had killed him, and then another." Soon, she said, it was general talk amongst the crowd that they had killed the Smiths. All around the tavern men were rejoicing and bragging about their work. This went on until two in the morning, she said.

To Robert's satisfaction, Graham specifically identified Thomas Sharp, Jacob C. Davis, and William Grover.

Robert let his eyes rest on the guilty murderers. They were slouched over, absorbing the incriminating testimony.

During a rough cross-examination, Miss Graham held her ground against Browning despite her fear, fatigue, and the fact that Browning tried to discredit her because of her membership in the Church.

Robert glanced at the clock on the wall as Graham was dismissed. It was four-thirty and his rear end had absorbed enough punishment on the cramped, hard, wooden bench.

But Lamborn called another witness, Benjamin Brackenbury.

Brackenbury was an eighteen-year-old boy who had driven one of the baggage wagons with Captain Jacob C. Davis' company of the Warsaw militia. He said that he was at the jail when the defendants ran out. The boy testified that he heard Grover say he had killed the Smiths, that Joe Smith was a "damned stout man," that he had gone into the room where Smith was, and that Smith had struck him twice in the face.

"Grover told me that he was the first man who went into the room where the Smiths were held prisoner," Brackenbury testified.

The smile returned to Robert's face, despite the hard bench.

Brackenbury also said that he saw the three wounded attackers—Wills, Voras, and Gallaher. Voras was wounded in the shoulder, Wills in the arm, and Gallaher in the face—"in the cheek, like as if a ball had taken the skin off."

Robert wondered where those three had fled to avoid the trial, and how difficult it would be to hunt them down.

The best Browning could do in his cross-examination was to get Brackenbury to admit that he was fifty yards away when the so-called murderers came running by, and that he—along with all the other militiamen—had drank a little whiskey out of the barrel.

The partial crowd inside the courthouse cheered as Browning attacked Brackenbury's admission of drinking whiskey; it was as though they had invented prohibition.

For the next three days Browning paraded a stream of defense witnesses in front of the court and jury. Browning had just one aim: to impeach the prosecution's key witnesses. The whole thing frosted Robert. There was no alibi evidence—none whatsoever. And during the three days, none of the defendants took the stand.

Robert felt a rising concern during the three days, however, that the minds of the jurors were already made up. He expected the worst. Even though each of the witnesses undermined the testimony of the prosecution witnesses somewhat, and even though Lamborn's cross-examination was particularly skillful, Robert felt the whole thing was a waste of time.

In Robert's view, the five defendants were as guilty as guilty could be. Had the original jury been held intact, there would be no doubt. But now the jury was filled with known Mormon-haters. To Robert, the mosaic of conspiracy on the part of Sharp, Alrich, Grover, Williams, and Davis was clear. Witnesses had agreed that they were present when the disbanding order was read, that a mob of militiamen marched to Carthage, had been seen going to the jail prior to the murders, were seen coming out of the jail after the murders, and had bragged about their foul deeds at a late evening supper in Warsaw.

*Hang them,* Robert said to himself. *Hang them!*

Robert tried to assess the feelings of the courtroom at his Friday lunch under the tree in the Carthage town square. A week ago citizens here feared an armed conflict. Now no one seemed apprehensive about the upcoming verdict. In fact, an eerie gloom prevailed. Sheriff Deming had told Robert and Katherine that he felt Judge Young had made a serious mistake in his closing instructions to the jury. Young failed to explain the theory of the prosecution's case—conspiracy.

"The prosecution's case depends upon the application of the complicated legal theory of conspiracy," Deming said. "Lamborn needed Young to go over that at the end, but he didn't do it."

At lunch, Henry was devouring dried pork, bread, and dark cheese. "They're gonna get off," he predicted. "In a couple of hours I'll be able to tell you 'I told you so'."

"I'm afraid you're right," Katherine admitted as she straightened Annie's bonnet.

"Hate to see you lose a cow over this, Robert," Henry added.

Robert's face reddened, thinking how much Henry resembled a preening rooster. "What if we round the killers up and hold our own trial? I'm keeping my cow. Those men are guilty and we all know it."

Henry didn't argue.

"I wonder how long the jury will deliberate?" Katherine asked herself.

Robert shook his head. "As complicated as all this is, they might need two or three days."

Robert was shocked beyond belief when the court reconvened at two o'clock sharp. The jury had been in deliberation for just more than two hours, and had time for lunch to boot. Robert sat between two men he didn't know, but who were obvious Mormon haters. From time to time they sipped corn whiskey from a small canning jar. They smiled, anticipating the verdict. Katherine and Sheriff Deming sat eight rows ahead of Robert.

The long-legged jury foreman arose. He was a wire-haired man with deep-set dark eyes named Jabez A. Beebe. His face carried a smirk, a new source of irritation for Robert. Beebee handed Judge Young a written verdict. It read:

*We the jury find the defendants not guilty, as charged in the indictments.*

Robert had expected the worst, but for a few seconds he was motionless and could not breathe. He felt as though life had been sucked out of him. It was impossible to grasp the true horror of the verdict—five men guilty of murdering Joseph Smith were going to be set free! He closed his eyes, his thoughts a swirling tempest of hate and regret. He began to shake. Satan and the secret combinations had won again.

Except for Robert, Katherine, Sheriff Deming, the prosecution lawyers, and the few prosecutions witnesses who were still in the building, the courtroom roared and stomped its festive approval.

The men seated next to Robert began to laugh and clap their hands.

Still feeling fuzzy, Robert narrowed his eyes and gave the man on his left a mad stare. He lowered his voice and spoke through his grinding teeth. "What are you laughing about?"

Through tobacco-stained lips the man said, "There's not a man in here that don't know the defendants done murdered Joe Smith. But it wasn't proven. The verdict of not guilty was right in law. And you won't be able to find an original Hancock County resident who will not stoutly sustain that verdict."

The man turned and let out a cheer. Robert said, "I ought to knock you on your rear end." The man returned an icy glare.

Katherine was sobbing in the arms of Sheriff Deming. Without comment, he patted her on the back.

Robert was further shocked when a man approached the sheriff and issued a blunt warning, half drowned out by the cheering of the spectators. "You're a marked man, Deming. Join our cause or suffer the consequences."

Deming gave the man an icy stare and let it pass. Robert, however, balled his fists. Deming held Robert back. "Let him go," Deming said. "He's not worth the trouble."

Out on the square Robert and Katherine had trouble locating Henry and Annie. It seemed to Robert that all the men and women of Carthage and

Warsaw were celebrating not only in the square but also in the streets. Drinks were flowing in the bars and taverns. Shots were fired in the air.

"What'd I tell you?" were Henry's first comments when they came together. "When do I get my cow?"

Robert blanched at Henry's coldness. "The men were guilty. I keep my cow."

"Who says?"

"Me, Henry. If you think you can take a cow from me, just try it. I'm not in a very good mood. And I'm tired of you treating our enemies like friends and our friends like enemies. You and your friends around here have maligned Mormons all I can stand. I can smell the garbage, so button up."

Henry was silent.

"Where's my horse, Henry? I'm going home. I've had enough of Carthage."

# 88

ROBERT'S MIND WAS A RAGING BLUR as he rode home on Lawless. Everything had gone wrong at Carthage from day one of the trial when the clerk called the case of *People v. Thomas Sharp, Mark Aldrich, Levi Williams, Jacob C. Davis, and William Grover.* Robert ground his teeth in anger as he thought about the judge caving in to the motion of the murderers' lawyers that he quash the jurors chosen by duly elected county commissioners. That had started a downhill slide for the prosecution.

He let Lawless loaf into a lazy walk. The sun peeked through drifting clouds in the west. Birds chirped in the swaying branches of trees; others hid under tall pokeberry and sweet rocket, pretty and fragrant. Reddish-looking Bobwhites scurried for cover, whistling their rallying call. A few exercised their wings, making a whirring sound. A dragonfly with a three-inch wingspan flew by.

Robert ignored all these beauties of nature.

*I'd like to have been in the room when that was all arranged,* he thought. He wondered where the clandestine meeting had taken place, and how much money had been paid to the judge. Or did threats do the job? Had it been done in one of the rooms in the Hamilton House where the judge and lawyers were staying? In the home of one of the rabid anti-Mormons in or around Carthage? Or right in one of the rooms of the courthouse? Did the judge sell his soul for a hundred dollars? A thousand? Ten thousand? Ten thousand or more dollars could be possible, given the number of anti-Mormons who would have contributed to a bribe fund.

There was a reason that the judge permitted the courthouse to be filled and surrounded by armed bands that were there to browbeat and overawe the administration of justice. Robert wondered if the judge had been compelled to allow those strange things to happen, or if he had been in collusion with them all along.

And where were the Mormon apostates during the trial? Funneling money to the judge and the defense attorney? Had Wilson Law and his gang been in town all along, but out of sight? Fearful that they might be arrested, or be subpoenaed to testify?

Robert wondered how those who testified in the trial would fare afterward. Would they be harassed, run out of town—even murdered? He hoped that prosecution witnesses like William M. Daniels, Eliza Jane Graham, and Benjamin Brackenbury were smart enough to stay far, far away from Carthage and Warsaw.

In Robert's opinion, Daniels had been more anxious for the glorification of the Prophet than to avenge his death, which destroyed his credibility as a witness. Although he became convinced Joseph was a Prophet when he saw him die, Daniels originally had been with the Warsaw troops who helped with the assassination.

He thought of Sheriff Deming, too. True, Deming was a man of influence and the commander of the Carthage militia. But the court had reduced him to ashes and he might not ever recover. He knew Deming to be sensitive, deeply religious, and opposed to mob activities. But all those things automatically put the sheriff in harm's way with the Mormon-haters around Carthage. From now on Deming would not be able to so much as twitch a muscle without drawing the ire of enemies and people who would threaten to kill him. Worse, the enemies would put untold pressure on him to join their side. Every strategy of the enemy was designed to demoralize, suppress, and kill. Anti-Mormons, in Robert's view, aimed to destroy the Church and all its followers with their relentless attacks on morality and truth.

Now more than ever, Robert hated the enemy. They were Satan's tools on earth.

"Hey! You on the horse!"

Robert's deep thoughts were interrupted by the intrusion of four dim figures on horseback, barely illuminated in their hiding place deep in the trees. All were armed and they looked like born killers. Chilled by the sight, he pulled Lawless to a stop.

"Mormon boy going home with his tail tucked beneath his legs?" said one. The man had a musket in his arms. He had lined up the muzzle with Robert's forehead.

"You want to try to knock me on my rear end now?" another asked, a smug smile crossing his lips.

Robert felt a knot in his stomach as he sent a blistering gaze at the four horsemen who rode out of the long, murky shadows of the trees. He recognized the man who had just spoken—he had sat next to him in the courtroom. A straw hat covered dark hair. The man was stocky and dark, almost Neanderthal, dressed in drab brown trousers and a tan shirt. He had olive skin and long mutton-chop sideburns.

"Not with those guns pointing at me," Robert said, his anger still pent up. "Even without the guns, I'd be outnumbered."

"Get off your horse," the man said, radiating a fiery clarity. He carried a standard-issue state militia Model 1842 musket rifle. He also had a large knife in his belt.

"Aim the rifle the other way and maybe I will," Robert answered as his eyes narrowed further. He did a reality check; any optimism was futile.

The man scoffed. "You're in poor position to make demands." He cocked the musket. "Get off the horse."

Robert dismounted as he continued his menacing stare at the men, his face a mask of repugnance. The four horsemen also dismounted. A third man, short and barrel-chested, took the reins from Robert and led Lawless to a tree and tied him up. The man in the straw hat advanced toward Robert, his visage ice cold and evil. He held a knife in his hand and then placed it back in its scabbard, smirking calmly.

"Hold him," the straw-hatted man told the others as he fouled the air with steamy curse words. The three men twisted Robert's arms behind him. "This will teach you to sass me."

The man drew the nine-pound musket back and then crashed it at Robert's face. Robert ducked out of the way but the man jerked it back, this time catching Robert squarely on the left eye. As the searing pain reached Robert's nerve center, the man pounded Robert's stomach. Robert fell to his knees gasping. The other three men were still holding his arms. A final blow, administered by the rifle, caught Robert on the side of his head. The men let him collapse to the ground.

"Don't ever come back to Carthage, Mormon boy."

The four men exchanged curse words.

Robert was nearly unconscious as the four horsemen sped away. As he staggered toward Lawless, he found that he could see out of his left eye with his eye open or shut. The blow had split his eyelid.

Ann Fleming flinched when she saw Thomas Sharp lead members of the Warsaw militia into her tavern, the Warsaw House. All of them, nearly fifty in number, were half drunk. She guessed a number of victory celebrations had already been held in Carthage.

Sharp burst through the door pointing to the tables. "Drinks are on the house, boys." He leaned over the bar to talk to Mrs. Fleming. "Still got some of that money we gave you for the trial? If not, we'll give you some more. And thanks for helping to save our hides."

Mrs. Fleming drew a deep breath. She did not dare betray Sharp and his friends, not now, not ever. "You're welcome. I'll set the bottles out." She remembered the men as not only having a taste for bourbon whiskey but also for Burgemeister Beer, brewed by the Warsaw Brewing Company.

Ann Fleming put on a friendly face but underneath she cringed at having to give service to a roomful of murderers. As she went to work waiting on her customers, she recalled her testimony at the trial. She had been instructed to be as brief as possible and do everything she could do to counter what Eliza Jane Graham had said.

"Yes," she had told the court, "I can remember those men in my tavern."

"Did you hear them say anything about killing the Smith brothers?" the defense lawyer had said.

"No."

She had testified that she did not remember seeing Sharp or Grover among them, either. But she did verify that there was a wounded man in the tavern. She had been told that it would be okay to say that, because all three of the wounded men had fled and therefore were not on trial.

From across the tavern's counter, William Grover looked at her long and pensively. "Here's a nice tip for you," he said as he flipped her a half dollar.

"Thank you," she said politely, forcing a smile. In the background, all the men were again bragging about how they had murdered Joe and Hyrum Smith—just like they did that night nearly a year ago.

Ann Fleming had long ago resolved in her mind that it was far better to submit to the demands of the murderers than to have her tavern destroyed either literally or by having it snubbed by everyone in town.

# 89

HANNAH NEARLY FAINTED WHEN SHE saw Robert stumble through the door. The entire left side of his face was swollen with ugly black and blue welts and he was staring at her through the slit eyelid. She was immediately overcome with horrified bewilderment.

"Oh! My Lord! What happened to you?" She wailed those words as she held both hands to her tummy. Robert said a quick prayer with the hopes this wouldn't cause the baby to come early.

"Four mobbers jumped me on the way home," Robert said in an embarrassed tone. "I guess one of them didn't like what I said to him at the conclusion of the trial."

Hannah's mind was still grappling with the shock of Robert's wounds. Caked blood clung to his skin. She began dabbing at his face with a clean wet rag. "The trial's over? I guess it would be too much to ask, but did they find them guilty?"

Before Robert could answer, Daniel, Elizabeth, and Harriett burst through the door without knocking. Robert had his back to them and

Hannah was still cleaning the wound.

"Robert!" Daniel exclaimed in a booming voice. "We're dying to know—how did the trial turn out?"

Robert turned, exposing the side of his battered face.

Elizabeth screamed. Harriet reeled, drawing her hands to her face.

Daniel stared at Robert in astonishment. "It looks like war finally broke out and you lost," he said. "What happened?"

Still wincing in pain, Robert related a quick rendition of the final week of the trial, the parade of witnesses, Lamborn's deficiencies, the trial's mournful conclusion, and how the mobbers had jumped him on the way home. Elizabeth ran to her house and found a salve she had made out of fried mutton tallow and turpentine and began applying it to Robert's face.

Robert studied Hannah, Daniel, Elizabeth, and Harriet as he told the story. He could see a morbid feeling settle over them. Not only had Joseph and Hyrum been taken from the members of the Church, but also their killers had been set free. While everyone in Robert's house shared this gloom, Robert suspected that at this very moment the taverns in Carthage and Warsaw were filled with the lustiest celebrations of the century.

"Tell us," Daniel said, "do you think the jury as it was composed would have convicted those five men if John Taylor and Willard Richards would have testified?"

Robert's head was throbbing but he had the right answer as far as Hannah was concerned. "Now that I look back on it, the jury would have let the killers off no matter what. The whole communities of Carthage and Warsaw approved of the murders. Half the population of those towns was involved."

Daniel grimaced and shook his head. "And what do you suppose would have happened if the jury would have reached a guilty verdict?"

"Civil war," Robert said flatly. "Those hotheads would've gone berserk."

Harriet looked mournfully at Robert. "They would have killed you if they hadn't won the verdict. They about did anyway."

"I'll get back at them," Robert warned. "I've got their faces etched in my memory."

"You stay away from Carthage from now on," countered Hannah. "The trial is lost, and Elias is gone forever. I don't want you there anymore."

Hannah felt Robert's icy stare, from one eye. His other eye was bandaged shut. "I mean it. It's over, done, final."

Days later, early on June eleventh—Hannah gave birth to her sixth child, a girl. She promptly named her Julia Ann, "Julia" simply because she liked the name, and "Ann" after her mother. The birth came one day after Hannah's thirtieth birthday and exactly on Elizabeth's thirty-first birthday. And that day—June eleventh—was the day Hannah and Robert and Elizabeth and Daniel celebrated their tenth wedding anniversary. Just two and a half months earlier, Joseph had turned nine; Lizzy was seven a week later.

The anniversary was celebrated over an evening meal at the Browett house. Robert was surprised by Hannah's spunkiness and willingness, but Hannah had quickly dismissed the idea that she should remain in bed. "If the Indian women can be back on their feet the same day, I can, too," she said.

"Your mother will be pleased that you named the baby Julia Ann," Elizabeth said as she took roast prairie chicken out of the oven. Elizabeth, as a midwife and herbalist, had been busy the past two months. In April, Elizabeth had lamented the loss of a newborn baby belonging to Edward and Annie Phillips—the baby died of canker two months after his birth. Days later Elizabeth delivered a daughter to Levi and Harriet Ann Roberts, and a week later the daughter of William and Mary Kay. In May, about the time the trial in Carthage was winding down, a daughter was born to Jacob and Louisa Butterfield.

Hannah smiled. She had already told Elizabeth that her mother's most recent letter confirmed the fact that Elder Woodruff had indeed delivered Hannah's letter to her in Apperley, Gloucestershire, England. Her aging mother had just turned sixty-two.

It didn't take long for Robert to turn the conversation to the recently concluded trial. He had been cursing the fact that it appeared that there would not actually be another trial in Carthage for the murder of Hyrum Smith. The first trial had been for the murder of Joseph. "Sheriff Deming will never be able to round up the witnesses again," Robert lamented. Judge Young—in Robert's opinion—had poured salt into the wounds of all Mormons when he freed the five defendants on only five thousand dollars bail and set the trial for June twenty-fourth.

"Did any Mormons get selected for the trial yet?" Daniel asked.

"Are you kidding?" Robert responded. He repeated what Henry and Katherine had told them two days earlier during a visit—that twenty-four persons had been selected as petit jurors but not a single one of them was a Mormon. "I'm willing to bet that not a single prosecution witness will show up for the trial—which will please the judge and everyone in Carthage and Warsaw."

Robert went on to admit that he dreamed about the trial and the results almost every night. "I can still see the smug faces of the five defendants and the defense lawyers," he said as he shook his head in anger.

"I don't think the Church is going to spend any more money on the whole thing," Daniel said. "Brigham Young has complained so much about lawyers and what they charge that I think everyone's ears are ringing."

When Katherine walked into the courthouse the day of the Hyrum Smith murder trial—June twenty-fourth—she sensed something bad was about to happen. Sheriff Deming, who until today had never worn a gun, showed up with a pistol strapped to his hip. That's because the courthouse was filled with the men who had killed Joseph and Hyrum Smith. The killers were free men and now sought to drive more nails in the coffins of Joseph and Hyrum.

Deming had earlier complained that none of the prosecution witnesses that had been subpoenaed were going to show up, and that Lamborn probably wouldn't either. But as sheriff, he had to be at the courthouse and do his duty. Deming also complained that it appeared Governor Ford and Lamborn were in some sort of collusion to literally give up on any further trial effort.

Katherine tried to make herself invisible. Notebook in hand, she cowered in a corner as an argument erupted between the sheriff and a man named Samuel Marshall. Marshall had originally been on the witness list for the Joseph Smith trial, but he had refused to appear. The argument was not only about the trial, but also over a contested land sale. There were harsh words and Marshall began cursing.

Suddenly, Marshall leaped at the sheriff, grasped him by the collar, and began beating him.

Katherine gasped, wondering if the sheriff would defend himself.

As the beating worsened, Katherine knew Sheriff Deming had no choice. In horror, she watched him struggle to draw his gun out of the holster.

*Bang!*

Samuel Marshall collapsed to the floor with a fatal stomach wound.

Katherine had the sinking feeling the next day that her employment in the sheriff's office was at an end. Not only did Judge Young dismiss the Hyrum Smith murder trial "for want of prosecution," but also—because he was pressured by the anti-Mormons—the judge quickly assembled a grand jury and indicted the sheriff for killing Sam Marshall.

"What are you going to do?" she asked the sheriff later that day.

Deming slowly shook his head. "My wife thinks I ought to resign."

"Why?" Katherine asked as they talked in his office.

"So that it doesn't appear that I used my office to prejudice my own trial," he responded.

"But that'll mean we'll have to have a special election and elect a new sheriff," Katherine wailed.

"The Mormons still control the vote," he countered.

"Who would run?"

"I've already talked to Jacob Backenstos."

Katherine nodded her approval. Although he was not a member, Backenstos was considered a friend of the Mormons. Katherine felt he would win the election easily.

# 90

ROBERT WENT TO BED IN A GRUMPY MOOD. All day long he and Daniel had argued about whether or not a Mormon vigilante posse ought to be organized to hunt down the murderers of Joseph and Hyrum. It was June twenty-sixth—tomorrow would be the first anniversary of the horrible event.

"Leave it alone," Daniel had warned. "Those men in Carthage and Warsaw are just looking for an excuse to raid Mormon settlements." He pointed to the necessity of the Church resorting to "whistling brigades" in town. Even nine-year-old Joseph had joined this junior militia. The boys carried whittling knives and scabbards and went around the city whistling and whittling on sticks to warn "ne'er-do-wells" out of town.

"See?" Robert said. "We let boys like my son be organized and get something done, but the men sit at home twiddling their thumbs!"

Robert knew that the boys didn't attack anyone, but let outside visitors know they were being watched. The roving guards jokingly referred to their targets as "black ducks." That included all non-Mormon visitors and even some of the disaffiliated Mormon leaders. Robert had given vivid description of Wilson Law and the other apostates to his son and the other boys. "You let me know if you see any of those men in town," he had said.

"I think Brigham Young is going to put an end to the junior militia," Daniel said. "It's drawing too much criticism."

"We've got to do something," Robert said. "Everyone goes to bed with one leg out of bed and with one eye open. We outnumber the non-Mormons. Why do we let them intimidate us so much?"

"Think about your newborn baby," Daniel counseled. "If there were a war, we'd want it to between the men. But the other side would start killing women and children. You know that as well as I do. You've got to purge yourself of your hatred. It's consuming you."

All these things were on Robert's mind as he went to bed. The city had lost its charter. Families out in the settlements were not safe. Enemies of the Church accused members of the Council of the Twelve of vile crimes, including counterfeiting. Worst of all, not one of Joseph and Hyrum's murderers had been convicted. Not one.

The bizarre image of Henry Eagles sitting on a steamy, lathered gray horse startled Robert. He had not been expecting a visit from Henry, but there he was with a big grin on his face.

"I've ridden out here to give you some good news," Henry said, his always wicked smile somehow surreal this time.

Robert leaped off his front porch, sensing something important. "What?" he asked.

"There's going to be a big celebration tonight at the Warsaw House," Henry began as he dismounted. "Word is that everyone who had anything to do with Joe Smith's death is going to be there."

Robert immediately perked up. "Tonight?" he asked as he glanced at the afternoon sun as though he were searching for any clue to substantiate Henry's claim. As always, the late June weather was hot and sticky.

"Exactly one year after the murders."

Robert was pleased that Henry used the term *murders*. "What time?"

"Midnight. Just like before, a year ago. Remember at the trial? That lady testified that the murderers met at the Warsaw House in the middle of the night and bragged about what they had done."

Robert nodded. "I remember."

"This is your chance," Henry said. "Round yourself up a mob of your Mormon buddies. I'll help you. Hurry—we've got time. We'll catch 'em off guard."

Robert began salivating. "Are you sure?"

"Doubly sure. Even your Mormon apostate friends are going to be there."

"Wilson Law?"

"Guaranteed."

Robert shook his head in disbelief. "Why are you telling me all this?"

"You know me—I like a good fight. Tell everyone to bring their rifles and pistols."

After he and Henry galloped into Nauvoo, Robert was amazed how quickly he was able to round up a group that volunteered to help. The story of the murderers holding a one-year anniversary party celebrating the death of the Prophet seemed to incite them equally. No one objected to joining the posse; rather, they were happy to do it. Robert soon had his mob following him— Thomas Bloxham, John Hyrum Green, Levi Roberts, John Cox, Edward Phillips, Joseph Hill, Jacob Kemp Butterfield, Charles Price, David Wilding, Richard Slater, Robert Pixton, John Cole, Robert Holmes, William Parsons, John Parry, Ezra Allen, John Cheese, and James Robins. Even Peter Maughan, the man who had married Mary Ann Weston Davis, joined them. Back at The Mound, Robert convinced Daniel to ride with them, and men like John Benbow, Thomas Kington, William Kay, and David Wilding. And other neighbors—William Blood, John Marriott, Robert Walton Burton, Hector Caleb Haight, William Lauder Payne, William Stewart, and Henry Wooley.

*Everything is clicking into motion so easily,* Robert thought as he led his Mormon mob to a swale covered with trees just outside Warsaw. Somehow the men had passed through De Moines City and Montebello along the Mississippi River without arousing suspicion, striking a southeasterly direction in a long trot. As the sun settled and darkness covered the grove, Robert began issuing orders.

"We'll surround the Warsaw House at one o'clock," he said in an authoritative voice. "By then they'll all be half drunk and they won't be able to offer much resistance."

Every man nodded obediently.

Visions of how the evening would proceed flashed through Robert's mind. The enormity of what he was doing almost overwhelmed him. He closed his eyes and willed himself to stay calm. "We'll have our own trial," he said. "John Benbow—you'll be the judge."

Benbow smiled. "More than happy."

Robert pointed to Thomas Kington. "Thomas—you're the jury foreman. Choose your jury."

Without hesitation, Kington quickly chose eleven other men.

Robert gave quick instructions to the others. They would be guards. He assigned some to guard the front door, others the back.

"Daniel," Robert said to his brother-in-law as he laughed. "You'll be the defense attorney."

Daniel returned the laugh. "There won't be much for me to do, will there?"

"No, my good friend," Robert said. "Not much at all."

"And what is your role?" Daniel asked.

"I'm the prosecutor and the executer."

"Executer?" Daniel asked.

Robert pointed to Judge John Benbow. "He'll hand out the sentences. I'll execute them."

"Let's see now," Benbow said, scratching his head. "Death by hanging is the stipulated sentence in the state of Illinois."

Robert held up a hand and slowly balled his fist. "I have a request. Before we hang them, let me do whatever I want with them. Break their arms, their jaws, their noses."

Henry seemed disappointed. "What about me? I alerted you to all this. What spoils do I get?"

Robert put his arm around Henry. "You get to help administer the beatings. Can you crack Thomas Sharp's jaw without breaking your knuckles?"

Henry balled his fists and laughed a wicked laugh. Above Robert's posse the stars were bright and the Milky Way came out like a long speckled cloud.

The door to the Warsaw House flew off its hinges when Robert burst through brandishing pistols in each hand. Dozens of cold gray eyes regarded him through a haze of cigarette, cigar, and pipe smoke. The celebrators stood stunned, wondering if Robert's appearance was some kind of joke. At the sight of Robert's weapons, one man dropped a whiskey bottle. It didn't shatter, but its contents flooded the wooden floor beneath the man's legs. Two others were wrenched out of a light sleep, or a drunken stupor. From a far corner rose the stench of another man disgorging his supper as the result of too much liquor.

"Don't anyone move!" Robert screamed as more of his Mormon mob leaped through the doorframe.

At the same time, Daniel crashed through the rear door, bringing with him more than a dozen armed men.

Robert chortled at the realization that he had caught the murderers completely off guard. None were armed. Most of them were glued to their barstools and chairs, their mouths wide open, and their eyes as big as saucers. Robert scanned the tavern room quickly. He guessed around a hundred men were there. The room seemed larger than it did the day he and Henry met Thomas Sharp, even with all the drunken bodies.

"All of you—over against that wall," he yelled, pointing at the north wall. Up high, the wall was gaily decorated with a banner that read:

FIRST ANNUAL CELEBRATION
DEATH OF JOE SMITH

"Who are you?" one asked as he stood.

Robert pulled the man to his face so closely he could smell the murderer's foul breath. He recognized the man as one of the five defendants, Levi Williams, the farmer from Green Plains. With his sunken cheeks, Williams looked like a haunted figure that might have been chiseled from Illinois granite. "We're the Mormon jury that *you* should have had during the trial. We brought our own judge, too."

Robert loved to live on the edge and had no intention of letting anyone do him out of any of his pleasures. Just for the sheer delight of it, Robert handed his pistols to Thomas Bloxham and threw his first punch. It landed squarely on Levi's nose, drawing an instant gush of blood. Robert drew his fist back and kissed it. He had thrown the blow without even feeling it.

"I know you!" stammered a surprised Wilson Law, spilling his whiskey as he rose to his feet. "You're a member of the Nauvoo Legion. I smell trouble."

Robert whirled at his old enemy. "What does trouble smell like? I never noticed it had an odor. You right sure you're not smelling yourself?" He leaped at Wilson and wrapped both his huge bony hands around the apostate's neck. There was no mistake: Wilson Law's face was indelibly printed in Robert's memory. "And you never did account for the hundreds of dollars you took for the rescue party last year, did you?"

Wilson couldn't answer. The former brigadier general of the legion was slowly turning blue from a lack of air and his vision began to blur.

"Did you use it for travel money to Carthage to murder my Prophet?" Robert screamed. He let go of Law's neck and let him collapse to the floor.

Robert whirled again, pointing wildly. He grabbed the closest oak chair and placed in on top of a round table. "John Benbow—you're the judge. You'll sit on this chair, up here where everyone can see you."

William Law stumbled to his brother's aid. "The trial's over," he said to Robert in a pleading voice. "You can't have another."

Robert swatted the older Law to the floor. "Wrong, buddy boy. Just you watch." Robert pointed to his mob. "All those selected for the jury, seat yourselves in a semi-circle on the right side of Judge Benbow."

# 91

"WHO DO YOU WANT TO TRY FIRST?" Judge Benbow asked the prosecutor from his bench—a chair atop a table stained with whiskey and beer.

Robert smiled in relief. After more than a year of hatred building up inside, he was finally letting it all out. "Wilson Law," he said.

"But this is an outrage!" Wilson protested as Robert dragged him to a barstool and plopped him on it. "I wasn't on trial—those men were!" He pointed to the five defendants, Thomas Sharp, Mark Aldrich, William Grover, Jacob Davis, and Levi Williams—who was still nursing his nose. A once-white handkerchief was soaked in red blood.

Robert ignored the remonstration and began the proceedings. He found a piece of white paper and pretended to read from it. "Every man in this room is hereby indicted for the murders of Joseph and Hyrum Smith, June twenty-seventh, exactly one year ago. You are charged with storming the Carthage Jail and either directly firing the shots or being an accessory to the fact. Look around you, gentlemen. Do you see men in attendance at this courtroom armed with muskets, rifles, and pistols? How do you like it? Do you see a tilted jury, made up of all Mormons? How do you like it?"

Fear plainly crossed Wilson Law's hard, chiseled face. With both hands, he was massaging his mangled neck.

Robert was not done. He turned and spoke to the jury. "The twelve men assembled here as a jury will hear the evidence and render a verdict of guilty. This is a rigged jury, just like the one in Carthage." Robert pointed to the stunned crowd. "The guilt of this crime hangs over you as a blight and a curse upon this generation of people, a bloodstain upon this dispensation. This is a foul blot that must be avenged."

"But where's my defense attorney?" Wilson asked meekly, his chest heaving with anxiety.

"My friend, Daniel Browett," Robert stated in a flat voice. "He's your attorney. He's the best I could find you. He's really favorable to my side, but that's just going to be the case. Not fair, but neither was the trial in Carthage. Let the games begin. I call my first witness, Levi Roberts."

Levi strolled toward Benbow's bench, staring at Robert.

"Levi Roberts—is it true or not true that both John Taylor and Willard Richards stated by affidavit that they saw Wilson Law in the group of men that stormed the jail, forced themselves up the stairs, and entered the room of the jail with smoking weapons in their hands?"

Levi's smile was wide. "Yes, sir. That is true."

"Thank you, Mr. Roberts. I call my second witness, John Cox."

John took Levi's place on the witness stand. An amazed look crossed the face of Wilson Law. He appeared as though he had missed something, or that things were going much too fast.

Robert was not a man to choke on details; he wanted the trial to be over quickly. "Mr. Cox, can you verify that the testimony of Levi Roberts is true, that John Taylor and Willard Richards signed such an affidavit?"

"No doubt about it. I testify to that effect," Cox answered.

"The jury will regard the testimony of these two men as true," Robert stated. "In the mouths of two or three witness shall the truth be established."

Wilson Law began his protest. "But those affidavits were never introduced as evidence in the Carthage court," he complained.

Defense attorney Daniel Browett smiled and shrugged his shoulders. Of course they weren't, by design of the opposition.

Hot anger flared within Robert. He pulled Wilson to his face, and nose-to-nose he said, "That's because John Taylor and Willard Richards were threatened with their lives if they came to Carthage to testify to the validity of their affidavits. You can blame the men right here in this room."

Robert stared at the ceiling for a few moments, thinking. "I suppose some of those threats actually came from you, Mr. Law." He pulled Wilson a little closer and a little tighter. "Is that true?"

"I will not answer that," Law stammered.

Robert turned to the jury again. "You will…"

"Just a minute," Judge John Benbow objected. "Instructing the jury is my job."

"Yes, your honor," Robert said as he released Wilson Law from his grip.

"Gentlemen of the jury, you will regard Mr. Law's statement as incriminating, because he would not answer. He probably issued such threats, but the prosecutor has no way of actually proving it."

Wilson was massaging his neck again.

Robert pointed a bony finger at Law. "The court not only charges you with murder, but conspiracy to commit murder!"

"What's the difference?" Wilson moaned.

"We let you hang by the neck three hours until dead, instead of just breaking your neck instantly," Robert said, the glare in his hazel eyes intense.

"Three hours?"

"There were three hours of darkness when the Savior hung on the cross," Robert stated. "That's what a son of perdition deserves—at least three hours suffering."

Wilson groaned again. "What's the point?"

"The true definition of a 'son of perdition' is one who would have crucified the Savior if he had the chance."

Wilson gasped this time, absorbing the meaning.

"You're a son of perdition, my ex-Mormon friend. You and the other apostates are in the same category, sons of perdition. You had a testimony of the gospel, and then denied it."

"But that doesn't make us sons of perdition," Wilson pleaded, fighting back tears.

"It wouldn't if you had just gone away and not battled against the Kingdom, and killed the Prophet. You should have just gone to Galena and stayed there, not causing a problem."

Wilson rose to his feet, screaming. "I'm not a son of perdition!"

Robert shoved him back into a chair, and then turned to Judge Benbow. "I rest my case, your honor. Here's the summary. That Wilson Law and the other Mormon apostates in this room were in Carthage during the incarceration of Joseph and Hyrum Smith is such a well known fact that we don't need to waste the court's time with that evidence. We know they had meetings with members of the Carthage Greys and members of the Warsaw militia, all in conspiracy to kill Joseph and Hyrum. The most damaging testimony is that of John Taylor and Willard Richards, which is irrefutable."

Benbow turned to the jury foreman, Thomas Kington. "Mr. Kington, is your jury ready to render a verdict?"

Kington huddled with the jury members for a few seconds. He stood and faced Judge Benbow. "Yes, sir. We have reached a verdict, your honor. That verdict is guilty on both counts. Guilty to murder in the first degree, and guilty to murder by conspiracy."

Benbow called the defendant to his bench. Wilson Law just stood there, dumbfounded, so Robert dragged him there.

"The jury has found you guilty. The court sentences you to death by hanging—the long and painful way, so that you will suffer even as the Savior suffered. Before your hanging, however, the court sentences you to a beating at the hands of the prosecutor."

Wilson Law's jaw dropped to the floor. "What?"

Benbow was quick to respond. "Just as the Savior was flogged, you will subject to a flogging of sorts. Whatever the prosecutor wishes to do."

Robert rolled up his sleeves. "I'll make this fair, Mr. Tough Guy. We'll have a match, a bare fisted fight. Just you and me." Robert pushed the jurors away. "Give us some room—about twenty or thirty feet square will do."

Wilson Law was smiling now. "And if I win?"

"If you win, you'll go free. I'll see that your sentence is remanded. In fact, I'll remand the sentence of every defendant in this room."

There was a general rumble in the room as the hundred or so murderers contemplating Robert's words.

"But I won't lose," Robert stated.

Wilson Law rolled up his sleeves. "I don't know about that."

Robert considered the insanity of Law's words and motioned to Daniel. "You're the referee. Do your job."

"Want me to recite Broughton's Rules?" Daniel asked.

"The short version," Robert said, displaying his impatience to get at Wilson Law.

Daniel held a hand in the air and quieted the crowd. "In the corner to my left I introduce the combatant Wilson Law. He's Irish, born in Ireland, but raised in Canada. Spent three years of his life in Nauvoo as a Mormon, denied the faith, and now lurks around various places in Illinois, from Galena to right here in Carthage and Warsaw. I'd guess him to weigh two hundred pounds, about the same as his opponent, and I'd guess him to be in his upper-thirties, a year or two older than Mr. Harris."

Daniel pointed to his right. "You all know the other combatant, our prosecutor. He's English, born in Gloucestershire. He came to Nauvoo in 1841 and has kept the faith. He has a temper and he holds grudges. He's held a grudge against you apostates for a long time, and now he holds a grudge against every murderer in this courtroom. I'd hate to be you, Mr. Law. In England, Mr. Harris did quite well as a pugilist, undefeated."

Wilson Law's concern began to show in his face but he did not flinch or back down, much to Robert's delight.

Daniel motioned to two other apostates, William Law—Wilson's brother—and Chauncey Higbee. "You two will be seconds. See this odd board in the floor? That's what we'll call the scratch line. If your man gets knocked down, you have thirty seconds to bring him to that line or the fight is over."

There was a combined gasp in the crowd, each of whom now had a vested interest in the contest. They watched as Wilson Law took off his shirt, displaying a sculptured torso and rippling muscles.

"Whom do you want for your seconds?" Daniel asked Robert.

Robert started to say Henry and Thomas Bloxham, but he stopped himself. "Why would I need seconds? I won't get knocked down."

Daniel found the tavern's dinner bell and rang it. "Round one!"

Robert chuckled to himself as Wilson Law drew his arms up into a classic fighting style and began circling him. One whack would do for just about anyone else on trial. It might take two whacks to lay Wilson on the floor.

"My brother's never been beaten in any kind of fight," William Law hissed from the sidelines. "He's the only one who ever threw Joe Smith, but Ole Joe never would admit it."

"Then the odds favor your brother," Daniel said. "The Prophet threw Robert one day—but of course that was wrestling. They never tried bare fists."

Wilson lunged at Robert, throwing a haymaker right. It missed its mark.

"I'll give you one more try," Robert said with a baritone laugh. He stared at Law's fleshy face punctuated by puffy cheeks and thick lips. His eyes were large and egg-shaped. They seemed to bulge from their sockets. "And then I'll do my damage. We've got a lot to do tonight. Nearly a hundred defendants."

This time Wilson jabbed at Robert with his left hand—two, three, four times. That was followed by the haymaker right again, which missed. Quick as a cat, Robert countered with a left cross of his own, which caught Wilson on the ear. Stunned, Wilson backed away as Robert chased him. There was a blinding combination of rights and lefts, all hitting their marks. One blow caught Wilson in the stomach and the air whooshed out of him. As he dropped his guard, Robert took a lightning quick aim and smashed blows to Wilson's ears, nose, and jaw. There was a cracking sound as bare knuckles found the jawbone. His jaw broken, Wilson collapsed to the whiskey-stained floor, bleeding from the nose and ear.

William Law stood stunned.

"I reckon there'll be a continuation of this trial," Robert gloated. "And you're next, William." He grasped the smaller of the Law brothers by the nape of the neck and led him to John Benbow's bench. "What do you say, Judge Benbow? Shall we try the rest of the apostates as a group?"

Benbow nodded his approval, breathing easier.

Daniel found the other apostates in a state of shock and led them to the bench: William Law, Chauncey Higbee, Francis Higbee, Charles Foster, Robert Foster, Joseph H. Jackson, Augustine Spenser, Henry O. Norton, and Sylvester Emmons.

"Each of you is named by both John Taylor and Willard Richards, so you are condemned," Robert said, scanning the faces of the men he hated. "You're all apostates, and you're all likely to be judged by the Savior to be sons of perdition. In my book, you're all sons of something else."

Robert grinned.

"William Law—I'm particularly disappointed in you," Robert said. "How can a man who rubbed shoulders with the Prophet as his trusted first counselor go astray as far as you did?"

William didn't answer. The implications of what his accuser had suggested were far reaching. He began to shake, fearing a death by hanging.

Robert slapped him in the face and the sound echoed throughout the large silent room. "I asked you a question!"

William drew deep, short breaths, unable to speak.

"Why did you believe your wife when she told those lies about Joseph? You knew they weren't true." Robert paused for an answer. William full well knew what he was talking about. William had rejected the principle of eternal marriage and so his wife, Jane, had asked Joseph if she could be sealed to him. Because Joseph said no, she reacted in the typical "woman scorned" fashion. She told William that Joseph had asked her to become a plural wife, which enraged William.

"I hated Joe Smith," William stammered. Fueled by whiskey, the words rushed out of him. "I knew my wife was lying, but I had had it with Joe, any way. He took all the glory positions for himself—mayor, president of the Church, head general of the Legion. He defied state laws when the Missourians tried to extradite him. He tried to kill Governor Boggs."

Robert did not waver after William's hollow explanations. He slapped him again. "You know that Joseph and Porter Rockwell didn't do that!"

William turned his head. "I know—I'm just too used to saying it."

"What else?" Robert asked. "Get it all out."

"Land sales," William said in a very low voice. "How could my brother and I make enormous profits when we had to compete with the Church?"

Robert whirled to face Judge Benbow. "I rest my case!"

Benbow turned to Kington and the jury. In unison they yelled, "Guilty!"

Robert shoved William to the floor, where William fell next to his bleeding, whimpering brother.

Attention next was turned to the Higbee brothers. Robert cursed them for their apostasy, telling them that their father—Elias Higbee, a faithful member of the Church—was undoubtedly rolling over in his grave at their deceitful and disgraceful actions. He cited their habit of giving business to the "house on the hill" and contracting a venereal disease.

"Guilty!" said the jury.

"And you!" Robert yelled at Dr. Robert D. Foster. "You've been a problem and a classic failure in morality from the beginning. Womanizer! If I had been the Prophet I would've excommunicated you long before your time. Joseph was too tolerant, too patient, too forgiving. How many times did you try to kill Joseph before you got the job done? How did you feel, firing at the helpless Prophet and his brother in the jail? What say ye, jurors?"

"Guilty!" On it went for Foster's brother, Charles, and Sylvester Emmons, editor of the *Nauvoo Expositor*. And the other Mormon apostates.

"Guilty as charged!"

Henry Eagles rushed to Robert's side. "Let me have a crack at some of these Mormons," he said.

"They're not Mormons," Robert said. "Far from it. One crack each at them for now; we'll do the real damage later, after we try all the others."

# 92

ROBERT HATED EVERYTHING THERE was to hate about Thomas Sharp. He hated his bulbous hooknose, the deep crease lines between his nose and mouth, the way he parted his hair on the left side, and the way he shaved his face but let the whiskers grow around his jowls and under his chin. Robert thought that even for a thirty-two-year-old man, Sharp was too cocky for his own good.

"You hate Mormons, don't you Mr. Sharp?" Robert began.

"You can read can't you?" was Sharp's tart reply. Sharp's hair looked like it had a can of secondhand lard poured over it, so complete was the sweat he had worked up.

"I wouldn't lower myself to read your scathing editorials," Robert said. He was well aware that Sharp's skill and persuasiveness were considerable. After the suppression of the *Expositor* in Nauvoo, Sharp had used his newspaper—the *Warsaw Signal*—to openly advocate killing Mormons with "powder and ball."

"Your version of frontier justice is barbaric," Sharp said as he hooded his eyes, looking for any possible escape route. There were none. Members of the Mormon mob had every exit blocked.

"You formed the anti-Mormon party. You have pounded it into the residents of Hancock County that Mormonism is a weird psychological obsession and that Joseph Smith was the evil genius behind it."

Sharp seemed to swell up. "Yes, I admit to all that. That spiritual wifery stuff is quite weird."

Robert grabbed Sharp by the shirt collar and pulled him to his face. "Your rote smirking at my Prophet and at my Church is linked to your own psychological compulsion to snobbery. You've stonewalled the truth about Mormonism and you'll never bring yourself to apologize. You're all alike, you Mormon-hater blue bloods. All you've wanted to do is sow fear and undermine a peaceful people."

"I just told the truth," Sharp whimpered.

"The news industry is the last place on earth you'd go for the truth about my Church," Robert countered. "Even Joseph Smith's exemplary personal life was subject to your gleeful jeers. You have a bleak, bankrupt vision of virtue. Why didn't you try reading the Book of Mormon and come to a spiritual conclusion about Mormonism?"

Sharp snorted his derision at the Book of Mormon.

"You're about to enter hell, Mr. Sharp," Robert threatened. "I might even make you dig your own grave."

Sharp began to shake. "The government will catch up with you for this. You're a dead man."

"You were in collusion with the Mormon apostates, weren't you?"

"How can you prove that?"

"Is your hearing impaired? Mr. Henry Eagles is beating confessions out of them now."

Henry's foot was on Robert D. Foster's head with plenty of pressure being applied. "Yes! Yes!" Foster was screaming. "We had it all arranged with the Warsaw boys!"

Foster's screams were loud enough for Sharp to hear clearly. The confession struck him like a blow and he began to cower in fear.

"And that's why you jumped on the wagon at Golden Point and made your impassionate speech, isn't it?" Robert pressed.

Sharp knew the kangaroo court was going to find him guilty regardless. "I'd say my speech was a success, wouldn't you?"

Robert pointed to a group of frightened Warsaw militia members, huddled at the north wall of the tavern. "You've condemned those men to hell, Mr. Sharp. They're all guilty of murder, and murdering men don't go to heaven."

Men against the wall trembled. Robert only knew a few of their names—James Wood, a blacksmith; Thomas L. Barnes, a quack doctor; Sylvester Bartlett, editor of the newspaper in Quincy; and Samuel Fleming, the Warsaw constable.

Robert turned to Judge Benbow. "I rest my case against Thomas Sharp your honor."

"Guilty!" shouted the jury.

From the north wall, Robert pulled three men from the crowd—William Voras, John Wills, and William Gallaher. "You three were the first men up the stairs at the Carthage Jail that day," Robert charged. "And you conveniently ran away before the trial began. Wonder why?"

The three young men trembled at the words.

With a swift, deft, powerful move, Robert ripped the shirt off John Wills. "Where'd you get that arm wound?" he asked the young Irishman. Robert spun Wills around to face the jury and to show the scar. "You got it at the jail because either Joseph or Hyrum Smith shot you in self defense, didn't they?"

Tears streamed down Wills' face. "Yes! Yes!" he admitted.

"Guilty!" screamed the jury.

Robert did the same to William Gallaher, exposing an ugly scar on his shoulder. "And this man? Look at that scar!"

With those words, he pulled the third man's face directly to his. "And look at the scars on this ugly face. Had part of your face shot away, didn't you boy? Didn't you Mr. V-o-o-r-h-e-e-s?" Robert stretched out the correct pronunciation of the Bear Creek hobbledehoy murderer's name.

"Guilty!" said the jury.

Jacob D. Davis erupted. He lurched to the center of the room and took the stance of a politician, like the state senator that he was. His normally fine features were contorted into a mask of disagreement. "This has gone far enough! This is not fair!"

Robert leaped at him and knocked the senator's beaver hat off his head, revealing a mass of dark, curly hair. "Fair? Let me tell you about fair! Sit down and listen!"

Robert pushed Davis into an empty chair.

"I came here from England seeking a haven of safety, and a place where I could join people like me and worship God as we please. Mr. Davis, this is America. In America, we have a constitution. It guarantees freedom of worship. You hate me because I believe a little differently than you do."

Davis sent Robert a frosty glare. "There are too damn many of you."

"But that's the American way, dummy. Majority rules. True, we Mormons can sway an election in Hancock County. And we had a powerful influence in the state elections, too. But that's fair, isn't it?"

Davis shook his head.

"In the election last August, the Mormon vote elected a Mormon county commissioner, beating out an anti-Mormon. What's not fair about that?"

No answer.

"That meant that two Mormons were now on the commission, along with one other man who was a Mormon sympathizer. One of their responsibilities was to select the grand jury for the Joseph Smith trial. The law required the commissioners to select a proportionate number of jurors from each township. The citizens of Nauvoo represented more than half the county population. Plus there were significant Mormon populations in several of the other townships. So it is fair to think that a lot of Mormons would end up on the grand jury. Correct?"

Davis, although steaming, was still silent.

"But your side—the anti-Mormons—did everything they could to intimidate the commissioners and the Mormons, even to the point of threatening us with civil war," Robert continued. "You issued death threat after death threat. The results showed it. Not one Mormon ended up on the list of twenty-three grand jurors that were chosen! Not one! Is that fair?"

Again, silence.

"Our county commissioners—bless their hearts—still did the best job possible under the circumstances. At least there were no anti-Mormons on the grand jury. I think it can be said that the grand jury at that point was deliberately composed of men who were either uncommitted or sympathetic to the Mormon cause."

Davis knew exactly where Robert was going with this. He ground his teeth in anger.

"And then what happened when the court convened?" Robert asked.

Davis smiled. "We got a better jury."

"Did you bribe Judge Young or threaten him with death?"

More silence.

"Or did you do both?"

Davis sneered. "Wouldn't you like to know?"

"Well, either way, it worked," Robert admitted. "The defense attorneys made a motion that the jury be dismissed and a new grand jury selected. Judge Young even went so far as to say that the jury must be composed of people who were sitting in the courtroom. Everyone knows that just about everyone admitted to the courtroom that day was a vehement anti-Mormon. So the new grand jury was composed entirely of anti-Mormon swine! Is that fair?"

"We got our verdict," Davis said.

"And we'll have ours," Robert retorted. He turned to Judge Benbow and Thomas Kington's jury. "I rest my case. What's the verdict on this man?"

Davis jumped to his feet. "This is not fair! Look at the armed men holding us hostage! The jury is all Mormon!"

"A reversal of tides, wouldn't you say?" Robert countered.

"Guilty!" cried the jury.

Robert was not done with the fairness issue. He turned to face the crowd of anti-Mormons stacked against the wall. "I am certain that it pleases all of you to know that the Mormons are planning to leave Hancock County and go somewhere out West. That means we will be selling our houses and farms, or abandoning them. The question for you is this—how many of you would be willing to give me a fair price for my new frame home just east of Nauvoo? Or a fair price for my farm?"

Not one hand went up.

"I'll re-ask the question," Robert said. "How many of you would be willing to take my house and my farm for nothing, after I am forced to abandon them?"

Every hand shot up.

Mark Aldrich's receding hairline and deep-set haunting eyes were the two features Robert noticed most as he started on the next witness. In minutes he had Aldrich in tears, begging for forgiveness for swindling money out of Mormon settlers at his real estate development in Warren, and for murdering Joseph Smith.

Robert was about to turn Aldrich over to Judge Benbow and the jury when a commotion was heard outside.

"You won't believe this, Robert," came a voice from near the front door.

Robert recognized the voice; it belonged to Levi Roberts. "Believe what?" he asked.

Levi barged through the door dragging a fine-dressed man. "This man says he is Governor Ford."

"My dear governor—what are you doing here?" Robert demanded. It was the governor all right. Robert remembered him from that day when Ford broke a horn off one of the wooden oxen that lined the baptismal font. There were the same thin lying lips, the long straight nosy nose, the eyes too close together, and the smartly combed brown hair over a not-too-smart skull.

"If you're the man in charge, I demand that your men release my aides outside," the governor stated in a huff.

Robert ignored Ford's authority and grabbed the governor by the lapel and spun him around. "I asked you a question—what are you doing here?"

Governor Ford quickly scanned the room with his blue eyes. "I was invited to a party," he admitted. "What's going on?"

Robert's mind was racing. He wanted to pepper the governor with questions, demanding explanations. "We're having our own trial."

Ford studied the men with guns. "You must be Mormons."

"Yes, we're Mormons," Robert stated. "As I said, we're having a trial. And you're next."

"What do you mean?" Ford asked, his face now a complex nest of worry lines and crow's feet.

"Shall we put him on trial?" Robert asked his fellow Mormons.

"Yes!" came the answer.

Robert shoved the governor into a chair. "I'm the prosecutor. You can be your own defense, since you're a former lawyer. And here's my first question."

"This is preposterous!"

Robert was thinking of John Taylor and the charges Taylor had leveled at the governor. "Not as preposterous as the murder of Joseph Smith. Now shut up!"

Ford was still scanning the large room of the Warsaw House, a makeshift courtroom. Men he recognized as members of the Carthage Greys and Warsaw militia were huddled in fear on one side of the room. Nearly a dozen Mormon apostates—men he called Wilson Law's gang—were cowering under guard of a wild-looking, dark haired Englishman. Wilson Law was bleeding from his nose, mouth, and ears. Twelve Mormon men were seated in a semicircle. Still another elderly Mormon was seated on a chair atop a table, staring down at him.

"You are charged with being an accomplice to the murders of Joseph and Hyrum Smith," Robert said.

Ford cursed and repeated his words. "This is preposterous!"

"Governor," Robert began, "I've always been curious. Has your compact with editor Thomas Sharp been a military alliance, or just an endorsement of

Sharp's murderous ideology?"

"I won't answer that," Ford said as he crossed his arms in a defiant gesture.

"Let's take it step by step, governor," Robert began. "We'll take it from the time the press of the *Nauvoo Expositor* was destroyed."

Ford's face was clouded with concern.

"Answer this question, governor. Really now, did the Nauvoo City Council and the mayor, Joseph Smith, break any law when we got rid of the nuisance of that newspaper? Answer that question according to the limitations of the Nauvoo Charter as authorized by the state legislature."

Ford slowly scratched his head. "Well, if you put it that way…"

Robert turned to the jurors. "Point number one is established."

"Where are you going with this?" the governor asked.

Robert simply asked his next question. "True, or not true, that you knew that mobs in Carthage and Warsaw met in the guise of citizens committees and passed inflammatory resolutions—resolutions that called for the extermination of Mormons from the county and from the state?"

Ford nodded. "Yes, I knew that."

"And did you not know that those mobs armed themselves and commenced hostilities against us?"

"Yes."

Robert patted himself on the back. This business of being a lawyer was a natural for him. "Governor, what you did next astonished all of us in Nauvoo. When you got into the middle of things, you activated the militia in Carthage and Warsaw, didn't you?"

"Well, yes. That's my job as governor when things get out of hand."

"Do you realize that when you activated the militia in those two communities, you enrolled the very men who wanted to kill Joseph and Hyrum Smith and gave them legitimacy, thus in a way legalizing their acts?"

Ford grimaced. "I had no choice. I didn't know which members of the militia were anti-Mormons and which were not."

"Don't give me that," Robert snorted. "You knew that ninety percent of the men in Carthage and Warsaw were Mormon haters."

"I suppose your right," admitted the governor.

Robert pointed to the specter of frightened men standing against the wall. "That even included Colonel Geddis, didn't it?"

Ford pulled his shoulders up. "Yes."

"At this point in time, after you activated the militia, did you—or did you not—disband the Nauvoo Legion?"

Ford thought for a moment. "Yes, I disbanded them. But I wanted to avoid an armed conflict."

"You gave no thought to a conflict between two forces, one armed, and one not armed? Is that your idea of a fair conflict?"

No answer.

Robert was on a roll. "The next thing you did was to request Joseph Smith to come to Carthage without an armed escort. Correct?"

"Yes."

"And you refused to interfere with the illegal move to put him in jail, correct?"

"Yes."

"And although you refused to interfere with the effort to put him in jail, you fully cooperated with the effort to have him come out of the safety of the jail. You sanctioned the use of force to have Joseph and Hyrum exposed to the mob for that little trip across the square to the courthouse, didn't you?"

Ford closed his eyes in a sign of admission.

"And contrary to your promise to help, you deliberately left Joseph and Hyrum in jail, didn't you?"

Silence.

"Before you left for Nauvoo, you dismissed all the troops from areas other than Carthage and Warsaw—men that might have been relied on to actually protect Joseph and Hyrum—and sent them home. Is that correct?"

"Yes, but ..."

"That left Joseph and Hyrum—and John Taylor and Willard Richards—under guard of the Carthage Greys, didn't it?"

Ford nodded, yes.

Robert pointed to the Carthage Greys against the wall. "Those men are the vilest anti-Mormons you could ever imagine. They are our most bitter enemies. They passed resolutions to exterminate us, to kill us. Those men had been placed under guard of General Deming only the day before. And you left them to guard the jail?"

"I did."

"That, sir, is preposterous!"

Ford slumped in his chair.

"The last piece of this conspiracy is that you left Carthage and came to Nauvoo, keeping us at bay while you delivered your treacherous little speech. Word was sent to the Warsaw militia to disband, thus freeing any Mormon sympathizers. That left a group of Mormon haters, about sixty men, ready and willing to run back to Carthage and take part in the killing."

Robert pointed to the men standing against the north wall.

Ford raised his eyes to take in the sight. Members of the Warsaw militia stood there speechless and trembling.

"Next came messages from the Carthage Greys and the Wilson Law gang. That was followed by steamy speeches from members of the anti-Mormon political party—Thomas Sharp and Mark Aldrich."

"I've heard that," Ford admitted, his thoughts a swirling tempest of fear and regret.

"And now what do we have?" Robert asked. "The recipe for murder. The recipe for conspiracy. As a result, the greatest individual in the history of the world—aside from the Savior himself and perhaps Adam, the first man—Joseph Smith, is dead."

"The greatest individual? Joseph Smith?" Ford pondered the words, scratching his head.

"And you, sir," Robert said, pointing, "are guilty of conspiracy!"

"Me?"

Robert whirled to face Judge Benbow. "The prosecution rests its case against Governor Ford."

Benbow's revulsion gave way to a broad smile. In his view, the governor was public enemy number one. "What say ye, honorable jurors?"

"Guilty!"

Ford jumped to his feet as a gesture of protest. "I'm going back to Springfield. Let me out of here!"

"Not without your due punishment," Robert said as he balled his fists.

"You're crazy!"

Robert's first blow caught the governor squarely on his fine pointed nose, sending a spray of blood. Cheers of approval from Robert's friends drowned out the screams of pain coming from the Illinois governor. The second blow broke several of the governor's ribs, and the third must have broken his jaw because he quit squealing through an open mouth.

# 93

ROBERT JERKED AWAKE WITH A VIOLENT motion. He lay in his bed a moment, taking stock, gasping for breath. He gained the realization that sweat was oozing from every pore. The bedding was soaked and his hair was a matted wet mass. Surely, a horse had kicked him in the head. He felt dizzy and exhausted, as though he hadn't slept at all.

"Wake up!" Hannah was saying as she poked at his ribs. Barely conscious, he felt her feet pushing at him. "Go check the baby. Go milk the cow. Wake Daniel up and get out to the fields."

Robert stretched and rolled his tongue through his parched mouth. He peeked out the window and tried to somehow gain control of his mind, to fuse together what he had experienced during the eerie night and the reality he now saw. The sun was barely up, meaning it was early—extremely early. It was June twenty-eighth, one of the longest days of the summer.

"Don't you dare go back to sleep," Hannah warned, probing her husband to his very core. "You've been kicking, hitting, squirming all night long. You ought to hear some of the things you've been saying. Sounded like you were re-living the trial all over again. What's wrong with you?"

Still in a fog and his head throbbing, Robert struggled to his feet. Little Julia Ann barely fussed, so he ignored her as he pulled on his trousers. His leg muscles were drawn up in knots.

"Don't make any noise in the kitchen," Hannah said. "Let me sleep another hour or two."

Robert stumbled into the kitchen, found a basin, and splashed water into his face. Feeling only partially revived, he limped outside to the well. Drawing water, he raised a bucket and let the contents wash over his rigid body, finally sending a chill that made him feel a little better. He lowered the bucket, filled it, raised it, and doused himself again.

A fearful bewilderment was sweeping over him. *Everyone has been one hundred percent correct,* he thought to himself. *The hatred that has built up inside me is consuming me. I've got to purge myself. This can't go on.*

He brought his knuckles to his face, examined them, and lowered them again. He found them normal, not swollen. *It must have been a dream,* he reasoned. *I really didn't hit those men. I wasn't at the Warsaw House last night. I wasn't the prosecutor. There was no trial. Thank God.*

"Riders coming."

Robert jerked his head up at Daniel's words. Five men on horseback were approaching from the direction of Nauvoo. The sun's orange ball was a third up from its eastern horizon. Robert shaded his eyes with a hand and said, "It's Brigham Young and some of the Apostles."

Robert and Daniel had been in their fields working since early morning. Hundreds of acres of prairie land near their farm had been enclosed in a circle of protection against possible raids from mobs. As the riders drew closer, Robert could identify the men: Brigham, John Taylor, Willard Richards, Heber C. Kimball, and Orson Pratt.

"Glad to see you working your farms," Brigham said as he dismounted a stout bay horse. "The crops along The Mound this year look good. Better than what we expected."

"Thank you," said Daniel as the men shook hands. "Just the right combination of rain and warm, sunshiny days I suppose."

Robert felt Brigham Young's eyes rake over him. "Brother Harris," Brigham said, "you look like a tornado hit you. Are you feeling well?"

Robert exhaled, telling himself to force the pictures of his nightmare out of his mind. The other Apostles were staring at him, too. "Just had a restless night," he said. "Once in while indigestion causes bad dreams."

"What did you eat?" John Taylor asked as he gave Robert a dubious look.

"I don't know exactly what it was," Robert said, "but it tasted like Governor Ford's dirty socks."

All the men laughed, much to Robert's relief. Immediately, he changed the subject. "How's Sheriff Deming doing?" he asked. For a brief moment, he wondered why the sheriff had not been in his dream.

Brigham Young was still searching Robert's face. "We're on our way to thank John Benbow," he explained. "Brother Benbow and some of his friends posted bail for the sheriff, same as they did for Joseph and Hyrum."

"How much this time?" Daniel asked.

"Ten thousand dollars," Willard Richards said. "Brother Benbow and the others had to swear to the lowest cash value of their property, so actually it amounted to more than twenty thousand dollars."

John Taylor seemed puffed up in anger. "Contrast that to the clemency extended by the court to Sharp, Williams, Aldrich, Grover, and Davis. They were admitted bail at only one thousand dollars each. They killed the Prophet in cold blood. Sheriff Deming killed Marshall in self defense."

Robert let a sly little smile come over him. "Well, brethren—we'll all just have to get over things like that and not let them bother us. Hatred can consume a man. You could have bad dreams if you dwell on things like that."

John Taylor blushed. "Brother Harris, you're absolutely right."

Daniel raised an eyebrow at Robert's remarks, and then turned to Willard Richards. "I hear your wife is not well. Give her our love."

"Thank you, Brother Browett," Elder Richards responded. "I will."

"Have you heard from Elder Woodruff?" Daniel asked Brigham.

"Yes, he's doing just great," Brigham answered. "I just wrote him a letter yesterday and gave him an update on the temple and the Nauvoo House."

Brigham paused and turned to scan Daniel and Robert's farm. "Won't be long until harvest time."

John Taylor sent Brigham a broad smile of agreement. "We'll need every bushel this year."

Brigham turned to Daniel and Robert. "May God bless this farm that you will have a productive harvest. Don't waste a kernel."

A premonition raced through Robert. "For the trip West?"

Brigham nodded. "It looks like this year's harvest will be the last for most of us. By spring, you'll be on your way to Oregon Territory or California."

John Taylor put on his most serious face. "Start preparing now," he warned. "We're meeting regularly, making plans. Every family will need a wagon, two or three yoke of oxen, two cows, two beef cattle, three sheep, and a thousand pounds of flour."

"And tents and tent poles, rifle and ammunition, bedding, cooking utensils," added Elder Richards. "We'll soon have a written list of the food you'll need to carry with you."

Robert stood sobered and speechless. All he'd heard previous to this were general comments about the possibility of someday having to leave Nauvoo. But today the brethren were being very specific. He'd heard only scanty news about an American explorer by the name of John C. Fremont, that Fremont had brought new knowledge of western territory back with him. Printed copies of his journal had made their way into St. Louis and Nauvoo.

"There's lots to do," Brigham was saying. "I'm going to be choosing leaders for the first company soon. Everyone ought to start building his covered wagons."

"Shouldn't be too difficult for you, Brother Browett," Willard Richards said. "As I recall, you were a cooper in England."

"I've made lots of barrels in my life and I've had experience in carpentry but I've never tackled a covered wagon," Daniel said.

"You're better off than most folks," Brigham said. "But we'll soon turn

Nauvoo into a vast wagon-building factory."

As Robert listened to all this he began having visions of what it would be like to trek into the American wilderness with a family of six children, one of them only a few months old. He shuddered at the responsibility and fear of the unknown.

"You're kidding," Robert said when he learned that Minor Deming had resigned as sheriff.

News of the sheriff's resignation had been brought to Robert and Hannah during a visit from Thomas and Dianah Bloxham.

"We're not kidding," said Thomas, Robert's brother-in-law. "We thought you'd like to know. We just heard about it this morning."

Thomas' appearance made Robert think about his dream again. He could still visualize Thomas riding off to the Warsaw House with him to hold the trial of the hundred or so murderers of Joseph and Hyrum. Robert shook himself back to reality. Sheriff Deming's resignation was going to be a sharp blow to the Mormons in Hancock County.

"Maybe you'd better go see Henry and Katherine again," Hannah suggested. "I'll bet that means she lost her job."

Dianah said, "If you go, tell Katherine hello for me."

Robert balked and held his hands in the air. "I've had enough of Carthage."

Dianah told him that a special election was going to be held in early August to choose a new sheriff. Dianah looked ill; the ague season always afflicted her.

"I feel sorry for Mr. Deming," Robert said, as Thomas went outside to watch the children at play. "You wouldn't believe what he went through during the trial—all the harassment. I'll bet it's been worse since, and has probably affected Katherine as well." Robert went on to tell details of his week in Carthage during the trial of the murderers of Joseph and Hyrum, wincing in remembrance.

"What is Mr. Deming like?" Dianah asked.

"He reminds me of your good husband, Sis," Robert answered. "He isn't a member of the Church, but might just as well be."

Robert went on to explain that Deming had become a sort of folk hero to all the Mormons since the martyrdom. When Joseph and Hyrum gave themselves up that day, it was Minor Deming—commander of the Hancock County militia units—who had personally met them outside Carthage and escorted them to town, trying to ensure their safety. In town, Deming had cordially introduced Joseph and Hyrum to his columns of troops in the town square, only to have the troops rudely greet them with hisses and foul cries. When Governor Ford disbanded the troops the day of the martyrdom, General Deming had urged the troops to go home and stay there. Deming openly deplored the murders of Joseph and Hyrum, drawing the wrath of the local citizens. Disregarding personal threats, Deming had restored order after the murders and personally tended to John Taylor. He also helped recover the bodies and provided eight reliable soldiers to escort the bodies back to Carthage.

"I voted for him for sheriff," Dianah said. "I hate to lose him."

The election had been held only two months after the murders. Prior to the trial, Robert explained, Deming had worked feverishly to arrest the men accused of the murders, even arresting a member of the state senate right on the floor of the senate. Since the trial, however, anti-Mormons had persecuted him relentlessly—culminating with the recent altercation in which Deming had to shoot one of the mobbers in self-defense.

"Do you really think Katherine will lose her position as special deputy?" Dianah asked.

Robert shrugged his shoulders. "It was temporary anyway."

"Katherine is better off at home anyway," Hannah said. "By now all the anti-Mormons in Carthage know who she is. They might start on her next—and Henry, too."

Robert snorted at the idea that Henry's old friends might turn on him. But he had to concede that it was possible. Virtually anything was proving possible in Hancock County, Illinois.

# 94

*September 1845*

ROBERT SLAPPED HIMSELF, WONDERING if he were dreaming again. There was the bizarre image of Henry again, sitting astride his steamy, lathered gray horse in front of the house. It was fairly early; the sun looked at about eight o'clock.

"Sheriff Deming's sick—very sick," Henry said, looking worn out from the long ride.

"What's wrong with him?" Robert asked, setting down his milk pail. For a moment he thought perhaps Henry had come to collect his cow.

"Consumption," Henry answered. "He's burning up with fever. Katherine sent me. Wants you and Daniel to give him a Mormon blessing. Trouble is, he's back at his home, in St. Mary's."

Robert groaned. St. Mary's was as far east from Carthage as Nauvoo was west. At least they wouldn't have to go through Yelrome where anti-Mormons were burning Mormon houses.

The conversation attracted Hannah's attention. She stepped out onto the porch with five children trailing behind. Lizzy held two-month-old Julia Ann in her arms.

"Thought you didn't believe in such things as blessings, Henry," Hannah said as she shielded her eyes from the morning sun.

Henry jumped off his horse and stretched his sore muscles. "I don't, but Katherine does. How about something to eat? I've ridden all night."

"Lucky for you I've got some leftover potatoes and eggs," Hannah said "Come on in."

"I'll go tell Daniel to saddle Bendigo," Robert said. He whistled for Lawless.

"Are you sure he'll be able to go?" Hannah asked. Elizabeth's baby was expected to come at any time.

On the way back to St. Mary's, Henry explained that Sheriff Deming's health seemed to go into decline right after that day in late June when Deming was attacked at the courthouse by men armed with pistols and knives. That resulted in the sheriff shooting the man named Marshall in the stomach. Marshall died, prompting an indictment against the sheriff by the anti-Mormons. Deming resigned as sheriff a few weeks later. In the August elections, Jacob Backenstos—a Mormon sympathizer—was elected.

"And Deming's health just kept going downhill?" Daniel asked.

"Straight downhill," Henry said. "Katherine says there hasn't been a day that they weren't harassed. The sheriff and his wife moved back to St. Mary's right after the election, but it didn't help. The fever's got him bad."

"How bad?" asked Robert.

"Flat in bed," came the answer.

Robert kicked Lawless in the flank and the three riders sped toward St. Mary's for a while, and then slowed to a walk again to rest the horses. The three men talked about the continued violence against Mormons in the outlying settlements and the fact that someday Brigham Young would likely lead an exodus of Mormons out of the state of Illinois.

"You should buy our farm, Henry," Daniel said.

"How much?" came the quick response, indicating to Robert that Henry had been thinking about such things.

"There's a committee in the City of Joseph working on property valuations," Daniel answered. "They'll come up with a fair price. They've appointed agents to work with, in fact."

Henry let a little smirk come to his face. "I have to be honest with you. There's a lot of talk around. Folks around here think we'll be able to take over most of the property for next to nothing, or nothing at all."

The remark irritated Robert. He'd heard that Church members had put more than twenty thousand acres under cultivation in the Nauvoo area and another ten thousand acres elsewhere in the county. Henry was probably right. Even if Church members were willing to take livestock in trade, very few farmers would get what their property was worth. Some would get nothing.

"Our farm is nearly all cultivated," Robert said, testing Henry. "It ought to be worth twenty or thirty dollars an acre."

"Not to me," Henry said. "I'll take my chances. If you don't sell it, let me have it for nothing, will you? After all, we're related."

Deming's farmhouse was located a mile west of St. Mary's, a pretty little frame whitewashed home with a picket fence. A large apple tree loaded with green apples stood out. A crowd had gathered, evident in the number of horses, carriages, and wagons surrounding the home. Robert trailed behind Henry as the three men trotted up to the fence and tied their horses.

Katherine burst out the door, tears coursing down her cheeks. "He's gone," she cried. "He died a half hour ago."

Robert's heart sank to his toes. "Who's in there?"

"Abigail and her children, and some of the neighbors," Katherine answered.

Daniel dismounted first. "The least we can do is give her some comforting words," he said.

Robert was impressed with the way Daniel handled the conversation with Abigail Deming, who was taking the death of her husband in a rough way. Daniel told her that Minor Deming was a son of God, that he lived with Heavenly Father before he came to this earth, and that her husband was now in a place called Paradise, where the Savior had gone after his death. Abigail in turned confided in Daniel, telling him that although she would let her own minister handle the funeral arrangements, she greatly appreciated the support of the Mormon community.

After nearly an hour passed, other friends and neighbors began to call and Robert and Daniel left for home and so did Katherine, Henry, and little Annie. Henry hitched his gray mare to his brown gelding and the Eagles family rode in their farm wagon all the way back to Carthage. Daniel kept the group moving at a fast pace; he was openly worried about Elizabeth. The last thing in the world he wanted to do was miss the birth of their first child.

Before Robert and Daniel left Carthage, Katherine fed them a meal while Bendigo and Lawless rested and fed on pasture grass. The conversation turned to the raids on Mormon settlements, a rehash of the trial of the murderers of Joseph and Hyrum, and events leading up to their deaths. That brought deep memories of Elias.

"There's something I haven't told you about that day," Henry said, rubbing his hands together in a nervous gesture.

After a tiring day of riding his horse all the way to St. Mary's and back to Carthage, Robert perked up. "About Elias?" he asked.

Henry nodded. Slowly, but with a dogged determination, he began to recount everything he and Elias had done the day Joseph and Hyrum were murdered, including delivering the message to the Warsaw militia at Golden Point, following the troops to the grove of trees near Carthage, the painting of their faces, and watching the anti-Mormons storm the jail.

"Afterward, when the mobbers came back to the trees, everyone started to run because they thought the Mormons were coming. It panicked me, too. I jumped on my horse and got out of there."

"But not Elias?" Robert asked.

"I wasn't thinking about him—only me," Henry said in a rare admission f guilt.

"So what happened?"

"As I was riding away, I heard a shot."

Katherine began to cry. "Henry—why didn't you tell anyone about this efore?"

Henry sort of ignored Katherine and continued to talk. "I was too afraid  look back, but I think I know what happened." He paused.

Robert had a premonition. "What do you think, Henry?"

Henry cleared his throat. "I think Elias was angry. I think he was so ngry about what he had seen; he must have tried to do something about it.  think he went after those men."

"And you think they shot Elias?"

Henry nodded. "And they must have taken his body with them, and one something with it to hide the crime."

There were a few moments of silence.

"Why did you take so long to tell us this, Henry?" Robert asked. Fifteen onths had passed. The explanation fit; long ago he had come up with a sim- ar scenario in his mind. The troops of the Warsaw militia were guilty not nly of murdering Joseph and Hyrum, but also Elias.

Henry shrugged his shoulders in embarrassment. "I was afraid they ould call me as a witness to the trial."

Daniel scratched at his chin. "Tell me, Henry. In your opinion, were hose five men guilty—the five who were on trial?"

Henry nodded again, this time emphatically. "Yes. Every one of them. 've been around Carthage and Warsaw enough that I know just about every- ody. I could have identified two or three dozen of them. Especially Sharp, )avis, Aldrich, Grover, and Williams. I even saw the three wounded men."

Robert thought for a few moments. He amazed himself that he did not ant to ride to Warsaw and start knocking heads together. "Well, at least /ary and Hannah can put their minds at rest. We can have a funeral for Elias now, without the body."

Daniel turned to Henry. "What are you going to do? Don't you thin you ought to go west with us?"

Katherine began to cry again.

"Why are you sobbing, Katherine?" Daniel asked.

"Don't answer, woman," Henry said.

"Let her talk, Henry," Robert said.

Katherine hesitated for a few moments and then said, "They're after u too. The same men who pestered Sheriff Deming. Just because I worked fc him."

"I told dish nose not to take that job," Henry said. "They're my ol friends. Now I've got no friends at all."

Robert's eyes took in little innocent Annie, only five years old. "You'v got one, Henry. That little girl. Think about her."

The words took their toll. Henry wiped away a tear.

# 95

ELIZABETH WAS IN LABOR AND HAD been that way for several hours when Daniel and Robert returned from Henry's place.

"She's being very stubborn," Harriet complained as Daniel rushed to the bed where Hannah sat holding Elizabeth's hands. "I sent for Patty Bartlett Sessions, but Elizabeth made her go home."

"What'd you do that for, silly woman?" were Daniel's first words to his wife as he tried to steady himself. This business of being a prospective father was a new emotion for him.

There were beads of sweat rolling off Elizabeth's forehead. "Let's save the money for our trip west."

Daniel displayed his growing concern. "But what if there're problems?"

"There won't be," she answered. "I can tell the baby's in the right position and I've got Harriet and Hannah to help me." On a nearby table lay all of Elizabeth's obstetrics tools and her satchel full of herbs and remedies.

Daniel could hear Robert on the porch. "Come in," he said in loud voice so he could be heard. "It's going to be a while."

Robert peeked through the doorway. "What about Dr. Brink—shall I go and get him?" He pulled a face, waiting for the reaction. Brink was a male doctor who had been sued for permanently injuring a woman during childbirth.

"Go back to Carthage or St. Mary's—wherever you've been," his sister steamed at him.

"I told them about Sheriff Deming, but not about Elias," Daniel said.

Hannah's back straightened and her eyes lit up at the name of her brother. "You have news this time?"

As Robert told Henry's story, Hannah rode an emotional trail—up one moment and down the next. Daniel could tell that she initially hoped to hear that he was alive but she quickly accepted the reality of his death.

"At least we know," Hannah said, wiping away tears. "You've got to tell Mary."

"Now?" Robert asked. "I might miss this big event."

"Go," said Elizabeth. "If it were Hannah—after six children—the baby might pop out any time. But I think I'll be two or three more hours, at least."

There was a lot on Robert's mind as he rode Lawless down Mulholland Street to his old log cabin, now the home of Mary Crook Eagles. He hoped Mary would greet the news favorably, despite the fact that Elias was dead. Robert thought of Brigham Young's talk at the grove Sunday when he promised a winter of peace in Nauvoo. The promise was probably given, Robert thought, to allow the Saints time to build their wagons, gather their crops, and leave Nauvoo in the spring or summer when the roads would be passable. Things in the surrounding communities, however, were already getting out of hand. People in the Highland Branch were being protected by order of the sheriff and there were new reports of mob attacks at Green Plains and Lima, to the south.

Robert wondered about Henry, Katherine, and Annie. For the first time in his life Robert thought that Henry had shown his first sparks of human decency these past few months, ever since the trial. From now on, Robert resolved, he would include Henry in his prayers. He would pray for a further softening of Henry's heart, that Henry would move his family away from Carthage and out of danger.

If the Saints did move west, out of Nauvoo, Robert wondered where the exact destination would be. Although it was anticipated that most members of the Church would remove to a new location, Nauvoo was still intended to be a place where Saints from the East and Europe could gather temporarily. The government of the United States seemed to be favoring the remote Oregon territory as the best place for the Mormons to relocate, although there was support for Mexican California, the Bay of San Francisco, north Texas, and even Nebraska territory.

Robert knew that Brigham Young and others had talked about and read about the travels of explorer John C. Fremont, who had mapped the Wind River Mountains and all along the Oregon Trail to the Pacific. That trip had included a westbound reconnaissance around the north end of a lake of salt. The *Nauvoo Neighbor* had published more than a dozen articles on the West, giving highlights of Fremont's expeditions. Robert suspected that Brigham Young knew more than he let on about the West, through the efforts of the Council of Fifty. Brigham had not only studied Fremont's writings, but also a book entitled *The Emigrants' Guide to Oregon and California* by Lansford W. Hastings.

Just a few days ago, Robert heard, two men named Orson Spencer and Charles Shumway had returned to Nauvoo from an exploring expedition along the upper Missouri River. The men, both Church members, shared the opinion that the route through Indian country would be relatively safe.

Robert passed by his old log home for a moment in order to get a good look at the nearly completed temple. The stonemasons had finished; a crew of carpenters was working inside. As soon as the baby was delivered, Daniel was scheduled to help them. Robert rode around the structure, one more time letting his gaze take in all the symbolism etched in limestone. To him, the sunstones represented the restoration of the gospel. Within his bosom there came a renewed appreciation of Wilford Woodruff and his efforts to preach the gospel in England to the United Brethren congregation, specifically to Daniel, Elizabeth, Hannah, and eventually to him. Robert laughed to himself, recalling how hardheaded he had been and how he had tried to throw Wilford out of his home.

Limestone carvings of the stars, moon, and sun made Robert think of the three degrees of glory represented in the final judgment of man, and the plan of salvation. Aboard his horse, Lawless, Robert thought of the wording in the seventy-sixth section of the Doctrine and Covenants:

*And the glory of the celestial is one, even as the glory of the sun is one. And the glory of the terrestrial is one, even as the glory of the moon is one. And the glory of the telestial is one, even as the glory of the stars is one; for as one star differs from another star in glory, even so differs one from another in glory in the telestial world.*

Robert thought of the godless people persecuting Church members in the surrounding communities—*These are they who are liars, and sorcerers, and adulterers, and whoremongers, and whosever loves and makes a lie. These are they who suffer the wrath of God on earth. These are they who suffer the vengeance of eternal fire.*

Robert said a prayer in his heart, hoping that Henry Eagles would not end up in the telestial glory in the final judgment. He prayed that even if Henry did not join the Church, he would at least end up in the terrestrial kingdom. *These are they who are honorable men of the earth, who were blinded by the craftiness of men.* The Prophet Joseph Smith had instructed the architect to place a moon at the base of each pilaster. Each moon had been carved in its quarter phase facing downward, with the image of a face carved into each curved edge.

Robert tried to key on the sunstones, which represented to him the celestial kingdom, or glory of the sun. He tried to visualize himself in that kingdom someday, sealed to Hannah and all his children. He wondered how many children would eventually come to them, and how many would live, and how many might die. Thus far he and Hannah were lucky. Other families had not been so fortunate. Child death was common not only in Nauvoo, but all along the American frontier, just as it had been in England.

He stared at the temple again, and at the pilasters. None of the thirty pilasters had decorations that resembled traditional Greek designs. This set the temple apart from all the other stately limestone structures in America, he had been told. The temple was the House of God, not a house of man. It wouldn't be long, he hoped—a few more months, perhaps—when the temple would be finished and he and Hannah could be endowed within the walls of the temple. Once most of the members had been endowed, then they could begin the trek west.

There was also symbolism to Robert in the carved stones that stood atop each pilaster. A pair of hands holding two trumpets above a man's face carved in a sun seemed to herald the restoration of the gospel in the latter-days—the final dispensation of times. Robert thought of Wilford Woodruff and the Apostle's dedication and hard work in preaching the gospel in England, specifically to the United Brethren congregation. That effort found people like Daniel and Elizabeth, and eventually Hannah and himself. He wondered how Elder Woodruff was doing in England these days. There seemed to be a steady stream of converts pouring into Nauvoo from the British Isles.

As Robert turned his horse toward Mary Eagles' home, he thought about Sheriff Minor Deming. A thought came to him that he ought to turn Deming's name into the Church so that a proxy baptism could be performed in Deming's behalf. After all, Deming was one of the most honorable men of the earth he had ever met. In his opinion, Deming was worthy of the celestial kingdom.

Mary Crooks Eagles took the news of Elias' death well and did not place any blame on Henry. "I blame myself as much as anyone," she said. "We should have taken up your offer to buy your little home here next to the temple, and forgotten about Carthage and the dairy."

"Do you want a coffin?" Robert asked in haste.

Mary shook her head. "I've thought a lot about what to do if it came to this," she said. "It would be an unnecessary waste. I don't suppose we even need to buy a lot in the Pioneer Cemetery. There's no one to put in it."

"What, then?"

The Pioneer Cemetery had been opened since 1842 and most of the people who had died in Nauvoo in the past two or three years were buried there, located southeast of the city on Parley Street.

"What if we have a private but nice little burial ceremony right here and put a memorial stone in the yard somewhere? The most important thing is for all of us to remember Elias in our hearts."

"Robert! You're just in time!" Daniel yelled, waving from his porch. "Elizabeth's lying-in time is about up. It'll happen any minute."

Robert waved back. "I'll tend to the horse. Let me know so I can come and see the baby."

The baby turned out to be a healthy boy. According to Elizabeth's instruments, the child weighed eight pounds two ounces and measured twenty-one inches. He had a light sprinkling of blond hair and good lungs.

"Well—what's his name?" Hannah asked. Elizabeth had toyed with the idea of naming a girl Sarah, after her mother, or Dianah, after her sister.

Elizabeth decided to have some fun before she divulged the name. "We've thought of John—after my brother in England. Or after John Benbow. Or Thomas—after Thomas Kington, or after my brother-in-law, Thomas Bloxham. Or how about Wilford? Or Joseph? Or Hyrum?"

Robert's head was swimming. "Which is it?"

"None of those," Elizabeth smiled. "How about a Biblical or Book of Mormon character?"

Hannah held up a hand and began reciting names and pointing to one finger at a time. "Adam?"

"Nope."

"Bartholomew? Benjamin?"

"Nope."

"Caleb? Clement? Cornelius?"

Elizabeth grinned and shook her head. She liked this game.

Hannah took a deep breath. "Help me out, Harriet."

Harriet tried the D's. "Daniel—it has to be Daniel!"

"Good guess, but no," Elizabeth said. And she said no to David, Darius, Enoch, Elijah, Ephraim, and Ezekiel.

Robert was out of patience. "Ecclesiastes! That's what I'm calling your boy no matter what," he said.

Elizabeth gasped. "No—I hate that name. His name is Moroni!"

"Moroni?" Hannah asked. "Perfect choice."

Daniel smiled. "That was my choice from the beginning, if it was a boy. I think he was the most important personality in the Book of Mormon."

Robert shrugged his shoulders. "That may be, but to me he's Ecclesiastes." He picked up the delicate baby and peered into his face. "Welcome to the world, Ecclesiastes."

# 96

*November 1845*

ORSON HYDE EXPRESSED REGRET that he had virtually no social life since his return to Nauvoo.

"You don't need to apologize," Daniel said during a brief visit to the Hyde home. It had been more than two weeks since Orson arrived. Daniel's main purpose for the visit, of course, was to see Rebecca, and he had brought Harriet with him. Elizabeth was at home with baby Moroni.

Orson had left Nauvoo in mid-June with an assignment from the Twelve to buy four thousand yards of canvas, purchase type to print the history of Joseph Smith, and to raise funds. In New York City, after raising the money, he had purchased Imperial Russia Duck canvas and had it shipped to Nauvoo via Pittsburgh. He was also successful in raising funds and obtaining the type and returned to Church headquarters in mid-October.

"Come in and sit down," Orson said, pointing to the parlor and a velvet ivan. "Rebecca will be down in a few minutes." He had just returned home after another meeting with the Twelve. Marinda and Mary Ann were keeping the loom humming, weaving carpet for the temple. Rebecca was upstairs changing her clothes. She had been outside storing pumpkins and squash in the cellar. "Congratulations on your first child. I suppose Elizabeth is very happy."

"Words can't express her happiness," Harriet commented.

Orson expressed his amazement at all the things that had happened in Nauvoo during his four-month absence. The harvest on the farms and in the gardens had been more abundant than usual, a gift from God in his opinion; there was enough grain stored to feed the Saints for two years and certainly enough for an exodus.

Workers on the temple had installed the windows, and at eventide the panes reflected the gold of the setting sun. "The tower is astonishing," Orson commented. "It seems to guide your eyes heavenward from the western portion of the temple."

Daniel agreed and gave an update of the carpentry work in the attic. Although the Twelve had already updated Orson on the October conference, Daniel told Orson how nice it was to meet on makeshift seats in the temple and listen to Church leaders encourage faithfulness and give detailed instructions about preparing to move. Nauvoo had been converted to a vast wagon-manufacturing venture with the clanging of hammers on iron and the rasping of saws on boards.

"What company are you in?" Orson asked.

"The Joseph Horne Company," Daniel answered. "Brother and Sister Robert Harris and their family are with us, and a lot of our friends."

Orson nodded his approval. More than twenty-five pioneer companies had already been organized by the Church with one hundred families in each company. Each company averaged about five persons per family, making each company consist of around five hundred persons.

"It's funny how things work out, isn't it?" Orson said.

A perplexed look came over Daniel. "What do you mean?"

"I was sent back east to buy canvas for a tabernacle to erect in front c the temple," Orson explained. "Instead, we're using all that canvas for covere wagons. In the wisdom of the Lord, my efforts are serving the Saints in a unexpected way."

A warm feeling came over Daniel. "That's why we came to town toda to buy some canvas and some parts for our wagon."

"You have an advantage over the rest of us since you are a skilled ca penter," Orson commented.

Daniel shrugged his shoulders. "I don't know—it's such a specialize craft. I've been able to make parts of the wagon, but it takes the combined ski of blacksmiths and mechanics as well."

For a few minutes they talked about how Daniel had either built c obtained things like wheels, tires, tongues, boxes, and double trees, and the their conversation turned to the continued persecution suffered at the han of anti-Mormons. The death of Minor Deming. Efforts by Sheriff Backenst to stop the burning of buildings in the county. The clash between Backenst and Porter Rockwell and their posse with a mob. Porter's shooting of Fran Worrell, one of the mob members. Efforts to indict Rockwell and Backensto Arrival of a Springfield delegation from Governor Ford, asking if th Mormons were ready to leave the state. Brigham Young's response—that l was willing to go if the Saints could sell their land at a fair price. The Octob conference and the circular sent out by the Church to all members, giving tl Saints instructions to begin the disposal of their properties. And the excon munication of the Prophet's brother, William Smith, for publishing a pan phlet against the Twelve.

"Have you got your farm sold?" Orson asked.

"No," came the answer. "We've had three different farmers come ar look at it, but nothing has come of it. Brother Harris' brother-in-law has al expressed some interest, but I don't think he has enough money."

"He's the one who has the wife who sat in on the trial?" Orson asked.

Daniel answered in the affirmative.

"Have you heard about Dr. Robert D. Foster?"

"Only that a few weeks ago he fired a shot at a Church member while on a steamboat," Daniel answered. It happened October twenty-fifth on the steamer *Sarah Ann.* When the boat landed Foster had a number of men try to haul a member of the Church named Robert Jackson Redding on board and kidnap him. Redding knocked the first man down; soon other members of the Church were helping. With sticks and stones they soon drove the whole crew on board. After the steamboat left, Foster shot his pistol at the Church members but no one was hit.

"This last incident happened just the other day," Orson explained. "Dr. Foster told one of the Church members that he regrets apostatizing. Foster said that at one time he loved Joseph Smith more than any man on the earth, and that he wished he could relive the past eighteen months of his life. He would stay in the Church. He wishes he were going west with us, and that right now he is the most miserable wretch that the sun shines upon, to quote him exactly."

Daniel thought about the other apostates such as William and Wilson Law, and what their lives were like right now. He suspected they were just as unhappy.

Rebecca came bounding down the stairs.

"Would you like to ride out and see the baby?" Daniel asked her.

She smiled and said yes.

On the way to see Elizabeth and the baby, Rebecca complained about her own barrenness. "I wish I were in a family way," she said. Leaves blown along the road made a snappy crunching sound as the wheels of the wagon passed by.

Daniel did a quick calculation. Rebecca had married Orson Hyde in April of 1843, two and a half years ago. She could have had two children in that time. "I guess there's just something wrong with us Browetts," he said. "We're not very prolific."

"Mama was," Rebecca said in a bitter tone.

Daniel nodded. "Yes, she was." Rebecca and Daniel had three brothers in England. Martha had produced seven children, two of whom had died in infancy back in England.

The Browett farmhouse was snuggled into its many maples like a cold chin into a fur coat. Rebecca shivered, buttoned up her coat, and tried to enjoy the rest of the ride.

"What do you think of my letter?" Governor Ford asked Shields, the state auditor, who had been reading it.

"The Mormons are making me weary," Shields said.

"Me, too," Ford replied. The letter to Brigham Young defended Ford against charges that he was just another Governor Boggs. "I'll be glad when they're all out of Nauvoo."

"You need to tell Mr. Young that if you hadn't sent your troops to occupy Nauvoo the anti-Mormons would have raised a mob of four or five thousand men and murdered everyone there," Shields said.

"Good idea," Ford said, making little notes on a piece of paper. "Do you think they'll believe me?"

"Who knows what they'll believe," Shields said. "You need to make reference to the gangs of thieves in Nauvoo, too. If I were you, I'd keep the troops there. They can keep a good eye on the Mormons, to make certain they'll actually leave in the spring."

# 97

*November 1845*

ROBERT FELT HIS MUSCLES TENSE up as he talked with Henry. The two men were in Henry's wagon, riding around the perimeter of Robert and Daniel's farm. Henry was trying to decide whether or not to buy it.

"If ole dish nose hadn't taken that job with Sheriff Deming," Henry was saying, "we wouldn't have to move out of Carthage." He had been telling Robert how the anti-Mormons had turned on him the past few weeks, especially since Sheriff Deming's death. Henry had even found a bullet wound in one of his cows. The cow was healing, but her milk production had been cut in half. On the first of October, Henry said, he had tried to attend an anti-Mormon meeting in the courthouse, but his old friends refused to let him in.

"They've known your wife was a Mormon ever since you moved there, Henry," Robert stated flatly. "You knew she was a member of the Church when you married her. It's silly to blame everything on her."

"I told the men of the Carthage militia that my wife has denied the Mormon faith, but they won't believe me. They want to hear it from her, personally," Henry explained.

Robert studied Henry with disgust. "Has she denied it?"

"Not yet, but she will if she wants to stay with me," Henry added.

"And what if she doesn't?"

A hard look came over Henry. "Then she can come and live with you."

Henry's words chilled Robert so he decided to change the subject. It was true that the anti-Mormons were turning up their viciousness. Robert and Henry had ridden from one end of the farm to the other and Robert had half expected to find one of his own cows shot. But they were merely lowing in a brown, wintry cornfield. John Benbow, whose farm was just a mile away, had recently reported fifteen wounded cattle. A few days earlier the farmhouse of a Brother Rice had been burned by anti-Mormons at Camp Creek, only two miles northeast. And that was on the heels of the death of Edmund Durfee who was shot and killed by a mob when Durfee tried to put out a fire near Solomon Hancock's barn. Grain fields had been burned in many locations and at last count, forty-four buildings. Frightened families had been scurrying to Nauvoo for protection. For a while Robert told Henry about Brigham Young's personal troubles—Brigham had gone into hiding because the anti-Mormons had issued warrants for his arrest on a charge of counterfeiting Elder Theodore Turley had actually been arrested.

Henry's next statement broke Robert's trance. "Why don't you just have Brigham print you some money for your farm, and give it to me for free?"

Robert took the time to explain that the anti-Mormons had tried to pin counterfeiting on Church leaders for years but that either non-Mormons or Mormons who had been cut off from the Church did actual bogus-making in Nauvoo.

"It's a nice farm, Henry, "Robert said. "You can have it—you just say the word and give us the money. Six dollars an acre." Robert had not told Henry but he doubted that Henry had the means to buy the farm either with cash or with a trade of some kind. The price did not include either house.

In the distance, Robert could see Daniel arriving with Rebecca. While Rebecca and Harriet disappeared into the Browett home, Henry drove the wagon toward the two nearly identical homes. The November wind whistled through a stand of willows, which were vibrating toys for the sparrows. Mallards flew into a half-frozen pond.

"Have you made a decision, Henry?" Daniel asked as he unhitched his horses.

"Yep," Henry answered. "I'll give you one calf as down payment and the remainder in two years. That includes both houses. Maybe I'll get me another wife to fill it."

Daniel snorted and ignored the inference to plural wives. "By then we'll be long gone, somewhere out West." He pointed toward a new covered wagon. "We've got one wagon almost done; we'll start on Robert's this week."

To Robert's surprise, Henry whistled and showed a keen interest in the wagon he and Daniel had been working on for the past few weeks. "You could haul a lot of milk in one of these," he said.

"Not milk, Henry," Daniel said as he ran his hand along the wagon box made of hickory, a durable hardwood, "but a lot of things we'll need for our new life out West."

The box was more than two feet deep and already had been tarred so that it could float across slow-moving rivers. The sideboards had been beveled outwards to keep the rain from coming in under the edges of the bonnet and to help keep out river water.

"Why two different sizes of wheels?" Henry asked as he tugged on his chin. His farm wagon had four standard-sized wheels.

"To be honest, this wagon is built the way a Church committee told us to build them, Henry, but that's a good question," Daniel answered. "The smaller front wheels allow for a little extra play, which lets the wagon take slightly sharper turns. Otherwise, I'd have to do a lot of extra carpentry work to keep the bed level during the turns."

Henry crouched and let his gaze take in the wagon spokes and rims. "No iron yet?"

"There're blacksmiths making tire irons in town," Robert answered. "We've got orders in for our two wagons. But there's a severe shortage of iron." All three men understood that iron tires protected the wooden rims and gave a much longer life. "Daniel learned how to make the wheels from Stephen Markham, Joseph Smith's main bodyguard."

"Lot of good Markham did Ole Joe Smith," Henry remarked. "What would Markham charge to come out and protect me?"

Robert laughed as the three men walked around the long tongue of the wagon and the neck yoke, singletree, and double trees.

"What are these?" Henry asked, pointing to thin strips of wood soaking in a wooden vat.

"Those are the bows to hold up the canvas bonnets," Daniel said. "I picked up our canvas today in town. Elder Hyde bought thousands of yards of canvas on his trip back east." Daniel pulled a bow out of the water and with two hands bent it into the shape he wanted. "We have to place the canvas kind of loose over the bows; too tight and they'll spring loose and tear the bonnet."

Robert noted Henry's rising interest. "We can build you a wagon, Henry. We'd be more than happy to take your family along."

Henry scratched his head. "But you don't even know where you're going."

Daniel smiled. "It's true. We don't, but the Lord does. And Brigham Young has a good idea."

Henry seemed to recoil at the remark. "That's doesn't sound like a good answer."

"They've been publishing articles in our newspapers here about the West for more than a year, Henry," Daniel explained. He went on to tell Henry about explorers such as William Wolfskill, Milton Green Sublette, Joseph Reddeford Walker, Captain B. L. E. Bonneville, and John C. Fremont.

"In fact, Fremont is on another exploring expedition right now," Daniel said. "The U. S. government finances him, and two years ago Fremont learned a lot about the West when he traveled into Oregon Territory, California, and the Salt Lake area."

"But you're talking area outside the United States," Henry said.

"True, the race is on to make Oregon part of the U.S.," Daniel acknowledged. "The newspapers claim that around five thousand settlers went into Oregon just this year and more are planning to make the trip next year." He also commented that the Church was ready to leave the United States if necessary. The government had never provided any protection against mob action, nor had it approved restitution of damages suffered in places like Missouri.

"And you're relying on newspapers to tell you where you're going?" Henry asked.

"Not at all," Daniel stated. "Brigham Young has sent out his own exploring parties. They've been making reports."

"It seems impossible to move all you Mormons out of Illinois and into the wilderness," Henry added, his greedy eyes scanning the farm again.

Robert explained that the Church had organized everyone into companies of one hundred families each. Already, he said, captains had been appointed for twenty-five companies. He laughed out loud as he recalled how nearly everyone wanted to be a member of a company that had a member of the Twelve as a captain. Each company had two captains of fifty families and also captains of ten. Brigham Young had met with all the captains of one hundred just this past Sunday. And The Twelve was meeting almost daily to tackle the exodus problem and to fine-tune the plans to leave by spring.

Henry was doing a quick calculation in his mind. "That's twelve thousand people," he exclaimed.

"And room for your family, too," Daniel commented.

Henry's broad jaw tightened. "But I'm not a Mormon ..."

"We can fix that," Daniel said, smiling.

Henry shook his head. "I know all about your view of heaven. I've gone down a different path. You know as well as I do that I'm not celestial material."

Daniel seemed to explode. "So what's your point, Henry? Neither am I and neither is Robert. Neither are any of us."

A huge blank came to Henry's face.

"That's why we need the atonement of Christ, Henry," Daniel said. "That's what can make us celestial. Christ has unfolded the gospel plan through his Prophets. You're problem is simple, Henry; you just don't have faith in Christ."

"I went to church as a boy, same as you," Henry answered. "I'm Christian, I just don't act like it."

"You believe in Christ—is that what you're saying?" Daniel asked.

Henry looked uncomfortable but he answered. "Yes, I suppose I do."

"Then you're saying you just don't believe Christ."

Henry furrowed his brow. "What do you mean?"

Daniel went for the juggler. "That's the message of the gospel, Henry. You've got to not only believe in Christ, but you've got to *believe* Christ. Christ says he can make you celestial but you seem to be standing there saying, 'no, he can't.' You've got to have faith that Christ can not only save you, but that he can exalt you. The gospel can work for you just as well as it can work for me or Robert, or Katherine. That's the good news of the gospel."

"I've never heard it put that way before," Henry said as he shifted his weight back and forth on his feet.

"Let me teach you the gospel," Daniel pleaded.

There was a long moment of silence. "I'll think about it," Henry said.

"Are you worried about taking a baby on a trip out in the wilderness next spring?" Rebecca asked Elizabeth as she gazed at her new nephew, Moroni Browett.

"Yes, of *course* I am," Elizabeth answered. "But I'm *more* concerned about staying here. The burnings, murders, and shooting livestock are getting closer and closer."

"Don't even mention those things," Hannah declared. Elizabeth watched as Hannah pulled little Julia Ann closer to her. Hannah's other children were outside playing on this mild November day.

"When does Elder Hyde think we'll have to leave?" Harriet asked.

Rebecca thought for a second. "Brigham Young has told Governor Ford that he's willing to lead the Mormons out of Illinois in the spring, as soon as the grass on the prairies will support livestock."

"Just so we don't have to travel in the heart of winter with our babies," Elizabeth moaned.

"I just wish I had a baby of my own," Rebecca said as Elizabeth handed her Moroni. He was wrapped in a striped blanket of blue and gray. "Maybe Orson would pay more attention to me."

Elizabeth ignored her sister-in-law's outward expression of jealousy. Orson's third wife, Mary Ann, had no children either, but Rebecca never mentioned that. Marinda, the first wife, lost her first child—a boy—who would have been ten years old now. A daughter, Laura, had been born a year later, followed by the birth and death of another daughter, Emily.

Rebecca's thoughts turned back to the exodus. She directed her question to both Elizabeth and Hannah. "Do both of your families have a thousand pounds of flour ready for the journey?"

Martha, Daniel's mother, pointed upstairs and answered for Elizabeth. "Our sacks of flour are stored upstairs where the mice can't get to them. How about yours, dear?" she asked her daughter. Martha, Harriet, and Elizabeth had also been drying peaches, apricots, apples, and pumpkins for the trip.

"Oh, yes," Rebecca answered. "Several weeks ago. Now we're spending all our time putting the finishing touches on the temple. I've been sewing robes and garments, and helping on the curtains, too. The painters are all finished painting the attic. In a few days the attic story will be dedicated."

"When will the endowments begin?" Martha asked.

"Orson thinks the middle of December," Rebecca answered. "But it'll take three or four months for everyone to be endowed, he thinks."

As Rebecca described the attic of the temple where she had helped divide the chamber with canvas partitions, and where the "sacred compartments" of the endowment ceremony would take place, Elizabeth suspected that Rebecca—along with Orson Hyde—would be among the first to be endowed in the soon-to-be-finished temple.

# 98

## *December 1845*

"I HAVE A PROPOSAL FOR YOU," Orson Hyde told Daniel when Daniel visited in December. Earlier they had been talking about the things the Quorum of the Twelve had learned about John C. Fremont's journal. Fremont had traveled extensively in the West in 1842-43. They had also talked about the endowment and the fact that a record one hundred six persons had received their temple ordinances yesterday, including Thomas and Margaret Kington; the day before, Theodore Turley and his wife. Days earlier, John Benbow and his wife had been endowed.

Suddenly, Daniel felt uneasy.

"I understand you still haven't sold your farm," Orson was saying.

"Our only possibility seems to be Henry Eagles, but we haven't received a penny down," Daniel acknowledged.

Orson had a serious look on his face. "There's no way all the Saints can leave Nauvoo at once. But it's imperative that a great number of us leave right away." He had been writing letters counteracting unfair media stories all over the nation.

Daniel pulled his face into a mask of puzzlement. "I thought we were going to wait for spring, when there would be grass for the animals."

"We're going to start the exodus right away, in early February."

"What?"

"The government's afraid that if we leave the United States we'll end up under the influence of the Mexican government or the British," Orson said.

"But isn't that the idea, to leave the United States, and go far away where we can have true freedom of religion?"

"Yes, but we hear that soldiers may be sent to prevent our leaving."

Daniel looked concerned.

"Brigham Young just received a letter from Governor Ford," Orson said. "The governor claims that regiments of the U.S. Army are going to be sent to Nauvoo in the spring to arrest Church leaders and possibly prevent the migration west. We'd be trapped between the anti-Mormons and the U.S. Army, and that would be a tragedy."

The words hit Daniel hard. "My wagon's nearly ready, and so's Robert's."

Orson set his jaw. "My proposal is this. Brigham says the first companies to leave will need extra wagons to carry feed for the animals."

To Daniel, this made sense. Grass would not be growing in Iowa until April. As he thought this out, he had a rising premonition. "And he wants my wagon?"

"Here's the plan," Orson began to explain. "If you agree, we'll take your wagon, and Brother Harris' wagon, and use them to haul feed. After we get the first companies across Iowa we'll send those wagons and teams back."

"Teams?" Daniel asked. Suddenly, he could see Bendigo and Lawless disappearing across the Mississippi, too. He wondered how he was going to explain this to Elizabeth, Harriet, and his mother—and to Robert, Hannah, and their children.

"If you think about it, it makes a lot of sense," said Orson. "This will give you more time to sell your farm and more time for your baby to gain size and strength. It'll probably be a rough trip across Iowa in February and March. I can't imagine how muddy the roads will be."

Daniel inhaled deeply. In a way, he was glad he and Robert had not purchased oxen yet. They couldn't afford them until they sold their farm. "And when will our wagons and horses be back?"

"By early May," Orson said. "You'll probably be able to catch up with the forward companies by July."

"Are you planning on leaving in one of the first companies?" Daniel asked the Apostle.

"Yes, unless Marinda complicates things. Her baby is due next month."

When Daniel returned to the farm, he was surprised to find Katherine and Annie at Robert's house.

"Henry threw her out," Robert said. "It came down to a choice between her and his Carthage anti-Mormon friends."

"Well, at least she didn't deny her faith," Daniel concluded, thinking how crowded Robert's house would be. During his last encounter with Henry, Henry seemed to manifest a little common sense, even a spark of interest in the gospel. Apparently Henry was back to his old ways, rationalizing worldly behavior, accepting false teachings, taking easy offense and being prideful. Henry had chosen Satan and his old friends in Carthage over a God-fearing woman like Katherine, and had rejected even his own little daughter.

"Henry pressured her, but she held fast," Robert said.

"What about the farm?" Daniel asked, still thinking about the contrast between Katherine and Henry. People like Henry were easily embittered by trials and adversity while others, like Katherine, were strengthened. It was a sad prospect to think that Henry was back in good stead with his old crowd and that his wife and child were inside Robert's house crying their eyes out.

"He still thinks he'll get it for nothing."

Henry Eagles sat in the Hamilton Tavern two days later, half drunk. Henry's drinking companions included George W. Thatcher, the clerk of the county commissioners. Henry's other Carthage friends seated around the table were a few members of the Carthage Greys, a situation that greatly pleased Henry. He was back in full acceptance with the old crowd.

"You're the only Mormon I've ever liked," Thatcher said.

Henry's eyes narrowed. "I keep telling you, I'm not Mormon."

"But you had a Mormon wife," Thatcher said, smiling.

"And she's gone," Henry said, sticking out his chest.

The other Carthage men laughed. Henry knew them by their full names now—Eli Williams, Edwin Baldwin, Albert Thompson, Thomas Griffith, and Ebenezer Rand.

"Well, from one Mason to another," Thatcher said as he raised his glass of whiskey, "I toast you for ridding yourself of your Mormon wife. What'd ya do with her?"

"She's somewhere back in Nauvoo, I suppose. After my brother-in-law gives me his forty-acre farm, she'll probably want me back."

"He's going to give you his farm?"

"He won't have any other choice once he leaves with all the other Mormons."

"What if they don't leave by spring?"

"I'd burn them out, except I want their houses, too."

"If you want to burn them out, I'll help you," said Edwin Baldwin.

"Me, too," added Thomas Griffith.

"I'll drink to that," said Ebenezer Rand.

As the group of men toasted Henry, a band of troopers rode up in front of the tavern.

"That's the marshal from Springfield," Thatcher said.

"What's he doing here?" Henry asked.

Thatcher looked relieved. "It was a well guarded secret, but he went to Nauvoo to arrest Brigham Young on counterfeiting charges. He took some local militia men with him."

Henry stood up and looked through the window in time to see the marshal and his prisoner dismount and walk toward the door. Hot steam spurted from the nostrils of every horse in the posse. The prisoner was dressed in a dark suit, a cap, and a dark gray cloak to protect him from the cold.

"Take a chair, Mr. Young," the marshal said as he walked through the door with his prisoner and three deputies.

Thatcher grimaced. To Henry, he whispered, "They've got the wrong man."

"That's not Brigham Young?" Henry asked.

Thatcher didn't answer. Instead, he walked straight toward the marshal and pointed to the prisoner. "This is a man named Miller, not Brigham Young."

The marshal wheeled and turned beet red. His eyes bored into the prisoner. "You're not Brigham Young?"

"I never told you I was Brigham Young, did I?" Miller said.

To Henry's eyes, the marshal looked devastated and did not believe Thatcher.

"No," the marshal admitted, "but one of my men professed to be acquainted with Mr. Young, and pointed you out as him."

Henry began to laugh and so did the other men in the tavern. As they did, a man Henry recognized as Sheriff William Backenstos walked into the tavern. He had been elected sheriff of Hancock County after the death of Minor Deming.

The marshal took in Backenstos with begging eyes. "I need some help here, sheriff." He pointed to Miller. "Is this man Brigham Young?"

Backenstos shook his head. "No, it is not."

"Then who are you?" the marshal asked Miller.

"William Miller," he replied with a wide smile. "I tried to tell you that you had made a mistake, even when we were still in Nauvoo."

"Well, I'm truly sorry," the marshal said. He turned to Backenstos and told the story of how he and the troops had suspected that Brigham Young was in the Nauvoo temple, and had watched as Brigham Young's carriage pulled up in front of the temple and Brigham—or Miller—came out and go into the carriage. The carriage driver called the passenger "Mr. Young." Miller was arrested immediately.

Henry pulled at Thatcher's coat. "You should have sent me to Nauvoo with the marshal. I wouldn't have made that mistake. You'll never find Brigham Young now. It'll be like looking for a needle in a haystack."

To the continuous laughter of the crowd, the marshal sent Miller away with Sheriff Backenstos.

"You can spend the night at my home," the sheriff said to Miller. "You can return to Nauvoo tomorrow on the stage."

Governor Ford shook his head in anger as he wrote a letter to Sheriff Backenstos.

"Does Sheriff Backenstos think you sent the marshal to arrest Brigham Young in Nauvoo?" auditor Shields asked the governor. Shields was scanning a scathing letter Backenstos had recently sent.

Ford dipped his quill and began writing. "Apparently so, but he's dead wrong. I don't want the federal government to get involved. I just want the Mormons out of Illinois."

"What about the fact that the marshal used state troopers?"

Ford sensed that no one in the world understood him and the problem he was having with the Mormons. "I didn't authorize it."

"It's probably a good thing the marshal took the troopers with him," Shields said.

Ford exhaled, wishing he could turn back the clock and prevent the Mormons from coming in Illinois that first winter. "The marshal would have been murdered by the Mormons, otherwise," he said, boiling over now. "There are a few other things the Mormons need to understand."

"Such as?"

"I'm putting them in my letter to Backenstos. Brigham Young may think he's quite cute and full of tricks, but he's tinkered with the U.S. government. This little event is going to put the Mormons and the U.S. government into a collision course, which is bad for us. I think the U.S. government is going to try to prevent the Mormons from going west of the Rocky Mountains. If the Mormons get far enough out West they could join the British and be more trouble than ever."

"Aren't the Mormons about ready to leave?" Shields asked.

"By spring," Ford said. "But I wish they'd leave now. Tomorrow wouldn't be too soon."

"A lot of your friends are picking up cheap property there."

That remark caused a sly smile to sweep across Ford's face. He cursed as he said, "I hope Nauvoo eventually becomes settled by no one other than Democrats. Democrats we can trust. No more Mormons."

# 99

*February 1846*

AT LEAST WE STILL HAVE OUR HORSES, Robert thought to himself as he watched Bishop George Miller cross the Mississippi River on a flat boat with six wagons. One of the wagons Miller was using was his; another belonged to Daniel. Elder Hyde had told Robert that both families would be blessed for the sacrifice they were making. Soon, Robert and Daniel would have to sell the horses, or trade them. Oxen were more suitable for pulling covered wagons across Iowa.

Yes, Robert concluded to himself, he was blessed. All of his family was in exceptionally good health and yesterday he and Hannah had received their endowments in the temple. So had Daniel, Elizabeth, Harriet, and Daniel's mother, Martha. In fact, a record five hundred twelve people had been endowed. Today—the seventh of February—another six hundred people were expected to be endowed, bringing the total endowed to more than five thousand six hundred adults. With members of the Twelve leaving, no more endowments would be given in the temple. A new temple would have to be built somewhere out west.

"I can't bear to look," Hannah lamented as Miller's flat boat got smaller and smaller, almost disappearing on the other side of the wide Mississippi River. "I don't think we'll ever see our wagons again."

Nearly a hundred wagons were lined up on Front Street and on Mulholland Street, waiting for flat boats to ferry them across. Children played in the wet snow. Babies cried. Oxen bawled; horses pawed nervously at the ground. In other parts of the city, strangers could be seen roaming around looking for bargains on left-behind furniture and other goods. It grated on Robert that so many Saints were being taken advantage of, so cheap were the prices. He thought of the men in his dream, those who were responsible for the deaths of Joseph and Hyrum. They, and others like them, were responsible for all this—the persecution of the Mormons, the leaving of homes and farms, and the sacrifices that were yet to come in the unknown American wilderness.

Robert and Hannah sat in their farm wagon with Daniel and Harriet. Elizabeth was at home with her baby. Earlier during this mild winter day, Brigham Young met with all the captains of the emigration companies and gave them loading instructions.

"At least this way we have a chance to sell our homes and the farm," Daniel said. Earlier they had talked about the fact that many of the Saints who had already crossed the river were leaving behind unsold property valued at hundreds, even thousands, of dollars. John Taylor was preparing to cross the river with his family, eight wagons, and a carriage. He was leaving behind a large two-story brick house, a brick store, and a printing office—all valued at more than ten thousand dollars.

"I can't bear to look," Hannah said as tears trickled down her cheeks. Wagon after wagon could be seen ferrying across the river on flat boats. A hundred other wagons waited for flatboats on the Nauvoo side of the river. "I can't decide if we're going to be better off waiting until spring or not. What if the Antis get braver? And the troops sent by Governor Ford are almost as bad."

"I know," Robert said. About five hundred state troopers were still patrolling Nauvoo, but many of them were anti-Mormons. "One of these days we're going to look up and find Henry among the state troopers."

"Wouldn't surprise me," said Daniel as Robert clucked Bendigo and Lawless into action and the wagon began moving away from the river. All eyes swept to the right as another wagon rolled by, loaded with logs.

An idea struck Robert. "Do you know what we ought to do, Daniel?"

"What?"

"Before the snow gets too deep again, let's find some trees to cut down and get busy building two more wagons," Robert said. His words reminded the group that there had been four-foot snowdrifts in Nauvoo not more than two weeks ago, followed by an unseasonable thaw. Now the streets were terribly muddy.

Harriet pulled her face into a contortion. "But our wagons will be back in a couple of months, won't they?"

Robert didn't divulge his innermost thoughts. He had a premonition that he wouldn't see his wagon again until spring or summer, and that would be somewhere beyond Iowa. "If so, we can always sell them to someone else," he said. "If not, what would we do? We wouldn't be prepared to leave."

"You're right," Daniel said. "Let's go home and get our axes." He thought for a moment. "I hope we can find iron for the tires. I think the Church used up all the iron in the whole state and all along the Mississippi."

"Then we'll use rawhide," Robert said.

Daniel nodded. The last few wagons completed in Nauvoo had used rawhide for a wrapping around the wheels, instead of iron.

With Brigham Young, Orson Hyde, and all the Twelve on the other side of the river—winding their way across Iowa—what would life be like here in Nauvoo? Could Joseph Young, the senior president of the Seventy, lead the remnants of the Church still in Nauvoo? Could he continue to organize the exodus? Could he keep the Saints safe from the anti-Mormons who were marauding all over Illinois? Could he see that the temple was finished and dedicated? And could he control the apostates and their efforts to lead away members of the Church? Men like John E. Page? John J. Strang and the "Strangites?"

These were the thoughts that reverberated in Daniel's mind as he drove into Nauvoo on this bitter cold morning in late February to say goodbye to Rebecca and the Hydes. He wondered how the Saints living out of wagon boxes were faring in Iowa. Now his own sister would be out there, out of the comfort of her warm home. Orson would have his wagons ready, loaded with a list of goods that Orson and the Twelve had recommended after weeks and weeks of deliberation. For every five persons the Twelve had specified a thousand pounds of flour, a bushel of beans, a hundred pounds of sugar, a musket or rifle, twenty-five pounds of salt, a few pounds of dried beef or bacon, tents, ten to fifty pounds of seed, farming tools, clothes, bedding, and cooking utensils.

Daniel was shocked to find Orson, Rebecca, and Mary Ann unloading their wagons in front of the Hyde home. Daniel's first reaction was to question whether or not the western movement of the Saints had been called off. But he could see other covered wagons moving towards the banks of the Mississippi, to the flatboats that functioned as ferries.

Timidly, Daniel asked the obvious. "Brother Hyde, why are you unloading?"

"Marinda's sick," Orson explained as he reached for a satchel of clothing. "I've been across the river visiting with Brigham Young. He tells me to wait until she feels better. She needs several days to recuperate, maybe weeks."

Elizabeth's reaction was typical of her. She jumped out of the Browett farm wagon with her eyes glued on the Hyde frame house. "May I go upstairs and see her?" she asked.

"Please do, and see if there is anything that you can do to help her," Orson replied. Marinda had delivered her third child, a boy, three weeks earlier. The Hydes had named him Frank Henry.

As Elizabeth bounced up the stairs Daniel said, "Will it be difficult to catch up with the others if you have to stay here long?"

"I don't know," Orson replied. "Brigham wants to keep the Twelve together. It's awfully tough going on the Iowa side—the wagons sink into the mud over the axles." As Daniel helped Orson unload, Orson explained the situation at the Sugar Creek encampment—shoveling away snow for places to pitch tents, cooking by campfires, and Church leaders dealing with the few individuals who were murmuring. Orson told Daniel not to bother unloading the big things like barrels of flour. Orson said he would leave them stored in the wagons and make certain they were well protected.

Daniel suspected Brigham Young needed all the help he could get to deal with the early problems of the Sugar Creek encampment and the trek west. Not all the Twelve were in Iowa. Lyman Wight was on his way to Texas with a group of Saints. Wilford Woodruff was still in England. William E. Smith—the Prophet's brother—still had not recognized Brigham Young as the head of the Church and was on his way to full apostasy. John E. Page had already apostatized and had joined the Strangites. But Brigham had the full loyalty of the others—John Taylor, Willard Richards, Heber C. Kimball, George A. Smith, Amasa Lyman, and Ezra T. Benson.

That left his brother-in-law, Orson Hyde, as the only member of the Quorum of Twelve Apostles in Nauvoo.

"I have one bit of good news to share with you," Orson said as the two men continued to unload satchels of clothing and household items.

Daniel said, "Good news is always welcome."

"We've received a letter from Senator Hoge of Illinois," Orson replied. "He says that the U.S. government will allow us to leave the United States if we please. They won't post soldiers to keep us in Nauvoo."

The statement intrigued Daniel. "Does that mean that Brigham Young and all the others are coming back until spring?"

Orson frowned and shook his head. "No, the exodus is on. But the letter said nothing about Brigham's proposal for us to build forts in Oregon."

Orson also told Daniel that he had recently met with a sea captain from

Boston who was in Nauvoo offering ocean passage from New York to California. Daniel laughed at the price—a hundred and fifty dollars per person for adults. Orson said, however, that Samuel Brannan had left New York with a group of Saints on the *Brooklyn* with plans to select a suitable spot near the Bay of San Francisco for a city.

"But what about the temple here in Nauvoo?" Daniel asked.

"At our last quorum meeting we prayed to the Lord that there would be a way for us to finish the temple and dedicate it as a completed edifice. It would be wonderful if it could be preserved as a monument to the Prophet Joseph Smith, but we really don't know what will happen to it after all the Church members leave. There's no hope anymore of the Catholics buying it."

Orson described the quorum meeting as very spiritual with prayers said over a scarlet and white altar in the temple.

For a few moments they talked about the fire on the temple roof and how it had burned a hole about ten by sixteen feet. An overheated stovepipe had caused it. The stove had been used to dry clothing in an upper room of the north side of the attic. Willard Richards had organized a bucket brigade to put it out.

"What are the latest projections on its completion date?" Daniel asked. He still marveled at the idea that the Church leaders were adamant about its completion, despite the fact that all worthy adults had received their endowment.

"We were hoping for April conference time."

"With all the Twelve headed west, who would dedicate it?"

Orson scratched his head. "Depends on how far west Brigham Young and the main companies are by then. He could delegate that responsibility."

"To just anyone?"

"That's about the time Elder Woodruff will return to Nauvoo—maybe he could do it."

Daniel smiled. "Or you."

Orson gulped. Yes, there was a possibility that Marinda's health and the health of her baby could delay him and his family leaving Nauvoo for two, three, or even four months.

# 100

*April 1846*

"I LAY CLAIM TO THIS FORTY-ACRE farm and both houses," Henry Eagles said to his four friends as they rode their horses around The Mound area that had been inhabited mostly by English immigrants.

The sun had set to the west, beyond Nauvoo, leaving the sky resplendent in orange and purple.

"So this is the farm owned by your brother-in-law?" Noah Reckard asked. Reckard and the other two friends of Henry were Carthage citizens and members of the Carthage Greys. Each of the four men cradled a musket across his lap. They had seen several abandoned farms and homes during their trip, with new squatters already taking over.

"And his brother-in-law, Daniel Browett," Henry said. "They farm together."

The farm was victim of neglect. No crops had been planted. Weeds infested most of the ground. Blue herons strolled on legs like sticks in the distance.

"And this is where your dish nose and your brat are staying now?" Reckard asked. He found the Browett and Harris homes with eyes that might have been on loan from the devil.

"No—they're in Nauvoo, staying with my brother's wife, Mary," Henry answered. "They'll be going west, too, I reckon."

Reckard pointed to the barn area, a quarter of a mile away. "Those must be their oxen, then."

Henry smiled. "Yep, they are."

Reckard returned a callous smile and patted his musket. "Then let's have a little fun, boys. How long's it been since we shot up a Mormon farm?"

Fred Loring and Leyrand Doolittle sat up straight on their horses. "Too long," one of them said. "Two less oxen won't hurt anything."

"No!" Henry exclaimed, holding up a hand as he felt a chill rake his flesh. "They need the oxen to pull their wagons. Until they leave, I can't take over their farm."

"Your Mormon friends can walk across Iowa for all I care," Loring said as he nudged his horse toward the Harris and Browett farm. "We could even make cemetery fodder out of them."

Henry spurred his horse a few galloping steps in front of the other three men. "No!"

"Get out of the way, Eagles," Doolittle warned, his rage at the boiling point. "You promised not to interfere with our fun."

"I'm not moving," Henry said in a dire tone. His senses were probing ahead of him like antennae. The men with him were not ordinary men. Like mad dogs, they would kill at the drop of a hat.

Doolittle raised his musket; so did Loring and Reckard. Their looks were of repugnance, cold and sadistic.

"There are plenty of other farms to shoot up," Henry said as he dismounted and reached for the reins of the other horses. "Try the Benbow farm again. All his cows are probably healed up by now." His voice was now thick with contempt.

"It'll send a message," Loring said as he dismounted with Doolittle and Reckard, sensing the confrontation. "It'll make the Mormons hurry a little more." Loring was tall, long-faced, and had a narrow, pointed nose.

"You're not shooting those oxen," Henry warned. "Don't rile me up. I'm mean as a tom turkey when I'm mad."

"You're more like a hen, Eagles," Loring countered.

Henry leaped at Loring, driving his head into his chest with such viciousness that there was an accompanying sharp snap of cracking ribs. At the same time, Henry's fist swung up into the man's jaw. Loring's expression went from shock to pain and terror. His face congested and flushed crimson as he was thrown backward and collapsed.

Reckhard swore, bitterly and vilely. He gave Henry a sinister stare and took a step backward, aiming his musket at him. His mouth was foaming with anger.

Doolittle's face also was contorted in rage and hate.

*Boom!*

Henry felt a burning sensation in the upper portion of his chest, near his right shoulder. He toppled backward and slowly sank to the ground. Waves of gnawing pain told him that the wound was serious. He closed his eyes and lay dead still. He was beginning to lose contact with reality.

"Shoot him again if he stirs," Reckard said without a shred of remorse.

"He looks dead to me," Doolittle said. "Let's get the oxen."

The three men from Carthage mounted their horses and galloped toward the two farmhouses.

Hannah sat straight up out of the wagon when she heard the gun shot.

"What was that?" she cried, her voice choking.

Hannah, Robert, Daniel, Elizabeth, and Harriet were returning from Nauvoo where they had attended a public meeting at the temple. Orson Hyde had spoken, saying that hundreds of families were now pouring into Nauvoo and fitting out for their travel campaign in the wilderness. Many new baptisms were reported. The shot had come from the direction of their farm, sending chills through everyone.

Robert slapped Bendigo and Lawless with the lines.

Hannah could see three riders approaching their houses from the east, bearing hard. From a standing position she pointed. "Look!"

Robert and Daniel stood in the wagon box and waved their arms and yelled. In seconds the three riders stopped in their tracks, turned to contemplate the approaching wagon, then sped off in the opposite direction, melting in the approaching darkness. Hannah could barely hear the thumping of the hooves.

"Who were those men?" Hannah asked as the wagon drew closer to the farm.

"Trouble, I'd say," Robert answered. "Good thing we got here when we did. I'll bet your mother is terrified, Daniel."

Martha Browett had been left to tend Elizabeth's baby and Hannah's six children.

When the wagon arrived at the farm, Robert stood again and folded his arms in a defiant gesture. "I don't see any sign of the three riders now," he reported as Martha and some of the older children emerged from the house.

In the back of his mind, Robert knew that the riders likely were anti-Mormons from Carthage. As far as he was concerned, the men would have done some severe damage to their homes and even their families had he and Daniel not scared them off, a fact that preyed on his mind. He gathered his children in his arms and gazed across the prairie where the three men had disappeared. When everyone had settled down he went into the house and got his musket and cleaned it, making certain it was in perfect order. The feel of the gun jarred his memory of the time when the ruffians from Carthage had accosted him on his way home and had slit his eyelid. If the three men came back, he was ready for them.

Henry had always wondered what it would be like to actually die. He felt terribly weak and his mouth was dry. He lay on his back and watched the moon.

He thought about crawling over to his musket, loading it, and aiming it at his head to finish the job. His life had been ruined—surprisingly, swiftly, unexpectedly, but ruined for sure. If he didn't die, he had nowhere to go. He was finished in Carthage, his former friends would see to that. He would be branded as a man who protected the Mormons, and he had a Mormon wife. He had made wrong choices all his life and he had another to make. Either kill himself or throw himself in with the Mormons, and that seemed worse than dying. He remembered Katherine and Annie. It seemed to him that perhaps they would want him to live, but they would want him to change, too. Even at death's door, he didn't want to change. With one hand he reached up and touched his wound and the warm blood. The blood was coming out of his shoulder, not his chest. With that realization, he rolled over and began to sit up. There might be a chance he could make it to Hannah's house before he fainted from a loss of blood.

Hannah was saying her evening prayers with Robert when she heard a strange sound on the front porch. She jumped to her feet.

"Did you hear that?" she squealed.

Quick as a cat, Robert retrieved his musket from under the bed and pulled back the hammer. Without answering Hannah, he jumped to the front door, listened for a second, and then burst onto the porch.

"Help me," a voice said from the dark.

"Bring a lantern, Hannah," Robert said as he kneeled down. "Someone's hurt out here."

"Who is it?" Hannah asked as she nervously fumbled with the lantern. She lit it and took it to Robert.

The body of a man lay on the porch, moaning. Robert rolled the man over and let the light spill over him.

"It's Henry!" Robert exclaimed. "He's been shot!"

Hannah screamed, plunging into a horrid gloom.

The light revealed a blood-soaked shirt and a strained look on Henry's almost-dead face. "Help me," he pleaded again.

"Quick," Robert said to Hannah. "Go get Elizabeth. I'll get him inside. We've got to stop the bleeding."

Henry was barely clinging to consciousness as Elizabeth treated his wound, stuffing it full of cayenne pepper to stop the bleeding. She drew out her instruments and prepared to search for the ball that had lodged somewhere in Henry's chest. In short spurts, Henry related the story of what had happened: his foray toward Nauvoo with four anti-Mormons, showing Robert and Daniel's farm to his friends, and his resistance to shooting the farm animals.

Hannah exchanged a knowing glance with Robert. In shocked grief she said, "If it hadn't been for Henry, we would have lost our oxen."

Robert nodded, putting the pieces together. The three men had shot Henry, probably because Henry had refused to maraud his home and Daniel's home. "That would have meant another delay in getting out of Illinois."

"They could have harmed our children, too," Hannah fumed, feeling her skin crawl.

Henry seemed to regain some strength. He opened his eyes and began to talk in a voice laced with sorrow. He clutched at Robert's arm. "Get Annie. Get Katherine. Bring them here."

Robert felt a sense of urgency. Henry could fill him on the details later. "I'll get Daniel and we'll leave right now. Don't worry, Henry. We'll get them."

As Robert rode through the darkness with Daniel in the wagon, he felt so anxious he began to get a headache. By the time they had traveled a couple of miles he began to have strong apprehensions. What if the three men were so angry with Henry that they had immediately turned their vengeance on Katherine and Annie? For forty-five agonizing minutes he worried while the horses trudged toward Carthage.

Just after they came over a gentle rise in the terrain, Robert's fears were confirmed. The evening was faintly lit in the distance with what was certain to be a fire.

"Oh, no!" exclaimed Daniel. "You don't suppose that's Henry's place?"

"I fear it is," Robert said as he coaxed the horses into a stern gallop.

The flames shimmered to the east, becoming larger and larger as they approached. Robert began to regret the fact that he had let Henry move to Carthage. If he had it to do all over again, he would beat Henry to a pulp, hogtie him, and force him to stay in Nauvoo. There wasn't much left of Henry's log cabin and barn. The logs and boards had collapsed to a smoldering pile of ash and flames.

Both Robert and Daniel began calling out Katherine's name. Bright moonlight revealed a grove of trees. At first there was no answer, only the popping from the hot coals of the fire.

Two figures emerged from the trees, that of a woman and a child. "Robert! Is that you?" a voice asked.

Almost at once tears streamed down Robert's cheeks, so complete was his relief. He could see none of the men who caused the havoc so he stood to wave. "Yes, it's me and Daniel. What happened?" He jumped out of the wagon and rushed to them. Katherine was carrying Annie in her arms. Annie seemed to be in complete shock and was sobbing. She had probably been sobbing for a long time, Robert surmised.

"It was terrible," Katherine whimpered. "I know the three men, they're Henry's friends. Where's Henry? Is he all right?"

"He's alive, but he's been shot," Robert answered. "It's just a shoulder wound. Elizabeth says he'll recover just fine, but he lost a lot of blood."

"I didn't know whether to believe the men or not when they said they had shot Henry," Katherine said as she boarded the wagon in the moonlight. "They were calling him all sorts of names and when they came here they killed three of our cows and then set the house and barn on fire. We lost everything. All we have is the clothes on our backs. If we can find the other three cows we'll be lucky."

"Looks like they didn't damage your wagon," Daniel said as he pointed. "What about your horse and mule?"

"Either shot or run off," Katherine said. "It was dark when the men got here, so I don't know."

"Let's get you home," Robert said as he turned his team of horses toward

Nauvoo. "We'll come back tomorrow and look for them."

As they traveled, Katherine related the horrid details of the attack Reckard, Loring, and Doolittle had approached the house firing shots into the air. Luckily, they let Katherine and Annie escape into the woods before they burned the house and barn and shot three of the cows. Katherine said that two of the cows died instantly but one collapsed to her front knees and bled for more than an hour before she turned over and died. The three men threatened Katherine repeatedly, telling her that if she didn't leave Carthage they would come back and kill both her and her daughter. They repeatedly cursed at her for her involvement in the trial, saying that if Minor Deming were not already dead they would kill him, too.

"I don't want you to go after the three men, Robert," Katherine said as they traveled under a full moon. "They've got more friends and they'll find a way to come after us."

Robert let out his breath as he thought the situation over. "Maybe you're right. We'll just pack up our things and leave Illinois."

# 101

THE AMAZING THING ABOUT HENRY EAGLES was the way he recovered from his gunshot wound. The first day or two he was in extreme pain and a fever made him half delirious, but thanks to Elizabeth's care and a visit by Dr. John Bernhisel, he began to mend quite nicely. But the better he got the more he talked about going his own way, leaving Nauvoo for parts unknown, which sorely distressed Katherine and Hannah.

"I don't want to travel with the Mormons," he would say to Katherine when no one else was listening. "Let's go down to St. Louis. We can take our three cows and start a dairy. Or we can sell the cows and strike out for western Missouri and settle there."

"But that'll put me right back smack dab into anti-Mormon country again," she would counter. "No thanks. I'm sticking with my people."

"I'm your people," he argued. "I'm your husband and Annie is my daughter."

"Your kind of people nearly killed not only Annie and me, but you, too," Katherine said. "You can't get that through your head?"

This argument continued for days into weeks, all the while Robert and Daniel continued their preparations to leave Illinois. They completed building their wagons—for the second time—and began loading them with the supplies they had been storing. Katherine began to feel left out, but she finally told Robert that she was leaving, too, with or without Henry. So while Henry was still recovering Robert began to fix up Henry's old milk wagon, placing a white canvas tarp over it and generally fixing it up to withstand the trip across Iowa. Robert and Daniel had found not only the three milk cows, but also Henry's horse and mule. The Eagles wagon probably wouldn't be the first or the last to be pulled by a mismatched team, one mule and one horse. Henry didn't quite know what to do, whether to thank Robert for fixing it up, or complain that he did.

Gestures of kindness further frustrated Henry.

"It's a good thing we're about the same size, Henry," Robert said one day. "I'll share my clothes with you. There's one boot maker in town. He's made us both a new pair of boots. We'll probably have them worn out by the time we walk across Iowa, but there'll be someone in one of the wagon companies who can repair them when we need it."

"I reckon I can pay for my own boots," Henry said, clearly embarrassed. "I've sold two of my cows." He patted his pockets. In them were twenty-two dollars.

Families who were assigned to the Daniel Browett Company kept coming to see Daniel and Robert, checking things over and having meetings. Every man that made up the company would come to see Henry and bring him little things like hard rock candy and buttermilk, and this further distressed Henry. He tolerated it, but he told Katherine one night he didn't like any of the men that would be in the company, men like Levi Roberts, John Cox, Edward Phillips, John Hyrum Green, Richard Slater, Robert Pixton, William Kay, John Gailey, and Thomas Kington. He sort of liked Thomas Bloxham, but only because Thomas had successfully resisted Mormonism, just as he had done.

"Do you know how many kids will be in Daniel's company if all those people join in?" he asked Katherine one evening. "Probably two or three or four dozen. It'll be a bloody nightmare."

"Better than the nightmare of sticking around here," she countered. "Daniel's a good leader. He got us from Liverpool to Nauvoo, didn't he?"

Henry didn't answer.

Katherine didn't know exactly what time he left, but Henry wasn't there the next morning. He left a little note saying that he was going to St. Louis and that he would find out in a few months where the Mormons were going and come and get her and Annie some day. He left her five dollars out of the twenty-two dollars he had from selling the cows. He must have traveled on foot, because he left Katherine the wagon, the horse, the mule, and the last remaining cow.

At first Hannah believed Henry would return but as the days passed it became evident he would not. No one had seen him board a steamboat in Nauvoo so she reasoned that he somehow must have made it to Warsaw or Quincy and caught a boat there. With all that had happened to her brothers she was glad she didn't have another on his way to Nauvoo. The inner stress caused by Elias' disappearance and possible murder, plus Henry's shooting and running away, was just about more than she could stand. She composed another letter to her mother in England, but decided not to say anything about Henry. In her heart, she believed Henry's note, that some day he would return and find Katherine and Annie. How that would happen, she didn't know. Her vision of where the Saints were going was blurred and distorted. Terms like the "Great Basin" and "Upper California" were confusing to her. She had no firm idea in her mind where they would be living once they got there. Their future home lay somewhere beyond Indian Territory, and she didn't know anything about that, either, except that there must be a lot of wild Indians. Communications from Brigham Young and others in the companies who had left Nauvoo in February and March indicated they were not even across Iowa yet, and Iowa was a big place just by itself. The next Zion was a year away, maybe more.

# 102

*May 1846*

DANIEL COULDN'T BELIEVE IT WHEN Rebecca told him she was dis appointed in the Nauvoo Temple dedication ceremonies.

"Why?" he asked as they strolled together toward Rebecca's home with Elizabeth and Harriet. Nearly three thousand Saints had attended the service Had it not been for the fact that Brigham Young and thousands of others wer still slugging it through Iowa in the mud, the attendance would have beer doubled.

To Daniel, the ceremony on this first day in May was perfect. Wilford Woodruff—who had returned to Nauvoo only two weeks earlier—gave the opening prayer. Rebecca's husband, Orson Hyde, gave the dedicatory prayer.

Speaking of blessings that will come in the next life, Orson stated, "Le thy Spirit rest upon those who have contributed to the building of this tem ple, the laborers on it, that they may come forth to receive kingdoms and dominions and glory and immortal power."

Rebecca pulled a long face. "I've heard so many stories about the Kirtland Temple dedication," she explained. "I expected something like that to happen here."

Daniel let his air out, understanding his sister now. He, too, had heard the stories connected with the dedication of the Kirtland Temple in March of 1836. The Prophet Joseph Smith had given the dedicatory prayer. The Lord's presence had been signified by the rushing sound of a mighty wind that filled the temple. The congregation had arisen simultaneously, inspired by invisible guidance. Many spoke in tongues and prophesied. Others saw magnificent visions. The Prophet had announced that angels filled the temple. Outside, astonished people in the neighborhood heard the unusual sounds from within the temple and saw a "pillar of fire" resting upon the temple. Some people inside the temple saw the Savior; others saw angels. The Savior appeared to the Prophet and made a solemn pronouncement: "I have accepted this house ... Yea, the hearts of thousands and tens of thousands shall greatly rejoice in consequence of the blessings which shall be poured out ..."

As a fitting climax, more heavenly visitors came to the Kirtland Temple. Moses appeared to Joseph Smith, committing the keys of the gathering of Israel from the four parts of the earth. The ancient prophet Elias also appeared, committing the dispensation of Abraham, telling Joseph that all generations would be blessed with the same blessing that Abraham had received. And the Prophet Elijah returned his priesthood keys also, restoring the power to bind all of Heavenly Father's righteous children in an eternal covenant in genealogical order.

"But didn't Orson say that something like that happened during the private dedication last night?" Daniel asked his sister.

"Yes," she acknowledged. "But I wanted to experience it, too. Why did that special experience have to be reserved for just Orson and the twenty or so other men in that special meeting?"

Orson had told her and Daniel that while the group of priesthood holders had engaged in prayer, asking Heavenly Father to accept the building, the "glory of the Lord shone throughout the room in matchless splendor like unto the rays of the sun, emanating from every side."

"I suppose it's a trial of our faith," Harriet explained as they strolled closer to the Orson Hyde home. "There's not anyone in the Church who would not like the opportunity to see the Savior, or see an angel for that matter."

Elizabeth said, "I don't know if we want the responsibility attached to seeing the Savior or an angel."

"What do you mean?" Rebecca asked.

"During the restoration, many priesthood bearers witnessed seeing an angel, but they fell away from the Church," Elizabeth explained.

Rebecca let a pained expressed cross her face, as though she did not understand.

"How about the Three Witnesses to the Book of Mormon," Elizabeth noted. "Oliver Cowdery, David Whitmer, and Martin Harris not only saw the plates from which the Book of Mormon was translated, but they saw an angel too. Those three men have never denied their testimony of the Book of Mormon, but none of them is active in the Church."

Daniel quickly thought of a recent Sunday gathering at the temple when Orson Hyde had reintroduced Luke Johnson to the members of the Church. Johnson, Marinda Hyde's brother—and therefore Orson's brother-in-law—had been one of the original members of the Quorum of Twelve Apostles before he fell away from the Church. Orson presented Luke Johnson's name for a rebaptism vote at the meeting and received it. Johnson's subsequent baptism had considerably weakened the position of the apostates. Orson, under guidance of the Spirit, had prophesied that Oliver Cowdery would soon realign himself to the Church.

"Sidney Rigdon is another example," Daniel added. "He saw the Savior but he tried to take over the Church last year."

Rebecca shrugged her shoulders. "I'm still disappointed."

Daniel stopped suddenly, and then turned to look at the Nauvoo Temple. It stood on the hill above them, a completed edifice now. Two nights earlier, he and Robert and their wives had met in the attic of the temple with other workers to celebrate its completion. There had been a feast of cakes and pies, and blessings of children, dancing, and music until midnight.

In the distance, Daniel could see Orson Hyde and Wilford Woodruff finally leaving the crowd that had assembled outside the temple and walking down the hill toward their homes. Daniel thought of the responsibilities that Orson had been given these past two or three months. Since the departure of Brigham Young and the other Apostles, Orson had responded well to his heavy load. Almost alone, Orson had stood his ground against apostates like John E. Page and James J. Strang, who were still in town drumming up support for the "Strangites," as they called themselves. Orson had also had to get in the middle of a property dispute that involved William Smith, Joseph's brother.

Like Daniel and Robert, several members of the Church had been asked to let early departing companies of Saints use their covered wagons. Now, two months later, the wagons had still not been returned and there was a host of murmuring that Orson had to deal with. Daniel understood the situation perfectly—the going in Iowa had been tough so far. The mud was deep and Brigham Young could only lead the exodus a few miles each day. Here it was May first and the covered wagons were still headed west. Daniel didn't expect his and Robert's wagons to be returned in time for their trip. Instead, Daniel and Robert had been busy building new wagons, and almost had them completed.

Orson also had the responsibility to sell property owned by the Church and by members of the Church. Unfortunately, those efforts were meeting with a lot of failure. Orson had given up trying to sell the temple to the Catholics and it looked like the Church would have to abandon it. While some private property was being sold for a few cents on the dollar, other homes and farms were being traded for livestock. But it looked like most homes and property would have to be abandoned. Saints from Canada had arrived in Nauvoo to prepare for the exodus. Most of them had moved into abandoned homes on a temporary basis.

A few minutes later Orson and Wilford caught up with Daniel.

"How soon can you cross the Mississippi?" Orson asked Daniel.

"Give me a deadline and we'll make it," Daniel answered. "Robert and I have been working for a farmer in Iowa, building a sod fence, in trade for oxen. Our wagons are complete, except for iron wheels."

"How about two weeks from now?" Orson said. He had his own sense of urgency. An anonymous anti-Mormon had mailed him a letter with a bullet in it, the message obvious.

"You point the way—we'll follow," Daniel smiled.

Wilford Woodruff showed a worried look. "Governor Ford's sent word that he plans to remove the state troops. It might happen right away."

"When he does, mobocracy is likely to be the only law around here," Orson added. "Keep your gun loaded."

"Marinda must be feeling better," Daniel said.

"Yes, she is," Orson answered. "But now I'm worried about Mary Ann. Her baby is due in three months."

"Do you still want us organized into companies?" Daniel asked the two Apostles. Daniel and Robert had originally been assigned to the Joseph Horne Company, but Brother Horne and his company had left in early February.

"As best you can, yes," Orson replied. "Got any ideas?"

"A number of the English converts are about ready to travel," Daniel said. "I think we can make up a company with them." He went on to name several families—Thomas Kington, John Benbow, Levi Roberts, John Cox, Thomas Bloxham, John Gailey, George Bundy, and William Kay. And, of course, Katherine Eagles and Mary Eagles.

Orson and Wilford discussed the names for a few minutes, made little notes, and confirmed their approval.

"When are you leaving, Elder Woodruff?" Daniel asked. He had already had several visits with Wilford since Wilford's return to Nauvoo on April thirteenth. Wilford's parents had moved from New England to Maine and were planning on making the trip west with him. Like so many of the Saints, Wilford had a young family to care for—Wilford, Jr., who would soon turn six; Phoebe Amelia, age four; Susan Cornelia, almost three; and baby Joseph, five months.

"Within ten days," he answered. "Your company is welcome to travel with us."

"I don't think we'll be ready that quickly," Daniel said. "Maybe we'll catch up with you."

While they walked toward the Hyde home, the three men continued their conversation. Orson and Wilford talked about their frustrations trying to find wagons and teams for all the poor, trying to sell property, what to do with additional English immigrants that were on their way to America and Nauvoo, and how to counteract apostate pressure.

Orson also told Daniel about the most recent letters from Brigham Young—that temporary settlements were being made in Iowa, one at the midpoint in the vicinity of Grand River called Garden Grove and another on the far side of Iowa near the Missouri River. Fields there were being cleared, plowed, and planted for the benefit of Saints arriving in later companies.

Daniel turned to look at the temple again. "It seems a shame to have to leave that beautiful building," he told the two Apostles.

Orson shrugged his shoulders. "At least it's dedicated now."

"Let it be said we built the temple with a trowel in one hand and a sword in the other," Wilford mused. "Mobs were troubling us the entire time."

"We quieted the naysayers," Orson added.

Daniel's mouth went dry. "If only the mobs will let us out of town now." The memory of Henry's shooting was still on his mind as well as all the other incidents of mob violence both within the city and in the surrounding areas. Brigham Young's decision to lead companies of Saints out of Nauvoo in February had certainly alleviated the ugly threats at that time, but more were coming now.

# 103

THE SKIES WERE GRAY, THREATENING RAIN the day the Daniel Browett Company left Nauvoo. Hannah was still wishing Henry were with Katherine and Annie, but he wasn't. Katherine would have to drive her horse-mule team across Iowa herself because there was a shortage of manpower, other than seventeen-year-old Job Smith. He was the nephew of George Bundy, but George was getting along in years and he and his wife needed Job.

Before the company gathered on the east bank of the Mississippi, Hannah ordered her wagon stopped on Mulholland Street in front of the temple, nor far from her original log house where Mary Eagles had been staying. Hannah's eyes had been boiling over with tears since early morning when her family left their farm at The Mound. She had barely recovered when they reached Nauvoo and the wagon rolled past their old log cabin where Mary Eagles had been staying. Mary was now traveling with Katherine and of course both Daniel and Robert had the responsibility to help them.

Robert crooned "hooo" and coaxed his two yoke of brown oxen into a stop as the temple came into full view. Hannah's words waxed melancholy. "I suppose the temple is a monument to our hard work. I dread what might happen to it after we are gone. At least we have our endowments."

To Hannah, the temple never appeared more beautiful. Its Egyptian style architecture, limestone walls, and its distinctive carved stones of the sun, moon, and stars stood as a divine sentinel against the Illinois landscape. She couldn't help but think of the Mormon people's commitment to God and their willingness to gather together, leave homes and families, face rancor and persecution in Missouri and Illinois, poverty, sickness, disappointment, and even death to fulfill what was to them a divine command. But they had done it. They had built a house suitable for God, a house where they had been taught and blessed by promises of salvation and exaltation.

Hannah let her gaze wander away from the temple to the collection of new businesses that dotted Mulholland Street. "Well, the temple sure looks wonderful, but I can't say the same for the way this street has changed this spring."

Nauvoo was slowly taking on the same appearance as Carthage, Warsaw, and other Illinois frontier towns. The high council had been dissolved; so had the city council. With no regulations, Mulholland and Main Streets had slowly been disintegrating into a collection of taverns, bars, bowling alleys, ten pin alleys, and grog shops. More than half the city residents were now non-Mormon. Instead of quiet, church-going people, the town was infested with reeling drunkards, boisterous laughter, giddy dancing, and mass confusion. Fences were nearly all down, gardens were laid waste, and fruit trees had been destroyed by cattle.

Robert gathered the lines to his oxen and slapped them down on their rumps. The wagon rattled, rocked, and bounced over the well-traveled Mulholland Street. "Try to remember Nauvoo the way it was, not the way it is today, or the way it'll be tomorrow," Robert counseled. He let his whip tickle the rear end of one of the oxen. "Let's go, Ford. Get up, Polk."

Hannah laughed. Robert had named the two oxen after Governor Ford and President Polk. Robert had tagged the lead yoke of oxen after two of the men who killed Joseph and Hyrum—Sharp and Alrich. Robert could order the governor, the president, and two of Joseph's killers all the way across Iowa.

"Pull hard Sharpie, pull hard, Aldy," Robert commanded. He had inserted a new cracker on his whip and it popped loudly as he lashed it out above the oxen's backs. Robert's dog, Duke, named after British royalty, trotted beside the wagon. Robert had purchased the second yoke of oxen from John Benbow. Benbow was not in the Daniel Browett Company; he was still trying to sell his large farm. From the last report, Benbow's nephew, Thomas, was the most likely prospect to take it over. But there was a concern that Thomas would not be safe if he remained in the Nauvoo area.

As Robert stroked the oxen down the hill, Hannah let her gaze take in the wagon company Daniel had organized. Mentally, she tried to count the number of people, but not the number of horses, mules, oxen, and cattle. She hoped there would be enough cattle to keep them alive until they reached the Great Basin, or where ever it was that Brigham Young would lead them.

Her own wagon held her, her husband, and her five children: Joseph, Lizzy, William, Thomas, Enoch, and Julia Ann. Daniel's lead wagon held four persons—Daniel, Elizabeth, baby Moroni, Harriet, and Daniel's mother, Martha. Also assembled were the families of Thomas Kington, Levi Roberts, John Cox, Richard Slater, Robert Pixton, Thomas Bloxham, John Hyrum Green, Edward Phillips, James Robins, George Bundy, William Kay, and John Gailey.

Hannah sat back on her wagon seat and heaved an audible sigh. According to her count, Daniel had seventy-two souls in his company. That didn't account for the collection of cows, beeves, sheep, pigs, and chickens that would be trailing along. Hannah recalled that there had been one hundred nine souls on the *Echo,* in 1841, the Mormon immigrant voyage that Daniel had been in charge of.

At the water's edge, the first wagon in the Daniel Browett Company was being ferried across the river. The May weather had lapsed into occasional, light showers. Morning sunlight shafted under dark clouds, lighting up the pink banks of the Mississippi River. The four oxen hooked to Hannah's covered wagon flinched nervously at the sight of the broad expanse of the river. George Bundy's mules pawed at the ground. The company's livestock, a collection of cows, calves, and sheep, mooed, bawled, and bleated, running this way and that. Hannah glanced warily at her children's shoes, wondering if they could stand the strain of a two hundred-mile walk. There was barely enough room in the wagon box for the baby, eleven-month-old Sarah Ann.

With a firm resolve, Hannah turned her face west. Soon she would find herself on the far brink of civilization. Behind her were Nauvoo and the Mormon settlements, still raw from the hands of the builders, prairies steaming from the first touch of spring plowing, and memories of plodding to Sunday meetings at the grove. She said a prayer in her heart, hoping also to leave behind intolerant people, murder, mayhem, and persecution.

As she crossed the Mississippi River and rode in the wagon as the oxen trudged up the west bank she wondered at the wilderness that lay before her. At least the muddy season was over; it had plagued those who had fled Nauvoo in February and March, led by Brigham Young. Ahead lay the lush prairies of Iowa and then the short grass country beyond that, and virtually unexplored deserts and mountains beyond that still. Mountains way out west were said to glisten like polished silver as they were approached. The thoughts of sleeping outdoors every night brought a mixed reaction to her mind. Sleeping under bright stars would be one thing, but huddling under the wagon or in a makeshift tent during a violent thunderstorm was another. Out there, too, were Indians, some friendly, but others hostile. The mosquitoes were already bad and apt to be worse, along with gnats, creeping varmints, and sure suffering from heat, thirst, and sheer exhaustion. There were breakdowns to come, too, changing diapers on the trail, feeding her children, and problems with animals. Already, the little collection of cattle and sheep were running off in all directions, confused and bewildered at their new surroundings.

Hannah tried to block all these things out of her mind. She turned to her husband and said, "It's hard not to look back, but I'm ready. Take me to a new Zion. Take me somewhere where we can be at peace, somewhere where the enemies of God can't find us."

CHAPTER NOTES

When Brigham Young began organizing the exodus from Nauvoo in late 1845, nearly everyone was assigned to a company with plans to leave in the spring of 1846. When Church members began leaving in haste in February, however, they were under orders to make their own plans for traveling. It is an invention of the author that many of the English immigrants left Nauvoo under the leadership of Daniel Browett. However, the author's research shows that the people mentioned in this final chapter left Nauvoo in May, just as depicted. And it is very likely that they traveled together.

John Benbow did not sell his farm to Thomas Benbow until August 1846. The selling price was only $2,000 for one hundred sixty acres, far less than market value.

# A FINAL WORD

Volume four, the next and final volume in the series, is entitled *The Mormon Battalion*. In real life, Robert Harris and Daniel Browett served in the battalion. Volume four details their service, helps the reader understand the Mexican-American war, and also chronicles the lives of Hannah and Elizabeth as they desperately battle poor living conditions at Winter Quarters.

# ABOUT THE AUTHOR

Darryl Harris received his B.A. degree in communications from Brigham Young University in 1966, after attending Idaho State University. He was graduated from Marsh Valley High School in 1959 and was raised in the small Idaho communities of McCammon and Arimo.

After being employed by the *Deseret News* in Salt Lake City and the *Post-Register* in Idaho Falls, and Evans Advertising in Salt Lake City, he began his own business, Harris Publishing, Inc., in Idaho Falls in 1971. The firm currently has 90 employees, counting those who work in the printing portion of the business—Falls Printing. Harris Publishing, Inc. publishes twelve magazine titles, including *SnoWest, SledHeads, Houseboat, Pontoon & Deck Boat, Riverjet, Potato Grower, The Sugar Producer, Mountain West Golf,* and *Idaho Falls*.

His church callings have including mission president (Korea Seoul), bishop, counselor in a bishopric, stake mission president, elder's quorum president, area public communications director (southeastern Idaho), and Sunday school teacher. He and his wife continue to reside in Idaho Falls. They have five children and sixteen grandchildren.